LIBRARY OF MONEY AND BANKING HISTORY

A HISTORY OF BANKING

IN ALL THE

LEADING NATIONS.

VOLUME II

A HISTORY OF BANKING

IN ALL THE LEADING NATIONS

WILLIAM GRAHAM SUMNER

EDITOR

FOUR VOLUMES

VOLUME II

[1896]

REPRINTS OF ECONOMIC CLASSICS

AUGUSTUS M. KELLEY · PUBLISHERS

NEW YORK 1971

First Edition 1896

(New York: The Journal of Commerce & Commercial Bulletin, *19 Beaver Street,* 1896)

REPRINTED 1971 BY
AUGUSTUS M. KELLEY · PUBLISHERS
NEW YORK NEW YORK 10001

I S B N 0 678 00554 0

L C N 68 30546

PRINTED IN THE UNITED STATES OF AMERICA
by SENTRY PRESS, NEW YORK, N. Y. 10019

A HISTORY OF BANKING

IN ALL THE

LEADING NATIONS;

COMPRISING

THE UNITED STATES; GREAT BRITAIN; GERMANY; AUSTRO-HUNGARY; FRANCE; ITALY; BELGIUM; SPAIN; SWITZERLAND; PORTUGAL; ROUMANIA; RUSSIA; HOLLAND; THE SCANDINAVIAN NATIONS; CANADA; CHINA; JAPAN;

COMPILED BY THIRTEEN AUTHORS.

EDITED BY THE

EDITOR OF THE JOURNAL OF COMMERCE AND COMMERCIAL BULLETIN.

IN FOUR VOLUMES.

VOLUME II.

PUBLISHED BY

THE JOURNAL OF COMMERCE AND COMMERCIAL BULLETIN,

19 BEAVER STREET, NEW YORK.

LONDON AGENTS:

EFFINGHAM WILSON, 11 ROYAL EXCHANGE, E. C., and

JOHN JONES, 11 TOKENHOUSE YARD, E. C.

1896.

TREATISES IN VOL. II.

A HISTORY OF BANKING IN GREAT BRITAIN,

BY

HENRY DUNNING MacLEOD, A. M.;

OF

BANKING IN THE RUSSIAN EMPIRE,

BY

ANTOINE E. HORN;

AND OF

SAVINGS-BANKS IN THE UNITED STATES,

BY

JOHN P. TOWNSEND, LL.D.

NEW YORK.
1896.

A History of Banking

IN

GREAT BRITAIN;

WITH A HISTORIC ANALYSIS OF THE PRINCIPLES GOVERNING BANKING, CURRENCY, AND CREDIT.

BY

HENRY DUNNING MacLEOD, A. M.,

Of Trinity College, Cambridge, and the Inner Temple;
Honorary Member of the Juridical Society of Palermo, and of the Sicilian Society of Political Economy;
Corresponding Member of the Société d'Économie Politique of Paris, and of the
Royal Academy of Jurisprudence and Legislation of Madrid.

::

NEW YORK.
1896.

CONTENTS.

PART I.

BANKING IN GREAT BRITAIN.

CHAPTER I.

BANKING IN ENGLAND.

SECTION I.

A Record of Beginnings.

SECTION II.

Foundation of the Bank of England.

SECTION III.

An Era of National Development.

SECTION IV.

State of the Irish Currency.

SECTION V.

FAILURE OF CURRENCY REFORM—INFLATION AND REACTION.

SECTION VI.

THE COMMITTEE ON BANKING OF 1840.

SECTION VII.

ON THE BANK ACTS OF 1844 AND 1845.

SECTION VIII.

COMMERCIAL CRISES.

SECTION IX.

MONETARY PANICS.

CHAPTER V.

THE THEORY OF VALUE.

SECTION I.

SECTION II.

SECTION III.

CHAPTER VI.

THE THEORY OF CREDIT.

SECTION I.

SECTION II.

PART II.

BANKING IN RUSSIA.

CHAPTER I.

THE EARLY STAGES OF MONEY AND CREDIT.

SECTION I.

PREFATORY.

SECTION II.

INTRODUCTION OF PAPER MONEY.

SECTION III.

FINANCIAL RECONSTRUCTION UNDER ALEXANDER II., AND THE FOUNDING OF THE STATE BANK.

CHAPTER II.

METHODS AND OPERATIONS OF THE STATE BANK.

CHAPTER VII.

THE PRECIOUS METALS.

CHAPTER VIII.

FOREIGN EXCHANGES.

CHAPTER IX.

THE DEBT AND FINANCES OF RUSSIA.

PART III.

SAVINGS-BANKS IN THE UNITED STATES.

BANKING IN GREAT BRITAIN.

CHAPTER I.

BANKING IN ENGLAND.

SECTION I.

A RECORD OF BEGINNINGS.

Banking Originates in Royal Rapacity—Goldsmiths Become Bankers—Cromwell Encourages Them—The King Seizes Their Treasure—His Promises of Compensation Never Honored.

BANKING, in the modern sense of the word, had no existence in England before 1640. Up to that date, merchants had been for a considerable time in the habit of depositing their bullion and cash in the Mint in the Tower, under the guardianship of the Crown. In that year, however, Charles I. being in great straits for money, in consequence of his fatal dissolution of the Parliament before it had voted supplies, seized upon the merchants' bullion and cash in the Mint, to the amount of £120,000. The merchants were in consternation, as the cash was the provision they had made to meet their bills with. They immediately met, and drew up and presented a strong remonstrance to the Council. They ultimately agreed to let the King have £40,000, upon receiving adequate security for its repayment with interest. The whole of the loan was ultimately repaid to them with interest.

But their confidence in the royal honor was gone; and henceforth they determined to keep their cash in their own houses, under the care of their own clerks and apprentices. But their treasures were no safer than before. The plebeian cashiers were more dishonest than the King. As the war went, these gentlemen of the quill were seized with a martial ardor; they deserted their desks in multitudes to join the army, and carried off their masters' cash with them. Others lent out their masters' funds to the goldsmiths clandestinely, at 4d. per cent. per day, which they kept to themselves. The goldsmiths lent out the money which came into their hands in great quantities to merchants and others, weekly or monthly, at high interest, and then began to discount mercantile bills. Finding this to be very profitable, they began to attract money from the general public by offering them interest at the rate of six per cent. and engaging to repay the sums placed with them on demand.

When a customer paid in money to his account, and when they discounted a merchant's bill, *i. e.*, bought the debt, or right of action to the money due to him, they simply gave them in exchange for it a credit, debt or right of action in their banks, which in the technical language of banking is termed a deposit. Moreover, in order to diminish the demand for actual money as much as possible, they agreed with their customers to make these credits or deposits as transferable as money itself, and to pay any person to whom their customers had transferred their credits, in the same way as to themselves. These credits or deposits, were transferred by means of paper documents, which were of two forms: 1. Either the goldsmith gave his customer a written promise to pay to himself, or to his order, or to bearer, on demand, a certain sum of money. These notes were in simple writing, and were called goldsmith's notes. 2. The customer might write a note to the goldsmith directing him to pay a certain sum to any person, or to his order, or to bearer, on demand; these notes were, at first, called cash notes, but in modern language they are termed cheques.

These two forms of documents were as transferable as money itself, and produced all the effects of money. By experience, the goldsmiths soon found that they could keep afloat an amount of credit several times exceeding the amount of cash they kept to meet the demands upon them; and this increased quantity of credit was in all its practical effects exactly equivalent to an increase of money of equal amount. People found it much more convenient to place their money with the goldsmiths, where they could have it back whenever they pleased with interest at six per cent., than to lend it out on real or personal security. The goldsmiths soon received the rents of all the gentlemen's estates which were transmitted to town. Five or six stood pre-eminent among their brethren; and Clarendon says, that they were men known to be so rich, and of such good reputation, that all the money in the kingdom would be trusted to their hands. These goldsmiths then, for the first time, came to be called bankers.

Several schemes for the foundation of joint stock banks, similar to those which existed in considerable numbers in Italy, were proposed under the government of Cromwell, but none of them were carried into effect. The goldsmith bankers however flourished; and their command of ready money soon brought them a much higher customer than the merchants. Notwithstanding the fame and strength of the Protector's Government, and his unquestionable sincerity in wishing to govern with free Parliaments, he and they were unable to agree better than his royal predecessor had done with them. They were jealous of his power, and kept him in a constant state of financial embarrassment. He then applied to the "Bankers," and they advanced him money, in anticipation of the supplies. They thus became almost indispensable to the Government.

The position the bankers had gained under the frugal government of Cromwell was not lost under his dissolute successor. The first care of the restored monarch was to disband the terrible republican armies. But they had to be paid off, and some hundreds of thousands of pounds were required to be got together in a few days. The slow receipts of the taxes were quite inadequate to effect this, and the Ministers were compelled to have recourse to the bankers; and they were so well satisfied with their proceedings that they declared that the King's affairs could not be carried on without their assistance. Their method of doing business with the Crown was as follows. As soon as the supplies were granted, they were sent for to attend the King. He having consulted his Ministers as to what immediate sums were needed, desired them to be called in, and they were then informed what ready money he would require to be provided by such a day. They were then asked how much they could lend, and what security they would require. Each answered according to his several ability; for there was no joint stock among them; one perhaps £100,000, another more, another less. They were desirous of having eight per cent. for their money, which the King and his Ministers were perfectly ready to give as a reasonable remuneration; but, upon further consideration, they determined to leave it to the King's own bounty, lest it might afterwards be turned to their disadvantage; mentioning at the same time, that they themselves paid six per cent. for it to their customers, which was known to be true. They then received an assignment for the first moneys that came in under the Act of Parliament, or tallies upon such other branches of the revenue as were least changed. But even this was no security; as the King and the Treasurer might divert these payments to other purposes. "Therefore," says Clarendon, "there is nothing surer, but that it was nothing but the unquestionable confidence in the King's justice and the Treasurer's honor and integrity which was the true foundation of that credit which supplied the necessities of the Government. The King always treated them very graciously as his very good servants, and all his Ministers looked upon them as very honest men." We shall now see how their confidence in the King's honor was repaid.

In 1667, the Government provoked a war with Holland. Parliament voted supplies of unexampled magnitude; but they were all embezzled by the courtiers, who made fortunes, while the seamen mutinied for want of pay and the ships were rotting. The Dutch destroyed Sheerness and Chatham, burnt the ships there, and attacked Tilbury; the sound of the enemy's guns was heard in London. The citizens were seized with the utmost alarm, and rushed to demand their money from the bankers. It was known that they had advanced large sums to the King, and the people believed that regular payments out of the exchequer could not be made. To quiet the public alarm, the King, in June, 1667, issued a proclamation that the payments out of the exchequer would continue as usual; but it was his steadfast resolution to preserve inviolable to all his creditors all the securities and assignments made for repayment of their advances, and that he held this resolution firm and sacred in all future assignments and securities to be granted by him upon any other advances of money for his service by any person on any future occasion. However, in 1672, the Court was in greater difficulties than ever, and the King declared that the Treasurer's staff should reward the ingenuity of the man who should discover an expedient for "raising the wind." The expedient hit upon was to shut up the exchequer. On the 2d January, 1672, a proclamation was issued stating that payment out of the exchequer would be suspended for one year; but a rent, or interest, at the rate of six per cent. was promised. The sum seized by the King was £1,328,526. So much for the King's proclamation of 1667.

The bankers, it is true, were not many; but the money they had belonged chiefly to their creditors, and there were 10,000 of them. The *coup de finance* was so cleverly done, that no one, except one or two intimate friends of the conspirators, had the slightest warning. The consternation was dreadful in the city. Numberless merchants were ruined. The distress was felt in all ranks of society. Widows and orphans who had no other means of subsistence had placed their all with the bankers. Many persons went mad; many died of a broken heart; many destroyed themselves. It was at first promised that the suspension should only be for a year; but year after year passed away and nothing was done, and neither the principal nor the interest was paid. What seems to be a most extraordinary circumstance was that no notice was taken of the transaction in Parliament. But the intensity of the public distress was too great, and the public indignation was too fierce to be entirely neglected. At length in April, 1676, the King was obliged to order the accounts of the creditors to be examined by the Chancellor of the Exchequer. This having been done, in April, 1677, the King issued letters patent granting to each of the goldsmiths' heirs and assigns, for the benefit of their creditors, in lieu and satisfaction of their debts, a yearly rent out of the hereditary excise equal to six per cent. upon the debt, with a clause of redemption upon payment of the principal and interest. These letters patent were printed and made public on the 23d of May, 1677, and a bill to ratify them was passed by the House of Lords; but by some misadventure (?) it did not reach the Commons before the end of the session and never became law. The rent, or interest, was paid till Lady Day, 1683, when it ceased, and none was paid during the reign of James II. At length, in 1689, the creditors, worn out with despair, petitioned the Court of Exchequer to make an order for the payment of their claims. In 1691, the Court gave judgment in their favor, and made an order on the exchequer for payment; but the judgment was reversed by Lord Somers on a technical point. But, in 1700, the Lords reversed the judgment of Lord Somers. This judgment of the Lords established the rights of the petitioners to their principal and interest; but they were not paid one farthing. In 1700, an act was passed that after the 31st December, 1701, the hereditary excise should be charged with interest at three per cent. on the principal until payment was made of one-half the debt. Thus ended this monstrous injustice. It was calculated that the bankers and their creditors lost £3,000,000. The principal was never repaid, and forms the first item of our National Debt.

SECTION II.

FOUNDATION OF THE BANK OF ENGLAND.

Financing of the War Against Louis XIV.—Failure to Borrow from the Bankers—Bank of England Established—First Issue of Notes Against Securities—Debasement of the Coinage—Lowndes' Report—Suspension by the Bank—A Fictitious Increase of the Bank's Capital—The Bank Made a Monopoly, and Exempted from the Usury Laws—The Bank "Rest" Introduced—Extension of Its Charter.

THE chief object which tempted the ambition of William of Orange to obtain the crown of England was to head the great European alliance against the overwhelming power of France. No sooner was William pretty firm on his throne than he declared war against Louis XIV. Parliament was eager for the war, and readily voted supplies; but they were scarce and difficult to be got in. The Government at first attempted the old plan of mortgaging the grants to be voted by Parliament, but they were not successful. In 1690, Parliament began the system of allowing money to be raised on short annuities, which was attended with good success. The increasing expense of the war, however, rendered this plan too burdensome; and, in 1692, a plan was brought forward for raising duties for the space of ninety-nine years to pay the interest of an intended loan of £1,000,000 upon a tontine scheme. The subscribers were to receive ten per cent. till 1700; and after that £7000 per annum was to be divided among the survivors till their number was reduced to seven; when, upon the death of each, his annuity was to lapse to the State. So low was the credit of the Government that only £108,000 was obtained on these tempting terms; and a clause was introduced by which the subscribers might receive fourteen per cent. upon any life they chose to nominate. But these schemes produced only £881,493. All these devices, however, failed of producing an adequate supply of money to support the war, which languished in consequence. The fatal proceedings of Charles II. seem to have ruined the bankers; or at least deterred them from making advances to Government in their former style. The Government was obliged to revert to the humiliating plan of borrowing from every one in the city on whom they could prevail to lend. They were obliged to solicit the Common Council of London for so small a sum as £100,000; and if they granted it, the Councilmen had to make humble suit to the inhabitants of their respective wards, going from house to house for contributions; and for these advances they had to pay in premiums, discount and commissions from thirty to forty per cent.

The inextricable financial difficulties of the Government turned attention towards a scheme for a public bank, such as existed in several of the Italian States. Mr. William Paterson, a Scotchman from Dumfriesshire, whose antecedents were gravely suspected, and who was so notorious for his Darien scheme, which ruined half Scotland, but who had traveled widely, and studied foreign financial institutions, proposed several schemes which proved abortive. At last, one succeeded. He proposed to raise and circulate £1,200,000 upon a fund of £100,000 a year. Some party jealousy came at the opportune moment to assist him. Mr. Michael Godfrey, brother of Sir Edmondbury Godfrey, and some merchants who were nettled with some transactions with the East India Company, now took Paterson up and in effect supplanted him; for, though he continued to advise and assist in the direction of the measure, Godfrey stood foremost in it, and was considered, both by the Ministers and the Parliament, as the efficient man on whom all depended, and to whom all acknowledgments were to be paid. The scheme succeeded. After the details had been settled in concert with the Ministers, it was brought before the Privy Council, and long and anxiously discussed in the presence of the Queen; and at last the Statute 1694, c. 20, was passed by which the Bank of England was established.

The Act, Statute 1694, c. 20, incorporating the Bank of England, received the royal assent on the 25th April, 1694; and its provisions, material to our present purpose, were as follows:

1. It provided that the sum of £100,000 a year should be appropriated to the encouragement of persons making a voluntary loan of £1,200,000 to the Government for the purpose of carrying on the war with France; such persons to be erected into a corporation, to be called the Governor and Company of the Bank of England, with all the usual privileges of a corporation.

2. The corporation was strictly forbidden to borrow or give security by bill, bond, covenant or agreement, under their common seal, for any sums exceeding £1,200,000, except they were permitted by act of Parliament.

Thus it will be seen that the bank advanced the whole of its capital to the State and received in exchange for it an annuity of £100,000; and also received the right to issue notes to the amount of the capital they had advanced to the Government, it being supposed that the annuity would be sufficient to support the credit of the notes. Now, the whole of the capital was advanced to the Government and put into circulation by them; and the bank was authorized to issue an equal amount of notes to be used in commerce. This, therefore, was an augmentation of the currency to the amount of £1,200,000. This was the first example of issuing notes based upon public securities—a most seductive but most dangerous principle, which was one form of Law-ism.

The immense benefit which accrued to the State by the establishment of the bank was shown by the increased vigor with which the war was carried on. Mr. Michael Godfrey, the Deputy Governor, published a pamphlet on the bank, written in a strain of the warmest congratulation upon the great success of the experiment, which he had taken so leading a part in promoting. He states that, whereas in the beginning of 1694, the Government bills were at a discount of £25 to £30 per cent., in addition to the public interest, the bank took them at par; and from the former heavy discount they had risen to a premium, so that they were then better than money; because there was seven or eight per cent. per annum benefit while they were kept, which never could have been done without the bank. He said that those who lodged their money with the bank had it as much at their disposal as if it were in the hands of the goldsmiths, or in their own chests; and he certainly countenances an accusation against the goldsmiths in contemporary pamphlets; for he says that if the money which had been lodged with them for four or five years past had been lodged with the bank, it would have prevented it from being so scandalously "clipped"; which he predicts would cost the nation some day a million and a-half or two millions to repair. He notes it as very surprising, and quite unexampled, that after the nation had been at war for six years, and had spent £30,000,000, besides great quantities of bullion being exported and captured by the enemy, that there had been so great a fall in the rate of interest, instead of a rise, as in all previous wars, which was entirely due to the bank; and he predicted that it would, in the course of a few years, reduce it permanently to three per cent. He says that, within thirty years of that time, the public had lost between two and three millions by the goldsmiths and scriveners breaking, which would not have happened if the bank had been established. Further, he affirms that there were some who were for having a forced currency of bills and tallies, thinking that they might pass as well as bank bills; but "they do not consider that it is nothing makes bank bills current but only because all those who desire it can go, when they will, and fetch their money for them"; and to force anything to pass in payment but money would soon end in confusion. He then enters into numerous arguments to show that any attempt at a forced currency would only end in damaging the public credit.

The Bank of England was a Whig project, and had been eminently successful in supporting the Government in the prosecution of the war. It had excited the warmest feelings of joy and congratulation among its friends, and the bitterest feelings of rage and indignation among its enemies and the enemies of the Government. But it received no monopoly of banking. The Government of William was composed of a mixture of Whigs and Tories. William not only reigned but governed. The resources of the Bank of

England were entirely devoted to supporting commerce. But the spirit of industry began to be developed in agriculture as well as in commerce, and many schemes were devised to found a bank in the interest of agriculture. The Tory portion of the Ministry determined to get up a rival bank on a much larger scale. The capital was to be £2,564,000, advanced to Government on the same principle as that of the Bank of England, but its trading capital, notes, etc., were to be advanced solely to land owners at three per cent. It was therefore called a land bank. It was warmly patronized by the Tory party. The Bank of England and all its friends opposed it with all its power; but the temptation was too great; and it was sanctioned by Act of Parliament in April, 1696. The time for receiving subscriptions was limited, as in the case of the Bank of England. The Lords of the Treasury subscribed £5,000 on behalf of the King; but, notwithstanding all the vaporing of the Tory party, the other subscriptions only amounted to £2,100 when the time came for its closing. It was therefore a total and complete failure; but its failure, combined with other circumstances which we have now to detail, exercised a most disastrous influence on the Bank of England.

We must now retrace our steps a little, and examine the condition of the coinage, which is necessary to understanding the subsequent history of banking; for controversies on the subject then began which have lasted almost until our own times, if indeed they are yet extinct. In April, 1690, the scarcity of silver coins occasioned great public inconvenience. The goldsmiths complained to the House of Commons that they had ascertained that immense quantities of silver bullion and dollars had been exported. That many Jews and merchants had recently bought up large quantities of silver to carry out of the kingdom, and had given three-halfpence per ounce above its regulated value. That this had encouraged the melting down of much plate and milled money, whereby for six months past no bullion had been brought to the Mint to be coined. These allegations were verified by a committee of the House. It was shown that the profit of melting down the milled money for exportation was about £25 per £1,000; that the Mint price of silver was 5s. 2d. per ounce, but it was generally sold for 5s. 3 1-2d. The House in consequence passed one of their useless laws against exporting bullion. The state of the coinage now became every day more disgraceful. By law, in 1666, it was enacted that every one might bring gold and silver bullion to the Mint and have it coined free of all expense. The guinea, then first coined, was intended by the Mint indentures to be equal to 20s. in silver. But there was no legal ratio established between the coins, so as to make them compulsorily taken by the public at that rate. They were left to be received by the public at such rates as they pleased. The guinea passed current at 22s. Quantities of base and counterfeit coin were in circulation. The silver coins were being constantly clipped, so that in 1694 they had lost nearly half their weight. By the end of 1694, guineas, which had been coined to be equal to 20s., rose to 30s. in the clipped and degraded coin. The exchange with Holland, which was reckoned in the degraded silver coin, fell to twenty-five per cent. below par, and it would have fallen still lower only it was shown that the real exchange was in favor of England. The exchange with Ireland fell so much that £70 there was worth £100 in England,

The frightful condition of the coinage may be judged of by the following facts. In the months of May, June and July, 1695, 572 bags of silver coin, each of £100, were brought into the Exchequer, whose aggregate weight, according to the standard, ought to have been 18,451 lbs; their actual weight was 9,480 lbs; showing a deficiency in the weight of the current coin in the ratio of 10 to 22. Bags of coin collected in various parts of the country showed a similar deficiency. A warm controversy arose whether the new money should be coined of the old standard weight, fineness and denomination; or whether it should be depreciated, or raised in value, as it was absurdly called. This controversy was keenly disputed then, and it was revived 116 years later, when the notes of the Bank of England were depreciated, and a strong party maintained that the standard of the coin should be depreciated to the level of the depreciated notes.

Mr. William Lowndes, the Secretary to the Treasury, was ordered to make a report on the coinage. In this, he enters into a long and, at the time, valuable investigation of the history of the coinage, and its successive depreciations in weight and fineness, in which he maintained the extraordinary hallucination that the successive frauds committed by the English kings in diminishing the bullion in the coin had raised its value. His doctrine was that by raising the *name* of the coin it thereby acquired increased *value.* His proposal was either that the new coinage should be made of a diminished weight; or that the same pieces should be rated at a higher price in tale; or that 60 pence were equal to 75 pence. Locke published a reply to this infatuated idea, showing that it was quite illusory.

All this time the Bank of England, with infantine simplicity, had received the degraded coin at its full nominal value. Its notes were payable to bearer on demand. As soon as the new coin came out, they were bound to pay them in full-weighted coin—that is, for every seven ounces they had received they were bound to pay twelve ounces. Such a state of things could have but one result; an immediate run upon the bank. Its success had enraged the private bankers and money-lenders, whose profits it had diminished. All its enemies now made a combined effort to destroy the Bank. They collected its notes in all directions, and on the 5th May, 1695, they suddenly presented them for payment. The directors, knowing the purpose for which these notes were presented, refused payment of them, but continued their payments to their ordinary customers. Their enemies ran about crying out that the Bank was destroyed. But the public, who quite understood the transaction, received their notes at first at their full value. The extreme scarcity, however, of silver continuing, compelled the Bank to make a general suspension. The managers gave notice that they could only pay ten per cent. on their notes once a fortnight; and as the demand continued they were unable to maintain even that payment, and a short time later they gave notice that they could only pay three per cent. every three months. On the 3d of August, bank notes were at a discount of fourteen and fifteen per cent. and exchequer tallies at thirty per cent. Fresh coin, however, continued to be issued from the Mint, and the exchanges, which were reckoned in the silver coin, were restored to par, although the bank notes were at a heavy discount.

Parliament met in October, 1696. At that time, bank notes were at a discount of twenty per cent. and exchequer tallies at forty, fifty and sixty per cent. discount, while at the same time the exchanges were at par. When the Bank of England was obliged to suspend payments in cash, it endeavored to retrieve its credit by making two calls of twenty per cent. each on its proprietors. These measures, however, were not successful, and Parliament had to take in hand the business of restoring the credit of the bank notes and exchequer tallies. By an Act of Statute, 1697, the capital of the bank was to be increased, and the subscriptions might be paid, four-fifths in exchequer tallies and one-fifth in bank notes, upon which the Crown would allow eight per cent. The time when the Crown might put an end to the corporation was prolonged to twelve months after the 1st August, 1710, and repayment of all Parliamentary debts. During the continuance of the corporation, no other bank, or any other corporation, society, fellowship, company, or constitution in the nature of a bank, should be erected or established, permitted, suffered, countenanced or allowed by act of Parliament within England. The bank was allowed to extend its issues of notes beyond the original capital of £1,200,000 to the amount of new capital which should be subscribed, provided that they were made payable to bearer on demand. We observe that the depreciated notes of the bank itself were taken at their full value at par, and treated as capital; the first practical instance on a great scale in this country of the doctrine that the *release of a debt* is in all respects equivalent to a *payment in money:* or the algebraical doctrine that $- \times - = + \times +$.

One reason probably that bank notes were at such a heavy discount was that there were none under £20; and those were of little use in current transactions. Montague, the Chancellor of the Exchequer, hit upon the plan of issuing bills upon the exchequer for £5 and £10. These bills passed, at first, at a small discount; but, upon the second issue of them, interest at £7 12s. per cent. was allowed upon them, and they were received at par in payment of taxes. They then rose to par. The Treasury was authorized to contract with any persons to cash these exchequer bills on presentment, allowing them a moderate premium. They were allowed ten per cent. at first; but the exchequer bills soon rose above par, and the interest upon them was reduced to four per cent. Under this act, upwards of £2,000,000 of exchequer bills were issued. The new subscription to the bank under this act amounted to £1,001,171 10s.; £200,000 being paid in bank notes and £800,000 in exchequer tallies. These large amounts were taken out of circulation and received at par in the subscription, which raised the value of the remainder; and in the course of the year bank notes which bore no interest were at par, and those which bore an interest were at a premium.

In 1709 the Government were in great pecuniary embarrassment. The produce of the taxes barely covered half of the expenses. The Ministry sought the assistance of the bank; and the following terms were accepted and ratified by Parliament: 1. The interest upon their original stock of £1,200,000 was reduced to six per cent., with an allowance of £4000 for managing the debt. 2. The bank was to advance a further sum of £400,000 at six per cent. interest. 3. The bank might double its then capital of £2,201,171 10s. at the price of £115 per cent. for the new stock. The bank agreed to circulate £2,500,000 of exchequer bills and receive an allowance of six per cent., one-half for interest and the other for repayment of the principal: that no more exchequer bills should be issued without the consent of the bank. 4. Their privileges as a corporation should be continued for twenty-one years from the 1st of August, 1711.

The Act of 1697 had only provided that no other bank should be erected or allowed by Act of Parliament; it did not prohibit private joint stock banks from being founded, nor any other corporation or company from setting up banking business. A company called the Mine Adventurers of England, at the head of which was Sir Humphrey Mackworth, who turned out to be a great rogue, commenced doing banking business of all sorts, issuing notes, etc. To put a stop to this it was enacted: "That during the continuance of the said Corporation of the Governor and Company of the Bank of England, it shall not be lawful for any body politic or corporate whatsoever, erected or to be erected (other than the said Governor and Company of the Bank of England), or for any other person united or to be united in covenants or partnership exceeding the number of six (now ten) persons in that part of Great Britain called England to borrow, owe, or take up any sum or sums of money on their bills or notes payable at demand, or at any less time than six months from the borrowing thereof."

The Bank of England was strictly forbidden to issue notes to a larger amount than their capital stock. That is, each loan to Government was attended with an augmentation of currency to an equal amount. Now, to a certain small extent, this plan might be attended with no evil consequences; but as a scientific principle it is utterly vicious. This is indeed one form of John Law's Theory of Money. His scheme of basing paper money on land, is sober sense compared to it; because in that, the quantity of paper money was limited to twenty years' purchase of the land. But in such a scheme as basing paper money on the public debt, there is absolutely no limit whatever. If this principle had been carried out to the present time, we should have had a national debt of about £800,000,000, and bank notes to the amount of £800,000,000.

At this time, no one had framed a definition of banking; but the issue of notes was considered to be so essentially "banking" that to prohibit that was supposed to be effectual in prohibiting banking. The clause quoted above was intended to disallow any bank being formed with more than six partners, so as to prevent any private company from being formed of sufficient power and influence to rival the bank; and it did have that effect for more than a century.

When we consider the unquestionable services the bank had rendered to the Government, which contributed so greatly to the success of the war and the pacification of Ryswick, and when we consider the terrific state of public credit when the Land Bank project failed, and the calamity of the Mine Adventurers, we need not be surprised that the Bank of England employed these circumstances for the purpose of securing a monopoly for themselves. Now, considering the ideas of the age, can we be surprised that they received it? Nevertheless, after making due allowances for these circumstances, it is one of the most deplorable acts which have come down to our times. The founders and contemporaries of the bank felt the benefit of its eminent services; but the consequences of this original sin fell with fearful force on their descendants of succeeding generations. The frightful convulsions and collapses of public credit which have taken place for more than a century, are chiefly due to this great wrong and violation of the true principles of trade. English banking has never recovered from its fatal effects to this day, and many years must elapse before it will arrive at the form to which it is tending, and which it would naturally have assumed, if its development had been left free to the skill and experience of men of business. We shall later show how much more wisely the people of Scotland acted with respect to their bank.

In 1713, the financial difficulties of the Government at the peace of Utrecht made it necessary to have recourse to the bank. It agreed to lend the Government £100,000, secured upon exchequer bills at three per cent., upon receiving an extension of their charter, which had still twenty years to run. By the Statute I. 1713, c. 11, its existence as a corporation was prolonged to twelve months' notice, to be given after the 1st August, 1742, and the payment of £1,600,000.

The excessive absurdity and inconvenience of the usury laws were even then felt, and the bank was exempted from their operation in 1716. In the quaint phraseology of the act, they were authorized "at their own good liking" to borrow, owe, or take up money at any rate of interest they pleased, above the legal rate, upon their bonds, bills, or any obligation under their common seal, or upon credit of their capital stock for any time, or to be paid upon demand. What portentous folly it was that anyone else might not observe "his own good liking" in the rate he paid for a loan of money. Yet this egregious folly was not relaxed till 1833, nor finally swept away till 1854. The Bank of France was similarly exempted from the usury laws after the panic of 1857. The bank's existence was prolonged indefinitely until all the public debts due to it were discharged.

In 1717, guineas were finally made current at 21s., although Sir Isaac Newton showed that their value in the markets of the world was only 20s. 8d. The effect of this was that, although gold and silver coin were equally legal tender, all the good silver left the country, being more valuable abroad than at home; and it became an established custom among merchants that all bills of exchange were understood to be payable in gold, as being the cheaper metal. The exchanges continued to be reckoned in silver, but were actually paid in gold, which rectified them; and, from this period, England became practically a gold monometallic country; although the law of bimetallism lingered on in the statute book for another hundred years.

Up to 1722, the bank divided the whole of its profits among the shareholders, and made no reserve for contingencies. The dividend varied from 18 1-4 per cent. in 1706 to 6 per cent. in 1722. The inconvenience was strongly felt, as well as having no friend to fall back upon in cases of emergency. These had hitherto been met by making calls on the proprietors. In this year the directors established a reserve fund, which is termed the REST.

When the charter had been renewed on former occasions, there had been many public discussions as to the expediency of the bank's monopoly. It had always purchased its privileges by aiding the Government. As the time was drawing near for the expiring of its charter, in 1742, these discussions became more frequent and animated, and several attempts were made to set up banks in such a manner as not to violate the clause in the Act of 1709. When the time for the renewal came, the Government were, as usual, in difficulties, and the bank agreed to lend them £1,600,000 without interest. To raise this sum, they made a call upon their proprietors, which raised their capital stock to £9,800,000. In consideration of this, their exclusive privileges were continued till twelve months' notice after the 1st of August, 1764. It was also determined to stop up all loop-holes in the Act of 1709; and the following clause was inserted in the Act, Statute 1742, c. 13, s. 5:

"And to prevent any doubts that may arise concerning the privilege or power given by former acts of Parliament to the said Governor and Company of *exclusive* BANKING; and also in regard to the erecting of any other bank or banks by Parliament, or restraining other persons from banking, during the continuance of the said privilege granted to the Governor and Company of the Bank of England, as before cited; it is hereby further enacted and declared by the authority aforesaid, that it is the true intent and meaning of the act that no other bank shall be erected, established or allowed by Parliament; and that it shall not be lawful for any body politic or corporate whatsoever, united or to be united, in covenants or partnership exceeding the number of six persons, in that part of Great Britain called England *to borrow, owe, or take up any sum or sums of money, on their bills or notes payable at demand, or at any less time than six months from the borrowing thereof,* during the continuance of such said privilege of the said Governor and Company, who are hereby declared to be and remain a corporation, with the privilege of *exclusive* BANKING, as before recited."

This clause demands the most earnest attention, because it is the one which contains the sole monopoly of the Bank of England, which has recently attracted considerable attention. It is a penal clause, and therefore of course to be construed strictly; and we must now examine its force and effect. All "Banking" consists in "Issuing" rights of action, or credit in exchange for money and securities. When a banker has once issued this right of action, credit or deposit, to his customer, the customer may transfer this right of action to any one else by two methods: (1) Either by the banker giving him his promissory note to pay the money to himself, or to his order or to bearer; (2) The customer may write a note to his banker, in modern language termed a cheque, directing him to pay a sum to some person, or to his order or to bearer. Now, Parliament undoubtedly intended to confer an absolute monopoly of banking on the Bank of England; and if it had been enacted in general terms that the bank was to have an absolute monopoly of "banking," such words would have been effectual. But, unfortunately for their own purpose, though fortunately for the country, they proceeded to define "banking," and they restricted their definition to only one of the two methods of circulating bank credits—that of bank notes. Consequently, the monopoly was restricted to that single method of circulating banking credits and left the other method,—by means of cheques,—untouched. The fact was that, at that time, the system of cheques was very undeveloped, and no one conceived that "banking" could be carried on without issuing notes, as indeed the fact was in those days. But subsequently cheques prevailed over notes; and when it was afterwards discovered that "banking" could be carried on without notes, the *lacuna* in the monopoly of the bank became clear to lynx-eyed economists, and ultimately led to the formation of joint stock banks in London.

In September, 1745, the rising in Scotland assumed formidable dimensions. The Chevalier captured Edinburgh, and the news produced a run upon the bank. Bank notes fell to a discount of ten per cent. A meeting of 1600 of the most eminent merchants was held, who pledged themselves to support the credit of the bank notes. In 1746, the bank again assisted the Government. The proprietors authorized the directors to cancel £986,000 of exchequer bills on receiving an annuity of four per cent., and to create new stock for the purpose. The capital of the bank then became £10,780,000, and was not further increased till 1782. In 1750, the interest on £8,486,000 of the Government debt was reduced to three per cent. In 1759, the bank began to issue notes for £15 and £10. In 1764, the bank's charter was renewed. The terms were an absolute gift of £110,000 to the nation, and a loan of £1,000,000, on exchequer bills for two years at three per cent. interest.

SECTION III.

AN ERA OF NATIONAL DEVELOPMENT.

Great Industrial and Engineering Progress Follows the Peace of 1763—Introduction of a Vast Canal System—Bank's Monopoly Prevents Required Increase in Note Circulation—Hence Came an Overwhelming Crop of Rotten Private Issues—Great Expansion of Foreign Trade—Suspension of Specie Payments—Bank Charter Extended Under Pitt's Administration.

THE termination of the seven years' war took place in 1763, when it is usually said that this country took that place in the scale of nations which she at present holds. After long and doubtful contests, in which victory often trembled in the balance, the star of England triumphed over that of France, both in the East and in the West. Coincidently with this, the industrial energies and mechanical genius of the nation burst forth with unparalleled splendor. Previously to this time, England was probably more backward in great public works than any State in Europe. She could show nothing to compare with the great engineering works of France and Spain. Spain owed the canal of the Ebro to the genius of Charles V. The first canal in France preceded the first canal in England by 150 years. The great canal of Languedoc was completed upwards of half a century before the smallest canal was begun in England. In Italy, Gerbert, the morning star of literature and science, was famous for his hydraulic works in A. D. 999. Those of Lombardy, executed in the eleventh century, are still the admiration of modern engineers. The first act for a work of this nature, however small, in England was passed in 1755. Facility, quickness and cheapness of transit are the very foundations of commercial greatness. Brindley, the father of the modern commercial greatness of England, completed the canal from Worsley to Manchester in 1762. This was as prodigious a stride in advance of the age as the opening of the railway from Manchester to Liverpool was in its day. The success of this was triumphant. Then commenced the great era of canal making. Within twenty-five years, the country was covered with such a network of canals as no other country but Holland can boast. Considering the comparative wealth of the country at the two periods, the period from 1770 to 1795 was fully as wonderful an effort in canal making as the period from 1830 to 1855 was in railway building. Concurrently with this prodigious extension of the facilities of transport, an equal extension of the powers of production took place. It would almost seem like a dispensation of Providence that at this particular period such an extraordinary outburst of mechanical genius took place. It would almost seem that these three men—Brindley, Arkwright and Watt—were specially raised up by Providence to elaborate those miraculous resources, which it is impossible to doubt carried this country triumphantly through that terrific contest which was then about to burst upon the world.

It was just at this period that the original sin of the monopoly of the Bank of England began to tell with full force on the country. Now were the seeds of future ruin, misery and desolation sown broadcast throughout the land. The prodigious development of all these industrial works demanded a great extension of the currency to carry them out. What was required was, to have banks of undoubted wealth and solidity to issue such a currency. Bank of England notes had no circulation beyond London. Its monopoly prevented any other great banks being founded either in London or the country, and it would not establish branches in the provinces. England required to have a currency, and as she could not have a good one, she had a bad one. Multitudes of miserable shopkeepers in the country—grocers, tailors, drapers—started up in all directions as "bankers," and issued their notes, inundating the country with their miserable rags, in many parts as low as a shilling. Burke says that, when he came to London in 1759, there were not twelve bankers out of London; in 1793 there were nearly 400. It is no doubt true that many of the most respectable banking firms of the present day took their rise at this time, but they were comparatively speaking few. The great majority were such as we have described. Nevertheless these great engineering works were executed by means of the notes of these bankers; and though afterwards they failed by scores, the solid works remained. In 1775, an act was passed to prohibit bankers from issuing notes of less than 20s., and two years afterwards of less than £5. In 1782, the unhappy war with our American colonies was fortunately terminated; and immediately a prodigious extension of foreign commerce, which had been previously unusually restricted, took place. The enormous markets thrown open led to extravagant overtrading, which was greatly fostered by incautious issues by the bank, and a very alarming drain of specie, which produced a crisis, threatened to compel them to stop payment. The directors however considered that, if they could restrain their issues for a short period, the returns in specie in payment of the exports would soon set in, in a more rapid manner than they went out. They made no communication to the Government, but they contracted their issues until the exchanges turned in their favor. The alarm felt by the bank was greatest in May, 1783. They then refused to make any advances to Government on the loan of the year;

but they did not make any demand for payment of the other advances to Government, which were then between nine and ten millions. They continued this policy up till October, when at length the drain had ceased from the country, and money had begun to flow in from abroad. At length, when the exchanges had turned in their favor, they advanced freely to Government on the loan; although at that time the cash in the bank was actually lower than at the time when they felt the greatest apprehension. It was then reduced to £473,000. Mr. Bosanquet said that the doctrine which guided the directors was this: that while a drain of specie was going on their issues should be contracted as much as possible; but that as soon as the tide had given signs of ceasing and turning the other way, it was safe to extend their issues freely. This policy was entirely successful, and it saved the credit of the bank.

In 1793, occurred the first of those great monetary panics which shook the country to its foundations, and have occurred periodically: but we think it better to defer notice of it until we come to treat of monetary panics in general. It was in 1793 that London bankers, after experiencing their ill effects in the great panic, discontinued issuing their own notes and restricted their customers to cheques. This proceeding attracted no notice at the time, but produced the most momentous consequences in English banking some forty years later.

The suspension of cash payments in 1797, which will be fully detailed hereafter, naturally produced the warmest discussions in Parliament. Sir William Pulteney spoke with great ability against the national evils and inconveniences of the monopoly of banking by one company, and moved for leave to bring in a bill to establish another bank, unless the Bank of England resumed cash payments by the 24th of June; but the interests arrayed against him were so strong that leave to bring in the bill was refused by a majority of fifty to fifteen. The arguments and ability of Sir William Pulteney in advocating the foundation of another bank produced a great effect, and during 1799 it excited great public interest. Meetings were held to promote it, and numerous pamphlets were published in support of it. The directors of the bank took alarm; and as the Minister was in want of a supply, they took advantage of his necessities to obtain a prolongation of their monopoly. The charter had still twelve years to run; but upon their advancing £3,000,000, without interest for six years, Mr. Pitt agreed to renew it for twenty-one years from 1812. In 1800, an act to effect this was passed.

SECTION IV.

STATE OF THE IRISH CURRENCY.

An Era of Theory—Bad State of the Irish Currency—Lord King's Law of Currency—A Parliamentary Committee on the State of the Currency of Ireland—Testimony Before the Committee—Strange Incongruities of Evidence—Recommendations of the Committee.

WE have now to enter upon a new era, as it were, in banking. During the eighteenth century, the bank had not been managed on theories, but by rule of thumb; and though there had been several commercial crises, there had never been any general monetary panics till 1793. But since 1800, the bank had been managed on a succession of theories, each of which was considered as the acme of human wisdom by its own generation, and was condemned as the *ne plus ultra* of human folly by the next.

A few years after the suspension of cash payments in 1797, bank notes suffered a serious depreciation, which gave rise to several important pamphlets on paper money; among others to Lord King's Law of Paper Money. This however passed away. The bank note recovered its value to a considerable extent, and discussion died out. In 1804, the Irish currency was in a dreadful state. The Bank of Ireland having been directed to suspend payments in cash at the same time as the Bank of England, issued notes with extravagant profusion. The foreign exchanges fell and the price of guineas rose. This led to the appointment of a committee of the House of Commons to inquire into the state of the Irish currency, of which we must give some account. In the space of six years after the suspension, the directors had increased their issues to nearly five times the amount they were before the restriction. For, while on the 1st of January, 1797, they were £627,917, by November, 1803, they were £2,911,628. The exchange between London and Dublin fell very rapidly in proportion to these increased issues.

At this time, the Irish shilling was 13d., and as both the Irish and English pounds were 240d., £100 sterling was equal to £108 6s. 8d. Irish currency.

The par of exchange between Ireland and England was called 8 1-3. Hence, when the exchange was *favorable* to Ireland, it was below 8 1-3; when it was *above* 8 1-3, it was adverse. During the first year of the restriction, the exchange between London and Dublin was 7, and therefore favorable to Ireland. But immediately after that it began to fall; at the end of 1798 it was 9 1-4; at the close of 1799 it had fallen to 14 1-4. After some fluctuations, in November, 1803, it stood at 19, and was therefore highly unfavorable to Ireland. At this time, the note issues of the Bank of Ireland were £2,911,-628. This extraordinary derangement of the exchanges was productive of the utmost mischief and confusion to all commerce; and, Lord King states, was repeatedly brought before Parliament in the debates as the Irish Bank Restriction Bill. It also forcibly attracted the notice of economists. In 1803 and 1804, Lord King and Mr. Parnell, afterwards Lord Congleton, published most able pamphlets supporting the doctrine that the depression of the exchange below the cost of transmitting bullion from one place to the other was the proof and the measure of the depreciation of the paper currency. Both these pamphlets deserve the most attentive study, because they most clearly and unanswerably establish the great fundamental law of paper money, which many persons most unjustly attribute to Ricardo, in 1809.

This great law which we have designated *Lord King's Law of Paper Money*, because he bore the most conspicuous part in establishing it, is this: "*A rise of the market or paper price of gold above the Mint price, and a fall in the foreign exchanges beyond the cost of sending bullion from one place to another, is the proof and the measure of the depreciation of the paper money.*" Lord King also showed most forcibly the fallacy of Adam Smith's doctrine, that as long as the issues of bank notes are confined to the discount of mercantile bills, founded upon real transactions and of undoubted solidity, they could not exceed the amount which would necessarily circulate if the currency were purely metallic, and therefore could not be excessive. This doctrine was stoutly maintained by the directors of the Bank of Ireland before the committee of the House of Commons, and by the directors of the Bank of England before the Bullion Committee of 1810. The doctrine is very specious, but is wholly delusive, and Lord King has the merit of having first shown its fallacy. In 1804, the extravagant issues of the country bankers and others reached such an intolerable height, that all the monetary transactions between Dublin and London were destroyed; while those between Belfast (where nothing but specie was tolerated) and London were perfectly regular. Lord Archibald Hamilton called the attention of the House very strongly to the evils of the excessive issues of paper. In 1797, when the first Irish restriction bill was passed, the issues of the Bank of Ireland were £600,000; they were then £2,700,000. While the par of exchange between Ireland and London was 8 1-3, it was then 17, 18, 19 and even 20. Thus an Irish gentleman who came to attend to his duty in Parliament, after he had allotted £500 for his expenses, found at the end of his journey that he had only £400 to receive. On the 2d of March, 1804, Mr. Foster moved for a committee to inquire into this monetary derangement. He said that guineas were then at a premium of 2s. 4d. and 2s. 6d. in the current paper of the country; and, to whatever causes it might be attributed, the whole bank paper of Ireland was then at a discount of ten per cent. There was scarcely anything in the shape of money to be seen; but a miserable coinage of adulterated copper and of counterfeit shillings, so bad that for a £1 note, even at its depreciated state, 26 or 27 of such shillings would be given in exchange.

The circumstances which caused the appointment of this committee and its report are deserving of great attention, because it was the first investigation by a Parliamentary Committee into the theory of the paper currency; and they are the antitype of what occurred afterwards in England, and gave rise to the appointment of the Bullion Committee in 1810. The evidence of the state of the currency of Ireland given before the committee was most extraordinary. Mr. D'Olier, a director of the Bank of Ireland, had some of the base currency in circulation weighed. He found that it took 126s. to the pound weight; such as remained of the old Mint issues weighed 94s. 6d. to the pound—the Mint weight being 62s. to the pound. He estimated that the best of the base silver shillings were not worth 6d. and the worst about 3d. The makers of the base coinage sold it to persons who had an opportunity of circulating it at the rate of 28s. to 35s. the guinea.

Mr. Roach said that, in the south of Ireland, the silver currency had entirely disappeared from circulation, and its place was supplied by the issue of silver notes. These, together with the increasing issue of bankers' notes of all descriptions, had enhanced the price of all articles of the export trade above their natural value, and had created a degree of false credit in the southern parts of Ireland, which increased the price of land and everything else. These issues of silver notes were constantly increasing, especially during the last twelve months. There was in reality a very good supply of real silver in the south of Ireland, which was hoarded and concealed, and which would again come into circulation, if these silver notes were suppressed. Traders almost universally issued notes for 3s. 9 1-2d. and 6s., payable to bearer at twenty-one days after date, to evade the law.

Mr. Colville, a director of the Bank of Ireland, said there might be some small proportion of Mint silver, greatly worn, in circulation in Dublin, but not more than two per cent. This had been gradually getting worse and worse for more than five years. Crowns and half-crowns, originally issued from the Mint, were not circulated, but kept as curiosities; and from the high state of the exchange, the best pieces were carefully picked out for exportation. There were at this time in Ireland seven bankers issuing notes; twenty-eight issuers of gold and silver notes; sixty-two issuers of silver notes; and 128 issuers of I. O. U.'s. In the Youghal district alone, there were seventy issuers of currency, of which sixty-two issued I. O. U.'s from 6s. down to 3 1-2d.

In the north of Ireland, where nothing but gold was current, the exchange at Belfast with London had always continued favorable to Belfast; and even while the exchange at Dublin was progressively sinking, the exchange at Belfast continued to rise. From 1794 to the end of 1798, the exchange had been invariably favorable to Dublin, being generally about 7 1-2, and sometimes even so high as 5; but at the end of 1798 it fell to 9; in December, 1799, it fell to 14; but it being expected that Bank of England notes would be substituted for those of the Bank of Ireland, it rose to 9. From this time, it gradually fell to 18 and 19 in January, 1804, when the matter was brought before the House.

The following figures exhibit the difference of the exchange on London between Dublin, where all the currency was paper, and Belfast, where it was all specie:

1802.	DUBLIN.			BELFAST.		
Average of	£	s.	d.	£	s.	d.
1st Quarter,	11	5	11	6	13	4
2d "	11	11	3	7	15	0
3d "	11	2	7	8	0	10
4th "	10	13	5	7	3	9
1803.						
1st Quarter,	11	1	9	7	12	6
2d "	13	8	11	8	8	8
3d "	15	17	0	7	12	6
4th "	15	8	7	5	12	6
1804.						
January 27,	18	0	0	6	0	0

At Newry, which was a kind of debatable land between specie and paper, the exchange upon London, according as bills were purchased with specie or bank notes, was as follows:

	SPECIE.			BANK NOTES.		
1803.	£	s.	d.	£	s.	d.
January,	7	17	6	12	17	6
April,	8	0	0	13	0	0
July,	8	10	0	13	10	0
October,	6	0	0	15	10	0
1804.						
January,	6	0	0	15	10	0

In 1696, the extremely depreciated state of the silver coinage had turned the exchanges greatly against the country. But it was a principle perfectly well understood at that time, that the real exchange between any two places could never vary by more than the cost of sending bullion from one place to the other. The question, therefore, before the committee was, to what could the extraordinary state of the exchange at Dublin upon London be owing? What could be the reason of the difference of the rates between

Dublin and Belfast? Some of the witnesses declared that it was owing to the over-issues of paper in Dublin. The directors of the Bank of Ireland indignantly denied that the bank's notes were depreciated. Mr. Colville being asked what could be the motive for so large an increase of its issues, from £600,000 to £3,000,000 in so short a time, said, that the course of exchange about two years after the restriction having become very high, and greatly against Ireland, the money of the country was carried out of it, for the purpose of paying the balance of remittances against Ireland; that as the gold decreased, it became necessary to supply its place with paper. This amount he placed at £1,200,000. He contended that it was a great error to suppose that the increased issues caused the raising of the exchange, as was often done. In his opinion it was directly the reverse, inasmuch as the paper enabled the gold which before stood in its place to be exported; and as far as it went in weight and measure, so far was it a clear and decided cause of preventing the exchange getting higher than it was. It was evident, he said, that the more paper issued by the bank in extension of loans enabled a greater drain of specie to take place, and consequently to strengthen the cause which kept down the rate of exchange. Mr. Colville repeatedly said that the state of the exchange was exclusively due to the fact that Ireland owed a great deal more money than she was able to pay. Mr. Colville's evidence was an amusing specimen of reasoning in a vicious circle. He decidedly held that the sole cause of the unfavorable state of the exchange was that Ireland owed a heavy balance of payments to Great Britain. And, being asked what was his criterion of such a heavy balance being due, he said it was the state of the exchange. That is, the *reason* why the exchange was unfavorable was that Ireland owed money; and the *proof* that Ireland owed money was that the exchange was unfavorable. Admirable logic! He admitted that the rate of exchange would be influenced if degraded and adulterated coin was the medium in which the balance of debt was paid; but he strenuously denied that such views in any way applied to Bank of Ireland paper.

The directors maintained that it was no proof that Bank of Ireland paper was depreciated because gold was bought at a premium. They maintained that buying gold at a premium was the effect and not the cause of the exchange, and, therefore, no proof of the depreciation of the paper. The theory of these gentlemen was that the exchange could only be depressed on account of money being remitted; and that it might be depressed to any extent in proportion to the money which had to be remitted. Now, if this theory was true, it happened, as may be seen from the above figures, that while the exchange was adverse to Dublin, it was highly favorable to Belfast. Therefore, while large remittances were being made from Dublin to London, there were at the same time large remittances being made from London to Belfast! The phenomena at Newry were more astounding still; for at that place, where payments were made both in specie and in paper, the exchange if paid in specie was favorable to Newry; but if paid in paper was favorable to London. Consequently, that reasoning would show that Newry was largely in debt to London, and London was largely in debt to Newry!

Mr. Colville fully admitted that, before the restriction, the bank was obliged to contract its issues during an unfavorable exchange and a drain of guineas; and also that the directors would have been very unfit for their business if they had not done so. The gist of the evidence of several of the witnesses was that, before the restriction, the directors had felt the necessity of contracting their issues during an adverse exchange, no matter how good the bills presented for discount were. But after the restriction, they adopted different principles. Then the doctrine of Adam Smith was brought forward, which we have noticed above as having been denounced by Lord King—viz., that the bank's issues could not be excessive, so long as they were advanced on mercantile bills of undoubted solidity, and based on a real transaction. This was a very plausible theory, and was stoutly maintained afterwards by the directors of the Bank of England before the Bullion Committee. But the very admission of the directors that it was incapable of being acted upon, so long as cash payments were maintained, was sufficient to condemn it.

In 1696, during the re-coinage of the silver money, the Bank of England stopped payment, and a difference of twenty per cent. arose between specie and paper, and between tallies and specie of forty per cent.; and it was universally said that bank notes and tallies were at a discount of twenty and forty per cent. respectively. There is no trace of any other language being applied to them. In 1804, the Bank of Ireland had suspended cash payments; and Irish bank notes and specie exchanged at a difference of ten per cent.; so that it required a guinea note and 2s. 6d. in specie to buy a guinea in specie. The statesmen and merchants of 1696 would have expressed this state of things by saying that Irish bank notes had fallen to a discount of ten per cent. But at this period, a new mode of expressing it was discovered. It was stoutly maintained that it was not the paper which was depreciated; but the gold which had risen in value! or was appreciated, as the jargon was. When those directors maintained that a rise in the price of gold was no more a proof of the depreciation of the note than the rise in the price of any other commodity, they did not remember that a bank note is a "promise to pay" gold, and is not a promise to pay anything else. The same opinions were expressed by other witnesses, who seemed to think that there could be no possible cause which influenced the rate of exchange, but the remittances to be made to or from the country. They totally forgot, what was fully understood in 1696, that a bad state of the coinage influenced the rate of exchange, as well as the remittances to be made. When we consider the nature of an exchange, and the state of facts proved with regard to the Irish coinage at that time, we might almost smile at these ideas, and attribute them to the peculiar modes of thinking which are sometimes prevalent on the western side of St. George's Channel. But when a precisely similar state of things took place in England with regard to the foreign exchanges, the very same doctrines were long and stoutly maintained by a very numerous party in this country.

One thing, however, made the investigation of the subject much simpler in Ireland than in England. In England, the use of bank paper extended throughout the whole country, and the exchanges were reckoned solely in bank notes. No part of the country used specie. But in Ireland, Dublin and the South used bank paper exclusively; Belfast and the North specie exclusively; and Newry used both specie and paper. The distinction between the two was therefore open and manifest. One very clear-headed witness, however, Mr. Marshall, Inspector-General of imports and exports of Ireland, controverted all these views. Upon considering the facts detailed above, he was clearly of opinion that Irish bank notes were depreciated from over-issue. Mr. Marshall also showed most clearly that the real exchange, arising from a balance of payments, was in favor of Ireland; and not adverse, as appeared by the nominal exchange. The exchange appeared to be against Dublin, because it was computed in bank notes, which, having ceased to represent the full quantity of specie for which they were issued, required an additional number of them to make up that quantity. This additional number swelled the exchange, and made it appear to be against Dublin, when it was in reality in its favor. The proof that the real exchange was in favor of Dublin was very simple. Bills of exchange purchased with specie in Dublin, or with Bank of Ireland notes equal in amount to specie at their market price, would then yield about £1 16s. 8d. more in London than they cost in Dublin. Whereas, if the exchange was unfavorable to Dublin, a merchant would always get more for his bill in Dublin than in London. This fact decisively proved that the real exchange was in favor of Dublin. Mr. Marshall then entered into a masterly analysis of the exchanges, showing that the depreciation of the note commenced when specie was flowing into Ireland; that it was always depreciated, whether specie was flowing in or flowing out, and had never been influenced by the balance of debt. He maintained that the high exchange which then existed arose like all other permanently high exchanges which ever existed, from the depreciated state of the currency in which bills of exchange were purchased.

The report of the committee condemned in the strongest terms the opinions of the Irish Bank directors and merchants, and adopted those of Mr. Marshall. It declared that the difference in the rates of exchange when paid in specie and in paper was due entirely to the depreciation of paper; that guineas were the true standard to which the value of the circulating paper was to be referred. It was not to be supposed that, by any circumstances, guineas could be ten per cent. higher in Ireland than in England, when the expense of conveying them from one country to the other was not so much as one per cent. From the official accounts it was certain that the balance of payments due to Ireland was about two and one-half millions; consequently the real exchange ought to be, and was, under par. The Irish Restriction Act was adopted purely for English considerations. There was no drain of specie; the exchange was highly favorable to Ireland; nor had the Bank of Ireland any reason to dread any alarming demand on it, as the Bank of England had. The committee attributed the unfavorable state of the exchange to the consequences of that restriction. It compelled the bank to refrain from sending gold, the only common medium between the two countries, into circulation. Paper was issued to supply the place of the gold so withdrawn; and at the same time the best and most effective check against the depreciation of paper—namely, convertibility into gold at the will of the holder—was removed. By being released from its engagements, the bank was encouraged to make excessive issues. The natural and constant effect of an adverse exchange, correcting itself by diminishing the issue of paper, was counteracted by this measure. When the exchange was so adverse as to draw gold out of the country, for every guinea drawn out of the bank an equal quantity of paper must be paid to buy the guineas. The directors would also be probably induced to lessen their discounts, so that the paper would be reduced in a greater degree than the gold withdrawn.

Mr. Colville admitted that, before the restriction, such was the practice of the Bank of Ireland and of every other bank. If prudence had not dictated such a course, necessity would have compelled a diminution of issues, by diminishing the stock of specie, which could only be replaced at a loss proportionate to the existing rise of exchange; and in fact, as well as in theory, the result of such practice always was, and must be, the redress of the unfavorable exchange. But the Restriction Act freed the directors from that necessity; and, so far from contracting their issues in consequence of the unfavorable exchange, they had increased them, which the state of the exchange would have prevented them from doing if they had not been relieved from the necessity of paying their notes in cash. The fact of the excessive issues of paper in 1753-4, and the adverse exchange which accompanied it, proved that excessive issues of paper produced a corresponding rise in the rate of exchange; and when the excess of paper was annihilated by the failure of the bankers, the exchange immediately became favorable. The reason was obvious: the nominal rates of exchange are influenced by the medium in which the payments are made, and the quantity of that medium necessary to effect a given payment must be increased as the value of the medium diminishes. This must equally take place, whether the payments are made in a degraded or adulterated coin or in a depreciated paper. The exchange between London and Holland in 1694 was a case in point. The currency of England was then degraded twenty-five per cent. below its proper value, and the exchange with Holland was twenty-five per cent. against England. As soon as the coin was reformed the exchange fell to par. If paper, therefore, by depreciation comes to represent a less quantity of money than it professes to do, it must make the exchange which it has to pay appear unfavorable, in the same manner as coin which contained less gold than it ought would do. And the removal of the degradation in the one case and of the depreciation in the other would have the same effect in bringing the exchange to its true state.

It was probable that this depreciation in Ireland arose almost entirely, if not solely, from excessive issues of paper. The rise in the exchange was concomitant with the extended issues of the bank. In March, 1797, the issues of the bank were under £700,000, and the exchange on Dublin was 5 1-2 to 6 3-4. In April, 1801, the paper was £2,266,000, and the exchange rose to 11 3-4 and 13. In January, 1804, the paper was £2,986,999, and the exchange rose to 17 and 18. How far these increased issues from the Bank of Ireland facilitated an increase from private bankers was not clearly proved, but it certainly did so to an immense extent; silver notes and I O U's especially, were issued with the greatest profusion. In 1799, the number of bankers issuing notes was eleven; in 1800, there were twenty-three; in 1801, there were twenty-nine; in 1802, there were thirty; and in 1803, there were forty. In 1799, the issues of the private bankers were £450,721; in 1800, £458,085; in 1801, £1,233,502; in 1802, £1,096,207; and in 1803, £1,457,283. These immense issues, along with the profusion of silver notes and the base and counterfeit coin, kept up the prices of all necessaries and manufactures, drove out of circulation what little good silver was in it, and above all kept up a high and unexampled rate of exchange against the kingdom, unwarranted in its height and continuance by any other great or adequate cause than that depreciation, which such extravagant issues had assisted. The total number of houses that issued tokens and notes, according to the best accounts they could procure, was considerably above two hundred. Mr. Beresford, a Dublin banker, estimated that the country issues had increased four-fold since the restriction.

The repeal of the Restriction Act, from which all these evils flowed, would undoubtedly be the great and effectual remedy for the high and fluctuating rates of exchange. The common medium of payment being thereby restored, the rise of exchange above par would be limited to the expense of transporting specie; and paper being convertible into gold, its depreciation would be prevented. The inconveniences, however, to which the Bank of Ireland and other banks would be exposed, if such a measure were suddenly adopted at the present rate of exchange, was a strong argument against its being done then. But there was no commercial reason against its being done, as the real exchange was undoubtedly in favor of Ireland. Seeing, however, that the repeal of restriction could not be expected at that time, other measures might be adopted to cure the evil. One was that the Bank of Ireland might give bills of exchange on London for its paper. This would certainly have the effect of rectifying the exchange. The bank objected to the difficulty and expense of establishing a fund for that purpose. But the argument had no weight, because the expense of this would not be so great as the bank was subject to before the restriction, in order to maintain the convertibility of its notes, and which they must again incur when the restriction should be removed. Besides, the Scotch banks had done the very same thing with the greatest success. The Scotch currency had never varied from par since they had organized a measure of this sort, even during periods of great discredit, and no restriction had been imposed upon them, as it was on the banks of England and Ireland.

The undoubted success of this measure in the case of the Scotch banks was a strong argument that the Bank of Ireland should do the same thing. And there was a stronger argument still why the Bank of Ireland should do it. The Scotch banks, of their own good sense and patriotism, organized this measure without a precedent, and provided a fund at their own expense. But the Bank of Ireland had now an opportunity of doing it without any risk, difficulty or expense. The sums to be remitted during that year from England to Ireland amounted to £5,000,000 Irish. This sum, or a portion of it, might be appropriated for that purpose. It might be paid into the Bank of England to the credit of the Bank of Ireland, and though no doubt it would be an expense to that bank, it would furnish a fund to draw upon, by which it would effectually control the exchange, and the evil of the expense would be temporary: the good would be permanent to the bank and to the public. But all the benefits derived from these remedies would be of little avail and of very short duration if they did not at the same time cure the depreciation of Irish paper by diminishing its over-issue. This consequence must necessarily follow from Bank of Ireland notes being made convertible into Bank of England notes, almost as they would be into gold, if the restriction were to cease. For, if their fund in London were too rapidly drawn upon at any time, they must immediately limit their issues to lessen the demand; the notes would become of equal value with the English notes, and therefore with guineas, so long as the English notes were at par. The committee did, in express terms, declare their clear opinion that it was incumbent on the directors of the Bank of Ireland, and their indispensable duty, to limit their paper at all times of an unfavorable exchange during the continuance of the restriction, exactly on the same principle as they would, and must have done, in case the restriction did not exist; and that all the evils of a high and fluctuating exchange were to be imputed to them if they failed to do so. The effect which making Bank of England notes procurable in Ireland would have on the exchange was clearly shown by the great fall in it in March, April and May, 1797, when Government passed Bank of England notes in Dublin. They recommended that the Irish currency should be equalized with the English, by making the Irish shilling 12d. before any new coinage was struck, and that the English copper coinage should be as current in Ireland as the silver and gold coinage.

This admirable report is the first Parliamentary investigation into the theory of a paper currency; and is the first authoritative declaration that it ought to be governed by the foreign exchanges. In this it fully adopted the truths demonstrated by Mr. Boyd, Lord King and Mr. Parnell, and is in entire accordance with the more celebrated Bullion Report of 1810. These two reports are the most masterly papers which were ever drawn by Parliamentary committees. This report did not discuss the new theory propounded, that the paper currency should be regulated by the discount of mercantile bills. The Bullion Committee did, and entirely condemned it.

SECTION V.

FAILURE OF CURRENCY REFORM—INFLATION AND REACTION.

Napoleon's Berlin Decree Starts a Great Commercial Speculation—Spread of Joint Stock Enterprises—The Bank Encourages Inflation—Country Banks Trebled in Number—They Issue £30,000,000 of Notes—Gold Bullion Rises—A War of Pamphlets—The Bullion Committee Appointed—Defeat of the Committee's Report—Great Inflation of Prices—A Violent Reaction and Failures—Suspension of Provincial Banks—The Peel Act of 1819—The Bank's Monopoly Broken in 1826—Private and Stock Banks Allowed to Issue—Withdrawal of £1 Notes.

IN 1807, speculation burst out with redoubled fury. Napoleon's Berlin decree, placing the whole of Great Britain under a paper blockade, and interdicting all commerce between all nations under his influence with Great Britain, was met with equally insane counter decrees by Great Britain. These decrees caused violent changes in the value of a multitude of commodities; and, as a natural consequence, immense speculation in them. The deposition of the House of Braganza from the throne of Portugal was followed by their emigration to the Brazils. This opened out the whole of the South American markets to British commerce, which had hitherto been closed against it. The speculation of the merchants swelled in proportion to the vastness of the markets opened up to them. A complete frenzy of speculation seized upon the nation. It spread from commerce to joint stock companies. The infatuation in 1720 was reproduced. Joint stock companies of every conceivable sort started up like mushrooms. At the same time the Bank of England fanned the flame of speculation beyond all the bounds of ordinary rashness. Sir Francis Baring said in his evidence before the Bullion Committee, that since the restriction, he knew of many clerks not worth £100 who had turned merchants, and got discount accounts from £5000 to £10,000 from the bank, which could not be done if it were not for the restriction. The paper discounted by the bank, which had been £2,946,500 in 1795, rose to £15,475,700 in 1809, and to £20,070,600 in 1810.

Along with this extravagant speculation, partly caused by it, and partly fanning it, a multitude of country banks started up in all directions and inundated the country with their notes, exactly as had happened before 1793. In the year 1797 they had been reduced to 270; in 1808 they had increased to 600; and in 1810, when the Bullion Committee was appointed, they amounted to 721; and the quantity of paper they put into circulation was supposed to amount to £30,000,000. At the same time the Bank of England had increased its issue to £21,000,000, a quantity declared by some of the most eminent witnesses far to exceed the legitimate wants of the country.

Concurrently with these extravagant speculations and issues of notes, the price of gold bullion rose rapidly, and the foreign exchanges fell with great rapidity—exactly the same symptoms as had been manifested in Ireland in 1804. Mr. Baring said that guineas sold for 26s. A celebrated war of pamphlets broke out. When the value of bank notes in 1797 had differed from specie, it had been universally said that bank notes had fallen to a discount. But in 1809, when exactly the same phenomena took place, an ingenious and powerful party made the wonderful discovery that it was not bank notes which had fallen, but gold that had risen! A host of writers, among whom one of the most distinguished was Ricardo, who now first appeared as a writer, maintained that bank notes were at a discount, which was caused by their excessive issues. The following figures, taken at intervals, are sufficient to show the rapid rise in the price of bullion and the fall in the foreign exchanges:

	Price of Sterling Gold.			Price of Silver.		Exchanges with Hamburg.	
	£	s.	d.	s.	d.	s.	d.
January, 1805	4	0	0	5	4	35	6
October, 1805	4	0	0	5	5	33	9
July, 1808	No quotation			5	3	34	9
February, 1809	4	10	0	5	3	31	0
May, 1809	4	11	0	5	5	29	6
January, 1810	No quotation			5	7	28	6

On the 1st of February, 1810, on the motion of Mr. Horner, the famous Bullion Committee was appointed.

The Bullion Report of 1810 has, from various circumstances, attracted so much public attention, as to have thrown completely into the shade the Report on Irish Currency in 1804. That report was soon so forgotten that the Directors of the Bank of England seem to have had no knowledge of it. The circumstances, however, of the derangement of the Irish currency in 1804 were precisely similar with those of the English currency in 1810. The same sets of opinions were delivered and adhered to stoutly by the professional witnesses in both cases, and the report of the committee in each case was precisely identical. In each case they condemned the doctrines and policy of the bank directors in the most emphatic manner. The report of the Bullion Committee of 1810 is written in a more methodical and scientific form, and is superior as a literary performance, but the principles adopted and enforced in it are absolutely identical with those of the report of 1804.

The witnesses examined before both committees consisted of the same varieties: bank directors, private bankers, general merchants and independent witnesses. The opinions given by the English bank directors and merchants were precisely similar to those of the Irish bank directors and merchants. The directors of both banks vehemently repudiated the idea that the bank paper was depreciated; they equally maintained that it was the price of specie which had risen; they both admitted that while they were liable to pay their notes in specie, they were obliged to regulate their issues by the foreign exchanges and the price of bullion; they both admitted that since the restriction they had paid no attention to their former rules, and they denied the necessity of so doing. They both denied that the issues of their notes had any effect on the exchanges, or were in any way the cause of the high adverse exchange, and they both denied that a limitation of their issues would have the slightest effect in reducing the exchanges to par. They both maintained that there could be no over-issue of their notes so long as they were confined to the discount of paper of undoubted solidity, founded upon real transactions. Nothing can be more remarkable than the perfect identity in sentiment in every point of opinion and policy between these two sets of directors; but we must remark what will detract considerably from the weight of their opinion, that they were all *interested* witnesses. In the first place, since the restriction on cash payments, and so being relieved of fulfilling their obligations, they had extended their discounts enormously, and as their profits upon their extended issues had been proportionate, the dividends of the proprietors had greatly increased. Secondly, they were in the position of semi-defendants; their policy was certainly impugned. The committee was a court of inquiry into their conduct; and it certainly was not likely that they would admit that the principles they were acting upon could be wrong, when they were so very lucrative to the proprietors of the bank. The same objection of interested testimony equally applies to that of the merchants; for they were interested in obtaining as large an amount of accommodation from the bank as possible; and a restriction on its issues would have curtailed their operations, speculative or otherwise; consequently, their interests were better served by the doctrines and policy of the bank directors. Both committees, however, examined witnesses of an independent position, who had no interest one way or the other; and in each case they totally disagreed from the opinions and the doctrines of the bank directors, and condemned their policy. And in both cases the committee, having examined all these witnesses of different shades and of opposite opinions, presented reports strongly condemning the opinions and practice of the directors of each bank, and called upon them to alter their policy; the report in the Irish case in language of great severity; that in the English case equally strong in fact, though milder in expression.

As this division of opinion on these financial questions exercised the most momentous consequences on the welfare of the country, it will be of advantage to state shortly and precisely the points upon which the respective parties were at issue.

The facts were, of course, easily ascertained and agreed upon. They were as follows:

1. That the Mint price of gold bullion, or the legal standard of the coin, was £3 17s. 10 1-2d. per ounce. 2. That the market price of gold bullion was then £4 10s. per ounce. 3. That the foreign exchanges had fallen to a great extent—that with Hamburg, 9 per cent.; that with Paris, 14 per cent. 4. That the increase of bank notes had been very great during the last few years; and was rapidly augmenting. 5. That specie had disappeared from circulation.

Upon this acknowledged state of facts the opposite issues maintained by the two parties were as follows:

The one party maintained—

1. (*a*) That the bank notes were depreciated.

(*b*) That the difference between the market price and the Mint price of gold bullion was the measure of the depreciation.

2. (*a*) That the extreme limit to which the foreign exchanges could, by the nature of things, fall in any case, was defined and easily ascertained, and consisted of the expense of freight, insurance and some other minute causes.

(*b*) That, in the then state of the foreign exchanges, there was a very large excess of depression over and above that limit, which was not attributable to any of these causes.

(*c*) That this residual depression of the exchanges, and the rise of the market price above the Mint price of gold, was caused by the excessive issues of bank notes in circulation.

3. That a diminution on the quantity of bank notes would increase the value of the domestic currency, would cause the foreign exchanges to rise to par, and cause the market price of gold to fall to the Mint price.

4. That the Directors of the Bank of England ought to follow the same rules in the extent of their issues during the restriction of cash payments as they had been obliged to do before the restriction—namely, by regulating them by the foreign exchanges. When the exchanges were favorable and bullion flowing in, they might enlarge them; when the exchanges were adverse, they must contract them.

In opposition to these principles the other party maintained:

1. (*a*) That it was not the bank notes which had fallen, but specie which had risen.

(*b*) That there was no difference between the price of bullion, whether paid in bank notes or in specie.

2. That the depression in the exchanges was in no way whatever attributable to the depreciation of the currency, but was entirely caused by the adverse balance of payments to be made by Great Britain, the remittances to the army, the Continental measures of Napoleon and other political measures.

3. That no diminution or increase of the issues by the bank could have any effect whatever on the foreign exchanges, either in raising or depressing them, or on the market price of bullion.

4. That since the restriction there was no necessity for observing the same rules in issuing their notes by discounts as before—*i. e.*, by observing the course of the foreign exchanges; but that the public demand was the sole criterion; and so long as they adhered to these rules there could be no over-issue.

With respect to the first point at issue between the two parties, after the previous full exposition of the principles involved in it, we need say very little about it here, as according to what has already been said, it is quite clear that it was a very fantastic opinion indeed to suppose that gold could rise in comparison to a "promise to pay" gold. There was one circumstance, however, different in the cases of England and Ireland. In the latter country, the bank notes were openly at a discount; there were two prices in every transaction—a money price and a paper price; and there were specie shops where guineas were openly sold for bank notes and several shillings over. In England, this was not the case, partly because Bank of England notes were received at their full nominal value in payment of taxes; but chiefly because it was held to be an indictable offence to sell guineas for more than 21s. Shortly before the Bullion Committee was appointed, a man named De Yonge was tried and convicted for the crime of selling guineas for more than 21s. This law only applied to heavy guineas. Light guineas, below 5 dwts. 8 grns. might be sold, and usually brought a bank note of £1, and 6s. or 7s. over. But though it was supposed to be an offence to sell heavy guineas openly for more than 21s., there was abundant evidence to show that when persons were dealing privately they made a difference between payment in gold and payment in notes. However, De Yonge's conviction was afterwards quashed. As Mr. Huskisson said, the doctrine of those persons who held that bank notes were not depreciated was, that bank paper was the real and fixed measure of all commodities, and that gold was only one of the commodities of which the value, like that of all others, was to be determined and ascertained by reference to this invariable standard and universal equivalent, bank notes. These views pervaded the whole of the mercantile evidence adduced, the reply to which is so obvious. A bank note was the promise to pay a certain specified weight of gold of standard fineness; it did not promise to be of the value of any amount of indigo, broadcloth, corn, or anything else. A £1 bank note professed to be of the value, and to be exchangeable for 5 dwts. 3 grns. of standard gold, and nothing else; and if it would only purchase 4 dwts. 8 grns., those who maintained that it was not depreciated, must also have maintained that 4 dwts. 8 grns. were equal to 5 dwts. 3 grns. There is no escape from this conclusion. Those who maintained that a £1 bank note, which was a promise to pay 5 dwts. 4 grns. was still a "Pound" when it would only purchase 4 dwts. 8 grns., ought also to have maintained that if the fifth part were to leak out of a pint bottle of wine, it was still a "pint of wine" because it was contained in a pint bottle. In each case the "promise to pay" and the "pint bottle" were only the outward sign of what the contents ought to be; in either case, it was the quantity of the substance, either of gold or of wine, they actually did contain, which was their true value. There was, however, one argument to show that there was no difference between specie and paper in transactions; for specie had totally disappeared from circulation; it had no existence. Bank notes and tokens were the sole circulating medium of the country. When people found that they could get no more for their good golden guineas than for the depreciated bank notes, they hoarded them; they either retained them locked up, or melted them down for exportation—the temptation to perjury being exactly 12s. per ounce. The explanation of this phenomenon is very simple. When bank notes are convertible into gold at the will of the holder they cannot fall to a discount; and if bankers issue too great a quantity of them the holders demand gold. But when bank notes are inconvertible, they take rank as a new independent, substantive currency, exactly like silver. Now the relative value of gold and silver purely depends upon the law of supply and demand; and when their relative values are fixed by law, if the legal, or artificial value does not agree with the market, or natural value, it invariably happens that the metal which is undervalued disappears from circulation. So, also, when heavy and light coins of the same metal circulated together, the heavy coins invariably disappeared from circulation, because the heavy coins were undervalued; and nobody would give six ounces of silver for what they could purchase with five ounces.

It was exactly the same with inconvertible bank notes. They could only preserve their relative value with gold by preserving certain relative proportions in their quantity. As soon as this relative quantity was exceeded their relative value fell; and as their relative value for gold was fixed by law, a change in their market value was followed by exactly the same consequences as a difference between the market and the legal value of gold and silver. The guineas which were undervalued were driven out of circulation, as has always been done under similar circumstances, and as always will be done to the end of time. Thus this iniquitous and ignorant law to force down the value of guineas brought its own punishment with it. It destroyed their existence as a circulating medium. But then it became literally true that there was no difference between specie and paper; the power of making an invidious distinction between specie and paper was effectually cured. *Solitudinem faciunt, pacem appellant.* When the inhabitants were massacred, the Russians proclaimed: *L'ordre regne à Varsovie.*

With respect to the second issue joined between the parties, the principal places with which London had established exchanges were Amsterdam, Hamburg and Paris. The witnesses examined by the committee proved that the whole expenses of freight, insurance, war risk, and every other charge, varied from about four to five and a-half per cent.; but beyond these there was a depression of twelve to fourteen per cent., totally unaccountable for by any of these causes. If it were true that this difference arose from a demand for gold on the Continent, it is quite evident that gold should equally have risen in the Continental markets. But those who alleged this cause should have been prepared with a proof of their assertions, which, however, they were totally unable to produce. On the contrary, it was proved that there was no alteration in the Mint price of gold in foreign places, and that the market price had experienced no rise at all in proportion to the rise in England.

Of all the witnesses examined by the committee, one foreign merchant alone maintained in opposition to the English witnesses, that the rate of exchange was in no way due to the balance of payments due by England, but that it was solely due to the depreciation of the bank notes in which payments were made.

With respect to the third issue joined between the parties, nothing can be clearer than that a diminution in the quantity of paper in circulation must have enhanced its value relatively to all other commodities, gold included. And as the market price of gold was determined solely with reference to the price paid for it in bank paper, and not in guineas, it is evident that a reduction in the quantity of paper must have reduced the price of gold when expressed in paper, and brought the real value of the bank note nearer its nominal value. And thus, by raising the value of the whole currency, if the diminution had been carried far enough, it must necessarily have raised the foreign exchanges to par, and so would have brought gold back again into circulation.

The fourth issue between the parties contains a perfectly new theory of the paper currency, which had been previously maintained by the directors of the Bank of Ireland. As this is a very important, but very delusive, theory of paper currency, we shall defer the discussion to a future chapter. The Bullion Report especially condemned it. Upon all this conflicting evidence the committee produced a most masterly report, probably the most able ever drawn up by a Parliamentary committee. It was the joint work of Mr. Horner, Mr. Huskisson and Mr. Henry Thornton—each a master in his own department. It is one of the great landmarks in economics, as containing the infallible principles upon which a paper currency must be regulated.

Nothing can be a more amusing example of reasoning in a vicious circle than the unanimous doctrines of the English merchants. They laid down as a dogma that an adverse state of the exchanges and an export of bullion could only be caused by a balance of payments being due by England; and *because* the exchanges were adverse, and an export of bullion had taken place, they maintained that it *must* be owing simply to a balance of payments being due by England, without the least investigation into the facts. But an inquiry into the facts entirely disproved this assertion; because it was decisively proved that when the exchanges were reduced to their true value in specie, that the real exchange was in favor of England, which we know must necessarily have been the case, from the enormous exports of English commodities to all quarters of the globe.

The committee decisively proved that an excessive quantity of inconvertible paper necessarily causes the exchanges to be apparently adverse, whatever the real exchange may be, and an export of gold. They thus showed that instead of there being only *one* cause of an adverse state of the exchanges and an export of gold, there were *two*. The committee then laid down the rule that the issues of paper must be governed and regulated by the state of the foreign exchanges and the market price of gold bullion. Unfortunately, however, they laid down no rule for carrying these principles into practical effect; and consequently their theory, correct as far as it went, was incomplete, and was never properly worked.

In 1856, we showed that besides the *two* causes of an adverse state of the exchanges, and an export of bullion, there is a *third*, which up till then had never attracted sufficient attention. By stating this new cause and devising a rule founded upon it, showing how the theory of the Bullion Report is to be carried into practical effect, we completed the theory of the Bullion Report; and by this rule the Bank of England and every bank in the world is now managed. Some proposals were made for remedying the evil by imposing a limit on the issues of the bank; but the committee entirely condemned the plan of imposing a cast-iron limit on the issues of the bank; because doing so would prevent the bank from rendering that assistance to commerce in times of trouble which repeated experience had proved to be necessary, and might very much aggravate the inconveniences of a temporary pressure. The only true and proper remedy for all these evils was, therefore, a resumption of cash payments. That, however, was an operation of the greatest delicacy, and it must be left to the discretion and prudence of the bank to carry it into effect. Parliament should merely fix the time, and leave it to them to carry it into effect. Under all the circumstances a period of two years seemed to be not longer than necessary, and at the same time sufficient to enable them to prepare for it.

This report contains the eternal and immutable principles which must regulate every paper currency which makes any attempt to conform to the value of gold; and if any legislation on paper currency be considered necessary, it must endeavor to enforce the practical application of the principles of this report; and just in so far as it deviates from or contravenes them, so it will be found to thwart and contravene the eternal principles of economics. All legislation, then, on the currency should have as its object merely to provide the best machinery for ensuring the practical application of the principles. The general principles laid down in this report are as complete a matter of demonstration as any in Euclid. The method of treating the subject is as scientific as any of the great discoveries in natural philosophy, which have excited the admiration of the world; nor could it fail to carry conviction to any one of ordinary intelligence who was capable of understanding the force of the arguments. No sooner was it published, than it was assailed by a whole multitude of pamphleteers, whose obscure memory it is not worth while now to revive. The interests affected by the report were too deep and extensive for it not to be attacked by every species of ridicule and acrimonious controversy.

In May, 1811, a debate of four nights took place on the report. Mr. Horner embodied the conclusions of the report in a series of sixteen resolutions. The first was negatived by a majority of 151 to 75. The next fourteen were negatived without a division; and the last was rejected by a majority of 180 to 45. Among the names of the majority was that of Robert Peel. Mr. Vansittart, the Chancellor of the Exchequer, in a speech of enormous length moved counter-resolutions to Mr. Horner. The purport of these was that there was no legal weight of bullion in the coins beyond what the caprice of each sovereign might dictate; that the bank notes were merely promises to pay these coins, and that they always had been, and at that moment were, held equivalent in public estimation to the legal coin of the realm, and were generally accepted as such in all pecuniary transactions to which such coin was lawfully applicable; and that the price of bullion and the state of the foreign exchanges were in no way owing to excessive issues of bank paper. Mr. Canning in vain attempted to persuade the Ministers to rest satisfied with the defeat of the Bullion Report; and, for the sake of the reputation of the House, not to make them pass a vote which no one outside of it could speak of without laughter. His amendment was rejected by a majority of eighty-two to forty-two, and Mr. Vansittart's resolutions were carried.

After the House had indulged in this wild freak,—the very saturnalia of unreason,—and given the bank so great an encouragement to pursue its wild career, it became evident to everyone who understood the subject, that the value of every man's property depended on the will of the bank. This was fraught with the most alarming consequences to every one with a fixed income; as, while the price of every article of necessity kept pace with the depreciation of the currency, anyone like a landlord, having a fixed rent to receive, was paid in a depreciated paper, while his tenants received the increased nominal prices of their commodities.

As matters were continually getting worse,—gold having risen to £4 16s. in March,—Lord King, who had distinguished himself some years before regarding paper money, issued a circular to his tenants, reminding them that their contract was to pay a certain quantity of the legal coin of the country, and that the present paper currency was considerably depreciated. He said that in future, he should require his rents to be paid in the legal gold coin of the realm; but that, as his object was merely to secure the payment of the real intrinsic value of the sum agreed to be paid, he should be willing to receive the amount in Portugal gold coin of an equal weight with that of the stipulated number of guineas, or in an amount of bank notes sufficient to purchase the weight of standard gold requisite to discharge the rent.

That such a demand was legal no one pretended to deny. But when this practical sarcasm was passed upon the resolution of the House of Commons, it drove that party wild. The most unmeasured abuse was heaped upon Lord King for *incivism.* Not only was the measure in every way legal, but nothing could have been more equitable. His tenants were receiving increased market prices for their produce, and only paid him in the same number of depreciated notes. It is quite clear that, if his tenants got an increase in the price of their products, owing to the depreciation, he ought to have received a proportionate increase in his rents. Lord Stanhope brought in a bill which, after being considerably modified, was ultimately passed, making it a misdemeanor to make any difference between specie and paper in payments. He mentioned several instances which he had been informed of in which 27s. were demanded for a guinea. Lord Holland also said that a £1 note and seven shillings were currently given for guineas. Admirable commentary upon the resolutions so triumphantly carried only two months before in the House of Commons, and then standing in their journals, that in public estimation guineas and bank notes were equal! This act was originally limited to the 24th March, 1812, but it was subsequently prolonged during the continuance of the Restriction Act.

The harvest of 1811 was extremely deficient, and that was the period when the power of Napoleon was at its height, and the Continental sources of supply were cut off. In August, 1812, corn reached its highest price during the war. The average price of wheat in England and Wales was then 155s.; some Dantzic wheat brought 180s.; and in some instances oats were at 84s. The advocates of the rival theories attributed this great rise in the price of cereals to different causes—one party almost entirely to the depreciation of paper, the other to the scarcity. Mr. Tooke was a distinguished advocate of the latter view, and in support of it urged forcible arguments from the corresponding rise which took place in France during the same period, where the currency was almost purely metallic. Mr. Tooke's powerful arguments derive additional force from his being a contemporary of the circumstances he describes. But we think he can hardly be correct in so entirely neglecting the effect of the depreciation of the paper currency as he does. We have abundant evidence that, before the gold coin and the bank note bill, there were very generally two prices in the country—a gold price and a paper price. After that act, gold totally disappeared from circulation, and there was nothing but a paper price. But, if any price had been paid in gold, would there not have been exactly the same difference in the price as before the act? If then such would have been the case, it is evident that when paid in paper, the paper was depreciated by exactly the difference that would have been between gold and paper. There does not appear to be the least reason to suppose that the scarcity was greater in 1812 than in 1800; in fact, the evidence seems to be all the other way; yet while corn only rose to 133s. in 1800, it rose to 155s. in 1812. Whence this difference? It was evidently due to the depreciation of the paper. In August, 1812, the price of gold was £4 18s. per ounce, at which the real value of the note was 15s. 11d. How is it to be supposed that the enhancement of prices when paid in paper, which was quite notorious before Lord Stanhope's Act, was actually annihilated by that act?

The principles of the Bullion Report having been decisively rejected by Parliament, and pronounced to be fallacious by the resolutions which declared twenty-one to be equal to twenty-seven, the bank took no measures to bring their notes to a nearer conformity to their nominal value; and the market or paper price continued to rise, till November, 1813, it stood at £5 10s.; the greatest height it ever reached. The long continuance of high prices, caused partly by a series of deficient harvests and partly by the depreciated paper in which prices were paid, gave rise to the belief that they would continue permanent. Immense speculations began in land jobbing; vast tracts of waste and fen land were reclaimed. It was at this time that the immense agricultural improvements in Lincolnshire were effected. Rents in most cases rose to treble what they were in 1792; all the new agricultural contracts entered into at this period were formed on the basis of these extravagant prices. Landlords and tenants increased their expenditure in a like proportion; family settlements were made on a commensurate scale. As a natural consequence, country banks multiplied greatly. In 1811 they were 728; in 1813 they had risen to 940; and the amount of their issues was supposed on the most moderate estimate to be about £25,000,000.

After the disaster of the French in the Russian campaign of 1812, and the battle of Leipzic in 1813, the ports of Russia and Northern Germany were thrown open to British commerce. This naturally gave rise to enormous speculative exports and overtrading. The harvest of 1813 was prodigiously abundant, so that the price of wheat, which in August, 1812, had been 155s. gradually fell till in July, 1814, it was only 68s. The exporting speculations were at their height in the spring of 1814, and the prices of all such commodities rose to, in many cases, double and treble what they had been before. Every branch of industry was affected by the preceding causes, and the natural and inevitable consequences soon followed. A violent revulsion and general depression of the price of all sorts of property, which entailed such general and universal losses among the agricultural, commercial, manufacturing, mining, shipping and building interests, as had never before been paralleled. As is always the case, the consequences of the wild speculations and engagements persons had entered into during the continuance of the fever, continued to be felt for many years afterwards. The disasters commenced in the autumn of 1814, continued with increasing severity during 1815, and reached their height in 1816-17. During these years, eighty-nine country bankers became actually bankrupt; probably four or five times that number ceased business, and the reduction of their issues of country paper was such, that in 1816 its amount was little more than half what it had been in 1814.

This discredit of country bank paper, similar to what had previously occurred in 1793 and 1797, caused a demand for additional issues from the Bank of England, to help to maintain public credit. This caused an extension of the bank paper by upwards of three millions; but so great was the abstraction of country bank paper, to certainly four times the amount of the increased issues of the bank, that the value of the whole currency gradually rose, so that while in May, 1815, the market or paper price of gold was £5 6s., the exchange on Hamburg 28·2, and the exchange on Paris 19·00, in October, 1816, the paper price of gold was £3 18s. 6d., the exchange with Hamburg was 38·00, and that on Paris was 26·10, and they remained at these prices with little variation till July, 1817. Hence at length was manifested the most complete triumph of the principles of the Bullion Report.

The great plethora of this worthless quantity of paper currency being removed, the value of the whole currency was raised almost to par; so near, in fact, that the smallest care and attention would have brought it quite to par; and if means could have been taken to prevent the growth of the rank luxuriance of country bank notes, cash payments would have been resumed at this period with the utmost possible facility, and, as a matter of course, without exciting the least comment.

On several previous occasions, the bank had intimated to the Government their perfect ability and readiness to resume payments in cash, but had always been prevented from doing so for political reasons. In 1815, when peace was finally restored, they prepared in good faith to be ready to do so as soon as they should be required; and during that year and 1816, they accumulated so much treasure that, in November, 1816, they gave notice of their intention to pay all their notes dated previously to the 1st January, 1812; and in April, 1817, all their notes dated before the first of January, 1816. When this was done, there was found to be scarcely any demand upon them for gold. The nation had got so accustomed to a paper currency, that they were most unwilling to receive gold for it. Mr. Stuckey, one of the largest bankers in the west of England, said that during this partial resumption of cash payments, it cost him nearly £100 to remit the surplus coin which accumulated upon him to London, as he could not get rid of it in the country, his customers all preferring his notes. Many persons who had hoarded guineas requested as a favor to have notes in exchange.

In March, 1814, the restriction was prolonged till July, 1816. Just after that, took place the Hundred Days. The expenses of the campaign made the Ministers dread a monetary crisis, and the restriction was prolonged till July, 1818. The partial resumption of cash payments was attended with perfect success; it caused no very great demand for gold; which continued to accumulate in the bank till October, 1817, when it reached its maximum, being £11,914,000. The bank gave notice that it would pay off in cash all the notes dated before the 1st of January, 1817, or renew them at the option of the holders. In the course of 1817, a very large amount of foreign loans was contracted for. Prussia, Austria, and other lesser states were endeavoring to replace their depreciated paper money by specie; and as money was abundant in England, a very large portion of these loans were taken up here. The effect of this began to manifest itself in April, 1817, when the exchanges with Hamburg and Paris began to give way and the market price of gold to rise. These phenomena gradually increased throughout 1818, until in January, 1819, the market price of gold was £4 3s., the exchange on Hamburg 33·8, and that on Paris 23·50. In July, 1817, the new gold coinage began to be issued from the Mint in large quantities. The consequence was, that a steady demand for gold set in upon the bank, and, in pursuance of its notices, the sum of £6,756,000 was drawn out of it in gold. Just at this time the British Government reduced the rate of interest upon exchequer bills. The very much higher rate of interest offered by Continental governments caused a great demand for gold for export; and in the beginning of 1818, a very decided drain set in. The bank directors, however, determined to set all the principles of the Bullion Report ostentatiously at defiance. While this great drain was going on, they increased their advances to the Government from £20,000,000 to £28,000,000; and though they knew perfectly well that the demand for gold was for export, they took no measures whatever to reduce their issues for the purpose of checking the export. At the same time, the issues of the country banks had increased by two-thirds since 1816. This demand for gold became more intense during 1818 and January, 1819; and it became evident that the bank would soon be exhausted if legislative interference did not take place. Accordingly, on the 3d of February, 1819, both Houses appointed committees to inquire into the state of the bank; and on the 5th of April they reported that it was expedient to pass an act immediately to restrain the bank from paying cash in terms of its notices of 1816-17. An act for that purpose was passed in two days. The report of the Commons stated that in the first six months of 1818, 125 millions of francs had been coined at the French Mint, three-fourths of which had been derived from the gold coin of this country. The act forbade the bank to make any payments in gold whatever, either for fractional sums under £5 or any of their notes, during that session of Parliament. The bank was, therefore, totally closed for cash payments. This was the second notable triumph of the principles of the Bullion Report. The first had proved the truth of its doctrine that a reduction of the paper currency would reduce the price of gold, and bring the exchanges to par. The second showed that an ostentatious defiance and contravention of its doctrines brought on a total suspension of cash payments.

The chief points of interest in these reports of the committees are the opinions of the witnesses respecting the great doctrines of the Bullion Report. The reports of neither House entered into any question of the theory of the currency; they were confined to recommending a certain course of action; but they examined a number of witnesses of the first eminence on the subject, and the result of their evidence is most extraordinary. In 1804 and 1810 the immense preponderance of commercial testimony scouted the doctrine that the issues of paper currency had any effect on the exchanges or the price of bullion, or should be regulated by them. Nevertheless, the reports of both committees were certainly in the teeth of the mercantile evidence. The Bullion Report had now been before the country for nearly nine years; and had caused more public discussion than almost any subject whatever, both in Parliament and in the press. It is perfectly manifest that if its principles were erroneous, the commercial world would only have been further strengthened against them. But what was the result now? The overwhelming mass of commercial evidence was entirely in their favor. The current of mercantile opinion was now just as strong in their favor as it had been formerly against them. A few old, antiquated fossils still stuck to the exploded fallacies to the last. What could be more triumphant than this? What could be more splendid testimony to their soundness and accuracy than the fact that they had converted the immense hostile majority of the commercial world? Notwithstanding that the Governor and the Deputy Governor of the bank had given strong evidence in favor of the doctrines of the Bullion Report, they were not able to carry the majority of the court with them, who persisted in the old opinions. On the occasion of some questions being sent to them for their consideration, the court took the opportunity of recording publicly their disapproval of the doctrines which were now in the ascendant. On the 25th of March they resolved:

"That this court cannot refrain from adverting to an opinion strongly insisted upon by some, that the bank had only to reduce its issues to obtain a favorable turn in the exchanges, and a consequent influx of the precious metals; the court conceives it to be its duty to declare that it is unable to discover any solid foundation for such a sentiment."

In pursuance of the reports of both Houses, the celebrated Act of 1819 was passed, commonly called Peel's Act, because he was Chairman of the Committee of the Commons, and the Ministry entrusted the bringing in of it to him.

The chief provisions of this Act, Statute 1819, c. 49, were:

1. The acts then in force for restraining cash payments should be continued till the 1st of May, 1823, when they were finally to cease.

2. That on and after the 1st of February, and before the 1st of October, 1820, the Bank of England should be bound, on any person presenting an amount of their notes, not less than of the value or price of sixty ounces, to pay them on demand at the rate of £4 1s. per ounce, in standard gold bullion, stamped and assayed by the Mint.

3. That between the 1st of October, 1820, and the 1st of May, 1821, it should pay in a similar manner in gold bullion at the rate of £3 19s. 6d. per ounce.

4. Between the 1st of May, 1820, and the 1st of May, 1823, the rate of gold bullion should be £3 17s. 10 1-2d. per ounce.

5. During the first period above mentioned it might pay in gold bullion at any rate less than £4 1s. and not less than £3 19s. 6d. per ounce; in the second period, at any rate less than £3 19s. 6d. and not less than £3 17s. 10 1-2d.; upon giving three days' notice in the *Gazette* and specifying the rate; but after doing so they were not to raise it again.

6. These payments were to be made in bars or ingots of the weight of sixty ounces each; and the bank might pay any fractional sum less than 40s. above that in the legal silver coin.

7. The trade in gold bullion and coin was declared entirely free and unrestrained.

The fantastic plan of paying in bars or ingots of gold bullion, instead of in gold coin, was a scheme of Ricardo's, who had by this time acquired great celebrity on account of the prominent part he took, in 1810, in proving that the bank note was depreciated, and the admirable evidence he gave before the committees of both Houses in 1819. But it proved a dead letter—it never took effect at all. Although the bank was permitted to pay its notes in bars of gold bullion at the rate of £4 1s. per ounce, they were actually at par. In August, 1819, the market price of gold fell to £3 17s. 10 1-2d., and continued at that rate till June, 1822, when it fell to £3 17s. 6d.

The accumulation of treasure became so rapid in the vaults of the bank in 1820, that early in 1821 the directors felt themselves in a position to resume complete payments in cash. An act was passed to enable them to do so on the first of May, 1821, instead of in 1823. By this time the Government had repaid £10,000,000 of the debt it owed to the bank, which all the witnesses agreed was a necessary preliminary to enable the directors to contract their own issues.

The Act, Statute 1819, c. 49, commonly called Peel's Act, has probably been the subject of more gross misapprehension and misrepresentation than any other act which was ever passed, even by grave historians who were culpably negligent in not accurately ascertaining the facts. The almost universal opinion is, that while bank notes were heavily depreciated, Peel's Act of 1819 compelled the bank at once to resume payments in cash at their full nominal value, thereby causing a great contraction of the currency, which it is alleged produced the dreadful agricultural distress in 1821 and succeeding years. The preceding narrative shows that this is a complete misstatement of the facts. The great contraction of the currency was caused by the failure of somewhere about three hundred country banks in 1815-16, and the destruction of about £12,000,000 of their worthless paper. This brought the bank note to all but its par value; and the bank of its own accord commenced a partial resumption of cash payments in November, 1816, and a further resumption in April, 1817; and there can be no doubt it would have completely resumed payment in 1818, without exciting the least comment, if it had not been so grossly mismanaged in that year. The Act of 1819 produced absolutely no contraction of the currency whatever. The bank note was at par in October, 1819, although the act allowed the bank to redeem their notes at £4 1s.; and the bank did not ultimately resume cash payments in pursuance of the Act of 1819, but in pursuance of an act passed at the instance of the bank itself in 1821. Mr. Turner, a director of the bank, says in a pamphlet: "With regard to the effect of Mr. Peel's bill on the Bank of England, I can state, from having been in the direction of the bank during the last two years, that it has been altogether a dead letter. It has neither accelerated nor retarded the return to cash payments." London bankers, as we have said, of their own accord, discontinued issuing their own notes in 1793; and proved that in such a place as London banking can be carried on without issuing notes, but only allowing their customers to draw cheques.

For a long time the consequences that might be deduced from this apparently unimportant change in the method of banking escaped notice. But about 1820 Mr. Joplin, a well-known writer on banking in his day, maintained that the monopoly of the bank was exclusively confined to issuing notes; and that there was nothing in its charter which prevented joint-stock banks being founded, and carrying on their business according to the then usual method of London bankers. He says:* "That public banks have not

* Supplementary Observations to the Third Edition of an Essay on Banking, 1823, p. 84.

hitherto existed, more especially in London and Lancashire, seems to have arisen from the want of a proper knowledge of the principles of banking, rather than from the charter of the Bank of England, which I find does not prevent public banks for the deposit of capital from being established. * * * That banks ought to be the permanent depositories of the capital of the country is an idea which no writer has hitherto entertained, and the silent operations of the Scotch banks have eluded observation. It has, in fact, always been hitherto considered that the proper business of a bank was to issue notes and discount bills at short dates. It is quite evident that the framers of the above clause (the monopoly clause) considered the business pursued by the Bank of England the only proper banking. It appeared to them that preventing banks with more than six partners from issuing bills at short dates or notes payable on demand was altogether conferring on the bank the privilege of exclusive banking as a public company. This it did, no doubt, according to their definition of the term, but it still leaves the most important part of banking open to the public. There is at this moment no legal impediment to the establishment of joint stock companies for trading in real capital. Both the letter and the spirit of the charter has reference to the circulation of bills and notes alone. A bank which traded only in capital would not in the least trench upon the monopoly of the Bank of England, nor be any infringement of its charter."

In this passage, Mr. Joplin shows that he had not well considered the nature of banking. He, as well as many others, consider that the private bankers and the joint stock banks of London trade only in real capital, *i. e.*, money; but this is a pure delusion. All London bankers discount bills by creating rights of action, or credit; the only thing is that these credits are circulated by means of cheques only, and not by cheques and notes. However, Mr. Joplin has the merit of being the first, as far as we are aware, who perceived that the charter of the Bank of England did not prevent joint-stock banks being founded so long as they did not issue notes. But, like many good ideas, it remained a considerable time unfruitful, and it was not till ten years later that the first joint-stock bank was founded in London.

In 1823, the Government endeavored to persuade the Bank of England to give up the privileges of their charter, so far as to permit joint-stock banks to be formed in the country. But the bank refused. Nothing further took place till 1826, when the disasters of the preceding year being very generally attributed to the improper management of the country bankers, the Ministers were powerful enough to compel the bank to give up its unjustifiable monopoly, and at length agreed to permit joint-stock banks to be formed beyond sixty-five miles from the metropolis. An Act, Statute 1826, c. 46, was passed for this purpose. The provisions which touch our present subject are:

1. Banks of an unlimited number of partners may be formed and carry on all descriptions of banking business by issuing notes and bills payable on demand, or otherwise, provided that such corporations or partnerships should not have any house of business or establishment as bankers in

London, or at any place within sixty-five miles of London; and that each member of such corporation should be liable for all its debts of every description contracted while he was a partner, or which fell due after he became a partner.

2. No such banking company was to issue or re-issue, either directly or indirectly, within the prescribed distance, any bill or note payable to bearer on demand; or any bank post bill; nor draw upon its London agents any bill of exchange payable on demand; or for any less sum than £50; but they may draw any bill for any sum of £50 or upwards, payable in London or elsewhere, at any period after date or after sight.

3. Such banking companies are forbidden by themselves or their agents to borrow, owe or take up in London, or at any place within sixty-five miles of London, any sum of money on any of their bills or notes payable on demand; or at any time less than six months from the borrowing thereof; but they may discount in London or elsewhere any bill or bills of exchange, not drawn by or upon themselves or by or upon any person on their behalf.

4. The Bank of England was authorized to establish branches at any place in England.

5. The rights and privileges of the Bank of England were to remain intact and unaltered, except so far as varied by the act.

The formation of joint-stock banks under this act proceeded very slowly at first; not more than four or five being formed in as many years. In fact, such banks could only be formed by influential persons; and, of course, such persons had already their own banker, whom they would naturally be unwilling to injure by the formation of so powerful a rival. The first joint-stock bank was formed at Lancaster; the second at Bradford, and a third at Norwich, before any one was founded in the great manufacturing towns. It was not till the prosperous years of 1833-4-5-6 that any remarkable increase took place in their numbers. In these years, however, they multiplied rapidly, more especially in 1836, when upwards of forty were established in the spring.

The great crisis and panic of 1825 was attributed to the excessive issues of £1 notes by the country bankers. These were suppressed by the Act, Statute 1826, c. 6. By this act:

1. The act repealing the Act, Statute 1777, c. 30, which prohibited promissory notes and bills under 20s. was repealed, thereby reviving the former act, but all notes of private bankers stamped before the 5th of February, 1826, or of the Bank of England stamped before the 10th of October, 1826, were exempted from its operation, and were permitted to be issued, re-issued and negotiated until the 5th of April, 1829.

2. Any person after that date making, issuing, signing or re-issuing any note or bill under £5 was subject to a penalty of £20.

3. Any person who published, uttered or negotiated any promissory or other notes, or any negotiable or transferable bill, draft or undertaking in writing for the payment of 20s. or above that sum and less than £5, or on which such sum should be unpaid, should forfeit the sum of £20.

4. These penalties were not to attach to any person drawing a cheque on his banker for his own use.

5. All promissory notes under £20 made payable to bearer on demand were to be made payable at the bank or place where they were issued.

When the Government determined to suppress the issue of £1 notes in England, they said it was their intention to extend the measure to Scotland and Ireland. However Scotland may have suffered from commercial over-trading, as all commercial countries must occasionally do, no banking panic had ever occurred such as those which had so frequently desolated England.

The Ministerial intentions raised a prodigious ferment in Scotland. Sir Walter Scott published three letters on the subject, under the name of "Malachi Malagrowther," which greatly fanned the public enthusiasm; and such an opposition was organized, that the Ministry were obliged to consent to appoint committees of both Houses on the subject. These committees sat during the spring of 1826, and investigated the whole subject of Scotch banking, which had been very little understood in England before that time; and the result was so favorable to the system of Scotch banking, that the Ministry abandoned their intention of attempting to alter it.

Although the act of 1775 had forbidden notes under £5 to be issued in England, it did not prohibit the circulation of Scotch £1 notes in England, and they had always circulated in the districts adjacent to Scotland, and even as far south as York. When the English £1 notes were suppressed, it seemed naturally to follow that the circulation of similar Scotch notes in England should also be suppressed. But the districts in which they had always circulated were as unanimous as Scotland itself against the measure. In 1828 the Ministry brought in a bill to restrain the circulation of the small Scotch notes in England. Sir James Graham presented a petition from the borderers, deprecating in the most earnest terms the withdrawal of the Scotch notes, to which they had been so long accustomed. For seventy years they said they had possessed the advantage it was now sought to deprive them of—namely, the Scotch currency. Seven-eighths of the rents of estates were paid in the paper currency of Scotland, and no loss had been sustained in consequence of it. After a debate of two nights the motion was carried by 154 to 45. The Act, Statute 1828, c. 65, provided that after the fifth of April, 1829, no corporation or person whatsoever should publish, utter, negotiate or transfer, in any part of England, any promissory note, draft, engagement, or undertaking in writing, payable to bearer on demand, for less than £5, or upon which less than £5 remained unpaid, which should have been made or issued, or purport to have been made or issued, in Scotland or Ireland, or elsewhere out of England, under a penalty of not less than £5, or more than £20.

The charter of the bank expired at the end of one year's notice to be given after the first of August, 1832, and this time the bank had done no such services to the Government as to be in a position to demand from it a renewal of its monopoly several years before it expired. Moreover, as Lord Liverpool said in 1826, these exclusive privileges were out of fashion. Many great monopolies were on the eve of breaking up; and the public mind was more roused and enlightened on the subject of banking from the discussions caused by the great panic of 1825. Before taking any steps towards a renewal of the charter, the Government determined to have an inquiry before a committee of the House of Commons. This committee sat for some months, and reported the evidence given before them at the end of the session. It was not reappointed, as the Government had made up their mind on the subject.

On the 31st May, 1833, Lord Althorpe moved a series of resolutions for the renewal of the bank charter—one of which was that, so long as the bank continued to pay its notes in gold, bank notes should be declared legal tender, except by the bank itself. Several members wished for further delay to consider the resolutions, as the session was nearly at an end. But Sir Robert Peel was decidedly of opinion that the resolutions should be passed at once. He held it desirable to continue the privileges of the bank, and that there should be but one bank of issue in the metropolis, in order that it might exercise an undivided control over the issue of paper, and give facilities to commerce in times of difficulty and alarm, which it could not give with the same effect if it were subject to the rivalry of another establishment [why not?]. He resisted at great length the proposition for making bank notes legal tender, as a departure from the principle of the Act of 1819 and the true principles which should govern a paper currency. It was decided by a majority of 316 to 83 to proceed with the resolutions. The plan of making bank notes legal tender was strongly opposed, but was carried by 214 to 156.

We have already shown that the public had at various times attempted to form rival banking companies to the Bank of England; and in 1709 and 1742 the Bank Acts had been framed to stop up various loop-holes which had been successively discovered. In 1742, the phraseology used had been supposed to be quite effectual for the purpose. At that time, the custom of issuing notes payable to bearer on demand to their customers in exchange for money and bills, was considered so essentially the fundamental idea of "banking," that to prohibit the issue of these notes was deemed an effectual bar upon the business of "banking." But in process of time—in 1793—the London bankers of their own accord discontinued the practice of issuing their own notes to their customers. The Act of 1742 was considered to be so effectual a bar against banking companies in general that it escaped public observation that the way of doing business by way of cheques enabled banking companies to elude the wording of the Act of 1742.

In 1796, when in consequence of the restrictive measures of the Bank of England, much distress was felt in London from the want of a circulating medium, an association of merchants and bankers was formed for the purpose of providing a circulating medium which should not infringe the privileges of the bank. The question was considered by them in what the bank's privilege of exclusive "banking" did consist, and they determined that, "The privilege of exclusive 'banking' enjoyed by the Governor and Company of the Bank of England, as defined by the acts of Parliament under which they enjoy it, seems to consist in the power of borrowing, owing, or taking up money on their bills or notes payable on demand." About the year 1822, Mr. Joplin and other writers detected the flaw in the monopoly of the bank, and maintained that a joint-stock bank of deposit was no infringement of the charter, and that such banks might be formed and carry on a very successful business without issuing notes at all, but by merely following the practice of the London bankers by adopting cheques only. It is somewhat remarkable that this discovery should have been allowed to lie unfruitful so long. When the Government first entered into negotiations with the bank in 1833, concerning the terms of the renewal of the charter, they, as well as the general body of the mercantile community, were persuaded that the monopoly forbade any banks of any description whatever, with more than six partners, being formed. In the course of the negotiation this point was brought under the notice of the Government, who took the opinion of their law officers upon so important a point. The opinion of the Crown lawyers was that the clause did not prohibit joint-stock banks of deposit being formed. The flank of the monopoly of the bank being, as we may say, turned in this extraordinary and unexpected manner, created the greatest consternation and alarm in that body, and they requested the Government to have the omission rectified. But Lord Althorpe decidedly refused anything of the sort, and told them that the bargain was that their privileges should remain as they were, and that he would not consent to any extension of them.

In order to remove all doubts upon the subject, the Solicitor General brought up a clause by way of rider, declaring the right to form such banks. He said that the basis of the contract with the bank was, that they were to enjoy whatever monopoly they already possessed, but nothing beyond it. He had examined the case with the utmost care, and there was no pretence for saying that such banks were an encroachment on the monopoly of the bank. The bank as originally founded was a bank of issue, and the monopoly first granted in 1697 must be held to refer to banks *ejusdem generis.* Such had been the uniform language of all the subsequent acts. The clause upon which their monopoly was founded was strictly confined to the issue of paper money. Joint-stock banks of deposit were legal at common law, and it rested with those who said it was forbidden to point out the act which prohibited them.

The chief provisions of the Act, Statute 1833, c. 98, were as follows:

1. The bank was continued as a corporation with such exclusive privileges of banking as were given by the act, for a certain time and on certain conditions, during which time no society or company exceeding six persons should make or issue in London, or within sixty-five miles thereof, any bill of exchange or promissory note, or engagement for the payment of money on demand, or upon which any person holding the same may obtain payment upon demand. But country bankers might have an agency in London for the sole purpose of paying such of their notes as might be presented there, but no such bill or note was to be under £5, or be re-issued in London or within sixty-five miles thereof.

2. For the purpose of removing any doubts that might exist as to what the exclusive privilege of banking which the Bank of England enjoyed consisted in, it was enacted that any body, politic or corporate, or society or company, or partnership, of whatever number they consisted, might carry on the business of banking in London, or within sixty-five miles thereof, provided that they did not borrow, owe, or take up in England, any sum or sums of money on their bills or notes payable on demand, or at any less time than six months from the borrowing thereof, during the continuance of the privileges of the Bank of England.

3. All the notes of the Bank of England which should be issued out of London, should be payable at the place where they were issued.

4. Upon one year's notice, to be given within six months after the expiration of ten years from the 1st day of August, 1834, and repayment of all debts due by Parliament to the bank, its privileges were to cease and determine at the end of the year's notice.

5. So long as the bank paid its notes on demand in legal coin, they were declared to be legal tender of payment for all sums above £5, except by the bank itself, or any of its branches. No notes not made payable at any of the branches were liable to be paid there, but the notes issued at all the branches were to be payable in London.

6. Bills and notes not having more than three months to run were exempted from the usury laws.

7. The Government was to pay off one-fourth of the debt due to the bank, and the proprietors might reduce the capital stock of the bank by that amount if they chose.

8. In consideration of these privileges, the bank was to give up £120,000 a year of the sum they received for managing the public debt.

By this act, declaring the common-law right to found joint-stock banks which did not issue notes, the second great breach on the monopoly of the bank was effected, and the joint-stock banks of London were founded. As the next renewal of the charter in 1844 was for the first time founded on certain specific theories of currency and banking, we shall defer mentioning and examining them for the present.

SECTION VI.

THE COMMITTEE ON BANKING OF 1840.

Testimony Before the Committee—Controversy on the Constituents of Currency—Author's Criticism of the Evidence.

PURPORT OF THE REPORT.

ELSEWHERE we have fully explained the meaning of the terms circulating medium and currency, which are always used as identical. We have shown that the term circulating medium, by its very meaning, necessarily includes money and credit in all its forms, both written and unwritten. We have shown that, in mercantile law, the term currency means anything whatever of which the property passes by delivery and innocent acquisition, and that, in its strict legal sense, it can only be applied to written securities for money; because, it is only such rights recorded on paper, which can be mislaid, lost, and stolen, and passed away by manual delivery; but that, if it is to be used as an economic term, denoting a certain class of economic quantities, it must include money and credit in all its forms, written and unwritten, as it was universally understood to do in all the debates in Parliament up to a certain time.

But the present monetary system of the country, as established by the Bank Charter Act of 1844, is founded upon a totally different definition of currency. And as that act is founded upon a peculiar definition of currency, and is expressly intended to carry into effect a peculiar theory of currency, we must critically examine this peculiar definition of currency, in order to see if it can be accepted, instead of the one as settled by the courts of law. We must also explain the particular theory of currency which the Bank Charter Act of 1844 is designed to carry out.

The disputes as to the meaning of currency were begun by Mr. Boyd, an eminent financial agent, who said, in a letter to Mr. Pitt: "By the terms circulating medium and currency, which are used as almost synonymous terms in this letter, I always understand ready money, whether consisting of bank notes or specie, in contradistinction to bills of exchange, navy bills, exchequer bills, or any other negotiable paper, which form no part of the circulating medium, as I have always understood them. The latter is the circulator, the former are merely objects of circulation." But he says iu the preface: "But, from the mere returns of bank notes (without that of the balances on the books for which the bank is also liable, and of the specie in its coffers) no accurate estimate can be formed of the positive difference between the present and the former circulation." Mr. Boyd, therefore, expressly includes banking credits, or deposits, under the term currency; and as his notion of currency was ready money, it is quite evident that cheques are also currency in his opinion, because mercantile law holds that bank notes, cheques, and deposits are all equally ready money. Now it is seen that Mr. Boyd had not well considered the meaning of the term circulating medium; because the circulating medium is the medium which circulates commodities. And bills of exchange are expressly created to circulate commodities; and it has been shown that bills of exchange possess the attribute of currency in all respects in the same degree as bank notes.

Mr. Thornton, an eminent banker, and one of the authors of the Bullion Report, immediately combatted Mr. Boyd's doctrine that bills of exchange form no part of the circulating medium. He says:* "A multitude of bills pass between receiver and lender in the country in the manner that has been described; and they evidently form in the strictest sense a part of the circulating medium of the country." In a note to this passage he says: "Mr. Boyd, in his publication addressed to Mr. Pitt on the subject of the Bank of England, propagates the same error into which many others had fallen, of considering bills as no part of the circulating medium of the country."

It will be seen in the progress of this work that it was necessary to clear away much confusion which had arisen from the want of a sufficiently full acquaintance with the several kinds of paper credit; and, in particular, to remove by a considerable detail, the prevailing errors respecting the nature of bills, before it could be possible to reason properly upon the effects of paper credit.

Those differences of opinion as to what the term currency includes appeared very strongly before the committee on the Bank Charter Act of 1832, but as they produced no practical result, we need not further advert to them. The question, "What the term currency includes?" was vehemently discussed before the committee on banking in 1840; and by this time a strong and influential party had adopted a certain definition which prevailed with Sir Robert Peel. The leaders of this party were Mr. Samuel Jones Loyd, afterwards Lord Overstone; Mr. George Warde Norman, and Colonel Torrens, and it will be best to let them explain their own views.

The question, "What does the term currency include?" was much discussed before the committee of 1840, but it is only necessary to state here the doctrines held by those witnesses whose opinions prevailed with Sir Robert Peel.

Mr. George Warde Norman, a director of the Bank of England, was asked:

Q. 1691. Are there any grounds for considering the deposits of the Bank of England as currency? No, I think not.

* Essay on the Public Credit of Great Britain.

1692. Do you consider that any deposits, merely in their character of deposits, can be considered as currency? No, I do not.

1693. Will you state what, in your opinion, forms the distinction between currency and deposits? I consider that, looking broadly at deposits and currency, they are quite distinct; they have little to do with each other. But I conceive that the use of deposits is one of the banking expedients which is available for economizing currency, along with a great many others. I do not consider them as currency or money. I ought to observe, perhaps, to the committee that I employ the words "money" and "currency" as synonymous. Deposits are used by means of transfers made in the books of bankers; and these afford the means of adjusting and settling transactions; and *pro tanto* dispense with a certain quantity of money; or they may be set off against each other, from one banker to another, to a certain extent, and thus produce the same effect. Still, they possess the essential qualities of money in a very low degree.

1694. Do you entertain a similar opinion as to bills of exchange? Yes, exactly. I think they are also used to economize currency. I look upon them as banking expedients for that purpose, but they do not possess fully the qualities which I consider money to possess.

1695. Will you explain the difference between the functions which money will perform, and those which bills of exchange or deposits will perform? To answer that question fully one must, I am afraid, take rather a wide view; but I look upon it that the three most essential qualities money should possess are, that it should be in universal demand by everybody, in all times and all places; that it should possess fixed value, and that it should be a perfect numerator. There are other qualities, but I think these are the most essential. Now, when I look at all banking expedients I find that they do not possess these qualities fully. They possess them in a very low degree; and, therefore, as we see took place in 1835, with a very large increase of the deposits of the bank, the circulation diminished; and there was every appearance of the effects of contraction; there was an increased influx of treasure; and I conceive from that there were lower prices. By a numerator I mean that which measures the value of other commodities with the greatest possible facility. If we look at all these banking expedients, we see that they possess the three qualities which I have mentioned in a very much lower degree.

1696. Will you state in what respect? I can only take them one by one. A bill of exchange is an instrument commonly payable at some future time, at a certain place and to some particular individual; it is of no use to any other individual, except it is indorsed to him. A man cannot go into a shop with a bill of exchange and buy what he wants; he could not pay his laborers with a bill of exchange. The same with a banker's deposit; he can do nothing of that sort with that; he can do with less money than he would otherwise employ if he has bills of exchange or bankers' deposits; but he cannot with bills of exchange or bankers' deposits do whatever he could with sovereigns and shillings. By a banker's deposit I mean a credit in a banker's books; nothing more nor less than that.

Mr. Samuel Jones Loyd, afterwards Lord Overstone, was asked:

Q. 2655. What is it that you include in the term circulation? I include in the term circulation metallic coin and paper notes promising to pay the metallic coin to bearer on demand.

2661. In your definition, then, of the word circulation, you do not include deposits? No, I do not.

2662. Do you include bills of exchange? No, I do not.

2663. Why do you not include deposits in your definition of circulation? To answer that question I believe I must be allowed to revert to first principles. The precious metals are distributed to the different countries of the world by the operation of particular laws, which have been investigated and are now well recognized. These laws allot to each country a certain portion of the precious metals, which, while other things remain unchanged, remains itself unchanged. The precious metals converted into coin constitute the money of each country. That coin circulates sometimes in kind; but, in highly advanced countries, it is represented to a certain extent by paper notes, promising to pay the coin to bearer on demand; these notes being of such a nature in principle that the increase of them supplants coin to an equal extent. Where those notes are in use the metallic coin, together with these notes, constitute the money or the currency of that country. Now, this money is marked by certain distinguishing characteristics: first of all, that its amount is determined by the laws which apportion the precious metals to the different countries of the world; secondly, that it is in every country the common measure of the value of all other commodities; the standard by reference to which the value of every other commodity is ascertained and every contract fulfilled; and, thirdly, it becomes the common medium of exchange for the adjustment of all transactions equally at all times, between all persons, and in all places. It has, further, the quality of discharging these functions in endless succession. Now, I conceive that neither deposits nor bills of exchange, in any way whatever, possess these qualities. In the first place, the amount of them is not determined by the laws which determine the amount of the precious metals in each country; in the second place, they will in no respect serve as a common measure of value, or a standard, by reference to which we can measure the relative value of all other commodities; and, in the next place, they do not possess that power of universal exchangeability which belongs to the money of the country.

2664. Why do you not include bills of exchange in circulation? I exclude bills of exchange for precisely the same reasons that I have stated in my former answer for excluding deposits. There is another passage in the same report which appears to me to show very clearly that the French Chamber have fully appreciated the distinction between bills of exchange and money: "Every written obligation to pay a sum due may become a sign of the money; the sign has acquired some of the advantages of circulating money; because, like bills of exchange, it may be transmitted by the easy and prompt method of indorsement. But what obstacles there are! It does not represent at every instant to its holder the sum inscribed on it; it can only be paid at a distant time; to realize it at once, it must be parted with. If one finds any one sufficiently trustful to accept it, it can only be transferred by indorsement. It is an eventual obligation which one contracts one's self, and under the weight of which, until it is paid, one's credit suffers. One is not always disposed to reveal the nature of one's business by the signatures one puts in circulation. These inconveniences led people to find out a sign of money still more active and more convenient, which shares, like the bill of exchange, the qualities of metallic money, because it has no other merit but to represent it, but which can procure it at any moment; which, like the piece of money, is transferred from hand to hand without the necessity of being guaranteed, without leaving traces of its passage. The note payable to bearer on demand, issued by powerful associations formed under the authority and acting under the continual observation of Government, has appeared to present these advantages. Hence banks of circulation."

2665. Under similar circumstances, will the aggregate amount credited to depositors in bankers' books bear some relation to the quantity of money in the country? I apprehend that it is dependent in a very great degree. I consider the money of the country to be the foundation, and the bills of exchange to be the superstructure raised upon it. I consider that bills of exchange are an important form of banking operations, and the circulation of the country is the money in which these operations are to be adjusted; any contraction of the circulation of the country will, of course, act upon credit; bills of exchange being an important form of credit, will feel the effect of that contraction in a very powerful degree; they will, in fact, be contracted in a much greater degree than the paper circulation.

2667. Sir Robert Peel: What are the elements which constitute money in the sense in which you use the expression "quantity of money?" What is the exact meaning you attach to the words "quantity of money—quantity of metallic currency?" When I use the words "quantity of money" I mean the quantity of metallic coin and of paper notes promising the pay in coin on demand which are in circulation in this country.

2668. Paper notes payable in coin? Yes.

2669. By whomsoever issued? Yes.

2670. By country banks as well as other banks? Yes.

2671. Chairman: Would this superstructure, consisting of sums credited to depositors in bankers' books and bills of exchange, equally exist, although no notes payable in coin on demand existed in the country? Yes, I apprehend that every question with respect to deposits, and with respect to bills of exchange, is totally distinct from the question which has reference to the nature of the process of substituting promissory notes in lieu of coin, and of the laws by which that process ought to be governed. If the promissory notes be properly regulated, so as to be at all times of the amount which the coin would have been, deposits and bills of exchange, whatever changes they may undergo, would sustain these changes equally, either with a metallic currency or with a paper currency properly regulated; consequently, every investigation respecting their character or amount is a distinct question from that which has reference only to the substitution of the paper notes for coin.

2672. There would be no reason why, if there were no notes payable in coin on demand, the amount of this superstructure should be less than it now is, with a mixed circulation of specie and of notes payable on demand? None, whatever. I apprehend that, upon the supposition that the paper notes are kept of the same amount as the metallic money, the question of the superstructure whether of deposits or of bills of exchange, remains precisely the same.

2673. That answer takes for granted that, in the first case the metallic currency, and in the second case the metallic currency plus the notes payable on demand, are the same in quantity? Yes.

2674. Sir Robert Peel: You suppose the notes payable on demand to displace an amount of coin precisely equal to these notes? They ought to do so under a proper regulation of the paper money, otherwise they are not kept at the same value as coin.

2675. Mr. Attwood: Would you consider that the superstructure of bills of exchange, founded entirely upon a metallic currency, might, at particular times, become unduly expanded? The answer to that question depends entirely upon the precise meaning of the word "unduly." I apprehend, undoubtedly, that it is perfectly possible that credit, and the consequences which sometimes result from credit—viz., over-banking in all its forms, and the over-issue of bills of exchange, which is one important form of over-banking—may arise with a purely metallic currency, and it may also arise with a currency consisting jointly of a metallic money and paper notes promising to pay in coin; and I conceive further, that if the notes be properly regulated—that is, if they be kept at the amount which the coin otherwise would be—whatever over-banking would have arisen with a metallic currency, would arise, and to the same extent, neither more nor less, with money consisting of metallic coin and paper notes jointly.

2676. May not over-banking and over-issue of bills of exchange, forming a superstructure based upon money composed of metal and paper notes, derange the certainty of the notes being duly paid in gold? I apprehend that if the paper notes be properly regulated, according to the sense which I have already attributed to that expression, and if a proper proportion of gold be held in reserve, the solidity of the basis cannot be disturbed; that is, that if there be a proper contraction of the paper notes as gold goes out, the convertibility of the paper system will be effectually preserved by the continually increasing value of the remaining quantity of the currency, as the contraction proceeds. At this period, and for a long time preceding, the greatest part of the circulating medium of Lancashire were bills of exchange, which sometimes had 150 endorsements on them, before they came to maturity.

Lord Overstone was asked:

Q. 3026. Does not the principal circulation of Lancashire consist of bills of exchange? As I contend that bills of exchange do not form part of the circulation, of course I am bound, in answer to that question, to say, No.

3027. Is there not a large quantity of bills of exchange in circulation in Lancashire? Undoubtedly, wherever a large mass of mercantile or trading transactions take place, there will exist a large amount of bills of exchange, and that is the case to a great extent in Lancashire.

3028. Do not the bills exceed, to an immense amount, the issue of notes payable on demand in Lancashire? Undoubtedly they do, to a great amount.

Mr. Hume had a long fencing match with Lord Overstone as to the distinction between bank notes and deposits. Lord Overstone admitted that a debt might be discharged either by the transfer of a bank note or by the transfer of a credit in the books of a bank; but he strongly contended that bank notes are money, and that bank credits, or deposits, are not.

3148. Do you consider any portion of the deposits in the Bank of England as money? I do not.

3150. Could 20,000 sovereigns have more completely discharged the obligation to pay the £20,000 of bills than the deposits did? Where two parties have each an account with a deposit bank, a transfer of the credit from one party to the credit of another party may certainly discharge an obligation in the same manner and to the same extent to which sovereigns would have discharged that obligation.

3169. Will not the debt between the two be discharged thereby? Yes.

3170. In the one case I have supposed that payment of £1000 was made by means of notes in circulation; payment was made by the delivery of these notes from one hand to another, and they are transported from place to place; but in the case of a payment made by means of a transfer in the books of the bank from one account to another, I ask you, are not these payments equally valid, and would not the debt be discharged equally in either case? In the one case, the debt has been discharged by the use of money; in the other case the debt has been discharged without the necessity of resorting to the use of money, in consequence of the economizing process of deposit business in the Bank of England.

3171. Can the debt of £1000 which one person owes to another be discharged without money being paid, or its value? A debt of £1000 cannot be discharged without in some way or other transferring the value of £1000, but the transfer of value may certainly be effected without the use of money.

3172. Was not the deposit transfer in the Bank of England to satisfy that debt of £1000 of the same value as the £1000 notes which passed in the other case? A credit in the Bank of England, I consider, is of the same value as the same nominal amount of money; and if the credit be transferred, the same value I consider to be transferred, as if money of that nominal amount had been transferred.

3177. Is there any fallacy in the statement that, in the accounts published by the bank, their liabilities are divided into two heads, circulation and deposits? I am not prepared to state that there is any fallacy in it.

3178. Have you not said that deposits do not, in any way whatever, possess the quality of money? If I have said so, I shall be glad to have the statement laid before me.

3179. Have you not in question 2663 enumerated certain distinguishing characteristics of money? I have.

3180. Have you not in the same question stated that deposits do not in any way whatever possess those characteristics? Yes, I have.

3181. Have you not, in answer to previous questions, admitted that for the discharge of debts, deposits have the characteristics of money? All that I have admitted is, I believe, that a deposit may, under certain supposed circumstances, be used to discharge a certain supposed debt.

Lord Overstone also said (3132): "Will any man in his common senses pretend to say that the total amount of transactions adjusted at the Clearing House are part of the money or circulating medium of the country?" Now this paragraph shows great looseness of idea. No one, of course, says that a transaction is money, but the operations of the Clearing House consist exclusively of the transfers of bank credits from one bank to another, and most undoubtedly these bank credits are part of the circulating medium of the country, and, as we shall shortly show, are included in law under the term "ready money." Lord Overstone further said (3082): "When I give a definition of 'currency,' of course it is currency in the abstract; it is that which currency ought to be; that definition properly laid down and properly applied, will include paper notes payable on demand, and it will exclude bills of exchange." Here again, Lord Overstone is absolutely in error. The term currency is, as we have shown, purely a legal term, and means anything of which the property passes by delivery and honest acquisition. Now bank notes and bills of exchange have each this property in common. Consequently they each are currency.

Lastly, we may quote Colonel Torrens, because he was not only one of the most influential of the sect, but it has been alleged that he was in reality the author of the scheme for dividing the bank into two departments, which Sir Robert Peel adopted in his Bank Act of 1844. He says: *

"The terms money and currency have hitherto been employed to denote those instruments of exchange which possess intrinsic or derivative value, and by which, from law or custom, debts are discharged and transactions finally closed. Bank notes, payable in specie on demand, have been included under these terms as well as coin; because, by law and custom, the acceptance of the notes of a solvent bank, no less than the acceptance of coin, liquidates debts and closes transactions; while bills of exchange, bank credits, cheques, and other instruments by which the use of money is economized, have not been included under the terms money and currency, because the acceptance of such instruments does not liquidate debts and finally close transactions."

Again, he says, in reply to some perfectly just observations of Mr. Fullarton:

"It is an obvious departure from ordinary language to say that, whether a purchase is effected by a payment in bank notes or by a bill of exchange, the result is the same. According to the meaning of the terms, money and credit, as established by the universal usage of the market, a purchase effected by a payment in bank notes is a ready money purchase [so is a purchase effected by a cheque], while a transaction negotiated by the payment of a bill of exchange is a purchase upon credit. In the former case, the transaction is concluded, and the vendor has no further claim upon the purchaser; in the latter case the transaction is not concluded, and the vendor continues to have a claim upon the purchaser until a further payment has been made in satisfaction of the bill of exchange. A bank note liquidates a debt; a bill of exchange records the existence of a debt, and promises liquidation at a future day. Mr. Fullarton not only inverts language, but misstates facts, when he says that the transactions of which bank notes have been the instruments must remain incomplete until the notes shall be returned upon the issuing bank, or discharged in cash. A bank note for £100 may pass from purchasers to vendors many times a day, finally closing on the instant each successive transaction. A bill of exchange may also pass from purchasers to vendors many times a day, but no one of the successive transactions of which it is the medium can be finally closed until the last recipient has received in coin or bank notes the amount it represents. Now it is the necessity of ultimate repayment which constitutes the main point of distinction—which marks the boundary between forms of credit and money. It is a necessity which applies to bills of exchange and cheques, but which does not apply to bank notes; and therefore, upon Mr. Fullarton's own showing, upon his own definitions and his own conditions, as to what constitutes money, bank notes come under the head of money; while bills of exchange and bankers' cheques, and such other instruments as require ultimate payments, transfers and settlements, do not come under the phrase money. * * * Upon Mr. Fullarton's own showing, money consists of those instruments only by which debts are discharged, balances adjusted, and transactions finally closed; and, therefore, Mr. Fullarton, unless he should choose to continue to contradict himself, must admit that bank notes are, and bills of exchange, cash credits, and cheques, are not money."

THE ECONOMICS OF THE REPORT.

We have given these long extracts in order that the reader may fully

* The Principles and Practical Operation of Sir Robert Peel's Act of 1844 Explained and Defended, p. 79.

understand the doctrines and principles of the influential sect whose views were embodied in the Bank Charter Act of 1844. He will at once see that they are based on an arbitrary definition of the term currency, which is in diametrical contradiction to the decisions of the courts of law, which we have cited in Chap. I., and the unanimous doctrines of economists and statesmen in all the Parliamentary debates on the subject; and we have now to examine the necessary logical consequences to which these doctrines lead.

Mr. Norman said that money or currency should possess fixed value, and be a perfect numerator. Now the value of money is the various commodities and services, or securities, it can purchase; and as the quantity of all these things which money can purchase constantly varies from time to time, from day to day and from hour to hour, how can money have "fixed value?" We have already shown in Chap. II. that neither money nor anything else can have "fixed value" unless everything has "fixed value." He said that he meant by a numerator that which measured the value of other things with the greatest facility; but does a cheque for £50, or a bill of exchange for £50, not measure the value of things with as great facility as a £50 bank note or fifty sovereigns?

It is not a little amusing to find the celebrated phrase of the Roman Catholic Church, *Quod semper, quod ubique, quod ab omnibus*, starting up and meeting us in a discussion on currency. In Lord Overstone's opinion, money and currency are identical, and include the coined metallic money, and the paper notes promising to pay the bearer coin on demand; and he says that the characteristic of their being money is, that they are received equally at "all times, between all persons and in all places." For the sake of shortness, let us designate this phrase by 3A—from the three Alls in it. Lord Overstone excludes bills of exchange from the designation of currency, because "they do not possess that power of universal exchangeability which belongs to the money of the country." This definition is fatal to Lord Overstone's own view. In fact, if it be true, there is no such thing as money or currency at all. In the first place, it at once excludes the whole of bank notes. The notes of a bank in the remote district of Cumberland would not be current in Cornwall; therefore, they are not 3A; therefore, they are not currency. Again, the notes of a small country bank in Cornwall would not be received in Cumberland; therefore, they are not 3A; therefore, they are not currency. Similarly, there are no country bank notes which would be generally received throughout England; therefore, no country bank notes are 3A; therefore, no country bank notes are currency. Till within the last sixty years or so, Bank of England notes had scarcely any currency beyond London and Lancashire; in country districts a preference was universally given to local notes; therefore, Bank of England notes were not 3A; they had not the power of "universal exchangeability"; therefore, they were not currency. Bank of England notes would even now not pass through the greater part of country districts in Scotland. If, therefore, the test of 3A and "universal exchangeability" be applied, the claims of all bank notes to be considered as currency are annihilated at once.

But the universality of Lord Overstone's assertion is fatal to his argument in other ways. On the Continent, silver is a legal tender as money. In England, silver, like copper, is merely coined into small tokens, called shillings, etc., which are made to pass current above their natural value, and are only legal tender to a very trifling amount: hence, silver in England cannot be used in the adjustment of all transactions; therefore, it is not 3A; therefore, it is not currency. There are other countries, such as India, where gold is not a legal tender; therefore, it fails to satisfy Lord Overstone's test; therefore, it is not currency. If, then, the test proposed by Lord Overstone is to be accepted, it is easy to see that there is no substance or material whatever which does not fail under it; and, therefore, there is no such thing as currency.

The fact is, that the only difference between a bank note and a bill of exchange is, that the note is the right to payment on demand, and a bill is the right to payment at a future time. For these reasons, a bank note possesses a greater degree of circulating power than a bill. In the Midland counties it used to be quite common for the banks to issue the bills they had discounted with their own indorsement on them, which made them bank notes, until the practice was declared to be illegal, and such instruments were declared to be bank notes. Moreover, there is not the same inducement to put a bill into circulation as a note; because the former increases in value every day until it is paid, while the latter does not. But it is to the last degree unphilosophical to maintain that these two obligations are of different *natures* because they are adapted to circulate in different *degrees*.

Colonel Torrens has adduced several legal and practical reasons in support of the views of his sect. The poet says:

> "Ah me! what perils do environ
> The man who meddles with cold iron."

So are the perils which environ the lay dreamer who meddles with mercantile law and practical business. All Colonel Torrens' reasons are absolutely fallacious both in law and practice. He includes bank notes in, and excludes cheques from, the title of currency; because, he says, by law and custom the acceptance of the notes of a solvent bank liquidates debts and closes transactions; whereas, the acceptance of bank credits and cheques does not liquidate debts and close transactions. In this Colonel Torrens is absolutely wrong, as any tyro in mercantile law could tell him. Bank notes, cheques and bank credits stand on exactly the same footing as to liquidating debts and closing transactions. No debtor can compel his creditor to accept an ordinary bank note, cheque or bank credit in payment of a debt; but if he chooses to do so voluntarily, they all equally liquidate debts and close transactions. Tender of a cheque is equally good tender of payment as the tender of an ordinary bank note. And when the bank has transferred the credit from the debtor's account to that of the creditor, it liquidates the debt and closes the transaction in all respects as if it had been a payment in money. If a creditor accepts payment by cheque and keeps the cheque an undue time, without presenting it for payment, and the bank fails, having sufficient credit on the debtor's account to meet his cheque, the debt between the creditor and debtor is liquidated and the transaction closed. And if the credit has once been transferred from the account of the debtor to that of the creditor, the debt as between the parties is liquidated, and the transaction closed, even though the bank should fail immediately afterwards.

But Colonel Torrens' statement of facts is equally erroneous as his statement of law. He alleges that a transaction by a bill of exchange is not finally closed until the bill has been paid in coin or in bank notes. It is the idea of Colonel Torrens, Mill and other dreamers, who have not the slightest knowledge of the mechanism of modern banking, that all bills of exchange and cheques are ultimately paid in coin or bank notes, at which all bankers and persons conversant with the mechanism of modern banking would make themselves very merry. In modern banking, probably not one bill of exchange in 10,000, and only a small proportion of cheques, are paid in coin or bank notes. An investigation instituted by some bankers after the late Gold and Silver Commission showed that only ·0025 per cent. of banking transactions are settled in coin. No doubt, 250 years ago, before the institution of banking, all bills were paid in money; but as soon as banking attained any magnitude, persons who had bill transactions must have been customers of the same bank; and in all such cases bills were paid and discharged by means of bank credits, and not by money. Before the institution of the Clearing House in 1776, all banking charges were settled by coin and bank notes; but when the Clearing House was instituted, and bankers' charges were settled by means of mutual exchanges of the securities, and it was only the inequality of these exchanges which was paid in bank notes, this, of course, enormously diminished the number of cheques and bills which were paid in money or bank notes; but in recent years almost all the banks, including the Bank of England, have entered the Clearing House, and even most of the banks which are not in the Clearing House themselves pass their cheques and bills through banks which are. And by a further improved system of clearing, no money or bank notes are used at all. In the year 1889, cheques and bills to an amount exceeding £7,000,000,000 were settled and discharged in the London Clearing House alone, without the use of a single coin or bank note; and besides that, there is a Country Clearing House and clearing houses in all the great towns. What becomes, then, of the foolish fancy of Torrens, Mill and so many others, that all cheques and bills are ultimately paid in coin and bank notes? They are all paid and discharged by bank credits. Thus, when Torrens and his sect maintain that the criterion of currency is that it liquidates debts, and closes transactions, and they maintain that bank credits, or deposits, are not currency, they are "hoist with their own petard." Because, as a fact in modern banking, all banking transactions are liquidated and closed by bank credits or deposits. Bank credits, or deposits, are now for all practical purposes the money of the country.

BANK CREDITS, OR DEPOSITS, ARE READY MONEY.

We show elsewhere that the term circulating medium means the medium which circulates commodities; and hence, *ex vi termini,* it necessarily includes money and credit in all its forms, both written and unwritten; because, if a person buys goods on credit, or by issuing a right of action, that credit or right of action circulates the goods equally, whether it is recorded on paper or not. So we have shown that money, and all rights to money recorded on some material, which can be lost or stolen, and passed away by manual delivery, are included under the term currency. A superficial difficulty, however, arises when the term currency is used as synonymous with circulating medium; because there is a vast mass of credits which have circulated goods, and are therefore circulating medium, which are not recorded on any tangible and transferable material, and therefore are not currency in its strict legal sense, such as book debts in traders' shops, and deposits or debts in bankers' books. The slightest reflection, however, will show that there is no real difficulty in the case. A right of action, credit or debt is exactly the same in its nature, whether recorded on paper or not. And it can be bought and sold or exchanged with perfect facility in either form. In Roman law, in which written instruments were not used, if it was wanted to transfer a debt, the creditor, the debtor and the transferee met together; the creditor transferred the debt orally to the transferee, and the debtor agreed orally to pay the transferee, instead of his original creditor. This was a valid transfer of the debt. The same mode of proceeding is equally a valid transfer of the debt in English law. But in many cases this is a clumsy and inconvenient way of transferring a debt. It is infinitely more convenient to write it down on paper, and then it can be transferred by manual delivery, like money or any other chattel. But whether the transfer be effected orally or by written document can make no possible difference in the nature of the right. Recording a credit, debt or right of action, therefore, on paper does not create any new right; it merely records an already existing right on paper. Payment, therefore, by means of a bank note, or cheque, or bank credit, termed a deposit, is absolutely the same. Now bank notes and cheques are currency in strict legal phraseology; but bank credits or deposits are not strictly currency in legal phraseology, because they cannot be lost, mislaid, stolen and passed away in commerce by manual delivery. So also of a book debt in a tradesman's books. If a trader buys goods from a merchant on credit, that credit has performed exactly the same function in circulating the goods as money; because we have shown that the word circulation means buying goods with money or credit, and the credit has been equally the medium of circulation or sale, whether it is recorded on paper or not; but it is not currency, because it cannot be dropped in the streets, stolen and transferred to some one else by manual delivery. Nevertheless, all these book credits in the books of bankers and traders are of exactly the same nature as if they were recorded on circulating paper, and they can always be recorded on paper at the will of the parties, when they become currency in the strictest legal sense of the term. If, then, we are compelled to adopt this barbarism, and employ the term currency to denote a certain class of economic quantities, synonymous with circulating medium, it must, by the laws of philosophy, be held to include bank credits or deposits, bank credits and verbal credits of all sorts.

And this is exactly what mercantile law does. It treats any form of credit payable on demand by a banker, whether it be a bank note, a cheque, or a bank credit, as money or cash. They are all equally, in the eye of the law, payment; that is, none of them are legal money; that is, a debtor cannot compel his creditor to take payment in them of a debt; but if a creditor chooses to do so of his own accord without objection, they all stand on exactly the same footing as payment.

The importance and the practical bearing of these investigations and decisions are evident. All banking "advances" are made, in the first instance, by creating bank credits or deposits in favor of the customer. These deposits are simply rights of action, or simple contract debts. Now, these rights of action, credits or debts, are the "goods and chattels" or property of the customer, which are exactly of the same value as money, because they can always be exchanged for money instantly on demand. But the customer wishes to use these credits as money and transfer them to some one else. This may be done by writing them down on paper either as notes or cheques. But it is evident that the property, or "goods and chattels," are identically the same, whether they are written down on paper or not. Now, many persons seeing a material bank note or cheque, are willing to admit that they are cash. But, from the want of a little reflection and ignorance of the mechanism of banking, they feel a difficulty with regard to what they see as deposits. They admit that a bank note or a cheque is an "issue" and "currency" and "circulation," but they fail to see that a bank credit is in exactly the same sense equally an "issue," "currency" and "circulation." When unreflecting persons see so many figures in a book they are sometimes startled at hearing them called wealth; but in fact it is not these figures in the ledger that are the wealth; these figures are only the evidence and the acknowledgment of so many rights of action, credits or debts in the persons of the creditors of the banker; these rights of action are just as much "issued" and in "circulation" as if they were notes; they are equally rights of action to demand gold, and it makes not the slightest difference in their nature whether they are recorded on paper or not. The figures in the book are a mere reminder to the banker that he is bound to pay them in gold if demanded. Thus these bank credits or deposits are a mass of exchangeable property, like so much gold, or corn, or timber, or any other; and their value depends upon exactly the same thing as the value of any thing else, whether they can be paid in gold on demand. And for this reason they are termed *Pecunia, Res, Bona, Merx,* in Roman law: *χρήματα, πράγματα, ἀγαθά, οὐσία,* in Greek law, and goods, goods and chattels, chattels, merchandise, vendible commodities and incorporeal wealth in English law. And in all the Parliamentary debates from 1797 till Sir Robert Peel's speech on introducing his Act of 1844, it was invariably assumed that money and credits of all sorts—*i. e.,* rights to demand money—whether written or unwritten, constitute the currency of the country. As Lord Tichfield expressed it: "When it was considered to how great an extent these contrivances (*i. e.*, credits of various forms) had been practiced in the various modes of verbal, book and circulating credits, it was easy to see that the country had received a great addition to its currency. This addition to the currency would of course have the same effect as if gold had been increased from the mines." This expression of Lord Tichfield's represents the unanimous doctrine of statesmen and economists until the time of Lord Overstone and his sect, and is amply confirmed by the decisions of the courts of law which we have so copiously quoted.

CONSEQUENCES OF LORD OVERSTONE'S DEFINITION OF CURRENCY.

We have now to point out the consequences to which Lord Overstone's definition of currency leads, which may somewhat surprise its advocates. Lord Overstone's dogma asserts that the fundamental essence of money or currency is that it "closes a debt." To this we reply, as was the fashion in the glorious old days of special pleading, (1) There is no debt to close; (2) It does not close the debt.

1. When money is exchanged for goods no debt arises, and if it be said that the money closes the debt which would have arisen on the sale of the goods, we reply that the goods equally close the debt which would have arisen on the sale of the money. It is simply an exchange; the money and the goods equally close the debt which would have arisen on either side. Therefore, if the essence of currency be to "close debt," the goods are currency for precisely the same reason that money is.

2. It is quite common in the city to close a debt with stock; therefore, by this dogma, stock is currency.

3. In numerous cases debts are closed by a payment in goods. Traders may exchange goods. Now, by the exchange of goods, the debt is closed as effectually as by money. Hence, by this dogma, the goods exchanged on each side are currency.

4. Two merchants may issue acceptances for the same amount payable on the same day. These merchants may chance to get possession of each other's acceptances. If so, each merchant may tender to the other his acceptance in payment of the debt due by himself. By this exchange, the

debts are closed on each side. Consequently, each acceptance, according to Lord Overstone's dogma, is currency. In the great Continental fairs merchants exchanged their acceptances by millions; the debts were closed; and therefore they were currency.

5. A merchant issues his acceptance, which gets into the hands of a banker. The banker issues notes, which get into the hands of the merchant. When the banker presents his acceptance to the merchant, the merchant pays the banker in his own notes. By this exchange the debt on each side is closed; hence, by Lord Overstone's dogma, the acceptance is equally currency as the notes.

6. Or the merchant issues an acceptance which gets into the hands of his own banker; when the acceptance falls due, the banker simply writes off the amount from the merchant's account. Both debts then are closed; and, according to Lord Overstone's dogma, the acceptance and the deposit are equally currency.

7. If two persons, A and B, are customers of the same bank, and A owes B a debt; A gives B a cheque on his account; B pays in the cheque to his account; the banker transfers the credit from A's account to B's, and the debt is closed by novation. Hence, by Lord Overstone's dogma, the deposit is currency. Thus Lord Overstone's dogma is transfixed by shafts drawn from his own quiver.

The same doctrine may be extended to other cases:

8. A person buys a ticket from a railway company; the company then is in debt to him for a journey. But when they have carried him to his journey's end, the debt is closed; therefore, according to Lord Overstone's dogma, the railway journey is currency.

9. A person buys an opera ticket; the manager is then in debt to him for a performance; when the person has seen the performance, the debt is closed; hence, by Lord Overstone's dogma, the performance of the opera is currency.

10. A person buys a postage stamp; the post office is then in debt to him for the carriage of a letter. When the letter is carried to its destination, the debt is closed. Hence, by Lord Overstone's dogma, the carriage of a letter is currency.

And the same principle may be applied to many other cases which will readily suggest themselves to the intelligence of the reader.

In the next place, by the unanimous consent of economists, a payment in money does not close the debt.

Economists affirm that the transaction is not closed until a satisfaction has been obtained for the one originally given; they therefore held that, in exchange for money, the exchange is not consummated. A baker, say, wants shoes; he sells his bread for money. But can he wear the money as shoes? Certainly not; he must exchange away his money for shoes. Consequently, the economists held that the exchange was not consummated or completed, and the debt closed, until the baker has got the shoes in exchange for the bread. For this reason, all economists, from Aristotle to the present time, have perceived and declared that money itself is only a species of credit, a general bill of exchange, as we have shown by a whole catena of writers. Hence, money and bills of exchange are fundamentally analogous. They are merely the evidence of a debt due to their possessor. And the payment of a bill of exchange in money is only the exchange of a particular and precarious right for a general and permanent one.

But, as economists, we have nothing to do with satisfaction and enjoyment, but only with exchanges; the exchange of goods for a bill is one exchange; the exchange of a bill or note for money is another exchange, and the exchange of money for goods is another exchange. Hence, a person who has received money for goods or services has no more got a satisfaction, in the economic sense, than the person who has received a bill of exchange.

SECTION VII.

ON THE BANK ACTS OF 1844 AND 1845.

Conditions Preceding the Acts—Peel's Vacillations—He Finally Embraces the "Currency Principle"—His Statement Before Parliament—Provisions of the Act of 1844—Scotch Bank Act of 1845—Irish Bank Act of 1845—Limited Liability Banks.

A FEW years after the Bank Restriction Act of 1797, the market price of gold in bank paper rose very considerably, and the foreign exchanges fell and produced great derangement in the foreign commerce of the country. The most sagacious observers of the day attributed the rise in the market price of gold and the fall in the foreign exchanges to the depreciation of the bank notes, caused by excessive issues. Many persons began to think how the bank was to be prevented from making these excessive issues of notes, which, being the only measure of value left in the country, caused the most violent changes in the value of all kinds of property. It was proposed by many that its issues should be limited by law. But Mr. Henry Thornton, M. P., one of the most eminent bankers in London, and one of the joint authors of the Bullion Report, says:* "It was the object of several former chapters to point out the evil of a too contracted issue of paper. The general tendency of the present, as well as the preceding one, has been to show the danger of a too extended emission. Two kinds of error on the subject of the affairs of the Bank of England have been prevalent. Some political persons have assumed as a principle that, in proportion as the gold of the bank lessens, its paper, or, as it is sometimes said, its loans (for the amount of the one has been confounded with that of the other), ought to be reduced. It has already been shown that a maxim of this sort, if strictly followed up, would lead to universal failure." We shall see afterwards whether this prognostication was verified.

This disturbance, however, passed away, and for several years the value of the bank note did not differ very much from par, and consequently these

* An Inquiry into the Nature and Effects of the Paper Credit of Great Britain, 245.

discussions slumbered. In 1804, a committee was appointed on the Irish currency in consequence of the excessive rise in Irish bank notes and the severe fall of the Dublin exchange. The committee condemned in the strongest terms the excessive issues of Bank of Ireland and other paper; and laid down most emphatically the doctrine that the issues of bank paper should be governed by the foreign exchanges, exactly as they were before the restriction. The most extravagant over-trading in 1808 and 1809 in England, fostered by the most reckless over-issues by the Bank of England, produced exactly the same phenomena, and led to the appointment of the Bullion Committee in 1810. The directors of the Bank of England maintained exactly the same doctrines as the directors of the Bank of Ireland. The directors of both banks acknowledged that before the restriction they regulated their issues by the state of the foreign exchanges; contracting them when the exchanges were adverse, and expanding them when the exchanges were favorable. But the directors of both banks maintained that they were in no way bound to follow such a rule after the restriction; and they all agreed in scouting the notion that their issues could have any effect on the exchanges. The directors of both banks stated that they regulated their issues solely by the discount of mercantile bills. The Bullion Report laid down that the issues of the bank should be regulated by the price of gold and the foreign exchanges; but how this was to be done they did not say. As in 1802, it was strongly urged that the issues of the bank should be limited by law. But the Bullion Report emphatically condemned the idea of imposing a cast-iron limit on the issues of the bank.

The report gave some statistics regarding the quantity of notes in circulation at different periods since the restriction. However, they said that the actual numerical amount of notes in circulation at any given time was no criterion whatever as to whether it was excessive. Different states of trade and different extents of commercial operations would require different amounts of notes. When public credit was good a smaller amount would be required than when public alarm was felt, and people had recourse to hoarding. Moreover, the different methods of doing business and economizing the use of the currency much influenced the amount which might be necessary at any period. The improved methods of business, the policy of the bank, the increased issue of country bankers, had all tended to diminish the quantity of notes necessary for commerce. Consequently, the numerical amount alone was no criterion whatever. A surer test must be applied; and that sure criterion was only to be found in the state of the exchanges and the price of gold bullion.

The experience of the crisis of 1793 had proved that an enlarged accommodation was the true remedy for the failure of confidence in country districts, such as the system of paper credit was occasionally exposed to. That it was true that the bank had refused the enlarged accommodation in 1793. But the issue of exchequer bills was the same in principle, and the good effect that followed that issue proved the truth of the principle, that if the bank had had the courage to extend its accommodation in 1797, instead of contracting it as they did, the catastrophe which followed might probably have been avoided. Some persons thought so at the time, and many of the directors since the experience of 1797 were now quite satisfied that the course adopted by the bank in that year increased the public distress, in which opinion the committee fully concurred. A very important distinction, however, was to be observed between a demand for gold for domestic purposes, sometimes great and sudden, and caused by a temporary failure of confidence and a drain arising from the unfavorable state of the foreign exchanges. A judicious increase of accommodation was the proper remedy for the former phenomenon, but a diminution of issues the correct course to adopt in the latter.

Some proposals had been made of remedying the evil by a compulsory limitation of the amount of the bank's advances or discounts, or of its profits or dividends. All these, however, were futile, because the necessary proportion could never be fixed; and even if it were so, might very much aggravate the inconveniences of a temporary pressure; and even if their efficiency could be made to appear, they would be most hurtful, and an improper interference with the rights of commercial property. Thus, the Bullion Report, the ablest commercial report ever presented to Parliament, absolutely condemned the plan of imposing a cast-iron limit on the issues of the bank.

Mr. Peel, who was chairman of the Committee of 1819, had become an entire convert to the doctrines of the Bullion Report, which he had voted against in 1811, contended in the debate on moving for the Act of 1819, that there was no test of the excess or the deficiency of bank notes, but a comparison with the price of gold. As the bank had repudiated the principles of the Bullion Report, they could not be expected to act upon them. It might, therefore, appear necessary to prescribe such a limitation of their issues as would secure the power of the bank over the exchanges. He himself thought this a very unwise plan, because it depended so much on circumstances whether or not there was an excess of circulation. There were occasions when what was called a run upon the bank might be arrested in its injurious consequences by an increase of its issues. There were other occasions when such a state of things demanded a curtailment. In the year 1797, when a run was made on the bank, but when the exchanges were favorable and the price of gold had not risen, it was proved that an extension of issues might, by restoring confidence, have rendered the original restriction unnecessary. On the other hand, if the run was the effect of unfavorable exchanges and the consequent rise in the price of gold, the alarm must be met by a reduction of the issues. It was, therefore, impossible to prescribe any specific limitation of issues to be brought into operation at any period, however remote. The quantity of circulation which was demanded in a time of confidence varied so materially from the amount which a period of despondency required, that it was an absolute impossibility to fix any circumscribed amount.

In the great monetary crisis of 1825, it was shown that the only method of arresting the run on the bankers, and saving their existence, was by greatly extending the bank's issues. For three days after the panic began, the bank restricted its issues with extreme severity; then, when every banker and merchant in London was in danger of stopping payment, the bank extended its issues with the greatest liberality; and in an instant the whole commercial world, mercantile and banking, was saved. Consequently, although the commercial crisis was alleged to have been greatly aggravated, if not originally produced, by the excessive issues of country bankers, no sane statesman breathed a word as to imposing a cast-iron limit on the issues of the Bank of England. Mr. Secretary Peel was convinced that the root of the evil lay in the monopoly of the Bank of England, and that if, in the year 1793, a set of banks had existed in this country on the Scotch system, it would have escaped the danger it was then involved in, as well as the calamity which had just occurred.

In 1793, upwards of 100 banks had failed. In seven years, from 1810 to 1817, 157 commissions in bankruptcy were issued against country bankers; in the crisis which had just occurred, seventy-six failures had taken place. But from the different ways of making compositions, etc., the number of failures should probably be estimated at four times the number of the commissions of bankruptcy. What system could be worse or more prejudicial to every interest in the country, than one which admitted of such an enormous amount of failures? Contrast what had been the case in Scotland, under a different system. Mr. Gilchrist, a manager of one of the Scotch banks, had been asked by the committee of 1819 how many failures there had been in Scotland within his recollection, and said, that there had been only one; that the creditors had been paid 14s. in the pound immediately, and, finally, the whole of their claims. These facts were a strong presumption that the Scotch system, if not quite perfect, was at least far superior to the one existing in England. The present system of country banking was most prejudicial in every point of view. He then described the misery caused by the failure of the country banks. He trusted that the institution of joint-stock banks would place the currency on a firmer footing. He most sincerely trusted that the great obstacle to the proposed institutions, the want of a charter, would be removed. He hoped that the directors of the Bank of England would seriously consider what advantage they would derive from refusing charters to these banks. He, himself, could not imagine what benefit they would derive from it; they, no doubt, had the right to prevent such charters being granted, but he hoped they would refrain from exercising their right.

On the renewal of the charter in 1833, Sir Robert Peel maintained the same opinion. He had, however, recanted his opinion as to the evil of the monopoly of the bank, and the expediency of adopting the Scotch system of a multiplicity of banks. He was of opinion that it was desirable to continue the privileges of the bank, and that there should be but one bank of issue in the metropolis, in order that it might exercise an undivided control over the issue of paper, and give facilities to commerce in times of difficulty and danger, which it could not give with the same effect if it were subject to the rivalry of another establishment. This, however, is an *obiter dictum*—a long way from proof.

Thus, up to 1833, all statesmen, financiers and economists held that the circulating medium or currency, the measure of value in which the price of commodities is expressed, consists of and comprehends money and credit in all its forms, both written and unwritten; that it had no definite fixed limit; that the sole test of its value is the price of gold and the state of the foreign exchanges, and that commercial crises, when they attain a certain degree of intensity, can only be alleviated and allayed by cautious and judicious but liberal extension of the issues of the bank. And as Sir Robert Peel is to play such a conspicuous part in the monetary legislation of the country, it is well to note the phases of opinion he underwent on the subject.

In 1811 he voted in the majority against the principles of the Bullion Report. In 1819 he had adopted to the full the principles of the Bullion Report; saw the necessity of leaving the bank free to assist commercial difficulties, and declared that at no period, however remote, would he ever consent to impose a cast-iron limit on the issues of the bank. In 1826 he was dead against the monopoly of the bank, which he declared was the root of all the evil in the banking system of England, and recognized the superiority of the Scotch system of a multiplicity of banks. In 1833 he was decidedly in favor of perpetuating the monopoly of the bank.

THE BANK ACT OF 1844.

In 1844, Sir Robert Peel cast all his own opinions and the opinions of the Bullion Report, and of all the soundest and most able economists and statesmen, to the winds. The bank in 1827 had at last adopted the principles of the Bullion Report, and had endeavored to carry them into effect. But the measures they adopted so utterly failed, and brought the bank into such discredit and up to the very verge of bankruptcy, that Sir Robert was naturally irritated and disgusted, and he delivered himself over, bound hand and foot, to the dogmas of Lord Overstone and his sect, which we have explained in a previous chapter. Hopeless of discovering any other method of controlling and curbing the mismanagement of the bank, Peel at length, after long hesitation and doubt, determined to impose a legal cast-iron limit on the bank's power of issue. If Peel had done this simply as a plain, practical measure; if he had said that the directors seemed so utterly incapable of managing the bank with unlimited powers of issue, that he saw no alternative but to try the effect of imposing a legal limit on their power, it might perhaps have been difficult to gainsay him. But, unfortunately, he founded his act upon a whole nest of theories. He adopted Lord Overstone's dogmatic heresy, that bank notes payable to bearer on demand alone are currency, to the exclusion of all other forms of credit, even cheques. He then adopted the theory which his supporters designate the "Currency Principle"—that is, that when bank notes are permitted to be issued, they should exactly equal the gold they are alleged to displace; and that for every five sovereigns drawn out of the bank, a £5 note should be withdrawn from circulation; and that any excess of notes above the gold they displace is a depreciation of the currency. He was aware that the doctrine was in diametrical contradiction to his own often-expressed opinion, and to the unanimous doctrine of every statesman in 1819. He then deliberately took away the power of the bank to act in support of commerce in a crisis, by propounding the astounding dogma that all commercial crises originate in excessive issues of notes by banks; and, therefore, he concluded that if he could prevent excessive issues by banks, he would thereby prevent the occurrence of commercial crises, and, therefore, there would be no need for the bank to have this power.

Now, it shows Peel's want of knowledge of the simplest mechanism of banking to suppose that the Act of 1844 really does carry out the "currency principle." It has been shown that, in order really to carry out the "currency principle" into effect, it would have been necessary to prohibit the Bank of England from discounting bills of exchange, because every bill a bank discounts is a violation of the "currency principle." The banks really constructed on the "currency principle" never discounted bills of exchange, and never made, and by no possibility ever could make, any profits. Secondly, if Peel had been acquainted with commercial history, he would have known that the "currency principle" is no preventive against commercial crises, because some of the very worst commercial crises on record took place in those very cities where the "currency principle" was really in force. Lastly, it was the very worst delusion of all to suppose that all commercial crises are produced by excessive issues of notes. Speculation originates with the mercantile community; and all rapid and sudden changes of price, all new fields of operation and new markets suddenly thrown open, naturally produce over-speculation. Banks, no doubt, may and do foster over-speculation and aggravate commercial crises; but the speculations do not originate with bankers; it is merchants who originate speculations, and who frequently drag bankers into them by the most unscrupulous, nefarious and (though not legally, yet morally) fraudulent means. To suppose that it is possible to prevent mercantile speculation and commercial crises by imposing an absolute limit on the currency, is as vain a delusion as that of the London alderman who declared that he would put down suicide.

On the 6th of May, 1844, Sir Robert Peel moved a resolution of the House that it was expedient to continue for a limited time certain of the privileges of the Bank of England, subject to any provisions that might be passed by any act for that purpose. In bringing this resolution forward, he gave a preliminary sketch of the evils of the paper currency as it then stood, and the methods he proposed for placing it on a sounder footing. After dwelling on the importance of a metallic standard, and exposing the absurdity of the theories which were so prevalent during the Restriction Act (by which he himself was beguiled), and the advantage of having a single standard of value, he addressed himself to the more immediate subject of consideration—the state of the paper circulation of the country, and the principles which ought to regulate it, remarking:

"I must state at the outset that, in using the word money, I mean to designate by that word the coin of the realm and promissory notes payable to bearer on demand. In using the word paper currency, I mean only such promissory notes. I do not include in these terms bills of exchange, drafts on bankers, or other forms of credit. (But unfortunately all judges do.) There is a natural distinction, in my opinion, between the character of a promissory note payable to bearer on demand and other forms of paper credit; and between the effects which they respectively produce upon the price of commodities and the foreign exchanges.

[There is no real difference on its effect on price between a note and a bill of exchange. They both aggravate prices, and thus by causing goods to be too dear to export they lead to an export of gold. An excessive importance was attached to notes in those days, because notes were almost the only credit payable to bearer in circulation. But at the present day cheques have, to a very large extent, superseded notes, and have increased at an enormously greater rate than notes, and cheques are in all respects absolutely identical with notes.]

"The one answers all the purposes of money, passes from hand to hand without indorsement, without examination, if there be no suspicion of forgery; and it is, in fact, what its designations imply it to be, currency or circulating medium (which words, though having radically different meanings, comprehend exactly the same quantities). * * * I think that experience shows that the paper currency—that is, promissory notes payable to bearer on demand—stands in a certain relation to the gold coin and the foreign exchanges in which other forms of paper credit do not stand. [Cheques and notes stand exactly in the same relation to the gold coin and the foreign exchanges; and, as we shall see, it was this extraordinary oversight which brought about the failure of the Bank Act of 1844.] There are striking examples of this adduced in the report of the Bullion Committee of 1810, in the case both of the Bank of England and of the Irish and Scotch banks. In the case of the Bank of England, and shortly after its establishment, there was a material depreciation of paper in consequence of excessive issues. The notes of the Bank of England were at a discount of seventeen per cent. After trying various expedients, it was at length determined to reduce the amount of notes outstanding. The consequence was an immediate increase in the value of those which remained in circulation, the restoration of them to par and a corresponding improvement in the foreign exchanges. [The troubles of the bank were not brought about by excessive issues, but by the shameful state of the coinage; and the bank having promised to pay twelve ounces of coin for every seven it had received, as soon as the new good silver coin came into general circulation, the exchanges were restored to par, while the note was at a discount of twenty per cent. and eleven months before the note was brought to par. Moreover, the notes were not reduced in amount. It is true that £200,000 were added to the new capital of the bank, but at the same time £800,000 in exchequer tallies were also added, and made the new capital exceed a million; and the bank was allowed to issue new notes to the full amount of its new capital, tallies and notes together; so that, in fact, the notes, instead of being reduced, were greatly increased.] In the case of Ireland, in 1804 the exchange with England was extremely unfavorable. A committee was appointed to consider the causes. It was denied by most of the witnesses from Ireland that they were at all connected with excessive issues of Irish notes. In the spring of 1804, the exchange of Ireland with England was so unfavorable that it required £118 10s. of the notes of the Bank of Ireland to purchase £100 of the notes of the Bank of England. Between the years 1804 and 1806, the notes of the Bank of Ireland were reduced from £3,000,000 to £2,410,000, and the effect of this, taken in conjunction with an increase of the English circulation, was to restore the relative value of Irish paper and the exchange with England to par. [At this time Bank of Ireland notes were inconvertible and the sole medium of paying the exchanges, and consequently excessive issues would necessarily cause a heavy depression of the exchanges.] In the same manner an unfavorable state of the exchange between England and Scotland has been more than once corrected by a contraction of the paper circulation of Scotland. [Not more than once. The cause of the Scotch notes falling to a discount was the optional clause, which in fact made them payable at six months after demand, at the will of the bank. As soon as the optional clause was abolished by law, the Scotch notes at once rose to par, and have never varied from it since.] In all these cases the action has been on that part of the paper credit of the country which has consisted of promissory notes payable to bearer on demand. There had been no interference with other forms of paper credit, nor was it contended then, as it is now contended by some, that promissory notes are identical in their nature with bills of exchange, and with cheques on bankers and with deposits, and that they cannot be dealt with on any separate principle."

It is well known now that all these ideas are entirely antiquated. They are in direct contradiction to the doctrines of Ricardo and the Bullion Report. All statesmen, economists and financiers of that time held that the actual amount of paper issues was no proof of excess; the sole criterion was the price of gold and the state of the foreign exchanges. All modern economists of reflection have reverted to the doctrines of Ricardo and the Bullion Report; and it is now well known that the true way of restricting paper currency, *i. e.*, credit, is not by imposing an arbitrary cast-iron limit on its amount, but by sedulously regulating the rate of discount by the bullion in the bank and the state of the foreign exchanges. The truth of this doctrine, which had not even been thought of in Peel's time, is now universally recognized, and it is the principle on which the Bank of England has been managed for more than thirty years.

Mr. Peel then proceeded to expatiate on the evils of the unlimited competition of issues :

"Are the lessons of experience at variance with the conclusions we are entitled to draw from reason and from evidence? What has been the result of unlimited competition in the United States? In the United States the paper circulation was supplied, not by private bankers, but by joint-stock banks established on principles the most satisfactory. There was every precaution taken against insolvency, unlimited responsibility of partners, excellent regulations for the publication and audit of accounts, immediate convertibility of paper into gold. If the principle of unlimited competition, controlled by such checks be safe, why has it utterly failed in the United States? How can it be shown that the experiment was not fairly made in that country? Observe this fact, while there existed a central bank (the United States Bank) standing in some relation to the other banks of the United States as the Bank of England stands to the banks of this country, there was some degree (imperfect it is true) of control over the general issues of paper. But when the privileges of the central bank ceased, when the principle of free competition was left unchecked, then came, notwithstanding professed convertibility, immoderate issues of paper, extravagant speculation, and the natural consequences, suspension of cash payments and complete insolvency. Hence, I conclude, that reason, evidence, and experience combine to demonstrate the impolicy and danger of unlimited competition in the issue of paper."

It is impossible to say which is the more remarkable—the evidence Sir Robert Peel omitted, or the evidence he adduced. What was the need for Sir Robert Peel to cross the Atlantic in search of an example of joint-stock banks with unlimited competition of issues? Why did he not cross the Tweed? On the north side of the Tweed there had existed joint-stock banks with unlimited issues for 150 years, and no central bank to control the others; the principle of free competition had been left unchecked, and the natural consequences, "suspension of cash payments and complete insolvency," had never occurred. In 1826, Sir Robert Peel had denounced the monopoly of the Bank of England in the severest terms, and lauded the Scotch system of competing banks with unlimited issues to the skies. Why had his zeal for the Scotch system cooled down to zero in 1844? But he carefully avoided saying one word about that case, because it militated against the theory he was determined to carry at all hazards—namely, that of one Central Bank of Issue. But the evidence he adduced was as great a misrepresentation of historical fact as what we have already quoted in a former section. The American banks, indeed, established on principles the most satisfactory! Why, John Law was the inspiring genius of American banking in 1834 till the subsequent crash. It was not because they were unlimited that was the cause of the catastrophe, but because the American legislatures fostered Law's wildest ideas of paper money. But as to the fact of the Central Bank of the United States exercising any due controlling influence over the other banks, we need only cite a passage from President Van Buren's message to Congress in 1839.

"I am aware that it has been urged that the control over the operations of the local banks may be best attained and exerted by means of a national bank. The history of the late national bank, through all its mutations, shows that it was not so; on the contrary, it may, after a careful consideration of the subject be, I think, safely stated that at every period of banking excess it took the lead; that in 1817 and 1818, in 1823 and in 1833, and in 1834, its vast expansions, followed by distressing contractions, led to those of the State institutions. It swelled and maddened the tides of the banking system, but seldom allayed or safely directed them. At a few periods only was a salutary control exercised, but an eager desire on the contrary exhibited for profit in the first place; and, if afterwards its measures were severe towards other institutions, it was because its own safety compelled it to adopt them. It did not differ from them in principle or in form; its measures emanated from the same spirit of gain; it felt the same temptation to over-issue; it suffered from, and was totally unable to avert, these inevitable laws of trade by which it was itself affected, equally with them, and at least on one occasion, at any early day, it was saved only by extraordinary exertion from the same fate that attended the weakest institution it professed to supervise. In 1837 it failed, equally with others, in redeeming its notes, though the two years allowed by its charter had not expired, a large amount of which remains at the present time outstanding."

Such was the language held by the Government regarding that bank which Peel held up as a model for that of England, and to whose abolition he attributed the destruction of American credit! And if we were to descend from the language of the Executive to that of private writers, such as Gallatin, Lee and Appleton, and others, we shall find that the most reckless mismanagement was the chief characteristic of that bank. When it stopped payment it was found to be utterly insolvent. So much for the value of it as an argument in support of Peel's views.

Sir Robert Peel then stated that it was the intention of the Government to increase as much as possible the power of a single bank of issue, and that bank should be the Bank of England. The bank was, therefore, to continue its privileges of issue, but it was to be divided into two departments—the one for the purpose of issuing notes, and the other for the ordinary business of banking. But the bank was to be deprived, once for all, of the power of unlimited issues. These were to take place in future on two foundations only: 1st. A fixed amount of public securities. 2d. Bullion. The amount of issues upon public securities was permanently fixed at £14,000,000; every other note was to be issued in exchange for bullion only, so that the amount of notes issued on bullion should be governed solely by the action of the public. Although he wished that there should only be a single bank of issue, yet existing interests were to be regarded, and those banks which were at that time lawfully issuing their own notes might remain banks of issue, but their amount was to be strictly limited to a certain definite average.

On the 20th oı May, Sir Robert introduced further resolutions, and proposed that, in the event of any country banks of issue failing, or withdrawing their notes voluntarily from circulation, the bank might, with the consent of the Crown, increase its issues to a definite proportion of the notes thus withdrawn. And further, that the bank should be obliged to buy all gold bullion presented for purchase at £3 17s. 9d. per ounce. It had only previously been giving £3 17s. 6d.; and a certain proportion was allowed on silver bullion, as the export of that was a proper remedy for the inconvenience of our standard differing from that of other nations. It was, therefore, of great importance to insure such a stock of silver in this country as might meet the wants of merchants, and prevent them having to send to the Continent for it. He proposed that the silver bullion on which the bank might issue notes should not exceed one-fourth of the gold bullion.

It was impossible for Sir Robert Peel not to see that his measure of 1844 was in express contradiction with his recorded sentiments in 1819 and 1833, the emphatically expressed doctrine of the Bullion Report, all the statesmen and financiers of that period and of 1819; that it was impossible to limit the issues of the bank to any fixed amount, because in time of commercial trouble, increased issues were indispensable. Sir Robert Peel knew that he was now taking away this power from the bank, and he was, accordingly, obliged to meet this objection. He said:

"It is said that the Bank of England will not have the means which it has heretofore had of supporting public credit, and of affording assistance to the mercantile world in times of commercial difficulty. Now in the first place, the means of supporting public credit are not means exclusively possessed by banks. All who are possessed of unemployed capital, whether bankers or not, and who can gain an adequate return by the advance of capital, are enabled to afford, and do afford, that aid which it is supposed by some that banks alone are able to afford. In the scond place, it may be a question whether there be any permanent advantage in the maintenance of public or private credit, unless the means of maintaining it are derived from the *bona fide* advance of capital, and not from a temporary increase of promissory notes, issued for a special purpose. Some apprehend that the proposed restriction upon issue will diminish the power of the bank to act with energy at the period of monetary crisis and commercial alarm and derangement. But the object of the measure is to prevent (so far as legislation can prevént) the recurrence of those evils from which we suffered in 1825, 1836 and 1839. It is better to prevent the paroxysm than to excite it, and to trust to desperate remedies for the means of recovery." Sir Robert Peel, therefore, deliberately took away the power of the bank to act on extreme occasions, because he fondly hoped that his act would prevent those extreme occasions from arising. We shall see how these hopes were fulfilled.

Sir Charles Wood followed Sir Robert Peel, whose mere *alter ego* he was, travelling over the same ground, and giving the same caricatured description of American banking as he had done. He, of course, was a zealous devotee of the "currency principle." He said: "It is not enough, then, to enact that the bank notes shall be convertible. The paper circulation must not only be convertible, but must vary in amount from time to time as a metallic circulation would vary. A system, therefore, of paper circulation is required which will attain this object, and insure a constant and steady regulation of the issues on this principle. This, and this alone, affords a permanent security for the practical convertibility of the notes at all times, and for the consequent maintenance of the standard." Thus, at length, the entire overthrow of the doctrines which had been held for half a century by the most experienced, the wisest, and the most sagacious statesmen, economists and financiers was effected, and doctrines which had been especially condemned and rejected, and which they had expressly declared would, if carried out, lead to universal failure, were exalted in their place. A nest of untried theories and facts set up against the lessons of experience and reasoning, and we shall see the result.

This was a striking instance of the mutability of fortune—

"Sic volvenda ætas commutat tempora rerum;
Quod fuit in pretio, fit nullo denique honore,
Porro aliut succedit et e contemptibus exit,
Inque dies magis appetitur, floretque repertum
Laudibus, et miro'st mortalis inter honore."

"Thus time, as it goes round, changes the seasons of things. That which was in esteem falls at length into utter disrepute, and then another thing mounts up, and issues out of its degraded state, and every day is more and more coveted, and blossoms forth high in honor when discovered, and is in marvellous repute with men."—(*Munro.*)

But we shall find that fickle Fortune rolled her wheel a full round in the not very distant future.

THE ORGANIZATION OF THE BANK.

The chief provisions of the Bank Charter Act, Statute 1844, c. 32, are as follows:

1. After the 31st August, 1844, the issue of bank notes by the Bank of England should be kept wholly distinct from the general banking business, and be conducted by such a committee of the directors as the court might appoint, under the name of the "Issue Department of the Bank of England."

2. On the same day the governor and company should transfer, appropriate and set apart to the issue department securities to the value of £14,000,000, of which the debt due by the public to the bank was to be a part; and also so much of the gold coin and gold and silver bullion as should not be required for the banking department. The issue department was then to deliver over to the banking department an amount of notes exactly equal to the securities, coin and bullion so deposited with them. The bank was then forbidden to increase the amount of securities in the issue department, but it might diminish them as much as it pleased, and increase them again to the limit defined, but no further. The banking department was forbidden to issue notes to any person whatever, except in exchange for notes, or such as they received from the issue department in terms of the act.

3. The proportion of silver bullion in the issue department on which notes were to be issued, was not at any time to exceed one-fourth part of the gold coin and bullion held at the time by the issue department.

4. All persons whatever, from the 31st August, 1844, were to be entitled to demand bank notes in exchange for standard gold bullion, at the rate of £3 17s. 9d. per ounce.

5. If any banker who, on the 6th May, 1844, was issuing his own notes, should cease to do so, it should be lawful for the Crown in council to authorize the bank to increase the amount of securities in the issue department to any amount not exceeding two-thirds of the amount of notes withdrawn from circulation.

6. Weekly accounts, in a specified form, were to be transmitted to Government, and published in the next "London Gazette."

7. From the same date the bank was relieved from all stamp duty on their notes.

8. The annual sum payable by the bank for their exclusive privileges should be increased from £120,000, as settled in 1833, to £180,000. And all profits derived by the bank from the increase of their issues above the £14,000,000, as prescribed by the act, shall go to the public.

9. After the passing of the act, no person other than a banker, who was lawfully issuing his own notes on the 6th May, 1844, should issue bank notes in any part of the United Kingdom.

10. After the passing of the act, it was forbidden to any banker to draw, accept, make or issue in England or Wales any bill of exchange, or promissory note, or engagement for the payment of money payable to bearer on demand, or to borrow, owe or take up in England or Wales any sum or sums of money on the bills or notes of such banker, payable to bearer on demand, except such bankers as were on the 6th May, 1844, issuing their own bank notes, who were allowed to continue their issues in such manner and to such an extent as afterwards provided. The rights of any existing firm were not to be affected by the withdrawal, change or addition of any partner, provided the whole number did not exceed six persons.

11. Any banker who ceased to issue his own notes from any reason whatever, after the act, was not to resume such issues.

12. All existing banks of issue were forthwith to certify to the commissioners of stamps and taxes the place and name and firm at, and under which, they issued notes during the twelve weeks next preceding the 27th April, 1844. The commissioners were then to ascertain the average amount of each bank's issues, and it should be lawful for such banker to continue his issues to that amount, provided that on an average of four weeks they were not to exceed the average so ascertained.

13. If any two or more banks of issue had become united during that twelve weeks, the united bank might issue notes to the aggregate amount of each separate bank.

14. The commissioners were to issue in the "London Gazette" a statement of the authorized issues of each bank.

15. If two or more banks afterwards became united, each of less than six partners, then the commissioners might authorize them to issue notes to the amount of the separate issues. But if the number of the united banks exceeded six, their privilege of issuing notes was to cease.

16. If any banker exceeded his authorized issue, he was to forfeit the excess.

17. Every bank of issue was to send a weekly account of its issues, which was to be published in the "London Gazette."

18. The mode of taking the average was laid down, and bankers were to permit their books of accounts to be inspected by a Government officer properly appointed, and to make a return to Government once a year, within the first fortnight in January.

19. The Bank of England was allowed to compound with private banks of issue, to withdraw their own notes and issue Bank of England notes, for a sum not exceeding one per cent. per annum, up to the 1st August, 1856.

20. All banks whatever, in London or within sixty-five miles of it, were allowed after the passing of the act to draw, accept or indorse bills of exchange, not being payable to bearer on demand.

21. The privileges of the bank were to continue till twelve months to be given after the 1st August, 1855, and repayment of all the public debts and all the other debts whatever.

THE SCOTCH BANK ACT OF 1845.

Sir Robert Peel having carried his Bank Charter Act of 1844 with scarcely a breath of opposition, and which was considered at the time to be the *ne plus ultra* of human wisdom, passed acts in 1845 to regulate banking in Scotland and Ireland. The chief provisions of the Scotch Bank Act of 1845, Act, Statute 1845, c. 38, are as follows:

1. All persons had been prohibited by the Act, Statute 1844, c. 32, from commencing to issue notes in the United Kingdom after the 6th May, 1844; and all such persons in Scotland as were lawfully issuing their own notes between the 6th May, 1844, and the 1st May, 1845, were to certify to the Commissioners of Taxes the name of the firm and the places where they issued such notes.

2. The commissioners were to ascertain the average number of such bankers' notes in circulation during the year ending 1st May, 1845.

3. Such bankers were authorized to have in circulation an amount of notes, whose average for four weeks was not to exceed the amount thus certified by the commissioners, together with an amount equal to the average amount of coin held by the banker during the same four weeks. Of the coin, three-fourths must be gold and one-fourth might be silver.

4. In case the bank exceeds the legal amount, it is to forfeit the excess.

5. If two or more banks unite, they are authorized to have an issue of notes to the aggregate amount of issues of the separate banks, as well as the amount of coin held by the united banks.

6. Notes of the Bank of England not to be legal tender in Scotland.

THE IRISH BANK ACT OF 1845.

The chief provisions of the Irish Bank Act, Act Statute, 1845, c. 37, are as follows:

1. All restrictions enacted by former acts, prohibiting banking partnerships of more than six persons to be formed and carry on business within fifty miles of Dublin, were repealed.

2. Interest was allowed to the Bank of Ireland on its capital of £2,630,769 at the rate of 3 1-2 per cent. per annum.

3. The bank was to manage the public debt of Ireland without any charge.

4. The bank might be dissolved at any time after twelve months' notice, to be given after the 1st January, 1855, and repayment of all Government debts.

5. Bank of England notes were not to be legal tender in Ireland.

6. All bankers issuing notes in Ireland were, within one month after the passing of the act, to give in a statement to the Commissioners of Taxes of their claim, and the name and place of the firm where they issued such notes, during the year preceding the 1st May, 1845; and if they were found to be lawfully issuing notes between the 6th May, 1844, and the 1st May, 1845, they might continue to issue notes to the amount of the average they issued during that year, together with the amount of gold and silver coin held by the banker.

7. If two or more banks united, they might issue notes to the combined amount of the separate banks, together with the coin held by the united bank. Three-fourths of the coin must be gold and one-fourth might be silver.

8. All bank notes under £1 prohibited, under a penalty of not less than £5 and not more than £20.

9. Bank notes above £1 and under £5 subject to certain regulations.

10. Any persons, except those specially authorized, issuing promissory notes payable to bearer on demand for less than £5, should forfeit £20.

11. All bank notes were to be for complete pounds.

Such are the acts which at the present time regulate the issue of bank notes in England, Scotland and Ireland; and we observe that, while the Bank of England was obliged to hold Government security for its fixed issue of £14,000,000, the country bankers in England were strictly confined to their fixed issue, and in Scotland and Ireland the banks might issue their fixed limit without any security, and in addition to that an amount equal to the gold and silver coin they hold. The English Bank Act was founded on certain specific theories of currency; but the Scotch and Irish acts were merely rough-and-ready methods of compelling the banks to hold a greater amount of specie in proportion to their liabilities than they had hitherto done. As the chief point of interest with regard to Sir Robert Peel's banking legislation is the operation of the act in a commercial crisis and a monetary panic, we shall defer the consideration of its practical working till the chapter on monetary panics.

Sir Robert Peel had also passed an act in 1844 to regulate the joint-stock banks in England; but having turned out a complete failure, it was totally repealed in 1857, and so does not require further notice. By this Act, Statute 1857, c. 49, the number of partners allowed in a private bank was increased to ten.

EXTENSION OF LIMITED LIABILITY TO BANKS.

The question of admitting the principle of limited liability into commercial partnerships had long been resisted with the fiercest acrimony in England. The old theory of the law was expressed by Lord Eldon, who said that a man who entered into a commercial partnership rendered himself liable "to his last shilling and his last acre" for the debts of the company. And this was no doubt true with regard to ordinary private trading partnerships. But many great companies had been formed and incorporated, and being corporations they were, *ipso facto*, endowed with the privilege of limited liability. A principle may reasonably apply to a private partnership, whose members all take an active part in the business, and have full knowledge of all transactions, which does not apply to a large joint-stock company, whose affairs are expressly left in the hands of a small committee, and the great majority of the members are specially debarred from all knowledge of its transactions. Now, as there are many great objects in commerce which can only be effected by a large company, it had long been the practice in granting acts to these companies to limit the liability of the shareholders. This was done in the case of the Bank of England; in railway and other companies, and in the charters granted to colonial banks. But for a very long time, the application of this principle to private partnerships in England was vehemently resisted. This resistance, however, was at length overcome in 1855, and in that year the Act, Statute 1855, c. 133, permitted the formation of joint-stock companies with limited liability,

But though the principle was allowed to other companies, joint-stock banks were still jealously excluded from it, from some unintelligible distinction being drawn between banking and other kinds of trading. However, as is usual in this country, what good sense and reasoning could not effect was at last brought about by several most dreadful calamities. In 1857, some joint-stock banks failed. At that time there was no method of calling upon the shareholders to contribute ratably in proportion to their holding, to discharge the debts of the company. But the creditors might single out any individual shareholders they thought worth powder and shot, and claim their full debts from them. The consequence was, that on the failure of a joint-stock bank, the responsible shareholders disposed of their property, and put the Channel between themselves and their creditors, until they could make terms with them. The terrible bank failures of 1857 at length compelled the legislature to concede limited liability to banks.

The chief provisions of this Act, Statute 1858, c. 91, were:

1. So much of the statute of 1857 as prevented banks being formed with limited liability was repealed.

2. All banks which issued promissory notes were to be subject to unlimited liability with respect to their notes, for which they are to be liable, in addition to the sum for which they are liable to the general creditors.

3. Every existing banking company might register itself under the act, upon giving thirty days' notice to each and all of its customers. Any customer to whom it failed to give notice retained his full rights as before.

This act, however, had a very limited success. It was adopted in very few instances. Banks do not readily change their constitution, and almost all the great banks had a pride in maintaining unlimited liability, and thought that adopting the act might endanger their credit. Not one of the London joint-stock banks, nor any of the Scotch banks—which, except the three chartered banks, were all of unlimited liability—brought themselves under the Act of 1858. But the stupendous catastrophe of the City of Glasgow Bank, in 1878, created such consternation among the shareholders of banks, that they made determined efforts to compel their directors to adopt the principle of limited liability. This was the case, especially in Scotland, where investment in bank shares was recognized by the law courts as a legitimate investment of trust funds. But banks do not recognize trusts. Consequently, unfortunate trustees were liable, not only personally for all losses sustained by the banks, but also to make good the losses of their clients. This created such alarm that the shares in the Scotch banks fell thirty per cent.

To facilitate the adoption of limited liability by banks, and also to preserve all reasonable security for creditors, the Act, Statute 1879, c. 76, was passed, which enacts:

1. That any unlimited company may increase the nominal amount of its capital by increasing the nominal amount of its shares; provided, that no part of such increased capital shall be capable of being called up, except in the event of and for the purpose of the company being wound up.

2. A limited company may declare that any portion of its still uncalled-for capital shall not be capable of being called up, except in the event of and for the purpose of the company being wound up.

3. All banks are subject to unlimited liability with respect to their notes in circulation.

The Bank of England and the three senior chartered banks in Scotland were created corporations before the Crown was authorized by act of Parliament to create trading corporations with unlimited liability. They therefore had always been limited banks, and did not require to avail themselves of the Act of 1879 to become so. But almost all the English joint-stock banks and all the other Scotch banks, without loss of time, registered themselves as limited companies under the Act of 1879, and the result has been to show that all the fears which had been entertained that limited banks would sustain a diminution of credit were entirely groundless.

THE DIFFERENCES IN PRINCIPLE BETWEEN SUPPORTERS OF THE BANK ACT OF 1844 AND THOSE OF THE BULLION REPORT AND THE BANK ACT OF 1819.

The supporters of the Bank Act of 1844 strenuously maintain that it is the complement of, and in strict accordance with, the principles of the Bullion Report and of the Act of 1819. Such statements are, however, entirely incorrect. Beyond the simple fact that both were desirous to maintain the convertibility of the note, the principles maintained by the framers of the Bank Charter Act of 1844 are in all other respects radically different from those of the Bullion Report and of the supporters of the Bank Act of 1819.

The following are the differences of principle between them:

1. In all the great Parliamentary debates and in the opinion of statesmen, it was invariably assumed that the term currency includes money and credit in all its forms, written and unwritten, although no specific definition of currency was ever attempted.

Lord Overstone and his sect, whose doctrines prevailed with Sir Robert Peel, maintained that the term currency includes money and bank notes payable to bearer on demand only, to the exclusion of all other forms of credit. Does the definition of currency by the framers of the Bank Act of 1844 agree with that of those who supported the Bank Act of 1819?

2. The Bullion Report declares that the mere numerical amount of notes in circulation at any time is no criterion whether they are excessive or not.

The dogma of the framers of the Bank Act of 1844 is that the notes in circulation ought to be exactly equal in quantity to what the gold coin would be if there were no notes, and that any excess of notes above that quantity is a depreciation of the currency. Does the dogma of the framers of the Bank Act of 1844 agree with the principles of the Bullion Report on this point?

3. The Bullion Report declares, and the supporters of the Bank Act of 1819 uniformly maintained, that the sole test of the depreciation of the paper currency is to be found in the price of gold bullion and the state of the foreign exchanges.

Ricardo says:* "The issuers of paper money should regulate their issues solely by the price of bullion, and never by the quantity of their paper in circulation. The quantity can never be too great or too little while it preserves the same value as the standard." The dogma of the framers of the Bank Act of 1844 is, that the true criterion of the depreciation of paper is whether the notes do or do not exceed in quantity the gold they displace. Is the dogma of the framers of the Bank Act of 1844 in accordance with the principles of the Bullion Report and of Ricardo on this point?

4. It was proposed to the Bullion Committee to impose a positive limit on the issues of the bank, in order to curb their power of mismanagement.

* Proposals for an Economical and Secure Currency, p. 3.

The Bullion Report expressly condemns any positive limitation on its issues; Peel himself in 1819 and in 1833 fully concurred in this opinion, and said that at no time, however distant, would he impose a positive limit on the issues of the bank. But, in 1844, Peel himself, by the Act of 1844, imposed a cast-iron limit on the issues of the bank. Was the dogma of Peel in 1844 in accordance with the doctrines of the Bullion Report and of himself in 1819 and 1833?

5. The Bullion Report, after discussing the most important monetary crises which had occurred up to that time, expressly declares that it is the proper policy for the bank in certain times of commercial crises to expand its issues to support commercial houses and avert a monetary panic. The history of commercial crises, both before and after the Bullion Report, has proved the indubitable wisdom of this doctrine.

The Bank Charter Act of 1844 expressly prevents this from being done. The consequence has been that on three several occasions since the passing of the Act of 1844 it has been found indispensable to suspend the act, in order to prevent every bank in England stopping payment, and probably nineteen merchants out of every twenty being ruined. Is the dogma embodied in the Act of 1844 in accordance with the principles of the Bullion Report?

The above are the glaring and radical differences of doctrine between the principles of the Bullion Report, the supporters of the Act of 1819, and those of the framers of the Act of 1844, and experience has fully demonstrated the superior wisdom of the principles of the Bullion Report and of the supporters of the Act of 1819, to those of the framers of the Bank Act of 1844.

SECTION VIII.

COMMERCIAL CRISES.

Accommodation Paper — Its Real Danger — Banking Risks of Mutual Accommodation Paper.

IN another part of this work we have explained the scientific and juridical principles and mechanism of solid credit, and shown how it augments the wealth of a country—meaning, by solid credit, that which is actually and punctually redeemed at maturity. But there is a reverse to the medal. If solid, and judiciously used, credit has conduced more to the wealth of the world than all the mines of gold and silver; its abuses, in the hands of incautious and unscrupulous persons, has produced the most terrible calamities of modern times—namely, commercial crises and monetary panics. We have now to contemplate the dark side of the picture, and to show how commercial crises and monetary panics arise; how they are to be dealt with and brought under scientific control, which has hitherto been the opprobrium of economics and of financial statesmanship.

We have shown clearly that all credit is the present right to, or the present value of, a future payment; and so long as the credit is actually redeemed at maturity, by the various methods described in another chapter, the credit is not excessive. But all credit created in excess of the future payment, and which is not fully redeemed at maturity, is excessive. And it is excessive credit which produces all commercial crises; and if they are not properly and judiciously controlled, and are allowed to obtain a certain magnitude and intensity, they are very apt to culminate in monetary panics.

The fact is, that commercial crises are innate in the gigantic system of credit which has grown up in modern times; and if they are not skilfully dealt with, they have a great tendency to develop into monetary panics; but if they are dealt with on the principles which repeated experience and reasoning have suggested, though periodical commercial crises cannot in the nature of things be avoided, yet they may be prevented from developing into monetary panics.

As all traders in modern times trade on credit, it must necessarily be that there are a considerable number of bad speculators among them. They create bills in excess of future profits; and if there were any methed of compelling them to incur and bear the loss at once, there would be comparatively little harm done. A few individuals would suffer, but there would be no general commercial crisis. But traders are not usually very willing to put up with a present loss. They always hope to recoup themselves by future and more fortunate speculations. Hope springs eternal in the human breast. Traders endeavor to acquire a good character with their bankers; and they keep their losses to themselves. They not only create fresh bills, by which they hope to retrieve their former losses, but they manufacture fictitious bills by cross-acceptances amongst each other for the express purpose of extracting fresh funds from their bankers to speculate with. Now, when a trader has established a good reputation with his banker, and is accustomed to have a discount account with him to a certain amount, it is very serious indeed for his banker to stop it. We have already explained that, at the present day, bills of exchange are almost universally paid, not by money, but by discounting fresh bills. If, therefore, a customer has his own acceptances to meet, and his banker refuses to discount fresh bills for him, it means nothing less than instant ruin.

Now a banker may have a very shrewd suspicion that his customer is overtrading; but, as he has no access to his customer's books, it may be very difficult for him positively to ascertain the fact. And if a banker acts upon insufficient grounds, and without sure cause ruins his customer, he will get himself into very bad odor, and may do himself much injury. Of course, the greater the merchant the more difficult it is to deal with him. And great merchants, who have numerous and powerful connections, can manufacture bills to an incredible extent to cover up losses, and keep themselves afloat by extracting fresh funds from their bankers to speculate with; until, when the final collapse comes, it is found that their assets are almost all eaten away, and left perhaps a shilling or two in the pound to meet the masses of paper.

ACCOMMODATION PAPER.

We must now examine more closely a species of credit which requires great attention; because it is the curse and the bane of commerce, and it has been the chief cause of those frightful commercial crises which recur periodically; and yet, though there can be no doubt that in the majority of cases it is morally fraudulent, it is of so subtle a nature that it defies all powers of legislation to cope with it. We have shown by the exposition of the system of cash credits in Scotland that there is nothing essentially dangerous and fraudulent in creating credit for the purpose of promoting future operations. On the contrary, such credits have been the most powerful method ever devised by the ingenuity of man for promoting the wealth and the prosperity of a country, and have accelerated the wealth and prosperity of Scotland by centuries. A certain species of this credit, however, having been grossly abused by unscrupulous persons for fraudulent purposes, and having produced the most frightful calamities, we must now examine and point out wherein the danger and the fraud of this particular species of credit consists.

When bills of exchange are given in exchange for goods actually purchased at the time, they are often called real bills; and it is often supposed that there is something essentially safe in them; because, as the goods have been received for them, it is supposed the goods are always ready to provide for the payment of the bills, and that only so much credit is created as there are goods to redeem it.

It is the inveterate error of a multitude of persons who will write upon the subject without the slightest knowledge either of mercantile law or of practical business, that the holder of a bill has a title to the goods for which it is given. This pestilent and mischievous delusion appears very strongly in Stanley Jevons. He says:* "What greatly assists a rise of prices started in a period of free investment is the system of credit, on which trade is necessarily conducted. By this system, a trader is not obliged to be the real owner of the goods in which he trades, but may buy freely by giving the promise of payment in, perhaps, three months' time. Thus, the goods really belong to the holder of his promissory note or bill. * * * Though the merchant does not own the goods, there must be some one to own them, to advance capital, or, as it is said, to discount the bills arising out of the transaction."

Thus Jevons holds that the merchant who buys goods on credit is not the real owner of them; that the person who holds the bill given for them is their real owner; or the person to whom he transfers it, such as the banker who discounts it, has the real title to the goods in respect of which it is given. But every lawyer and banker in the world would laugh at such ideas. Nothing is more common than for uninformed persons to say that a trader who buys goods on credit trades on borrowed capital. Such an idea, however, is a pure delusion. When a trader buys goods on credit and gives his bill for them, the goods become his actual property just as much as if he had paid for them in money. The bill of exchange is payment for the goods, just as money is. A purchase on credit is just as much a sale or an exchange as a purchase with money. What the trader has to do after having bought goods with his bill is to pay the bill when it becomes due.

Mr. Henry Thornton long ago pointed out the fallacy of supposing that there is any security in real bills because they are given in exchange for goods, or that the holder of the bill has any title to the goods.†

When a wholesale dealer buys a quantity of goods from a merchant on credit, he perhaps sells those goods to fifty different retail dealers, and takes their bill for them. These very goods are sold by the retail dealers, per-

* Investigations in Currency and Finance, p. 31.

† Essay on Paper Credit, p. 30.

haps, to hundreds of their customers, and consumed by them, before the bill given by the wholesale dealer becomes due. How in the name of common sense is the holder of the bill to follow the goods into the hands of hundreds of customers, who will most probably have consumed them before the bill becomes due? How, even, is he to ascertain their names? But, suppose that the wholesale dealer does not divide the goods into parcels and sell them to different dealers, but sells them in a lump to some other single person and takes his bill for them; then a new bill must be created to transfer the goods, and if the same goods are transferred in a lump a dozen different times, a new bill must be created on each transfer. Hence, there will be a dozen bills relating to the very same goods, and perhaps every one of these bills may have been discounted with a banker: which banker has a title to the goods? Every banker in the world would laugh at the idea that he has any title to the goods for which a bill has been given, which he has discounted. Nor have any of the bills any relation to any specific money, such as the purchaser of the goods may receive in payment for them. They are nothing but pure rights of action against the person of the debtor. Every lawyer and every merchant knows that every bill is a separate and independent article of merchandise, exactly like money itself, and that it is bought and sold solely on the belief that the acceptor will have the means of extinguishing it when it becomes due.

Mr. Thornton also points out the fallacy of making a distinction between the security of real bills and accommodation bills, *qua* accommodation bills. After describing an accommodation bill, he says:

"They agree; inasmuch as each is a discountable article, each has also been created for the purpose of being discounted, and each is perhaps discounted in fact; each therefore serves equally to supply means of speculation to the merchant. So far, moreover, as bills and notes constitute what is called the circulating medium or paper currency of the country and prevent the use of guineas, the fictitious and the real bill are upon an equality, and if the price of commodities be raised in proportion to the quantity of paper currency, the one contributes to that rise exactly in the same manner as the other."

The fact is, that in a real bill goods have already been purchased wherewith to redeem it; in an accommodation bill goods are to be purchased to redeem it. And if each transaction is equally sound and judicious, there is exactly the same security in the one bill as in the other. In fact, we may say that all commercial credit is of the nature of accommodation paper; because, in this case, a credit is always created for the express purpose of buying goods to redeem it. There is, therefore, clearly nothing in the nature of accommodation paper worse than "real paper," and when it is carefully used, nothing more dangerous. Cash credits, which have been one of the safest and most profitable parts of Scotch banking, and which have done so much for the prosperity of the country, are all of this nature. They are created, as we have seen, for the express purpose of stimulating future operations out of which the credit is to be redeemed. There is, therefore, nothing more atrocious, vicious and criminal in the one species of paper rather than in the other; or, if there is, it must lie in the difference between *has been* and *is to be.*

Nevertheless, as it is indubitably certain that most, if not all, of those commercial crises and monetary panics which have so frequently convulsed nations, have sprung out of this species of paper, it does merit a considerable portion of the obloquy and vituperation which has been heaped upon it. It is, therefore, our duty to investigate the method in which it is applied, and to point out wherein its true danger consists.

The security supposed to reside in real bills, as such, is, as we have seen, exaggerated. But there is at least this to be said for them, that as they only arise out of the real transfers of goods, their number must be limited by the very nature of things. However bad and worthless they may be individually, they cannot be multiplied beyond a certain limit. There is, therefore, a limit to the calamities they can cause. But we shall show that with accommodation paper the limits of disaster are immensely and indefinitely increased, frequently involving in utter ruin all who are brought within their vortex.

THE REAL DANGER OF ACCOMMODATION PAPER.

We must now explain wherein the difference between real and accommodation paper consists, and wherein the danger of accommodation paper lies. Suppose that a manufacturer or wholesale dealer has sold goods to ten customers, and received ten *bona fide* trade bills for them, he discounts these ten bills with his banker. The ten acceptors of these bills having received value for them, are the principal debtors to the bank, and are bound to meet them under the penalty of commercial ruin. The bank has their names as acceptors or real principal debtors on the bills, and its own customer as security on each of them. The bank also keeps a certain balance of its customer's in its hands, proportionate to the discount allowed. Even under the best of circumstances, an acceptor may fail to meet his bill. The banker then debits his customer's account with the bill and gives it to him back. The drawer has an action against the acceptor, because it is a real debt due to him. If there should not be enough, the customer is called upon to pay the difference. If the worst comes to the worst, and its customer fails, the bank can pursue its remedy against the estates of both parties, without in any way affecting the position of the other nine acceptors, who, of course, are still bound to meet their own bills.

In the case of accommodation bills there are very material differences. To the eye of the banker there is no visible difference between real and accommodation bills. They are, nevertheless, very different, and it is in these differences that the real danger of accommodation paper consists. In accommodation bills, the person for whose accommodation the drawing, indorsing or accepting, as the case may be, is done, is bound to provide the funds to meet the bill, or to indemnify the person who gives him his name. In a real bill the acceptor is the principal debtor, who is bound to provide funds to meet the bill, and the drawer is a mere surety. In the most usual form of accommodation, that of an acceptance, the drawer is the real principal debtor, who has to provide funds to meet the bill, and the acceptor is a mere surety, and if he is called upon to meet the bill he is entitled to sue the drawer, as the principal debtor, for the amount. Now, suppose as before, A gets ten of his friends to accommodate him with their names as acceptors, and discounts these bills with his banker, it is A's duty to provide funds to meet every one of the ten bills. There is, in fact, only one real principal debtor and ten sureties. Now, these ten accommodation acceptors are ignorant of each other's proceedings. They only gave their names to the drawer on the express understanding that they were not to be called upon to meet their bill; and, accordingly, they make no provision to do so. If any one of them is called upon to meet their bill, he has an immediate remedy against the drawer. In the case of real bills, then, the bank has ten real principal debtors, who would each take care to meet his own acceptance, and only one surety. In the case of accommodation bills, the bank has only one real principal debtor to meet the acceptances of ten. Thus, there is only one real principal debtor and ten sureties. Furthermore, if one of ten real acceptors fails to meet his bill, the bank can safely press the drawer, because it will not affect the position of the other nine acceptors. But if the drawer of the accommodation bills fails to meet any one of the ten acceptances, and the bank suddenly discovers that it is an accommodation bill, and it is under large advances to the drawer, it dare not for its own safety press the acceptor, because he will of course have immediate recourse against the drawer as his debtor, and the whole fabric will probably tumble down like a house of cards. Hence, the chances of disaster are much greater when there is only one person to meet the engagements of ten, than when there are ten persons, each bound to meet his own acceptance.

The real danger to a bank, then, in being led into discounting accommodation paper is that the position of principal and surety is reversed. It is deceived as to who the real debtor is and who the surety is, being precisely the reverse to what they appear to be, which makes a very great difference in the security of the holder of the bills. In fact, the parties are not governed by the contract visible on the face of the bills, which the banker believes in; but by a latent contract, collateral to the bills, of which he knows nothing. To advance money by way of cash credit, or by loan with security, is quite a different affair; because the bank then knows exactly what it is doing; and as soon as anything occurs amiss, it knows the remedy to be adopted. Moreover, it never permits the advance to exceed a certain definite limit; but it never can tell to what lengths it may be inveigled into in discounting accommodation paper until some commercial reverse happens, when it may discover that its customer has been carrying on some great speculative operation with capital borrowed from it alone. This is the rationale of accommodation paper pure and simple.

We have now to examine a species of accommodation paper still more subtle and still more dangerous; and this because, though it is really and in its very nature accommodation paper, yet it is not so in technical jurisprudence.

MUTUAL ACCOMMODATION PAPER—ITS DANGER TO A BANK.

We have shown that the real genuine distinction between real and accommodation paper is, that real paper is based upon a simultaneous transfer of goods, the proceeds of which are expected to redeem the bill at maturity; and in accommodation paper, bills are created, not based upon any past or simultaneous transfer of goods, but for the express purpose of purchasing goods in the future to redeem the bills. If these two species of transactions are done with equal care and judgment, and with the full knowledge of all parties of the real nature of the transaction, there is nothing more dangerous or improper in one species of paper than in the other. We have now to deal with a species of paper which is in its real nature accommodation paper, because it consists of paper not founded on any past or simultaneous transfer of goods, but consists of paper created for the express purpose of purchasing goods after it has been created; but yet in jurisprudence it is not accommodation paper, because it is held to be given for good and valuable consideration; and therefore, though in very many cases it is a moral fraud, yet it is not a legal fraud; and it is to this species of paper that most of the great commercial crises are due. We have now to explain how very much more dangerous to a bank this species of paper is than the worst calamities which can happen from real paper.

We have already pointed out the very common error that all bills of exchange are paid in money. Bills in modern usage are very seldom paid in actual money; only in a very few isolated instances; they are paid by discounting fresh bills. Thus, in ordinary times, debts are always paid by creating new debts. No doubt, if the banker refuses to discount the new bills, the customer must discharge his bills in money. But then no trader ever expects to have to do that. He has usually a fixed discount limit, and if he brings good bills he has little less than an absolute right to have them discounted. And if the banker suddenly calls upon him to meet his bills in money, it might oblige him to sell his goods at a great sacrifice, or might cause his ruin. However, it is always supposed that the bills discounted are good ones; that is, they could be paid in money if required. Thus, though in common practice very few bills are really ever paid in money, it is manifest that the whole stability of the bank depends upon the last bills discounted being good ones. Now, suppose that a customer for a considerable time brings good bills to his banker and acquires a good character with him, and so throws him off his guard. Owing, perhaps, to some temporary embarrassment, or wishing to push his speculations, he goes to some of his friends, and gets them to accept bills without having any property to meet them. He then takes these accommodation bills to his banker. The banker, trusting to his good character, discounts the bills. In course of time these accommodation bills must be met, and the way he does it is to create fresh similar bills. The drawer may be speculating in trade and losing money every day. But his bills must be met; and there is no other way of meeting them but by constantly creating fresh accommodation bills. By this means the customer may extract indefinite sums from his banker, and give him in return—so many bits of paper. Now, when discounts are low, and times are prosperous, this system may go on for many years. But at last a crisis comes. The money market becomes "tight." Bankers not only raise the rate of discount, but they refuse to discount so freely as before. They contract their issues. The accommodation bills are in the bank, and they must be met. But if the banker refuses to discount fresh bills, they must be met in money. But all the property the speculators may have had may have been lost twenty times over; so when the crisis comes they have nothing to turn into money. Directly the banker refuses to meet his customer's bills by means of his own money, he wakes to the pleasant discovery that, in return for the money he has paid, he has got so many pieces of paper! This is the rationale of accommodation paper; and we see how entirely it differs from real paper. Because with real paper and *bona fide* customers, though losses may come, yet directly the loss occurs there is an end of it. But with accommodation paper, the prospect of a loss is the very cause of a greater one being made; and so on in an ever widening circle, until the canker may eat into the banker's assets to any extent almost.

It is also clear that if a trader, having got a good character and a high position in commerce, may do so much mischief to a single banker, his capacity for mischief is vastly increased if, from his high position and old standing, he is able to discount with several banks, for then he is able to diminish greatly the chances of detection.

From these accommodation bills to forged bills there is but one step. It is but a thin line of division between drawing upon a man who is notoriously unable to pay, and drawing upon a person who does not exist at all, or forging an acceptance. In practical morality, and in its practical effects, there is none. Traders do not even take the trouble to get a beggar to write his name on their bills, but they invent one. The case of traders in a large way of business, dealing with a vast number of small country connections, affords great facilities for such rogueries. They begin by establishing a good character for their bills. Their business gradually increases. Their connections, as they say, gradually extend all over the kingdom. The banker, satisfied with the regularity of the account, cannot take the trouble of sending down to inquire into the acceptor of every small bill. The circle gradually enlarges, until some fine morning the whole affair blows up. The ingenuity sometimes exercised by traders in carrying out such a system is absolutely marvellous.

It is in times of speculation in large commodities that accommodation paper is peculiarly rife. In a great failure of the harvest, when great importations were required, and it was expected that prices would rise very high, every corn merchant wanted to buy as much as possible. But if no real sales had taken place, there could be real trade bills. They therefore proceeded to manufacture them in order to extract funds from bankers to speculate with. No banker in his senses would actually advance money for them to speculate with, with his eyes open. Nevertheless they must have funds. This they did by cross-acceptances. One merchant drew on another, who accepted it; he then in turn drew upon his drawer, who accepted in his turn. They then went and discounted these cross-acceptances with as many bankers as possible, in as many different parts of the country as possible, so that their proceedings might not come too much under the notice of any particular bank. In the Crimean war there was a great and sudden demand for shipping; an enormous amount of accommodation paper was manufactured by the Liverpool ship owners and discounted all over the kingdom. The results were frightfully disastrous.

Whenever great speculation in commodities may take place, again the same things will recur. And the quantities of accommodation paper manufactured on such occasions is something astonishing. But this paper is discounted by banks creating fresh credits in the form of deposits. So, these deposits swell up; and they are only so many bank notes in disguise; and then the public holds up its hands in astonishment at the vast sums the banks have to trade with; whereas it is not solid money at all, but only paper. But this immense augmentation of the circulating medium, or currency, raises prices all round. The insurmountable objection, therefore, to this species of paper is the dangerous and boundless facility it affords for raising money for speculative purposes. And there is much reason to fear that this pernicious system prevails to a much greater extent than is commonly supposed. Even in quiet times it has been said that it is surmised that one-fourth of the paper in circulation is accommodation paper; and in times of great speculation the proportion is far greater than that.

The Legislature has imposed rigid limits on the issues of banks, and many persons think that it might be possible to curb the creation of this pestilent kind of paper by law. But, unfortunately, such a thing is not possible. The difficulty consists in determining what is really accommodation paper. As a matter of economics, all these cross-acceptances are pure accommodation paper; but they are not so in jurisprudence.

The whole question turns on the consideration. An accommodation bill in law is a bill to which the drawer, acceptor or endorser, as the case may be, puts his name without consideration for the purpose of benefiting or accommodating some other party, who is to provide the funds to meet the bill when due. But the consideration may be of many sorts. It does not by any means necessarily imply a sale of goods at the time. Moreover, a bill may be an accommodation bill at the time it is created; but if any consideration is given for it during the period of its currency, it ceases to be an accommodation bill. Moreover, the consideration may be of many sorts. If A draws a bill upon B, who accepts it for A's accommodation for the express purpose of enabling him to get it discounted by a bank, that is a pure accommodation bill. But if B draws an exactly similar bill upon A, who accepts it for the accommodation of B, to enable him to get it discounted by a bank, then neither of the bills is an accommodation bill, but they are each of them given for a good consideration. To an unlearned reader this may seem somewhat strange doctrine: but it is nevertheless firmly established law.

This doctrine, which is quite unanswerable, shows how impossible it is to deal legislatively with this kind of accommodation paper. At least they must be very poor rogues who cannot manufacture any amount of *bona fide* bills they please. Two ragamuffins have only to get as many bills as they please—if they can only pay for the stamps. One engages to pay £1000 to the order of the other. That would be an accommodation bill. The second then engages to pay £1000 to the order of the first. These are no longer accommodation bills; but are two good *bona fide* bills; each given for a good consideration. If two such bills are good, then two thousand or any larger number are equally good. Bankers would look askance at such paper; but Westminster Hall declares them all to be *bona fide* bills given for a good consideration. Stated in the above form, the doctrine may appear somewhat startling to some. But when we consider the principle of the case, and not the accidental circumstance that the two persons who may do it are insolvent, the difficulty disappears; for it is just what happens every day in banking. It is quite common for a banker to discount the simple promissory note of his customer. The note given by the customer is the consideration for the deposit, credit or right of action created by the banker; and the right of action or deposit created by the banker is the consideration given to purchase the note of the customer. Each, therefore, is the consideration for the other. Each party gives value to the other. It is precisely the same in principle in the other case. If the issuers of the bills are able to purchase goods with them, they may be paid off at maturity. If they cannot do so, the re-exchange of the securities is the mutual payment of each debt; precisely in the same manner as when two bankers exchange notes, or when a merchant pays his acceptance to a banker in the banker's own notes. The two contracts are extinguished by compensation. The accident that both the creators of the bills are insolvent does not affect the juridical principles of the case.

Now, in times of great speculation, these cross-acceptances are manufactured to an enormous extent among merchants. And the more cross-acceptances they can manufacture and get discounted by bankers, the more funds the adventurers have to speculate with. But such things are always sure to be overdone. As soon as any new and extensive market is suddenly opened up, multitudes of speculators are sure to rush in and create vast amounts of paper which can never be redeemed. And when this is done on a sufficiently large scale, a commercial crisis is produced. And if this commercial crisis is not properly and judiciously met, and it reaches a certain degree of intensity, it produces a monetary panic in which merchants and bankers fall together. All commercial crises, therefore, originate in the over-creation of credit, and this is innate in the modern system of credit.

Suppose that at any time the commercial world started with a perfectly clean slate. When such multitudes of persons are trading on credit, it must inevitably happen that a considerable number will speculate unsuccessfully and create an excess of credit, which cannot be redeemed by fair means. All excess of credit may be considered as so much virus or poison in the body commercial. However, by various tricks and devices known to traders, they can keep themselves afloat many years after they are utterly insolvent; and thus the poison constantly accumulates. Then perhaps a fever of speculation takes place, giving rise to the creation of vast masses of speculative paper; and then the poison, having accumulated to a sufficient extent, bursts forth in a tumor, or an abscess, called a commercial crisis. Now, it is clear that these things cannot take place in a day; it takes a certain time for a sufficient amount of excessive credit to be generated and accumulate in the body commercial to produce a commercial crisis. During the last 130 years, in which the credit system has attained its gigantic development, a commercial crisis has usually returned in periods of ten years, or thereabouts, and sometimes oftener. But on each occasion the circumstances which brought it about are perfectly well known. And because the spots on the sun's disc have also a period somewhat approaching to ten years, it gave rise to the Bedlamite craze of Stanley Jevons that commercial crises and monetary panics are due to spots on the sun's disc and conjunction of the planets!

One cannot fail also to be surprised that Sir Robert Peel, with all his long and extensive experience, should have conceived the idea that all commercial crises originate in excessive issues of bank notes, and that if the quantity of notes could only be restricted to the quantity of gold there would be if there were no notes, commercial crises would be prevented. Excessive issues of notes have, no doubt, in many cases fostered and aggravated commercial crises; but they do not originate with bankers. They always originate with the mercantile community; and no restrictions on the issues of banks can, by any possibility, prevent their occurrence, as will be shown in the following chapter.

SECTION IX.

MONETARY PANICS.

The Panics of 1764, 1772, 1782, 1793—Remarkable Remedy of the Latter—The Panic of 1797—The Bank Suspends—£1 and £2 Notes Issued—The Famous Panic of 1825—Speculation its Cause—Opposition to £1 and £2 Notes—The Crisis of 1838-39—The Panic of 1847—Its Instant Remedy by Releasing the Bank Restriction—Sir Robert Peel's Review of the Workings of the New Bank Act—Parliamentary Committee of 1848—The Author's Currency Discoveries—The Panic of 1857—The Panic of 1866—Overend, Gurney & Co.'s Great Failure—The Crisis of 1890—The Barings' Suspension.

ALL commercial crises originate, as we have seen in the preceding chapter, in the over-creation of credit, in credit created which cannot be redeemed, and not in spots on the sun's disc or conjunctions of the planets. It is the express business of merchants and traders to speculate. And in the vast numbers of the mercantile community who are always speculating, a considerable number must speculate badly, especially in times of great changes in price, and consequently over-creations of credit are constantly accumulating, and in process of time they come to a head and burst in a commercial crisis. Commercial crises are, therefore, innate in the colossal system of modern credit and are unavoidable.

A monetary panic is a general run upon bankers for gold. It is not the business of bankers to speculate themselves, but to judge of and control the speculations of others. No doubt bankers are often duped and deceived into supporting bad speculations; but they do not originate them,—which shows the fallacy of Sir Robert Peel's fancy, that all commercial crises originate in excessive issues of bank notes. But when a commercial crisis attains a certain magnitude and intensity, there is great danger of its developing into a monetary panic, or a general run for gold upon bankers. Monetary panics, in this country at least, have been invariably produced by bad banking legislation, or by bad management of the Bank of England; sometimes by both. Monetary panics are, therefore, generally speaking, avoidable.

Ever since the prodigious development of the system of credit, from the latter end of the seventeenth century, there have been periodical commercial crises which, after a certain degree of tension, have deepened into monetary panics, accompanied by great failures of banks, and very severe runs for gold on those banks which were able to stand their ground. And it has been a subject of sore perplexity to know how these monetary panics are to be controlled, and the proper action of the Bank of England during their continuance. There have been, and still are, two conflicting theories on the subject: 1. That in periods of great commercial crisis, the issues of the Bank of England should be rigorously restricted, and give no aid to commercial houses. This may be called the restrictive theory. 2. That, at such periods of extreme commercial pressure, the issues of the Bank of England should be liberally expanded so as to support all commercial houses which can prove themselves to be solvent. This may be called the expansive theory. In the series of commercial crises and monetary panics which have taken place during the last 140 years, each of these theories has been tried, and we have now to examine the circumstances of each crisis *seriatim*, and show the effect of each theory upon it. The experience on the subject has now been ample and abundant, so as to enable us to come to a definite conclusion.

THE MONETARY PANIC OF 1764.

The first great monetary panic in modern times which we need notice, took place in 1764 in Holland and neighboring countries. The banks of Amsterdam, Hamburg and Nuremberg did not issue notes in the discount of bills. They were pure examples of what is called by a certain party the "Currency Principle." That is, those banks did not issue any credit except in exchange for specie. Thus, the credit they issued was exactly equal in amount to the specie it displaced. This principle was that advocated by the supporters of the Bank Act of 1844, and of Sir Robert Peel, who considered it as the panacea for all commercial crises.

The seven years' war had just come to an end; and changes from peace to war or from war to peace, causing great fluctuations in price, are great promoters of commercial crises. The Neufvilles, two bankers at Amsterdam, were among the principal merchants and speculators, who had connections all over the Continent. At length their embarrassments became so great that the bankers at Amsterdam could no longer support them, and they failed for 330,000 guineas on the 29th July, 1763. Before the news of the actual stoppage reached Hamburg, the bankers of that town were thrown into the utmost consternation by hearing that it was intended at Amsterdam to allow the Neufvilles to fail. On the 4th August, 1763, the bankers at Hamburg met to consider how the tottering state of credit in that town was to be supported. They said: "We received a fatal express with the terrible news that you, the gentlemen of Amsterdam, would leave the Neufvilles to sink, by which we were all thunderstruck; never dreaming that so many men in their senses in your city would take such a step—a step which will infallibly plunge all Europe into an abyss of distress, if not remedied by you while it is time. We therefore send this circular and general letter to you by express, to exhort and conjure you, as soon as you receive this, to undertake still to support the Neufvilles, by furnishing what money they want, and giving them two or three persons of unquestionable probity and skill for curators, that their affairs and their engagements may be concluded and terminated without causing a general ruin, which will otherwise infallibly happen. If you do not, gentlemen, we hereby declare to you that our resolution is taken—that is to say, that though we represent a very respectable body of rich and respectable men, we have unanimously resolved to suspend our own payments, as long as we shall judge it proper and necessary, and that we shall not acquit them or the counter protest that shall come from you, or any whatever. This is the resolution we have unanimously taken, and from which we will not depart, happen what will. The fate of the general commerce of all Europe is, at present, absolutely in your hands; determine, gentlemen, whether you should crush it totally, or support it."

The letter, however, came too late to exercise any influence, as the Neufvilles had been allowed to fail six days previously. A general failure took place; eighteen houses in Amsterdam immediately stopped payment. A much greater number in Hamburg immediately followed, and no business was transacted for some time except for ready money. The failures were equally general in many of the other chief cities of Germany. This crisis extended to England; and Smith says, that the bank made advances to merchants to the amount of a million. Thus this first great commercial crisis was in direct contradiction to the doctrines of the devisers of the Bank Act of 1844, for it occurred in places where the "currency principle" was in full force; and the Bank of England acted on the expansive theory.

THE MONETARY PANIC OF 1772.

In 1772, the first great monetary panic took place in England, in which the Bank of England was called upon to take a prominent part in supporting commercial credit. The preceding two years had been distinguished by the most extravagant over-trading. On the 10th June, Heale & Co., bankers in Threadneedle street, stopped payment, involving many others. The Bank of England and some merchants came forward to support credit; which had the appearance for a few days of being successful. But, in ten days' time, a general crash ensued. The whole city was in consternation. There had not been such a prospect of general bankruptcy since the South Sea scheme. By the liberal advances of the Bank of England, the panic was at length allayed. But the bankruptcies of that year amounted to the then unprecedented number of 525. These speculations had been general throughout Europe; and in 1773 the crash extended to Holland. About the beginning of the year, the failures in that country were so alarming, and so extensive, that they threatened a mortal blow to all credit, public and private, throughout Europe. They were caused by great speculative dealings in trade, as well as in the public funds of different countries. The losses were estimated at £10,000,000—an immense sum for that period. Thus, the circumstances of this great crisis were like those of the first, in direct contradiction to the doctrines on which the Bank Act of 1844 is based; because English commerce was only saved by the expansive theory—by liberal advances by the Bank of England; and the crisis extended through countries in which the currency principle was in full force.

THE MONETARY PANIC OF 1782.

As we have remarked at pages 17 and 18, in 1782, the unhappy war with America was fortunately terminated, and immediately a prodigious extension of the foreign commerce, which had previously been unusually restricted, took place. The enormous markets thrown open to the merchants led to the most extravagant overtrading, which was greatly fostered by very incautious issues by the bank; and this led to a very alarming drain of specie from the bank, which produced a crisis, threatening to compel them to stop payment. The directors, however, considered that if they could only restrain their issues for a short period the returns in specie in payment of the exports would soon set in in a more rapid manner than they went out. They determined therefore to make no communication to the Government, but for the present to contract their issues until the exchanges turned in their favor. The alarm felt by the bank was greatest in May, 1783. They then refused to make any advances to the Government on the loan of that year, but they did not make any demand for payment of their other advances to Government, which were then between nine and ten millions. They continued this policy up to October, when at length the drain had ceased from the country, and money had begun to flow in from abroad. At length, in the autumn, when the favorable signs had begun to appear, they advanced to Government freely on the loan; although, at that time, the cash in the bank was actually lower than at the time when they had felt the greatest alarm. It was reduced to £473,000. The doctrine which Mr. Bosanquet stated guided the directors was this: That while the drain was going on, their issues should be contracted as much as possible; but as soon as the tide had given signs of ceasing and turning the other way, it was safe to extend their issues freely. This was the policy they acted upon, and it was entirely successful, and the credit of the bank was saved.

THE MONETARY PANIC OF 1793.

Mr. Tooke states from his own personal recollection that there had been an enormous and undue extension of commercial speculation, not only in the internal trade and banking of this country, but also throughout Europe and the United States, for some years previous to 1792. The amount of bank notes in circulation, which was under six millions in 1784, had increased to nearly eleven millions and a-half in 1792. At length, in the autumn of 1792, commercial failures began both here and abroad, as well as in America. The average of bankruptcies during the ten months had been fifty, in November they suddenly rose to 105. This unusual number created much uneasiness, but they diminished greatly in December. In January, 1793, they rose again. The French Revolution was now advancing with rapid strides; the King had been a prisoner ever since the 10th August. In November, the convention published what was tantamount to a declaration of war against every established government in Europe. Great Britain thought it time to arm. The militia were called out; on the 13th December Parliament met; and the King called the attention of the Houses to the increasing political ferment of the country, which had shown itself in acts of riot and rebellion. He said that the agitators were evidently acting in concert with persons abroad, and that it was impossible to see without the most serious uneasiness the evident intention of the French to excite disturbances in foreign countries, wholly contrary to the law of nations. Under these circumstances, it became necessary to augment the military and naval forces of the country. An angry correspondence inflamed the passions of both nations; and on the execution of the King, the British Government expelled the French Ambassador, and the convention instantly declared war. The declaration of war, though it must evidently have been foreseen, gave a shock to credit, which was already staggering. On the 15th of February, a house of considerable magnitude, deep in corn speculations, failed; and on the 19th the bank refused the paper of Lane, Son & Fraser, who stopped next morning, to the amount of nearly one million, involving a great number of other respectable houses. In the meantime the panic spread to the bankers. It began at Newcastle. The partners in the banks at Newcastle were opulent, but their private fortunes were locked up. They issued notes which allowed interest to commence at some months after date; and then they were payable on demand; when the run came they were unable to realize, and stopped payment. The panic immediately spread throughout the country. It was computed that there were nearly 400 country banks at that time; of these 300 were much shaken, and upwards of 100 stopped payment. The Banks of Exeter and the west of England almost alone stood their ground. They issued notes payable at twenty days' sight; with interest commencing at the date of the note, and ceasing on the day of acceptance. The best contemporary authorities are unanimous in attributing this terrible disaster to the inordinate multiplication and reckless operations of these country "bankers," which had been established in almost every town and even village in the country.

This great pressure extended to the London bankers as well as those of the country. One of them says that the extraordinary state of credit had obliged every person connected with trade and money transactions to gather in and husband every resource to meet all demands. That for six weeks back every man of money and resources had been straining every nerve to support himself and immediate friends, and could not give that support to others which they would have been disposed to do. All these circumstances naturally produced a demand on the Bank of England for support and discounts. But the bank being thoroughly alarmed, resolved to contract its issues. Bankruptcies multiplied with frightful rapidity. The Government urged the bank to come forward and support credit; but they resolutely refused. Sir Francis Baring greatly blames the directors for their action on the occasion. He says that they first accommodated themselves to the crisis; but their nerves could not stand the daily demand for guineas; and, for the purpose of checking the demand, they curtailed their discounts to a point never before experienced; and that, if they determined to reduce their issues, they should have done it more gradually. Their determination and the extent to which they carried it, came like an electric shock.

He says that there are three different causes for a great demand for guineas: 1. For export; 2. For the purpose of hoarding, from want of confidence in the Government and in the circulating paper; and 3. To enable country banks to discharge their demands while confidence in the Government and in the bank remained entire.

That every measure ought to be taken to prevent and mitigate the first cause except prohibition and bankruptcy. We may reserve the second till we come to 1797. That the third ought to be viewed not with indifference, but with a disposition to spend almost their last guinea. He shows, from the state of the exchanges, that it was quite impossible that the guineas could have left the country, as the loss on exporting them to Amsterdam was £3 6s. 3d.; and to Hamburg, £4 2s. 6d. per cent.; and it was notorious that large quantities of gold and silver were coming in from France. The cause of this was the continued depreciation of the assignats. Under these circumstances, he says that the directors acted quite wrongly; they ought to have seen that the guineas would have very soon come back to them, and that, in fact, they ought to have followed the precedent of 1783, which had been so successful.

When the bank adopted this perverse course, universal failure seemed imminent. Sir John Sinclair remembered the precedent of 1697, when Montague had invented exchequer bills to sustain public credit, and thought that a similar plan might be followed in this crisis. The Minister desired him to propose a scheme for the purpose, which he presented on the 16th April. A committee of the House of Commons was immediately appointed.

In the meantime a director of the Royal Bank of Scotland came up with the most alarming news from Scotland. The public banks were wholly unable, with due regard to their own safety, to furnish the accommodation necessary to support commercial houses and the country bankers; that unless they received immediate assistance from Government general failure was inevitable. Numerous houses which were perfectly solvent must fall unless they could obtain temporary relief. Mr. Macdonald, M. P. for Glasgow, stated that the commercial houses and manufactories there were in the greatest distress from the total destruction of credit; that this distress arose from the refusal of the Glasgow, Paisley and Greenock banks to discount, as their notes were poured in upon them for gold.

The committee recommended that exchequer bills to the amount of £5,000,000 should be issued under the directions of a board of commissioners appointed for that purpose, in sums of £100, £50 and £20, and under proper regulations. After considerable doubts were expressed by Mr. Fox and Mr. Grey as to the policy of this extraordinary measure, which was unknown to the constitution, and might subvert our liberties, the bill passed. No sooner was the act passed than the committee set to work. A large sum of money (£70,000) was sent down to Manchester and Glasgow, on the strength of the exchequer bills, which were not yet issued. This most timely supply, coming so much earlier than was expected, operated like magic, and had a greater effect in restoring credit than ten times the sum would have had at a later period. When the whole business was concluded, a report was presented to the Treasury. It stated that the knowledge that the loans might be had operated in many instances to prevent them being required. The whole number of applications was 332, and the sum applied for was £3,855,624; of which 238 were granted, amounting to £2,202,000; forty-five for sums to the amount of £1,215,100 were withdrawn, and forty-nine rejected. The whole sum advanced was repaid; two only of the parties assisted became bankrupt; all the others were ultimately solvent, and in many instances possessed of great property. A considerable part of the sum was repaid before it was due, and all the rest with the utmost punctuality. So much scrupulous care was taken to preserve secrecy as to the names of the applicants, that they were not known to that hour except to the commissioners and their own sureties. After all expenses were paid, the transaction left a clear profit to the Government of £4,348.

Whatever were the prognostications of its futility and danger before it was done, its success was perfect and complete. The contemporary writers all bear witness to the extraordinary effects produced. Macpherson says that the very intimation of the intention of the Legislature to support the merchants operated like a charm all over the country; and in a great degree superseded the necessity of the relief by an almost instantaneous restoration of confidence. Sir Francis Baring concurs in this view, and adduces the remarkable success of the measure as an argument to show the mistaken policy of the bank. The panic was at length happily stayed. The failures up to July had been 932; in the remaining five months they were reduced to 372. Gold continued to flow in; and in the last six months of 1793, and during the two following years, money became as plentiful as in time of peace, and four per cent. interest could scarcely be got.

After careful deliberation, the Bullion Report warmly approved of it, censured the proceedings of the Bank of England, and especially cite it as an illustration of the principle they laid down, that an enlarged accommodation is the true remedy for that occasional failure of confidence in the country districts to which our system of paper credit is unavoidably exposed. Notwithstanding all this weight of testimony, practical and theoretical, in favor of the happy effects of this measure, some rigid doctrinaires afterwards condemned the proceedings as a violation of the true principles of economics. Even some who helped to devise it afterwards changed their opinion on the subject. Lord Sidmouth, in 1811, observed that he was, on consideration, inclined to doubt of its wisdom and policy. Lord Grenville also said, from experience and reflection, he was convinced the measure was founded on wrong policy; as one of those who were concerned in the measure, he was perfectly ready to avow his error; for he was perfectly satisfied in his own mind that it was unwise and impolitic.

The reply to these objections seems to us to be perfectly plain and simple. In the first place, if it were a violation of the true principles of economics, it immediately resolves itself into a question of loss of capital. It is quite easy to show that all great errors in economics are destructive of capital. They may be estimated in money. Was this measure a pecuniary loss to the country? But what would have been the loss to the country if it had not been adopted? The simple result would have been that every bank in the country would have stopped payment, and nineteen out of every twenty merchants would have been ruined. Who can estimate the destruction of capital that would have ensued in the general wreck of public credit? It might have endangered the safety of the State. But there are other arguments which appear to us to be conclusive as to its propriety. The general loss of credit was chiefly caused by a thorough want of confidence in the circulating medium, or the currency of the country. The miserable notes of the majority of country bankers were utterly blown upon. The indispensable necessity was a solid currency. Now, what was it that caused such an unsafe currency to be in circulation? It was nothing but the unjustifiable monopoly of the Bank of England. It was this monopoly, which was itself the most flagrant violation of the true principles of economics, which was the cause of the bad state of the circulating medium. This monopoly prevented the formation of solid banks in the country. Consequently, the measure of the Government in providing a solid currency, in which everybody had confidence, was merely the correction of the error which led to these deplorable results. An undesirable one it may be, but yet no better one was possible under the circumstances. The superior wisdom of the Bullion Report, one of the wisest and most masterly reports ever presented to Parliament, and one of the great landmarks of economics, corroborated by the subsequent series of monetary panics, infinitely outweighs the morbid doctrinairism of Lord Sidmouth and Lord Grenville. This crisis alone is amply sufficient to decide between the merits of the restrictive theory and the expansive theory. While the restrictive theory, if it had been persevered in, would have involved the whole mercantile and banking community in absolute ruin, the expansive theory instantly saved them. We shall find the experience of this monetary panic amply borne out by the experience of all subsequent monetary panics.

It was at this period, as far as we can ascertain, that London bankers introduced a slight, and to all appearance, an unimportant change in the method of doing business, which was yet followed by the most momentous consequence in the history of banking. The panic extended, as we have seen, to London bankers. Now, when bankers issue notes in a dense population like London, it gives great facilities to their enemies to work them injury. Their enemies had only to go and buy up their notes in all directions, and then go and present them suddenly for payment, and the bankers, not being prepared for such a sudden demand, may be ruined. Now, in that unique and unrivalled collection of banking documents in the possession of Messrs. Child and Co., the latest note of a London banker in it is dated April, 1793. From this time, London bankers wholly ceased to issue their own notes; and exclusively allowed their customers to circulate their bank credits by means of cheques. This slight change in the method of doing business ultimately produced a result which no one could have foreseen. The business of "banking" was considered so essentially to consist in issuing notes, that to prevent persons from issuing notes was considered as effectual to prevent them from "banking." Accordingly, the monopoly clauses of the Bank Charter Act conferred upon the bank the monopoly of issuing notes. But about thirty years after London bankers had shown that banking business could be carried on in London without issuing notes, persons began to scrutinize the privileges of the Bank of England, and they maintained that its privileges were exclusively confined to issuing notes.

By a fortunate accident, the opportunity which this method offered of circumventing the monopoly of the bank was not discovered for many years afterwards. If it had been, there cannot be any doubt but that Parliament would have put it down very quickly. When it was discovered and acted upon, the age of such monopolies had passed away, and the demand of the bank to have it provided against was refused.

THE MONETARY PANIC OF 1797.

We must now be very minute in detailing the circumstances of the monetary panic of 1797, in which the restrictive theory was carried out to the bitter end, and resulted in the stoppage of the bank. Sir Francis Baring and

Mr. Tooke, two financial authorities of the very highest eminence, both agree that nothing could be more satisfactory than the financial condition of the country during 1794 and part of 1795. Both agree that the circumstances of the embarrassments which led to the catastrophe in 1797 began in the latter part of 1795. Mr. Tooke places the commencement rather earlier than Sir Francis Baring. He states that the winter of 1794–95 was one of the severest on record; and that in the spring or summer of 1795 apprehensions began to be felt for the growing crops. The prices of all sorts of corn advanced rapidly. The spring of 1795 was very cold and backward, the summer wet and stormy, and the harvest unusually late. Wheat, which was at 55s. in January, rose to 108s. in August. The same scarcity was general throughout Europe and America. France was in a still worse position than England; and the Government, still further to embarrass her and afford relief to England, seized all neutral vessels laden with corn and bound for France. It also employed agents to buy corn in the Baltic ports, where its price had already been greatly raised in consequence of large purchases on account of the French Government.

Sir Francis Baring also states that the method in which the Government contracted the loan that year tended much to aggravate the evil. He says, that in former wars it had been usual for the Government to contract with none but the most respectable moneyed men, who had the undoubted power to fulfill their engagements. On this occasion the Minister contracted with men who did not possess those powers; and, in order to make good their payments, they were obliged to have recourse to operations on foreign places, which deranged the exchanges, and had a still greater effect in raising the rate of interest in this country. These causes alone were sufficient to create a monetary pressure; but though they were inconvenient, there would have been nothing to create alarm in them. They were, however, aggravated and intensified by other circumstances, which we must now relate.

The enormous abuses which might be perpetrated by an unscrupulous government, and the dangerous power which so potent an engine as the Bank of England would confer upon them, had been clearly foreseen by its antagonists at the time of its foundation, and had inspired them with a well-grounded jealousy. Stringent precautions were taken in the first Act of 1695 to prohibit the bank from making any advances to Government without the express permission of Parliament. It had been the custom, however, time out of mind, to advance for the amount of such Treasury bills as were made payable on the bank, up to the amount of £20,000 or £30,000, when it was usual for the Treasury to send down orders to set off such advances against the accounts to which they properly belonged. If ever these advances reached £50,000, it was a subject of complaint. In the American war these limits had been much exceeded, and sometimes reached £150,000. Mr. Bosanquet was governor of the bank in 1793, and the legality of such proceedings excited grave doubts in his mind. After consulting with his brother directors, they agreed that it was a serious question whether the penalties provided in the act did not extend to such transactions. They, therefore, thought it would be expedient to apply to the Government to obtain an act of indemnity to relieve them from any penalties they might have incurred, and to permit such transactions to a certain limited amount. Mr. Bosanquet, who conducted the negotiation with Mr. Pitt, expressly says that Mr. Pitt proposed to bring in a clause which should indemnify the directors to advance to a limited amount. He says that it was originally intended that the penalty should be taken off only in case the advance on Treasury bills should be restrained within a limited sum. This limited amount was intended to be fixed at £50,000 or £100,000. Mr. Bosanquet, however, went out of office, and was unable to attend further to the negotiation. Mr. Pitt was much too keen not to see at once the enormous facilities Government would obtain if this act was passed. Accordingly, he pressed it quickly through Parliament; but he took care to omit any clause of limitation (Act, Statute 1793, c. 32). Never had such a formidable engine been placed in the hands of a Minister. He was now armed with the unbounded power of drawing upon the bank; with nothing to restrain him, unless the directors should take the audacious step of dishonoring his bills. The bank was henceforth almost at his mercy, and then he plunged headlong into that reckless career of scattering English gold broadcast over Europe.

No sooner had Mr. Pitt obtained this surreptitious power over the bank than he set all bounds of moderation at defiance; and, sure of being able to command unlimited supplies at home, he proceeded to send over enormous amounts of specie to foreign powers. In 1793, the subsidies and sums paid to foreign governments amounted to £701,475. In 1794, the foreign subsidies were £2,641,053; in 1795 they amounted to £6,253,140. Thus, in three years, the sums sent abroad amounted to upwards of nine millions and a-half. These were, however, not the totals of the specie sent abroad on other accounts. In 1793, it was £2,715,232; in 1794, £8,335,592; in 1795, £11,040,236. These great remittances had the inevitable effect of making the foreign exchanges adverse, and excited the greatest alarm in the bank parlor. At the same time that this great drain of specie was going on, the Treasury bills increased to an unprecedented amount, and the demands for accommodation from the commercial world were equally pressing. Nothing could be more unpleasant than the position of the directors, placed between these powerful parties contending for accommodation, which it was daily becoming less in their power to give. So early as the 11th December, 1794, the directors foresaw the ensuing pressure, and made representations to Mr. Pitt. In January, 1795, it became necessary to adopt a firmer attitude; and, on the 15th, they passed a resolution that a foreign loan of six millions and a home one of eighteen millions being about to be raised, the Chancellor of the Exchequer must be requested to make his financial arrangements for the year without requiring further assistance from them; and more particularly, that they could not allow the advances on

Treasury bills at any one time to exceed £500,000. Mr. Pitt promised to reduce them to that amount by payments out of the first loan. He, however, paid little regard to these remonstrances; and, on the 16th April, they were compelled to remind him that he had not kept his promise, that the sum should be reduced. They told him that they had come to a resolution that they would not, in future, permit the advances to exceed the stipulated sum. Mr. Pitt pretended that he had forgotten the circumstance in the multiplicity of business, and promised that the sum should be immediately paid. Nevertheless, no reduction took place in the amount; another remonstrance was equally ineffectual, and on the 30th July, the directors informed him that they intended, after a certain day, to give orders to their cashiers to refuse payment of all bills, when the amount exceeded £500,000. Mr. Pitt was not prepared to comply with this request, and on the 6th of August he applied to them for another advance of two millions and a-half; but they refused to take his letter into consideration until he had made satisfactory arrangements with them for the repayment of the other advances. After some further communication, he persuaded them to agree to the loan for £2,000,000.

The act of Mr. Pitt had, in fact, deprived the directors of all control over the bank. The foreign exchanges began to fall rapidly towards the end of 1794, and in May, 1795, had reached such a depression as to make it profitable to export bullion; and this circumstance, as well as the knowledge that several foreign loans were in progress, should have warned the directors of the necessity of contracting their issues. Such was the course of the directors in 1783. Instead of that, their issues were greatly extended. In the quarter, from January to March, 1795, they stood higher than they had ever done before; though we must, in common fairness, acquit the directors of the whole blame. The amount of their issues, in August, 1794, was little more than ten millions; in February, 1795, it had increased to fourteen millions; but this was chiefly caused by the bills which were drawn on the Treasury on behalf of foreign governments and made payable at the bank. The directors had then to choose between endangering their own safety, or making the Government bankrupt.

All these concurrent causes began to produce their full effect in the autumn of 1795. The drain commenced in September, and proceeded with alarming rapidity. On the 8th October the bank made a formal communication to Government, that it excited such serious apprehensions in their minds as to suggest an absolute necessity that the advances to Government must be reduced. They reminded him of the warning they had given in the beginning of the year as to the danger of the foreign loans, which had been fully verified, and that numerous other payments must be shortly provided for. That the market price of gold was then £4 4s. per ounce. Under these circumstances, the bank could lend no further assistance to the Government. On the 23rd of the same month, the directors, having heard of a new loan, waited on Mr. Pitt, who professed that he had not at the time the most distant idea of one. On the 18th November, the governor informed Mr. Pitt that the drain continued with unabated severity; and that the market price of gold was £4 2s. per ounce; and said that rumors were in circulation that another loan was intended, notwithstanding Mr. Pitt's denial of it so lately. Mr. Pitt said that, since their last interview, the successes of the Austrians had been so great against the French, that he was of opinion that it would highly conduce to the common cause to aid them with another loan not exceeding two millions; but he added that if such a course would be hazardous to the bank, every other consideration should be overlooked and the loan abandoned.

Parliament met on the 29th October, in the midst of great public excitement and dissatisfaction. The King was saluted with loud groanings and hootings, and volleys of stones were flung at his carriage, as he went to open the session. The speech said that for some time past he had observed with the greatest anxiety the very high price of grain, and that this anxiety was much increased by the deficiency of the harvest this year. A committee of the House of Commons was immediately afterwards appointed to consider the high price of corn. In December the House came to strong resolutions as to the necessity of diminishing the consumption of wheat as much as possible, and the members of both Houses signed an engagement to diminish the quantity by at least one-third, and to use their influence to persuade others to do the same; and an act was passed offering heavy bounties on the importation of corn.

The project of a loan going on, and it now being proposed to be £3,000,000, the directors, after a very solemn deliberation on the 3d of December, came to the unanimous resolution that, if the loan proceeded, they had the most cogent reasons to apprehend very momentous and alarming consequences from the actual effects of the last loan, and the continued drain of specie and bullion. In answer to this representation, Mr. Pitt solemnly promised them that he would lay aside all thought of it, unless the situation of the bank should so alter as to render such a loan of no importance to them.

The directors at last found it necessary to choose between making the Government bankrupt, and taking stringent measures to restrict their accommodation to the merchants. They resolved to fix beforehand the amount of advances they could make day by day; and gave notice that if the applications on any day exceeded the sum so resolved to be advanced, a *pro rata* proportion of each applicant's bills should be returned, without regard to the respectability of the party or the solidity of the bills. As matters continued to get worse, the directors had several communications with Mr. Pitt in January and February, 1796; but the project of the foreign loan being much dwelt upon with great earnestness by Mr. Pitt, on the 11th February they came to a resolution which was communicated to him the same day: "That it is the opinion of the court, founded upon its experience of the effects of the late Imperial loan, that if any further loan or advance of money to the Emperor, or other foreign State, should, in the present state of affairs take place, it will, in all probability, prove fatal to the Bank of England. The court of directors do, therefore, most earnestly deprecate the adoption of any such measure, and they solemnly protest against any responsibility for the calamitous consequences that may follow thereupon." Mr. Pitt replied that after the repeated promises he had made that no further loan should be made without communication with the bank, and a consideration of their circumstances, he saw no occasion for these resolutions, and that he should consider them as having been made in a moment of needless alarm.

We have already seen from Mr. Pitt's conduct with respect to the affair of the clause relating to the advance on Treasury bills, that he was not bound by any very scrupulous notions of honor. On this occasion, he departed still more widely from the right path; for, notwithstanding all his solemn promises, so frequently and emphatically made, the directors discovered that remittances were still continuing to be clandestinely made. In several interviews with him, the governor of the bank stated that he apprehended these remittances were being made. Mr. Pitt did not offer any explanation, and it was afterwards ascertained that they were being made.

The stringent measures adopted by the bank to contract its issues, caused much complaint amongst mercantile men, and a meeting of bankers and merchants was held at the London Tavern, on the 2d of April, who resolved that an alarming scarcity of money existed in the city of London, which was caused chiefly, if not entirely, by an increase in the commerce of the country, and the great diminution of mercantile discounts by the bank. They resolved that if means could be found to augment the circulating medium without infringing the privileges of the Bank of England, so as to restore the amount to what it was before the contraction of discounts, it was the duty of every friend of trade to give such a plan the most earnest support. The meeting appointed a committee to prepare a plan for such a purpose. Mr. Boyd drew up a long report on behalf of the committee, which proposed that a board of twenty-five members should be appointed by Parliament, who should be authorized to issue promissory notes, payable at six months after date, bearing interest at 1 1-4d. per £100 per day, upon receiving the value in gold, silver, Bank of England notes, or bills of exchange having not more than three months to run. The committee had an interview with the Chancellor of the Exchequer on the subject, and he informed them that the directors of the bank had proposed as a remedy that the floating debt should be funded, which plan he determined to try before adopting their scheme.

Mr. Pitt had never fulfilled his promise so often repeated to the directors, that the advances on Treasury bills should be reduced to £500,000; on the 14th June they were as much as £1,232,649. At the end of July he sent an earnest request to have £800,000 more at once, and a similar sum in August. They were induced to consent to the first, but refused the second advance. Mr. Pitt said that the first advance without the second would be of no use to him, and begged them to reconsider their decision. The directors, thus pressed, were driven to assent to it, but they accompanied it with a most serious and solemn remonstrance, which they desired should be laid before the Cabinet. They said that nothing under present circumstances could induce them to comply with the demand, except the dread of a worse evil following the refusal; and they said that this advance would incapacitate them from granting any further assistance during the year. They closed their remonstrance by saying: "They likewise consent to the measure in a firm reliance that the repeated promises so frequently made to them, that the advances on the Treasury bills should be completely done away, may be actually fulfilled at the next meeting of Parliament, and the necessary arrangements taken to prevent the same from ever happening again, as they conceive it to be an unconstitutional mode of raising money, which they are not warranted by the charter to consent to, and an advance always extremely inconvenient to themselves."

However, in November, Mr. Pitt made a fresh demand on them for £2,750,000 on the security of the land and malt taxes of 1797, which was granted on condition that the advances on Treasury bills, amounting to £1,613,345 were paid out of it. Mr. Pitt took the money, but never paid off the bills. The directors sent again on the 1st February, 1797, to demand payment of them, as they then amounted to £1,554,635, and would in a few days be increased by £300,000 more. Mr. Pitt made many excuses for the non-payment, and promised to make an endeavor to do so; but he dropped a hint that another large sum of bills had come in from St. Domingo. Upon being pressed as to the amount, he said that it was about £700,000. The governor expressed the greatest apprehensions, and begged him to delay the acceptance as long as he could. Mr. Pitt then hinted that he should want a large sum for Ireland, which he said would be about £200,000. The governor assured him that the drain of cash had been continuous and severe of late, and that such a demand would be very dangerous.

The enormous failures of the country bankers in 1793 had been followed by a diminution of the issues of country banks to a very large extent. Mr. Henry Thornton, after instituting extensive inquiries in different parts of the country, stated as the result that the country bank notes were reduced by at least one-half, and that the wants of commerce had caused a very large quantity of guineas to be drawn into the country to supply their place. Meantime, as we have already observed, although the foreign exchanges had become favorable, the bank still continued to adhere, with the utmost severity, to its policy of restriction throughout the autumn of 1796; and during the last three months of that year they were no higher than they had been in 1782, though commerce was many times larger than it had been in that year. Commercial payments had to be made in some medium in which the public had confidence. As the public could not get notes, they made a steady and continuous demand for guineas. The bullion in the bank in March, 1796, was £2,972,000; in September, £2,532,004; and in December, £2,508,000, when a drain set in more severely than ever.

At this period, the political situation of the country was in the most gloomy condition. The warlike combinations of Mr. Pitt had totally failed, and all Europe was now smarting under the consequences of their suicidal policy in meddling with the French republic. Mr. Burke had pronounced, in 1790, that France was, in a political light, expunged from the system of Europe. That it was doubtful whether she would ever appear on it again. That *Gallos quoque in bellis floruisse audivimus* would possibly be the language of the next generation. So much for political prophecy! That country which had been supposed to offer so easy a prey to surrounding nations, and whose epitaph Mr. Burke had so kindly and sagaciously suggested, was now the most powerful State in Europe. She had quelled internal dissensions in oceans of blood, and poured forth her armies in resistless torrents to avenge herself on the haughty States which had presumed to meddle with her internal condition. Great Britain, which had commenced the war with every other State in Europe as her ally, was now left alone. The Directory had subdued Spain by artifice and negotiation, and concluded a treaty with her, offensive and defensive, at St. Ildefonso, on the 19th of August. The campaign of Napoleon in the north of Italy in 1796 is generally allowed to be equal, if not superior, in brilliancy to any subsequent one. By a series of marvellous victories he drove the Austrians out of Italy, and in the beginning of 1797 Rome was only saved from conquest by absolute submission at Tolentino, and within a month Venice was annihilated, and Austria sued for peace at Leoben. This great reverse of circumstances had strengthened the party which had always been advocates for peace in England, and Mr. Pitt was compelled to make overtures for peace in October, 1796. A British Envoy was sent to treat with the Directory, and he stayed in Paris for two months; but, as neither party was sincere, the treaty came to nothing. The fact was that peace was the furthest thing possible from the thoughts of the Directory. After the conquest of La Vendée, they had an army of 100,000 men set free under a general who is usually acknowledged to have been the equal of Napoleon in military talent, and who was burning to emulate his exploits in Italy. While the pretended negotiations for peace were going on, the Directory were organizing an immense expedition for the invasion of Ireland. The orders to sail were transmitted to it several weeks before the British Envoy was expelled from Paris, and it actually sailed two days before he left. Fortunately this great Armada was, like its predecessor, dispersed by a tempest; a few straggling vessels reached Ireland in the last week of December, but the rest were obliged to put back to France.

This terrible menace, which had been so long hanging over the country, and whose destination it was vain to conceal, inspired the utmost alarm, and there was a continual demand for guineas for Ireland. The year 1797 commenced with the most gloomy apprehensions and depression. The country bankers discerned that the first burst of the tempest would fall on them, and determined to provide for it, by obtaining as much specie as they could from London; and, accordingly, the drain from the bank continued with increased rapidity after the beginning of the year. Mr. Pitt had hinted in his interview with the governor of the bank, on the first of February, that a loan for Ireland would probably be required, which was not likely to exceed £200,000; but soon afterwards, the directors were struck with dismay on hearing that the amount required was £1,500,000. On the 10th of February, the directors came to a resolution that, before they could entertain any proposal for the Irish loan, the Government must pay off the debts to them amounting to £7,186,445, of which they handed him in the details. At that time, the banks of Newcastle had a more than usual demand upon them for cash. In addition to the manufactories and collieries, the number of troops stationed in that part of the country had been considerably augmented. The banks had imported an extra supply of cash to meet their purposes, and were negotiating for more, when an event happened which brought on the crisis. A French frigate ran into one of the Welsh harbors and landed 1,200 men. At the same time an order came down from the Government to take an inventory of the stock of the farmers all along the coast, and to drive it into the interior if necessary. These circumstances created a perfect panic among the farmers. On Saturday, the 18th day of February, being market day, the farmers, who at that time of the year had the principal part of their rents in their hands, actuated by the terror of an immediate invasion, hurried into Newcastle the produce of their farms, which they sold at very low prices; and immediately rushed to the banks to demand specie. Seeing the universal panic, the banks came to an agreement to stop payment on the Monday, which they accordingly did. On the 21st February the state of the bank became so alarming, that the directors resolved that the time had come when they must make a communication to the Government. The quantity of bullion had been rapidly diminishing, and the constant calls of the bankers from all parts of the town for cash showed them that there must be some extraordinary reason for it. Mr. Pitt was aware that this proceeded from the general fear of invasion, which he thought was magnified much beyond anything to warrant it. It was agreed that a frigate should be sent over to Hamburg to purchase specie. On the 24th of February the drain became worse than ever, and inspired them with such alarm for the safety of the house that they sent a deputation to Mr. Pitt to ask him how long he considered that the bank should continue to pay cash, and when he should think it necessary to interfere. Mr. Pitt said it would be necessary to prepare a proclamation to put a stop to cash payments, and to give Parliamentary security for the notes. But in that case it would be necessary to appoint a secret committee of the House to look into the affairs of the bank. The deputation assured him that the bank would readily agree to this, and it was resolved to call a meeting of the chief bankers and merchants of London to come to some resolution to support public credit in this alarming crisis.

The news of the stoppage of the Newcastle banks spread like wildfire throughout the country, and soon reached the metropolis. The drain upon the bankers' coffers now became a run. The first serious apprehensions that danger was imminent were felt on the 21st of February; but the drain then became unexampled, till on Saturday, the 25th, the cash was reduced to £1,272,000. Before this the directors, in utter bewilderment at the state of the country, had used the most violent efforts to contract their issues. In five weeks they had reduced them by £2,000,000. On the 21st of January the issues were £10,550,830; on the 25th of February they were £8,640,250. But even this gave no true idea of the curtailment of mercantile accommodation; for the private bankers were obliged for their own security to follow the example of the bank. In order to meet their payments, persons were obliged to sell their stock of all descriptions at an enormous sacrifice. The three per cents. fell to 51, and other stock in proportion. On Saturday, the 25th, the court felt that the fatal hour was at last come, when they must for the first time since the institution of the bank come to a total suspension of payments. A meeting of the Cabinet was held on Sunday at Whitehall, and an order in council was issued, requiring the directors of the Bank of Er.gland to suspend all payments in cash, until the sense of Parliament could be taken on the subject. The King the next day sent a message to Parliament to inform them of the step that had been taken; and recommended the subject to their most serious and immediate attention. Mr. Pitt moved that the message should be taken into consideration next day; and he should propose that a select committee be appointed to investigate the state of the bank's affairs, which he believed were in the most solid condition. The directors of the bank had the order in council printed and widely circulated, and issued a notice of their own to say that the general concerns of the bank were in the most affluent and prosperous condition, and such as to preclude every doubt as to the security of the notes. At this time the cash in the bank was reduced to £1,086,170. The relief produced at the instant, by the definite determination to suspend cash payments and extend their issues of paper, was very great. Within one week it increased its accommodation by nearly two millions. On the same day, a resolution was entered into by 4000 of the merchants in the city to combine to support the credit of the notes.

Both Houses of Parliament appointed committees to examine into the affairs of the bank. The committee of the House of Commons reported that the outstanding obligations of the bank on the 25th of February were £13,770,390, and the total amount of their assets were £17,597,280; leaving a surplus of £3,126,890 over and above the debts of the Government, amounting to £11,686,800, which paid them three per cent. Both Houses reported that it was advisable, in the public interest, that the suspension o. cash payments should be continued for a limited time, and a bill for tha purpose was accordingly brought in. After some debates, which threw very little light on the subject, the Act, Statute 1797, c. 45, was passed. Its chief provisions were: 1. A clause of indemnity to the bank and all connected with it for anything done in pursuance of the order in council. 2. The bank was forbidden to make any payments in cash to any creditors, except in certain cases, and protected from all law proceedings. 3. The bank might issue cash in payments for the army, navy or ordnance, in pursuance of an order from the Privy Council. 4. The bank was to make no advance above £600,000 for the public service, in cash or notes, during the restriction. 5. If any person deposited any sum, not less than £500, in gold, in exchange for notes in the bank, it might repay three-fourths of the amount. 6. It might advance £100,000 in cash to the bankers of London, Westminster and Southwark, and to the Bank of Scotland and the Royal Bank of Scotland, £25,000 each. 7. Payment of debts in bank notes to be deemed as payment in cash, if offered and accepted as such. 8. No debtor was to be held to special bail unless the affidavit stated that payment in bank notes had not been offered. 9. Bank notes were to be received at par in payment of taxes. 10. The bank might issue any cash it received since the 26th of February, upon giving notice to the Speaker of the House of Commons and advertising in the "London Gazette" and on the Royal Exchange. 11. The act to continue to the 24th of June.

An act was also passed to enable the bank to issue notes under £5 (Statute 1797, c. 28), and, by chapter 32, this was extended to the country banks; but they were to continue liable to pay money on demand for them; and on failure of doing so within three days after demand any justice of the peace might cause the amount and costs to be levied by distress. All banking companies and bankers in Scotland might issue notes payable to bearer on demand for any sum under 20s.

An event of such portentous magnitude as the suspension of cash payments by the Bank of England could not fail to give rise to the most conflicting opinions as to the necessity of the measure, of the course of conduct of the directors which led to it, and as to the policy which ought to have been adopted under the drain which occurred in the last week of February, 1797. Many men of great eminence and ability changed their opinions in after times, when they came to look back upon the subsequent events. In examining this question, so as to form a just estimate of the conduct of the directors, we must remember that they were not masters of their own policy. They were distracted by two antagonistic claims, both of which they conceived it impossible to satisfy at the same time—namely, that of the Chancellor of the Exchequer and the demands of commerce. They considered that if they advanced to the Government they must contract their issues to the merchants; and, as the Minister was the more powerful and imperious party of the two, they were obliged to yield to his power.

Several of the directors, being examined before the committees, unanimously attributed the necessity of stopping payment to the enormous amount of their advances to Government, and gave it as their decided opinion that if the Government had repaid those advances, as they ought to have done, the great catastrophe would have been avoided. It may, therefore, be taken as admitted on all hands that, if they had been repaid by Government, they would have very greatly extended their advances to the merchants. The real question therefore is whether, considering that they were under such advances to Government, it would have been prudent to be more liberal in their accommodation to merchants? Mr. Henry Thornton was very strongly of opinion that the excessive contraction of the bank notes had produced the most injurious effects in shaking public credit of all descriptions; that the excessive reduction of notes had caused an unusually severe demand for guineas; that the great public distrust was directed against country bank notes, and that the bank ought to have extended its issues to supply the place of the country notes. Mr. Walter Boyd, an eminent merchant and financial agent, was very clearly of opinion that the restriction of the issue of notes by the bank was the chief cause of the forced sale and depreciation of the public securities; and if the bank had only maintained its issues at the same height as they were in December, 1795, the drain of specie from the bank, as well as the embarrassments of the mercantile world, would have been avoided, and a great portion of the fall which public securities had experienced would have been prevented. Mr. George Ellison, who was secretary to an association of a large number of country banks, considered that the quantity of coin in the country was greater than it was in 1793, but that a very considerable part was hoarded away, owing to the public alarms that were abroad. He attributed the great public distrust to the remembrance of the conduct of the bank in 1793, when it suddenly contracted its discounts just at the period when they were most wanted.

The Committee of the Lords called the attention of the House very strongly to these opinions, but they did not venture themselves to pronounce an opinion on their justness. The Committee of the Commons went considerably nearer to approving of them. In the year 1810, the governor of the bank being examined before the Bullion Committee, stated that after the experience of their policy of restriction, many of the directors repented of the measure, and the Bullion Committee explicitly condemned the policy of the bank both in 1793 and 1797.

The directors of the bank, acting in the midst of such unprecedented circumstances and so tremendous an emergency, are entitled to have their conduct examined with all forbearance. But, taking all these circumstances into consideration, we cannot fail to acquiesce in the opinion expressed by so many eminent bankers and merchants at the time, by the subsequent avowal that experience had led many of the directors to repent of the policy they then pursued, and by the emphatic judgment of the Bullion Committee, that the policy pursued by the bank in this momentous crisis was erroneous, and that the severe restrictions they attempted to place upon commerce very greatly contributed to bring on the calamity which subsequently overwhelmed them. Nothing, in short, could be more unhappy than their management of their issues. When the exchanges were violently adverse, so that it was extremely profitable to export gold, they enlarged them to an extravagant extent; and when the exchanges were extremely favorable, so that gold was flowing in, they restricted them with merciless severity. The issues of notes, which were £14,000,000 when the exchanges were against the country, were reduced to £8,640,250 when the exchanges had for several months been eminently favorable. It is perfectly certain that the directors who managed the bank in 1783 would have acted very differently to the directors who managed it in 1797. In 1783, as soon as the exchanges became favorable, the directors expanded their issues, though the cash in the bank then was less than half what it was in 1797. It appears from the entire evidence in the reports, that it was this excessive restriction of notes which drained their vaults during the autumn of 1796, and that if they had been more liberal in their issues, their vaults would have been much better replenished with cash. It was a pregnant instance of the truth well known to all bankers, that an excessive restriction of credit causes and produces a drain of gold.

This great catastrophe was the second notable penalty which the country paid in four years for the unjustifiable monopoly of the bank. Never was there a more unfortunate example of monopolizing selfishness. It would neither establish branches of its own in the country, nor would it permit any other private company, of power and solidity, to do so, whose credit might have interposed and aided in sustaining its own. Moreover, when a failure of confidence was felt in the country notes, it refused to issue notes of its own to supply their place. The power of issuing, which plays so important a part in commerce, was absolutely forbidden to powerful and wealthy companies, and left in unbounded freedom to private persons—a vast number of them nothing but small shopkeepers, with no adequate capital or property to support their issues, and whose credit vanished like a puff of smoke in any public danger. The bank consequently was left alone to bear the whole brunt of the crisis, solitary and unsupported, and finally succumbed.

From the foregoing considerations, as well as the weight of authority on the subject, we can scarcely doubt that the suspension of cash payments was brought about at that particular time by the erroneous policy of the directors. But it appears open to much doubt whether any management, however skilful, could have prevented such an event at some period of the war. Several of those who concurred in the measure at the time, after their judgment had been corrected by subsequent experience, expressed their regret at having done so. Sir Robert Peel, in 1844, said it was a "fatal" measure. Notwithstanding, however, the concurrence of so many weighty authorities—and this is peculiarly a case where great authorities carry much weight—we cannot help thinking that it was fortunate that it occurred at this early period. The alarm and dangers which preceded its stoppage were comparatively slight compared with those which menaced the country after that event. The mutinies in the fleet, the rebellion in Ireland, a great army being gathered together, avowedly for the invasion of England, under the command of a more fortunate, though probably not a greater soldier than Hoche, were probably dangers of such portentous magnitude as to render it in the last degree improbable that any paper currency convertible into gold could have survived them.

That Montague was a greater financier than Pitt can, we think, scarcely be doubted, and the carrying through the recoinage of the silver, in the midst of so much public distress, was a financial operation of which the skill, audacity and success must ever be regarded with admiration. But it must be remembered that the crisis in that reign lasted a much shorter time than the revolutionary war, and was never fraught with so much real danger to the independence of the country. At that period, there was no paper credit except the notes of the Bank of England and a few London bankers; and William was at the head of a great European confederacy against one overgrown power. So that the circumstances of the two periods were in no way parallel, but rather, we may say, reversed. The confederacy against England at the latter period was far more menacing and formidable than the alliance against France. The fortunes of the British Empire were apparently at their lowest ebb in 1798; the state of Venice in the war of Chiozza was scarcely more desperate; and there seemed to be but one thing wanting to complete the destruction of the country—the loss of public credit. However great and invaluable are the blessings of a solid paper currency in the time of peace, there does not appear to be any instance of its having successfully withstood the danger of an invasion by a foreign enemy. The banks at Edinburgh, no doubt, survived two rebellions; but they took refuge in the impregnable fortress of the Castle of Edinburgh, which the insurgents were never able to capture. And at a later period, when banking was confessedly founded on a better system, and obtained the confidence of the country to a much greater degree, it could not have withstood the dread of invasion if it had not been for the timely assistance of the Bank of England. And if it could not do so in that country, where the danger was remote, it is morally certain that it could not have done so in England, where not only was it of much inferior stability, but was the very part of the Empire aimed at, and the first exposed to danger. Moreover, the constant power of producing public embarrassments by demands for gold, would have been a powerful weapon in the hands of the enemy, in which they would have found many to support them from political sympathy.

The scarcity of guineas, which led to the supposed necessity of issuing the order in council, also rendered a more abundant supply of the circulating medium necessary, and an act was immediately passed suspending till the first of May the Act, Statute 1775, c. 51, restraining the negotiation of small promissory notes. In a few days the bank caused to be prepared and issued

£1 and £2 notes; and to supply still further the demand for small currency, they issued a notice that they had imported a large number of Spanish dollars, which were to be current at 4s. 6d. However, it was discovered that the dollars were undervalued by 2d. each, so their current value was enhanced by 3d. These dollars were stamped with a small king's head. The bank having put the dollars into circulation at 1d. each above their market value, the bullion merchants were not slow in seizing the advantage and imported an immense quantity of similar dollars, which they stamped in a similar manner. They were called in on the 31st October, 1797, by which time the bank had put 2,325,099 into circulation. It at first attempted to refuse payment of the illegitimate ones, but they were executed in so close an imitation of the legitimate ones, that it was impossible to detect them, and they were obliged to pay them all.

Parliament met again on the 2d of November, and on the 15th the House of Commons appointed a secret committee to inquire whether it was expedient to continue the restriction. They presented a resolution of the directors stating that the condition of the bank's affairs was such that it could with safety resume its usual functions. The committee, however, recommended that, in consequence of the state of public affairs, it was advisable that the restriction should be continued for a further period. After a short debate an act was passed to continue the restriction until one month after the conclusion of a definite treaty of peace.

THE MONETARY PANIC OF 1825.

The monetary panic of 1825 was the next instance in which the two conflicting theories—the restrictive theory and the expansive theory—were brought into contrast. The harvest of 1823 was deficient both in quantity and quality, and prices rose considerably in the beginning of 1824, old wheat being then at 78s.; later in the year, however, they declined; but the harvest of 1824 being inferior, they rose again. The bank had for some years been accumulating treasure to meet the anticipated deficiency of the country issues expected to follow the suppression of the £1 notes. When the unhappy change in the policy of the Government took place this great amount of bullion was rendered comparatively useless, and the country banks began to extend their issues in 1824; and in 1825 they exceeded what they were in 1818. In January, 1824, the bullion in the bank was £14,200,000.

During the preceding year an adjustment of rents, to meet the altered state of prices, had taken place; and the old stocks having been gradually worked off, the energy of the people began to revive. The enormous amount of cash in the bank, for which there was no immediate use, enabled the Government to carry through a great financial operation—the reduction of the interest upon nearly one-quarter of the public debt. The navy five per cents. were reduced to four per cent., and the four per cent. stock was reduced to three and a-half. This operation, only equalled and exceeded in our own time by the vast and successful transaction carried through by Mr. Goschen, had a very considerable influence in curtailing the incomes of many persons who could ill afford it to a very inconvenient extent, and prepared them to look out for more favorable investments for their money. Notwithstanding the unhappy and severe distress of the agricultural portion of the community, Mr. Tooke says that the trading and manufacturing interests had never been in a more regular, sound and satisfactory state than in the interval from 1821 to 1824. At the close of the session of 1823, the King congratulated Parliament on the flourishing condition of all branches of our commerce and manufactures and the gradual abatement of agricultural distress.

At the close of 1824 the seeds of the disasters which ensued at the end of 1825 were sown. The royal speech opened Parliament with the same strain of congratulation as had closed the preceding session; and the same congratulations were used at the close of the session of 1824. Towards the end of that year, it became visible that in some of the leading articles of consumption the supply was falling short of the demand, which gave rise to a spirit of speculation; and, as in all similar cases, a few early purchases which were successful induced extensive imitation. At the end of 1824 and in the beginning of 1825, this had amounted to positive infection, numbers of persons being induced to go out of their own line of business to speculate in articles with which they had no concern whatever, but induced by representations of their brokers to do so in hopes of realizing great and immediate gains. Just at this period occurred one of those events which have so often lured the commercial world to their destruction. The long contest between Spain and her South American colonies had now finally terminated in favor of the colonies. We have already noticed the great commercial catastrophe brought about in 1810 by the extravagant speculations on the opening of Brazil to British trade. Precisely the same course occurred in 1824. The recognition of the independence of the South American States and Mexico opened out a boundless field for speculation and for the consumption of British manufactures. The spirit of speculation was aggravated to the utmost by the visions of wealth which was to be extracted from the gold and silver producing countries; and immense schemes were formed for working the mines with British capital. However, the long struggle for independence had inspired the British people with much sympathy for the juvenile republics; and when they wanted to borrow money to support their public credit the British were only too eager to lend it. It was alleged that £150,000,000 of British capital was then sunk in different ways in Mexico and South America.

Although the symptoms of a coming mercantile catastrophe were plainly evident in the beginning of 1825, the speech put into the King's mouth declared the utmost gratification at the continuance and the progressive increase of the public prosperity. "There never was a period," it said, "in the history of this country when all the great interests of the nation were at the same time in so thriving a condition, or when a feeling of content and satisfaction was more widely diffused through all classes of the British people." The speech of Lord Dudley and Ward was exactly in the same strain. After contrasting the suffering the nation had gone through during the last thirty years, he said it was his good fortune to ask their lordships to carry to the foot of the throne their unmixed aid and, he hoped, their unanimous congratulations upon a state of prosperity such as he believed was unequalled in this country and had never been surpassed in any age or nation. And yet, though the whole debate was in this strain, no sooner was it ended than the Lord Chancellor called the attention of the House to the dangerous extent to which the mania for joint-stock companies had gone, and said he would move for leave to bring in a bill to restrain the system. Within seven weeks after that Lord Lauderdale called the attention of the House to the "fury for joint-stock companies which had taken possession of the people," and said that the schemes already subscribed for amounted to £200,000,000.

The following extract from the Annual Register of 1824 contains a description of the rising of the joint-stock mania. After stating that the "mines of Mexico" was a phrase which opened visions of boundless wealth to the imagination, and how the mania spread from foreign enterprises to home ones, it says: "In all these speculations only a small instalment, seldom exceeding five per cent., was paid at first, so that a very moderate rise in the price of the shares produced a large profit on the sum actually invested. If, for instance, shares of £100 on which £5 had been paid rose to a premium of £40, this yielded on every share a profit equal to eight times the amount of the money which had been paid. This possibility of enormous profit, by risking so small a sum, was a bait too tempting to be resisted. All the gambling propensities of human nature were constantly solicited into action, and crowds of individuals of every description—the credulous, the suspicious; the crafty and the bold; the raw and the experienced; the intelligent and the ignorant; princes, nobles, politicians, placemen, patriots, lawyers, physicians, divines, philosophers, poets, intermingled with women of all ranks and degrees, spinsters, wives and widows—hastened to venture some portion of their property in schemes of which scarcely anything was known except the name." As a specimen of the madness of the speculations, we may quote the price of mining shares. The Anglo-Mexican, on which £10 was paid, were at £43 on the 10th of December, 1824; on the 11th of January, 1825, they were at £150. The Real del Monte, with £70 paid, were at £550 in December and at £1350 in January, and others in similar proportion. The price of most other commodities doubled and trebled.

Now what was the conduct of the Bank of England during this period? The bullion which stood above £14,000,000 in the beginning of January, 1824, was reduced to £11,600,000 in October. The exchange on Paris had been falling ever since the close of 1823. The last time it was above par was in June, 1823, and since then the fall had been continuous. The decrease in bullion had been steady, uniform and rapid ever since March, 1824. Now, when it was known that immense sums were leaving the country, and the exchange falling lower, what did the bank do? It increased its issues. During the month of October, 1824, they were increased by £2,300,000. While every consideration of common sense and prudence demanded a rapid contraction when the speculative fever was plainly declared, instead of doing what they could to check it, they added fuel to the flames. But the directors seemed determined to set all the principles of the Bullion Report at defiance, and the drain upon them proceeded with increased severity. In April, 1825, the bullion was diminished by upwards of £4,000,000; and their issues were £3,600,000 higher when they had only £6,650,000 of bullion than when they had £14,000,000.

The speculative fever was at its height in the first four months of 1825, when it had spent its force and came to an end in the natural course of things. Vast numbers of persons who had embarked in these wild schemes, with the hope of selling out of them before the inevitable crash came, were now called upon for their subscriptions. Vast quantities of capital having been already absorbed, had the inevitable effect of raising the rate of interest. Successive calls compelled the weaker holders to realize; and while the calls for ready money were immediate and pressing, the prospect of returns was distant and uncertain. Accordingly, after May and June, the decline was rapid. The South American loans and the Mexican mining schemes proved almost universally total losses. In the meantime, that slack water which, as Mr. Tooke observes, always precedes a great turn in the tide of prices, took place. The increase of commodities, which speculation had caused, could no longer be kept from being realized; prices fell as rapidly as they had risen. The obligations of the speculators now became due, and the sale of commodities had to be forced to meet them. Universal discredit now succeeded; goods became unsalable; so that stocks which are usually held in anticipation of demand, were wholly unavailable to meet the pecuniary engagements of the holders. Merchants, who had accepted bills for only half the value of the goods consigned to them, were unable to realize even that half, or even to obtain advances on security of the bills of lading; and even the advances already made were peremptorily called in. The usury laws, which limited interest to five per cent., greatly aggravated the distress; nobody would lend money at five per cent. when its real value was so much greater; hence, numbers who would gladly have paid eight or ten per cent. interest, were obliged to sell goods at a difference of thirty per cent. for cash, compared with the price for time.

The bankers in the country had followed exactly in the steps of the Bank of England. While the fever was raging, they had increased their issues and liabilities by speculative advances on commodities. The persons to whom these advances had been made had no means of repaying them, but "the promises to pay" the bankers had advanced them remained in circulation and must be met. The bankers foresaw the coming storm and endeavored to provide funds to meet it. The Bank of England itself had its eyes open to the suicidal career it was following in May, and then endeavored violently to contract its issues. This sudden change of policy only aggravated the general feeling of discredit. During the autumn, everything portended the approach of the impending catastrophe.

The following table shows the progressive decrease in the bullion at the bank during 1824 and 1825:

1824.	£	1825.	£
Jan. 31, . . .	13,527,850	Jan. 29, . . .	9,490,420
Feb. 28, . . .	13,800,390	Feb. 26, . . .	8,857,730
March 27, . .	13,871,280	March 26, . . .	8,152,340
April 24, . . .	13,405,550	April 30, . . .	6,659,780
May 29, . . .	12,887,840	May 28, . . .	6,131,300
June 26, . . .	12,809,140	June 25, . . .	5,482,040
July 31, . . .	11,814,720	July 30, . . .	4,174,830
Aug. 28, . . .	11,763,550	Aug. 27, . . .	3,626,570
Sept. 25, . . .	11,811,500	Sept. 24, . . .	3,496,690
Oct. 30, . . .	11,433,430	Oct. 29, . . .	3,150,360
Nov. 27, . . .	11,323,760	Nov. 26, . . .	3,012,150
Dec. 24, . . .	10,721,190	Dec. 31, . . .	1,260,890

The inevitable *contre coup* of the undue expansion of credit in the spring began to press heavily on the country banks in the autumn of 1825. It gradually became severer during the month of November. On the 29th of November it was announced in the London papers that Sir William Elford's, a large bank at Plymouth, had failed, and that was immediately followed by the fall of Wentworth & Co., a great Yorkshire firm. By the 3d of December the panic had fairly set in, and the whole city was thrown into the most violent state of alarm and consternation. On that day (Saturday) some of the directors were informed that Pole, Thornton & Co., one of the leading city banking houses, was in difficulties; and at a hurried meeting held the next day it was resolved to place £300,000 at their disposal upon proper security. During that week, the utmost attention was paid to the position of that house, which fought it through the following week, though it was privately known to the governor that, if the storm did not abate, they must fail on the following Monday morning. Instead of abating, however, it became more furious than ever on Monday; and Pole & Co. stopped payment, and the ruin of forty country banks, which were connected with them, was expected. The fall of this great banking house was the signal for a general run upon the London bankers; and three or four more gave way, and spread universal consternation among the country banks, sixty-three of which stopped payment; though several paid 20s. in the pound, and eventually resumed business.

From Monday, the 12th, to Saturday, the 17th December, was the height of the crisis in London. Mr. Richards, the deputy governor of the bank at that time, said: "On Monday morning the storm began, and till Saturday night it raged with an intensity that it is impossible for me to describe. On the Saturday night it had somewhat abated. The bank had taken a firm and deliberate resolution to make common cause with the country as far as their humble efforts would go; and on Saturday night it was my happiness when I went up to the Cabinet, reeling with fatigue, to be able just to call out to my Lord Liverpool, and to the members of his Majesty's Government then present, that all was well; that was, I believe, on the evening of Saturday, the 17th of December. Then, in the following week, things began to get a little more steady; and by the 24th, what with the £1 notes that had gone out and other things, people began to be satisfied; and then it was, for the first time in a fortnight, that those who had been busied in that terrible scene could recollect that they had families who had some claim on their attention."

As the crisis was evidently approaching, at the end of November, the papers discussed the probable policy of the bank, and it was generally anticipated that it would continue to contract its issues, and let the evil work its own cure by the fall of those houses which had been imprudent in their speculations; and this was the course adopted by the bank, and to which they adhered as matters grew worse; and they were supported in it by public opinion. On the day after Pole & Co. fell, another house of equal magnitude, Williams, Burgess & Co., stopped payment. The panic then became universal; and the directors thought that they would certainly have to stop payment; they sounded the Government as to a restriction act; but the Government absolutely refused it, and it was resolved that the bank should pay away its last sovereign. The Mint was kept constantly at work day and night; but it could not supply coin with sufficient rapidity, so that it kept constantly diminishing. On the Saturday, the coin in the bank's vaults scarcely exceeded one million; but fortunately, when the Saturday evening came, the tide had receded, and the directors were able to assure the Ministry that all danger was over. The great pressure had produced its necessary effect in such circumstances. The great increase in the value of money here had turned the exchanges in favor of the country; the directors expected remittances from Paris, and they fortunately came earlier than was expected. On the Monday following, the 19th, about £400,000 came from France; and the demand having sensibly abated, the supplies from the Mint fully equalled the sums drawn out of the bank—or rather exceeded them.

Mr. Huskisson said afterwards in the House of Commons that, during forty-eight hours, Monday and Tuesday, December 12th and 13th, it was impossible to convert into money to any extent the best securities of the Government. Persons could not sell exchequer bills, nor bank stock, nor East India stock, nor the public funds. Mr. Baring said, that men would not part with their money on any terms, nor for any security. The extent to which the distress had reached was melancholy to the last degree. Persons of undoubted wealth were seen walking about the streets of London, not knowing whether they should be able to meet their engagements for the next day. The exchanges had, however, turned in favor of the country; and on Wednesday, the 14th, the bank totally changed their policy, and discounted with the utmost profuseness. They made very large advances on exchequer bills and securities of all sorts. Mr. Harman said: "We lent by every possible means and in modes we had never adopted before. We took in stock as security; we purchased exchequer bills, and we made advances on exchequer bills; we not only discounted outright, but we made advances on deposit of bills of exchange to an immense amount; in short, by every possible means consistent with the safety of the bank; and we were not on some occasions over-nice; seeing the dreadful state in which the public were, we rendered every assistance in our power." This audacious but prudent policy was crowned with the most complete success; the panic was stayed almost immediately. On Friday evening, the 16th, the "Courier" said: "We are happy to think that the worst is over, though there are still great demands upon the bank, particularly from the country." On the next day the same paper said: "Although public confidence is on the return in the metropolis, and things are resuming their usual course, yet, as might be expected, this has not yet communicated itself to the country." In fact, the London panic was completely allayed in this week by the profuse issue of bank notes. Between Wednesday, the 14th, and Saturday, the 17th, the bank issued £5,000,000 of notes.

The waves of discredit, however, were propagated through the country, and throughout the following week the demand still continued great from the London bankers for their country correspondents. During the course of it, it came to the remembrance of some of the directors that there was a chest of their £1 notes which had never been used. As soon as this was discovered, it occurred to them that they might be used to stay the panic in the country districts and the discredit of the country notes. Upon communicating this idea to the London bankers, it was eagerly approved of and the sanction of the Government asked for the experiment. The Government consented and the notes were sent off to the country bankers without delay, and produced instantaneous relief. At Norwich, when the Gurneys showed upon their counter piles of bank notes, it at once stopped the run in that part of the country. By the 24th of December the panic was completely allayed all over the country, and the amount of the £1 notes which the bank issued was under £500,000. By the beginning of 1826 the credit of the banking world was completely restored.

The circumstances of this famous crisis are the most complete and triumphant examples of the unquestionable truth of the principles of the Bullion Report and of Sir Francis Baring, already quoted. When the drain of treasure from the bank was severe and increasing, and notoriously for exportation on account of foreign loans, the bank, with infatuated obstinacy, had extended their issues instead of contracting them, in defiance of the clearest warnings of the Bullion Report. After six months' continuance of this fatal policy, they at last reversed their course and greatly contracted their issues. In the course of the autumn the drain for exportation ceased, but continued for internal purposes; the demand for gold was entirely to support the tottering credit of the country bank notes. Now, as the country bankers were only too glad to withdraw their own notes and substitute gold for them, there was not the slightest danger of an increase of Bank of England notes adding to the general amount of paper currency in the country, but just the reverse; consequently, it was just the precise case in which Sir Francis Baring and the Bullion Committee said that it was the duty of the Bank of England to extend its issues of paper to support general credit. There was not the smallest danger that an extension of issues would, under such circumstances, turn the foreign exchanges against the country. The character of the demand was declared in the most unmistakable manner. On Thursday, the 15th, a meeting of merchants and others took place at the Mansion House, when it was stated that Sir P. Pole & Co. had a surplus of £170,000 after payment of all claims against them, besides large landed property belonging to Sir Peter Pole, and about £100,000 the private property of other members of the firm. Williams & Burgess had enough to pay 40s. in the pound.

Now, if the course which was adopted on the Wednesday had been adopted on the Monday, the whole of that terrific crisis might have been saved. Mr. Vincent Stuckey, one of the most eminent of the country bankers in the kingdom, says: "My opinion was that the crisis at that time was brought on by excessive issues; but when the panic came country bank paper was bought in for Bank of England paper, and therefore all that was immediately wanted was an exchange of paper. I stated in a letter I wrote upon the subject to the bank on the 14th of December, 1825, that they would not have to increase the sum total of circulation, but that all they would have to do was to exchange A for B; and in my letter I recommended them to issue a million of paper a day, which they did; for otherwise most of the banks in London as well as in the country must have stopped." And, accordingly, they did issue, and all contemporary evidence proves that it was this profuse issue of £5,000,000 of paper in a few days that stopped the panic and saved the whole banking and mercantile community from ruin. If they had persevered in the restrictive policy for three days longer, the total and entire destruction of commercial credit would infallibly have ensued. In short, if they had followed the precedents of 1793 and 1797, so strongly condemned by the Bullion Report, all credit, both banking and mercantile, would have been destroyed. They followed the principles laid down in the Bullion Report, and the country was saved. This panic adds another to the previously conclusive ones of the truth of the expansive theory in a monetary panic, and the mischief and fatal erroneousness of the restrictive theory.

When the causes of this terrible calamity came to be discussed, there were not wanting many who laid the whole blame on the excessive issues of the bank as well as the excessive issues of the country banks. But, though it is indisputable that the bank acted on the most erroneous principles, in not contracting its issues when the great drain of bullion was going on, it is a mere delusion for men to attribute the consequences of their own wild and extravagant mania to the Bank of England or to any bank. The errors of all the banks put together were trivial, compared to the outbreaks of speculative insanity which seized upon all classes. Was it the issues of some banks which led a respectable bookselling firm to risk £100,000 in a speculation in hops and ruin themselves, and drag down Sir Walter Scott along with them?

The bank had committed many errors before, as serious as those of 1825, without leading to any such disaster. In fact, it was the nature of the speculations which men had rushed into headlong, that must inevitably have brought about that great catastrophe, if there had not been a bank note in existence. The speculative mania of 1694 took place before the bank was founded; the great South Sea Bubble mania took place when there were no country banks at all; and no one accused the Bank of England or the London bankers of having made too profuse issues then. The great railway mania of 1845-46 took place after it was fondly supposed that the Bank Act of 1844 had effectually secured the country against the recurrence of similar calamities. The worthless character of a great portion of the country paper had greatly aggravated the intensity of the calamity; in fact, it began with the country banks; and the great commercial failures did not commence until after the banking panic had subsided. The Government and the bank, at last learning wisdom from repeated convulsions, which seemed to recur periodically, became sensible that it was imperatively necessary to provide a currency of a more solid description for the country; and that the frightful evils of the monopoly of the Bank of England must come to an end.

Parliament met on the 3d of February, 1826, and six paragraphs of the speech from the throne were occupied with the commercial catastrophe. It said that part of the remedies to be applied consisted in placing the currency and circulating credit of the country on a firmer foundation. Lord King said that the causes of the calamity were partly to be attributed to the Government; in a greater degree to the country banks; and in a still greater degree to the monopoly of the Bank of England. There was no period of distress during the last thirty or forty years in which the conduct of that establishment had not been injurious, and in every way aggravated it. It was a most faulty machine. It was impossible that a bank so incorporated could do good. If the purpose was to erect an establishment to do mischief, they would erect it on the very principles of the bank. They would give it a monopoly; remove from it all fear of rivalry; and connect it with the Government. He lamented that the pressure of the country gentlemen and the country bankers had been too powerful to be resisted by the Ministry in

1822, and had forced them to continue the issues of £1 and £2 notes to keep up prices and encourage speculation. The Earl of Liverpool chiefly blamed the excessive issues of the country bankers, and said that the small notes must be gradually withdrawn and a metallic currency substituted. He said that he was perfectly satisfied, and had entertained the conviction for years, that the country had grown too large, and that its concerns had become too extensive to allow of the exclusive privilege of the Bank of England. Its privileges had operated in a most extraordinary, and, as he thought, unfortunate manner for the country. Any small tradesman, a cheesemonger, a butcher, or a shoemaker, might open a country bank, but a set of persons with a fortune sufficient to carry on the concern with safety were not permitted to do so.

The Ministry took upon themselves to prohibit any more stamps being issued to the country banks for £1 and £2 notes. The Chancellor of the Exchequer said that these notes were to be deprecated as an infringement of the Act of 1819, which no one could deny was passed, if ever any act was, with the unanimous approbation of all the parties of which Parliament was composed; an act which had solemnly been resolved upon as the only measure which could enable the country to meet any future danger by placing the circulating medium on a permanent and stable footing. No man could insinuate that that act was not the result of the deliberate conviction of almost every individual of every party in that House. He then detailed the continual evil and insecurity of the small notes, and said that he always had regretted, and still regretted, the step taken by Parliament, in 1822, which permitted them. The intention of the Government was, therefore, to suppress them as soon as possible in England, and subsequently in Scotland and Ireland. He moved a resolution that no fresh notes were to be issued by country bankers in England under £5; and that those printed before the 5th February, 1826, might be issued, re-issued and circulated until the 5th April, 1829, and no longer.

The opinions as to the causes of this great catastrophe, expressed in Parliament and the country, were, of course, most conflicting, but the great preponderance of opinion was adverse to the small note issues. Mr. Baring, who defended the country bankers from the accusations levelled against them, said that their small notes were bad as a permanent system, and they ought to be called in. Even although they might sometimes be of almost indispensable use to the country, still, if the misery which had been caused by their use among the poorer classes was taken into consideration it was a sufficient reason why the nuisance should be abated, and it was his opinion that the House had not got rid of this deluge of paper at the time when it had the power to do so, and that it had not resisted, as it ought to have resisted, the importunity of the country bankers, that these small notes should be abolished as soon as practicable.

Mr. Huskisson described the frightful nature of the panic during forty-eight hours (Monday and Tuesday, December 13th and 14th), and said that it had been truly observed that the bank, by its prompt and efficacious assistance, had put an end to the panic and averted the ruin which threatened all the banking establishments in London, and, through them, the banking establishments and moneyed men all over the country. The conduct of the bank had been most praiseworthy, and had, in a great degree, saved the country from a general convulsion. The bank, through its prompt, efficacious and public-spirited conduct, had had the countenance, advice and particular recommendation of the Premier and Chancellor of the Exchequer. He admitted that the commercial distress in Scotland was very great, but that did not prove that the system of Scotch banking did not afford greater securities than the English system, and that it was desirable to introduce it into this country. He then described the wild spirit of speculation which had seized the country, and which produced a rise of prices so rapid as had never been equalled. He might mention, as an instance, the price of nutmegs, which rose in one month from 2s. 6d. to 12s. 6d. a pound; and speculation in other spices caused a corresponding rise in their prices. The mania extended equally to other articles of consumption; merchants, traders, shopkeepers, clerks and apprentices partook equally of the frenzy of vieing with each other in their endeavors to secure a monopoly of each article. And this state of things took its rise, not among the wild, insane and bedlamite schemers, but among those who were considered the sober, steady merchants and traders of the metropolis. And all this took place at a time when money was rapidly leaving the country. Now, if when it was leaving the country so rapidly, it was still hawked about at a greatly lowered rate of interest, that showed that there must be something wrong in the currency. And to what would any sober man say such a state of things must come at last? The bank at last was obliged to provide for its own safety by narrowing its issues, which checked the spirit of speculation, and, as a necessary result, those country banks which had been most rash and immoderate in aiding these speculations by advances were ruined. The ruin of these bad and unstable banks had affected even the stability of the most solvent ones. A general panic ensued, and seven or eight hundred country banks had asked for assistance from the Bank of England. She had 700 or 800 drains for gold suddenly opened upon her. Was this a safe or proper condition to leave the country in? Certainly not. It was his opinion—an opinion not hastily formed, but the result of long and anxious observation—that a permanent state of cash payments and a circulation of £1 and £2 notes could not co-exist. If there were in any country a paper and a coin currency of the same denomination, the paper and the coin could not circulate together—the paper would drive out the coin. Let crown notes be made, and a crown piece would never be seen; make half-crown notes, and no half-crown would remain in circulation. Allow £1 notes to circulate, and we should never see a sovereign. One of the great evils they were called on to correct was the excessive issue of paper. This had been the cause of the greatest distress; it had caused the ruin of thousands of innocent persons. Nothing but disgrace and danger could attend the deviation from the true principles of currency, which Parliament had solemnly recognized. If they wished to prove the value of a steady, unchangeable currency, they had it in the example of France, which had twice been invaded by a foreign army, her capital had been taken, and she had been obliged to pay a large sum to foreign countries for corn, but she had a steady metallic currency; and, however the great contractors might have suffered, the great body of the people had remained uninjured. This was due to the excellent footing upon which the currency of that country was established. If this measure was adopted, every country banker would be obliged to have as great a regard to the exchanges as the Bank of England, and be compelled to provide for his own safety, without leaning on the bank in times of danger Now was the time to withdraw these small notes, when the bankers were smarting under the consequences of their over-issues. They had, at present, a large amount of gold and bank notes; if they allowed the favorable time to pass by, the small notes would soon be issued again. It would be advantageous to the public to have chartered joint-stock banks, established under a proper system, with only a limited liability. This would, no doubt, induce many persons of great fortune and credit to take shares in them; but the bank objected to the extension of limited liability, and stipulated that the banks of Scotland and Ireland should not have this privilege. Some thought that the currency should be even more purely metallic than was now proposed, and that notes of a higher denomination should be suppressed. For himself, he entirely differed from Mr. Ricardo as to the true basis of the currency; and he believed that if Mr. Ricardo, ingenious as he was, had been sole director of the Bank of England, it would, before now, have stopped payment. He thought Mr. Ricardo's view of the currency quite erroneous.

Sir John Newport, as a banker himself, considered the issue of small notes to be most injurious to all connected with them, as affording the most dangerous facilities for extravagant speculation. It had been said that a considerable portion of the commerce of the country could not be carried on if these notes were abolished. He was quite willing to accept that alternative and abandon a portion of our commerce rather than continue them. He did not believe that such would be the case. Now was the best time to abolish this pernicious system, when so many of the country bankers had failed.

Mr. Secretary Peel was convinced that the root of the evil lay in the monopoly of the Bank of England, and that if, in the year 1793, a set of banks had existed in this country on the Scotch system, it would have escaped the danger it was then involved in, as well as the calamity which had just occurred. In 1793, upwards of 100 banks had failed. In seven years, from 1810 to 1817, 157 commissions in bankruptcy were issued against country bankers; in the crisis which had just occurred, seventy-six failures had taken place. But from the different ways of making compositions, etc., the number of failures should probably be estimated at four times the number of the commissions of bankruptcy. What system could be worse or more prejudicial to every interest in the country than one which admitted such an enormous amount of failures? Contrast what had been the case in Scotland, under a different system. Mr. Gilchrist, a manager of one of the Scotch banks, had been asked by the committee of 1819 how many failures there had been in Scotland in his recollection, and said, there had only been one; that the creditors had been paid 14s. in the pound immediately, and finally the whole of their claims. These facts were a strong presumptive proof that the Scotch system, if not quite perfect, was, at least, far superior to the one existing in England. The present system of country banking was most prejudicial in every point of view. He then described the terrible misery caused by the failure of the country banks. He trusted that the institution of joint-stock banks would place the currency on a firmer footing. He most sincerely trusted that the want of a charter, the great obstacle to the proposed institutions, would be removed. He hoped the directors of the Bank of England would seriously consider what advantage they would derive from refusing charters to these banks. He himself could not imagine what benefit they would derive from it; they, no doubt, had the right to prevent such charters being granted, but he hoped that they would refrain from exercising such right. He eulogized highly the conduct of the directors during the late crisis; he could not conceive it possible for any body of men to have acted better; or to have exercised more judgment, discretion and liberality than they had done—of which he hoped they would give a further instance, by not opposing the grants of charters to the proposed new banks. He fully concurred with Mr. Huskisson, that it was impossible to maintain coin in circulation if paper of the same denomination were allowed to circulate along with it. Now was the most favorable opportunity of getting rid of the small notes. It would be impolitic and unsafe to wait the moment of returning prosperity, as the country bankers would be more reluctant to agree to it, and more able to oppose it. To stand gazing on the bank, in idle expectation, now that the river was passable, would be an irreparable mistake. The Ministers carried their proposals by 222 to 39; and a motion to continue the small notes of the Bank of England was rejected by 66 to 7.

THE MONETARY CRISIS OF 1838-9.

In 1827, the directors of the bank had become convinced of the truth of the principles laid down by the Bullion Committee for regulating their issues of paper, and had formally rescinded the resolution of the directors of 1819 condemnatory of them. Mr. Horsley Palmer, the governor of the bank, being asked by the Committee on the Bank Charter Act, in 1832, by what principle in ordinary times the bank was guided in the regulation of its issues, said, that in a period of full currency, and consequently with a par of exchange, the bank considered it desirable to invest two-thirds of its liabilities of all sorts in interest-bearing securities and one-third in bullion. The circulation of the country being then regulated by the action of the foreign exchanges, the bank was extremely desirous to avoid using any active power of regulating the circulation, but to leave that entirely in the hands of the public. The action of the public was fully sufficient to rectify the exchanges without any forced action of the bank in buying and selling securities. He thought it desirable to keep the securities very nearly at the same amount; because, then the public could always act for themselves in returning notes for bullion for exportation when the exchanges were unfavorable; and, if there was a great influx of gold, the bank could always reassume its proportion by transferring part of the bullion into securities. He considered that the discount of private paper was one of the worst means which the bank could adopt for regulating its notes, as it tended to produce a very prejudicial extension of them. He condemned strongly the practice of the bank, during the restriction, with respect to the extensive discounts of mercantile paper at five per cent. when the market rate was so much higher, which necessarily led to an excessive issue.

For several years after the renewal of the bank charter, in 1833, the harvests were unusually abundant, which caused all sorts of agricultural produce to be ruinously depressed. Wheat fell continuously through 1834 and 1835, till in the last week in December, 1835, its price was 36s. the imperial quarter. As all agricultural contracts were framed on the expectation that wheat would not be much less than 70s. a quarter, this long-continued depression produced the most severe distress. At the same time, however, all the manufacturing interests were in a state of unexampled prosperity from the abundance and cheapness of food. The continued low price of corn caused less to be sown in 1835, and the spring of 1836 was unfavorable. From these causes, the price of wheat rose in 1836, and the harvest time being wet and cold, wheat rose to 61s. 9d. in the autumn.

The extraordinary prosperity enjoyed by the commercial interests in 1833-34-35, gave rise to an immense amount of speculation and dabbling in foreign loans, as if people had forgotten 1825. The unexpected success of the first railway gave rise to a considerable amount of speculation in the formation of railways. An immense extension of the joint-stock banking system multiplied banking credits to an enormous extent, reduced the rate of interest, and immensely extended credit. On the 14th August, 1834, Lord Wharncliffe called the attention of the Ministry to the prodigious extension of joint-stock banks and their branches, and the insufficient capital they were trading with. The important subject of joint-stock banking was brought before the House of Commons in 1836, and a committee was appointed to inquire into it. The committee sat during the session and made two reports. The fever of speculation reached its acme in the spring of 1836.

Mr. Poulet Thompson, President of the Board of Trade, said in the House of Commons on the 6th of May, 1836: "It is impossible not to be struck with the spirit of speculation which now exists in the country, but I believe that there is a great difference in the state of things from what took place in 1825. The spirit of speculation was then turned to foreign adventure of the most extraordinary description; but now speculation is directed to home objects, which, if pushed too far, may be very mischievous, though the consequences may not be quite so mischievous as in 1825. But, really, on turning to any newspaper or any price current, and observing the advertisements of joint-stock companies upon every possible subject, however unfit to be carried on in the present state of society, every man must be struck with astonishment at the fever which rages at this moment for these speculations. I felt it my duty some time ago to direct a register to be kept, taking the names merely from the London and a few country newspapers of the different joint-stock companies, and of the nominal amount of capital proposed to be embarked in them. The nominal capital to be raised by subscription amounts to nearly £200,000,000, and the number of companies to between 300 and 400. * * * The greater part of these companies are got up by speculators for the purpose of selling their shares. They bring up their shares to a premium, and then sell them, leaving the unfortunate purchasers who are foolish enough to invest their money in them to shift for themselves. I have seen also with great regret the extent to which joint-stock banks have sprung up in different parts of the country. I believe, indeed, that great good has arisen from joint-stock banks, but the observations I have made with regard to other companies are equally applicable to many of the joint-stock banks that are springing up in different parts of the country, and the existence of which can only be attended with mischief."

The Bank of England had adopted the principles of the Bullion Report in 1827. The method they adopted of carrying them into effect was, to keep their "securities" as nearly as possible even; and to keep their bullion and cash equal to one-half of the securities—the bullion, cash and securities, being together equal to their liabilities. The bank was got into this normal condition in October, 1833, when its liabilities, *i. e.*, its notes and deposits, were £32,900,000; the securities were £24,200,000, and the bullion, £10,900,000. Some transactions with the East India Company and speculations in South American stock occurred to derange these proportions in 1834, and caused an export of specie; but in 1835 the foreign exchanges became favorable, and the drain was arrested. But, in the meantime, the bank had totally lost all power of preserving the proportion between the bullion, securities, and liabilities it had professed to adhere to. The following table, taken at intervals, exhibits this very clearly:

			Liabilities.	Securities.	Bullion.
1833, Oct.	1,	. .	£30,937,000	£22,640,000	£10,527,000
1834, March	11,	. .	31,372,000	24,777,000	8,901,000
" July	15,	. .	37,554,000	31,735,000	8,298,000
" Sept.	9,	, .	31,058,000	26,643,000	7,010,000
1835, Jan.	13,	. .	33,071,000	29,165,000	6,608,000
" May	5,	. .	29,417,000	26,179,000	5,951,000

This was the lowest point which the amount of bullion reached, and the drain was arrested. The above table shows how totally deranged the proportions were to what the directors considered to be a proper position for the bank. From that time bullion continued to flow in, till in March, 1836, it slightly exceeded eight millions; but even then, the securities were three times the bullion, instead of twice, as they ought to have been. The amount of bullion in the bank was at its height in March, 1836, and then began steadily to decline again; in the middle of July it had fallen below six millions, when the bank thought it necessary to endeavor to stop it; and it raised the rate of discount to four and a-half per cent. This however had no effect in stopping the demand for discount. In September the bullion barely exceeded five millions and the bank raised the rate of discount to five per cent. Now the bubbles blown in the preceding year and spring of 1836 were fast bursting on all hands.

The drain on the coffers of the bank proceeded at a rapid rate, both from external and internal causes. President Jackson had determined that the charter of the National Bank of the United States, which expired in 1836, should not be renewed, and that the currency of that country should be placed on a sounder footing than it had hitherto been by forming a sound metallic basis. Operations to effect this purpose soon commenced. Immense quantities of American securities of all sorts were imported into England, and negotiated for the purpose of remitting the specie to America. The improperly low rate of discount in this country, favored by the inordinate multiplication of banks, enabled a great quantity of these securities of various descriptions to be realized in England, and the cash was remitted to America.

The joint-stock banks had been blowing the bubble of credit to the utmost tenuity, by re-discounting most of the bills they discounted. This most objectionable practice, which renders the position of the bank which adopts it dependent on the good will of the discounter, adds greatly to any peril in times of discredit. The Bank of England at length (but too tardily, as has almost invariably been the case) awoke to the impending danger, and determined to strike a blow at the distended state of credit. It not only raised the rate of discount to five per cent. in August, but absolutely refused to discount any bills indorsed by any joint-stock bank of issue. This was a great blow at the vast amount of American securities afloat in the country, as most of these bills had been purchased by the joint-stock banks, and re-issued with their endorsement upon them. In the autumn of 1836, the symptoms of the coming storm were very apparent, especially in Ireland. One very large joint-stock bank, the Agricultural and Commercial, was known to be in difficulties early in the autumn, and it made several applications to the other joint-stock banks in Ireland and England and Scotland for assistance, which they all refused. It also made a call upon its shareholders, which was not responded to. The other Irish banks, foreseeing a stoppage of the Agricultural and Commercial, had been laying in a stock of gold to meet the run which would necessarily follow the failure of a bank with so many ramifications. The sum in gold which the Irish banks laid in to provide for the run was estimated to be not less than £2,000,000, all of which came from the Bank of England. Much of this was required on account of the extraordinary differences of opinion, which were given by the most eminent counsel, as to whether Bank of England notes were legal tender in Ireland. Three very eminent lawyers held that they were legal tender, and three equally eminent held that they were not. The Bank of Ireland itself thought that they were not, and were still less inclined to make the experiment, when there was such a difference of opinion among the lawyers. The other banks followed the example of the Bank of Ireland and provided gold.

The catastrophe which had been foreseen took place on the 14th of November, when the Agricultural and Commercial Bank stopped payment, which was immediately followed by a general run upon all the banks in Ireland; but it was well met, from the care which had been previously taken to provide specie. So great was the state of discredit, that even Bank of England notes were at a heavy discount in Dublin. The Bank of Ireland would only take them in very small quantities from their customers at a discount of 2s. 6d. each. During all this time the diminution of bullion in the Bank of England had been going on rapidly. At the beginning of October it had £5,035,000 in bullion to meet £29,869,000 of liabilities; at the end of November its liabilities were £30,941,000, and its bullion £3,640,000. During December its bullion slightly increased, and in January diminished again. In November, the Northern and Central Bank, with its head office in Manchester, and thirty-nine branches in the manufacturing districts, became seriously embarrassed, and applied to the Bank of England for assistance, which the bank at first refused; but, upon consulting the leading bankers in London, their opinion was that the stoppage of so extensive a concern in the manufacturing districts would very probably bring on a general panic. The bank, therefore, determined to advance the sum of £500,000 to enable it to meet its engagements; which, upon suddenly discovering that these were more extensive than had at first been represented, was further increased to £1,370,000.

Early in January, a London banking house applied for assistance to the bank, and on the other London bankers giving their guarantee to the bank, it made advances sufficient to enable that house to meet its engagements. The difficulties attending the American houses, both in London and Liverpool, became now so pressing, that they also were obliged to apply to the bank. Persons were appointed to look into their affairs, who represented that if assistance were given to them to meet their outstanding engagements, they would ultimately prove solvent. As an additional reason for granting this assistance, it was stated, that if these American houses were permitted to stop payment, their concerns were so vast and so extended through the north of England, that a general destruction of credit would ensue. After full consideration, the bank determined to attempt to carry these houses through their embarrassments, and for this purpose it advanced the enormous sum of £6,000,000. This great operation was, however, successful, though the final liquidation of the account was retarded by the great prostration of American credit in 1839. The advance made to the banking interests in England were all repaid, principal and interest, with one very trifling exception. The bank thus followed, for a second time, the principles of the Bullion Report, and there can be no doubt averted a calamity only second in magnitude to the catastrophe of 1825.

The assistance of the bank was only intended to be of a temporary nature, to give time for the withdrawal of the great mass of unsound paper from circulation. This having been effected to a large extent, the result followed which always has been the case—a great influx of gold to fill the vacuum caused by the great annihilation of this unsound paper currency. During the whole of 1837, bullion rapidly flowed into the bank, and in December it reached the sum of £10,500,000. The position of the bank on the 13th of March, 1838, was as follows: Liabilities, £31,573,000; securities, £21,046,000; bullion, £10,527,000.

Thus, after the long period of nearly five years, the bank was at length brought back again into what the directors had laid down for themselves as the normal position; and it enabled credit to pass through a crisis which would have been tenfold more severe, and would infallibly have ended in a monetary panic, if it had not been met by that "judicious increase of accommodation" which the Bullion Report declared to be the proper remedy for a temporary failure of credit. Thus was seen the most magnificent triumph of the principles of the Bullion Report and of the truth of the expansive theory in a commercial crisis. After, no doubt, many errors of management, when the great commercial crisis at length declared itself, the bank met it boldly and promptly by the most audacious application of the expansive theory, and averted a monetary panic.

THE MONETARY CRISIS OF 1839.

From 1832 to 1837, there had been a series of seasons of remarkable abundance. For some years a series followed of extreme scarcity. The crop of 1838 was the worst which had been known since 1816; that of 1839 was scarcely, if at all, better. This great deficiency rendered it necessary to import foreign corn to the value of £10,000,000; a considerable portion of this required to be remitted in specie. But, just at this period, a number of concurrent causes happened to create a great demand for gold for foreign countries. During the preceding years, America, France and Belgium had carried the extension of paper credit to most extravagant lengths. In America, the fatal system of issuing bank notes upon "property" and "securities" had been carried to a length almost worthy of Law. In France and Belgium, joint-stock banks had been extensively formed. This great extension of paper currency had the very same effect as the excessive issues of paper in England had; it drove bullion out of those countries, and was one of the great causes which, together with the fortunate destruction of the extravagant paper credit in England in 1837, caused such an influx of gold to this country up to March, 1838. But in this year these bubbles burst. In the autumn of 1838 the Bank of Belgium failed; and a severe run upon the banks in Paris took place. This revulsion of credit and extinction of paper issues in those countries caused a current of bullion to set in towards them which came from the Bank of England. In the beginning of 1838, when the bullion in the bank had been rapidly increasing for several months, the commercial world thought it was time for the bank to make use of the treasure in its vaults. And with extraordinary fatuity, although the exchanges were unfavorable, it reduced the rate of interest from five to four per cent., and while every one else was exporting bullion to America in consequence of the destruction of paper in that country, it conceived the extraordinary idea of doing a little business on its own account and exported a million to America, when every consideration of common sense showed that it ought to have kept the tightest grip possible upon its bullion. Of all acts of mismanagement in the whole history of the bank, this is probably the most astounding.

The bullion in the bank kept a pretty even amount till December, 1838. On the 18th of that month the liabilities were £28,120,000; the securities, £20,776,000, and the bullion, £9,794,000. From this date a rapid and steady drain set in, which continued with unabated severity till October, 1839. When the bank lowered its rate of discount to four per cent. in February, 1838, the market rate had fallen lower still, and in summer was about three per cent From that time forward it began to rise, and at the end of autumn was level with the bank. While everything was symptomatic of an impending drain of bullion, the bank on the 29th of November suddenly lowered its rate to 3 1-2 per cent. for advances upon bills of exchange, East India bonds, exchequer bills and other approved securities. The market rate of interest was now decidedly higher than that of the bank, and the consequence was an immediate pressure for accommodation on the bank. The securities which in December, 1838, were £19,536,000, mounted up in January, 1839, to £27,594,000, and the bullion fell from £9,522,000 to £8,826,000. The following table exhibits the progressive diminution of bullion:

		Liabilities.	Securities.	Bullion.
1838, Dec.	18, . .	£28,120,000	£20,776,000	£9,794,000
1839, Jan.	1, . .	28,136,000	22,377,000	9,048,000
" "	15, . .	30,305,000	24,529,000	8,336,000
" Feb.	12, . .	26,939,000	22,628,000	7,047,000
" March	12, . .	26,088,000	22,143,000	6,580,000
" April	9, . .	29,039,000	22,173,000	5,213,000
" "	30, . .	26,475,000	24,536,000	4,455,000
" May	14, . .	25,711,000	24,098,000	4,117,000

Up to this time the bank seemed to have been struck with actual paralysis. Notwithstanding the continuous rise in the market rate of interest and the unmistakable drain of bullion that had set in, they, on the 28th of February, issued a notice continuing the same rates on the same securities as in the previous November. And it was not until the 16th of May that they suddenly raised it to five per cent. The above figures show how completely the directors had belied their own principles of keeping the bullion at one-third of the liabilities. On the 14th of May, 1839, instead of being one-third, it was less than one-sixth. The market rate had advanced considerably more rapidly, so that the bank rate was yet below it. The drain still continued. On the 28th of May the bullion stood at £3,910,000, and the liabilities were upwards of £24,500,000. But the directors seemed so utterly blind that on the 30th of May, the time for shutting the books for the dividends, they still offered advances at five per cent. till the 23d of July, on the same securities as have been last mentioned. However, on the 20th of June they at last became alarmed, and issued notices that the rate of discount would be 5 1-2 per cent., and no securities would be received except bills of exchange. On the 16th of July the liabilities were £28,-860,000, the securities were £28,846,000 and the bullion £2,987,000. The directors at last awoke to the fact that the bank was rapidly drifting into bankruptcy. On the 13th of July they gave notice that they would be ready to receive tenders for the purchases of some terminable annuities, but the minimum price they fixed was so high that no sale took place.

Besides raising the rate of discount in May, the bank sold public securities to the amount of £760,000, and it authorized bills upon Paris to be drawn on its account to the amount of £600,000. These measures had the effect of arresting the drain for a short time. But when these bills became due the bank was in no better position to meet them, and it then became necessary to create a larger credit in Paris to meet the first. The position of the bank was, of course, well known to all the foreign dealers in exchange; and in June it was generally expected abroad that the bank would have to suspend payments in specie. In consequence of this, all long-dated bills upon this country were sent over for immediate realization and the values withdrawn as speedily as possible. To counteract this drain, as well as to meet the payments of the first credit which had been created on behalf of the bank, it was obliged in July to organize a measure of a much larger nature. The house of Baring entered into an agreement with twelve of the leading bankers in Paris to draw bills upon them to the amount of £2,000,-000; and as each of them had only a fixed credit at the Bank of France that bank agreed to honor their acceptances in case they should be presented there and exceed their usual limits. An operation of a similar one to the amount of £900,000 was organized with Hamburg. As soon as any bill was drawn on account of one of these operations the bank transferred an equal amount of the annuities it had offered for sale in July to two trustees, one for the drawers and the other for the acceptor. Out of this second credit, the bills which fell due from the creation of the first credit were paid. This measure had the effect of gradually arresting the drain of bullion, which reached its lowest point in the week ending the 2d of September, 1839, when it was reduced to £2,406,000. From that time, it began slowly to increase, and in the last week of the year it stood at £4,532,000; the liabilities being £23,864,000 and the securities £22,098,000. The operations ensuing from this foreign credit extended over nine months—from July, 1839, to April, 1840; and the highest amount operated upon was in November, 1839, when it was £2,900,000.

The figures we have quoted, showing the proportion between the bullion and the liabilities of the bank, are sufficient to show either that there was some natural impossibility in adhering to the rule the directors had laid down for themselves in 1832, or that they had not sufficient firmness to contract their securities in time of pressure to maintain it. The flagrant disproportion which these figures had assumed, which would scarcely be safe in an ordinary banking house, but which were to the last degree perilous in the Bank of England, which was known to be the last resource of every bank in the kingdom in times of difficulty, turned the attention of writers to devise some plan by which, if possible, the bank should be compelled to maintain the proper proportion between bullion and liabilities. Colonel Torrens appears to have been the originator of the idea, which was eventually adopted, of dividing the bank into two distinct departments, independent of each other—one for the purpose of issuing a regulated amount of notes and the other for carrying on the business of banking. This plan was first started in 1837, and was much canvassed and discussed by several eminent writers on the subject, such as Mr. Tooke, Mr. Norman and others, and was the prominent feature in the Bank Charter Act of 1844.

The great commercial and monetary crisis the country had passed through within the few preceding years attracted much public attention, and several petitions were presented to Parliament; and, in 1840, the Government determined to institute an inquiry into the whole system of paper issues. On the 10th of March the Chancellor of the Exchequer moved for a committee for that purpose. He reminded the House that the bank charter would terminate in 1844, and he thought it expedient that they should not postpone inquiry into the subject until the last moment. That, whatever might be the difference of opinion among the most intelligent men as to what part of the difficulties they had gone through were to be attributed to the Bank of England or other banks, still they were very strongly of opinion that the present system required revision and alteration. Leaving out of consideration former transactions, the difficulties and embarrassments which the country had gone through within the last few years had led the most important bodies and the largest of the manufacturing towns to make complaints, in calm and temperate language, and to express an anxiety that the House should institute an investigation into their complaints and endeavor to provide adequate remedies.

The chief points of interest connected with the report and evidence were: 1. The principle propounded in 1832 for the management of the bank, for the purpose of carrying into effect the principles of the Bullion Report, was totally condemned. 2. The great modern heresy that bills of exchange form no part of the circulating medium or currency, which was first asserted before a Parliamentary committee in 1832, was now maintained by the great majority of the commercial and banking witnesses. 3. This seems to have been the first adoption by mercantile men of what became the reigning banking fallacy for a time, but which is now utterly exploded, of what is known by the name of the "Currency Principle." This principle is: "That when bank notes are permitted to be issued, the number in circulation should always be exactly equal to the coin which would be in circulation if they did not exist."

The advocates of this principle maintain that it is the only true method of regulating a paper currency and of preserving the paper of equal value with the gold coin. This theory sounds remarkably specious and plausible, and from the eminence of the persons who adopted it, acquired for a time much importance. Nevertheless, there never was a greater delusion palmed off upon the credulity of mankind, and could never have emanated from or been believed in by any one who had an accurate knowledge of the mechanism of banking.

THE MONETARY PANIC OF 1847.

The Bank Charter Act of 1844 was passed amid universal applause, and was supposed to have put an end forever to commercial crises and monetary panics. We have now to see how these hopes were realized. The harvests of 1842-3-4 were extremely abundant; the bullion in the bank accumulated very rapidly in these years, and a very large quantity of money which the nation must otherwise have spent in food was set free for commercial purposes. Other circumstances occurred at the same time to liberate a large quantity of the capital of the country from its accustomed use and to render it applicable to commercial purposes, which have been very clearly and ably pointed out by Mr. James Wilson. He shows that the rapidity and certainty of conveyance reduces very greatly the amount of stock it is necessary at all times to keep on hand when communications are slow and uncertain; that the amount of goods in transit is much larger with a slow conveyance than with a quick one. For example: When Manchester supplies London with manufactured goods, if it takes seven days by canal for these goods to reach London, it is clear that there must always be seven days' consumption of goods on the way. If the same transit is accomplished by railway in one day, it is only necessary to have one day's consumption on the way; and the capital employed in producing the other six days' consumption is liberated and may be employed in promoting other commercial operations. When we consider the enormous economy of capital required in the same amount of business which was effected by the introduction of more rapid modes of communication, whether by railways or steamers, we shall understand how greatly they increased the national resources. There can be no doubt that the economy of national capital effected by the extension of railways far exceeded the losses which occurred from unsuccessful speculation in them. Now, these operations were beginning to have their full effect in saving the national capital simultaneously with the good harvests of 1842-3-4, and helped to swell the quantity of disposable capital to an unprecedented extent.

An attentive consideration of these circumstances is absolutely necessary, because they show the fallacy of the doctrine that the price of goods must vary exactly with any increase or decrease of the amount of the currency, whereas there is no necessary relation between the two whatever. The particular methods of doing business have the most important influence on the quantity of currency necessary to carry it on with; and a clumsy or more ingenious method of transacting business may make the most important changes in the quantity of money necessary to circulate any given amount of commodities without causing any alteration in the price of these commodities. The Act of 1844 having placed an absolute limit upon the discretion of the bank in issuing notes, Sir Robert Peel said that he thought that banking business could not be too free and unrestrained. The extraordinary accumulation of capital arising from the circumstances we have just detailed lowered the market rate of discount to one and three-quarters and two and a-half per cent. on the best bills, and the Bank of England immediately conformed to the market rate on the passing of the act, and reduced its rate from four per cent. to two and a-half for the best bills. The day the act came into operation, indeed, the whole of the discounts were done at one and three-quarters; and they continued at that rate for a fortnight, when some were done at two per cent.; and up to the 26th October a considerable portion were done at two and a-quarter. From this date, however, up to October, 1845, the rate was two and a-half. In November, 1845, the rate was suddenly raised to three and a-half, and continued at that figure till August, 1846, when it was lowered to three per cent.; these rates being governed by the flow of bullion, which diminished from fifteen and a-half millions when the Act of 1844 passed, to thirteen and a-half millions in

November, 1845; after which it increased again to above sixteen millions in August, 1846, and then began steadily to decline till it reached its minimum in the great crisis of October, 1847.

The first failure of the potato crops in Ireland, in 1845, and the railway mania of that year, are too well known to need repetition here; nor had they anything to do properly with the management of the bank, whose sole proper duty it was to look after its own affairs and preserve its own stability. The calamity of 1846 was far more severe and extensive than that of the preceding year. It was absolutely certain that an immense quantity of bullion would require to be exported in payment of the grain which it would be necessary to import. Accordingly, from the middle of September, 1846, a steady and continuous drain of bullion set in, but the bank made no alteration in the rate of discount until the 16th January, 1847; when the bullion had fallen to £13,949,000, it raised the rate of discount to three and a-half; and on the 23d, the bullion having been further diminished by £500,000, it raised the rate to four per cent. Henceforth, the drain continued rapidly, but the bank still continued to make no alteration until the 10th April, when, its treasure being reduced to £9,867,000, the rate of discount was raised to five per cent. Here we have the same inveterate blunder committed by the bank as on so many previous occasions—an immense drain of bullion, and yet none but the most feeble, inefficient and puerile means taken by the bank to raise the value of money here. But the operation of the bank at this time is an excellent example of the self-acting nature of the Act of 1844. We need only observe that the banking capital of the bank was £14,000,000 of notes based upon public securities, together with notes representing as much bullion as there is in the issue department. Consequently, the notes held in reserve must always be equal to the difference between the notes in circulation, or held by the public, and the sum of £14,000,000 added to the quantity of bullion.

Now, we have seen that the intention of the framers of the Act of 1844 was that, as the bullion diminished, the notes in the hands of the public should be diminished in conformity with the "currency principle." Let us now see: 1. How the bank was inclined to act on the principle. 2. Supposing that they were disinclined to do so, how far the act, by its own self-acting principles, compelled them to do so.

The table on the following page shows the utter futility of the idea that, as the bullion diminished, the act could compel a reduction of notes in the hands of the public; for the notes in circulation were within an insignificant trifle as large in amount when the bullion was only £9,867,000 as when it was £16,366,000. Consequently, nothing could be a more total and complete failure of the Act of 1844, on the very first occasion on which its services were required.

Now, let us recall to our readers' attention what Mr. S. J. Loyd had pointed out as the fatal defect of the bank rule of 1832, which we have just given. He said that under it the whole bullion in the bank might be drained

	BANK NOTES.		Total Amount of Bullion.	Minimum Rate of Discount Per Cent.
	Held by the public.	Held in Reserve by the Bank of England.		
1846.				
August 29	20,426,000	9,450,000	16,366,000	3
October 3	20,551,000	8,809,000	15,817,000	"
November 7 . . .	20,971,000	7,265,000	14,760,000	"
December 19 . . .	19,549,000	8,864,000	15,163,000	"
1847.				
January 9	20,837,000	6,715,000	14,308,000	3
" 16	20,679,000	6,546,000	13,949,000	3 1-2
" 30	20,469,000	5,704,000	12,902,000	4
February 20 . . .	19,482,000	5,917,000	12,215,000	"
March 6	19,279,000	5,715,000	11,596,000	"
" 20	19,069,000	5,419,000	11,232,000	"
April 3	19,855,000	3,700,000	10,246,000	"
" 10	20,243,000	2,558,000	9,867,000	5

out without any contraction in the circulation, and it was especially supposed that the Bank Act of 1844 had distinctly provided against this defect. In fact, the whole theory of the framers of the act was, that for every five sovereigns which left the country, a £5 note should be withdrawn from circulation; and that if the directors failed to do so of their own accord, the "mechanical" action of the act would compel them to do so. But what was the actual result? The bank had lost £7,000,000 of treasure, and its notes in circulation were only reduced by £200,000; the whole of the reduction had been thrown on its own reserves. Hence, the Bank Act of 1844 was open to exactly the same charge as the bank rule of 1832! Mr. F. T. Baring, ex-Chancellor of the Exchequer, who maintained that the act had been successful on several points, yet allowed that it had completely failed on this point:* "I find that the amount of bullion in the bank on September 12, 1846, was £16,354,000; and on the 17th of April, 1847, it was reduced to £9,330,000, being a diminution of £7,024,000. Now, I take the same dates with respect to the circulation of notes, and I find that on September 12, 1846, the amount was £20,982,000, and on April 17, 1847, it was £21,228,000, being an increase of £246,000. * * * I must say that I never entertained the idea that it would have been possible under the operation of this act to have shown such a set of figures. * * * I believe, if we look back, we shall find that the operation of the deposits and the question of the reserve was not sufficiently considered, either by those who were favorable or those who were opposed to the bill. I cannot find in the evidence before the committee of 1840 more than a few sentences leading me to suppose that danger arising from such a cause was contemplated or referred to; yet this was a most important con-

* Hansard Parl. Debates, Vol. 95, p. 615.

sideration; for it was by the reserve the bank was enabled to do what was contrary to the spirit of the bill when gold was running out, not to reduce their circulation by a single pound. I do not think that the system works satisfactorily in this respect; and in fact, the point did not receive anything like a sufficient consideration. Perhaps it was impossible before the bill was in practical operation to see how the reserve of notes would operate; but it certainly never entered into the contemplation of anyone then considering the subject that £7,000,000 in gold should run off, and yet that the notes in the hands of the public would rather increase than diminish."

The number of notes held in reserve in the banking department, under the system of 1844, correspond to the amount of bullion held by the bank before the division. When, therefore, the public saw that the whole banking resources of the bank were reduced to £2,558,000, a complete panic seized both the public and the directors. The latter adopted severe measures to check the demand for notes. The rate was not only raised to five per cent., but this was only applicable to bills having only a few days to run, and a limit was placed upon the amount of bills discounted, however good they might be. Merchants who had received loans were called upon to repay them without being permitted to renew them. During some days it was impossible to get bills discounted at all. These measures were effectual in stopping the efflux of bullion; and a sum of £100,000 in sovereigns, which had been actually shipped for America, was relanded. During this period, the rate of discount for the best bills rose to nine, ten and twelve per cent. During all this time, the price of wheat continued steadily to rise, notwithstanding the monetary pressure, and at the close of May the price on one occasion reached 131s. in Windsor market. The foreign exchanges, which had been adverse to the country during the latter part of 1846 and the beginning of 1840, from the immense quantity of foreign corn which was imported, became favorable in the middle of April, partly owing to the great monetary pressure. The pressure passed off after the first week in May, having lasted about three weeks, and bullion began to flow in after the 24th of April, until at the end of June it amounted to £10,526,000, the notes in circulation being £18,051,000 and the notes in reserve £5,625,000. The conduct of the bank in keeping down the rate of discount when a rapid drain was going on, and the foreign exchanges unfavorable, was the exact counterpart of what it had done on so many previous occasions, and excited much comment and adverse criticism by the whole commercial community of London. The market rate rose decidedly above it, so that a rush for discounts was made to the bank, which were no sooner granted than the gold was immediately drawn out.

On the 27th of May, the Chancellor of the Exchequer brought the subject of the monetary pressure before the House, and stated that he had numerous deputations to him respecting a suspension of the Act of 1844, which the Government was not prepared to adopt. However, he meant to assist the bank so far as to dispense with the aid the Government usually had from the bank at Quarter day. With this view, he intended to raise the interest on exchequer bills, which were then at a greater depreciation than any other kind of Government security, to 3d. per day. On the 10th, he brought in a resolution to allow all persons who had subscribed to the eight million Irish loan a discount of five per cent. on any installment paid in before the 18th of June, and four per cent. if paid in before the 10th September.

On the 9th of August the first of the frightful catalogue of failures began. Leslie, Alexander & Co. stopped payment, with liabilities amounting to £500,000. On Wednesday, the 11th, Coventry & Sheppard stopped for £200,000; and King, Melville & Co. also for £200,000; and several other minor firms made the total failures in the first week amount to £1,200,000. In the next week Giles & Co. failed for £100,000; and the total in the second week was £300,000. In the following week Robinson & Co. failed for £110,000, the senior partner of the firm being the governor of the Bank of England. Week after week followed, each one increasing in severity, until at last the total exceeded £15,000,000. In the middle of September, Saunderson & Co., the eminent bill-brokers, stopped payment, being much involved with the great houses in the corn trade. The exchanges, which had been brought to par in April by the monetary pressure in that month, were, in consequence of the increasing severity of the crisis, become decidedly favorable, and on the 25th September bullion began to flow in. During the whole of September the commercial calamities were falling fast and thick. Almost all the firms connected with the Mauritius, such as Reid, Irving & Co., failed—principally from having their funds locked up in sugar plantations. This was accompanied by immense failures in the India trade, the credit given in that trade being commonly of unusual length, which affords dangerous facilities for stretching it to too great a length. The railway works which had been sanctioned in the session of 1845-46 were now in full operation, causing an immense demand for ready money. Almost every tradesman in the kingdom, from Land's End to John o' Groat's, was deep in railway speculations. The extravagant delirium of prosperity in 1845-46 had caused great numbers of them, not only to go far beyond their means themselves, but to trust their customers beyond the bounds of ordinary credit. There can be no doubt whatever but that commercial credit of all sorts and descriptions, among all classes of traders, was in all probability in a more unhealthy state than it had ever been before; and that an unprecedentedly large portion of the community were entangled in obligations, of which there was no prospect of their ever working themselves free. Sharp and severe as the remedy was, therefore, it unquestionably was the best thing that could happen, that this unhealthy superstructure should be cleared away, and that commerce should be reconstructed upon an improved and renovated basis.

The extreme pressure may be considered to have begun on the 23d of September, when the bank adopted more stringent measures for curtailing the demand upon its resources. Ever since the 25th of June the diminution of bullion had been going on rapidly; on the 2d of October it was reduced to £8,565,000; the notes in circulation being £18,712,000, and the reserve £3,409,000. The rapid diminution of their resources showed the directors that the time had come when they must think of their own safety; and on that day they gave notice that the minimum rate of all bills falling due before the 15th of October would be five and a-half; and they refused altogether to make advances on stock or exchequer bills. This last announcement created a great excitement on the stock exchange. The town and country bankers hastened to sell their public securities to convert them into money. The difference between the price for consols for ready money, and for the account of the 14th October, showed a rate of interest equivalent to fifty per cent. per annum. Exchequer bills were sold at 35s. discount. Everything became worse day by day. On the 18th of October the bank rates of discount varied from five and a-half to nine per cent. At this time the bullion was £8,431,000; the notes in circulation £19,359,000; and in reserve £2,630,000. The following week, from Monday the 18th to Saturday the 23d, was the great crisis. On that Monday, the Royal Bank of Liverpool, with a paid-up capital of £800,000, stopped payment, which caused the funds to fall two per cent. This was followed by the stoppage of the North and South Wales Bank, also of Liverpool; the Liverpool Bank, the Union Bank of Newcastle, heavy runs upon the other banks of the district, and other bank failures at Manchester and in the west of England. As the whole of the commercial world knew that the resources of the banking department were being rapidly exhausted, a complete panic seized them. A complete cessation of private discounts followed. No one would part with the money or notes in his possession. The most exorbitant sums were offered to, and refused by, merchants for their acceptances.

The continued and ever increasing severity of the crisis caused deputation after deputation to be sent to the Government to obtain a relaxation of the act; and on Saturday, the 23d of October, the final determination of the Ministry to authorize the bank to issue notes beyond the limits prescribed by the act was taken and communicated to the bank, who immediately acted upon it, and discounted freely at nine per cent. The letter itself was not actually sent till Monday, the 25th. It stated that the Government had expected that the pressure which had existed for some weeks would have passed away as the one in April had done, by the operation of natural causes; that, being disappointed in this hope, they had come to the conclusion that the time had come when they ought to attempt by some extraordinary and temporary measure to restore confidence to the mercantile community. That, for this purpose, they recommended the directors of the Bank of England in the emergency to enlarge the amount of their discounts and advances upon approved security; but that, to restrain this operation within reasonable limits, a high rate of interest should be charged which, under the circumstances, should not, they thought, be less than eight per cent. That, if such a course should lead to any infringement of the law, they would be prepared to propose to Parliament, on its meeting, a bill of indemnity. This letter was made public about one o'clock on Monday, the 25th, and no sooner was it done than the panic vanished like a dream! Mr. Gurney stated that it produced its effect in ten minutes! No sooner was it known that notes might be had than the want of them ceased! Not only no infringement of the act took place, but the whole issue of notes in consequence of this letter was only £400,000; so that while at one moment the whole credit of Great Britain was in imminent danger of total destruction, within one hour it was saved by the issue of £400,000.

The extraordinary and disastrous state of public credit at this period may be judged of by the aid afforded by the Bank of England to different establishments from the 15th of September to the 15th of November, as follows: 1. It advanced £150,000 to a large firm in London, who were under liabilities to the extent of several millions, on the security of debentures of the Governor and Company of the Copper Miners of England, which prevented them from stopping payment. 2. It advanced £50,000 to a country banker, on the security of real property. 3. It advanced £120,000 to the Governor and Company of the Copper Miners, which prevented them from stopping payment. 4. It advanced £300,000 to the Royal Bank of Liverpool on the security of bills of exchange, over and above their usual discounts; but this was inadequate, and the bank, having no further security to offer, stopped payment. 5. It advanced £100,000 to another joint-stock bank in the country. 6. It advanced £130,000 on real property to a large mercantile house in London. 7. It advanced £50,000 to another mercantile house on the security of approved names. 8. It advanced £50,000 on bills of exchange to a joint-stock bank of issue, which soon after stopped payment. 9. It advanced £15,000 on real property to another mercantile house in London. 10. It saved a large establishment in Liverpool from failing by forbearing to enforce payment of £100,000 of their acceptances falling due. 11. It assisted another very large joint-stock bank in the country by an advance of £800,000 beyond its usual discount limit. 12. It advanced £100,000 to a country banker on real security. 13. It advanced to a Scotch bank £200,000 on the security of local bills and £60,000 on London bills. 14. It assisted another Scotch bank by discounting £100,000 of local and London bills. 15. It advanced £100,000 to a large mercantile house in London on approved personal security. 16. It assisted a large house in Manchester to resume payment by an advance of £40,000 on approved personal security. 17. It advanced £30,000 to a country bank on real property. 18. It assisted many other houses, both in town and country, by advances of smaller sums on securities not usually admitted; and it did not reject in London any one bill offered for discount except on the ground of insufficient security. The far larger portion of this assistance was given before the 23d of October.

A general election had taken place in the autumn of 1847; and the

Ministry, having taken upon themselves the responsibility of authorizing the Bank of England to violate the Act of 1844, lost no time in calling a meeting of the new Parliament. It met on the 18th of November, and after a few preliminary days were occupied in swearing in the members, the speech from the throne was delivered on the 23d. The first paragraph stated as a reason for calling them together that the embarrassments of trade were so alarming, that the Queen had authorized the Ministry to recommend to the Bank of England a course which might have led to an infringement of the law. Happily, however, the power given to infringe the law, if necessary, had allayed the panic.

On the 30th of November the Chancellor of the Exchequer moved for a committee to inquire into the causes of the recent commercial distress and how far it had been affected by the Act of 1844. He spoke of the panic in the spring. He said that he had seen no reason to change the opinion he had then expressed, that it was mainly owing to the imprudence of the bank, which, having full warning of the various demands it would have upon it, was too tardy in raising the rate of discount and had lent out, over the period when the dividends became payable, the money they had provided for that purpose, so that they were not in possession of adequate funds when they were required. The low state of their reserve then excited consternation. The bank then took the severe step of reducing the amount of discounts. They pulled up as suddenly as they had unwisely let out their reserve before. With respect to the panic in October, he said that the severe pressure in the money market had abated when the bank failures in Liverpool and the north of England took place, which renewed the alarm. After describing the great pressure on the banks in the country, the Chancellor said:

"The Bank of England were pressed directly for assistance from all parts of the country and indirectly through the London bankers, who were called upon to support their country correspondents. The country banks required a large amount of notes to render them sure against possible demands—not so much for payment of their notes as their deposits. Houses in London were constantly applying to the bank for aid. Two bill-brokers had stopped, and the operations of two others were nearly paralyzed. The whole demand for discount was thrown upon the hands of the Bank of England. Notwithstanding this, the bank never refused a bill which it would have discounted at another time; but still the large mass of bills which, under ordinary circumstances, are discounted by bill brokers, could not be negotiated. During this period we were daily, I may say hourly, in possession of the state of the bank. The governor and deputy governor at last said that they could no longer continue their advances to support the various parties who applied to them; that they could save themselves—that is, they could comply with the law—but that they could not do so without pressing more stringently on the commercial world. At this crisis a feeling as to the necessity of the interposition of Government appeared to be generally entertained; and those conversant with commercial affairs, and least likely to decide in favor of the course we ultimately adopted, unanimously expressed an opinion that, if some measures were not taken by the Government to arrest the evil, the most disastrous consequences must inevitably ensue. Evidence was laid before the Government which proved not only the existence of severe pressure from the causes I have stated, but also that it was aggravated in a very great degree by the hoarding on the part of many persons of gold and bank notes to a very large extent, in consequence of which an amount of circulation which under ordinary circumstances would have been adequate, became insufficient for the wants of the community. It was difficult to establish this beforehand, but the best proof of the fact is in what occurred after we had interfered. As soon as the letter of the 25th October appeared and the panic ceased, thousands and tens of thousands of pounds were taken from the hoards, some from boxes deposited with bankers, although the parties would not leave the notes in their bankers' hands. Large parcels of notes were returned to the Bank of England cut into halves, as they had been sent down into the country; and so small was the real demand for an additional quantity of notes that the whole amount taken from the bank when the unlimited issue was given was under £400,000. The restoration of confidence released notes from their hoards and no more was wanted, for this trifling quantity of additional notes is hardly worth notice. * * * Parties of every description made application to us with the observation, 'We do not want notes, but give us confidence.' They said: 'We have notes enough, but we have not confidence to use them; say you will stand by us and we shall have all we want; do anything, in short, that will give us confidence. If we think we can get bank notes we shall not want them. Charge any rate of interest you please; ask what you like'—(Mr. Spooner, No! No!) I beg pardon of the honorable gentleman, but I may be permitted to know what was actually said to me. I say that what I have stated was the tenor of the applications made to me. Parties said to me: 'Let us have notes; charge ten or twelve per cent. for them; we don't care what the rate of interest is. We don't mean, indeed, to take the notes, because we shall not want them; only tell us that we can get them, and this will at once restore confidence.' We have been asked what was the change of circumstances which induced us to act on Saturday, when we declined acting a day or two before. I reply that the accounts which we received on Thursday, Friday and Saturday were of a totally different description from those which had been previously brought to us. It was on Saturday, and not before, that this conviction was forced upon us; and it was not till then that we felt it necessary to sanction a violation of the law."

The persons applying generally said that it was necessary to place a limit on the amount to be authorized, which they proposed should be £2,000,000 or £3,000,000, but the Government thought that the limit should be placed on the rate of interest, and accordingly this was the method adopted.

Sir Robert Peel felt particularly called upon to defend the Act of 1844. After defending himself from some minor charges, he protested against singling out individual members of Parliament and making them responsible for the acts of the whole Legislature. He said that some persons alleged that the Act of 1844 had been passed without due inquiry; but he recounted the committees that had sat for five years, and had asked, on the whole, upwards of 14,000 questions—questions and answers without end—but with no practical result from those apparently interminable investigations. The last committee had closed its labors without any practical results. At last, the Ministry determined to bring forward a measure on their own responsibility, which had been carried by extraordinary majorities; but, nevertheless, if it could be shown that the Act of 1844 could be amended that it ought to be done. Sir Robert remarked:

"There has been some misrepresentation respecting the objects of this act. I do not deny that one of the objects contemplated by the act was the prevention of the convulsions that had heretofore occurred, in consequence of the neglect of the Bank of England to take early precautions against the withdrawal of its treasure. I did hope that, although there was not imperative obligation on the Bank of England to take those precautions, that the experience of 1825, 1836 and 1839 would have induced that establishment to conform to principles which the directors of the bank acknowledged to be just, and which they had more than once professed to adopt for their own regulation. I am bound to say, that in that hope, that in that object of the bill, I have been disappointed. I am bound to admit, seeing the extent of commercial depression which has prevailed, and the number of houses which have been swept away—some of which, however, I think, were insolvent long before the bill came into operation, and others of which became insolvent in consequence of the failure of those who were connected with them, and were imprudent in their speculations—I am bound to admit that that purpose of the bill of 1844 which sought to impress, if not a legal at least a moral obligation on the bank, to prevent the necessity for measures of extreme stringency by timely precautions, had not been fulfilled. I must contend that it was in the power of the bank, if not to prevent all the evils that have arisen, at least to diminish greatly their force. If the bank had possessed the resolution to meet the coming danger by a contraction of its issues, by raising the rate of discount, by refusing much of the accommodation which they granted between the years 1844 and 1846—if they had been firm and determined in the adoption of these precautions, the necessity for extrinsic interference might have been prevented; it might not then have been necessary for the Government to authorize a violation of the Act of 1844. * * * The bill of 1844 had a triple object. Its first object was that in which I admit it has failed—namely, to prevent by early and gradual, severe and sudden contraction, and the panic and confusion inseparable from it. But the bill had at least two other objects of at least equal importance—the one to maintain and guarantee the convertibility of the paper currency into gold; the other, to prevent the difficulties which arise at all times from undue speculation being aggravated by the abuse of paper credit in the form of promissory notes. In these two objects my belief is that the bill has completely succeeded. My belief is, that you have had a guarantee for the maintenance of the principle of convertibility such as you never had before; my belief also is, that whatever difficulties you are now suffering, from a combination of various causes, the difficulties would have been greatly aggravated if you had not wisely taken the precaution of checking the unlimited issues of the notes of the Bank of England, of joint-stock banks and of private banks."

Sir Robert Peel then entered into a most able description of the true evils the country was suffering from, which arose from the enormous destruction of capital, by the dearth of food, the unusual absorption of capital in one channel of commerce, and the construction of railroads which were not yet remunerative. He showed the absurdity of having cheap money while capital was scarce. The whole of his remarks are so admirable, that we regret that their length prevents us from giving them entire. He cordially approved of the course the Government had taken in not issuing the letter sooner than they did, and in doing it when they did. The true remedy for the state of things under which the country was suffering was individual exertion, the limitation of engagements, the cessation of all demands which could be postponed; an earlier issue of the latter would have relaxed those exertions. But to that pressure a panic succeeded, which could not be provided against or foreseen by legislation; which could not be reasoned with, and which could only be met by a discretionary assumption of power by the Government suitable to the emergency. Whether any modification of the Act of 1844 was desirable was a question for future consideration. His own opinion was in favor of the maintenance of the great principles of that measure. If the identical restrictions were not imposed upon the bank as were then in force, still there must be some restrictions; for, after the experience of 1825, 1836 and 1839 he, for one, would not be content to leave the regulation of the monetary concerns of this country to the uncontrolled discretion of the bank. In 1844, the general conviction was that it ought not to be so left, and he knew no better mode of imposing restriction than that which was devised by the Act of 1844.

The committee appointed by each House began to sit in February, 1848. The Governor, Mr. Morris, and the Deputy Governor, Mr. Prescott, were examined at great length before each committee, and expressed their unqualified approbation of the Act of 1844, and the manner it had worked. The object of the act was to place the circulation of this country exactly in the same position as it would have been if the currency had been entirely metallic.

Mr. Morris was asked: "Your opinion is, then, that with regard both to the contraction of the currency and the expansion of the currency, they would both have taken place precisely in the same mode, and to the same degree had the currency been purely metallic?" Mr. Morris: "Yes, I have not the slightest doubt upon the subject." These gentlemen testified that the object of the act was to secure the convertibility of the note, which it had effectually done. That the bank acted erroneously in the spring of 1847 in not raising their rate of discount sooner, which much contributed to the monetary pressure in April. They said that the Government letter of the 25th October was not sought for by them, nor issued in any way at their instance; that they had no fear whatever for the bank, and that it was not required to maintain the solvency of the bank; but, nevertheless, it had the best effects in allaying the commercial panic. That the panic would have inevitably occurred even without the Act of 1844; but the act brought it on sooner, and probably made it less severe. That the great merit of the act was, that when the pressure did come, the bank was in possession of £8,000,000 of treasure; that if the bank had been left free it would probably have followed the course of dangerous liberality, which it had done on so many occasions previously. That though the Government letter did relieve the panic, it would probably have passed away without it. They earnestly deprecated any alteration in the act, except that they thought the permission to issue notes on silver too limited.

Mr. S. Gurney agreed in blaming the management of the bank during the first three months of 1847, and said that if the bank had commenced restrictive measures much earlier, the pressure of April would have been mitigated. He said that in October the rapid diminution of the reserve caused a very general distrust among the public as to how they were to obtain circulating medium. The wealthy and more powerful took care to very largely over-provide themselves, infinitely beyond the necessities of the case. The consequence was that the notes in the hands of the public amounted to nearly £21,000,000, of which he had no doubt that four or five millions were locked up and inoperative, in consequence of the alarm and fear of not being able to get bank notes at all. In illustration of this, he said that his own house was largely called upon for money on Saturday, the 23d, not from the distrust of the house, but from doubts that the bank notes were to be had at all. They applied to the bank for discount to a large amount, which was agreed to, but they were told the rate must be ten per cent. Upon remonstrating with the governor, and saying it would have the worst effect if it became known that their house was paying ten per cent. for money, the rate was finally agreed upon at nine per cent. At this rate they took £200,000. On Monday, the 25th, however, the demand was very heavy, and they took £200,000 more. It was a case of difficulty with the bank, under its reduced reserve and the limitation of the act, and a final decision was postponed until two o'clock. At one o'clock, however, the letter from the Government was announced, authorizing the relaxation. Its effect was immediate. Those who had sent notice for their money in the morning sent word that they did not want it, and that they had only ordered payment by way of precaution. After the notice they only required £100,000 instead of £200,000; the alarm passed off, and by the end of the week they had to ask the bank, as a favor, to be allowed to repay the money they had taken. Mr. Gurney stated that the experience of the last two years had altered his opinion respecting the act, and that he thought it necessary that there should be a relaxing power somewhere.

Thus it is seen that this occasion demonstrated, as all previous ones had done, that the restrictive theory in a very severe commercial crisis brings universal failure; and that the expansive theory is indispensable to preserve the existence of merchants and banks.

THE TRUE AND SUPREME POWER OF CONTROLLING CREDIT AND THE ISSUES OF THE BANK.

It was in the autumn of 1855 that I discovered what I conceive to be the true method of controlling credit and the paper currency; showing how the principles of the Bullion Report are to be carried into practical effect, and thus completing the theory of the paper currency which is now universally accepted. As soon as I came to examine critically the Bank Charter Act of 1844, and the ideas, concepts and theories upon which it is founded, I saw at once—as every mercantile lawyer would—that its very basis, the definition of currency, upon which it is founded, is absurd, and in diametrical contradiction to a whole series of decisions of the courts of law, and to the doctrines previously held by all statesmen and economists. That its very aim and object was to enforce a theory which had been uniformly condemned by all the most eminent financial authorities of former times; by the Bullion Report; by Sir Robert Peel himself on several previous occasions; and confuted by the uniform practical experience of all preceding monetary panics. All preceding financial authorities of the highest eminence—the Bullion Report, Sir Robert Peel himself—had condemned the restrictive theory in a commercial crisis; and had declared that, after it had attained a certain degree of intensity, it was indispensable to adopt the expansive theory to avert universal failure. These doctrines were founded upon irrefragable reasoning, and ample and uniform experience.

In 1764 the bank had advanced a million to support commerce in the great crisis of that year. In 1793 the bank had adopted a rigorously restrictive system, and persevered doggedly in this course in defiance of the repeated advice of the highest financial authorities; at length, when universal failure was imminent, the Government came forward and, following the precedent of Montague in 1697, issued a moderate amount of exchequer bills, and commerce instantly was saved. In 1825, for three days, the bank adopted the rigorously restrictive system; and when it had pulled down several powerful and wealthy banks, and commerce was on the very brink of universal failure, it suddenly adopted the expansive system, and commerce was saved. In 1836-38, when a commercial crisis and a monetary panic were impending as severe as any which had happened before, the bank with great skill, wisdom, courage and audacity at once boldly adopted the expansive system, and the monetary panic was averted. Nevertheless, in defiance of all this unanimous consent of financial authorities, and the uniform experience of commercial crises and monetary panics, Sir Robert Peel, in flat contradiction of his own repeatedly expressed opinions, enforced the restrictive theory by law, by imposing a cast-iron limit on the power of the bank to issue notes. And why did he do this? Because he evolved a fantastic theory out of his own inner consciousness that commercial crises are solely due to the excessive issues of bank notes. Now, any banker and practical man of business would have told him that such an idea was a fond delusion. As a matter of positive fact, one of the most terrible commercial crises of modern times took place at Amsterdam and Hamburg in 1764, where there were no bank notes except those issued in exchange for specie.

The fact is that the Bank Act of 1844 is founded upon a whole nest of definitions and theories which are pure moonshine. In 1847 the whole of Sir Robert Peel's anticipations and theories were blown to the winds by the monetary pressure in April, and the monetary panic in October, when it was found indispensable to abandon the restrictive theory and to adopt the expansive theory, just in the old, old way; and the mercantile community was saved from universal ruin thereby. Nevertheless, although all the theories upon which the Bank Act is founded are erroneous, and were shattered to pieces by the rude experience of facts, on the very first occasion on which they were really tested, there was one great, solid, practical benefit derived from it. When the monetary panic actually came, the bank possessed an ample store of gold to meet it. In April, 1847, the directors had proceeded exactly in the way of their predecessors. They allowed their gold to ebb away without taking any efficient measures to prevent it. It was evident that at that time they had not perceived the true way of stopping it—*i. e.*, by a bold and rapid raising of the rate of discount. Now, whatever might be the theoretical errors of the act, statesmen saw that at all events it compelled the bank to keep a greater store of gold to meet the panic when it did come, which it was wholly out of their power to touch.

And it was hopeless to expect that the Government or Parliament would consent to any alteration of the act while it secured that inestimable practical benefit—or at least until a better method was discovered of attaining the same practical end.

Now let us recall to the reader the state of the question. The witnesses before the Irish Committee of 1804 and the Bullion Committee of 1810 maintained that there is only one cause of an export of bullion—namely, a balance of payments to be made on account of goods imported. But the Bullion Committee showed that there is a second cause—namely, a depreciated paper money. Thus it was established that there are two causes of an export of bullion. The Bullion Report laid down as a doctrine that, in order to prevent the export of bullion on account of a depreciation of the paper money, it was indispensable to regulate the amount of paper money by the market price of bullion and the state of the foreign exchanges. But they gave no rule or principle by which this was to be done. They emphatically laid down that the absolute quantity of paper money was no criterion whether it was excessive or not. The sole criterion was the market price of bullion and the state of the foreign exchanges. In 1819 the directors of the bank repudiated the doctrines of the Bullion Report, and strenuously denied that the amount of their issues could have any effect on the price of gold or on the foreign exchanges. In 1827, however, they became convinced of the truth of the doctrines of the Bullion Report; they expunged the resolution of 1819 from their books, and made an attempt to regulate their issues by them. But the scheme they adopted turned out a complete failure, and was condemned by Lord Overstone, who was no doubt a practical banker of the first eminence; and the proof was that in 1836 and 1839 they brought the bank to the very verge of bankruptcy. The specific indictment which Lord Overstone brought against the scheme of the directors was, that under it every single sovereign might be drawn out of the bank, and yet not a single note be withdrawn from circulation. Then the sect of which Lord Overstone was the most influential member maintained the dogma, which they termed the "currency principle"—which is, that when bank notes payable to bearer on demand are permitted to be issued, they ought to be exactly equal in quantity to the amount of gold they displace; and that for every five sovereigns drawn out of the bank a £5 note ought to be cancelled. This they held to be the sole criterion whether paper was excessive or not. This scheme, it was alleged, would secure the country from all future monetary troubles; it was supposed to be the *ne plus ultra* of human wisdom; and the Bank Act of 1844 remodeled the bank so as to carry this principle into effect. But the experiences of April and October, 1847, shattered all these theories to pieces. For it was found, on both these occasions, that vast quantities of gold were drained away from the bank, and not a single bank note was withdrawn from circulation. This shows how much easier it is to criticise the schemes of others which are seen in operation than to devise one's own.

In 1854, I was led to take up the subject of political economy, or economics. On examining the current text-books on the subject, I found that they had not the remotest conception of the juridical and mathematical principles of credit, or of the mechanism of the colossal system of mercantile and banking credit. I therefore undertook to write a treatise on the subject. I carefully studied all the Parliamentary debates and all the Parliamentary reports on the subject, the different principles which the directors had adopted for the management of the bank, and the history of the various commercial crises and monetary panics which had occurred up to that time. On examining the doctrines of the sect which embodied the Act of 1844, and the act itself, I at once perceived—as any mercantile lawyer would—that the definition of currency on which it is founded is absurd—that all the theories on which it is based are pure moonshine—and, furthermore, that the act itself does not carry out the theory it professes to adopt. In order really to carry out the "currency principle" into effect, it would be indispensable to prohibit the bank from discounting bills of exchange; because every time the bank discounts a bill of exchange it violates the "currency principle." Moreover, its principles were in diametrical contradiction to the doctrines of all the great financial authorities of previous times and of the Bullion Report. The experience of the monetary panic of 1847 proved to demonstration that the doctrines of the Bullion Report are correct, and those of the Bank Act of 1844 erroneous. Nevertheless, there was one inestimable practical merit of the Act of 1844—it insured a store of gold to meet the panic when it did come, and prevented the directors from allowing their gold to be all drained away, as they had uniformly done previously, and as they would have done in 1847, if they had not been stopped by the provisions of the act. In the eyes of practical statesmen this single merit would outweigh all the fantastic theories upon which it is founded.

The problem, therefore, was to discover a method which should protect and preserve the store of gold in the bank as effectually as the Bank Act of 1844 had indisputably done; and at the same time emancipate the bank from the fantastic theories which held it in thraldom, and permit it to act in commercial crises and monetary panics in accordance with the principles of the Bullion Report and of all former financial authorities, which had been proved to be true by uniform experience, and further confirmed by the experience of 1857 and 1866, shortly to be described. In this I claim to have perfectly succeeded. While I was reflecting on this complex problem, and hitherto saw no solution to it, a very sudden and severe monetary drain took place in the autumn of 1855. One day, during this drain, happening to be on duty at the bank, a customer came in and wanted me to do something. Having been only a few months in the bank, and therefore a perfect neophyte in banking, I had not the remotest idea what he wanted me to do; and, accordingly, I set him to talk, in order to give myself time to think. He then made this revelation to me. He said that when the rate of discount between two monetary centres differs by more than sufficient to pay the cost of sending bullion from one to the other—as was the case then between London and Paris—bullion dealers and others, who have had no operations necessitating remittances of gold, fabricate bills for the express purpose of exporting bullion from the cheaper centre to the dearer for the purpose of reaping the profit during the currency of the bills. Not only that, but foreign merchants and bankers hurry over their bills for discount and take away the gold. To take an extreme case. Suppose that London bankers perversely maintained their rate of discount at two per cent., while the rate in Paris was ten per cent. The meaning of that would be that persons could buy gold for two per cent. in London and sell it at ten per cent. in Paris. What would be the consequence? First, every post from foreign parts within a certain distance would bring over shoals of foreign bills to be discounted in London, and the proceeds immediately remitted abroad. Secondly, bullion dealers and others would immediately fabricate bills for the purpose of having them discounted, drawing out the proceeds and remitting them abroad.

Now, both these classes of persons do not want bank notes at all—they want nothing but solid gold. The error upon which the whole theory of the Bank Act made shipwreck was the popular one, that when a banker discounts a bill he hands over bank notes in exchange for it over the counter in the first instance. But a banker never discounts or purchases bills of exchange with bank notes in the first instance. It is the very essence of "banking" that a banker in the first instance purchases a bill of exchange by creating a credit or a deposit in his customer's favor in his books. Then after, but not before, this credit or deposit has been created in his favor in the banker's books, the customer may either (1) have notes in exchange for it, or (2) may draw out the gold by means of a cheque. Now, persons engaged in the operations above described have no use for notes; their great object is to obtain credits or deposits in the books of bankers; and as soon as they have succeeded in obtaining these they instantly draw out all the gold and export it. Thus the whole of the gold may be drained away from the banks, and not a single note be withdrawn from circulation; which plays utter havoc with the brain-spun theories of the Bank Act of 1844.

The express object of that act was to compel a £5 note to be withdrawn from circulation for every five sovereigns that were drawn out of the bank. And it was stoutly maintained that, if the directors perversely refused to do this, the mechanical action of the act would compel them to do so. It is now proved decisively, by a simple statement of facts and abundant practical experience, that by a due course of mismanagement every single sovereign may be drawn out of the banking department of the bank, and yet not a single note withdrawn from circulation, as all but happened in the great panic of 1857, and would actually have happened within an hour if the doors of the bank had been opened on the morning of the 13th November, and the act had not been suspended on the previous evening. Thus the Bank Act of 1844 is open to exactly the same fatal defect as the former scheme of the directors. The outside public only see the contests between bankers and merchants on the question of accommodation; but, as a matter of fact, it is the bullion dealers who are the natural enemies of bankers. Bullion dealers import and export bullion for profit, just as merchants do other merchandise. Like every one else, they buy in the cheapest market and sell in the dearest. And if they see that English bankers are willing to sell them their gold at two per cent., when the market price is ten per cent., they are quite ready to fool them to the top of their bent, and buy every ounce of gold they possess; thus draining away the bullion basis of the paper currency, and leaving the entire currency so many pieces of paper. This is so perfectly well understood now that there is no need of giving any further examples. It is very remarkable that, though this circumstance must have been known to hundreds of business men, yet it has never before, that we are aware of, found its way into print; it was never on any occasion alluded to in the Parliamentary debates; it was never mentioned by a single witness before the Parliamentary committees, nor in any Parliamentary report; and yet it is decisive of the whole question, and it gives the key to the solution of the whole difficulty.

It is now demonstrated that instead of there being only one cause of the export of bullion, as maintained by the witnesses before the Bullion Committee—or two, as proved by the Bullion Report—there are in reality three causes: 1. Payments due for goods imported. 2. A depreciated paper money. 3. A difference in the rates of discount between two monetary centres more than sufficient to defray the cost of the transport of bullion from one to the other. This last discovery puts the coping-stone on the theory of the Bullion Report, and renders it absolutely complete; and shows how the principles of the Bullion Report are to be carried into practical application. The theory of credit and the paper currency is now complete.

Ricardo and the Bullion Report utterly denied that the absolute quantity of paper at any time is any criterion of its being defective or excessive. They maintained that the only criterion of the legitimate quantity of paper—*i. e.*, credit—is the market price of bullion and the state of the foreign exchanges. And their doctrines, after having been temporarily submerged by the fantastic theories of Lord Overstone and his sect, who beguiled Sir Robert Peel away from his sager mentors, have now re-emerged triumphant, and are now universally acknowledged to be true by all practical men of business in the world. I published these doctrines in my "Theory and Practice of Banking" in 1856; and from that time forward these principles have been understood and acted upon by the directors of the bank, and they received the most satisfactory confirmation; because in the Committee of the Commons on the great monetary panic of 1857, Mr. Norman, who had been one of the leading supporters of Lord Overstone's dogmas and of the Bank Act of 1844, candidly acknowledged that the directors of the bank had found the rate of discount amply sufficient means of controlling their issues.

THE MONETARY PANIC OF 1857.

The crisis we have last considered was the inevitable termination of a multiplicity of derangements of the proper course of commerce. No one conversant with commercial history could fail to foresee that the entanglements of so large a portion of the public with railway speculations, and the losses caused by the failures of the harvest, must produce a crisis. We have seen that this panic gave a fatal blow to the prestige of the Bank Act of 1844, which was enacted in express contradiction to the unanimous opinions of the most experienced authorities of former times whom it professed to follow. They had invariably protested against imposing a cast-iron limit on the issues of the bank. The experience of the crisis of 1847, amply confirming that of 1793, 1797 and 1825, and also proving the wisdom of the action of the bank in 1836, showed that such a restriction cannot be maintained in the paroxysm of a great crisis without endangering the existence of the whole mass of commercial credit.

The crisis we are now going to describe was of a very different nature. It burst upon the world in the most unexpected manner. It gave no premonitory symptoms which were apparent to any but very watchful and experienced eyes; and when it did come it revealed a depth of rottenness in the commercial world which appalled every one, and proved to be of much more severe intensity than that of 1847. The supporters of the Act of 1844 were much crestfallen by its failure in 1847, but they took courage again after the Crimean war. The act had been subjected to the test of a great commercial crisis and had failed. It was now subjected to the test of a war, and many of its opponents predicted that it would fail again; but it did not. Its effects during the Crimean war were probably salutary; but the war did not proceed to any such lengths as to test its powers severely. Peace was restored before the resources of the country were in any measure strained.

For several weeks preceding, the "Economist" reported the money market to be as tight as it could well be. But on the 29th December it said: "The money market continues as stringent as it can well be. Paper at long dates cannot be discounted on any terms. The great extent of our trade, as indicated by the returns for November, confirms the suspicion awakened by the continued demand for money, that trade has received no serious check from the advance in the rate of discount, and is still more extensive than prudence warrants, or in the end will be justified."

In the course of 1855 the directors began to perceive that the rate of discount was the true method of protecting the reserve of the bank. The following table—showing the bullion in the bank and the rate of discount during 1855—shows a most marked difference in the action of the bank in 1855 and during former periods:

1855.		Bullion in the Issue Department.	Rate of Discount.
		£	
January	4	13,180,835	5 per cent.
"	20	11,880,560	"
February	22	12,313,230	"
March	22	13,479,975	"
April	12	14,392,500	4 1-2 per cent.
May	3	14,791,785	4 per cent.
"	17	15,336,510	"
"	31	16,337,685	"
June	14	17,056,945	3 1-2 per cent.
"	28	17,429,435	"
July	19	16,631,890	"
August	9	15,601,590	"
September	6	14,368,010	4 per cent.
"	13	13,668,005	4 1-2 per cent.
"	27	12,695,250	5 per cent.
October	4	12,368,255	5 1-2 per cent.
"	18	11,205,855	6 per cent. for bills not longer than 60 days.
November	8	10,741,320	7 per cent. for bills not longer than 95 days.
December	6	10,580,570	"
"	27	10,369,595	"

This most judicious conduct on the part of the bank, which merited nothing but the most unqualified commendation, excited a great clatter among a certain number of people who think that money is to be created *ad libitum* by writing "promises to pay" on bits of paper, when there is no money to pay them with, and who think it possible to send one's money abroad and also to have it at home. The papers were filled for weeks with letters and articles exhibiting all the rank follies which were once prevalent on the subject of the price of corn, and which have been so admirably exposed by Adam Smith. But not many years afterwards a marked change for the better took place. The majority of writers then began to understand that the rate of discount is the true and supreme regulating power of the paper currency; and instead of assailing the bank with howls of execration when it did its duty in raising the rate of discount, they generally commended it. This was great, real and sound progress in the spread of economic science.

At the end of 1855 the Queen exercised the power reserved in the Act of 1844 to enable the Bank of England to extend its issues to not more than two-thirds of the amount of those of any banks of issue that might cease to issue notes. From the passing of the act up to this period, forty-seven banks, whose authorized issues amounted to £712,623, ceased to issue their own notes; and on the 13th December, 1855, the Queen in Council issued an order authorizing the Bank of England to increase its issues to the amount of £475,000 upon public securities. But this is not the *bona fide* increase in the issuing power of the bank; for in the year 1854 the Clearing House was organized on a better plan; and whereas before that an average amount of £200,000 of bank notes was required to adjust its transactions, by the new system these were totally dispensed with, and no notes at all are now used. Moreover, by the admission of the joint-stock banks to the Clearing House they were saved from keeping an enormous amount of notes to meet the "bankers' charges," which no one who was not behind the scenes could estimate. These notes, therefore, now became available to the bank to use for commercial purposes; and consequently are to be considered as so much additional power of issue to the bank, which thus had in reality acquired an increased power of issue far exceeding a million.

For several months after the beginning of 1856 the money market continued in a state of great "tightness" and the bullion in the bank scarcely varied. The lowest was on the 26th of April, when it stood at £9,081,675; after that it gradually rose, and the rate of discount fell in summer to about 4 1-4 to 4 1-2; but in October the bullion fell very considerably again, and discount rose to 7 and 8 per cent., and a pressure followed of about the same severity as in 1855 and continued with very little variation to the end of the year. On December the 4th discount was 6 1-2; on the 18th, 6 per cent., and it continued so till the autumn of 1857. These rates were, of course, very much higher than the average ones of former times, and they were one ground of accusation brought by many against the act; but in truth they were its very merit. The directors had now learned from experience, and it was these very variations which preserved the security of the bank.

In August nothing seemed amiss to the public eye. "Things were then pretty stationary," said the governor of the bank. "The prospects of the harvest were very good; there was no apprehension that commerce at that time was otherwise than sound. There were certain far-seeing persons who considered that the great stimulus given by the war expenditure, which had created a very large consumption of goods imported from the East and other places, must now occasion some collapse, and still more those who observed that the merchants, notwithstanding the enhanced prices of produce, were nevertheless importing, as they had done successfully in the previous years. But the public certainly viewed the trade as sound, and were little aware that a crisis of any sort was impending, far less that it was so near at hand.' The bullion at this time was £10,606,000, the reserve £6,296,000 and the minimum rate of discount 5 1-2, when on the 17th of August the bank entered into a negotiation with the East India Company to send one million of specie to the East.

Things were in this state when, about the middle of September, news came of a great depreciation of American railway securities. It was found that for a long time they had been carrying on an extravagant system of management and paying dividends not earned by traffic. The system had at last collapsed; and, of course, an enormous depreciation of their stock followed, to the amount of nearly twenty per cent. It was supposed that as much as eighty millions of this stock was held in England, and that the effects of this fall would be very serious. On the 25th of August the Ohio Life and Trust Company, with deposits to the amount of £1,200,000, stopped payment. The panic spread throughout the Union. Discount rose to 18 and 24 per cent. On the 17th of October news came that 150 banks in Pennsylvania, Maryland, Virginia and Rhode Island had stopped payment. The drain was then beginning to be severe on the Bank of England. On the 8th October the bullion was £9,751,000, the reserve £4,931,000, and discount was raised to 6 per cent. On the 12th the rate at Hamburg was 7 3-4, and bullion was flowing to New York; discount was then raised to 7 per cent. About this time rumors strongly affecting the Western Bank of Scotland were abroad. On the 19th discount was raised to 8 per cent. The commercial disasters were increasing in America. In one week the Bank of France lost upwards of a million sterling. The bullion in the bank had sunk to £8,991,000, and the reserve to £4,115,000. Discount was raised to 7 1-2 in Paris and 9 per cent. in Hamburg. On the 20th a deputation from the Western Bank of Scotland applied for assistance, but the bank was afraid to undertake so enormous a concern. The Borough Bank of Liverpool was also in difficulties, and after some time the bank agreed to assist them to the amount of £1,500,000, on condition of their winding up; but the arrangements fell through in consequence of the Liverpool bank closing its doors before it was completed.

On the 13th October a general run took place on the New York banks in consequence of the severe measures of restriction they were obliged to adopt to protect themselves. Eighteen immediately stopped, and soon afterwards, out of sixty-three banks, only one maintained its payments. This immediately reacted on Liverpool and Glasgow, which were much involved with American firms. By the 19th October, the failures began to be numerous in this country. Uneasiness greatly increased in London. On the 28th, the principal discount house applied to the bank for an assurance that they would give them any assistance that they might require. On the 30th, an express came for £50,000 (sovereigns) for a Scotch bank, part of £170,000, and £80,000 for Ireland. On the 5th November discount was raised to 9 per cent. The great house of Dennistoun, with liabilities of nearly two millions, stopped payment on the 7th, and the Western Bank closed its doors on the 9th. Failures in London rapidly increased. Purchases and sales of stock were enormous, much beyond what they had ever been before. The bullion in the bank had sunk to £7,719,000, and the reserve to £2,834,000. On the 9th, discount was raised to 10 per cent. On the 10th of November, a large discount house applied to the bank for £400,000. The Bank of France raised its rate to 8, 9 and 10 per cent. for one, two and three months. Another English bank was assisted. The City of Glasgow

Bank then stopped. On that day the discounts at the bank were £1,126,000. On the 10th and 11th, upwards of one million sterling in gold was sent to Scotland, and there was a great demand for Ireland. On the 11th, Sanderson & Co., the great bill-brokers, stopped payment, with deposits of three and a-half millions. On the 12th, the discounts at the bank were £2,373,000. On the 11th, in consequence of these sudden demands for Scotland and Ireland, the bullion was reduced to £6,666,000 and the reserve to £1,462,000.

As the failures in London became more tremendous, discounts became more and more contracted. The stunning news of the stoppage of so many banks created a banking panic. Private banks stopped discounting altogether. The only source of discount was the Bank of England. The public, however, and the directors knew that the precedent of 1847 must be followed; and though they made no direct application to the Government for the suspension of the act, they laid the state of the bank continually before them and continued to discount as if they knew the act must be suspended. Then private persons, being unable to obtain discounts, began to make a run for their balances. When universal ruin was at last impending, the Government, on the 12th of November, sent a letter to the bank to say that, if they should be unable to meet the demands for discounts and advances upon approved securities, without exceeding the limits of their circulation prescribed by the Act of 1844, they would be prepared to propose to Parliament a bill of indemnity for any excess so issued. In order, however, to prevent the temporary relaxation of the act from being extended beyond the necessities of the case, the rate of discount was not to be reduced below the then present rate, ten per cent. The issue of this letter immediately calmed the public excitement. But on the evening of the 12th the total banking reserve of the bank and all its branches was reduced to £581,000.

To show the state the bank was reduced to, the governor gave in a paper to the Parliamentary committee with the following figures, showing its reserve on the 11th and 12th November.

On Wednesday, November 11th, the reserve consisted of:

Notes in London	£375,005	
Notes at branches	582,705	
		£957,710
Gold coin in London	£310,784	
Gold coin at branches	97,665	
		408,449
Silver coin in London	£44,046	
Silver coin at branches	51,948	
		95,994
Total reserve		£1,462,153

On Thursday, November 12th, at night, the reserve consisted of:

Notes in London	£68,085	
Notes at branches	62,545	
		£130,630
Gold coin in London	£274,953	
Gold coin at branches	83,255	
		358,208
Silver coin in London	£41,106	
Silver coin at branches	50,807	
		91,913
Total reserve		£580,751

That is to say, the total reserve in London on the evening of the 12th was £384,144! Such were the resources of the Bank of England to commence business with on the morning of the 13th! "Truly," said the governor, "it must have entirely ceased discounting, which would have brought an immediate run upon it; and the bankers' balances alone were £5,458,000. It is easy to see that the bank could not have kept its doors open an hour." The governor of the bank said that the panic of 1857 was not so great as that of 1847, but that the real commercial pressure was more intense. This is proved by the fact that, while in the former year the issue of the letter immediately allayed the panic, and by that means stopped the demand for notes, and there was only required an issue of £400,000 in notes to surmount all difficulties, which did not exceed the statutory limits; in 1857 the issue of the Government letter produced no cessation of the demand for advances. The statutory limit was £14,475,000 of notes issued on securities, and there were issued in excess of them:

Nov.	13	£186,000	Nov. 23	£397,000
	14	622,000	24	317,000
	16	860,000	25	81,000
	17	836,000	26	243,000
	18	852,000	27	342,000
	19	896,000	28	184,000
	20	998,000	30	15,000
	21	617,000		

Being a total of £7,376,000.

On the meeting of Parliament, an act was passed permitting a temporary suspension of the Bank Act till February 1st, 1858, provided that the directors did not reduce their discount below ten per cent. On the 24th December they reduced it to eight per cent., thereby reviving the operation of the act.

This great crisis of 1857, far exceeding in intensity that of 1847, added another proof upon proof that, in a great commercial crisis, the restrictive theory will bring about the universal failure of merchants and bankers; and that the expansive theory is the only one which can save both.

THE MONETARY PANIC OF 1866.

In 1858, the inevitable consequence followed from the crash of 1857. The enormous mass of false trading being cleared away, money naturally flowed into the bank, and the quantity of bullion gradually and steadily increased up to the end of the year. The bank now learned to adopt much higher rates of discount than formerly. In 1847, it kept the rate at five per cent. while the bullion was under £10,000,000; in 1858, the rate of five per cent. was maintained till the bullion exceeded £15,000,000—a great advance in sound principle.

In my "Dictionary of Political Economy," Art. "Banking in England," § 254, published not long after this great crisis, we said: "This year (1858) passed away in great tranquillity, persons not having forgotten the lesson of 1857. But we cannot doubt, judging from all former experience, that an uneasy spirit will soon be abroad again; we cannot doubt that the brood of speculators are now anxiously casting about to see if they can plant the seeds of the next crisis; and it is the duty of those who are now at the head of monetary affairs to be on the watch to counteract all such attempts as they can detect; and in the meantime, the most interesting question, in a banking point of view, is—What is to be the next mania?

Time in due course gave an answer to this question. There is nothing special to arrest our attention during the next few years. The rates of discount continued generally moderate throughout 1859 and 1860. In February, 1861, it rose for a short time to eight per cent., but soon subsided again. The unhappy civil war in America then being imminent, created natural apprehension as to our cotton supplies, and most persons could foresee that this would lead to monetary complications. These, however, were for the future. During 1861 and 1862, the money market was, generally speaking, extremely easy; the issue of paper by both the belligerent governments having the inevitable effect of driving bullion over to this country; consequently, trade flourished surprisingly, and the price of money was very easy So things went on until October, 1863, when every one began to foresee a disturbance in the money market. In the first place, the rapid rise in the price of cotton, from the failure of the supply from the Southern States of America, forced up the price to a great height. The world had to be searched to produce the supply. Immense quantities came from the East Indies, from Egypt, from the Brazils, besides other quarters. This vast trade, being suddenly created, had to be paid for in cash. Consequently, a great drain of silver began towards the East, which was obtained from Paris and Hamburg—the great marts for silver as London is for gold. The Italian Government also contracted a loan at this time. The law of limited liability began to operate at the same time, and the number of new companies being formed under it inspired uneasiness. The Bank of France lost great quantities of specie. The Bank of England raised its rate twice in one week from five to six and then to seven. The Bank of France also raised its rate to seven, and spoke of issuing 50-franc notes; on the 2d of December the bank raised its rate to seven, and on the 3d to eight. At the same time a great fall took place in the Russian exchange, in consequence of certain Government measures not having succeeded. In consequence of these circumstances, the reserves of the bank were considerably strengthened after a short time. But in January, 1864, a fresh export of specie began, and continued with great severity till the middle or end of May, so that discount varied from eight to seven and six, and again up to nine. With a few fluctuations, this great pressure continued all through the summer. Having fallen to six per cent. in June, it gradually rose again to nine in September. After that it gradually fell to five per cent. in June, 1865. Already in March, 1864, the number of new companies formed under the limited liability principle gave great uneasiness. Up to that time, it appeared there were 263 companies formed, with a nominal capital of £78,135,000, of which twenty-seven were banks and fourteen discount companies. In August, 1864, the long-dated acceptances of the new financial companies began to press on the market and lay the foundations of the crisis of 1866. In April, the Bank of England was admitted into the Clearing House, thereby still further economizing the use of bank notes. On the 8th of September, the bank raised its rate to nine per cent., and this measure stopped the foreign drain, lowered the price of foreign commodities and strengthened their reserves. The price of cotton was greatly lowered, owing to the expected peace in America; and this rise in the rate of discount, striking on a falling market, produced an immense curtailment of business in all directions. On the 20th of June, 1865, the rate of discount reached its minimum—three per cent. On the 5th of August it was raised to four, and then gradually and continuously, with very slight fluctuations, till it culminated in the crisis of May, 1866. In November, a strong foreign drain began; the exchange fell, and this growing stronger in January, 1866, the bank raised its rate on the 6th. This had some effect in arresting the drain, but it did not bring in fresh supplies from abroad. At this period, the National Provincial Bank transferred its head office to London, and in consequence was, by the Statute of 1826, obliged to give up its issues of notes, which amounted to £442,371. Several other banks having ceased to issue since the Bank of England was last authorized to increase its issues of notes, the bank was now permitted to increase its issues on securities to £15,000,000. The high rate of interest here caused a good deal of foreign money to be invested in long-dated bills.

Towards the end of January, the difficulties began, which brought on the panic of May. In consequence of there having been no Parliamentary inquiry, as might have been expected, the circumstances of this panic have never been fully explained. But it may be stated, generally, that these finance and discount companies had advanced enormous sums of money to promote great enterprises, such as railways and other schemes which could never repay their cost until completed, which might take years. The first company that failed was the Joint Stock Discount Company, in February. This spread a general feeling of alarm, as the doings of this company were merely a type of a large amount of business, which was known to have been engaged in by numerous other companies. In March, Barned's Bank, at Liverpool, stopped payment, with liabilities of upwards of three and a-half millions. Several great railway contractors suspended, involving in discredit the companies with whom they were known to have "financed." On the 3d May, the bank raised its rate of discount to seven per cent. Every one now felt that the long-dreaded crisis was at last come. The air was thick with rumors. Every one knew that it was now merely a question of weeks, perhaps of days, when the storm would burst. On the 8th of May, the bank raised its discount to eight per cent. The advocates of the Bank Act, in their usual strain, proclaimed that on no account whatever must the act be suspended. Such a thing was not to be thought of. These wise persons were quite oblivious of 1847 and 1857. Credit was then tottering, and received a blow from the report of the speech of the Emperor Napoleon III., said to have been addressed by him to a meeting at Auxerre, in which he expressed his detestation of the treaties of 1815. This, in the feverish political state of the Continent, was held to mean that he was determined on war.

It is possible that this excitement might have passed off, as the bank had a fair reserve in the Banking Department, and abundance of bullion in the Issue Department. On the 9th of May, the bank revised its discount to ten per cent. On this day, however, occurred the event which it is probable produced the great panic. The Mid-Wales Railway Company had accepted bills of exchange to the amount of £60,000, which were held by three parties—Bateman; Overend, Gurney & Co., and the National Discount Company. The company had dishonored the bills, and actions had been brought against them by the three parties above named. As ill fortune would have it, judgment in these actions was delivered on the 9th of May in the very height of the excitement. The Court of Common Pleas held unanimously that the railway company had no authority whatever to accept such bills; and, consequently, that they were absolutely invalid and so much waste paper. For some time back, it was known that Overend, Gurney & Co. were very deep in with contractors and other parties. Moreover, they held forged bills to a large extent on another firm. Their shares were pressed on the market and were going down. This fall in their shares produced a steady withdrawal of their deposits. The judgment in the case of the Mid-Wales Railway converted this into a complete panic. And on the afternoon of the 10th of May the terrible news spread through London that the great establishment of Overend, Gurney & Co. had stopped payment, with liabilities exceeding £10,000,000—the most stupendous failure that had ever taken place in the city. This news only spread about after banking hours; but every one could foresee what the effects would be next morning. The Chancellor of the Exchequer said next evening, in the House, that the oldest inhabitant in the city declared that the excitement was without a parallel. Early in the evening, he was questioned as to whether Government had authorized the bank to issue notes in excess of the legal limit. The Chancellor replied that he had not yet done so, but that he had received a deputation from the private bankers, and was expecting one from the joint-stock banks on the subject. Very soon afterwards this came, and the members of the Cabinet having retired to a committee room and consulted, the Chancellor, later in the evening, announced, amidst the loudest cheers from all parts of the House, that the Government, following the precedents of 1847 and 1857, had informed the bank that, if they thought proper to make advances beyond the legal limit the Government would bring in a bill of indemnity. He also stated that the bank had advanced £4,000,000 that day.

The announcement of the suspension of the Bank Charter Act produced the best effects next morning. The bank raised its rate to ten per cent., and everything calmed down; and though, subsequently to this, some other stoppages took place, yet the knowledge that the bank had the power to issue notes on good securities abated the panic. On the 18th of May, the Chancellor of the Exchequer stated that the bank had advanced £12,225,000 in five days. The sum that was paid away during the panic will probably never be known, but it was something fabulous. We were informed, on good authority, that one bank alone paid away £2,000,000 in gold in six hours. Establishments, whose names need not be particularized, stopped payment, whose liabilities according to their last published balance sheet amounted to £37,222,716; besides several others whose liabilities were not stated, but which would probably bring up the sum total to £50,000,000. Besides these actual stoppages, several other banks connected with the East confessed to immense losses. Thus, the Bank of Hindostan, China and Japan stated its profits at £23,485, and its losses at £87,796, with a further expected loss of £70,000; the Asiatic Bank stated its profits at £61,494, and its losses at £142,000; the Bank of Queensland stated its profits at £10,373, and its losses at £42,071. What losses the other banks made we, of course, have no means of knowing, but they were probably very heavy.

In the great crisis and panic of 1866, the law that the rate of discount is the most powerful method of controlling the exchanges, seemed for some time to be at fault. From the beginning of that year the difference in the rates of discount at London and Paris was constantly two per cent.; and gradually increased to three, four and even six per cent.; and, while the storm was raging in England the Bank of France was in a state of the greatest serenity. The high rates in England were totally unable to prevent a severe foreign drain; and the Bank of France rapidly gained large quantities of bullion while its rate of discount was only four per cent. This remarkable, and indeed unprecedented, phenomenon led many persons to question the truth of the law; and even to maintain that the rates of discount in different countries ought to be quite independent of each other. But, it is to be remembered that the rate of discount, although in modern times the most powerful, is only one of several causes which influence the flow of bullion which may at any time act in the same or contrary directions. On this occasion, it was for a short period overpowered by other causes. The principal of these was the utter discredit into which England had fallen. It was fully expected that the Bank of England would stop payment, and that there would be a general stoppage of the other banks, involving the whole mercantile community in ruin. The high rate of discount failed to attract supplies, because it was feared that the whole principal would be lost. In consequence, large quantities of long-dated bills on England were hurried over and realized at any sacrifice, and the proceeds remitted abroad. But as soon as these temporary causes had ceased to act, large supplies of bullion poured in, and the equilibrium between credit and bullion was restored. As was well pointed out in a pamphlet by Mr. Fowler at the time, it was only that a longer period than usual was required to produce the effect on the exchanges than had been found needful on former occasions.

With respect to the Bank of France, the explanation is also easy. There was no commercial crisis in France, but strong expectations of war. Consequently, mercantile enterprise was curbed, and specie naturally flowed into the Bank of France. Also, in anticipation of war, the Government of Italy suspended cash payments and issued paper money. This, of course, necessarily drove specie out of the country, and it also naturally went to the Bank of France. Thus, it is seen how necessary it is to have a knowledge of the circumstances at any period to understand the operation of the laws of economics. Thus we see that true science is vindicated by experience, and the history of banking since 1866 has amply confirmed the truth of this doctrine, which was first demonstrated in the first edition of my "Theory and Practice of Banking" in 1856, and has since then made its way to universal acceptance. The Bank of France was exempted from the operation of the usury laws in France to enable it to adopt it, and by a sedulous attention to this principle, the notes of the Bank of France, which were for several years inconvertible after the war of 1870, circulated exactly at par with specie, and in fact every bank in the world is now managed on this principle.

THE CRISIS OF 1890.

The recent crisis, from which we are only now emerging, which was only prevented by the splendid management of the Bank of England from culminating in the most terrible monetary panic recorded in history, amply confirms all the principles and doctrines enunciated in this work.

After the severe crisis of 1878, when the country only escaped a monetary panic by the skin of its teeth, things went pretty smoothly for several years. But soon after that the great Argentine Republic, of immense extent and boundless resources, which was constantly receiving a vast immigration, especially from Italy, got into the hands of an unscrupulous "ring," who created loan after loan for the ostensible purpose of developing the resources of the country. Most unfortunately, the great house of Baring Brothers & Co., one of the leading merchant-bankers of the world, constituted themselves one of the principal agents for floating these loans with the public. Argentina was advancing by leaps and bounds, and for several years these loans were received with great favor. But when loan after loan was launched with boundless profusion, people began to take alarm, and they ceased to be taken up by the public. Added to this, one of the usual South American revolutions took place; and the crew who were chiefly responsible for the loans, and who according to popular report, had feathered their own nests to the tune of millions, were driven from power, which of course, was a fatal blow to Argentine credit. Rumors and reports got about affecting many great houses, but as yet no one ventured to question the stability of the great house of Baring Brothers & Co. But, at last, on the 8th November, the appalling intelligence was made known to the governor of the bank that this great house was in the extremest danger of stopping payment, with liabilities to the amount of £21,000,000; and that the most energetic measures must be taken without a moment's delay to avert the catastrophe.

The magnitude of the panic which would have ensued if this house had been allowed to shut its doors, may be gauged by the fact that, in 1866, the liabilities of Overend, Gurney & Co., which was up to that time the most stupendous failure in the city, were only £10,000,000; whereas those of Baring Brothers & Co. were £21,000,000. Moreover, Overend, Gurney & Co.'s liabilities were entirely internal, whereas the paper of Baring Brothers & Co. was held by millions in foreign countries. It is not too much to say that, if this house had been allowed to stop, it would have produced a monetary panic throughout the whole world. Now, at this time, the whole available resources of the bank, under the Bank Act of 1844, to meet the awful calamity, were just about £10,000,000, which would have been nothing but a drop in the bucket. In this emergency, the Chancellor of the Exchequer was summoned in hot haste to give counsel in the city. Popular report attributes the measures taken chiefly to the wisdom of Mr. Lidderdale, the governor. With magnificent energy, the bank itself being utterly unable to meet the crisis unaided, the joint-stock banks in London, the provinces, and in Scotland were summoned to combine, and a guaranteed fund of £15,000,000 was subscribed for.

Moreover, the news of the danger would not improbably have brought on a panic and a run for gold. Vast quantities of stock were thrown on the market, which reduced it lower than it had been for years, and far different from the halcyon days when Mr. Goschen effected his conversion. It is also said that some of the joint-stock banks contemplated ceasing to discount, which would have at once brought on a panic—and were only dissuaded from so doing by the peremptory and energetic remonstrances of the governor. But to insure against a possible panic, it was necessary to have a provision of notes; and as, under the Bank Act of 1844, additional notes could only be issued against an equal amount of gold, several millions of gold were required to be got together without a moment's delay. The rate of discount was six per cent., and the bank did not dare to raise it higher; because, with its exceedingly restricted power of issue, raising the rate of discount would have been the very thing to aggravate the panic, and bring on the bank a demand for gold and notes. Accordingly, the bank contracted a loan for £3,000,000 for a short period with the Bank of France; and £1,500,000 with St. Petersburg, and obtained £500,000 from other quarters. It had, therefore, the power to issue £5,000,000 in notes and felt itself secure. By these energetic means, in such splendid contrast to the proceedings of the bank on former occasions, it was at length announced that all the liabilities of Baring Brothers & Co. were protected; but at the cost of the liquidation of this world-renowned firm; and the frightful monetary panic was averted, which would have thrown all former ones into the shade.

The nearest parallel to this crisis was that of 1838, when the greatest American houses were in danger, and the bank promptly and instantly advanced £6,000,000 and averted a monetary panic. The circumstances of this great crisis suggest the following reflections:

1. It dissipates the last vestiges of Peel's hallucination, that all commercial crises are due to excessive issues of bank notes, and that if these could be suppressed commercial crises could be prevented.

2. Although in ordinary times, the rate of discount is the true supreme power of controlling credit and the paper currency, it is utterly too slow to attract millions of gold, if required to be got together in a few days.

3. That while the bank is bound down to such a narrow restriction of its power of issuing notes, raising the rate of discount too much will aggravate the panic, and bring on a run for notes and gold.

4. That to give full play and efficacy to the power of the rate of discount, it must be free and uncontrolled, and trusted as the sole controlling power, without any restriction in the power of issuing notes.

5. It also demonstrates the absurdity of not only restricting the power of issuing notes, but also of locking up half the resources of the bank out of the power of the directors. While the bank was busily scouring the world to scrape up £5,000,000 of gold, it actually had £10,000,000 of gold in its own vaults, which it was unable to touch.

6. It demonstrates that the Bank of England is utterly too small a machine to meet such a crisis alone, when it would have had the whole banking and mercantile community on its shoulders at once. To meet such tremendous crises, as all future ones will be, the Bank of England must act together with all the other banks in the country to support the mercantile community.

7. It proves that while commercial crises in our modern system of credit

are unavoidable, monetary panics are preventable, and are brought about by bad banking legislation and bad management of the bank.

8. It gives the *coup de grâce* to the restrictive theory; and shows that, when a great commercial crisis is imminent, the banks must act together instantly and promptly, and energetically support the mercantile community, and not wait till half the city is in ruins, as on former occasions.

The bank on this occasion was saved by the energetic measures of Mr. Lidderdale, who is entitled to the gratitude of the whole banking and mercantile community in the world for his bold, prompt and energetic measures, which were the only ones possible under the circumstances. But it is too degrading to be repeated. Of course our excellent friends, the French, were jeering and gibing, and mocking at the Bank of England having to be taken in tow by the Bank of France. If the Bank of England had had the whole of its resources at command; if it had had a reserve of £20,000,000 of gold instead of £10,000,000, with unlimited powers of issue, it, with the assistance of the other banks, might have tided over the crisis with perfect security, by means of the rate of discount alone. If the present Bank Act had been in force in 1838, the bank could never have saved the American merchants, and there would have been a panic, as in 1847, 1857 and 1866. All these things show the indispensable necessity of a thorough and scientific reform of the entire banking system of the country.

CONDITION OF JOINT-STOCK BANKS (1) OF ENGLAND AND WALES AND (2) OF IRELAND, OCTOBER 19, 1895.

	* England and Wales.	† Ireland.
Market Value of Entire Paid-up Capital	£169,160,609	£19,523,600
Capital Subscribed	208,409,130	25,299,231
Capital paid up	58,420,470	7,109,231
Total Capital Liability (callable and reserved)	149,772,634	18,190,000
Reserve Fund	28,232,285	3,079,082
Dividend and Undivided Profits	2,480,373	413,188
Notes in Circulation	27,160,504	5,830,468
Acceptance Liabilities	18,329,659	244,700
Miscellaneous Liabilities, Credits, Rebate, etc.	3,777,014	262,769
Deposit and Current Accounts	485,277,381	43,612,697
Total Liabilities	£623,777,686	£60,552,135
Cash in hand and Money at Call and Short Notice	144,163,223	10,642,282
British Government Securities	82,519,223	7,129,308
Bonds, Stocks and other Investments	50,848,435	10,515,297
Discounts	43,509,726	5,950,084
Advances, Loans, Bills and other Securities	280,097,543	25,021,244
Buildings, Cover for Acceptances, Sundries	22,639,536	1,293,720
Total Assets	£623,777,686	£60,552,135

* 100 banks and 2,677 branches. † 9 banks and 1,008 branches.

SECTION X.

GENERAL CONCLUSION.

I NOW may conclude by some remarks on the existing banking system of England. On its foundation in 1694, the Bank of England received no monopoly in its favor, and not till 1708; and this monopoly, with some modifications, has endured to the present day. The Bank of Scotland, founded in 1695, at first received a monopoly in its favor for twenty-one years; but it was not renewed; and at the very notion of the bank claiming a monopoly of banking, the Scotch rose up with their usual democratic fervor, and scouted the idea that a single company should possess a monopoly of banking. Since then, banking in Scotland has been allowed to develop itself freely and spontaneously, so as to meet the growing requirements of the country. And though there have been some terrible catastrophes, such as the Ayr Bank, the Western Bank and the City of Glasgow Bank, these disasters never shook the solid system of the older and well-managed banks. There have also been commercial crises, as there must necessarily be in every commercial country; but there have not been any such monetary panics as those which have shaken England to its foundations—a very good proof of what has been advanced, that although commercial crises are innate and inevitable in the modern system of credit, yet the monetary panics are brought about by bad banking legislation and bad management of the bank, and that they are preventable.

Under the circumstances, I think that the monopolies conferred on the Banks of Scotland and England were justifiable as temporary measures, in consequence of the subject not being properly understood, and the number of wild, reckless speculations which were abroad. I think that the monopoly of the Bank of England was justifiable up to 1742; or at latest up to 1762; but after that it has been nothing but an unmitigated evil. For it was after 1762 that the industrial energies both in England and Scotland burst forth with unparalleled splendor; and they required an immense extension of banking accommodation. This was supplied in Scotland by the chartered banks throwing out branches in all directions, and carrying banking accommodation into all the principal towns of the country; and these, of course, were not independent institutions, governed by their own will; but they were integral parts of their head offices, and under the supervision and control of their experienced managers and directors. But in England, when the very same accommodation was required to develop the multiplied industries—canal making, agricultural and manufacturing—with which the country was teeming, the Bank of England would neither establish branches of its own in the various provincial towns, nor would it permit powerful and local solid banks to be founded in them. The consequence was that hundreds of country traders sprung up as bankers to supply the indispensable currency. The majority of them were perfectly unfit from their want of capital and experience to do so; and they were all perfectly independent of each other, without any central control and supervision. No doubt great things were effected by them; but when terror and alarm came in 1793 and 1797, they were swept away in multitudes. These local banks being, the majority of them, not possessed of any sufficient capital to bear such a strain, flung themselves for support on the Bank of England. Thus, in 1797, there were Mr. Pitt, the whole mercantile world, and hundreds of country banks all tugging at the money bags of the Bank of England. Thus, the bank, by its unjustifiable monopoly, not only prevented solid banks being founded, capable of maintaining themselves, but brought hundreds of country banks on its shoulders; and the directors, dazed and confused, were wholly unable to manage the bank under such an unexampled strain, and thus brought on a stoppage. Up till 1762, I think that the bank was adequate for the wants of the country.

It would be impossible to over-estimate the services of the Bank of England to the State—it was a great pillar of State. It was entirely owing to the reorganization of the finances, and the extension of solid credit by the bank, that under the masterful and sagacious guidance of William, England gradually rose from the nadir of her degradation under the two last Stuarts, when she was scarcely better than a wretched little island in a stormy sea, and very little more than an appanage of the Crown of France. It was the Bank of England alone that enabled William to prosecute his Continental wars; that supplied the funds for Marlborough's immortal campaigns, when the name of England was heard for the first time on the Continent with terror and respect, after an eclipse of half a century, and which steadily led her onward through the matchless Ministry of Pitt, till in 1763 she attained that place in the scale of nations which she has since held.

But statesmen are mostly purblind; they live from hand to mouth; their energies are exhausted in providing for the wants of the moment, and maintaining themselves in power; and they usually fail to see that many institutions which may have been useful in their day have become inadequate and insufficient under changing circumstances. Things, they think, will last their day; after them the deluge; until at the last the organization comes down with a crash, and then they are compelled to pay attention to it. After 1762, one such pillar as the Bank of England became wholly insufficient for the expanding wealth and commerce of England. It required many such. In the natural course of things a multitude of joint-stock banks would have grown up to meet the wants of expanding commerce. Decades of years passed away, and still the Ministers allowed the solid progress of commerce to be throttled in the grasp of a single joint-stock company. And instead of the gradual formation of powerful institutions, which would have given additional support to the State and to each other, multitudes of small banks sprung up, which not only were no support to each other, but which in moments of danger threw themselves on the single bank, and were an additional source of embarrassment to it and aided to bring it down. It seems to me a deep blot on the financial statesmanship of Mr. Pitt that he always steadfastly resisted the formation of powerful banks.

I do not share the opinion of Sir Robert Peel, that the suspension of cash payments in 1797 was a "fatal" measure; on the contrary, I believe that it was absolutely indispensable. Nor did the suspension of cash payments to the public in any way involve the necessity of the depreciation of the bank note. In 1797, the Scotch banks, without any protection from legislation, agreed among themselves to suspend cash payments to the public. But they rigorously maintained their system of exchanges among themselves. By this means no single bank could continue to over-issue, because it would have been called upon to redeem its over-issues. This state of matters continued for twenty years; and during that period the Scotch bank notes never sustained any depreciation beyond that of the Bank of England note, which they were bound to follow. When the time came they resumed payments in cash to the public without the slightest trouble or difficulty. And why was this not the case in England? The reason was this, the Clearing House of London was a purely private institution, to which the Bank of England was not admitted. Now, from the evidence given before the Parliamentary committees, the management of the bank was most reckless during this period, and we know that she must have sustained immense losses. Now, when the notes she issued never came back to her in due course, what did she do? No outsider, of course, knew what these losses were. But to cover them up, she had nothing to do but to issue fresh torrents of paper, which were continually aggravating and inflating the channel of circulation, and sending up prices.

If banking had been allowed to develop itself in England in its natural course, as it did in Scotland, there would have been a considerable number of joint-stock banks in London who would have established a clearing house; and every bank would have been obliged to redeem its over-issues in specie, and by this system of exchanges, the excessive issues would have been removed from circulation and the notes would have been kept at par, even though inconvertible with respect to the public, as the Scotch bank notes were. But the Bank of England not being in the Clearing House, was never called to account for its over-issues, and so could issue unlimited torrents of inconvertible notes, which fell to a ruinous discount, shaking the value of all property.

Moreover, the unparalleled increase of manufactures, agricultural improvements, in consequence of the enhanced price of cereals and stock, commerce and population demanded an increased amount of currency, and country banks multiplied in all directions. In 1814, there were 900 country banks pouring forth torrents of paper currency; and this flood of paper, combined with the excessive issues of the bank itself, at last reduced the bank note to 14s. 6d. But in 1814-15-16 hundreds of these banks failed, and many millions of their notes were withdrawn from circulation. In consequence of this, the bank note rose almost to par, and if the bank had been managed with common prudence, it would have risen quite to par, and cash payments would have been resumed in the ordinary course of business without the least disturbance.

The circumstances of this period afford one lesson of great importance. It is this: Governments and States should never issue paper money themselves. When States and Governments once begin to issue paper money, they never can resist the temptation to issue it in boundless quantities, so that it soon begins to depreciate, they have no power to redeem it, and the depreciation is incurable. Even those statesmen in 1813, who were most anxious to revert to cash payments, were constrained to allow that in process of time the argument passes over to depreciation. When depreciation has continued a certain time, all contracts and engagements are made in the depreciated paper and under inflated prices, and to compel them to redeem their debts in solid cash would be ruinous to all debtors. If the depreciation in 1814 had been brought about by issues of State paper money, England would have been in exactly the same position as Russia, Austria and many other States which have indulged in that fatal practice and were never able to resume cash payments. But in England this paper currency was supplied by the banks; and when the depreciation of the notes seemed absolutely hopeless, the failure of hundreds of banks withdrew many millions of paper currency from circulation, and enabled the remainder to right itself suddenly, at the cost of terrific suffering to those who had entered into engagements, based upon the inflated prices of this rotten paper. The sufferings endured for many years, and were produced by the disappearance of this rotten paper, and not by the Bank Act of 1819, as is so often ignorantly asserted.

When governments want funds for public purposes, they should apply to the banks, and not issue paper money themselves. It is the duty of banks to supply the paper currency of the country, and not the Government; and to take measures to keep it at its par value by properly adjusting the rate of discount. The Government has no power to keep its paper money at par value by raising the rate of discount. In the dreadful calamities of 1870-71, the Government of France did not issue their own paper money; they applied to the Bank of France, and by the admirable management of the bank, its inconvertible notes, which for a short time suffered a very small depreciation, soon recovered, and for years circulated at an absolute par value with specie. When the Government wants accommodation, the banks should treat it exactly as they would do any other customer. They should grant it the accommodation required, if advisable, and charge it the market price for it. And it is the business of the banks, and they alone can take measures, to maintain their notes at their par value, even though inconvertible to the public, and then they would avoid the curse of irredeemable paper money. But if the Government issues torrents or inconvertible paper money it will drive all specie out of the country, and affect all values with the most ruinous fluctuations.

And so the bank went on till 1826, when the great catastrophe of 1825 awoke the sleepy Ministry from their lethargy, which nothing but such a cataclysm could have done; and it was the clearly expressed opinion of all statesmen that the Bank of England was far too small a machine for the requirements of the country, and that its monopoly was an intolerable evil which must come to an end, and that the Scottish system of banking was far superior to the English. The bank was coerced into giving up a part of its monopoly, and allowing joint-stock banks to be formed in the provinces at a distance of not less than sixty-five miles from London, on the condition that they should do no business in London or within sixty-five miles therefrom. Now, this was not the Scottish system of banking, which is to have the head offices in the leading cities, Edinburgh and Glasgow, with a network of branches in all quarters of the country, all under one management. But the provincial joint-stock banks of England were, on a large scale, only a number of isolated banks, and forbidden to have their head offices in London.

But a few years afterwards, another most important breach was effected in the supposed monopoly of the bank. And now we see the important historical consequences of a total misconception of the nature of banking. In former days, it was understood that the express business of banking was to issue notes; and that was supposed to be the definition of banking. Now, that was not strictly accurate. The business of a bank is to create and issue rights of action, credits, debts (termed deposits) to its customers. And their customers might circulate these rights of action either by means of notes or cheques. No doubt, in the early days of banking, when it was a luxury of the rich, notes vastly predominated over cheques. Still, these documents are identical and their sole function is to circulate banking credits. Nevertheless, notes were conspicuous in the public eye, while cheques escaped observation.

In 1742, when the words of the monopoly clause were tightened, the bank's privilege was defined to consist in issuing notes. But the use of cheques instead of notes gradually increased; and their greater safety than notes, in masses of a dense population, made London bankers discontinue issuing notes in 1793 of their own accord, and restrict their customers to the use of cheques. Thus it was shown, what had never been dreamed of before, that in such places as London banking could be carried on without the use of notes at all.

In process of time persons who were anxious to establish joint-stock banks in London began to scrutinize the words of the monopoly clause, and they found that it did not prohibit the formation of joint-stock banks which should carry on their business in the then mode of London bankers without the use of notes. This opinion was declared to be correct by the Law Officers of the Crown, who pronounced that such banks were perfectly legal at common law. Thus the second great breach was effected in the monopoly of the bank, and joint-stock banks were founded in London. But still this was not the Scottish system of banking. All these banks, London and provincial, were merely isolated and local banks, having no communication with each other.

I will now explain in what the essential superiority of Scotch banking consists. Money always has a tendency to accumulate in agricultural districts, or the supply exceeds the demand; and in manufacturing districts the demand exceeds the supply. Now, in Scotland, all the banks have some branches in the agricultural districts and other branches in the manufacturing districts. Consequently, the branches in the agricultural districts remit their surplus money to the head office, which transmits it to the manufacturing districts. And all this is done under one management, which does not conflict with its separate parts. But this could not be done in England, where all the banks are purely local. Consequently, banks in the agricultural districts had to send up their surplus money to establishments in London, and so lose their absolute control over it; and banks in the manufacturing districts remitted their bills to this establishment in London to be discounted and had the money sent down to them. Thus the monetary nervous system was severed into three parts, under three managements, instead of being all under one management, as in Scotland. These London establishments were the great discount houses, of which the chief was Overend, Gurney & Co. The danger of this system was that the agricultural banks lost all control over their own money, which was involved in the speculations of the London discount house; and the manufacturing banks were dependent for their very existence on their bills being discounted by the London house. The great panic of 1866, which brought about the fall of Overend, Gurney & Co., contributed greatly to break up this system.

Since then, a far more healthy and natural system has been growing up. The Act of 1826 provided that if the provincial banks formed under it chose to establish their head offices in London and do London business they must give up their issues of notes in the provinces. The National Provincial Bank was a great provincial bank, with a large multitude of branches and an issue of £450,000 of notes in the provinces. But, in course of time, it found it expedient to establish its head office in London, even at the cost of giving up its issues in the provinces. This was similar to a genuine Scotch bank, with its head office in the capital and branches in every part of the country. Besides that, several banks in the southern counties agreed to amalgamate and open their head office in London, under the name of the Capital and Counties Bank, giving up, of course, their provincial issues. Moreover, the process of healthy amalgamation has been proceeding rapidly. Banks in Birmingham and Manchester have amalgamated with London banks; provincial banks have amalgamated with each other, and several private banks have amalgamated with joint-stock banks. Thus the banking system of this country has been gradually, and in recent times even rapidly, assuming the natural system—*i. e.*, the system it would have assumed if it had been allowed to develop itself free from the monopoly of the Bank of England. And the more rapidly the process of amalgamation proceeds the better; till at last the system will be reduced to the natural one—namely, a comparatively small number of very powerful banks instead of a vast multitude of small ones.

Then as this system proceeds with an accelerated pace, the great question will come of the restoration of the power of issuing notes to these great banks. The Bank Act of 1844 was of service in its day as a temporary measure until fuller knowledge and experience was obtained on the subject, and to give statesmen and financiers time to think upon devising a better system. But every one knows that it is utterly unsuited to the gigantic development and magnitude of modern commerce. All the theories upon which it is founded are utterly disproved; and Sir Robert Peel's extraordinary hallucination that all commercial crises originate in excessive issues of notes, which every one knew to be fallacious in his own day, has been scattered to the winds by 1847, 1857, 1866 and the crisis of 1890. Was it excessive issues of notes that tempted the great house of Baring to wreck its splendid name in wild speculations in South American securities?

The experience of every commercial crisis for the last 130 years has incontestably demonstrated the indispensable necessity of the expansive theory in a great commercial crisis, in accordance with the unanimous doctrine of all the great financial authorities of former times, and given the *coup de grâce* to the restrictive theory which is enacted by the Bank Act of 1844.

The great question will have to be considered of the restoration of the power of issuing notes to the banks of great power and undoubted solidity. No doubt, the unlimited power of issuing notes has left very evil memories in this country, somewhat similar to the horror of banking caused in France by the catastrophe of Law's Mississippi scheme. But that was owing to the erroneous nature of the system so long maintained by our purblind statesmen of allowing a single joint-stock bank to have a monopoly of banking in London, and preventing solid and powerful joint-stock banks being formed in the provinces, while every tinker and tailor, grocer and cheesemonger might issue unlimited torrents of notes at his own sweet will. But the question stands in a wholly different position at the present day There is nothing more odious and intolerable than privileges and monopolies in banking. No English-speaking race will tolerate a dominant bank. When the monopoly of the Bank of Scotland expired, and when it growled because another bank was founded, the republican spirit of the Scotch utterly scouted the idea that one set of persons should have a monopoly of banking. Sir Robert Peel, who in 1826 was keen in favor of the Scotch system of an equality of banks, in 1844 completely turned his back on himself, and cited the example of the United States. But unfortunately the Bank of the United States had failed, utterly insolvent, six years before; and its action and its influence had been condemned in the severest terms by the President and every independent writer in the country. The people of the United States will not tolerate a dominant bank. No English colony will tolerate a dominant bank. But the system exists in England, and therefore it must be dealt with cautiously, temperately and tenderly. If, during the long period of its monopoly, the bank had extended its branches into all the great provincial towns, as the Bank of France has done, the case might have been different. But it lost the opportunity and it can never return. By the breaches in its monopoly a vast number of joint-stock banks have grown up in London and the provinces, daily growing in magnitude and some even approaching in magnitude to the bank itself. The bank is therefore no longer the absolutely supreme power; it is only *primus inter pares.* Now, a bank in this position is wholly unable to bear the stupendous strain cast upon it in the crisis of 1890. The system of banking ought to be an aristocratic republic. All banks ought to act together as they wisely did in that year. The Bank of England, under present circumstances, is quite incompetent to support the whole banking and mercantile interests, as it used to have to do in former times. The banks must unite to support the mercantile community, as they did for the first time in the recent crisis, and to be able to do this effectually they should be on an equality.

There is nothing more odious and intolerable to English-speaking people than peculiar privileges and monopolies in banking. We freely admit that according to the prevailing ignorance on the whole subject, and according to his lights, the Bank Act of 1844 was probably the best thing that Sir Robert Peel could have done. But circumstances have changed. Floods of light have been thrown on the subject. The whole system of banking has been rapidly assuming a much healthier and more stable form, and the one it would have assumed in the course of nature, if it had not been forcibly prevented by law. Why then cling with fetish superstition to an act which is demonstrated to be founded on a whole series of erroneous theories, is in flat contradiction to all experience both preceding and subsequent to itself, and has failed in all the purposes it was intended to effect except one? The Bank Act of 1844 prohibited any new banks, private or joint-stock, formed after its date, from issuing notes; so that we have now a number of joint-stock banks which have the right to issue notes; and a great number of others, far larger and more powerful, which are prohibited from issuing notes. The National Provincial Bank was for many years allowed to issue notes to an unlimited extent; and never abused its rights. Now it is the greatest bank in England next to the Bank of England; and because it has greatly increased the solidity of the banking system by removing its head office to London, it has had to suppress an issue of £450,000 of notes in the provinces.

The fact is that the still prevailing feeling with respect to notes arises from the dangerous system on which they were formerly allowed to be issued, and a total misconception of the nature of banking. No one would dream of reviving the old system of allowing every small trader in the country to issue notes *ad libitum*. In fact, it was only tolerated in former times because powerful banks were not allowed to be formed. Again, banking is almost universally supposed to consist in "borrowing money from one set of persons and lending that same money to another set of persons." And Mill supposes that issuing notes is an extension of a banker's business—which is, no doubt, the popular idea. But as we have fully shown, this is a pure fallacy and delusion. The essential business of all banks is to issue circulating rights of action, credits or debts to their customers, recorded in the first instance as entries in their books, termed deposits, and their customers may circulate these rights of action, credits or debts, either by means of notes or cheques. It lies with the customer to determine whether he will circulate these credits by notes or cheques, and not with the banker. And notes and cheques are absolutely identical in law and economics. As a matter of fact, notes of late years have been constantly diminishing both in absolute and relative importance as compared with cheques. We believe that there is not a single bank in England, private or joint-stock, which has the right of issuing notes, which has in circulation anything like their legal maximum. The total amount of banking credits in the United Kingdom may be taken in round numbers as about £1,000,000,000. It is these banking credits which are, for all practical purposes, the current money of the country. And the amount of these banking credits, circulated by means of notes, is absolutely insignificant, as compared with those which are circulated by means of cheques. In Scotland, with banking credits to the amount of £95,000,000, there are only £5,000,000 of notes in circulation; because in recent times cheques have come greatly more into use in Scotland, and have superseded notes. A similar cause has greatly diminished the circulation of notes in England. And yet notes alone are the subject of alarm, and are held to be currency; and cheques are wholly overlooked and neglected; and it is supposed that it is only necessary to provide for the safety of notes. The truth is that banks must provide for the safety of the whole of their liabilities both notes and deposits. Now, while banks were few in number and confined to the rich, and moreover were isolated from each other, notes were the most convenient form of circulating banking credits. But now that banks have multiplied in number, and entered into relations with each other by means of clearing houses, when population has so vastly increased, and almost every one keeps a banking account, cheques have not only superseded notes to a vast extent, but have increased to an enormous amount; so that the quantity of notes is constantly diminishing and the quantity of cheques is constantly increasing; and both are equally currency and banking liabilities. It is not then in issuing notes at the present day that the great danger of bad banking consists; but in granting the original credit; and when the credit is once granted, it is wholly immaterial whether it is circulated by notes or cheques; the liability and the danger is exactly the same in either case.

Now there are certain circumstances, especially in commercial crises and in country districts, where the issue of notes is indispensable. To suppress £1 notes in Scotland would at once destroy one-third of the business of the banks, compel them to shut up multitudes of their branches, deprive large extents of thinly peopled districts of all banking accommodation, and compel the banks to keep double the quantity of gold they are now required to do under the present system. It is sometimes alleged that £1 notes tend to increase a panic; this no doubt was the case under the former system. But it is not the case when notes are issued by powerful and well organized banks like those of Scotland. When the Western Bank was known to be failing, the demand for gold was absolutely insignificant. When its customers drew their balances they took them in the bank's own notes and paid them into other banks. The other banks then called upon the Western Bank to meet its notes in the Clearing House in the usual way. This bank stopped payment, not from any run for gold, but from being unable to meet its exchanges. A certain number of banks still kept an insignificant amount of notes in circulation, which can only be done by the option of their customers. And it shows that their customers find notes more convenient than cheques. But the customers of non-issuing banks also want notes; and these banks are obliged to get them from the Bank of England. This is not only a heavy expense to themselves, but a severe strain on the resources of the Bank of England, because all the notes issued to the non-issuing banks are so much subtracted from the banking power of the Bank of England. Now, why should the customers of such splendid institutions as the National Provincial Bank, the London and County Bank, the Capital and Counties Bank, and many others, be deprived of the right of having the notes of these banks if they choose to have them? These banks are permitted to create banking credits to any unlimited amount they please; but directly it is proposed to allow their customers the choice between notes and cheques it sends a tremor of alarm through every old woman in the country of either sex.

Thus the whole question now stands on a totally different footing to what it did in former times. The subject, supposed to be so complicated and incomprehensible, is now reduced to the most perfect simplicity and the strictest scientific demonstration, which is now perfectly well understood. It is perfectly well recognized now that the whole mystery of banking consists in keeping strong reserves of specie as compared to total liabilities, notes and deposits, and steadily adjusting the rate of discount by the bullion in the bank and the state of the foreign exchanges. That is the whole secret of banking, and it was the ignorance and neglect of these principles which has been the cause of all the monetary panics during the last century.

It is the rate of discount, and not a cast-iron limit imposed on the issues of notes by the Bank of England, which is the true, sole and supreme controlling power of credit and the paper currency, and which is the true method of carrying into effect the principles of the Bullion Report and of Sir Robert Peel himself until 1844. It is these principles combined with the power to issue notes adequate to meet a commercial crisis, together with placing all the great leading London banks on an absolute equality, and so enabling them to act together instead of in antagonism to each other, as was too often the case formerly—though they cannot prevent commercial crises, which are innate in the modern system of credit, yet will forever avert a monetary panic.

It is then the very essence of banking reform that all joint-stock banks should be placed on an absolute equality like the Scotch banks, as Sir Robert Peel and all the statesmen of 1826 desired. But in order to effect this thorough and effectual banking reform, one thing is indispensable. It is that Government should pay off the public debt to the Bank of England. It is this debt which bars all reform. The act provides that all the privileges of the bank shall remain untouched until all the public debts to it are discharged. Chancellors of the Exchequer are apt to vaunt of the millions of the public debt they have paid off. It would have been infinitely more to the public advantage if they had paid off the comparatively trifling debt due to the bank. At all events, that is the point which all persons who are anxious to promote banking reform must steadily keep in view, and bring their influence to bear on the Government to effect. All mere tinkering with the present system, such as permitting the bank to issue two or three more millions of notes on public securities, is wholly ineffectual. It is not only utterly vicious and dangerous in itself, but the more it is extended the more dangerous it becomes. As a matter of fact, in a great monetary panic, this kind of property becomes absolutely unsalable and inconvertible. In the crisis of 1890, the action of the bank alone saved the world from the most terrific monetary panic recorded in history. But it ought not to be repeated. It is neither consistent with the dignity of this great mercantile country, nor with common sense, that the Bank of England should expose itself to the mockery and jeers of our not too ardent friends abroad, by running about to scrape up a few millions of gold on the Continent; when she had double the quantity required stored up in her own vaults which she could not touch. England ought to be sufficient for herself. Fortunately, the crisis took place in a time of profound peace. We fervently hope that we may maintain perpetual peace with our neighbors across the Channel. But who can tell how long this may last? Every one knows that the furies of revolution permeate every country on the Continent, and that they are only kept under restraint by the overwhelming hand of force. But this very force is an intolerable burden upon nations, and in process of time may break down from its own weight. How could the bank have effected its recent operation if we had been at war?—and in a period of war it would have been certain to happen.

No doubt, the proposal to restore the power of unlimited issues to the bank rouses alarm in many persons who have heard by dim tradition how the bank misused its powers during the present century. But these persons forget that the bank had powers of unlimited issues for more than a century, and used them with consummate skill. It was the suspension of cash payments in 1797, and the power of the bank to issue unlimited quantities of paper money that debauched the minds of the directors. Then, instead of controlling their issues by rule of thumb, which they had observed with the greatest success during a century, they maintained that they were no longer bound by these practical rules, but issued paper money and notes on certain theories which they formed out of their own imagination, each of which was supposed to be the perfection of wisdom by its inventors, and condemned as utterly erroneous by the succeeding generation. Adam Smith started the theory that it was perfectly safe to issue any amount of notes on the discount of good mercantile bills. This theory was maintained with exceeding pertinacity by the directors of the Bank of Ireland and the Bank of England; but it was utterly condemned by the Bullion Report, and by Mr. Horsley Palmer, the Governor of the Bank in 1832, who said that it was the worst method that could be conceived. Mr. Horsley Palmer, then, and his directors concocted a new theory, which was equally supposed to be the perfection of wisdom. But this theory utterly broke down in practice; and Lord Overstone, who certainly was a practical banker of the highest eminence, said that the wonder was, not that this theory had broken down in practice, but that it should ever have been thought of at all. Lord Overstone then concocted a wholly new set of theories of his own, which were embodied in the Bank Act of 1844—which was again supposed to be really the perfection of wisdom; and, by putting the bank in a strait waistcoat, had forever put an end to commercial crises. But, alas! the logic of facts blew all these theories to the winds; and showed that the very act which was supposed to have prevented all commercial crises, not only did not prevent them, but was the very thing which, when they reached a certain degree of intensity, surely and certainly, in exact fulfillment of the predictions of the highest authorities of former times, brought on a monetary panic. Thus the Bank Act of 1844 has gone the way of all its predecessors.

Many persons have implicit confidence in the consummate practical wisdom of Sir Robert Peel. But these persons are probably not aware that Sir Robert Peel had three totally different states of mind on the subject. In 1811 he was one of the majority who carried that unique vote that 27 equals 21. In 1819, he was converted, and became the ardent adherent of the doctrines of the Bullion Report, Horner, Huskisson, Ricardo, Thornton; and maintained these doctrines till 1844, when he delivered himself over, bound hand and foot, to the theories of Lord Overstone, Colonel Torrens and that sect. And we have shown that the doctrines of Lord Overstone were diametrically antagonistic to those of the Bullion Report.

In 1856, we demonstrated that all these great directorial banking theorists had entirely missed the true method of controlling credit and the paper currency—which is the rate of discount. And before the committee on the panic of 1857, Mr. George Warde Norman, who was an ardent adherent of the Bank Act of 1844, acknowledged that it was amply sufficient for all purposes. This is now universally recognized to be true; and the bank has been managed with the greatest success on this principle ever since 1857. Thus it is evident that the question of restoring the power of unlimited issues to the bank, when the true principle of controlling credit, which is acknowledged to be amply sufficient, is universally recognized and acted upon, stands upon a totally different footing now from what it did when the directors were deluded by a series of fantastic theories which utterly broke down in practice.

The power of unlimited issues is absolutely indispensable to enable the bank to meet a great emergency promptly and successfully, when millions of notes have to be issued without delay to avert a monetary panic, and perfectly safe when done under a high rate of discount, so as to prevent the exchanges being turned against the country. It is the completion and the coping-stone of the doctrines of the Bullion Report; and the theory of banking, credit, and the paper currency is now absolutely complete.

It has long been the fancy that the whole business of credit, banking, commercial crises, and monetary panics is pure haphazard empiricism and rule of thumb; and not capable of being brought to strict scientific demonstration. Considering the stupendous advance of modern times—when science is advancing by leaps and bounds and bringing under its dominion every department of human knowledge, and bringing under its sway subjects which would have been beyond the dreams of the most sagacious and far-seeing philosophers of the last century,—it would be fatuous to suppose that the human intellect is incapable of bringing economics, or the science of commerce or exchanges,—which is a pure science of facts—under the strictest scientific demonstration, if the same general methods are adopted as have been employed in every other department of knowledge which has been brought under scientific control and adapted to the peculiar circumstances of economics. It was the essential glory of Bacon, the founder of inductive philosophy, to foresee and proclaim with the voice of a trumpet that the same methods and principles by which the physical sciences were to be constructed were to be applied to the construction of all other sciences. And has not every economist of note, J. B. Say, John Stuart Mill, and hosts of others, maintained that economics can only be erected into a positive, definite science by following the same principles and methods by which the physical sciences have been constructed?—and if it has not hitherto been done, it is only from the inaptitude of those who have attempted it.

But the science of pure economics—that is, of commerce or exchanges, including credit, banking, the foreign exchanges, commercial crises and monetary panics—has now been brought to the strictest scientific demonstration, and its principles are now universally recognized and acknowledged to be true. Economics is a pure science of variable quantities. It is a science of causes and effects measured numerically, produced by the properties of men; and its types and standards of reasoning are to be found in the sciences which treat of the causes and effects measured numerically, produced by the properties of material substances. The special science of variable quantities, termed economics, must be governed by the rules which govern the science of variable quantities in general. The principles which govern the varying relations of economic quantities must be the same which govern the varying relations of the stars in their courses. The same general method of investigation is common to them all. In all, the inductive logic reigns supreme. A new inductive science is created, and a new monument raised to the everlasting glory of the monarch of philosophy.

It only remains to bring banking legislation into harmony with the demonstrated and acknowledged principles of economic science. Nor is it any part of our duty to suggest how that is to be done. Our duty is solely to set forth the true scientific principles of the subject. It is the part of the highest and most responsible statesmen and financial authorities to determine and devise the measures by which banking legislation is to be brought into harmony with demonstrated economic science. The wisdom of statesmen, in this country at least, has been usually Epimethean. It would redound to the immortal honor of a powerful government for once to display Promethean wisdom, and bring the banking system of this country into harmony with demonstrated scientific truth, before another catastropne arrives, and to create a system which would last to the end of time.

CHAPTER II.

BANKING IN SCOTLAND.

The Beginnings of Banking—The First Bank Charter—Attempts at Monopoly in Banking—Creation of the Royal Bank—Great Over-Issue of Notes—Their Consequent Depreciation—Statute of 1765, to Cure the Depreciation—Currency Restored to Par Permanently—The Notorious Ayr Bank—Great Revival of Prosperity, from Sound Banking—Suspension of Gold Payments by the Three Public Banks—A Clearing House Established—Eulogium by the House of Lords on Scottish Methods.

UP till 1695, there were no such persons as "bankers" in Scotland. The records of commerce are so scanty, that we are unable to say whether the custom of discounting bills of exchange had been introduced into Scotland before then. But if there were any persons who discounted bills of exchange, they did so with the money itself, and therefore they were technically money lenders or bill discounters, and not "bankers," who, as we have shown, invariably purchase money and debts by issuing their own circulating credit in exchange for them.

The successful institution of the Bank of England led to the project being formed to establish a bank in Scotland. Mr. John Holland, a merchant of London, was the author of the scheme, and he got eleven Scottish merchants to join him. On the 17th July, 1695, they obtained an act of the Scottish Parliament, authorizing the Crown to grant them a charter of incorporation. They were however purely a private company, and had no connection with the State. The authorized capital was £100,000, and they received a monopoly for twenty-one years.

As the Scots were supposed to know nothing about banking, it was provided that, for a certain number of years, the governor and twelve directors should be English, and the deputy governor and twelve directors should be Scots. However, it was soon found that the Scots took so kindly to the business that the arrangements were changed, and all the directors were

Scots; but thirteen trustees were chosen to manage the English business and affairs in London. The first call was for £10,000. The bank at first received no money from the public. They found that, on the subscription paid in by their shareholders, they could maintain £50,000 of their notes in circulation, which John Law justly said was equivalent to an augmentation of capital to the country. Their notes were at first for £100, £50, £20, £10 and £5.

In 1696, they opened branches at Glasgow, Aberdeen, Dundee and Montrose, but not finding them to pay withdrew them. In 1704 they began to issue £1 notes. It appears that, up to this time, their profits were very large. A rival pamphlet states the dividends at thirty-five, forty and fifty per cent., and accordingly these profits attracted competition. In 1716, the monopoly of banking granted by their charter expired, and no attempt was made to renew it. Several bodies of persons tried to force an amalgamation with them, but their offers were steadily refused.

At the time of the Union a considerable number of persons, both civil and military, were creditors of the Crown; and the equivalent sum stipulated by the act of Parliament was not sufficient to discharge their claims. In 1714, they obtained an act of Parliament to constitute their debts; but no Parliamentary provision was made to satisfy them till 1719, when £10,000 was set apart for the purpose, to be paid annually in preference to all other claims. The act of 1719 empowered his Majesty to incorporate the proprietors of the debt into a body politic or corporate, with powers to do and perform all matters appertaining to them to do, touching or concerning the said capital sum, and the yearly sum payable in respect thereof, as his Majesty by the said letters patent should think fit to grant. In pursuance of this act, the proprietors were incorporated in 1724.

This was one of the bodies of persons who tried to force themselves on the Bank of Scotland. When they were repulsed by the bank, they petitioned the King to grant them powers of banking. This petition came to the knowledge of the bank in 1726, and they did everything they could to oppose it. A cry was got up against them that they were hostile to the House of Hanover; that they charged too high interest for their loans; that they were too particular in the securities they required; that they would not lend on their own stock, and other things. To all these various charges they, or a friend for them, replied. They said that such a thing as two banks in one country was never heard of, and that if Scotland had two banks, England should have ten. By this time they had called up three-tenths of their capital, or £30,000, and they alleged that that was sufficient to circulate all the credit that could be required in Scotland. They very justly said: "For the quota of credit in a banking company must be *proportioned to the stock of specie in the nation*, learned and understood by long experience, and not extended to a capital stock subscribed for, which cannot in the least help to support the company's credit, if the specie in a nation decay."

The last call which had been made was partly paid up in the bank's own notes, just as the subscription to the new stock of the Bank of England had been partly paid up in its own notes. An outcry was raised against this, but the directors well answered: "But the objectors do not at all consider this point. For the payments are many of them made in specie, and bank notes are justly reckoned the same as specie, when paid in on a call of stock; because, when paid in, it lessens the demand on the bank. Thus the directors, from their own mercantile instinct, and equally innocent of Roman law and the profound principles of algebra which were not then discovered, perceived the great doctrine of Roman law that the *release of a debt* is in all respects equivalent to a *payment* in money: or that $- \times - = + \times +$. It was also said: "A certain stock of specie circulating in the country is needful for currency of payments in markets, and among the meaner sort of people, bearing a due proportion to what is running on paper credit upon the faith of the banking company. Notwithstanding the opposition of the Bank of Scotland, the charter with the powers of banking was issued to the Equivalent Company on the 8th of July, 1727, with a capital stock of £151,000.

Granting that all the charges against the Bank of Scotland were futile and groundless, we may well rejoice that its monopoly was not allowed to continue. A writer who professed to be independent of either bank touched the right point in reply to a statement on behalf of the old bank: "The power of monopolies is, I believe, an exploded doctrine. Did ever any nation make an exclusive bank perpetual, or for longer than twenty-one years—or, if such an instance can be given, was the measure right? * * * If the old bank should reply, 'We are in possession, and what have we done to have our possession disturbed?' the answer upon the abstract question is plain by another question, '*What have we, the other subjects, done to be secluded; or by what law are we secluded from the advantages you enjoy*'?" The writer then says, after comparing the rival companies: "The obvious reflection which arises from comparing these two is, that these candid and fair dealers have also dealt profitably for themselves, as is but reasonable. They have taken very good payment for all the services they have done to the nation; and what title they, or any other set of men, have to an hereditary or indefeasible monopoly of banking, is hard to understand. * * * As ready as our Parliament was at the Union to accommodate petitioners, *a perpetual monopoly of banking was a thing so manifestly pernicious, that no private* man could have the assurance to aim at it, far less could any parliament be so unthinking as to grant it."

On the south of the Tweed, there was found a parliament so unthinking as to grant a monopoly of banking to a single company for 130 years, and the consequences fully justified the opinions of the sagacious Scot. A monopoly in banking is as utterly pernicious as any of the monopolies which the parliaments of Elizabeth and James I. rebelled against. Scotsmen may feel justly proud that they resisted it from the beginning. Scotland was allowed to develop her system of banking by the talents of her native men of business, unmeddled with by Parliament; and it is now recognized and admitted by all persons of authority that she possesses the best organized system of credit and banking in the world. The alarm and jealousy created by the new bank soon wore off, as it was discovered that, so far from injuring the old bank, the inevitable consequence followed, which an enlarged experience of commerce would have enabled us to predict; it increased the prosperity of both banks. The stock of the old bank rose to 400 per cent. and that of the new bank also rose very high.

The Royal Bank, as it was named, had only been in existence two years when it invented a further development of the system of banking which, in the unanimous judgment of all persons who know that country, has done more to develop its resources and promote its agricultural and general prosperity than any cause whatever. This is the system of cash accounts, or cash credits, of which we have given a full exposition elsewhere. This system deserves the most attentive consideration, because it is entirely of the nature of accommodation paper, which has fallen into such disrepute in England from the enormous abuses of it which have taken place. It also realizes all the advantages which are practicable from the schemes of land banks, which were devised by the seething brains of Chamberlen, Briscoe, Law and others. It has advanced the wealth of Scotland by centuries. It is a striking instance of the aphorism of Demosthenes: "If you were ignorant of this, that credit is the greatest capital of all towards the acquisition of wealth, you would be utterly ignorant"; and of the aphorism of Daniel Webster: "Credit has done more a thousand times to enrich nations than all the mines of all the world."

In 1731, the Bank of Scotland again tried to establish branches at Glasgow, Aberdeen and Dundee; but, after two years, was obliged to discontinue them, and the plan was not tried again till 1774. The unlimited power of issuing "promises to pay," placed in the hands of hostile parties who had not acquired sufficient practical experience of the subject, naturally led to great over-issues. To protect themselves from the consequences of these over-issues, as well as from the attacks of each other, the Bank of Scotland, in 1730, introduced a clause into their notes, making them payable at the option of the directors at the end of six months after demand, with the legal interest up to that time. This practice was adopted by all the other banks; for the manifest advantages of banking were so strikingly displayed that, after the expiring of the monopoly of the Bank of Scotland, banking companies started up in all directions, and inundated the country with their notes. When the holders of the notes demanded payment of them, the companies threatened to take advantage of the optional clause, unless the demanders would content themselves with a part of what they wanted. Moreover, as there was no restraint on the amount of their notes, many of the companies issued notes for 10s., 5s. and even lower than that. In Perthshire, there were notes for 1s. and even for 1d.; and the Perth

Banking Company was founded partly to put an end to that nuisance. The inevitable consequences followed; these paper notes drove all the gold and silver out of the country, and the exchange with London fell. Adam Smith says: "While the exchange between London and Carlisle was at par, that between London and Dumfries would sometimes be four per cent. against Dumfries, though this town is not thirty miles from Carlisle. But, at Carlisle, bills were paid in gold and silver; whereas, at Dumfries, they were paid in Scotch bank notes; and the uncertainty of getting these notes exchanged for gold and silver coin had thus degraded them four per cent. below the value of coin." At this time, owing to the degraded state of the English coin, the foreign exchanges were against England; and the market price of gold was £4 per ounce; so that the whole depreciation was about six and a-half per cent. Thus, we see that the Scottish bank notes were practically inconvertible; and, in reality, bills of exchange were payable six months after demand—a circumstance of great importance, and one which must be specially observed, as this instance was brought forward by Sir Robert Peel in introducing the Bank Act of 1844, and he was not rightly informed of the circumstances.

The manifest consequences of this state of matters followed. All the gold left the country, as it always does from an excessive issue of inconvertible paper, and the banks were all obliged to employ agents in London to collect money for them at an expense of seldom less than one and a-half or two per cent. Adam Smith says: "This money was sent down by the wagon, and insured by the carriers at an additional expense of three-quarters per cent., or 15s. on the £100. These agents were not always able to replenish the coffers of their employers as fast as they were emptied. In this case, the resource of the banks was to draw upon their correspondents in London bills of exchange to the extent of the sum they required. When these correspondents afterwards drew upon them for the payment of this sum, together with the interest and commission, some of these banks—from the distress into which their excessive circulation had thrown them—had sometimes no other means of satisfying this draft but by drawing a second set of bills either upon the same or upon some other correspondents in London; and the same sum, or rather bills for the same sum, would in this manner make more than two or three journeys, the debtor bank always paying the interest and commission upon the whole accumulated sum. The gold coin which was paid out, either by the Bank of England or by the Scotch banks, in exchange for that part of their paper which was over and above what could be employed in the circulation of the country, being likewise over and above what could be employed in that circulation, was sometimes sent abroad in the shape of coin; sometimes melted down and sent abroad in the shape of bullion, and sometimes melted down and sold to the Bank of England at the high price of £4 per ounce. It was the newest, the heaviest and the best pieces only which were carefully picked out of the old coin, and either sent abroad or melted down at home; and while they remained in the shape of coin, those heavy pieces were of no more value than the light, but they were of more value abroad or when melted down into bullion at home."

At this period, the Scottish banks had got themselves into a very alarming condition, from their ignorance of the true principles of regulating a paper currency, as well as of the effect of an excessive issue of inconvertible paper in depressing the exchanges and causing an export of gold; and not perceiving that, while in this state, bringing gold into the country was like pouring water into a sieve, like the toil of the Danaides. They had been far too prodigal in granting cash credits and allowing them to be converted into dead loans, without observing the rules which were specially applicable to them. And everything seemed to show that matters would get worse, as numerous other companies were forming to add to the currency, which was already excessive. United in a common danger, the two principal banks agreed to combine their influence and obtain an act to put a stop to the abuse. By their influence the Act, Statute 1765, c. 49, was passed, suppressing all notes under 20s. and prohibiting these to be issued with the optional clause, and enacting that all such notes should be payable to the bearer on demand. The banks also curtailed their cash credits very extensively and called up fresh capital. Owing to these combined measures, silver immediately reappeared in circulation; the value of the Scottish currency was restored to par, and from that time to the present, although the issue of bank notes was absolutely free until 1845, the Scottish currency has never varied from par.

The Bank of Scotland and the Royal Bank continued to be the only chartered banks in Scotland till 1746. In that year the British Linen Company was incorporated for the purpose of carrying on the manufacture of linen and banking in connection with it. The company, however, soon found, what ample experience has since confirmed, that the same company should never carry on banking and another business at the same time. They soon found it expedient to discontinue their linen manufacture and confine themselves to banking; and it has since become one of the most powerful and wealthy of the Scottish banks, but it did not introduce any new feature into Scottish banking. These three banks, the Bank of Scotland, the Royal Bank and the British Linen Bank, are the only banks in Scotland which are constituted with the full powers and privileges of a corporation—that is, their liability is limited to the amount of their subscription; and the members are not liable, in their private capacity, for the debts of the corporation beyond their subscribed stock.

In 1770, that abominable system of accommodation paper, which is the sure precursor of mercantile convulsion, was first fully manifested on a great scale. The Scottish banks had learned a very wholesome lesson, and contracted their issues within the bounds of prudence. This was a source of prodigious annoyance and vexation to a multitude of speculators and adventurers. The increased prudence which the banks exercised in granting advances, not only alarmed but enraged their projectors in the highest degree. Adam Smith (*Wealth of Nations*, Bk. II. ch. 2) gives a long account of the circumstances of the country at this period, and describes the foundation of a new bank, the notorious Ayr Bank, which was designed to remedy the distress which was owing, its projectors said, to the ignorance, pusillanimity and bad conduct of the banks, which did not give a sufficiently liberal aid to the spirited undertakings of those who exerted themselves in order to beautify, improve and enrich the country. This new bank comprised the Duke of Hamilton and many other proprietors of immense wealth, and it was based upon the fallacy that, because the capital and property of its proprietors was undoubted, it might therefore issue notes to any extent without depreciation. It was the avowed principle of this bank to advance upon any reasonable security the whole capital which was to be employed in these improvements, of which the returns are the most slow and distant, such as the improvements on land. This bank accordingly issued its notes with the utmost profusion, and very soon found them coming back on it for payment. To meet these demands, it began to draw upon London; and when the bill became due, it paid it by another bill, together with interest and commission. It continued to exist for two years, and it had then £200,000 of its notes in circulation and £600,000 in drafts upon London, for which it paid eight per cent. in interest and commission, while it gained five per cent. on its own notes.

The exports of 1771 and 1772 rose to a height which they did not again reach till 1787. While commerce was in this apparently prosperous, but in reality, bloated and diseased condition, on the 10th June, 1772, a partner in one of the great London banks, Neale & Co., decamped with £300,000. This man was a Scotsman named Forsyth, who had a large Scottish connection; these were blown upon by the failure of their London agent, and a complete commercial panic set in. The Ayr Bank had branches in Edinburgh and Dumfries. On the 17th a run began on its Edinburgh branch, and it stopped payment on the 25th, along with a crowd of speculators. The whole of Scotland was shaken to its foundation. The liabilities of the Ayr Bank amounted to £800,000. There had been no disaster similar to it since the Darien scheme, and there was none like it again till the failure of the Western Bank. The credit even of the other banks was almost gone. Besides the three public banks, only three private ones survived. It is said that the winding up of this unfortunate bank was not completed until 1830.

By the Act, Statute 1774, c. 32, the Bank of Scotland was authorized to double its capital. At this time the least fear of any Jacobite rising had died away. The measures taken after the suppression of the rising in 1746 had introduced peace and civilization into the remotest districts of the Highlands. Scotland shared in the great outburst of industrial energy which had developed itself in England, and had been the cause of the immense multiplication of country bankers. In this year, the Scottish banks began to throw out branches in all directions to promote agricultural improvements, and henceforth Scotland increased in wealth by gigantic strides produced by the system of cash credits. By the Act, Statute 1784, c. 12, the capital of the Bank of Scotland was raised to £300,000. By the Act, Statute 1792, c. 25 it was raised to £600,000; and by the Act, Statute 1794, c. 19, it was raised to £1,000,000; and by the Act, Statute 1804, c. 23, it was raised to £1,500,000, of which £1,000,000 was called up. All this shows how the industry of the country was increasing.

The news of the suspension of cash payments by the Bank of England in 1797 reached Edinburgh on the 1st March. The managers of the public banks met at Sir William Forbes' to consider what was to be done. It was agreed to follow the example of the Bank of England and suspend all payments in cash. A public meeting of the principal inhabitants was called by the Lord Provost, and attended by the Lord President of the Court of Session and the other dignitaries. The meeting came to the unanimous resolution to support the credit of the banks and to receive their notes as specie. This resolution was advertised in the papers and sent to all the principal towns. This resolution caused a little commotion at first, but it soon subsided; and during all the period of the revolutionary war the suspension of cash payments continued; and not a single action was ever brought against them to enforce payment, although they were unprotected by any act of Parliament; and in a short time business proceeded more prosperously than ever. By the admirable system of the Clearing House, which the Edinburgh banks had adopted in 1776, the Scottish bank note currency never varied from par with the Bank of England note. The next occurrence which we may mention was the foundation of the Commercial Bank in 1810. At this time the high Tory *regime* was at its highest and palmiest state, and the banks were alleged to carry their politics into their business. Whig bills of exchange were looked upon with very cold and unfavorable eyes. The Whig party then determined to found an opposition bank, which was named the Commercial, which has since attained as high an estimation as any of the older ones in public opinion. This bank subsequently obtained a charter, but the liability of its shareholders was specially declared to be unlimited.

The long and dreadful catalogue of failures in England in 1825, chiefly caused by the monopoly of the Bank of England preventing large and solid banks being founded, and which were attributed to the issues of £1 notes by the country bankers, caused the Ministry to intend to abolish £1 notes in Scotland and Ireland at the same time as they did those of England. But this raised such a ferment, headed by Sir Walter Scott, that the Government consented that committees of both Houses should be appointed to consider the subject. The result was so eminently favorable to the Scottish banking system, which had been freely developed by practical men of business without the interference of the Legislature, that the attempt was abandoned. The report of the Lords said that: "With respect to Scotland, it is to be remarked that during the period from 1766 to 1797, when no small notes were by law issuable in England, the portion of the currency of Scotland in which payments under £5 were made continued to consist almost entirely of notes of £1 and £1 1s.; and that no inconvenience is known to have resulted from this difference in the currency of the two countries. This circumstance, among others, tends to prove that uniformity, however desirable, is not indispensably necessary. It is also proved by the evidence and by the documents that the banks of Scotland, whether chartered or joint-stock companies or private establishments, have for more than a century exhibited a stability which the committee believe to be unprecedented in the history of banking; that they supported themselves from 1797 to 1812 without any protection from the restriction by which the Bank of England and that of Ireland were relieved from cash payments; that there was little demand for gold during the late embarrassments in the circulation, and that, in the whole period of their establishment, there are not more than two or three instances of failure. As, during the whole of this period, a large portion of their issues consisted almost entirely of notes not exceeding £1 or £1 1s., there is the strongest reason for concluding that, as far as respects the banks of Scotland, the issue of paper of that description has been found compatible with the highest degree of solidity; and that there is not, therefore, while they are conducted upon their present system, sufficient ground for proposing any alteration with the view of adding to a solidity which has so long been sufficiently established." The report of the committee was adverse to any legislative interference with the system of Scottish banking. This report is somewhat too *couleur de rose*, inasmuch as it takes no notice of the dreadful catastrophe of the Ayr Bank. It is known as a fact that a whole multitude of joint-stock and private banks started up in Scotland during the period of great industrial energy after 1766, but we are not aware that there is any record of their numbers. But, in 1826, besides the three public chartered banks with forty-four branches, there were twenty-two joint-stock banks with ninety-seven branches, and eleven private bankers in Scotland, or in all 194 banking offices.

No interference with Scottish banking took place till 1845, when Sir Robert Peel, having carried his Bank of England Charter Act and Joint-Stock Banking Act, which has since been totally repealed, with scarcely a breath of opposition, determined to regulate those of Scotland and Ireland as well. The principal provisions of this Act, Statute 1845, c. 38, are as follows:

(1.) All persons had been prohibited by the Statute 1844, c. 32, from commencing to issue notes after the 6th May, 1844, in the United Kingdom, and all such persons in Scotland as were lawfully issuing their notes between the 6th May, 1844, and the 1st May, 1845, were to certify to the Commissioners of Stamps and Taxes the name of the firm and the places where they issued such notes.

(2.) The commissioners were to ascertain the average number of such bankers' notes in circulation during the year preceding the 1st May, 1845.

(3.) Such bankers were authorized to have in circulation an amount of notes, whose average for four weeks was not to exceed the amount thus certified by the commissioners, together with an amount equal to the average amount of coin held by the banker during the same four weeks. Of the coin, three-fourths must be gold and one-fourth silver.

(4.) In case the bank exceeds the legal amount, it is to forfeit the excess.

(5.) If two or more banks unite, they are authorized to have an issue of paper to the aggregate amount of issues of the separate banks, as well as the amount of the coin held by the united bank.

(6.) Notes of the Bank of England not to be legal tender in Scotland.

The reader will see that there are some striking points of difference between the restraints laid upon the English and Scottish banks; for, while the former are bound down to an absolute fixed limit of issue, the latter are permitted to issue to any amount, provided they hold an equal amount of coin above their authorized issue. Moreover, if any number of banks unite, they may have an aggregate authorized issue equal to that of the separate banks; but in England, if the number of partners of the united bank exceeds ten, they forfeit their power of issuing notes altogether. This absurd restriction as to the number of partners in a bank was never in force in Scotland, and is simply one of the methods by which the banking system of England was sacrificed to the Bank of England. It must be observed that the coin required to be held against the amount of notes in circulation above their authorized issue is in no way appropriated to their payment of these notes; it is merely a rough-and-ready method of compelling them to hold a greater amount of gold in proportion to their general liabilities. Whether this act has in any way conduced to the greater security of the Scottish banks, we will not take upon ourselves to say. All we can say is, that the two most dreadful calamities in Scottish banking, many times exceeding that of the Ayr Bank, have occurred since it was enacted. But it is the cause of one great nuisance. All payments in Scotland are made at two fixed terms—the 15th of May and the 11th of November. To effect these payments the banks have to issue millions of notes, which are emitted and get into circulation in the morning and are retired before evening. But for this one day's issue of the notes it is necessary to have an equal amount of gold to back them. So millions of gold are sent down to Scotland from the Bank of England, and having lain a short time in the vaults of the Scottish banks, are trundled back again to London. The terrible catastrophe of the City of Glasgow Bank in 1878 produced a complete change in the constitution of all the joint-stock banks in the United Kingdom. Their shareholders compelled them to adopt the principle of limited liability. But we shall defer the consideration of this question to a later chapter.

The following table exhibits the position of all the Scottish banks on the 19th October, 1895:

Condition of Joint-Stock Banks of Scotland, October 19, 1895; Including 10 Banks and 1008 Branches.

Market Value of Entire Paid-up Capital	£26,890,500
Capital subscribed	29,135,000
Capital paid up	9,302,000
Total Capital Liability (callable and reserved)	19,833,000
Reserve Fund	5,717,879
Dividend and Undivided Profits	936,415
Notes in Circulation	6,733,523
Acceptance Liabilities	2,981,638
Miscellaneous Liabilities, Credits, Rebate, etc.	1,177,174
Deposit and Current Accounts	93,489,068
Total Liabilities	£120,337,697
Cash on hand and Money at Call and Short Notice	22,165,770
British Government Securities	10,486,946
Bonds, Stocks and other Investments	20,581,096
Discounts	16,389,601
Advances, Loans, Bills and other Securities	44,354,351
Buildings, Cover for Acceptances, Sundries	6,359,933
Total Assets	£120,337,697

CHAPTER III.

THE THEORY AND MECHANISM OF BANKING.

ON THE MEANING OF THE WORD BANK.

BEFORE we proceed to explain the mechanism and effects of banking, we must ascertain the meaning of the word bank, because great misconception prevails respecting it. At one time, there was considerable discussion in Italy as to the origin of the word Banco. Many writers said it came from "abacus," a calculating machine. But Muratori entirely disapproves of such a derivation. "To me, on the contrary," he says, "the word seems to have come from the German word banck, which is a very ancient word in that language"; and he says that the term was first used for a store of goods in the town of Brescia. Ducange also says: "Bank is of Franco-German, or Saxon, origin; no other is to be sought for." There is no doubt whatever that these learned authors are right. The word banck in German has two meanings: (1). A heap or mound, like a sand-bank; hence a store, like the goods in a shop. (2) A bench or seat; because the surface of a sandbank is usually smooth and level. Many writers who are not acquainted with the technicalities of business suppose that the word bank as a place of business comes from the second of these meanings; because they suppose that the "banco" was the counter upon which the money-changers kept their money. But the technical meaning of the word banking, and the invariable meaning of the term as used by the Italian economistes, and the invariable meaning of the word when it was first introduced into English, conclusively prove that the preceding opinion is erroneous; and that, as a technical term in commerce, it is derived from the first of the meanings given above—*i. e.*, a heap or mound.

The word bank originated in this way. In 1171, the City of Venice was at war both with the Empires of the East and the West. Its finances were in a state of great disorder, and the Great Council levied a forced loan of one per cent. on all the property of the citizens, and promised them interest at the rate of five per cent. Commissioners were appointed to manage the loan, who were called "*Camera degli Imprestiti.*" Such a loan has several names in Italian, such as "*Compera,*" "*Mutuo,*" etc.; but the most usual name is "*Monte,*" a joint-stock fund. This first loan was called the "*Monte Vecchio,*" or the old loan; subsequently two other similar loans were contracted, and called the "*Monte Nuovo*" and the "*Monte Nuovissimo.*" In exchange for the money, which became the actual property of the Government to be employed for public purposes, the citizens received stock certificates, or credits, which they might transfer to any one else; and the commissioners kept an office for the transfer of the stock and the payment of the dividends. At this time, the Germans were masters of a great part of Italy, and the German word banck, meaning a heap, or mound, came to be used simultaneously with monte, and was Italianized into banco, and the public loans were called indifferently monti and banchi.

It was this office, the Chamber of Loans, which such multitudes of writers have supposed was the famous Bank of Venice. But this is a complete mistake. It was in no sense a bank, in the modern meaning of the word; it was simply the National Debt office; similar to the National Debt office of the Bank of England; it was the origin of the funding system. Thus in the "Volpone" of Ben Jonson, the scene of which is laid in Venice, Volpone says: "I turn no monies in the public bank"—meaning, "I do not dabble in the Venetian funds." So an English writer, Benbrigge, in 1646, speaks of the "three bankes" at Venice—meaning the three public loans or monti. So in Florian and Torriani's Italian Dictionary, published in 1659, it says: "Monte, or standing bank, or mount of money, as they have in divers cities in Italy." That the word *banco* in Italian means a public debt might be proved by numberless quotations. Thus a recent writer, Cibrario, says (*Economia Politica del medio evo*): "Regarding the theory of credit, which I have said was invented by the Italian cities, it is known that the first bank or public debt (*il primo banco o debito publico*) was erected in Venice in 1171. In the thirteenth century paper money is mentioned at Milan; the credit was paid off. A monte or public debt (*un monte o debito publico*) was founded in Florence in 1336." This passage shows that banco is the equivalent of monte, and of a public debt. At Genoa, during the wars of the fourteenth century, the Bank of St. George was formed of the creditors of the State.

Every economist in the south of Europe knows that the word bank means a public debt. Thus the distinguished Spanish economist, Olozaga, speaking of the Venetian loans, says: "El Monte Vecchio (Banco Viejo). * * * el Monte Nuevo (Banco Nuevo)." So Baretti's Italian Dictionary 1839, says: "Monte, a bank where they lend or take money at interest." So Evelyn speaks of the Monte di Pietà at Padua, where there is a continual bank of money to assist the poor. So Blackstone says: "At Florence, in 1344, Government owed £60,000, and being unable to pay it, formed the principal into an aggregate sum, called metaphorically a mount or bank." Every one acquainted with the writings of the Italian economists knows that they invariably use the words monte and banchi as absolutely synonymous; but I am informed by my friend Professor Loria of Sienna that the word monte is not used now in Italian for a bank. This was also the meaning of the word bank when it was first introduced into English. Thus Bacon says: "Let it be no bank or common stock." So Gerard Malynss says: "Mons Pietatis, or bank of charity. In Italy there are Montes Pietatis; that is tc say, mounts or banks of charity." Benbrigge, in his *Usura Accommodata,* 1646, says: "For their rescue may be collected *Mons Pietatis sive Charitatis,* or banks of piety or charitatis, as they of Trent fitly call it." Again, "For borrowers in trade for their supply, as their occasion shall require, may be erected *Mons Negotionis* or banke of trade." Tolet says: "*Mons fidei,* a banke of trust which Clement XII. instituted at Rome; he that put his money into this banke was never to take it out again"; for which the lender received seven per cent. interest, like the subscribers to the original Bank of England stock. He also speaks of *Mons Recuperationis,* or banke of recovery, in which the interest was twelve per cent. The difference between these two, which were public debts, was that the first was a perpetual annuity, and the second a terminable annuity, in which the higher rate of payment was repayment of the principal.

In the time of Cromwell, several proposals were made for erecting public banks. Samuel Lambe, a London merchant, recommending them in 1658, says: "A bank is a certain number of sufficient men of estates and credit joint together in joint stock; being as it were the general cash keepers or treasurers of that place where they are settled, letting out imaginary money (*i. e.*, credit) at interest at two and a-half or three per cent. to tradesmen or others, who agree with them for the same, and making payment thereof by assignation, and passing each man's account from one to another with much facility and ease." So Francis Cradocke, a London merchant who was appointed a member of the Board of Trade by Charles II., strongly advocated the introduction of banks into England, and says: "A banke is a certain number of sufficient men of credit joined together in a stock, as it were, for keeping several men's cash in one treasury, and letting out imaginary money (*i. e.*, credit) at interest for three or more in the hundred per annum, to tradesmen or others that agree with them for the same; and making payment by assignation, passing each man's account from one to another, yet paying little money." And he says that, "the aforesaid bankers may furnish another petty bank (or mount) of charity." Thus these writers perfectly well understood the nature and constitution of a bank. They knew well that the function of a bank is to advance imaginary money, or credit, and not metallic money, as is the popular delusion of the present day. In a little tract, entitled "*A Discourse Concerning Banks,*" and supposed to be by a director of the Bank of England, we find this description: "There are three kinds of banks; the first for the mere deposit of money [like those of Venice, Amsterdam, Hamburg, etc.]; the second for profit. The banks of the second kind, called in Italy *Monti* [*i. e.,* public debts], which are for the benefit of the income only, are the Banks of Rome, Bologna and Milan. These banks were made up of a number of persons who, in time of war or other exigencies of State, advanced sums of money upon funds granted *in perpetuum,* but redeemable. * * * The third kind of banks, which were both for the convenience of the public and the advantage of the undertakers, are the several banks of Naples, the Bank of St. George at Genoa, and one of the banks of Bologna. These banks having advanced sums of money at their establishments, did not only agree for a fund of perpetual interest, but were allowed the privilege of keeping cash."

The Bank of England was of this last kind. It was a company of persons who advanced a sum of money to the Government and received in exchange for it a perpetual annuity, or a right to receive forever a series of annual payments from the State. This annuity is in legal phrase termed a bank annuity; in popular language, "The Funds." There has only been one instance in England of a bank which did not receive cash from the public. Some time after the foundation of the Bank of England, a company of persons united to advance a million pounds to the Government. They were incorporated as the "Million Bank." This company existed till nearly the end of the last century, and thus it resembled the original Bank of Venice. Thus, from these passages, and many more might be cited if necessary, it is perfectly clear that the word bank, as a term in commerce, is the equivalent of monte; and meant a joint-stock fund contributed by a number of persons. So when the word bank was introduced into our American colonies before the Revolutionary War, Professor Sumner says ("History of American Currency," p. 6, n.): "Bank, as the word was used before the Revolutionary War, meant only a batch of paper money, issued either by the Government or a corporation. The impression seems to have remained popular that the essential idea of a bank is the issuing of notes. * * * The notes issued in 'banks,' or masses, as loans were pure paper money." So, in a valuable history of the notes issued in the United States, it says that an issue of paper money to the amount of £50,000, authorized to be issued by the Treasury, was styled a bank.

The essential feature of all these "banks" was this: The subscribers advanced the money as a loan or *mutuum;* it thus became the absolute property of the borrowers, and in exchange for their money the lenders received a credit—*i. e.*, a certificate, or promise to pay interest, which they might transfer to anyone else. And those persons whose business it was to trade like these banks—*i. e.,* to buy money and in exchange for it to issue credit of various sorts—were termed "bankers," and only those. Thus, as a technical term in business, to "bank," means to issue credit.

ON THE MEANING OF THE WORD BANKER.

Here, again, great misconception prevails as to the meaning of the word banker and the nature of the business of banking. Gilbert says: "A banker is a dealer in capital; or, more properly, a dealer in money. He is an intermediate party between the borrower and the lender. He borrows of one party and lends to another; and the difference between the terms at which he borrows and those at which he lends forms the source of his profit." So a report of the House of Commons says: "The use of money, and that only, they regard as the province of a bank, whether of a private person or incorporation, or the banking department of the Bank of England." Notwithstanding the apparently high authority of these passages, which have misled so many unwary persons, these descriptions of the nature of the business of banking are entirely erroneous. In former times, there were many persons who acted as intermediaries between persons who wanted to lend and those who wanted to borrow. They were called "money scriveners." The father of John Milton was a money scrivener, but no one ever called a money scrivener a banker. At the present day, many firms of solicitors act as intermediaries between persons who wish to lend and others who wish to borrow. They may have some clients who wish to lend and other clients who want to borrow; and they act as agents between them. The first set of clients may entrust their money to the firm to lend to the second set, and the solicitors receive a commission on the sums which pass through their hands. But no one ever called a firm of solicitors who transact such business "bankers"; which shows that there is an essential distinction between the business of money scriveners and such a firm of solicitors and the business of "bankers." Solicitors who transact such agency business do not acquire any property in the money which passes through their hands. They receive it merely as a bailment or a depositum. They are only the custodians or the trustees of the money; and it is only entrusted to their custody for the express purpose of being applied in a particular way. The actual property in the money passes directly from the lender to the borrower through the medium of the trustees or bailees, and if the latter appropriated the money in any way to their own purposes it would be a felony, and they would be liable to be punished for embezzlement. But the case of a banker is wholly different. When his customers pay in money to their account they cede the property in the money to the banker. The money placed with him is not a depositum or a bailment; it is a *mutuum* or *creditum;* it is a "loan" or sale of the money directly to himself. The banker is not the bailee or trustee of the money, but its actual proprietor. He may trade with it or employ it in any way he pleases for his own profit or advantage. The banker buys the money from his customer, and in exchange for it he gives his customer a credit in his books, which is simply a right of action to demand back an equivalent amount of money from his banker at any time he pleases, and the customer may transfer this right of action to any one else he pleases, just like so much money.

When the client of a solicitor entrusts money to him, to lend to some one else, he retains the property in it until the arrangement with the borrower is completed; and then the property in the money is transferred directly from the lender to the borrower, without in any way vesting in the solicitor. But when a customer pays in money to his banker, the property in it instantly and, *ipso facto,* vests in the banker; and the customer has nothing but a right of action against the person of the banker to demand back an equivalent sum. So long as the money remains in the possession of the customer, it is a *jus in rem;* but when he has paid it into his account he has nothing but a *jus in personam.*

Galiani says (*Della Moneta,* p. *323*): "Banks began when men saw from experience that there was not sufficient money in specie for great commerce and great enterprises. The first banks were in the hands of private persons with whom persons deposited money; and from whom they received bills of credit (*fedi di credito*), and who were governed by the same rules as the public banks now are. And thus the Italians have been the fathers and the masters and the arbiters of commerce; so that in all Europe they have been the depositaries of money, and are called bankers." So Genovesi says (*Delle dezioni di Economia Civile,* part II., ch. 5, § 5): "These monti (banks) were first administered with scrupulous fidelity, as were all human institutions made in the heat of virtue. From which it came to pass that many placed their money on deposit, and as a security, received paper, which was called and is still called bills of credit. Thus private banks (*banchi*) were established among us, whose bills of credit acquired a great circulation, and increased the quantity of signs and the velocity of commerce." And this was always recognized as the essential feature of banking. Thus Marquardus says (*De Jure Mercatorum,* Lib. II., ch. 12, § 13): "And by 'banking' is meant a certain species of trading in money, under the sanction of public authority, in which money is placed with bankers (who are also cashiers and depositaries of money) for the security of creditors and the convenience of debtors, in such a way that the property in the money passes to them; but always with the condition understood that any one who places his money with them may have it back whenever he pleases."

A "banker" is therefore a person who trades in the same way as the public banks did; they acquired the property in the money paid in; and in exchange for it they gave bills of credit; which circulated in commerce exactly like money and produced all the effects of money. And, moreover, when they bought or discounted bills of exchange, they did it exactly in the same way; they bought them by issuing their own credit, and not with money. And experience showed that they might multiply their bills of credit several times exceeding the quantity of money they held; and thus for all practical purposes multiply the quantity of money in circulation. Thus the essential business of a banker is to create and issue credit to circulate as money. In the neighborhood of the Royal Exchange, many firms announce themselves as "Money Changers and Foreign Bankers." Thus they show that they know that money changing is not "banking." By foreign bankers they mean that, in exchange for specie, they will give their customers bills of credit on their foreign correspondents.

The following is a true definition of a "banker": A banker is a trader who buys money and credits, debts or rights of action, payable at a future time, by creating and issuing credits, debts or rights of action, payable on demand, as will be more fully exemplified further on.

ON THE CURRENCY PRINCIPLE.

We must now explain the meaning of an expression which has acquired much importance, and which must be clearly understood before we come to the exposition of the system which the Bank Charter Act of 1844 was designed to carry out.

The express function of a bank being to create credit, it has sometimes been maintained that a bank should only be allowed to create exactly as much credit as the specie paid in, and no more; and that its sole function should be to exchange credit for money and money for credit; and thus the quantity of credit in circulation would always be exactly equal to the money it displaced. This doctrine is that which is distinctively known by the name of the CURRENCY PRINCIPLE. It is the doctrine which the supporters of the Bank Act of 1844 asserted to be the only true one, and which that Bank Act was especially designed to carry out. The doctrine is supposed to be of modern origin, and the latest refinement in the theory of banking. But this is far from being the case; it was first formulated in China in 1309. That country had been plagued for 500 years with the excessive issues of inconvertible paper by the banks. The author of a work named *Toao-Min*, exhibiting the evil consequences of excessive issues of paper money, and speaking of the times before such mischief arose, said: "Then it was ordered that, at the offices of the rich merchants who managed the enterprise, when the notes were paid in, the money came out; when the bills came out the money went in; the money was the mother, the note was the son. The son and the mother were reciprocallv exchanged for the other."

Several banks have been constructed on this principle, such as those of Venice, Amsterdam, Hamburg, Nuremberg and others. These places, small in themselves, were the centres of a great foreign commerce, and as a necessary consequence large quantities of foreign coin of all sorts, of different countries and denominations, were brought by the foreigners who resorted to them. These coins were moreover greatly clipped, worn and diminished. The degraded state of the current coin produced intolerable inconvenience, disorder and confusion among the merchants, who, when they paid or received payment of their bills, had to order or receive a bagful of all sorts of different coins. The settlement of these bills, therefore, involved perpetual disputes—which coins were to be received and which were not, and how much each was to count for. In order to remedy this intolerable inconvenience, it became necessary to institute some fixed and uniform standard of payment, so as to insure regularity of payments and a just discharge of debts. To effect this purpose, the magistrates of these cities instituted a Bank of Deposit, into which every merchant paid his coin of all sorts and countries. They were weighed, and the bank gave him credit in its books for the exact bullion value of the coins paid in. The owner of the credit was entitled to have it paid in full-weighted coin on demand. These credits, therefore, insured a uniform standard of payment, and were called "bank money," "*Moneta di Banco,*" and it was enacted that all bills upon these cities above a certain small amount should be paid in bank money only. As this bank money was always exchangeable for coin of full weight on demand, it was also at a premium, or *agio,* as compared with the worn, clipped and degraded coin in circulation. The difference was usually five to nine per cent. in the different cities. The term *agio* is misleading, because it is evident that it was the "*Moneta di Banco,*" which was the full legal standard, and the current coin was at a discount. These banks professed to keep all the coin and bullion deposited with them in their vaults. They made no use of it in the way of business, as by discounting bills. Thus the credit created was exactly equal to the specie deposited, and their sole function was to exchange credit for money and money for credit. These banks were examples of the currency principle. They were of no use to commerce further than to serve as a safe place to keep the money of the merchants, and to insure a uniform standard for the payment of debts. They made no profits by their business, and no bank constructed on the currency principle can by any possibility make profits. The merchants who kept their accounts with the bank paid certain fees to defray the expenses of the establishment.

These banks were banks of deposit, because the money and bullion placed with them were merely placed there for safe custody and keeping. But they were not banks in the true sense of the word, because the money deposited with them did not become their absolute property to deal with as they pleased. They were simply trustees of the money. They were, however, banks in a certain sense; because the primary meaning of *banco* is a store, and they were stores of money. They were not the bankers, but the treasurers of the merchants; and they were obliged to take a solemn oath that they would keep in their vaults all the money deposited with them. Nevertheless, both at Venice and Amsterdam, they violated their solemn oaths, and advanced large sums to the Government, which ultimately led to their ruin.

ON THE MECHANISM OF BANKING.

Banks of the nature of those of Venice, Amsterdam, Hamburg and others, founded on the "currency principle," never existed in England; and we must now explain the mechanism of the great system of banking—or the great system of the commerce in credits, debts or rights of action, as it has been carried on in England.

It was during the great civil war, as we have already explained, that the goldsmiths of London first began to receive the cash of the merchants and country gentlemen for safe custody, on condition of repaying an equal sum on demand, and to discount bills of exchange with their own promissory notes; that commenced the business of banking. Now, this money was not placed in their hands to be locked away in their cellars, as plate and jewelry are often given into the custody of a banker for mere safe custody as a *depositum*, and to be restored in specie. The money was sold to the banker to become his actual property, according to the well-understood custom of bankers; that is, it was a *mutuum* or *creditum;* and was to be restored only *in genere*. The goldsmith bankers agreed not only to repay the money on demand, but also to pay six per cent. interest upon it. Consequently, in order to make a profit, they were obliged to trade with it.

We must now explain how a banker makes a profit by the money his customers sell to him. Suppose that customers pay in £10,000 to their accounts. They cede the absolute property in the money to the banker; it is a *mutuum* or *creditum*. The banker buys the money from his customers, and in exchange for it he gives them an equal amount of credit in his books; that is, he creates rights of action against himself to an equal amount, giving his customers the right to demand back an equal amount of money at any time they please, and also the right to transfer their rights of action to any one else they please, exactly as if they were money, and the banker agrees to pay the transferee the same as his own customer. This right of action, credit or debt, entered in the banker's books is, in banking language, technically termed a deposit. After such an operation his accounts would stand thus:

LIABILITIES.		ASSETS.	
Deposits . .	£10,000	Cash . . .	£10,000

Now, though his customers have rights of action against the banker to demand exactly an equal sum of money to what they have paid in, yet persons would not pay money to their banker if they meant to draw it out immediately; just as no one would spend all the money he has at once. Nevertheless, some will want to draw out part of their funds; but if some customers want to draw out money, others will, probably, pay in about an equal sum. Observation shows that, in ordinary and quiet times, a banker's balance will seldom differ by more than one thirty-sixth part from day to day. The banker's cash is, therefore, like a column of gold with a slight ripple on the surface; and, if he retains one-tenth in cash to meet any demands which may be made on him, that is ample and abundant in all ordinary times. If, then, in the above example, the banker retains £1000 in cash to meet any demands upon him, he has £9000 to trade with and make a profit by; and it is just in the method in which bankers trade that so much misconception exists. It is commonly supposed that, when a banker has the £9000 to trade with, he employs it in purchasing bills of exchange to that amount, and that he receives a profit only on the £9000; but that is a complete misconception of the nature of banking. A banker never buys bills of exchange with money. That is the business of a bill-discounter or money-lender. The way in which a banker trades is this: He sees that £1000 in cash is sufficient to support £10,000 of liabilities in credit; consequently, he argues that £10,000 in cash will bear liabilities to several times that amount in credit. One of the most eligible methods of trading for a banker is to buy or discount good commercial bills; and he buys these bills exactly in the same way as he bought the cash—that is, by creating credits in his books, or debts or rights of action against himself to the amount of the bills, deducting at the same time the interest or profit agreed upon, which is called the discount. A banker, therefore, invariably buys a bill of exchange with his own credit and never with cash, exactly in the same way that he bought the cash. That is, he buys a right of action payable at a future time by issuing a right of action payable on demand; and this right of action or credit is also in banking language termed a deposit—as the right of action created and issued to buy the cash.

Suppose that the banker buys £40,000 of bills of exchange at three months, and that the agreed-upon profit is four per cent.; then the sum to be retained on these bills is £400. Consequently, in exchange for bills to the amount of £40,000 he would create credits, debts or rights of action—technically termed deposits—to the amount of £39,600. Hence, just after discounting these bills, and before his customers began to operate upon them, his accounts would stand thus:

LIABILITIES.		ASSETS.	
Deposits . .	£49,600	Cash	£10,000
		Bills of exchange .	40,000
			£50,000
		Balance of profit .	400

The balance of £400 being his own property or profit. By this process the banker has added £39,600 in credit to the previously existing cash, and his profit is clear; he has not gained four per cent. on the £9000 in cash, but four per cent. on the £40,000 of bills he has bought. This is what the business of banking essentially consists in; and thus the correctness of the definition of a banker given above is manifest.

It is also evident that a banker's profits depend upon the quantity of credit he can maintain in circulation in excess of the cash he holds in reserve. Thus it is seen that the very essence and nature of a bank and a banker is to create and issue credit payable on demand; and this credit is intended to circulate and perform all the functions of money. A bank is therefore not an office for borrowing and lending money, but it is a manufactory of credit. As Mr. Cazenove well said: "It is these banking credits which are the loanable capital;" and, as Bishop Berkeley said, "a bank is a gold mine." So we ought not to speak of the money market, but of the credit market.

ON THE LEGAL RELATION BETWEEN BANKER AND CUSTOMER.

It must be carefully observed that the legal relation between banker and customer is simply that of debtor and creditor.

When a customer pays in money to his account with his banker, he cedes the absolute property in the money to the banker and receives in exchange for it a right of action, or credit or debt, to demand an equivalent sum of money any time he pleases, but not the identical money. In speaking of banking, it is too often implied that the money placed with the banker still belongs to the customer. But this was decisively refuted by Lord Chancellor Cottenham. It must therefore be carefully observed that a banker in no way resembles the treasurer of a public fund, or a solicitor or a money scrivener, who are only trustees or bailees of the money placed with them by their clients. If a banker were the mere trustee of the money placed with him, he would have no right to use it for his own private profit.

It is often the custom of persons to say that they have so much money at their banker's; but such an expression is wholly erroneous and misleading; they have no "money" at their banker's; they have nothing but an abstract right of action to demand so much money from their banker, which they give in exchange to their banker for money. As a consequence of this relation between banker and customer, if a customer were to leave a balance at his banker's for six years without operating on it, or receiving interest for it, the banker might, if he chose to be so dishonest, refuse to pay it, because the statute of limitations does not apply to trusts. Another consequence of this relation is that a cheque is a bill of exchange and not a draft. It is an order addressed by a creditor to his debtor, and not one addressed to his trustee or bailee. To call a cheque a draft is to mistake the relation between banker and customer.

ON THE LEGAL CONTRACT BETWEEN BANKER AND CUSTOMER.

It has been shown that the legal relation between banker and customer is simply that of debtor and creditor. Nevertheless there is an important distinction between an ordinary debtor and a banker debtor. At common law, an ordinary debtor is not bound to accept a bill drawn upon him by his creditor without his own consent, even though he admits the debt; nor, if the creditor assigns the debt, is he bound to pay the transferee. The debtor has simply engaged to pay his creditor, and no one else. Nor has the transferee any right of action against him, because there is no privity of contract between the debtor and transferee; and the creditor has no power to stipulate that the debtor shall pay the transferee unless he expressly consents to do so. The transferee can only sue the debtor under the name of the transferer, or the transferer can sue the debtor as the trustee of the transferee. If, however, the debtor had entered into an obligation, under seal, promising to pay the assignee or bearer; or if he had accepted a bill payable to order, or to bearer, then the transferee might sue him in his own name, because the consent of the debtor had created a privity of contract between himself and the transferee. But the case of a banker debtor has always been different. When persons have money in their own possession they can transfer it to any one else, any moment they please. Persons, therefore, would not place their money with bankers unless they had exactly the same facility of transferring their right of action against their banker as they had of transferring the money itself.

Consequently, from the very first institution of banking, it was always the fundamental contract that customers might either demand payment themselves from their bankers, or that they might transfer their right of action made payable to order, or to bearer, or to anyone else as freely as their money; and the bankers agreed to pay the transferee as readily as their own customers. By the very nature therefore of the consensual contract, termed the custom of bankers, a banker having funds of his customer is in the position of an ordinary debtor who has accepted a bill payable to order or to bearer. Hence, while the simple admission of funds by an ordinary debtor in no way compels him to accept, or to pay, a bill drawn upon him without his own consent, the simple admission of the possession of funds by a banker operates *ipso facto* as a legal acceptance of any bills or cheques drawn upon him by his customer, and gives the holder of them a right of action against him.

ON THE MEANING OF DEPOSIT IN THE TECHNICAL LANGUAGE OF MODERN BANKING.

The word *depositum* is one of that class of Latin words which, in classical Latin, meant a material thing, but which in modern times has come to mean only an abstract right. A *depositum*, in Roman law, means anything which is placed in the gratuitous charge or custody of some person for the sole purpose of safe-keeping, without the property in it passing to him, or his being allowed to use it in any way for his own advantage, or even being allowed to retain it as a security for a debt due to him.

It is part of the duty of a London banker to take charge of his customer's plate, jewelry and securities, if required to do so. This plate, jewelry and securities so committed to their charge for safe custody is what in Roman law is called a *depositum.* The banker acquires no property in such a *depositum;* he can make no use of it for his own advantage; he receives no remuneration for keeping it, and he has no lien on it if his customer becomes indebted to him. So, if a customer tied up a sum of money in a bag and placed it in the custody of his banker, it would be a *depositum;* and the banker would be bound to redeliver the specific bag of money to him on demand, untouched. It is said that in the 1893 crisis in America, numbers of customers withdrew their balances from their current accounts, tied them up in bags and redelivered them to their bankers to keep for them as *deposita;* and then of course the bankers could not touch them. It is almost universally supposed by lay writers that when a customer pays in money to his account with his banker, it is a deposit; and that the deposits of a bank are the cash held in reserve. This, however, is a pure delusion. When a customer, in the ordinary way, pays in money to his account with a banker, he loses all property in it; the banker acquires the absolute property in it to use for his own advantage; such money, therefore, is not a *depositum;* it is a *mutuum* or a *creditum.* If the money so paid in were a *depositum,* it would mean that the banker acquired no property in it; that the property in it remained with the customer who placed it in his banker's hands for pure safe-keeping, and that he could demand back that specific sum of money at any time he pleased. But every person who thinks knows that such ideas are erroneous.

In exchange for the money the banker makes an entry of an equal sum in credit in favor of his customer; that is, he issues a right of action to him. And it is this entry of a credit or right of action in his customer's favor which in the technical language of modern banking is termed a deposit; that is, he buys the money by creating a deposit. So when a banker discounts a bill for a customer, he buys a right of action from him exactly in the same way as he bought the money. He creates a credit in his books in his favor; or he issues a right of action to him. This credit, or right of action, is the price the banker pays for the bill. And this credit or right of action created to purchase the bill is termed a deposit, equally as the right of action created to purchase the money. The money and the bills are the banker's assets. The deposits are the rights of action he has created to purchase his assets. Every advance a banker makes is done by creating a deposit. His depositors are those persons who have rights of action against him to pay money, or his creditors. A deposit is simply a banking credit.

IN BANKING LANGUAGE A DEPOSIT AND AN ISSUE ARE THE SAME.

It must therefore be observed that, in the technical language of modern banking a deposit and an issue are the same thing. A deposit is simply a credit in a banker's books. It is the evidence of the right of action which a customer has to demand a sum of money from the banker. As soon as the banker has created a credit, or deposit, in his books in favor of a customer he has issued to him a right of action against himself.

The word issue comes from exitus, a going forth; and in mercantile law to issue an instrument is to deliver it to any one so as to give him a right of action against the deliverer or issuer. It in no way increases the banker's liability to write down this credit, or deposit, on paper in the form of a bank note or cheque. Such documents are only made after the credit or deposit has been created; and their sole purpose is to facilitate the transfer of the credit or deposit to some one else. Now, as every advance a banker makes is by issuing a right of action against himself to his customer, and as a banker has an unlimited right of buying any amount of debts or obligations from his customers which he thinks prudent, every banker has the right of unlimited issue. Bank notes and cheques, then, do not increase a banker's liability. The liability is created as soon as the banker has entered the amount to his customer's credit in his books. The note, or cheque, is merely a convenient method of transferring from hand to hand the pre-created liability which has already been issued. Deposits, then, instead of being so much cash, as is so commonly supposed, are nothing but the credits or rights of action the banker has created as the price to purchase the cash and bills which figure on the other side of the account as his assets. A sudden increase of deposits is, therefore, nothing more than an inflation of credit, exactly similar to a sudden increase of bank notes. Deposits are nothing but bank notes in disguise.

ON THE METHOD OF UTILIZING BANKING CREDITS.

The banker, then, having issued these credits, deposits or rights of action against himself to his customers, they cannot, of course, transfer them by manual delivery in that form to any one else. In order to be capable of manual delivery they must be recorded on paper or some other material. And this might be done in two forms: 1. The banker might give his customer his own promissory notes, promising to pay a certain sum to his customer, or to his order, or to bearer on demand. 2. The customer might write a note to his banker directing him to pay a certain sum to a certain person, or to his order, or to bearer on demand. These orders were formerly called cash notes, but they are now termed cheques. These paper documents do not create new liabilities; they merely record on paper the credits, debts or deposits which have already been created in the banker's books, and their sole use is to facilitate the transfer of these rights of action to other persons. There is one juridical distinction between bank notes and cheques. A bank note is the absolute obligation of the banker to pay it; a cheque is only the contingent obligation of the banker to pay it, provided that the customer has sufficient credit on his account to pay it. If, however, he has, then the obligation of the banker is absolute. The holder of a cheque with funds to meet it on the drawer's account has the same right of action against the banker as upon one of his own notes. So far as regards economics, bank notes and cheques are absolutely identical. They are both equally circulating medium or currency. Bankers' notes were at first merely written on paper like any other promissory notes, and they were for any sums the customer might require. In 1729, Child & Co. introduced the practice of having their notes partly printed and partly written like a modern cheque. They were not, like modern bankers' notes, for fixed definite sums; but, like modern cheques, for any sum that might be required.

London bankers appear to have issued their own notes till about 1793, when perhaps the panic of that year may have shown them the danger of having large amounts of their notes in the hands of the public, which their enemies might collect and present for payment. In 1793, they discontinued issuing notes of their own accord, but they were never forbidden to do so until the Bank Act of 1844. Most erroneous conclusions have been drawn from the fact of the London bankers having voluntarily discontinued issuing their own notes. Lay writers, who know nothing of the mechanism of banking, have asserted that the London banks are, like the banks of Venice, Amsterdam, etc., pure banks of deposit; that they do not create credit, and that their whole business is to "lend" out the money they "borrow" from their customers. All such ideas are, however, pure delusions. Bankers now, as ever, make all their advances by creating credits or deposits in their books. But instead of giving their customers two methods of circulating these credits, by means of notes or of cheques, they are now restricted to one method—cheques. But whether a bank credit is circulated by means of a note or a cheque makes no possible difference in economics.

The Bank Charter Act of 1844 allowed the banks which were then issuing notes to continue to do so to a certain limited amount, but forbade any new bank to commence doing so. A considerable number of the banks which issued notes in 1844 have disappeared, and the notes of private banks have diminished by several millions. Many ill-informed writers have drawn the conclusion from this circumstance that the currency of the country has been diminished by so much. This, however, is a pure delusion. The system of banking has enormously increased since then, and the amount of banking credits has increased by scores of millions, and these increased banking credits being circulated by cheques are currency in exactly the same way as notes.

OPERATIONS BY MEANS OF NOTES AND CHEQUES.

When, therefore, a banker has created a credit or deposit in favor of his customer, he can put this credit into circulation either by means of the banker's own note or by means of a cheque, and when he does so, the following different results may take place: 1. The customer himself or the holder of the note or cheque may demand payment of it; if they do so, the banker's liability is extinguished. It is a resale of money to the holder of the note or cheque, and the banker buys up the right of action against himself. 2. The note or cheque may circulate in commerce and effect any number of transfers of commodities or payments exactly like an equal sum of money; and it may ultimately fall into the hands of a customer of the same bank, who pays it into his own account, and the whole series of transactions is finally closed by the mere transfer of credit from the account of the drawer to that of the holder, without the necessity of any coin. 3. The note or cheque may, after performing a similar series of operations, fall into the hands of a customer of another bank. So the banker becomes debtor to the customer of another bank. But if the bank A becomes debtor to the customers of bank B, the chances are that about an equal number of the customers of bank A will have about equal claims against bank B. If the mutual claims of the customers of each bank are exactly equal, the respective documents are interchanged, and the credits are readjusted among the accounts of the different customers without any payment in money. Thus, if the mutual claims among any number of bankers exactly balanced, any amount of credits, however large, might be settled without the use of a single coin. Formerly, if the mutual claims did not balance, the differences only used to be paid in money or bank notes. But now, by an ingenious arrangement of the Clearing House, which will be described shortly, the use of coin and bank notes is entirely dispensed with, and all the banks which join in the clearing are really and practically formed into one huge banking institution for the purpose of transferring credits among each other, just as credits are usually transferred from one account to another in the same bank, without a single coin being required.

HOW CREDIT IS CAPITAL TO A BANKER.

It is now seen how credit is capital to a banker. For what is the commodity which a banker deals in and makes a profit by? He opens his place of business and has an array of clerks with their desks, ledgers, etc. He then gives notice that he is ready to buy gold from any one who has it to sell. And what is the commodity with which he buys the gold—what does he give in exchange for it? His own credit. The commodity he gives in exchange for the gold is a right of action to pay an equivalent of gold on demand, *i. e.*, his own credit. He then gives notice that he is ready to buy good commercial debts—which are credits or rights of action—which any one has got to sell. And what does he buy these credits, debts, or rights of action with? Again, with nothing but his own credit—with rights of action against himself. His own credit is the commodity with which he buys these other credits. The banker charges exactly the same price for his credit as if it were money. The only commodity the banker has to sell is his own credit, for which he charges exactly the same price as if it were money. Hence he makes exactly the same profit by selling his credit as if he were selling money. Now, as we have seen, anything which gives a profit is capital. Hence, as a banker's credit produces him exactly the same profit as money would, it is evident that his credit is capital to him just as much as money is.

Again, credits, debts or rights of action are goods, chattels, commodities, merchandise. Now, under the term circulating capital, Smith expressly includes the goods or commodities in shops. The trader buys them at a lower price from one person and sells them at a higher price to another person, and so makes a profit by them; and thus the goods in the shop are capital to him. And Adam Smith expressly includes bank notes or banking credits and bills of exchange under the term circulating capital. So a banker buys the goods or commodities termed credits, debts or rights of action from one person, his own customer, and sells them at a higher price to another person—namely, the acceptor or debtor. The debt the banker buys is increasing in value every day from the time he buys it until it is paid off. These goods or commodities termed debts in the portfolio of a banker produce him a profit just in the same way as the goods, commodities or merchandise in the shop produce profits to the trader. Hence the bills in the portfolio of a banker are circulating capital, exactly in the same way as the goods, commodities or merchandise in the shop of a trader are circulating capital.

ON THE SCOTTISH SYSTEM OF BANKING.

The credits, or rights of action, created by bankers in the operations which we have been describing, were employed to buy commercial bills which arose out of the transfer of commodities; and it has been shown that they create credit to several times the amount of the cash in their possession. And some writers suppose that this is the limit of legitimate credit. It is very commonly imagined that credit can only be used to transfer existing commodities. We have now to describe a species of credit of a totally different nature, invented in Scotland, to which the marvelous progress of that country is mainly due. It is credit created, not for the purpose of transferring or circulating commodities already in existence, but for the express purpose of calling new products into existence. It is entirely of the nature of accommodation paper; and it will show that there is nothing in the nature of accommodation paper more dangerous or objectionable than there is in real paper, as it is called; but, on the contrary, that they stand on exactly the same footing of security; and also that credit is equally applicable to call new products into existence as to transfer those already in existence.

When, after a long period of inactivity, the energies of a people are suddenly turned into an industrial direction, they find innumerable enterprises which would be profitable if only they possessed the means of setting them agoing. The quantity of money which was sufficient for a non-industrial people is now found to be wholly inadequate for the increased demand for it; and the only consequence will be that, if there is a greatly increased demand for the existing quantity of money, the rate of interest will rise enormously; and to such an extent as to preclude all possibility of profit from such enterprises, even if effected. It is, therefore, invariably found, that whenever this takes place, multitudes of schemes are set afloat for increasing the quantity of money. For many centuries after the Conquest, England was essentially a feudal and military—an agricultural and pastoral people. Its law was almost entirely feudal, and related to the tenure of land. Merchants and commerce were held in very subordinate esteem, and commercial law had no existence. In the sixteenth century, the energies of the nation were absorbed in religious controversies; and in the first half of the next century in constitutional struggles and politics. At length, in the reign of Charles II., men, weary of polemics and politics, began to devote themselves more to industry and commerce; and this was greatly stimulated by the manifest advantages of banking which had just been introduced into England. Among fields of enterprise at that period, none seemed more promising than agriculture. But unfortunately all the available specie was absorbed in commerce; none was to be had for agriculture; or, at least, only at such rates as to be practically prohibitive. In no species of industry are the profits so moderate as in agriculture. Hence, if capital has to be borrowed to effect improvements in agriculture, it is requisite that it should be at a very low rate of interest. The usual rate of interest in the time of Charles II. was ten per cent., and few improvements in agriculture could bear that. But by the introduction of banking and the foundation of the Bank of England, the rate of interest in commerce was reduced to three per cent. It was this real want, and the enormous advantage which banking had been to commerce, which gave rise to the schemes of Asgill, Briscoe, Chamberlen, Law, and others, for the purpose of creating paper money based upon land; and to found land banks, to assist agriculture, as the mercantile banks had assisted commerce, which were so rife at this period.

One of these schemes was attempted to be carried out in 1696. The Ministry of William III. was not, as is now the case, formed exclusively of one party of the State. William III. reigned and governed; and the Ministry was his Ministry, and not that of the Parliament, as it is now. His Ministry was partly Whig and partly Tory. The Whig portion of it, who were in close connection with the mercantile community of the city, succeeded in founding the Bank of England in 1694, which was essentially a Whig project, and intended to assist the finance of the Government and commerce. The immense benefit of the Bank of England was so evident that the Tory portion of the Ministry endeavored to found a bank which should also assist Government, and besides that, be specially for the benefit of agriculture. It was attempted to be founded in 1696, and it was called the Land Bank. But the attempt did not succeed, and its failure was one of the causes which produced the stoppage of the Bank of England in 1697. There were, no doubt, defects in the scheme which fully accounted for its failure; but the want was very real, and the idea was perfectly sound. Among the projectors of a scheme for basing paper money on land, the most celebrated was John Law. He has given an elaborate exposition of his theory in a work entitled "Money and Trade Considered"; and he laid a scheme before the Parliament of Scotland in 1705, which they fortunately rejected, or there would have been a catastrophe in Scotland as great as that of the Darien scheme in 1699. Law had the opportunity of reducing his theory to practice in France in 1720, under the name of the Mississippi scheme. This is not the place to give an account of Law's scheme. But ten years after its failure in France, the Scotch banks, by the admirable invention of cash credits, pushed credit to the utmost extent of its legitimate limits, and realized all that was practicable in the schemes of Asgill, Briscoe, Chamberlen and Law. And it is to these cash credits that the principal progress of Scotland in agriculture and all public works is due, as well as the personal wealth of its merchants. Moreover, after the end of the Seven Years' War in 1763, an ingenious merchant devised a scheme of land banks in Germany, and it is to these land banks that the principal part of the progress of agriculture in central Europe is due.

ON CASH CREDITS.

The Bank of Scotland was founded in 1695 with unlimited powers of issue, both in amount and denomination. At first it only issued notes of £100, £50, £10 and £5. Though several times urged to do so, they did not issue £1 notes at first, but in 1704 they began to do so. The bank received a monopoly of banking for twenty-one years; but in 1716, when the monopoly expired, it was not renewed. In the year 1727 the proprietors of the Equivalent Fund were endowed by royal charter with powers of banking, and they assumed the name of the Royal Bank. In the very contracted sphere of commerce in Scotland at that time there were not sufficient commercial bills in circulation to exhaust the credit of the banks. They had, as it were, a superfluity of unexhausted credit on hand; and the bank devised a new scheme for getting its credit into circulation, which was the most marvelous development of credit ever imagined. It agreed, on receiving sufficient guarantees, to open credits of certain limited amounts in favor of trustworthy and respectable persons. A cash credit is a drawing account created in favor of a person who pays in no money, which he may operate upon precisely in the same manner as on an ordinary account; the only difference being that, instead of receiving interest on the daily balance of his account, as used formerly to be the case in Scotland, he is charged interest on the daily balance at his debit. A cash credit is, therefore, an inverse drawing account. Cash credits are applicable to a totally different class of transactions to those which give rise to bills of exchange, one difference being that bills of exchange arise out of the transfers of commodities, and are payable in one sum at a fixed date; whereas cash credits are not issued on the transfer of commodities or on any previous transactions. They are expressly intended to promote the formation of future products. They are not repayable at any fixed date; but they are a continuous working account which continues open as long as the operations are satisfactory.

It is a condition of all cash credits that the persons to whom they are granted should accept all advances in the bank's own notes.

If every future commercial profit has a present value, which can be brought into commerce and exchanged, the same is equally true of the land and of every commercial work or enterprise. The present value of every future profit from land or any commercial work can be brought into commerce and bought and sold exactly like the present values of the future profits of traders; and if the credit be strictly limited and redeemed by the future profits of the land or commercial work, credit may be created to purchase the present value of these future profits from land and commercial public works, exactly in the same way as it is created to purchase the present values of the future profits from traders.

CASH CREDITS GRANTED IN AID OF PERSONS.

Every man in business, however humble or however extensive, must necessarily keep a certain portion of ready money by him to answer immediate demands for small daily expenses, wages and other things. This could, of course, be much more profitably employed in his business, where it might produce a profit of fifteen or twenty per cent., instead of lying idle. But, unless the trader knew that he could command it at a moment's notice, he would always be obliged to keep a certain amount of ready money in his till, unless he were able to command the use of some one else's till. Now, one object of a cash credit is to supply this convenience to the trader, and to enable him to invest the whole of his capital in his business; and, upon proper security being given, to furnish him with the accommodation of a till at a moment's notice, in such small sums as he may require, on his paying a moderate interest for the accommodation. Almost every trader in Scotland has a cash credit at a bank, by which he can draw out such sums as he may want for his daily business, and replace such as he does not want before the close of the bank hours. Almost every young man in Scotland commencing business does it by means of a cash credit. Thus, for instance, lawyers, or writers to the signet, commencing business, have occasion for ready money from day to day before they can get in payments from their clients. It is a great bar to any young man to commence the business of a solicitor without capital, which must either be furnished to him by his friends or others. It is an immense advantage to him and to them to have it supplied by a bank, by means of a cash credit, on a mere guarantee, a mere contingency, which they never would give if they thought there was any danger of its being enforced. So the great employers of labor, manufacturers, builders, ship-builders and others, have cash credits by which they can pay their laborers. These credits are granted to all classes of society; to the poor as freely as to the rich. Everything depends upon character. Young men in the humblest walks of life may inspire their friends with confidence in their steadiness and judgment, and they become sureties for them on a cash credit. This is in all respects of equal value to them as money; and thus they have the means placed within their reach of rising to any extent that their abilities and industry permit them. Multitudes of men who have raised themselves to immense wealth began life with nothing but a cash credit. As one example among thousands, Mr. Monteith, M. P., told the committee of the House of Commons in 1826 that he was a manufacturer, employing at that time 4000 hands, and that, except with the merest trifle of capital lent him, and which he soon paid off, he began the world with nothing but a cash credit.

The banks usually limit their advances to a certain moderate amount, varying from £100 to £1000 in general, and they take several sureties in each case. These cautioners, as they are termed in Scottish law, keep a watchful eye on the proceedings of the customer, and of inspecting his account with the bank and of stopping it at any time if irregular. These credits are not meant to degenerate into dead loans, but they are required to be operated upon by constantly paying in and drawing out. The enormous amount of transactions carried on by this kind of account may be judged of by the evidence given before the committee of the Commons in 1826. It was then stated that on a credit of £1000 operations to the extent of £50,000 took place in a single week. Others stated that on a cash credit of £500 operations to the amount of £70,000 took place in a year. One witness stated that in a very moderately sized country bank operations to the amount of £90,000,000 took place in twenty-one years, and that the whole loss to the bank during that period was £1200. At that time, it was conjectured that there were about 12,000 cash credits guaranteed by about 40,000 sureties, who were interested in the integrity, prudence and success of the customers. The witnesses before the Lords declared that the effects of these were most remarkable on the morals of the people.

ON CASH CREDITS GRANTED TO PROMOTE AGRICULTURE AND THE FORMATION OF PUBLIC WORKS.

We have now to consider the way in which the Scottish system of cash credits has been applied to promote agriculture and the formation of all manner of public works.

The two Scottish banks which were first founded applied their cash credits to assist the industry of traders, and tended much to foster it. Agricultural industry had not then awoke. The Scots were a fierce, turbulent people, who thought a great deal more of harrying their neighbors than of peaceful agriculture. The land was bound down under the fetters of the feudal system. But, after the suppression of the rebellion in 1746, the feudal system was to a great extent broken up, and a great spirit of enterprise awoke; and then, for the first time, Scotland became an industrial nation. At this time, there were in many parts of Scotland large tracts of reclaimable land and multitudes of people, but they remained unemployed, because there was no money in the country to set their industry in motion. Now, suppose that a proprietor of one of these tracts of land had had £10,000 in money, and that he employed it in paying wages to laborers and in buying seed to sow; then, in course of time, the value of the produce of the land would replace the sum expended in bringing the land into cultivation. Then the money so employed would have been expended as capital. But at that time there was, comparatively speaking, no money in the country. It was just then emerging from the bonds of feudalism. The chiefs had vast tracts of lands, and no doubt lived in a state of rude abundance, from their herds and flocks and the natural produce of the soil. But commerce had never penetrated into these Highland strongholds; and consequently the greatest chiefs were very seldom blessed with the sight of coin. But at this period began the transition from feudalism to industrialism, in which money was absolutely indispensable. It was at this time that the banks, having habituated the people during forty years to receive their £1 notes in all respects as money, and having acquired their thorough confidence, threw out branches in all directions, and sent down boxes of their £1 notes. Farmers at that time had no votes in Scotland, and consequently the landlords had no motives to keep their tenants in political thraldom, as was too much the case in England. They adopted every means possible to develop the resources of the soil. And as it was not to be expected that the farmers would lay out their capital and industry on the soil without security of tenure, it became the custom, almost universal in Scotland, for landowners to grant their tenants leases of nineteen years; and in many cases, for particular reasons, much longer than that. Upon the security of these leases, and also upon that of personal friends, the banks everywhere granted cash credits to the farmers, the advances being made exclusively in their own £1 notes. From the strong constitution of the banks, and the universal confidence they had acquired, their notes were universally received as cash; and though they were demandable in cash at the head office, no one ever dreamt of demanding payment for them. With these advances in £1 notes, the farmers employed the laborers in reclaiming the land, bought seed and sowed the crops. The notes were employed in exactly the same way as money would have been, and they produced exactly the same effects as money would have done. The land was reclaimed, and sown, and stocked; and, in a few years, bleak and barren moors were everywhere changed into fields of waving corn, and they produced a continuous series of profits. With the value of the produce, the farmers gradually repaid the loans and reaped a profit.

Now, if it be admitted that money expended in agricultural improvements is used as productive capital, how can it be denied that credit, employed in exactly the same way, and which produces exactly the same effects as money, and produces exactly the same profits, is also equally productive capital? The £1 notes were universally received by the people as of exactly the same value as money; and therefore they were in all respects money; they produced exactly the same profits that money did. Now, as we have seen, that capital is anything which produces a profit, it is evident that the £1 notes were just as much productive capital as the money. The only difference was that, in using money, the employer made capital of the realized profits of the past; in using credit he made capital of the expected profits of the future. But the results are exactly the same in either case. Every one acquainted with Scotland knows perfectly well that the prodigious progress in agriculture made in that country during the last 140 years has been almost entirely effected by means of these cash credits. Not only has almost the entire progress in agriculture been effected by these cash credits, but all public works of every description—roads, canals, docks, harbors, railways, public buildings, etc., have also been made by the same means. It was stated to the committee of the House of Commons in 1826, that the Forth and Clyde Canal was executed by means of a cash credit of £40,000 granted by the Royal Bank. So when a road has to be made, the trustees obtain a cash credit, and pay it off out of the rates. So when a railway, a dock, a harbor, a public building, a canal, is to be made, the directors obtain a cash credit and so pay the wages of the men.

It is thus seen how credit is applied to the formation of new products equally well as to the transfer of existing ones. Credit is purchasing power equally as money; and it may be applied to purchase labor to form new products equally well as to transfer existing ones. The principle of the limit, however, being exactly the same in both cases—namely, that it is the present value of the future profit. When money is used to produce a profit, it is expected that the profit will replace the money advanced; when credit is used to produce a profit, it is expected that the profit will redeem the debt incurred. Hence credit can do whatever money can do; but we have shown that credit is the inverse of money. Hence, in mathematical language, all the propositions which are true with respect to money are equally true with respect to credit, only with the sign changed.

Exactly the same effects were produced in England by the use of bankers' notes. The success of the Bridgewater Canal had exactly the same effect as the success of the Liverpool & Manchester Railway eighty years later. The period from 1776 to 1796 was just as great an era in canal making as the subsequent period in railway building, considering the wealth of the country at the respective times. In the course of twenty years, England, from being the most backward country in Europe in water communication, was covered with a network of canals such as no other country but Holland can boast. These canals were made by the notes issued by the country bankers. Burke says that when he first came to London there were not twelve bankers out of London. In 1793 there were 400. However, these bankers, not having the solid constitution of the Scottish Banks, were swept away in multitudes in the panics of 1793 and 1797. But, nevertheless, though the bankers were swept away, the solid results of their issues of notes remained. Thus it is now clearly demonstrated that credit may be used as productive capital, exactly in the same way and in the same sense, and for all the purposes, that money is.

THE SCOTTISH SYSTEM OF CASH CREDITS.

All these marvelous results, which have raised Scotland from the lowest depth of barbarism up to her present proud position in the space of 200 years, are the children of pure credit. It is no exaggeration, but a melancholy truth, that at the period of the revolution in 1688, and the foundation of the Bank of Scotland in 1695—partly owing to such a series of disasters as cannot be paralleled in the history of any other independent nation; partly owing to its position on the very outskirts of civilization, and far removed from the humanizing influence of commerce; divided into two nations, aliens in blood and language—Scotland was the most utterly barbarous and lawless country in Europe. And it is equally undeniable that the two great causes of her rapid rise in civilization and wealth have been her systems of national education and banking.

Her system of banking has been of infinitely greater service to her than mines of gold and silver. Mines of the precious metal would probably only have demoralized her people, and made them more savage than they were before. But her banking system has tended immensely to call forth every manly virtue. It has taught them industry, steadiness and moral rectitude. In the character of her own people, Scotland has found wealth infinitely more beneficial to her than all the mines of Mexico and Peru. The express function of the banks was to create credits, incorporeal entities, created out of nothing, for a transitory existence; and, when they had performed their functions, vanishing again into the nothing from whence they came. And has not this credit been capital? Will anyone, with these results staring him in the face, believe that there are some persons who are supposed to be economists who maintain that the results of credit are purely imaginary? That credit conduces nothing to production and the increase of wealth? That credit only transfers existing capital? But even if it did no more than that, it has been shown that circulation or transfer is one species of production; as is indeed now admitted by all economists of note, and that these persons who say that credit is capital are such puzzle-headed dolts as to maintain that the same thing can be in two places at once!

Circulating credits of all kinds have exactly the same effects as money, both in circulating existing commodities and in promoting the formation of new products. And they may be used as productive capital, exactly in the same way and in the same sense that money is. It must be observed that all these cash credits are for a distinct purpose, quite different from the discount of mercantile paper. The marvelous results they have produced are due to a system of pure accommodation paper. They are not founded on any previous transactions; nor are they for the purpose of transferring existing commodities. They are created for the express purpose of bringing new products into existence which, but for them, would either have had no existence at all, or at all events would have been deferred for a very long period, until solid money could have been accumulated to effect them. They are founded on exactly the same principles as the discount of mercantile bills. In discounting mercantile bills, the banker merely buys up the right to a future payment to be made out of the profits of the transaction. In creating cash credits the banker merely buys the right to a future payment to be made out of the future profits of the land or other public works.

The invention of cash credits has advanced the wealth of Scotland by centuries. We have an enormous mass of exchangeable property created out of nothing, by the mere will of the bank and its customers, which produces all the effects of solid gold and silver; and when it has done its work, it vanishes again into nothing, at the will of the same persons who called it into existence. What the Nile is to Egypt, that has her banking system been to Scotland; and it was fortunate for her that the foundations of her prosperity were laid broad and deep before the gigantic fallacy was dreamt of that the issues of banks should be inexorably restricted to the amount of gold they displace; that no increase of money can be of any use to a country; and before Mill had proclaimed to the world that to create credit in excess of specie is robbery!

The reader will now perceive the gigantic utility of the £1 note system to Scotland; and comprehend the consternation and fury of the Scottish people when various attempts have been made by Parliament to suppress them. When Parliament suppressed £1 notes in England, in consequence of the evils they were alleged to produce, owing to the bad organization of the English banking system, before the monopoly of the Bank of England was first broken up in 1826, it was intended to have suppressed them also in Scotland. But all Scotland rose up against it; and, headed by "Malachi Malagrowther," raised such a commotion that an inquiry was granted which first made the Scottish system of banking understood, and the attempt was abandoned. Still, however, constant jeers and gibes were addressed to the Scotch people by persons who knew nothing about the subject, about their fatuous attachment to their "dirty £1 notes." But the Scotch knew their value to the country far better than their assailants. The Scotch knew that the prosperity of their country was bound up with the cash credits; and cash credits were bound up with the issue of £1 notes. To have suppressed the Scotch £1 notes at that time would have destroyed two-thirds of the business of the banks. The extent of commerce in Scotland at that time was not sufficient to support the public banks. It was stated that at that time two-thirds of the business of the Scottish banks consisted in cash credits, though we are informed that now, in consequence of the great development of commerce, the ratio of cash credits to the mercantile business of the banks has considerably diminished.

Happily, however, no such attempts will ever be made again, now that the subject is better understood. Parliament is, however, justified in taking any measures it may be deemed necessary to secure their perfect safety and convertibility. So completely has the tide of opinion changed, that the question now is whether £1 notes can be reintroduced into England. But, with the present transitional state of banking in England, it is premature to discuss that question.

ON THE CLEARING HOUSE.

One of the great improvements in modern times, in the organization of credit, is the institution of clearing houses; and as the effect of these, like everything else in banking, is the subject of great misconception, we must explain their operation. It is usually stated that the Clearing House is an example of the principle of compensation, like that effected by the foreign merchants at the Continental fairs. In foreign treatises the Clearing House is usually called a *Maison de Compensation,* or *de Liquidation.* This, however, is a complete error.

It has been shown that if any number of customers of the same bank have transactions among themselves, and give each other cheques on their accounts, any number of transactions may be settled by mere transfers of credit from one account to another without a single coin being required, so long as the receiver of the cheque does not draw out the money. Such transfers are novation. The clearing system is a device by which all the banks which join in it are formed, as it were, into one huge banking institution, for the purpose of transferring credits from one bank to another without the use of coin; just in the same way that credits are transferred in the same bank from one account to another without the use of coin. The Clearing House is, therefore, not a *Maison de Compensation,* but it is a *Maison de Novation.* Every banker has every morning claims on behalf of his customers against his neighbors, and they have claims on behalf of their customers against him. These claims are called bankers' charges. Formerly it was the custom for every banker to send out his clerks the first thing in the morning to collect these charges, which had to be paid in money or bank notes. Having collected these charges, he credited his customer with the sums due to him. Now, when the banker had paid the charges against him, there was of course so much credit extinguished. The money and bank notes collected by the banker became his actual property, but he was obliged to create an equal amount of credit on behalf of his own customers; so that, on the whole, an exactly equal amount of credit was recreated to what had been extinguished. And so the final result was that there was exactly the same amount of credit in existence. But each of his neighbors had also claims on behalf of their customers against him. Consequently, every banker was obliged to keep a large amount of money and bank notes to meet these claims. By this a very large amount of money and bank notes had to be retained for the purpose of meeting these bankers' charges; it was simply transferred and re-transferred from bank to bank; it never got into general circulation at all so as to affect business or prices, and it could be made no other use of.

It was stated before the House of Commons, many years ago, that one bank alone, the London and Westminster, was obliged to keep £150,000 in notes for this sole purpose. And if one bank alone, then comparatively in its infancy, was obliged to keep such a sum in notes idle for this purpose, what would have been the sum necessary to be retained at the present day by all the banks, if it were not for the Clearing House? To remedy this inconvenience, an ingenious method was devised, it is said, by the banks at Naples in the 16th century. The banks instituted a central chamber to which each sent a clerk. These clerks exchanged their different claims against each other, and paid only the difference in money. By this means the different credits were readjusted among the different customers' accounts just as easily as before; and a large amount of money and notes were set free for the purpose of circulation and commerce; and were in fact, for all practical purposes, equivalent to so much increase of capital to the banks and to the country.

This system was first adopted in this country by the banks in Edinburgh. And we have now to show that no permanent extinction of credit takes place as in compensation; the final result is only a transfer of credit, that is a novation. Suppose that a customer of the Commercial Bank has £100 in notes of the Royal Bank paid to him. He is then creditor of the Royal Bank. He pays these notes into his account with the Commercial Bank. He desires the bank as his agents to collect the proceeds of these notes from the Royal Bank, and to place the amount to his credit. Suppose that, in a similar way, a customer of the Royal Bank has £100 in notes of the Commercial Bank paid to him. Then he is creditor of the Commercial Bank. He pays these notes into his account with the Royal Bank, and constitutes them his agents to collect the proceeds from the Commercial Bank and place them to his credit. Each bank is then debtor to the customer of the other. The full way of proceeding would be for each bank to send a clerk to the other to collect the notes in money. Each bank then having obtained payment of the notes in money would place to the credit of its customer, and put the money which would become its own property into its own till, just as if the customer had paid in the money himself. In this case it is evident that there is no permanent annihilation or extinction of credit; because by the process each bank, instead of being debtor to the customer of the other, becomes debtor to its own customer. Thus it is evident that in each case there is a novation, and not a compensation. This method of settling the claims of the customer would require £200 in money.

The same result may be obtained in a much simpler way. Let the agents of the two banks meet. The agent of the Commercial Bank says to the agent of the Royal Bank: "In consideration of your giving up to me the notes held by your customer by which I am debtor to him, and so releasing me from my debt to him, I agree to credit my customer with their amount, and so become debtor to him." This is a novation. The agent of the Royal Bank says to the agent of the Commercial Bank: "In consideration of your giving up to me the notes held by your customer, by which I am debtor to him, and so releasing me from my debt to him, I agree to credit my customer with this amount, and to become debtor to him." This is also a novation. The agents of the two banks then exchange notes, and each bank having received £100 in its own notes—that is, being released from its debt to the customer of the other, which, as we have seen, is equivalent to a payment in money—enters the amount to the credit of its own customer. By this means, each bank, instead of being debtor to the customer of the other, becomes debtor to its own customer, and the use of £200 in money is saved. The release of the debt of each bank to the customer of the other is the consideration for the creation of the debt to its own customer. No doubt the £100 of notes from each bank are withdrawn from circulation and replaced in its own till. But an equal amount of credit is created and placed to the credit of each customer, so that upon the whole the quantity of credit remains exactly the same. Thus, the debt of each bank to the customer of the other is extinguished by the new debt created in favor of its own customer. And the whole transaction consists of two novations.

The reason why the operations of the merchants at the Continental fairs were compensations in which both credits were extinguished, and the operations of the Clearing House are novations, in which new credits are created, which pay and extinguish the prior ones, but create an equal amount of new credits, so that the whole amount of credit remains exactly the same as it was before, is this: In the case of the merchants they were principals; they were mutually indebted to each other; when, therefore, they exchanged their mutual debts they were canceled and extinguished, and no new debts were created to replace them. But, in the case of the Clearing House, the banks are not principals, they are only agents for their customers; consequently, when they receive their own notes, and so are released from their debts to the customer of the other, they are bound to create an equal amount of credit in favor of their own customer, which cancels and extinguishes the former debts, but leaves exactly the same amount of credit existing. Hence, the Clearing House is a *Maison de Novation,* and not a *Maison de Liquidation* or *Compensation.*

The system of clearing was adopted by the city bankers in 1776, but the Bank of England was not admitted to it. Nor were the joint-stock banks admitted to it till 1854; when the charges of the joint-stocks pressed so heavily on the private bankers that they were obliged to admit them. The Bank of England was not admitted till 1864. The charges of the London bankers consist of cheques and bills of exchange, and not in notes; but that makes no difference in the principles of the case. A cheque or bill on a bank by a customer who has funds on his account to meet it is in all respects equivalent to a note of the banker himself. They collect the cheques and bills due to their customers and rearrange the credits due to the various parties exactly in the same way as if they were notes. Before 1864, the differences payable by the banks were settled by bank notes, and it is said that about £250,000 were required for that purpose. But in 1864, when the Bank of England was admitted, the system of clearing was further improved, so that the use of coin and bank notes is now entirely dispensed with. Every clearing bank keeps an account with the Bank of England, and the inspector of the Clearing House keeps one also. Printed lists of the clearing banks are made out for each bank with its own name at the top, and the others placed in alphabetical order below it. On the left side is the debtor's column and on the right side the creditor's. The clerk of the Clearing House then makes up the accounts between each bank, and the difference only is entered in the balance sheet according as it is debtor or creditor. A balance is then struck between the debtor and creditor side, and the paper delivered to the clerk, who takes it back to his own bank. The balance is then paid to or received from the Clearing House. If the bank is debtor it gives a white ticket to, and if it is creditor it receives a green ticket from, the Clearing House. By this most ingenious system not a single coin or bank note is used, and the sums transferred by this means at the present time are about £7,000,000,000 a year.

HOW MERCANTILE BILLS OF EXCHANGE ARE PAID.

We have now to show how erroneous are the ideas of those writers who, like Torrens and Mill, and the sect who supported the Bank Act of 1844, think that all bills of exchange are paid in money or bank notes.

All merchants and traders not only buy goods on credit, but they also sell them on credit. Hence, they are not only indebted on their own acceptances to those from whom they have bought goods, but they hold the acceptances of those to whom they have sold goods. Now, a merchant knows when his own acceptances are coming due, and if he has not sufficient funds on his account to meet them, he has only two methods of providing for them. He must either sell his goods in the market or he must discount the acceptances he holds with his banker. The latter is, of course, the preferable plan. Accordingly, when his balance is low, and his own acceptances are falling due, he simply takes a batch of the acceptances he holds and discounts them with his banker, who buys them by creating a credit, debt, right of action or deposit in his favor, and thus increases his balance. The merchant, of course, makes his own acceptances payable at his banker's; consequently, on the day they mature and become debts, they are simply cheques; and the whole mass of bills and cheques pass through the Clearing House; and, as we have shown in the description of the operations there, the whole transactions are settled by pure transfers of credit, without the use of a single coin or bank note. Hence, in our present highly organized system of credit, bills of exchange are not paid in money or bank notes at all, except only in a very few isolated cases; but they are paid exclusively by the constant creation of new banking credits. Hence, in our present system, the constant creation of banking credits is a matter of vital necessity. If the London bankers were suddenly to give notice that next day they would stop discounting, the result would be that nineteen out of twenty merchants would be ruined. But more than that. As the merchants would, of course, exhaust all their means to maintain themselves, they would instantly draw their balances, and thus the bankers would draw upon themselves a run for gold. It is perfectly well understood by all bankers that "an excessive restriction of credit causes and produces a run for gold." And thus bankers and merchants will all come down in one universal crash.

ON THE TRANSFORMATION OF TEMPORARY CREDIT INTO PERMANENT CAPITAL.

We shall now give an example of the doctrine that the release of a debt is in all cases equivalent to a payment in money, which may surprise some of our readers, and of which we have not seen the slightest notice anywhere else.

When it is published to the world that the Bank of England has a paid-up capital of £16,000,000, and that the several joint-stock banks have paid-up capital of some millions, most persons take it for granted that the banks have these sums paid up in hard cash. Nevertheless this is a profound error. Of course it is impossible for any outsider to have any precise knowledge as to how much of these amounts was ever paid up in actual money. But it may probably be said with safety that not so much as one-half of these various amounts was ever paid up in real money, but by another method which we shall now describe; by which it will appear that at least one-half of these millions of "capital" was never anything more than the bank's own credit turned into "capital." To explain this, we may observe that the first subscription to the Bank of England was £1,200,000; paid of course in actual money. It was advanced to Government, and the bank was allowed to issue an equal amount in notes, which were of course an augmentation of the currency. In 1696, the bank stopped payment, and its notes fell to a discount of twenty per cent. In 1697, Parliament undertook the restoration of public credit; and it was determined to increase the capital of the bank by £1,000,000. But not one penny of this was paid up in actual money. The act directed that £800,000 of the subscription should be paid up in exchequer tallies or exchequer bills; and the remaining £200,000 in the bank's own depreciated notes, which were received at their full value as cash. Thus, of its first increase of capital, £200,000 consisted of its own depreciated notes. The bank was authorized to issue an additional amount of notes equal to its increase of capital. At subsequent increases of capital the subscribers might pay up any amount they pleased in the bank's own notes, which were always held as equivalent to a payment in money, and an increase of capital. In 1727, the Bank of Scotland increased its capital. The subscription was paid up partly in the bank's own notes. An outcry was made against this. But the directors justly answered, "But the objectors do not at all consider this point, for the payments are many of them made in specie; and bank notes are justly reckoned the same as specie, when paid in on a call of stock; because when paid in, it lessens the demand on the bank." Hence the directors clearly understood that the release of a debt is in all respects equivalent to a payment in money. The bank had issued its notes, and was, of course, debtor to the holders of them. These debts were negative quantities. The subscribers might either pay in money, which was $+ \times +$, or release the bank from its debts, which was $- + -$; and the effect of either transaction was exactly the same. At every increase of capital the same operations would be repeated; payment in money and in the bank's own notes would always be treated as equivalent. And hence, at every fresh increase of capital, a certain amount of the bank's own temporary credit was turned into permanent capital. Thus we see that the Parliament of England and the directors of the Bank of Scotland, who were probably equally innocent of Roman law and algebra, simply from their own mercantile instinct treated the release of a debt as in all respects equivalent to a payment in money.

Banks, therefore, which issue notes may increase their capital by receiving their own notes in payment, by which they turn their own credit into capital. But banks which do not issue notes may increase their capital exactly in the same way. A customer of the bank who has a balance to his credit is in exactly the same position as a noteholder. If he wishes to subscribe to an increase of capital he simply gives the bank a cheque on his account. This is equally a release from a debt as a payment in the bank's own notes, and an increase of capital. If the customer has not sufficient on his account to pay for the stock he requires, he may bring the bank bills to discount. The bank discounts those bills by creating a credit or deposit in his favor; which, of course, is a negative quantity exactly like a bank note. The customer then gives the bank a cheque on his account—that is, he releases the bank from the debt it has created, and that debt released becomes increase of capital. This is the way in which the capital of all joint-stock banks is increased; and it may go on to any extent without any payment in money. And, consequently, it is wholly impossible for anyone who has not had access to the books of the bank to ascertain what proportion of the capital consists of payment in money, and what proportion consists of the bank's own temporary credit turned into permanent capital.

CHAPTER IV.

DEFINITIONS OF ECONOMIC TERMS.

I.—DEFINITION OF ECONOMICS.

ECONOMICS is the science of exchanges, or the science which treats of the scientific principles and mechanism of commerce in its widest extent and in all its forms and varieties.

The word economics is compounded of the Greek words *οἶκος* and *νόμος*. *Οἶκος* in Greek means property of every description. Throughout the whole range of Greek literature, from Homer to Ammonius, the word *οἶκος* is used as absolutely synonymous with *πλοῦτος* and *χρῆμα*, to denote wealth of every sort. It is the technical term in Attic law for a person's whole substance, or estate, of every form. It includes not only such property as lands, houses, money, jewelry, corn, cattle, and such things of a material form; but also such property as consists only in the form of abstract rights—such as rights of action, debts, bank notes, bills of exchange, the funds, shares in commercial companies, the goodwill of a business, copyrights, patents, and many other kinds of abstract rights, which are termed in law incorporeal wealth.

Νόμος in Greek means a law; hence economics is the science which treats of the exchanges of all kinds of property which constitute commerce. Hence it may be defined as the science which treats of the principles and mechanism of commerce in all its forms. It is sometimes called the theory of value, or the science of wealth; or it may be called the science which treats of the laws which govern the relations of exchangeable quantities. Michel Chevalier did me the honor to say that he considered this to be the best definition of the science which has yet been proposed. Pure economics, then, is the science which treats of exchanges—of all exchanges, and of nothing but exchanges. And it is a fundamental law of the philosophy of science that when the concept of the science is once determined, all questions and problems in the science must be stated in accordance with that concept, and no other. Thus, economics being the science of exchanges, all economical questions and problems must be stated in the form of an exchange and in no other, such as that of addition or subtraction, or any other.

II.—DEFINITION OF WEALTH, OR OF AN ECONOMIC QUANTITY.

Next, after clearly explaining the nature and purpose of a science, it is necessary to define clearly all the technical terms used in it. In almost every science a considerable number of the definitions used are taken from words of common discourse which have a variety of meanings But in a formal scientific treatise it is indispensably necessary to select one of these divers meanings as suitable for the science, and to use it uniformly in that sense throughout the work. Nor is it sufficient to enumerate a number of isolated objects under a term or definition. As pointed out by Bacon long ago, a scientific definition essentially requires some principle or quality which is common to all the objects which are classed under it. It is not sufficient to allege that lands, houses, jewelry, money, cattle, corn, labor and services, debts, rights of action, the funds, etc., are wealth, without clearly defining the quality or principle which is common to them all, and which constitutes them wealth—*i. e.*, that which constitutes the essence of wealth. This is what Whewell calls the colligation of facts. It is also a principle in framing definitions that, when once the quality, or principle, is agreed upon, which is the basis of the science, all quantities whatever which have that quality in common must be included in the definition, however diverse they may be in nature or form, and even though they possess no other quality in common but that single one. So Bacon earnestly inculcates as the foundation of all true science a careful collection of all kinds of instances in which the given nature, or quality, is found:* "The investigation of forms proceeds thus: a nature, or quality, being given, we must first of all have a muster or presentation before the understanding of all known instances which agree in the same nature, or quality, though in substances the most unlike. And such collection must be made in the matter of a history, without speculation." This is what Plato designates as the one in the many—*i. e.*, the same quality appearing in quantities of the most diverse forms. What, then, is the common property, or principle, which constitutes things wealth?

III.—ARISTOTLE'S DEFINITION OF WEALTH.

Ancient writers for 850 years unanimously held that exchangeability, or the capability of being bought and sold or exchanged, is the sole essence and principle of wealth, and that everything whatever which can be bought and sold or exchanged is wealth, whatever its nature or its form may be. Thus

* Nov. Org., Bk. II., Aph. 11.

Aristotle says, "Nicomach Ethics," Book V.: "χρήματα δὲ λέγομεν πάντα ὅσων ἡ ἀξία νομίσματι μετρεῖται."—"And we call wealth all things whose value can be measured in money." So Ulpian, the eminent Roman jurist, says: "*Ea enim res est quæ emi et venire potest.*"—"For that is wealth which can be bought and sold."

All the most eminent modern economists have come to agree in this definition. Thus Mill says:* "Everything, therefore, forms a part of wealth which has a power of purchasing." Here we have a perfectly good general concept, or definition, which contains only one general idea, and it is therefore fitted to form the basis of a great science. It is a concept as wide and general as the dynamical definition of force. That single sentence of Aristotle's is the germ out of which the whole science of economics is to be evolved, just as the huge oak-tree is developed out of the tiny acorn.

A quantity means anything which can be measured; hence, an economic quantity means anything whatever whose value can be measured in money, or which can be bought and sold or exchanged. The sole criterion, then, of anything being wealth is, can it be bought and sold? Can it be exchanged separately and independently of anything else? Can its value be measured in money? This criterion may seem very simple; but, in fact, to apply it properly, to discern what can and what cannot be bought and sold separately and independently of anything else, or to perceive all things whose value can be measured in money, requires a thorough knowledge of some of the most abstruse branches of law and commerce.

IV.—THE THREE SPECIES OF WEALTH, OR OF ECONOMIC QUANTITIES.

Having, then, adopted exchangeability, or the capability of being bought and sold, as the sole essence and principle of wealth, we have next to discover how many different orders or species of quantities there are which satisfy this definition. First, there are material things of all sorts, such as lands, houses, money, jewelry, corn, cattle, etc., which can be bought and sold, or whose value can be measured in money. Everyone now admits all these things to be wealth, and therefore we need say nothing more about them here. There are, however, two other orders of quantities of a totally different nature—one of which may be typified by the term labor, and the other by the term credit—which can be bought and sold, or whose value can be measured in money; and in modern times there has been a vast amount of controversy as to whether they are to be admitted as wealth or not, and it is these species of quantities which we have now to consider.

V.—ANCIENT DIALOGUE SHOWING THAT LABOR IS WEALTH.

There is a very remarkable work of antiquity extant which is the earliest treatise that we are aware of discussing an economical question. It is a

* Preliminary Remarks, p. 5.

dialogue called the "Eryxias; or, On Wealth," and is frequently bound up with the works of Plato. It is attributed to Æschines Socraticus, one of the most distinguished disciples of Socrates. Critics, however, unanimously pronounced it to be spurious, without being able to assign it to any definite author. High authorities consider it was probably written in the early Peripatetic period. This dialogue is to the following effect: The Syracusans had sent an embassy to Athens, and the Athenians had sent a return embassy to Syracuse. As the Athenian ambassadors were entering the city on their return, they met Socrates and a party of his friends, with whom they entered into conversation. Erasistratus, one of the envoys, said he had seen the richest man in all Sicily. Socrates immediately started a discussion on the nature of wealth. Erasistratus said what he thought upon the subject, as everyone else did, and that to be wealthy meant to have much money. Socrates asked him what kind of money he meant, and he instanced the moneys of several countries. At Carthage they used as money leather discs in which something was sewn up, but nobody knew what it was, and he who possessed the greatest quantity of this money at Carthage was the richest man there. But at Athens he would be no richer than if he possessed so many pebbles from the hill. At Lacedæmon they used iron as money, and that useless iron. He who possessed a great quantity of this iron at Lacedæmon would be rich, but anywhere else it would be worth nothing. In Ethiopia again they used carved pebbles as money, which were of no use anywhere else. Among the nomade Scythians a house was not wealth, because no one wanted a house, but greatly preferred a good sheepskin cloak. He showed that if anyone could live without meat and drink, they would not be wealth to him, because he did not want them.

Socrates showed that money is only wealth because it is exchangeable—because it can purchase other things. Where it is not exchangeable, where it cannot purchase other things, it is not wealth. He then asked why some things are wealth and other things are not wealth. Why are some things wealth in some places and not in other places? And at some times, and not at other times? He showed that whether a thing is wealth or not depends entirely upon human wants and desires; that everything is wealth which is wanted and demanded; that things are only wealth, *χρήματα*, where and when they are *χρήσιμα*—that is, where and when they are wanted and demanded; and that nothing is wealth when and where it is not wanted and demanded. Thus we see that though some persons might be puzzled at the meaning of the word wealth, there is no possibility of mistake when we refer to the Greek, because *χρῆμα*, which is one of the most usual words in Greek for wealth, comes from *χράομαι*, to want or demand. Consequently, the word *χρῆμα*, wealth, means simply anything whatever which is wanted and demanded, no matter what its nature or its form may be.

It is, then, human wants and desires which alone constitute anything wealth. Anything whatever which people want and demand and are willing to pay for is wealth. Everything, therefore, which can be bought and sold is wealth, whatever its nature or its form may be; and anything which no one wants or demands is not wealth.

Socrates then showed that gold and silver are only wealth in so far as they enable us to obtain or purchase what we want and demand; and that if anything else will enable us to purchase what we want and demand in the same way that money does, it is wealth for the very same reason that gold and silver are. He then instanced persons who gained their living by giving instruction in the various sciences. He said that persons are able to purchase what they want by giving this instruction, just as they are able to do with gold and silver. Consequently, he said that the sciences are wealth —*αἱ ἐπίϭτημαι χρήματα οὖϭαι*; and that those who are masters of such sciences are so much the richer—*πλουϭιώτεροί εἰϭι·* Now, in instancing the sciences as wealth—that is, of course, a general term for labor, because labor in economics is any exertion of human ability or thought which is wanted, demanded, and paid for—thus the author of this dialogue showed that labor is wealth.

Socrates showed that the mind has wants and demands as well as the body, and that the things which are wanted and demanded for the mind and are paid for are equally wealth as those things which satisfy the wants and demands of the body and are paid for. Thus all of the great professions—law, physic, surgery, engineering, and many others—are great estates, which produce utilities, which are as much wealth as the utilities which satisfy the wants of the body.

Now, labor cannot be seen nor handled; it cannot be transferred by manual delivery; but it may be bought and sold; its value may be measured in money; therefore it satisfies Aristotle's definition of wealth. If any person wants any other to do any labor or service for him, and pays him for it, its value is measured in money as exactly as if it were a material chattel. Suppose that a person gives fifty guineas for a watch or a horse, and also fifty guineas for the opinion of an eminent advocate; the value of the opinion is measured in money as exactly as the value of the watch or the horse; and therefore they are all equally wealth.

So if a person earns an income of some thousands a year as the manager of a great mercantile company—banking, insurance, railway or any other—his services are as much wealth to him as corn or cattle to a farmer, or goods to any trader. Hence, the author of this dialogue showed that personal qualities in the form of labor are wealth, which no one perceived till Adam Smith; and thus he anticipated by about 2176 years one of the great extensions which Smith gave to the science.

VI.—MODERN ECONOMISTS INCLUDE LABOR UNDER THE TERM WEALTH.

It has been shown that the economists expressly excluded labor, or services,.from the term wealth. But, in accordance with the author of the

"Eryxias," Smith enumerates under the term fixed capital:* "The acquired and useful abilities of all the inhabitants or members of the society. The acquisition of such talents, by the maintenance of the acquirer during his education, study, or apprenticeship, always costs a real expense, which is a capital fixed and realized, as it were, in his person. These talents, as they make part of his fortune, so do they likewise that of the society to which he belongs." So also he says: "The property which every man has in his own labor, as it is the original foundation of all other property, so it is the most sacred and most inviolable. The patrimony of a poor man lies in the strength and dexterity of his hands."

J. B. Say dwelt with emphatic force on the doctrine that personal qualities are wealth. Among many other passages, he says:† "He who has acquired a talent at the price of an annual sacrifice enjoys an accumulated capital; and this wealth, though immaterial, is nevertheless so little fictitious that he daily exchanges the exercise of his art for gold and silver."

"Since it has been proved that immaterial property, such as talents and acquired personal abilities, forms an integral part of social wealth, you see that utility, under whatever form it presents itself, is the source of the value of things; and what may surprise you is that this utility can be created, can have value, and become the subject of an exchange, without being incorporated with any material object. A manufacturer of glass places value in sand; a manufacturer of cloth places it in wool; but a physician sells us a utility without being incorporated in any manner. This utility is truly the fruit of his studies, his labor, and his capital. We buy it in buying his opinion. It is a real product, but immaterial."

Say calls all species of labor and services immaterial wealth, because they are vendible products, but not embodied in any matter. This is an excellent name, and we shall adopt it to distinguish this order of economic quantities from material things and abstract rights.

We must, however, guard against an erroneous expression of Say's. He says that the manufacturers of glass and cloth place value in sand and wool. This, however, is an error. The artisans place their labor in sand and wool, but it is the demand of the consumer which alone gives value to the glass and the cloth.

Senior has a long and eloquent passage to the same purpose:‡ "If the question whether personal qualities are articles of wealth had been proposed in classical times, it would have appeared too clear for discussion. [We have already seen that the question was discussed in classical times.] In Athens everyone would have replied that they, in fact, constituted the whole value of an *ἔμψυχον ὄργανον*. The only differences in this respect between a freeman and a slave are, first, that the freeman sells himself, and only for a period and to a certain extent; the slave may be sold by others and absolutely; and secondly, that the personal qualities of the slave are a

* Wealth of Nations, Bk. II., ch. i.

† *Cours, Considérations Générales.*

‡ Political Economy, p. 10.

portion of the wealth of his master; those of the freeman, so far as they can be made the subject of exchange, are part of his own wealth. They perish, indeed, by his death, and may be impaired or destroyed by disease or rendered valueless by any change in the custom of the country which shall destroy the demand for his services [thus Senior sees that value depends on demand and not upon labor]; but subject to these contingencies they are wealth, and wealth of the most valuable kind. The amount of revenue derived from their exercise in England far exceeds the rental of all the lands in Great Britain."

So also Senior says: "Even in our present state of civilization, which, high as it appears by comparison, is far short of what may be easily conceived or even of what may be confidently expected, the intellectual and moral capital of Great Britain far exceeds all the material capital, not only in importance but in productiveness. The families that receive mere wages probably do not form a fourth part of the community; and the comparatively larger amount of the wages even of these is principally owing to the capital and skill with which their efforts are assisted and directed by the more educated members of the society. Those who receive mere rent, even using that word in its largest sense, are still fewer; and the amount of rent, like that of wages, principally depends on the knowledge by which the gifts of nature are directed and employed. The bulk of the national revenue is profit; and of that profit the portion which is merely interest on material capital probably does not amount to one-third. The rest is the result of personal capital, or, in other words, of education. It is not in the accidents of the soil, in the climate, in the existing accumulation of the instruments of production, but in the quantity and diffusion of this immaterial capital that the wealth of a country depends. The climate, the soil, and the situation of Ireland have been described as superior, and certainly not much inferior to our own. Her poverty has been attributed to the want of material capital; but were Ireland now to exchange her native population for seven millions of our English north-countrymen, they would quickly create the capital that is wanted. And were England north of the Trent to be peopled exclusively by a million of families from the west of Ireland, Lancashire and Yorkshire would still more rapidly resemble Connaught. Ireland is physically poor, because she is morally and intellectually poor. And while she continues uneducated, while the ignorance and the violence of her population render persons and property insecure, and prevent the accumulation and prohibit the introduction of capital, legislative measures, intended solely and directly to relieve her poverty, may not, indeed, be ineffectual, for they may aggravate the disease the symptoms of which they are meant to palliate, but undoubtedly will be productive of no permanent benefit. Knowledge has been called power; it is far more certainly wealth. Asia Minor, Syria, Egypt and the northern coast of Africa were once among the richest, and are now among the most miserable countries in the world, simply because they have fallen into the hands of a people without a sufficiency of the immaterial sources of wealth to keep up the material ones."

So Mill says:* "The skill and energy and the perseverance of the artisans of a country are reckoned part of its wealth no less than its tools and machinery." And why not the skill and energy and perseverance of other classes as well as of artisans? He also says: "Acquired capacities, which exist only as a means, and have been called into existence by labor, fall exactly, as it seems to me, within that designation." So Madame Campan inscribed over the hall of study in her establishment at St. Germain: "Talents are the ornaments of the rich and the wealth of the poor." So Cardinal Newman says:† "If gold is wealth, power, influence; and if coal is wealth, power, influence, so is knowledge."

We have, then, already found two distinct kinds of things which can be bought and sold, or whose value can be measured in money: (1) Material things which can be seen and handled, such as money, corn, cattle, lands, houses, etc., which can be transferred by manual delivery. (2) Things like labor and knowledge, which can neither be seen nor handled, but which can be bought and sold; and though these two kinds of things have nothing in common besides the capability of being bought and sold, they are each for that reason comprehended under the term wealth.

VII.—DEMOSTHENES SHOWS THAT PERSONAL CREDIT IS WEALTH.

But personal qualities may be used as purchasing power in another method besides that of labor. If a merchant enjoys good "credit," as it is termed, he may go into the market and buy goods, not with money, but by giving his promise to pay money at a future time—that is, he creates a right of action against himself. The goods become his property exactly as if he had paid for them in money. It is a sale or an exchange. The right of action is the price he pays for the goods; it is termed a credit—in French, a *créance*—because it is not a right to any specific sum of money, but only a right of action to demand a sum of money from the merchant at a future time. Hence, a merchant's credit is purchasing power, exactly as money. The merchant's purchasing power is his money and his credit. They are both, therefore, equally wealth, by Mill's definition. When a merchant purchases goods with his credit, instead of with money, his credit is valued in money, because the seller of the goods accepts his credit as equal in value to money; his credit is valued in money exactly as his labor may be. Hence, by Aristotle's definition of wealth, which is now universally accepted, the merchant's personal credit is wealth.

So Demosthenes says:‡ "*δυοῖν ἀγαθοῖν ὄντοιν πλούτου τε καὶ πρὸς ἅπαντας πιστεύεσθαι, μεῖζόν ἐστι τὸ τῆς πίστεως ὑπάρχον ἡμῖν.*"—"There being two kinds of wealth—money and general credit—the greater is credit, and

* Principles of Political Economy, Bk. I., ch. iii. † Historical Sketches, Free Trade in Knowledge, p. 50.

‡ Against Leptines, 484, 20.

we have it." So also again.* "*εἰ δὲ τοῦτο ἀγνοεῖς ὅτι Πίϭτις ᾽Αφορμὴ τῶν παϭῶν ἐϭτι μεγίϭτη πρὸς χρηματιϭμὸν πᾶν ἂν ἀγνοήσειας.*"—"If you were ignorant of this—that credit is the greatest capital of all toward the acquisition of wealth, you would be utterly ignorant." Thus Demosthenes shows that personal credit is *ἀγαθά*—wealth, property, goods, and chattels—and *ἀφορμή*, or capital.

Thus, though personal credit, like labor, can neither be seen nor handled nor touched, yet it can be bought and sold, or exchanged; its value can be measured in money; it is purchasing power, and therefore it is wealth. And as we have seen that Adam Smith declares that a man's labor is his most sacred possession, of which no person has the right to despoil him, so to all bankers, merchants and traders, their credit is their most sacred possession, of which no one has the right falsely to despoil them. Hence the personal credit of all bankers, merchants, and traders is an integral and colossal portion of the national wealth—just as the industrial faculties of workingmen of all kinds are. So also the credit of the State, by which it can purchase money and other things by giving persons the right to demand a series of future payments from it, is national wealth.

VIII.—MODERN ECONOMISTS INCLUDE PERSONAL CREDIT UNDER THE TERM WEALTH.

It has been shown that the economists steadfastly refused to admit that personal credit is wealth; because they alleged that, to allow that would be to maintain that wealth can be created out of nothing. But contemporary, general, and mercantile writers were entirely against them on that point. Thus Daniel de Foe says:† "Credit is so much a tradesman's blessing that it is the choicest ware he deals in, and he cannot be too chary of it when he has it, or buy it too dear when he wants it: it is a stock to his warehouse; it is current money in his cash-chest." So that keen metaphysician, Bishop Berkeley, who has many searching questions on economics in his "Querist," asks (Quest. 35): "Whether power to command the industry of others [*i. e.*, credit] be not real wealth?" So Melon says:‡ "To the calculation of values in money there must be added the current credit of the merchant and his possible credit."

So Dutot says:§ "Since there has been a regular commerce among men, those who have need of money have made bills, or promises to pay money. The first use of credit, therefore, is to represent money by paper. The usage is very old; the first want gave rise to it. It multiplies specie considerably; it supplies it where it is wanting, and which would never be sufficient without the credit; because there is not sufficient gold and silver to circulate all the products of nature and art. So there is in commerce a much larger amount in bills than there is in specie in the possession of the merchants.

* For Phormion, 958.

† The Complete English Tradesman, ch. xvii.

‡ *Essai Politique sur le Commerce*, ch. xxiv.

§ *Réflexions sur le Commerce et les Finances*, ch. i., art. 10.

A well-managed credit amounts to tenfold the funds of a merchant, and he gains as much by his credit as if he had ten times as much money. This maxim is generally received among all merchants. Credit is, therefore, the greatest wealth to everyone who carries on commerce."

So Smith says:* "Trade can be extended as stock increases, and the credit of a frugal and thriving man increases much faster than his stock. His trade is extended in proportion to the amount of both [*i. e.*, his stock and his credit], and the sum or amount of his profits is in proportion to the extent of his trade, and his annual accumulation in proportion to his profits." So Junius says: "Private credit is wealth"; and Franklin says: "Credit is money." Smith expressly includes "natural and acquired abilities" under the term fixed capital. Now, mercantile character or personal credit evidently comes under the designation of "natural and acquired abilities." Hence personal credit is included by Smith under the term capital.

No person has more explicitly declared that personal credit is wealth than Mill. He says, in the preliminary remarks: "Everything, therefore, forms a part of wealth which has a power of purchasing." He then says:† "For credit, though it is not productive power, is purchasing power."

"The credit, which we are now called upon to consider as a distinct purchasing power." He also says:‡ "The amount of purchasing power which a person can exercise is composed of all the money in his possession, or due to him (*i. e.*, the bank notes, bills, and credits he has), and of all his credit. Credit, in short, has exactly the same purchasing power with money." And many other passages to the same effect. Now, if Mill lays down as the fundamental definition of wealth, "Everything that is purchasing power is wealth," and if he says, "Credit is purchasing power," then the necessary inference is that credit is wealth. That is a syllogism in which Mill is safely padlocked, and from which there is no escape.

IX.—ON ABSTRACT RIGHTS AS WEALTH.

But there is yet another or a third order of quantities which can neither be seen nor handled, but which can be bought and sold, or exchanged, and whose value can be measured in money; and these are abstract rights of various sorts—rights and rights of action. Suppose that a person pays in a sum of money to his account at his banker's, what becomes of that money? It becomes the absolute property of the banker. The customer cedes the absolute property in the money to the banker, but he does not make him a present of it. He gets something in exchange for it—and what is that something? In exchange for the money the banker gives his customer a credit in his books, which is a right of action to demand back an equivalent sum of money whenever he pleases. But it is not a title to any specific sum of money in the banker's possession. It is a mere abstract right of action

* Wealth of Nations, Bk. I., ch. x.

† Principles of Political Economy, Bk. III., ch. xi. § 3.

‡ Ibid., Bk. III., ch. xii. § 3.

against the person of the banker to demand a sum of money from him. The transaction is a sale or an exchange; the banker buys the money from his customer by issuing to him in exchange for it a right of action; and the customer buys this right of action with gold. Furthermore, the banker agrees that his customer may transfer this right of action to anyone else he pleases, by means of a bank note or cheque. So this right of action may pass through any number of hands, and effect any number of exchanges, exactly like an equal amount of money, until the holder demands payment of it, and it is extinguished. When the holder of the cheque demands payment of it from the banker, the banker buys up the right of action against himself with gold; and the holder of the cheque sells his right of action for gold. The transaction is therefore a sale or an exchange, and an act of commerce. Hence the whole series of these transactions are sales or exchanges. When the customer pays in money to his account it is an exchange; when he pays away his cheque in commerce it is an exchange; every time the cheque is transferred it is an exchange; and, finally, when payment is demanded from the banker it is an exchange. All these transactions are acts of commerce.

This right of action is termed a credit; because anyone who chooses to take it in exchange for goods or services knows that it is not a title to any specific sum of money in the banker's possession; but it is only an abstract right to demand a sum of money from him; and the person who takes it only does so because he has the belief or confidence that the banker can pay if required. It will be convenient to state here that this right of action is also termed a debt; and that both in law and common usage the words credit and debt are used quite indiscriminately to mean a creditor's right of action against his debtor. The reason of this will be explained in a future section. Similarly, when a merchant sells goods "on credit," as it is termed, to a trader, he cedes the property in the goods to the trader, exactly as if he had sold them for money. And in exchange for the goods the trader gives the merchant his promise to pay, or a right of action to demand money at a future time—say three months after date. This right of action is also termed a credit or a debt. It is the price the trader pays for the goods. And if it be recorded on paper in the form of a bill of exchange, it may be exchanged against other goods, and circulate in commerce, exactly like an equal sum of money, any number of times, until it is paid off and extinguished. Again, suppose that the State wants to borrow money for any public purpose—such as a war or for some great public work. It buys money from those who are willing to sell it, and in exchange for the money it gives them the right to demand a series of payments from the State, either forever or for a certain limited time. This right to demand a series of future payments is termed an annuity, and is the price the State pays for the money. In popular language, they are termed the funds. And the owners of these rights may sell them again to anyone they please. They are salable commodities, just like any material goods.

Suppose, again, that a person subscribes to the capital of a joint-stock company—banking, railway, insurance, canal, dock, or any other. He pays the money to the company, which is a distinct person, quite separate from any individual shareholders, and receives in exchange for it the right to share in the future profits of the company. These rights are termed shares; and they are also salable commodities; they may be bought and sold like any material chattels. So, when a trader has established a successful business, he has the right to receive the future profits to be made by the business. This right to receive the future profits is a property quite distinct and separate from the house or shop, and the actual goods in them. It is additional to them. It is the product of labor, skill, thought, and care as much as any material chattels, and is a part of the trader's assets. It is termed the goodwill of the business, and is a salable commodity.

Thrale, the great brewer, appointed Johnson one of his executors. In that capacity it became his duty to sell the business. When the sale was going on, says Boswell, "Johnson appeared bustling about, with an inkhorn and pen in his button-hole, like an exciseman; and on being asked what he really considered to be the value of the property which was to be disposed of, answered, 'We are not here to sell a parcel of vats and boilers, but the potentiality of growing rich beyond the dreams of avarice.'" This latter phrase was merely Johnsonese for the goodwill of the business. The price realized was, we are told elsewhere, £135,000.

When the banking house of Jones, Loyd & Co. sold their business to the London and Westminster Bank, it was said in the papers that the price paid was £500,000. Similarly, every successful business has a goodwill attached to it which is a salable commodity and an asset of the trader's.

Now, these abstract rights cannot be seen nor handled nor touched. But they can be bought or sold or exchanged. Their value can be measured in money. They can be transferred from one person to another as easily as any material chattels. Therefore, they satisfy Aristotle's definition of wealth. They all possess that quality of exchangeability which ancient writers unanimously, and modern economists now at last agree, is the sole essence and principle of wealth. And, therefore, by the fundamental laws of natural philosophy, these abstract rights are all wealth.

X.—GENERAL RULE OF ROMAN LAW THAT RIGHTS ARE WEALTH.

Now, in the Pandects of Justinian, which are the great code or digest of Roman law, it is laid down as a fundamental general rule: "*Pecuniæ nomine non solum numerata pecunia, sed omnes res tam soli quam mobiles, et tam corpora quam jura continentur.*"—"Under the term wealth, not only ready money, but all things, both immovable and movable, both corporeal things and rights are included." So the eminent Roman jurist Ulpian says:* "*Nomina eorum qui sub conditione vel in diem debent, et emere et vendere solemus. Ea enim res est quæ emi et venire potest.*"—"We are accustomed

* *Liber* 34, *ad Edict.*

to buy and sell debts payable at a certain event or on a certain day. For that is wealth which can be bought and sold."

So it is also said:* "*Æque bonis adnumerabitur si quid est in actionibus.*"—"Rights of action are properly reckoned as goods." So also:† "*Rei appellatione et causæ et jura continentur.*"—"Under the term property both rights and rights of action are included."

So Sir Patrick Colquhoun says:‡ "The first requisite of the consensual contract of *emptio et venditio* is a *Merx*, or object to be transferred from the buyer to the seller, and the first requirement is that it should be *in commercio*—that is, capable of being freely bought and sold. Supposing such to be the case, it matters not whether it is an immovable or a movable, corporeal or incorporeal, existent or non-existent, certain or uncertain, the property of the vendor or another: thus a horse or a right of action, servitude or thing to be acquired, or the acquisition whereof depends on chance. A purchaser may buy of a farmer the future crop of a certain field; wine which may grow next year on a certain vineyard may be bought and sold at so much a pipe, or a certain price may be paid, irrespective of quantity or quality, and the price would be due, though nothing grew, or for whatever did grow. In the second case the bargain is termed *emptio spei*, and in the first and last *emptio rei speratæ*, which all such bargains are presumed to be in cases of doubt. The cession of a right of action being legal in the Roman law, the right of A to receive a debt due by B may be sold to C."

Thus it is clearly seen that abstract rights of many various sorts, including rights of action, which in law, commerce, and economics are termed credits, or debts, are expressly included under the terms *Pecunia* (wealth), *Res* (property), *Bona* (goods or chattels) and *Merx* (merchandise) in Roman law.

XI.—GENERAL RULE OF GREEK LAW THAT RIGHTS ARE WEALTH.

For nearly 500 years after Constantine removed the seat of government from Rome to Constantinople, the language of the Court was Latin, but the people were Greek. Consequently, as the official language was Latin, it was unintelligible to the mass of the people. The great code of Roman law, termed the Pandects, was published in A.D. 530, but all the pleadings in the courts were carried on in Greek. The Latin Pandects soon fell into desuetude; they were superseded by Greek treatises, translations, and compilations. The Latin Institutes of Justinian did not hold their place in the curriculum of legal education for more than ten years. They were superseded by the paraphrase of Theophilus, one of the Professors of Law who were charged with the compilation of the Institutes; and this paraphrase became the text-book for the education of law students throughout the Eastern Empire. At last, in the ninth and tenth centuries, under the Basilian dynasty, all the Pandects, Institutes and Legislation of Justinian were set aside as obsolete. A reformed digest or code was published in Greek,

* Digest, 50, 16, 49. † Digest, 50, 16, 23. ‡ Summary of Roman Law. Digest, 18, 34, § 1, 2.

which was called the *Basilica,* which may mean either the Imperial Constitutions or the Code of the Basilian dynasty, like the *Code Napoléon,* and this henceforth became the law of the Eastern Empire, and has remained to the present time as the common law of all the Greek population in the East, and is the common law of the modern Kingdom of Hellas. And the Roman definition of wealth is adopted and confirmed.

Thus it is said:* "*τῷ ὀνόματι τῶν Χρημάτων οὐ μόνον τὰ χρήματα, ἀλλὰ πάντα τὰ κινητὰ καὶ ἀκινητὰ, καὶ τὰ σωματικὰ καὶ Δίκαια δηλοῦται.*"

"Under the term *χρήματα*, or wealth, * * * rights are included." Also† "*τῇ τοῦ πράγματος προσηγορίᾳ καὶ Αἴτιαι καὶ τὰ Δίκαια περιέχεται.*" Under the term *πράγματα*, goods and chattels, both rights of action and rights are included.

Thus it is seen that by express enactment in Greek law, the words *χρήματα* and *πράγματα* include rights and rights of action. These rights and rights of action are also included under the terms *'Αγαθά* (goods), *περιουσία* (estate), *'Αφορμή* (capital), *Οὐσία* and *Οἶκος* (wealth), and other similar words; they are also called *οὐσία ἀφανής* (invisible wealth). And these words include all the three orders of economic quantities.

XII.—GENERAL RULE OF ENGLISH LAW THAT RIGHTS ARE WEALTH.

It is exactly the same in English and every other system of law; abstract rights or property are included under the term "Goods," "Goods and Chattels," "Chattels," "Merchandise," "Vendible Commodities," "Incorporeal Chattels," and "Incorporeal Wealth" in English law. And under similar terms in every other system of jurisprudence. And under wealth and capital in economics.

A chattel means any property of any sort which is not freehold.

Thus Sheppard says:‡ "All kinds of emblements, sown and growing, grass cut; all money, plate, jewelry, utensils, household stuffs, debts, wood cut, wares in a shop, tools and instruments for work, wares, merchandise, carts, ploughs, coaches, saddles and the like; all kinds of cattle, as horses, oxen, kine, bullocks, goats, sheep, pigs; and all tame fowl, swans, turkeys, geese, capons, hens, ducks, poultry and the like, are accounted as chattels. All obligations, bills, statutes, recognizances, judgments shall be as a chattel in the executor. All right of action to a personal chattel is a chattel."

So in Ford's case§ it was resolved by Popham, Chief Justice of England, and the Court, that: "Personal actions are as well included within the word 'goods' in an Act of Parliament as goods in possession." So Lord Chancellor Hardwicke said:‖ "The chattels are * * * the debts (*i. e.*, rights of action) due and to be due, * * * and debts come within the words and meaning of the act, and would pass in a will thereby."

* Basil., II., 2, 214.

† Basil., II., 2, 21.

‡ Grand Abridgment, Part I., s. v., Chattels; also Touchstone, Vol. II., p. 468.

§ 12 Co. 1.

‖ Ryall v. Rowles, 1 Vesey, 348.

Burnet, J., said: "A bond debt is certainly a chattel * * * the conclusive case is Ford's case, that personal actions are included in the word goods in an Act of Parliament as goods in possession." Parker, L. C. B., said: "But goods and chattels include debts (rights of action). * * * Goods and chattels comprehend things-in-action in the construction of any Act of Parliament." Lee, C. J., said: "The inquiry is whether choses-in-action are not included under goods and chattels? And I agree, choses-in-action will be included herein."

So Blackstone says:* "For it is to be understood that in our law, chattels, or goods and chattels, is a term used to express any property, which having regard either to subject-matter, or quantity of interest therein, is not freehold." * * * "Property, or chattels personal, may be either in possession or action. * * * Property in action is where a man has not the enjoyment (either actual or constructive) of the thing in question, but merely a right to receive it by a suit or action-at-law." So Mr. J. Williams says:† "Personal estate is divided in English law into chattels real and chattels personal; the latter are again divided into choses-in-possession and choses-in-action."

We are dealing exclusively with the commerce in rights of action—*i. e.*, their creation, transfer and extinction—which constitutes the great system of credit; and, therefore, we shall henceforth confine our attention to them. Rights of action, then, being now shown to be goods and chattels, it is absolutely necessary to observe that it is the abstract right of action itself which is the "goods" or "chattels," and not any material upon which it may be written down. Rights of action, *i. e.*, credits, or debts, may be bought or sold with perfect facility even in the abstract state. It is, however, very usual to write them down on paper in the form of bank notes, cheques, bills of exchange, and other instruments. By doing this they become capable of manual delivery, and are transferable from hand to hand like money or any other material chattel. Abstract rights of action are incorporeal chattels; but when written down on paper they become corporeal chattels or material commodities, exactly like money. Hence, the reader must observe that writing a right of action down on paper in no way alters its nature. Doing so is merely a convenient form of rendering it capable of being transferred in commerce. But it is exactly of the same nature and effect whether written down on paper or not.

XIII.—MODERN ECONOMISTS INCLUDE RIGHTS OF ACTION, *i. e.*, CREDITS, OR DEBTS, UNDER THE TERM CIRCULATING CAPITAL.

It has been shown that the economists steadfastly refused to admit credits, or debts, *i. e.*, rights of action, to be wealth. But it has been shown in the introduction that Smith expressly classes bank notes and bills of

* Bk. II., Pt. I., ch. v.

† Encyl. Brit., vol. xviii., art. Personal Estate.

exchange under the term circulating capital; hence Smith expressly recognizes the three orders of exchangeable quantities, and that credits are wealth and capital. Thus Smith expressly includes money under the term circulating capital. And under money he includes bank notes, bills of exchange, etc., which he terms paper money—which term is not quite correct because, though under certain circumstances, bank notes and bills of exchange may be, and in an immense number of cases are money, as will be seen further on, still they are not absolutely money. But they are all included under the term paper currency. Among several passages, it will be sufficient to quote one here:* "Suppose that different banks and bankers issue promissory notes payable to bearer on demand to the extent of one million, reserving in their different coffers £200,000 for answering occasional demands. There would remain therefore in circulation £800,000 in gold and silver, and £1,000,000 in bank notes; or, £1,800,000 of paper and money together." He also observes that credits in the Bank of Amsterdam were termed bank money. Thus we see that Smith in this and numerous other passages places paper credit exactly on the same footing as money, as independent property, and of the same value as gold and silver.

So J. B. Say says:† "The exclusive possession, which in the midst of society clearly distinguishes the property of one person from that of another in common usage, is that to which the title of wealth is given [not unless this property is exchangeable]. * * * Under this title are included not only things which are directly capable of satisfying the wants of man, either natural or social, but the things which can satisfy them only indirectly —such as money, instruments of credit (*Titres de créance*) and the public funds." Thus Say expressly includes instruments of credit and the funds, which are mere rights of action, under the term wealth; and he also includes bills of exchange, bank notes, and bank credits—which are all credit—under the term capital. Thus he says that if a bank can maintain in circulation a greater quantity of notes than it retains specie in reserve, it augments by so much the capital of the country. So he also says:‡ "We must include under capital many objects which have a value, although they are not material. The practice of an advocate or notary, the custom of a shop, the representative of a sign-board, the title of a periodical work, are undoubtedly property (*Biens*); they may be bought and sold, and be the subject of a contract, and they are also capital, because they are the fruit of accumulated labor." How are bank notes and bills of exchange, which Say admits to be capital, the fruit of accumulated labor?

So Mill says:§ "We have now found that there are other things such as bank notes, bills of exchange, and cheques [which are credit] which circulate as money, and perform all the functions of it." He also designates bank notes as productive capital.

* Wealth of Nations, Bk. II., ch. ii.

† *Traité d'Economie Politique*, p. 1.

‡ *Cours d'Economie Politique*, Part IV., ch. v.

§ Principles of Political Economy, Bk. III., ch. xii., § 1.

Whately is the only English economist that we are aware of who has drawn especial attention to incorporeal property. He says:* "The only difficulty I can foresee as attendant on the language I have been now using, is one which (*i. e.*, defining political economy as the science of exchanges) vanishes so readily on a moment's reflection as to be hardly worth mentioning. * * * In many cases, where an exchange really takes place, the fact is liable (till the attention be called to it) to be overlooked, in consequence of our not seeing any actual transfer from hand to hand of a material object. For instance, when the copyright of a book is sold to a publisher, the article transferred is not the mere paper covered with writing, but the exclusive privilege of printing and publishing. It is plain, however, on a moment's thought, that the transaction is as real an exchange as that which takes place between the bookseller and his customers who buy copies of the work. The payment of rent for land is a transaction of a similar kind, though the land itself is a material object; it is not this that is parted with to the tenant, but the right to till it, or to make use of it in some other specified manner. Sometimes, for instance, rent is paid for a right of way through another's field, or for liberty to erect a booth during a fair, or to race or exercise horses."

And Whately says in a note to this passage: "This instance, by the way, evinces the impropriety of limiting the term wealth to material objects." Thus in this passage is found the first dim perception, that we are aware of, that all exchanges consist of the exchange of rights against rights, as will be shown further on.

The stupendous importance of this doctrine, that rights and rights of action are goods, chattels, merchandise, vendible commodities and wealth, consists in this: that modern commerce is almost exclusively carried on by means of rights of action, credits, or debts. Money is only used to such an infinitesimal degree that it may almost be neglected. The principal use of money in commerce now is to keep such a stock of it as may be necessary to maintain the convertibility or value of the circulating credits. Moreover, in recent times, rights in the form of securities of various sorts, and rights of action in the form of public and private debts, form a most important article of import and export between countries, and have exactly the same effects on the foreign exchanges and the movements of bullion as material goods, as will be shown further on.

XIV.—THERE IS NO SUCH THING AS ABSOLUTE WEALTH.

The preceding considerations show that there is no such thing as absolute wealth—that is, there is nothing which is in its own nature, and in all circumstances, in all places and in all times, wealth. The sole essence and principle of wealth is exchangeability. For anything to be exchangeable it

* Lectures on Political Economy, p. 6.

is necessary that someone besides its owner should desire and demand it, and be willing to give something to obtain it. It is only, therefore, human desires and wants, and the capacity to give something to obtain it, that constitute anything wealth. Things are wealth only in those places and in those times where and when they are wanted, demanded, and paid for; and consequently they cease to be wealth when they cease to be wanted and demanded. Therefore, the very same things may be wealth in some places and not in others; and at some times and not at others; and become wealth more or less as the demand for them increases or decreases. Hence the amount of wealth in any country is simply the mass of exchangeable commodities in it.

XV.—ECONOMICS, OR COMMERCE, CONSISTS OF SIX DISTINCT KINDS OF EXCHANGE.

It has now been shown that, for 1300 years, ancient writers unanimously held that exchangeability is the sole essence and principle of wealth. That anything whatever which possesses the principle or quality of exchangeability; everything whatever which can be bought or sold or exchanged; everything whose value can be measured in money, is wealth, no matter what its form or its nature may be. The ancients also showed that there are three distinct orders of quantities which possess the quality of exchangeability, or whose value can be measured in money—namely, (1) material things; (2) personal qualities, both in the form of labor and credit; (3) abstract rights. And reflection will show that there is nothing which can be bought and sold, or whose value can be measured in money, which is not of one of these three forms; either it is a material thing or it is a personal service or quality, or it is an abstract right. Hence, as it is positively known that there is nothing which possesses the quality of exchangeability, or whose value can be measured in money, beyond these three orders of quantities, the science is now complete.

Now, if all material things be symbolized by the word money; if all personal services be symbolized by the word labor, and if all abstract rights be symbolized by the word credit, these three distinct orders of economic quantities may be symbolized by the words money, labor, and credit. And all commerce in its widest extent, and in all its forms and varieties—that is, the science of pure economics—consists in the exchanges of these three orders of quantities. There being, then, three, and only three, distinct orders of economic quantities, it is evident that they may be combined two and two in six different ways. These six different kinds of exchange are: 1. A material thing for a material thing; as when gold money is given in exchange for lands, houses, corn, jewelry, etc. 2. A material thing for labor; as when gold money is paid as wages, fees, or salary, for any service done. 3. A material thing for a right; as when gold money is given to purchase a bank credit, a bill of exchange, copyrights, patents, shares in commercial companies, the funds, or any other valuable right. 4. Labor for labor; as when persons agree to perform certain amounts of reciprocal services for each other. 5. Labor for a right; as when a person performs services for another, and is paid in bank notes, cheques, or bills of exchange. 6. A right for a right; as when a banker buys one right of action, such as a bill of exchange, and gives in exchange for it a credit in his books, which is another right of action; or when a person purchases copyrights, patents, or any other abstract right, and gives in exchange for them bank notes, cheques, or bills of exchange.

The economists only admitted material products to be wealth, and only treated of one species of exchange—that of products for products. Beccaria admitted that services are wealth, and said that all exchanges consist of the exchanges of products for products, products for services, and services for services, thereby admitting three kinds of exchange. But, as a matter of fact, there are three orders of economic or exchangeable quantities, and therefore there are six distinct kinds of exchange. The business of banking consists in the exchanges of credit for money, and of credits for credits. An operation "on credit" is one in which one or both of the quantities exchanged is a credit or debt. The system of credit means the commerce in rights of action, credits, or debts, and is the subject-matter of this work.

XVI.—ON THE MEANING OF THE WORD PROPERTY.

There being, then, three orders of quantities which possess the quality of exchangeability, they must, by the laws of natural philosophy, by the unanimous doctrine of ancient writers, and at last by the acknowledgment of all modern economists, all be included under the term wealth. The next thing to be done is to find a general term which will include them all. And this general term will be found in the word property. And when we understand the true and original meaning of the word property, it will throw a blaze of light over the whole science of economics and clear up all the difficulties which the word wealth has given rise to. In fact, the meaning of the word property is the key to the whole sciences of jurisprudence and economics. Most persons, when they hear the word property, think of some material things, such as lands, houses, cattle, corn, money, etc. But that is not the true and original meaning of the word property. Property, in its true and original meaning, is not anything at all material or otherwise, but it is the ownership or absolute right to something. Savages have very feeble notions of abstract rights. Their ideas of wealth are something which they can lay hold of—something which they can only acquire by violence and which they can only retain by bodily force. They have no idea of abstract rights separated from anything material. So in archaic jurisprudence, wealth or property is described as anything material, which can only be retained by manual force and transferred by manual delivery. In early Roman jurisprudence a person's possessions were called *mancipium;*

because they were supposed to be acquired by the strong hand, and if not held with a very firm grasp would probably be lost. But as civilization and firm government succeed, men's ideas are transferred from the actual material things to the personal rights in them. Thus, in the course of time, the word *mancipium*, which originally meant the material things which were held by the hand, came to mean the absolute right to them; and in early Roman law, *mancipium* came to mean absolute ownership. Thus Lucretius says:* "*Vitaque mancipio nulli datur, omnibus usu.*"—"And life is given in absolute ownership to none, but only as a loan to all."

In process of time the word property came to be denoted by a term which meant a pure abstract right. All the possessions of the family belonged to the family (*domus*) as a whole; but the head of the house (*dominus*, δεσπότης) alone exercised all rights over them. He alone had the absolute ownership of his *familia*, or household, including his wife, children, slaves and all its possessions. Hence this right was called *dominium*, δεσποτεία, and *dominium* was always used in Roman law to denote absolute ownership. So long as the *patria potestas* subsisted in its pristine rigor, no member of the family could have any individual rights to things; but in the times of the early emperors the extreme rigor of the *patria potestas* was relaxed. In some cases individual members of the family were allowed to have rights to possessions independently of the head of the house and its other members, and this right was termed *proprietas*. Sometimes the *dominus* granted the exclusive rights to certain things to his sons and slaves. This right was termed *peculium*. The emperors Augustus, Nero, and Trajan enacted that the sons of the family might possess in their own right, and dispose of by will, as if they were *domini*, what they acquired in war. This was termed *castrense peculium*. This right of holding possessions independently of the other members of the family was considerably extended by subsequent emperors, and was always called *proprietas*. *Proprietas*, therefore, in Roman law, meant the absolute and exclusive right which a person had to anything independently of anyone else, and was synonymous with *dominium*. Neratius, a jurist of the time of Hadrian, says: "*Proprietas, id est, dominium.*"—"Property, that is, ownership." So Gaius says: "*Non solum autem proprietas per eos quos in potestate habemus adquiritur nobis.*"—"Not only, therefore, do we acquire absolute property through those whom we have in our power." So also Justinian: "*Transfert proprietatem rerum.*"—"Transfers the property in the goods"; and in other instances too numerous to cite.

Thus the word *proprietas* in Roman law never meant a material thing; it meant exclusively the absolute right to it; the thing itself was termed *materia*.

* *De Rerum Naturâ*, III., 971.

XVII.—MEANING OF THE WORD PROPERTY IN ENGLISH.

So also in early English the word property invariably meant a right and not a thing. Thus grand old Wycliffe says: "They will have property in ghostly goods where no property may be, and have no property in worldly goods where Christian men may have property." So Bacon invariably uses the word property to mean a right and never a thing. He says one of the uses of the law "is to dispose of the property of their goods and chattels." He explains the various methods by which property in goods and chattels may be acquired. So he speaks of the "property or interest in a timber tree." In Comyns' great digest of the law there is not a single instance of the word property being applied to material things. He uses it invariably to mean absolute ownership. Thus up to the middle of the last century property was invariably used to mean absolute ownership, and was never applied, at least in any work of authority, to material substances.

Every jurist knows that the true meaning of the word property is a right and not a thing. Thus Erskine says:* "The sovereign or real right is that of property, which is the right of using and disposing a subject as our own, except so far as we are restrained by law or paction." This meaning of property has been understood by economists as well as by jurists. Thus Mercière de la Rivière, one of the most eminent of the French economists, says:† "Property is nothing but the right to enjoy. * * * It is seen that there is but one right of property—that is, a right in a person, but which changes its name according to the nature of the object to which it is applied." Nor is the word property in any way restricted to the rights to material substances, but it is also applied to the rights to abstract rights.

Thus landed property means rights to lands and houses; real property means rights to realty; personal property means rights to personal chattels. Funded property is the right to demand a series of payments from the State; literary property is the right to the profits from works of literature; artistic property is the right to profits from works of art; dramatic property is the rights to the profits from dramatic representations; newspaper property is the right to the profits from publishing certain newspapers. So there are many other kinds of incorporeal property, such as shares in commercial companies of all sorts, the goodwill of a business, a professional practice, patents, tithes, advowsons, shootings, fisheries, market rights, and many other kinds of valuable rights. So, when a person has sold goods "on credit," and has acquired a right of action in exchange for them, termed a credit, or a debt, he has a property in this right of action and can sell it like any material chattel.

This appears still more clearly in the law of Scotland, in which what is termed real property in England is termed heritable rights, because the rights to them pass to the heir; and what is termed personal property in England

* Institutes of the Law of Scotland.

† *L'Ordre Naturel des Sociétés Politiques*, ch. xviii.

is termed movable rights in Scotland, because the rights to them pass or move to the executor; and under the term movable rights, credits, debts, or rights of action are included. Hence, abstract rights are the subjects of property exactly in the same way as material chattels. When the Socialists and Communists wish to destroy property it is not the material things they wish to destroy, but the exclusive rights which private persons have in them.

We shall find further on that there is a whole class of words which, like *mancipium*, in early times and in classical Latin meant material things, have in the progress of civilization and jurisprudence and in modern mercantile law come to mean abstract rights; and by a reverse process, most unfortunately, many words which really mean abstract rights have been perverted to mean material things, to the great confusion of jurisprudence and economics.

The word property means absolute, entire, and exclusive ownership. It is the absolute right to deal with the objects material, immaterial, and incorporeal in any way the owner pleases, except in so far as he is restrained by law.

The term property comprehends:

1. The *jus possidendi*, or the right of possession of the object.
2. The *jus utendi*, or the right of using it in any way the owner pleases.
3. The *jus fruendi*, or the right of appropriating any fruits or profit from it.
4. The *jus abutendi*, or the right of alienating or destroying it.
5. The *jus vindicandi*, or the right of recovering it, if found in the wrongful possession of anyone else.

Property or dominion, then, does not mean any single right, but an aggregate or bundle of rights; it comprehends the totality of rights, which can be exercised over anything.

XVIII.—ON THE RIGHT OF PROPERTY AND THE RIGHT OF POSSESSION.

But though all property is a right, it must be observed that all rights are not property. There is an essential distinction between the right of property and the mere right of possession or of use. Thus, where one person lends his horse or a book or other chattel to another; or delivers goods to him as a common carrier by sea or land, to be carried from one place to another; or deposits goods or valuables with him as a warehouseman for the mere purpose of being safely kept, or by way of pledge or lien; or hires a house, a horse, or land or plate or any chattel; or finds valuable goods,—in these and other cases he has the mere right of possession of the various things, and he can bring an action against anyone who deprives him of their possession; but he has no right to use the goods except in the way and for the specific purpose for which they were delivered to him. He has, therefore, only a specific right to hold them, and not the absolute ownership in them, to deal with them in any way he pleases. Some of the most subtle and important doctrines in economics are based entirely on the distinction between right of property and right of possession.

XIX.—APPLICATION OF THE POSITIVE AND NEGATIVE SIGNS TO PROPERTY.

Economic quantities or economic rights are, then, of three distinct orders: (1) Rights or property in some material thing which has been already acquired; (2) rights or property in labor or services; (3) rights or property in something which is only to be acquired at some future time.

Now, we observe that the first and the third of the economic quantities or rights enumerated above are inverse or opposite to each other. Property, like Janus, has two faces placed back to back. It regards the past and the future.* We may buy and sell a right to a thing which has already been acquired in time past; and we may also buy and sell a right to a thing which is only to be acquired in time future.

Now, it is one of the innumerable applications of the algebraical signs + and −, that if any point in time be taken as 0, then time before this epoch and time after this epoch are denoted by the opposite signs, + and −, which sign is used to denote either time being a matter of pure convention. Let us denote time present by 0, time past as + and time future by −. It will then be represented thus: + 5, + 4, + 3, + 2, + 1, 0, − 1, − 2, − 3, − 4, − 5, etc.; and it is evident that the totality of time from any year preceding the given era 0, to any year subsequent to the given era, will be the sum of the positive and negative years. Thus, if we take the Christian era as 0—years before it as positive and years after it as negative—then the total period from the foundation of Rome to the present time will be + 753 years, together with − 1893 years, or 2646 years altogether.

Hence, the products which have already been acquired in the past or positive years may be termed positive products; and the products which are to be acquired in the future or negative years may be termed negative products. Now, in all mathematical and physical sciences, it is invariably the custom to denote similar quantities, but of opposite qualities, by the opposite signs + and −. Hence, as a matter of simple convenience, and following the invariable custom in mathematical and physical science, if we denote property in a product which has been already acquired in time past as positive, we may, as a mark of distinction, denote property in a product which is only to be acquired in time future as negative. Now, property in a thing which has already come into possession in time past is corporeal property; and, as we have assumed above, time past as positive, corporeal property may be termed a positive economic quantity; and, as property in a thing to be acquired at some future time is incorporeal property; and, as we have above denoted time future as negative, incorporeal property may be

* See Maynz, I., 197, on *Droits Futures.*

aptly designated as a negative economic quantity. And, as in all mathematical and physical sciences, the whole science comprehends both positive quantities and negative quantities, so the whole science of economics comprehends both positive economic quantities and negative economic quantities, both corporeal property and incorporeal property. By this means we double the field of economics as usually treated, and we do in economics what those have done in the various mathematical and physical sciences who introduced negative quantities into them. By this means we are enabled to obtain the solution of problems which have hitherto baffled all economists, and it is by this means only that the theory of credit can be explained.

XX.—EVERY SUM OF MONEY IS EQUIVALENT TO THE SUM OF THE PRESENT VALUES OF AN INFINITE SERIES OF FUTURE PAYMENTS.

The investigation of the theory of the value of land demonstrates a proposition of great importance in economics. It is seen that the £100,000 given to purchase the estate in land expected to produce £3000 a year, is in reality the sum of the rights to its future products forever. Each annual product has a present value, and the value of the land is simply the sum of this infinite series of present values. But the same is evidently true of every sum of money. Hence, every sum of money is not only equal in value to a certain quantity of material goods, or to a certain quantity of services, but also to a perpetual annuity. An annuity is the right to receive a series of future payments. The lowest form of an annuity is the right to receive a single future payment, such as a bank note, a cheque, or a bill of exchange. The highest form is the right to receive an infinite series of future payments, such as the land or the funds. And there may be also the right to receive a limited number of future payments intermediate between the other two, which is called a terminable annuity. Hence, an annuity or the right to receive a series of future payments is an economic quantity, which may be bought or sold or exchanged, or whose value may be measured in money, like any material chattel. As when a sum of money is given to purchase land, or the funds, or municipal or other obligations, such as railway debentures. So an annuity may be paid to secure a certain sum of money at a given time, or on a given contingency, such as a life or fire insurance.

It is thus seen that economics comprehends three great departments: (1) material things, (2) personal qualities, (3) annuities.

The first school of economists restricted their attention to the first of these departments and refused to take any notice of the other two. Adam Smith, J. B. Say, and J. S. Mill have given much attention to the second, and treated labor as a marketable commodity; they have also noticed the existence of the third department, but they never made any attempt to exhibit the commerce in rights. And yet, at the present day, it is the most extensive of any, because it comprehends the whole theory of the value of land, the funds, mercantile credit, banking, the foreign exchanges, shares in commercial companies, and all other incorporeal wealth.

XXI.—PERSONAL CREDIT—A SUCCESSFUL TRADER IS AN ECONOMIC QUANTITY, ANALOGOUS TO THE LAND.

Now, a person exercising any profitable business or profession is an economic quantity exactly analogous to land. The land has produced profits in the past, but it has equal capacity to produce profits in future. So a merchant or a professional man may have accumulated a quantity of money as the fruits of his skill, industry, and ability in the past. But, over and above his accumulated money, he has the same skill, industry, and ability to earn profits in the future. His capacity to earn profits in the future is exactly the same as his capacity to have earned profits in the past. And, of course, he has the right or property in his expected profits of the future. And he may trade in two ways—he may trade, with the money he has already acquired, the profits of the past; or he may trade by purchasing goods by giving in exchange for them the right or property to demand payment at a future time out of the profits he expects to earn in the future. Personal character used to trade in this way as purchasing power is termed credit. And, as we have seen that anything which has purchasing power is wealth, it follows that money and credit are equally wealth. But it is evident that money and credit are inverse and opposite to each other. Hence, if money is a positive economic quantity, credit is a negative economic quantity.

XXII.—ALL ANNUITIES ARE NEGATIVE ECONOMIC QUANTITIES.

Hence, it is seen that all annuities or rights to receive a series of future payments, whether the right be to receive a single future payment or a limited or an infinite number of them, are negative economic quantities. These negative economic quantities comprehend all mercantile and banking credit, such as bank notes, cheques, bills of exchange, and all instruments of credit; exchequer bills, navy bills, dividend warrants, etc.; the land, the funds, terminable annuities, shares in commercial companies, the goodwill of a business, a professional practice, copyrights, patents, tolls, ferries, market rights, advowsons, benefices, shootings, fisheries, leaseholds, policies of insurance of different kinds, and many other valuable rights; amounting in value to scores of thousands of millions in this country, of which there is scarcely a notice in the usual text-books on economics.

XXIII.—WEALTH IN ECONOMICS IS AN EXCHANGEABLE RIGHT.

It follows from the preceding considerations that the true definition of wealth in economics is an exchangeable right. Now, there are three kinds of rights or property which can be bought and sold, or whose value can be measured in money.

I. Corporeal or material property or rights. There may be the right or property in some specific material substance which has already come into existence, and has come into the actual possession of the owner. This species of property in Roman and English law is termed corporeal property, because it is the right to certain specific *corpus*. It is also called material property, because it is the right to certain specific matter. Hence, we term this species of property corporeal or material wealth.

II. Immaterial property. The property which a man has in his own mental and intellectual qualities, in his own labor, or in his capacity to render any sort of service. As Smith says: "The property which every man has in his own labor, as it is the original foundation of all other property, so it is the most sacred and inviolable." Now, a person may sell the right to demand some labor or service from him. As all these services, though they require some bodily instrument to give effect to them, are in reality operations of the mind, we may call them immaterial property, or immaterial wealth, as J. B. Say, the French economist, does.

III. Incorporeal property. There is lastly a third kind of property or right, wholly separated and severed from any specific *corpus*, or matter in possession. It may either be in the possession of someone else at the present time, and may only come into our possession at some future time; or it may be even not in existence at the present time. Thus we may have the right or property to demand a sum of money from some person at some future time. That sum of money may no doubt be in existence at the present time, but it is not in our possession; it may not even be in the present possession of the person bound to pay it. It may pass through any number of hands before it is paid to us. But yet our right to demand it at the proper time is present and existing, and we may sell or transfer that right to anyone else for money. We may also have the right to something which is not yet even in existence, but will only come into existence at a future time. Thus, those who possess lands, cattle, fruit, trees, etc., have the right or property in their future produce. This produce is not in existence at the present time; it will only come into existence at a future time; but the right or property to it when it does come into existence is present and existing, and may be bought and sold like the right to any material product. This species of property is called in Roman law and English law incorporeal property, because it is a right, but separated from any specific *corpus*. Hence, it is called incorporeal wealth. But all these three different kinds of rights possess the quality of exchangeability; they can all be equally bought and sold or exchanged; the value of each of them can be measured in money; they are all equally merchandise, or articles of commerce. They are each, therefore, *Pecunia, Res, Bona, Merx; χρήματα, πράγματα, οἶκος, οὐσία, ἀγαθά*, etc., goods, chattels, merchandise, vendible commodities, wealth, in the jurisprudence of all nations. And, as it is the quality of exchangeability which alone constitutes anything wealth, and is the sole quality which economics regards, it follows that all these three kinds of rights are equally wealth in economics. And all the fundamental concepts and definitions, and all the laws of economics, must be enlarged and generalized, so as to comprehend indifferently the exchanges of these three orders of rights.

XXIV.—ECONOMICS, OR COMMERCE, IS THE SCIENCE OF THE EXCHANGES OF RIGHTS.

We have found that the true meaning of wealth in economics is an exchangeable right, and that there are three orders of these exchangeable rights; hence, these three orders of rights may be exchanged in six different ways.

1. The right or property in a material thing may be exchanged for the right or property in another material thing, as when the property in so much gold is exchanged for the property in so much corn or cattle, timber, jewelry, etc.

2. The right or property in a material thing may be exchanged for the right to demand so much labor or service, as when the property in so much gold is exchanged for the right to demand so much labor in any form.

3. The right or property in a material thing may be exchanged for the right to an abstract right, as when the property in so much gold is exchanged for the right to a bank note, cheque, bill of exchange, the funds, or any other incorporeal property.

4. The right or property in so much labor or service may be exchanged for the right to demand so much labor or service from someone else, as when persons agree to perform reciprocal services for each other, which are estimated as equivalent.

5. The right or property to demand so much labor or service may be exchanged for an abstract right, as when labor or service of any kind is paid for in bank notes, cheques, or bills.

6. The right or property in one abstract right may be exchanged for the right or property in another abstract right, as when a banker buys or discounts a bill of exchange, which is an abstract right, by giving in exchange for it a credit in his books, termed in banking language a deposit, which is another abstract right; or, as when a publisher buys the copyright of a work by giving bills of exchange for it.

Thus it is seen that all exchanges are of rights against rights, and these six kinds of exchange constitute commerce in all its forms and varieties, or the science of pure economics.

XXV.—ON MONEY AND CREDIT.

In the early ages of the world there was no such thing as money. When persons traded, they exchanged the products directly against each other; as is the custom at the present day with savage people. Thus in Iliad, vii., 468, we have:

"Νῆες δ' ἐκ Λήμνοιο παρέσταααν οἶνον ἄγουσαι"

. . . .

"ἔνθεν ἄρ' οἰνίζοντο κάρη κομόωντες Ἀχαιοί,
ἄλλοι μὲν χαλκῷ, ἄλλοι δ' αἴθωνι σιδήρῳ,
ἄλλοι δὲ ῥινοῖς, ἄλλοι δ' αὐτῇσι βόεσσιν,
ἄλλοι δ' ἀνδραπόδεσσι."

"From Lemnos' isle a numerous fleet had come
Freighted with wine. . . . .
. . . All the other Greeks
Hastened to purchase, some with brass and some
With gleaming iron ; some with hides,
Cattle and slaves."

This exchange of products against products is termed barter. And the inconveniences of this mode of trading are obvious. What haggling and bargaining it would require to determine how much leather should be given for how much wine! how many oxen or how many slaves! In the Homeric poems there is not the faintest allusion to anything of the nature of money. But even in those days it had been discovered that it would greatly facilitate commerce if the products to be exchanged were referred to some common measure of value. There are several passages in the Iliad which show that, while traffic had not advanced beyond barter, such a standard of reference was used. We find that various things were frequently estimated as being worth so many oxen. Thus in Iliad, ii., 448, Pallas's shield, the ægis, had one hundred tassels, each of the value of one hundred oxen. In Iliad, vi., 231, Homer laughs at the folly of Glaucus, who exchanged his golden armor, worth one hundred oxen, for the bronze armor of Diomede, worth nine oxen. In Iliad, xxiii., 703, Achilles offered as a prize to the winner in the funeral games in honor of Patroclus, a large tripod, which the Greeks valued among themselves at twelve oxen, and to the loser a female slave, which they valued at four oxen. But it must be observed that these oxen did not pass from hand to hand like money. The state of barter continued; just as at the present day it is quite common to exchange goods according to their value in money, without any actual money being used.

XXVI.—ON THE NECESSITY FOR MONEY.

The necessity for money arises from a different cause. So long as the products exchanged were equal in value there would be no need for money. If it could always happen that the exchanges of products or services were exactly equal, there would be an end of the transaction. But it would often happen that when one person required some product or service from another person, that other person would not require an equal amount of product or service from him in return; or even perhaps none at all. If, then, such a transaction took place between persons with such an unequal result, there would remain over a certain amount of product or service, due from the one to the other. And this would constitute a debt; that is to say, a right or property would be created in the person who had received the less amount of service or product to demand the balance due at some future time. And at the same time a correlative duty would be created in the person of the other, who had received the greater amount of product or service, to pay or render the balance due when required. Now, among all nations and persons who exchange or traffic with each other, this result must inevitably happen. Persons want some product or service from others; while those others want either not so much, or even perhaps nothing at all, from them. And it is easy to imagine the inconveniences which would arise if persons could never get anything they wanted, unless the persons who could supply these wants wanted something equal in value in return at the same time.

In process of time all nations hit upon this plan; they fixed upon some material substance, which they agreed to make always exchangeable among themselves, to represent the amount of debt. That is, if such an unequal exchange took place among persons, so leaving a balance due from one to another, the person who had received the greater amount of service or product gave a quantity of this universally exchangeable merchandise to make up the balance; so that the person who had received the lesser amount of service or product might obtain an equivalent from someone else. Suppose a wine-dealer wants bread from a baker; but the baker wants either not so much wine, or even no wine at all, from the wine-dealer. The wine-dealer buys the bread from the baker, and gives him in exchange as much wine as he wants, and makes up the balance by giving him an amount of this universally exchangeable merchandise, equivalent to the deficiency; and if the baker wants no wine at all, he gives him the full equivalent of the bread in this merchandise. The baker wants perhaps meat, or shoes, but not wine. Having received this universally exchangeable merchandise, from the wine-dealer, he goes to the butcher or the shoemaker, and obtains from him the equivalent of the bread he has sold to the wine-dealer. Hence the satisfaction that was due to him from the wine-dealer is paid by the butcher or shoemaker.

This universally exchangeable merchandise is termed money; and these considerations show its fundamental nature. Its function is to represent the debts which arise from unequal exchanges among men, and to enable persons who have rendered any sort of services to others, and have received no equivalent from them, to preserve a record of these services; and of their rights or title to obtain an equivalent product or service from someone else, when they require it.

XXVII.—ARISTOTLE, BISHOP BERKELEY, THE ECONOMISTS, ADAM SMITH, THORNTON, BASTIAT, MILL, AND JURISTS HAVE SEEN THE TRUE NATURE OF MONEY.

The true nature of money is now apparent. It is simply a right or title to demand some product or service from someone else.

Now, when a person accepts money in exchange for products, or services rendered, he can neither eat it, nor drink it, nor clothe himself with it; nor is it any species of economic satisfaction for the service he has done. He only agrees to accept it in exchange for the services he has rendered, because he believes, or has confidence, that he can purchase some satisfaction which he does require at any time he pleases. Money is therefore what is termed credit. A whole series of writers from the earliest times have perceived that the true nature of money is merely a right or title to acquire a satisfaction from someone else—*i. e.*, a credit. Thus Aristotle says:* "*ὑπὲρ δὲ μελλούσης ἀλλαγῆς (εἰ νῦν μηδὲν δεῖται, ὅτι ἔσται ἐάν δεηθῇ) τὸ νόμισμα οἷον Ἐγγυητής ἐστιν ἡμῖν. δεῖ γὰρ τοῦτο φέροντι εἶναι λαβεῖν.*"—"But with regard to a future exchange (if we want nothing at present, that it may take place when we do want it) money is as it were our security. For it is necessary that he who brings it should be able to get what he wants."

So a London merchant, F. Cradocke, in the time of the Commonwealth, says: "Having now pointed out the inconvenience of these metals (gold and silver) in which the medium of commerce, or universal credit, hath formerly been placed. * * * Now that credit is as good as money will appear, it is to be observed that money itself is nothing but a kind of security which men receive upon parting with their commodities, as a ground of hope or assurance, that they shall be repaid in some other commodity; since no man would either sell or part with any for the best money, but in hopes thereby to procure some other commodities or necessary." So an old pamphleteer in 1710 saw the same truth. He says:† "Trade found itself unsufferably straightened and perplexed for want of a general specie of a complete intrinsic worth, as the medium to supply the defect of exchanging, and to make good the balance where a nation or a market, or a merchant demands of another a greater quantity of goods than either the buyer hath goods to answer, or the seller hath occasion to take back." So the great metaphysician, Bishop Berkeley, says in his "Querist":

"21. Whether the other things being given, as climate, soil, etc., the wealth be not proportioned to industry, and this to the circulation of credit, be the credit circulated by what tokens or marks whatever?"

"24. Whether the true idea of money, as such, be not altogether that of a ticket or counter?"

"25. Whether the terms crown, livre, pound sterling, are not to be considered as exponents, or denominations; and whether gold, silver and paper are not tickets and counters for reckoning, recording and transferring such denominations?"

"35. Whether power to command the industry of others be not real wealth? And whether

* Nicomach, Eth., B. V.

† An Essay on Public Credit, p. 25.

money be not in truth tickets or tokens for recording and conveying such power? and whether it be of consequence what material the tickets are made of?"

"426. Whether all circulation be not alike a circulation of credit, whatsoever medium—metal or paper—is employed; and whether gold be any more than credit for so much power?"

It is one of the special merits of the economists that they clearly saw the true nature of money. Among many others, Baudeau, one of the most eminent of them, says:* "This coined money in circulation is nothing, as I have said elsewhere, but effective titles on the general mass of useful and agreeable enjoyments, which cause the well being and propagation of the human race. It is a kind of bill of exchange or order, payable at the will of the bearer. Instead of taking his share in kind of all matters of subsistence and all raw produce annually growing, the sovereign demands it in money, the effective titles, the order, the bill of exchange, etc." So Edmund Burke† speaks of gold and silver as "the two great recognized species that represent the lasting credit of mankind." So Smith says:‡ "A guinea may be considered as a bill for a certain quantity of necessaries and conveniences upon all the tradesmen in the neighborhood." So Henry Thornton, the eminent banker, one of the authors of the Bullion Report, says:§ "Money of every kind is an order for goods. It is so considered by the laborer when he receives it, and it is almost instantly turned into money's worth. It is merely the instrument by which the purchasable stock of the country is distributed with convenience and advantage among the several members of the community."

This great fundamental truth was also very clearly seen by Bastiat. He says: ‖

"You have a crown piece. What does it mean in your hands? It is, as it were, the witness and the proof that you have at some time done work which, instead of profiting by, you have allowed society to enjoy in the person of your client. This crown piece witnesses that you have rendered a service to society; and, moreover, it states the value of it. It witnesses, besides, that you have not received back from society a real equivalent service, as was your right. To put it into your power to exercise this right when and where you please, society, by the hands of your client, has given you an acknowledgment or title, an order of the State, or token, a crown piece, in short, which does not differ from titles of credit, except that it carries its value in itself (?), and if you can read with the eyes of the mind the inscription it bears, you can see distinctly these words: 'Pay to the bearer a service equivalent to that which he has rendered to society, value received and stated, proved and measured by that which is on me.' After that you cede your crown piece to me. Either it is a present or it is in exchange for something else if you give it to me as the price of a service. See what follows; your account as regards the real satisfaction with society is satisfied, balanced, closed. You rendered it a service for a crown piece, you now restore it the crown piece in exchange for a service; so far as regards you, the account is settled. But I am now just in the position you were in before. It is I, now, who have done a service to society in your person. It is I who am the creditor for the value of the work which I have done for you, and which I could devote to myself. It is into my hands now that this title of credit should pass, the witness and the proof of this social debt; you cannot say that I am the richer, because if I have to receive something it is because I have given something. * * * ¶ It is enough for a man to have rendered

* *Introduction à la Philosophie Economique.* † Reflections on the French Revolution.

‡ Wealth of Nations, Bk. II., ch. ii. § An Enquiry into the Nature and Effects of the Paper Credit of Great Britain, p. 80.

‖ *Œuvres*, Vol. II., *Maudit Argent*, p. 80. ¶ *Harmonies Economiques, Capital*, p. 209.

services, and so to have the right to draw upon society by the means of exchange for equivalent services. That which I call the means of exchange is money, bills of exchange, bank notes, and also bankers. Whoever has rendered a service and has not received an equal satisfaction is the bearer of a warrant either possessed of value, like money, or of credit like bank notes, which gives him the right to draw from society when he likes, and under what form he will, an equivalent service. * * * † I take the case of a private student. What is he doing at Paris? How does he live there? It cannot be denied that society places at his disposal food, clothing, lodging, amusements, books, means of instruction—a multitude of things, in short, of which the production would demand a long time to be explained and still more to be effected. And in return for all these things, which have required so much labor, toil, fatigue, physical and intellectual efforts, so many transports, inventions, commercial operations, what services has the student rendered to society? None! He is only preparing to render some. Why, then, have these millions of men who have performed actual services, effectual and productive, abandoned to him their fruits? This is the explanation: The father of this student, who was an advocate, a physician, or a merchant, had formerly rendered services—it may be to the people of China—and had received not direct services, but rights to demand services, at the time, in the place, and under the form which might suit him the best. It is for these distant and anterior services that society is paying to-day; and wonderful it is! If we follow in thought the infinite course of operations which must have taken place to attain this result, we shall see that everyone must have been remunerated for his pains, and that these rights have passed from hand to hand, sometimes in small portions, sometimes combined, until in the consumption of this student the whole has been balanced. Is not this a strange phenomenon? We should shut our eyes to the light if we refused to acknowledge that society cannot present such complicated transactions, in which the civil and penal laws have so little part, without obeying a wonderfully ingenious mechanism. This mechanism is the object of political economy."

So Mill says: "The pounds or shillings which a person receives weekly or yearly are not what constitutes his income; they are a sort of ticket or order, which he can present for payment at any shop he pleases, and which entitles him to receive a certain value of any commodity that he makes choice of. The farmer pays his laborers and his landlord in these tickets. as the most convenient plan for himself and them."

It is so clearly understood that money is, in reality, nothing more than the right or title to demand something to be paid or done that some jurists expressly class it under the title of incorporeal property. Thus Vulteius says: "*Nummus in quo non materia ipsa, sed valor attenditur.*"—"Money, in which not the material, but the value is regarded." That is, we desire or demand other things for the direct satisfaction they give us; but we only desire money as the means of purchasing other things.

Gold and silver money, therefore, may be justly termed metallic credit.

Thus it is seen that writers of all classes, philosophers, merchants, bankers, economists, and jurists, are all perfectly agreed upon the nature of money. It represents indebtedness or services due to the owner of it, and it represents the right or title which its owner has to demand some product or service in recompense for some service he has done for someone else.

† *Harmonies Economiques, Organisation Naturelle*, p. 25.

XXVIII.—ON SUBSTANCES USED AS MONEY.

The necessity for money has arisen among all nations, the most barbarous as well as the most civilized. As soon as the members of any community, however barbarous, begin to exchange among themselves, unequal exchanges must necessarily arise, and therefore indebtedness is created. And some substance is hit upon to represent these services due, and the rights which its holders have to demand some product or service, in satisfaction of the services they have done to someone else. A great many different substances have been used by different nations to represent this universal want. The Hebrews, we know, used silver. No money was in use in the times of the Homeric poems; but some time after them, though we cannot say when, copper bars or skewers were used as money throughout Greece, which Pheidon of Argos, in the eighth century, B. C., superseded by silver coins. The Æthiopians used carved pebbles; the Carthaginians used leather discs with some mysterious substance sewn up in them. Throughout the islands of the Eastern Ocean, and in many parts of Africa, shells are still used. In Thibet and some parts of China, little blocks of compressed tea are used as money. In the last century dried cod was used in Newfoundland, sugar in the West Indies, tobacco in Virginia. Smith says that in his day nails were used as money in a village in Scotland. In some of the American colonies powder and shot; in Campeachy, logwood, and among the North American Indians belts of wampum were used as money. We read of another people who used cowries as small change, and the skulls of their enemies for large sums. It is said that in Virginia, in 1667, the proprietors were reduced to such straits as to use dried squirrel-skins as money, and many other things have been used in various countries for the same purpose.

But when we consider the purposes for which money is required, it is easily seen that no substance possesses so many advantages as a metal, The use of money being to preserve the record of services due to its possessor for any future time, it is clear that money should not alter by time. A money of dried cod would not keep very long, nor would it be easily divisible. Not many bankers would care to keep their accounts in dried cod, tobacco, sugar, logwood, or dead men's skulls. One of the first requisites of money is that it should be easily divisible into very small fragments, so that its owner should be able to get any amount of service he pleases at any time. Taking these requisites into consideration, it is evident that there is no substance which combines them so well as a metal. Metal is uniform in its texture. It can be divided into any number of fragments, each of which shall be equal in value to any other fragment of the same weight; and, if required, these fragments can always be reunited, and form a whole again of the value of all its parts, which can be said of no other substance. All civilized nations, therefore, have adopted metal as money; and of metals gold, silver, and copper have been chiefly preferred.

XXIX.—THE CHINESE INVENTED PAPER MONEY.

We have now to treat of a material used as money which, in latter times at least, has had incomparably more influence in the world than all the gold and silver—namely, paper.

The Romans invented the business which in modern language is termed banking. The Roman bankers invented cheques and bills of exchange, but they did not invent bank notes. The use of cheques and bills of exchange by the Romans was extremely narrow, restricted to the immediate parties, and they were never made transferable, as far as we are aware, so as to get into general circulation and serve the purposes of money.

The invention of paper to be used as circulating money is due to the Chinese. In the beginning of the reign of Hiantsong of the Dynasty of Thang, about the year 807 A. D., there was a great scarcity in the country. The Emperor ordered all the merchants and rich persons to bring their money into the public treasury, and in exchange for it gave them notes called *fey-thsian,* or flying money. In three years, however, this money was suppressed in the capital, and was current only in the provinces. in 906 A. D. Thait-siu, the founder of the Soung Dynasty, revived this practice. Merchants were allowed to deposit their cash in the public treasuries, and received in return notes called *pian-thsian,* or current money. The convenience of this was so great that the custom quickly spread, and in 997 there was paper in circulation to the amount of 1,700,000 ounces of silver, and in 1021 it had increased to 2,830,000 ounces. At this period a company of sixteen of the richest merchants were permitted to issue notes payable in three years. But at the end of that time the company was bankrupt, which gave rise to much public distress and litigation. The Emperor abolished the notes of this company and forbade any more joint-stock banks to be founded. Henceforth the power of issuing notes was kept in the hands of the Government. These notes were also called *kiao-tsu,* and were of the value of an ounce of silver. In 1032 there were *kiao-tsu* to the value of 1,256,340 ounces in circulation. Subsequently banks of this nature were set up in each province, and the notes issued by one provincial bank had no currency in any other. These were the first bank notes on record—that is to say, notes issued in exchange for money, or convertible into money, and not paper money or paper created without any previous deposit of specie. Besides these bank notes the Chinese issued paper money to a vast amount.* It would be too long here to give a complete history of the paper money of China, but we have given some full notices of it elsewhere.† But it may interest our readers to know the process of its manufacture.

About 1288, Marco Polo traveled in China, and discovered the existence of this paper money. In Book II., c. 18, he gives an account of its manufacture. He says that it was made in Kambalu. The inner rind of the mul-

* Klaproth, *Journal Asiatique,* Vol. I., p. 256.

† Dictionary of Political Economy, art. Currency, p. 666.

berry-tree was steeped and pounded in a mortar, and then made into paper, resembling that made from cotton, but quite black. It was then cut into pieces nearly square but of different sizes. The smallest were of the value of a denier tournois, the next for a Venetian groat, others for two, five, and ten groats, others one to ten gold besants. Several officers had to subscribe their names and place their seals on each note, which was then stamped with the royal seal dipped in vermilion. Counterfeiting was a capital offence. It had then a forced currency, and no one dared to refuse it on pain of death. Caravans of merchants arrived with their goods, which they laid before the King, who selected what he pleased, and paid them in this money. When anyone wished to exchange old money for new, it was done at the mint at a charge of three per cent. If anyone wanted gold or silver for manufacture, he could obtain bullion at the mint in exchange for the paper. Marco Polo mentions many cities where he observed this money in circulation.

Credit and paper, either payable in specie or inconvertible, now forms the great circulating medium or currency of the world, and as we shall show hereafter, amounts to nearly one hundred times the quantity of specie in this country.

XXX.—THE FUNCTION OF CREDIT IS TO BRING INTO COMMERCE THE PRESENT VALUES OF FUTURE PROFITS.

The true function of credit is now apparent.

It is a very common idea that credit is the "goods" which are "lent," or the "transfer" of them. Such ideas are wholly erroneous. In all cases whatever, a credit is the present right to a future payment. And the true function of credit is to bring into commerce the present values of future profits.

When an estate in land is sold, the present value of all its future profits is expressed, and brought into commerce by the money paid for it. The total amount of the shares in any commercial company—banking, insurance, railway, or any other—denotes the value of the existing property of the company, together with the total present value of their future profits. So the money paid for the goodwill of a business, a copyright, patent, a professional practice, etc., is the present value of the future profits. So when a merchant or trader trades on "credit," he brings into commerce the present value of a future profit. He buys the goods or the labor, and gives as their price the right to demand a sum to be paid out of the expected future profits. So when the State contracts a loan for any public purpose it buys the money, and gives as its price the right to demand a series of payments out of the future income of the people. So when municipal corporations and other public bodies contract loans for public purposes, they buy money by giving as its price the right to demand a series of payments out of the future revenues of their constituents. That is, they bring into commerce the present value of their future income. So credit in all its forms, and to whatever purpose it is applied, simply brings into commerce the present value of a future profit. The famous French wit, Rivarol, well said: "Man conquers space by commerce, and time by credit."

XXXI.—THE FUNDAMENTAL CONCEPT OF MONETARY SCIENCE.

The preceding considerations now enable us to perceive the fundamental concept of monetary science.

We have seen that writers of all classes are agreed as to the fundamental nature of money. It represents debts which are due to persons who have done services to others, and have received no equivalent services in return. It merely represents the right to demand these equivalent services when they please; and its special function is to measure, record, and preserve these rights for future use, and to transfer them to anyone else. If all the services exchanged in society exactly balanced, there would be no need for money. Supposing, then, that there was nothing but metallic money in use, the following axiom is evident: The quantity of money in any country represents the quantity of debt which there would be if there were no money. But as we have seen that, in civilized countries, these debts, or rights, are recorded in the simple form of rights against particular persons, whether written or unwritten, as well as in metallic coin, which are rights against the general community, the terms circulating medium, or currency, include these debts in both forms. Hence, it is clear that the circulating medium, or currency, represents nothing but transferable debt; and that whatever represents transferable debt is circulating medium, or currency, whatever its nature or form may be, either metal or paper, or anything else. Consequently this proposition necessarily follows: Where there is no debt there can be no currency.

All erroneous theories of currency have been founded on not perceiving the fundamental nature of currency; and the greatest monetary disasters the world has ever seen have been produced by violating this fundamental axiom.

XXXII.—ON THE DISTINCTION BETWEEN MONEY AND CREDIT.

It has now been shown that money and credit are essentially of the same nature, money being only the highest and most general form of credit. They are each a right or title to demand some product or service in future. Nevertheless, there is a very important distinction between money and credit, which must now be pointed out. In economics all money is credit, but all credit is not money. No one can compel anyone else to sell him anything for money or credit. When, therefore, anyone has taken money in exchange for anything, it is in reality only credit, because he only takes it in the belief that he can exchange it away for something else. But suppose that a sale has taken place, and that a debt has been incurred thereby, public policy requires that the debtor should be able to compel the creditor to accept something in discharge of his debt. It would cause infinite misery if creditors could arbitrarily refuse anything they pleased in payment of their debts. Hence, in all countries the law declares that, if a debt has been incurred, the debtor can compel the creditor to accept some specific thing in payment of it. Whatever that something is which a debtor can compel a creditor to accept in payment of a debt which has been incurred, is money or legal tender. From this it follows that some things may be money in some cases and not in others. Gold coin in this country is money or legal tender in all cases, and to any extent. Silver is only money or legal tender to the amount of 40s. If a creditor chooses to accept of payment of a larger amount than 40s. in silver, it is entirely of his own free will.

In England, as between the public and the Bank of England, bank notes are nothing but credit. The bank cannot compel anyone to receive its notes, and any holder of its notes can compel the bank to cash them on demand. Between private persons, a bank note for £5 is not money or legal tender for that exact amount of debt. But in debts above £5, bank notes are money or legal tender. But even this is only so long as the bank pays its notes in cash on demand. If the bank were to stop payment, its notes would cease to be legal tender in any case. In Scotland and Ireland, Bank of England notes are not legal tender in any case.

If two persons are mutually indebted to each other in equal amounts at the same time, each may compel the other to accept the debt he owes as legal tender for the debt which is due to him. Each debt is therefore money or legal tender, in respect of the other, and neither party can demand specie from the other. So, if a creditor voluntarily accepts payment from his debtor in a country bank note without indorsement, he makes it money even though the bank should fail; or, if he voluntarily accepts a cheque from his debtor, and has the credit transferred to his own account, he makes it money, and it is a final closing of the transaction even though the bank should fail immediately after. This is a principle of supreme importance in modern commerce, as will be shown more fully hereafter.

XXXIII.—REASON WHY PAPER CAN SUPERSEDE MONEY.

The reason why paper can supersede money is now apparent.

An order to receive a coat could never serve as a substitute for a coat, because it cannot serve the same purpose as a coat. An order to receive meat or bread or wine cannot supersede meat, bread, or wine, because it cannot serve the same purpose as meat, bread, or wine; and so on regarding orders for other material chattels. An order for such things can never serve as a substitute for the things themselves; because they are heterogeneous quantities of a totally different nature, and cannot serve the same purpose as the things themselves. But an order to pay money can serve the same purpose as money, because they are homogeneous quantities. A piece of money, like a piece of paper, is nothing more than an order to receive a useful, material chattel; and, provided that the order is sure to be obeyed on demand, it is of no consequence whether it be of metal or paper. Consequently, the exchange of paper for money is nothing more than exchange of a particular right for a general right. As Daniel Webster, the eminent American jurist, said: "Credit is to money what money is to goods." That is, credit is an order for money and money is an order for goods. To be useful, money must be exchanged away for other things just as paper is. And if paper can be exchanged away for exactly the same things that money can, paper has exactly the same value as money. As the Italians say: "*Che oro vale, oro è.*"—"That which is of the value of gold is gold."

XXXIV.—THE SAME QUANTITY MAY REQUIRE TO BE REGARDED IN DIFFERENT ASPECTS IN DIFFERENT SCIENCES.

We have now a most important observation to make. The same quantities may be common to different sciences and require to be regarded in different aspects in each. Thus jurisprudence and economics are inseparably allied; and money and bank notes, bills of exchange and abstract rights, are both juridical and economical quantities; but they differ in some respects according as they are regarded in a juridical or an economical aspect. Thus, in jurisprudence, money is the absolute payment and satisfaction of a debt, and a closing of the transaction; and bills of exchange are not the closing of the transaction, unless they are accepted as such. Also, in jurisprudence, money is corporeal property; abstract rights and rights of action are incorporeal property; but if these rights and rights of action are recorded on paper, parchment, or any other material, they become corporeal or material property, just like money. But, in economics, a payment in money is not the closing of the transaction. The economists held that a complete exchange is the obtaining a satisfaction for a satisfaction. In economics, money is only an abstract right recorded and preserved in gold to obtain a satisfaction. Money, in economics, is only a bill of exchange in gold. So in economics, rights, whether purely abstract or recorded on paper, are exactly of the same nature. A piece of money is no more an economic satisfaction than a piece of paper. Hence in economics, money and rights of action, whether written or unwritten, are of exactly the same nature. They are all simply rights to demand something in future; hence, as many jurists have seen, they are all, in economics, equally incorporeal property, or credit. But, as they all possess the quality of exchangeability, they are all equally wealth.

XXXV.—THERE IS NO NECESSARY RELATION BETWEEN THE QUANTITY OF MONEY IN ANY COUNTRY AND THE QUANTITY OF COMMODITIES AND THEIR PRICE.

We have now to demonstrate a proposition of the greatest importance in economics, and on which errors of the most serious nature are very prevalent. Many writers on economics have supposed that the quantity of money in a country bears some necessary relation to the quantity of commodities in it; and many more think that the prices of commodities are determined by the ratio which the quantity of metallic money bears to the quantity of commodities. That this is a very serious error may easily be shown. Suppose that A and B are mutually indebted; that A owes B £10, and B owes A £13. Then, it is quite clear that their debts may be settled in three different ways:

1. Each may send a clerk to demand payment of his debt from the other in money; this method would require £23 in money to discharge the two debts.

2. A may send £10 to B to discharge his debt, and B may send back to A the same £10, with £3 additional, to discharge his debt. This method would require £13 to discharge the two debts.

3. They may meet together and set off their mutual amounts of debt and pay only the difference in money. By this means the two debts would be discharged by the use only of £3.

Now, it is quite clear that a very different quantity of money would be required to carry on any given amount of business, according as either of these methods of settling debts was adopted. Between the first and the third methods there is a difference of £20. These £20 would not influence prices, but would only be required to settle debts in a clumsy way. So that it is clear that by a simple change in the method of doing business, £20 might be withdrawn from its employment, and set free to be applied to new transactions. The adoption of the third method of settling debts in the place of the first would in no way affect prices, because these amounts of money would have to be retained for the sole purpose of settling debts, and would in no way enter into the sales of commodities, and therefore in no way affect their prices. At the same time, it would greatly alter the ratio between money and commodities. Now, when these transactions are multiplied by millions, it is evident that there may be large quantities o money in a country which may exercise no influence on prices; and the ratio between money and commodities may vary greatly, according as one or other of these methods of doing business is adopted. Now, if a country which habitually used the first method were to change its custom and adopt the third method, it is quite evident that a very large quantity of money might be disengaged from its usual employment and applied to promote new operations; and, therefore, for all practical purposes, it would be equivalent to an addition to the previously existing quantity of money, as by this improvement in the method of settling debts many times the same quantity of business might be done on the same basis of specie. Hence, the various methods of economizing the use of money are, for all practical purposes, to be considered as an increase of the resources of the nation.

But the methods of proving this proposition are by no means exhausted. I was examined as a witness before the Gold and Silver Commission of 1887, and I somewhat startled the Commission by saying that, though every system of credit must rest on a basis of specie, there is no necessary relation between the basis of specie and the superstructure of credit raised upon it. The proof of this is extremely simple, and may be best illustrated by a practical example. Before bankers discounted bills of exchange, there used to be fairs at the great Continental cities, Lyons, Nuremberg, and many others, held every three months. Merchants in France and other countries did not make their bills payable at their own houses, where they must have kept large sums in specie to meet them, but they made them payable only at these great fairs. In the meantime their bills circulated throughout the whole country, and performed all the functions of money. On a fixed day of the fair the merchants met together and exchanged their acceptances against each other. By the principle of compensation, which will be more fully described in a future chapter, these acceptances exchanged, reciprocally paid, discharged, and extinguished each other. Boisguillebert, the morning star of French economics, says that at the fair of Lyons 80,000,000 of bills paid and discharged each other without the use of a single coin. Hence, when all debts balance each other they may all be settled without the use of a single coin. Now, this is equally true whether there were 80 or 800 or 8000 millions of debts to be settled. Hence, it is evident that so long as the debts to be settled exactly balance, there is no use for any money, however large they may be in actual amount. In such a case money is only required in case there should be any undischarged balances of debts.

Again, suppose that creditors and debtors have accounts at the same bank. The debtor gives his creditor a cheque on his account. The creditor pays it into his own account; and the banker transfers the credit from the account of the debtor to that of the creditor, and this is a complete payment of the debt without the use of money. This operation is termed a novation. Now, it is evident that the larger a bank is, the more of its customers will deal with each other, and the greater will be the number of transactions settled by means of novations, without the use of money. But the system has been carried to a greater degree of refinement still, by a device called the clearing system, which will be more fully described in another chapter.

XXXVI.—ON BARTER.

When material products are exchanged directly for material products the transaction is termed barter.

XXXVII.—ON SALE OR CIRCULATION.

To understand economics as a science, we must revert to the original concept of it by its founders, the economists, as the science of exchanges, or of commerce, to which all the most intelligent economists in the world are now reverting, as the only one by which it can be created into a science, after the temporary confusion into which it was thrown by the unfortunate system of J. B. Say and John Stuart Mill, which is rapidly sinking into oblivion.

The economists only admitted an exchange to be where a material product was exchanged for material product, *i. e.*, a barter; that is, where each side obtained a satisfaction. But, in modern times, such exchanges are comparatively rare. Persons usually want to obtain things from others, while these others want nothing from them. To obviate the inconveniences which would arise if no one could get what he wanted, unless he could supply the other party at the same time with what he wanted, people hit upon the plan of adopting some particular commodity, which should be universally exchangeable. The buyer, therefore, gave the seller in exchange for his product an equivalent in this universally exchangeable merchandise, so that he could get any satisfaction he pleased from anyone else who could render it. This universally exchangeable merchandise is termed money. The person who has got the money has not got a satisfaction; his desire is not consummated or completed. In order to obtain a satisfaction, he must exchange away the money for some product he does desire. Hence, the economists termed a sale a demi-exchange. Le Trosne says:* "There is this difference between an exchange and a sale, that in an exchange everything is consummated or completed (*consommé*) for each party. They possess the thing which they desired to procure, and they have only to enjoy it. In the sale, on the contrary, it is only the purchaser who has attained his object, because it is only he who is in a position to enjoy. But everything is not ended for the seller." And again: "Exchange arrives directly at its object, which is completion (*consommation*); it has only two terms, and is ended in one contract. But a contract in which money intervenes is not completed (*consommé*), but it is necessary that the seller should become a buyer, either himself or by the interposition of the person to whom he transfers the money. There are, therefore, to arrive at completion (*consommation*), which is the ultimate object, at least four terms, and three contractants, of whom one

* *De l'Intérêt Sociale*, p. 905, 916.

intervenes twice." When, however, the person who had sold his product for money, and, therefore, furnished a satisfaction to the other party, had himself exchanged away the money and obtained a product for it, he, too, had acquired a satisfaction, which he could enjoy, and the exchange was completed (*consommé*). For this reason, money was called the medium of exchange. This "sale" the economists termed circulation. Sale or circulation, therefore, the economists defined to mean the exchange of a product for money. Circulation, therefore, meant purchase with money; in contradistinction to exchange of products, or barter.

But credit is used in all respects in the same way as money to purchase or circulate commodities. Hence, sale or circulation always denotes an exchange in which one or both of the quantities exchanged is money or credit. The sum total of these sales is properly termed the circulation. Hence, any sum of money or credit may add considerably to the circulation, because every time it is transferred it is a sale, and, therefore, it augments the circulation. Just in the same way, the circulation of a newspaper is not properly the number of copies sold, but the number of its readers. Hence, the circulation is the quantity of money and credit multiplied into the number of their transfers.

As the use of money and credit is to set industry in motion; and, inasmuch as they have no use unless they do that, their beneficial effects are not measured by their actual amount, but by the industry which they generate. Money lying locked up in a box, or credit unused, only represents latent power, and not actual power. They may be called power or wealth in the latent state, they resemble the steam-engine of a mill which is not going, and which is of no use until it is set in motion. And, as the produce of the mill is measured by the quantity of the motion of the engine, so the useful effect of money and credit is measured by their quantity of motion, which is called the circulation. The circulation, which is the sole test of their useful effect, is, therefore, the product of their amount multiplied into the velocity of their circulation. The quantity of motion of the engine is called its duty. Hence, the circulation of money and credit may be called its duty. It is so essential to have a clear conception of the useful effect produced by any amount of money or credit, that we may add another illustration. The effect produced by any body in motion is measured by its weight or mass multiplied into its velocity, which is termed its momentum. If the mass be diminished, yet by increasing its velocity, the effect or momentum may still be the same. If a body weighing 100 lbs. move with a velocity 1, its momentum will be 100; but if we diminish the weight to 50 lbs., and can double its velocity, the effect or the momentum will still be the same—100. The useful effects of money and credit are exactly analogous. Their useful effect is the result of their combined amount and velocity of circulation, which is termed circulation. If we can make £50 circulate with twice the velocity of £100, the useful effect or circulation will be the same. Hence, it may be said that the circulation is the momentum of money and credit.

XXXVIII.—ON EXCHANGE.

An exchange is the interchange of things of a like nature; either products for products, or money or credit for money or credit. Thus we speak of the foreign exchanges or the value of the money of one country in terms of the money of another. Or we ask for the change (*i. e.*, the 'change or exchange) of a £5 note or a sovereign. A bill of exchange is a right of action to be exchanged at the proper time for money. So we exchange one book for another, or a picture for a statue. So in "Lear," when Albany throws down his glove to the traitor Edmond, the latter, throwing down his own, says: "There's my exchange"; and a little further on Edgar says to Edmond: "Let's exchange charity." So in "Hamlet," Laertes says: "Exchange forgiveness with me, noble Hamlet." When the interchange is between products and money or credit, the one who gives the money or credit is said to buy the product, and the one who gives the product is said to sell it, and the quantity of money given is termed the price. When the exchange is between money or credit for money or credit, each side is said to buy and sell, and each quantity of money or credit exchanged for the other is termed the price of the other. Thus we buy a horse or a house or land or a bill of exchange with money or credit. An officer formerly bought a commission in the army, but he exchanged from one regiment into another.

XXXIX.—ON THE MEANING OF CIRCULATING MEDIUM AND CURRENCY.

We have now to consider two terms, circulating medium and currency, which are both of comparatively recent origin, which have in recent times given rise to many controversies, but which are admitted to be synonymous, and, consequently, if we can positively determine the meaning of one of them, that will also necessarily determine the meaning of the other. The term circulating medium does not occur in Adam Smith. It seems to have come into use in the last decade of the last century. The first occasion on which we have met with it is in the debate on the Bank Restriction Act of 1797. Mr. Fox said:* "He wished that gentlemen, instead of amusing themselves with new terms of 'circulating medium' and the like," etc., which shows that it must then have been of very recent origin. Mr. Pitt, in his reply, said: "As so much had been said on the nature of a circulating medium, he thought it necessary to notice that he did not, for his own part, take it to be of that empirical kind which had been generally described. It appeared to him to consist of anything that answered the great purposes of trade and commerce, whether in specie, paper, or any other term which might be used." It is quite evident, therefore, that Mr. Pitt included under the term circulating medium or currency, money and credit in all its forms. Which continued to be the invariable usage in all Parliamentary debates,

* Parliamentary History of England, Vol. XXIII., p. 340.

until Lord Overstone perverted men's minds with a fantastic definition of his own, which he beguiled Sir Robert Peel into adopting.

The verb to circulate, like many others in English, has both an active and a neuter meaning. 1. It means that which circulates commodities, *i. e.*, which causes commodities to circulate, where it is an active verb. 2. That which circulates itself, where it is a neuter verb. Smith uses the word circulate in both senses in different passages. Thus, speaking of gold and silver, he says: "Their use consists in circulating commodities. The great wheel of circulation is altogether different from the goods circulated by it. The revenue of the society consists altogether in these goods and not in the wheel that circulates them." In these two passages circulates is active. A little further on, he speaks of the different sorts of paper money, but he says that the circulating notes of banks and bankers are best known, where circulates is neuter. In the following sentence both senses occur: "Let us suppose, for example, that the whole circulating money of some particular country amounted at a particular time to one million sterling, that sum being sufficient for circulating the whole annual products of their land and labor."

The ordinary meaning of words in scientific language leaves no possible doubt as to which is the true meaning of circulate, in the expression circulating medium. A medium, in scientific language, means some middle thing by which something else is effected. Thus, money is termed the medium of exchange, because it is the medium by which exchanges are effected. Hence, the circulating medium is the medium by which the circulation of commodities is effected. Now, it has just been shown that by circulation the economists meant sales. And how are sales effected? By the means or medium of money and credit. Buying with money effects the circulation of commodities; but buying with credit equally effects the circulation of products; in whatever form the credit may be, either written or unwritten. Hence, money and credit are equally circulating medium; and the total amount of the circulating medium means the total amount of money and credit in all its forms.

XL.—ON. THE MEANING OF CURRENCY.

The meaning of the word currency, which all writers admit to be synonymous with circulating medium, is much more recondite, and has given rise to protracted controversies in modern times, which, however, we shall not notice at present. We shall in this section merely explain the true meaning of the word. The word currency is, in fact, a technical term in mercantile and constitutional law, and the following is the true meaning of "current" and "currency" in English law: It is a general rule of law that a person cannot transmit to another any better title to a thing than he has himself. As it is said:* "*Nemo plus juris ad alium transferre potest quam ipse haberet.*"—"No one can transfer to another a greater right than he has him-

* Digest, 50, 17, 54.

self." It is also a general rule of law that, if a person loses a thing or has it stolen from him, he does not thereby lose the property in it. Consequently, he can not only recover it from the finder or thief, but also from anyone else in whose possession he may find it, even though that person bought it or took it in pledge honestly and in good faith and gave full value for it, and not knowing that it was not the lawful property of the seller or pledger. This right of recovery is termed the *Jus vindicandi* in Roman law. But to this rule of law, money always was, from the very necessity of the case, an exception. If the true owner of the money finds it in the possession of the finder or thief, he can reclaim it. But if the finder or thief has once purchased goods with it, and the shopkeeper has taken it honestly, in the usual way of business, and without knowing it has been stolen, he can retain it against the true owner, even though he should be able to identify it. That is, the person who acquires money honestly, in the way of business, has a good title to it, even though the transferer had not. Thus it is said in law that "the property in money passes by delivery." Thus, after the money has once been passed away in commerce to an innocent receiver, the true owner has lost his *Jus vindicandi*. It is this peculiarity which affects the property in money, which passes by delivery, which is denoted by the words "current" and "currency" in English law. And when an Act of Parliament declares that any instrument shall be "current," it means that the property in it shall pass by delivery to the innocent purchaser. This quality of currency is also called negotiability. And when the representatives of money, such as bank notes, cheques, bills of exchange, etc., came into use, the law merchant applied the same principle of currency to them. They are like money so far as this, that the property in them passes like the property in money. Thus, if they are lost or stolen the true owner may recover them if he can find them in the hands of the finder or thief, but if the finder or thief succeeds in passing them away for value in the ordinary course of business to an innocent purchaser, that innocent purchaser acquires the property in them, and may retain them against the true owner and enforce payment of them from all the parties liable on them. This doctrine has been affirmed in a whole series of cases in the courts of law which we shall notice shortly. It follows from this that in strict law this principle of currency can only be applied to those rights of action which are recorded on some material. An abstract right cannot be lost, mislaid or stolen or passed away in commerce. For a right of action to be currency in strict law, it must be recorded on some material, so as to be capable of being carried in the hand, or in the pocket, or put away in a drawer, or dropped in the street, or stolen from the drawer or the pocket and carried off by the finder or thief, and transferred in commerce.

So far, then, as regards mercantile law there is no difficulty; the meaning of the word is perfectly clear. But if the word currency is used to denote a certain class of economic quantities, synonymous with circulating medium, a difficulty arises; because there is an immense mass of credit which has produced exchanges, and has circulated commodities, and is, therefore, circulating medium, which is not recorded on any material at all, in such a way that it can be lost or stolen and carried off, and transferred in commerce by manual delivery. Thus the gigantic mass of banking credits and the book debts of traders have all effected a sale or circulation, and therefore they are all circulating medium; but they have not the attribute of currency in a legal sense, because they cannot be mislaid, lost or stolen and picked up and passed away in commerce by manual delivery. So also private debts between persons, termed verbal credits; they only arise from the transfer of goods or money, and they exist equally whether they are recorded on paper or not. They are equally circulating medium. Private debts among traders affect prices and effect sales exactly like so much money. Consequently, though they are not currency in strict law, yet if that word is still to be retained as a scientific term denoting a certain class of economic quantities, synonymous with circulating medium, they must all be included under that term, because they can all be recorded on paper at pleasure and put into circulation, when they do actually become currency in strict law; and their nature and effects are exactly the same, whether they are recorded on paper or not.

In the great discussions in Parliament which arose out of the suspension of cash payments by the Bank of England, no attempt was made to define the term currency; but all the speakers assumed that it comprehended money and credit in all its forms. This truth was well expressed by Lord Titchfield in the House of Commons in the debates of 1822. Speaking of the various forms of credit used as substitutes for money, he said:* "When it was considered to how great an extent these contrivances had been practised in the various modes of verbal, book, and circulating credits, it was easy to see that the country had received a great addition to its currency. This addition to the currency would have the same effect as if gold had been increased from the mines."

XLI.—THE DIFFERENT FORMS OF CURRENCY.

Adopting, then, the terms circulating medium and currency as absolutely identical and synonymous and as designating a certain class of economic quantities, its different forms are: 1. Coined money—gold, silver, and copper. 2. The paper currency—bank notes, cheques, bills of exchange, promissory notes, exchequer bills, dividend warrants, and all orders and promises to pay money. 3. Simple debts of all sorts, not recorded as circulating paper, such as credits in bankers' books termed deposits, book debts of traders and private debts between persons; because all these debts may be recorded on paper at the will of the parties and thrown into circulation; moreover, simple debts can be transferred with perfect facility without being

* Parliamentary Debates, N. S., Vol. IX., p. 868.

recorded on paper. All these denote that a transaction has taken place and are a title to future payment. From these considerations it follows that the circulating medium or currency of any country is the sum total of all the debts or titles to future payment belonging to every individual in it—that is, all the money and credit in it.

Postage stamps must also be included under the term currency. They are a most usual form of remittance; they pass in small payments, and since the post-office is bound to cash them, they are in fact penny notes. Though the point has not been actually decided at law, there can be no doubt that if anyone were to steal postage stamps, and they were taken honestly in payment, it would be held that they possess the attribute of currency; hence they are in every sense strictly currency.

XLII.—ON PRICE.

When any economic quantity is exchanged for any other economic quantity, each is termed the value of the other. But when one or both of the quantities exchanged is money or credit, it receives a special name—it is termed price. Price, therefore, always is value expressed in money or credit. Now, the value of money is any other economic quantity which can be obtained in exchange for it—either a material chattel, or a service, or a right, such as a debt. If money be taken as the fixed quantity, the more of the other quantity which can be obtained in exchange for it, the greater is the value of money. The less of the other quantity which can be obtained for it, the less is the value of money. Or if the other quantity be taken as the fixed quantity, the less the money given for it, the greater is the value of money; and the more the money given for it, the less is the value of money. Hence it is seen that the value of money varies inversely as price.

But credits, or debts, are commodities or merchandise, which are brought into commerce and bought and sold or exchanged like any other merchandise. Now, when any commodities or merchandise are brought into commerce they are always divided into certain units for the convenience of sale. Coals are sold by the ton, corn by the quarter, tea and sugar by the pound, cloth by the yard, wine and other liquids by the gallon, quart, or pint, etc. So, for the convenience of commerce, bullion is divided into units called coins. In a similar way, when the commodity or merchandise termed credit or debt is brought into commerce it must, for the convenience of trade, be divided into units. The unit of credit or debt is the right to demand £100 to be paid one year hence. The sum of money given to purchase the unit of debt is also termed its price. And as in all other sales, the less the quantity of money given to purchase the unit of debt, the greater is the value of money; and the greater the quantity of money given to purchase the unit of debt, the less is the value of money. Hence the value of money, with respect to debts, varies exactly in the same way as it does with respect to any other merchandise. But in the commerce of debts it is not usual to estimate the value of money by the quantity of debt it will purchase. As money naturally produces a profit, it is clear that the value or price of a debt to be paid only one year hence must be less than the actual amount of the debt. The difference between the present value or the price of the debt and the amount of the debt is the profit made by buying it. This difference or profit is termed discount.

XLIII.—THE VALUE OF MONEY VARIES INVERSELY AS PRICE, AND DIRECTLY AS DISCOUNT.

To discount a debt is to buy it by paying down the present value of its amount payable at a future time. Hence it must be observed that the term value of money has two distinct meanings in commerce. There are three great branches of commerce; the commerce in material commodities, the commerce in labor, and the commerce in debts. And the expression "value of money" has two distinct meanings, as it is applied to these three branches of commerce. In the commerce of material commodities and in the commerce of labor it means the quantity of the commodity or of the service which money can purchase; in the commerce of debts it means the discount or profit made by buying the debt.

XLIV.—ON INTEREST AND DISCOUNT.

Profits made by trading in debts are made in two ways:

(1) When the person who buys the debt agrees to defer receiving the profit until the end of the time agreed on.

In this case the profit is termed interest. Thus, when a person buys a debt of £100 payable one year hence, at £5 per cent. interest, he pays down the £100, and receives in exchange for it the right to demand £105 at the end of the year. The debt is the price of the money, and the money is the price of the debt. When the debtor pays the debt he brings the £105 in money to his creditor, and buys up the right of action against himself. Thus every "loan" of money, as it is called, is a sale or an exchange; the lender transfers the property in the money to the "borrower," and in exchange for it receives the right of action to demand the principal and interest at the end of the year. This right of action is a new creation of property, and is the credit, or the debt. All "loans" of money are sales or exchanges; they are acts of commerce, and, therefore, enter into the science of economics.

(2) Where the difference, or profit, is retained at the time of the purchase of the debt.

In this case the profit is termed discount. But discount itself is of two kinds: (*a*) In the ordinary books of algebra it is said that discount is where the profit is retained at the time of the purchase; and the sum paid for the debt is such a sum as, improved at the given rate of interest, should be equal to the full amount of the debt at the end of the period of advance. It is, therefore, the present value of the sum agreed upon at the agreed upon rate of profit. This may be called algebraical discount. It is used by insurance companies in determining the present value of future payments and in some other cases. (*b*) But this kind of discount is never used by bankers and dealers in money. In banking it is invariably the custom to retain the full amount of the profit agreed upon at the time of purchasing the debt. Thus, if a banker discounts a bill of £100 for a year at five per cent., he deducts and retains the full £5 at the time of the purchase, and gives his customer a credit for £95. That is, he creates a right of action of £95 to purchase the right to £100 at the end of the year. As this method of discount is invariably used in banking and money lending, it may be termed banking discount.

The rate of interest or discount is the ratio of the profit to the amount of the debt, made in some given time, as the year. The profits made by interest and algebraical discount are exactly equal, but banking discount is more profitable; because in the example given in the former case, a profit of £5 is made on the advance of £100, in the latter case on the advance of £95.

So long as the rate of discount is low, there is not much difference in the profits by way of interest or banking discount. But as the rate increases, the profit increases at a very rapid ratio, as may easily be seen. If a person "lends" £100 at twenty per cent. interest, he advances £100, and at the end of the year receives £120, which is a profit of twenty per cent. If he discounts a bill for £100 at twenty per cent., he advances only £80, and at the end of the year receives £100, which is a profit of twenty-five per cent. If he lends £100 at fifty per cent. interest, he advances £100, and at the end of the year he receives £150, which is a profit of fifty per cent. If he discounts a bill of £100 at fifty per cent., he advances only £50, and at the end of the year receives £100, which is a profit of 100 per cent. So, discounting a bill of £100 at sixty per cent. is a profit of 150 per cent. If a person lends £100 at 100 per cent. interest, at the end of the year he receives £200, which is a profit of 100 per cent. If he discounted a bill of £100 at 100 per cent., he would advance nothing, and at the end of the year he would receive £100, or his profit would be infinite.

It would be out of place here to investigate the whole theory of banking discount; but we have given a full exposition of the subject in our Theory and Practice of Banking and Elements of Economics.

XLV.—ON PAYMENT AND SATISFACTION.

The words payment and satisfaction are often supposed to be synonymous, but they are not so. The word payment means anything whatever which is taken in exchange for anything else. It originally came from the Sanskrit *paç*, which is the same word as the Greek *πήγω*, Doric *πάγω*, *πήγνυμι*. In old Latin this was *pago* or *paco*, the same as *paciscor*, and also *pango, pegi* or *panxi, pactum;* to covenant, agree with, or come to terms with. Thus it is said in the Laws of the XII. Tables: "*Rem ubi pagunt, orato.*"—"If they come to terms, let it be settled as agreed upon." "*Ni pagunt, in comitio aut in foro ante meridiem causam conjicito.*"—"If they do not come to terms, bring on the cause before midday either in the comitium or the forum." Hence, *pacare* is to come to terms with, to appease; hence the Italian *pagare* and our pay.

When one person has parted with anything else to another person, or done him a service, he is entitled to receive from him some equivalent, unless it was meant as a donation. But at the same time he has the right to accept anything he pleases as an equivalent. Thus, where two persons agree to exchange any material products, each is payment for the other; because each product satisfies and appeases the claim of the other for an equivalent. When goods are paid for in money, it is sometimes supposed that it is only the money which is payment for the goods. But the goods are equally payment for the money, because each person has got what he agreed to take in exchange for his product. So when money is paid as wages for work done, the money is payment for the work, but the work is equally payment for the money. So when persons agree to exchange different kinds of work, each is payment for the other. So when a merchant agrees to take a trader's bill at three months in exchange for goods, the bill is payment for the goods; it appeases the claim of the merchant because he has agreed to take a right of action in exchange for the goods. And the goods are equally payment for the right of action. When the bill becomes due, the trader has to pay his bill; that is, he has to appease the claim which the holder of the bill has for money. And when he pays the bill he buys up the right of action against himself.

The money is the payment for the right of action; and the right of action is payment for the money. Hence to pay means simply to appease. When a man pays his debt he appeases the right or claim which his creditor has to demand a sum of money from him. When he pays his rent he appeases the right which the owner of the house or land has against him for compensation for its use. But it does not follow that a payment is a final closing of the transaction. The only legal word which denotes a final closing is satisfaction. If a bill is taken in exchange for goods it is payment; but it is not satisfaction (unless it is expressly received as such) until the bill itself is paid. If, however, the owner of the bill neglects to follow up his legal remedy, the bill becomes not only payment, but satisfaction; by doing so the owner of it has made it money. And economists go further; they say that money itself is only a higher order of bill; that, though when a person has received money it is payment, yet it is not satisfaction until he has exchanged away the money for some object he desires. Thus, though a shoemaker is paid when he has got money for his shoes, yet he has not got a satisfaction until he has got bread or meat or clothing or something else he desires for the money.

XLVI.—ON CAPITAL.

Adam Smith's use of the word capital strikingly exemplifies the defect of his definitions. He enumerates as capital—(1) Material things; (2) personal qualities; (3) abstract rights, such as bank notes, bills of exchange, etc., which are credit. That is, he enumerates all the three orders of economic quantities as capital. Now, when we are told that all these things are capital we have no more notion of what capital is than if we were told that they are all abracadabra. We do not want an enumeration of what things are capital; but we want a definition of what capital is.

The word capital is derived from the Latin *caput*, which means the source of a spring or the root of a plant—namely, the source from which any increase flows. Thus Plautus says: "*O scelerum caput.*"—"O source, or fountain, of crimes." "*Perjurii caput.*"—"O fountain of perjury." Stephen, in his Thesaurus, thus defines the word: "*Κεφάλαιον—Caput unde fructus et reditus manat.*"—"Capital, the source from which any profit or revenue flows." So Senior says: "Economists are agreed that whatever gives a profit is properly termed capital." And de Fontenay says: "Wherever there is a revenue you perceive capital." This is a good general definition; and the "whatever gives a profit" must be interpreted in as wide and general a sense as the "anything whose value can be measured in money" is in the definition of wealth. The definition of capital is, therefore, this: "Capital is an economic quantity used for the purpose of profit."

XLVII.—ANY ECONOMIC QUANTITY WHATEVER MAY BE USED AS CAPITAL.

Now, as Aristotle pointed out, any economic quantity whatever may be used in two different ways—(1) The proprietor may use it for his own personal enjoyment; (2) he may trade with it—*i. e.*, he may use it so as to produce a profit. When any economic quantity whatever is used so as to produce a profit—*i. e.*, is traded with—it is termed capital.

Economic quantities, it has been shown, are of three distinct orders—(1) Material things; (2) personal qualities, both in the form of labor and credit; (3) abstract rights. And each of these quantities may be used in either of the above ways.

I. Material Things.—Suppose that a person has a sum of money. If he expends it on his own personal gratification or household expenses, such money is not used as capital, because he makes no profit by it. But if he lends it out at interest, or if he buys goods with it for the purpose of selling them again at a profit, or if he buys into the funds, or the shares of any commercial company, then he uses his money as capital; and the goods are also capital, because he intends to sell them again at a profit; and the funds and the shares are also capital, because they produce him an annual revenue. So, if the owner of land lives on it himself and uses it for his own personal enjoyment, he does not use the land as capital. But if he lets it out to farmers or to builders to build houses upon and receives a rent for so doing, then he uses the land as capital. Some great noblemen possess large tracts of land upon which part of London is built; that land yields them enormous revenues, and therefore it is capital to them. And so any material thing whatever may be used as capital. So, if a person spends money merely on a general education, of which he makes no profitable use, that money is not used as capital. But if he spends his money in acquiring a professional education, such as that of a schoolmaster, an advocate, a physician, a surgeon, or an engineer, or any profession by which he intends to earn an income, then he uses the money as capital. And the professional knowledge which he has thus acquired is capital to him, because he makes an income by trading with it.

II. PERSONAL QUALITIES.—Personal qualities may also be used in both ways. But personal qualities are of two forms; they are of the form (*a*) of labor and (*b*) of credit.

(*a*) *Personal Qualities as Labor.*—If a man digs in his own garden for his amusement, or if he sings, acts, or gives lectures for the delectation of his friends, such labor is not used as capital. But if he sells his labor in any way for money, then he uses his labor as capital. Thus Huskisson said he had "always maintained that labor is the poor man's capital." So Mr. Cardwell, speaking to his constituents, said: "Labor is the poor man's capital." So a writer in a daily paper said: "The only capital they possess is their labor, which they must bring into the market to supply their daily wants." And speaking of them the "Economist" said: "They have no capital but their labor." So Froude said in "Oceana": "And the land would be within the reach of poor men who have no capital except their labor." So Cardinal Manning said: "I claim for labor the rights of capital. It is capital in the truest sense. * * * The capital of money and the capital of strength and skill must be united together." So his knowledge, skill, and abilities are capital to anyone who earns an income as an advocate, physician, actor, engineer, or as manager of a great commercial company, or in any other profession. His services are wanted, demanded, and paid for by his clients; their value is measured in money; hence they are *χρήματα*, or wealth; and as he makes an income by their employment they are capital. This income is measurable and taxable, just in the same way as if he made an income by selling corn, cattle, or any other material chattels. All modern writers admit that labor is a marketable commodity which can be bought and sold like any material chattel, and consequently it is wealth; and as a person can sell his labor for a profit, and make an income thereby, it may be used as capital.

(*b*) *Personal Qualities as Credit.*—So personal credit may be used in two ways. If a person buys goods on credit for his own enjoyment, as for household use, such credit is not used as capital. But a merchant may use his credit for the purpose of profit, and therefore as capital. He may use it for the purpose of purchasing goods or materials or in employing labor, by giving a promise to pay at a future time, instead of actual money. He sells the goods and makes a profit by so doing, just as if he had paid for them in money. Or he may employ laborers by means of his credit, and sell the products for more than they cost, and so make a profit; in these ways he uses his personal credit as capital. When personal qualities, either in the form of labor or of credit, are used in this way to produce a profit, they are termed personal capital.

III. RIGHTS.—When personal credit is used as a purchasing power, a right of action or an economic quantity of the third order is created. And as this right of action may be bought and sold or exchanged, like any material chattel, it is a marketable commodity. The traffic in these rights of action is the most colossal branch of modern commerce. It is in buying and selling these rights of action that bankers make their profits. But as the commerce in these rights of action is the subject-matter of this work, we shall say no more about them here. But any other right may be used as capital. If a man buys the funds or shares in any commercial company, or municipal or other obligations, such as railway debenture stock, all these and many other classes of rights produce him a profit, hence they are capital to him. So the copyright of a successful work is capital to the author, and if he sells it to a publisher it becomes fixed capital to him. There is a class of traders whose especial business is to buy and sell rights, such as shares in all kinds of commercial companies and public securities; they keep a stock of this kind of property on hand, just as other traders keep a stock of material goods. These persons are termed stock jobbers.

XLVIII.—THERE IS NO SUCH THING AS ABSOLUTE CAPITAL.

It has been shown that there is no such thing as absolute wealth—that is, there is nothing which is in its own nature wealth, and that whether anything is wealth or not depends entirely upon human wants and desires. So, also, it must be carefully observed that there is no such thing as absolute capital. As Mill justly observes, the distinction between capital and non-capital does not lie in the kind of commodity, but in the mind of the owner; that is, that whether anything is capital or not, in no way depends on the nature of the thing itself, but solely and exclusively on its method of use.

Many writers, from an imperfect consideration of the subject, say that capital is simply the accumulation of the products of past labor. But this is a vital error which must be carefully guarded against; because all the accumulated products of past labor are not capital, but only that portion of them which is traded with or used for the purposes of profit. Moreover, many things may be used as capital which are in no way the accumulated products of past labor. As Senior says: "Economists are agreed that whatever gives a profit is properly termed capital." Now, it has been shown that any economic quantity may be used as capital. Not only may many material products be used as capital which are not the products of past labor, such as the land, but personal qualities both in the form of labor and credit may be used as capital. Now, how is labor itself the accumulated product of past labor? How is personal credit the accumulated product of past labor? Also incorporeal quantities may be used as capital or for the purposes of profit, as well as any material chattels. Now, how are banking credits, bank notes, cheques, bills of exchange, etc., the accumulated product of past labor? In fact, in this great civilized country the enormously greater amount of capital is purely personal and incorporeal.

Some statisticians, indeed, endeavor to estimate the amount of capital in the country. But it is evident that such attempts are wholly futile. How can they form any estimate of the amount of capital unless they tell us what they reckon as capital? Because it is utterly impossible to estimate the amount of economic quantities which are being used as capital at any given instant. The very same quantity may be used as capital at one instant and as income at the next. And it has been shown that persons trade with, and make capital of, not only the realized profits of the past, but also the expected profits of the future.

CHAPTER V.

THE THEORY OF VALUE.

SECTION I.

I.—VALUE DEFINED.

VALUE, in its original sense, is a desire or affection of the mind toward some object: it means esteem or estimation. To bring value into economics, a person must not only have an estimate of some object or property of his own, but he must have a desire or value for something which is in someone else's possession, and be willing to give some of his own property in exchange for it. One person, however, cannot acquire an object which another person possesses without giving him in exchange for it some object which that other person desires, demands, and values; hence, economic value necessarily requires the concurrence of two minds.

If a person brought a cargo of tobacco to a nation of non-smokers, it would have no value among them, because no one among them would desire or demand it. If a person brought a cargo of wine to a nation of teetotallers, it would have no value, because no one among them would desire or demand it, and therefore no one would buy it. However much a person may wish to sell his product, he cannot do so unless someone else will buy it, and in that case it would have no economic value. Hence, for an exchange to take place, there must be the reciprocal desire or demand of two persons, each for the product of the other. When, however, two persons each desire or demand to obtain the product of the other, and when they have agreed as to the quantity of their own product which they will give in exchange to acquire the product of the other, each product may be said to be the measure of the desire of its owner to acquire the product of the other. The two products, therefore, measure the desire, demand, or value of their respective owners to obtain the product of the other; and when two persons have agreed upon the quantities of their products to be exchanged, the two products are said to be equal value; each product is the value or the demand for the other. And this is the only kind of value with which economics is concerned.

The Greek word for value is *ἀξία*, which is derived from *ἄγω*, one of whose meanings is to weigh, or be of the weight of. Thus Demosthenes, speaking of some golden goblets, says:* "*ἄγουσα ἑκάστη μνᾶν.*"—"Each one weighing a mina." And he says of the sword of Mardonius:† "*ὃς ἦγε τριακοσίους δαρεικούς.*"—"Which weighed three hundred darics." So Homer says:‡ "*κὰδ δὲ λέβητ' ἄπυρον, βοὸς ἄξιον, ἀνθεμόεντα θῆκ' ἐς ἀγῶνα φέρων.*"—"And he offered, too, as a prize, a new caldron, ornamented with flowers, worth an ox." Hence *ἀξία* meant equality, weight for weight, as when two quantities placed in a balance are of equal weight.

So in Latin *æstimatio* means exactly the same as *ἀξία*; it means the quantity of money (*æs*) given for anything. Thus Cicero§ speaks of: "*æstimatio frumenti.*"—"The value of the corn to be furnished." So Cæsar‖ speaks of: "*æstimatio rerum et possessionum.*"—"The value of their goods and chattels." So Catullus says, 12, 11: "*Quod me non movet æstimatione.*"—"Which does not affect me on account of its value." So Le Trosne says¶ that value is a new quality which products acquire when men live in society. "Products acquire, then, in the social state, which arises from the community of men among each other, a new quality. This new quality is value, which makes products become wealth. Value consists in the ratio of exchange, which takes place between such and such a product, between such a quantity of one product and such a quantity of another product. Price is the expression of value; it is not separate in exchange; each thing is reciprocally the price of the merchandise; in a sale the price is the money."

Hence it is clear that value is a ratio or an equation; like distance and an equation, it necessarily requires two objects. The value of anything is always something external to itself. Hence a single object cannot have economic value. A single object cannot be equal or distant. If an object is said to be equal or distant, we must ask—Equal to what? or, Distant from what? So if any quantity is said to have value, we must ask—Value in what? And as it is absurd to speak of absolute or intrinsic distance, or absolute or intrinsic equality, so it is equally absurd to speak of absolute or intrinsic value. It is impossible to predicate that any quantity has value, without at the same time implying that it can be exchanged for something else; and of course everything it can be exchanged for is its value in that commodity. Hence any economic quantity has as many values as quantities it can be exchanged for; and if there is nothing for which it can be exchanged, it has no value.

---

* Against Androtion, 617, 21. † Against Timocrates, 741, 7. ‡ Iliad, XXIII., 885. § Ver. 2, 53.
‖ *Bell. Civil.*, 3, 1. ¶ *De l'Intérêt Sociale*, ch. i., sec. 4.

II.—EXAMPLES OF VALUE.

Any economic quantity may have value in terms of any other. Suppose that A as above is ten guineas; then B may be any one of the other three species of economic quantities. It may be a watch, or so much corn, or wine, or clothes, or any other material chattel. Or it may be so much labor, instruction, or amusement, or service. Or it may be a right of action, or a debt, or the funds, or a copyright, or any other abstract right. Each of these species of property is of the value of ten guineas, and it follows that each of them is equal in value to the other; because, things which are equal to the same thing are equal to each other. The value of the money in the pockets of the public is the products, services and rights it can purchase. The value of the goods in the warehouses of merchants and traders is the money in the pockets of the public.

The value of an incorporeal right is the thing promised which may be demanded. The value of a £5 note is five sovereigns; the value of a postage stamp is the carriage of a letter; the value of a railway ticket is the journey; the value of an order to see the play is seeing the play; the value of a promise to cut a man's hair is the cutting of the hair; the value of an order for milk, bread, wine, soup, coals, etc., is the milk, bread, wine, etc. If I want a loaf of bread which costs a shilling, what difference does it make to me whether I have a shilling or the promise of the baker to give me a loaf? It is clear that in this case the shilling and the promise are of exactly the same value to me. Suppose that the price of cutting a man's hair is a shilling; what difference does it make to me whether I have a shilling or the promise of the hairdresser to cut my hair? In this case it is clear that the shilling and the promise are exactly equal value to me. In short, in the case of every product and service, the money to purchase it with, and a promise to render the product, or service, are of exactly equal value in each separate case.

Now, what is money by the unanimous consent of economists? It is nothing but a general right, or title, to demand a product or service from any person who is in the habit of rendering them at any time; and as there is always some person who can render them, if another cannot, money has general and permanent value; while each of these promises has only particular and precarious value. Each of these separate rights, then, is of exactly the same nature as money; but it is of an inferior degree. But they are, each of them, economic quantities, or wealth, for the very same reason that money is. Is it not clear that if a person had his pockets full of promises by solvent persons to render him all the products and services he might require, he would be exactly as wealthy as if he had so much money? And he can always sell, or exchange, any of these orders for orders for a different thing. Hence we see the perfect justice of the doctrine of all jurists that rights are wealth.

III.—ON NEGATIVE VALUES.

Value, then, being the desire, or affection of the mind, toward some object, may be of two forms; either the desire to acquire some object, or the desire to get rid of it. As these desires are inverse and opposite, they may be denoted by opposite signs; if the desire to obtain something be termed positive value, the desire to get rid of something may be termed negative value. Thus if we consider a piece of land just in the fit state to be cultivated, to be in the state o, it may be covered with primeval forest, with marshes and fens, with jungle, and huge bowlders, or any other obstructions to cultivation. It may require a considerable sum of money to clear away all these obstructions and bring it into a fit state for cultivation, which we have denoted by o; the sum necessary to clear away all these obstructions, and bring it into the state o, may be termed its negative value. So if the state of a person in health be denoted by o, he may fall into illness and require the services of a physician; or he may meet with an accident and require the services of a surgeon to bring him into a state of health. As the fees paid to the physician or surgeon are paid for removing obstructions to health, they may be termed negative values.

If we consider persons in the enjoyment of perfect security as to their persons and property as o, and if people were perfectly honest and never attacked their neighbors' persons and property, there would be no use for the police; hence all sums spent on the police, which are spent merely for the purpose of warding off attacks on person and property, may be termed a negative value.

Now, it is evident that all the sums spent on negative values, or on removing obstructions, are just so much subtracted from positive values, or the acquirement of wealth, or enjoyments. We thus see what a gigantic obstruction to progress and wealth these European armaments are; and what an immense advantage in progress of wealth it is to America to be free from them; and to devote all the money and people employed in Europe on negative values to the increase of positive values. It was the observation that there are two kinds of value, positive value and negative value, to which we first drew attention, which led Stanley Jevons, as he acknowledged, to designate economics by the somewhat fantastic title, as the calculus of pleasure and pain.

IV.—THERE MAY BE A GENERAL RISE OR FALL OF PRICES; BUT NOT OF VALUES.

Price is the value of any economic quantity in money or credit. Now, if money or credit be very greatly increased or decreased in quantity, the prices of all other economic quantities may rise or fall, but they will still preserve their relations among each other. If a loaf of bread and a pound of meat each cost a shilling; and if in consequence of a great increase in the quantity of money or credit they each rise to two shillings; or if in consequence of a great decrease in the quantity of money or credit they each fall to sixpence, the loaf of bread is still of the value of a pound of meat. Hence there may be a general rise or a general fall of prices. But there can be no such thing as a general rise or a general fall in values. Everything can no more rise or fall in value with respect to everything else, than, as Mill says, a dozen runners can each outrun the rest, or a hundred trees can each overtop each other. To suppose that all things could rise relatively to each other would be to realize Pat's idea of society where everyone is as good as his neighbor, and a great deal better, too. The opposite case of everything falling in value with respect to everything else would be analogous to everyone thinking himself inferior to everyone else; which, according to human nature and St. Paul, would be an impossible case.

V.—NOTHING CAN HAVE FIXED VALUE UNLESS EVERYTHING HAS FIXED VALUE.

As value is the ratio in which any two quantities will exchange, it is clear that the value of A with respect to B varies directly as B; that is, that it increases or decreases according to the greater or less quantity of B that A can purchase. And the value of B in terms of A varies directly as A; that is, it increases or decreases according as B can purchase more or less of A. It is also clear that if from any cause whatever the value, or ratio, between A and B has changed, the value of both of them has changed. It is manifestly as absurd to say that the value of A has changed with respect to B, but the value of B has remained the same, as it would be to say that a railway station has remained at the same distance from a train, while the train has increased its distance from the station. Moreover, it is as absurd to say that a quantity has changed its own value, or kept its own value fixed, without stating the quantities with respect to which its value has changed or remained fixed, as it would be to say that an object has changed or preserved its distance, or its ratio, fixed, without saying its distance from what or its ratio to what. Hence it is clear that nothing can have fixed or invariable value unless everything else has fixed and invariable value as well. Because, though a quantity may retain its value unchanged with respect to a certain number of quantities, yet if its value has changed with respect to other quantities, its value has changed. From this it will be seen that it is utterly futile to seek for a currency, or circulating medium, of fixed or invariable value.

SECTION II.

VI.—ON THE ORIGIN, SOURCE, OR CAUSE OF VALUE.

WE now come to the second branch of our inquiry—What is the origin, source, or cause of value? Or, in the language of Bacon—What is the form of value? And whence does it originate?

Now, when we are to search for the cause of value, it is necessary to understand what we are searching for. There are three distinct orders of quantities, each containing many varieties, which all have value. We have to discover some single cause which is common to them all; and ascertain what that single cause is by genuine induction. Bacon says:* "But the induction which is to be available for the discovery and demonstration of sciences and arts, must analyze nature by proper rejections and exclusions, and then, after a sufficient number of negatives, come to a conclusion on the affirmative instances." Also:† "What the sciences stand in need of is a form of induction which shall analyze experience and take it to pieces, and by a due process of exclusion and rejection lead to an inevitable conclusion." The first step in this process of induction is to make a complete collection of all the different kinds of quantities, of whatever nature they may be, which have value‡—"For whoever is acquainted with forms [*i. e.*, causes] embraces the unity of nature in substances the most unlike. From the discovery of forms [causes] results truth in theory and freedom in practice."

Bacon earnestly inculcates as the foundation of all true science a careful collection of all kinds of instances in which the given nature is found:§ "The investigation of forms [causes] proceeds thus: a nature [such as value] being given, we must first of all have a presentation before the understanding of all known instances which agree in the same nature though in substances the most unlike; and such collections must be made in the manner of history, without premature theory." Bacon then exemplifies his method by an investigation into the form, or cause, of heat. He gives tables of the divers instances agreeing in the nature of heat; also where it

---

* Nov. Org., Bk. I., Aph. 105.

† *Distributio Operis.*

‡ Nov. Org., Bk. II., Aph. 3.

§ Nov. Org., Bk. II., Aph. 11.

appears in different degrees:* "The work and effect of these tables I call the presentation of instances to the understanding; which presentation having been made, induction itself must be set to work; for the problem is upon a review of instances, all and each, to find such a nature as is always present or absent with the given nature, and always increases and decreases with it; and which is, as I have said, a particular case of a more general nature. We must, therefore, make a complete solution and separation of nature; not, indeed, by fire, but by the mind, which is a kind of divine fire. The first work, therefore, of true induction (so far as the discovery of causes) is the rejection or exclusion of the several natures which are not found in some instances where the given nature is present, and are found in some instances where the given nature is absent; or are found to increase in some instances where the given nature decreases, or to decrease where the given nature increases. Then, indeed, after the rejection and exclusion has been duly made, there will remain at the bottom, all light opinions vanishing in smoke, a cause affirmative, solid and true and well defined."

As an indispensable part of induction is the rejection of erroneous causes,† "I must now give an example of the exclusion and rejection of natures, which, by the table of presentations, are found not to belong to the form or cause [of value], observing in the meantime not only each table suffices for the rejection of any nature, but even any one of the particular instances contained in any one of the tables. For it is manifest from what has been said, that anv one contradictory instance overthrows a conjecture as to the cause."

VII.—INVESTIGATION OF THE FORM OR CAUSE OF VALUE.

Bacon has exemplified his process of induction by investigating the form, or cause, of heat; our present task is to investigate the form, or cause, of value. Following the example of the mighty master, we must begin by making a complete collection of all the instances of value. That is, we must enumerate all the different kinds of quantities, with all their varieties, which have value. These are:

I. Corporeal or material quantities. Under this species are comprehended the following varieties: lands, houses, trees, cattle, flocks and herds of all sorts, corn and all other fruits of the earth, furniture, clothes, money, minerals of all sorts, jewelry, pearls, manufactured articles of all sorts, fish, game.

II. Immaterial quantities; comprehending labor of all sorts—agricultural, artisan, professional, scientific, literary, trade secrets, news.

III. Incorporeal quantities; comprehending rights of action, credits or debts, the funds, shares in commercial companies, copyrights, patents, the goodwill of a business, a professional practice, tolls, ferries, tithes, advowsons, rents, shootings, fishings, market rights, and all other valuable rights.

* Nov. Org., Bk. II., Aph. 16.

† Nov. Org., Bk. II., Aph. 18.

We must now investigate the cause of value in all these different kinds of quantities, and in all their varieties, and in each one separately. We must first, by a due course of rejections and exclusions, eliminate all accidental and intrusive ideas which may in some cases be associated with value, and in other cases not; and after completing this course of rejections and exclusions, we must end by an affirmative; and discover that single general cause, which is common to all these different classes of quantities, which, being present, value is present; which, when it increases, value increases; which, when it decreases, value decreases; and which, being absent, value is absent.

VIII.—MATERIALITY IS NOT NECESSARY TO VALUE.

Now, in examining these three classes of cases which all have value, we observe that the whole class of immaterial quantities, and the whole class of incorporeal quantities, have value, but have no materiality. Hence it is evident that materiality is not necessary to value; it is only in some cases the accident of value.

IX.—PERMANENCE, OR DURABILITY, IS NOT NECESSARY TO VALUE.

We also observe that some things which have value last forever, like the land, the funds, precious stones, statues, coins. Other things may last a very long time, such as houses, watches, pictures. Other things have a very much less degree of durability, such as clothes, animals. Others have a very short degree of durability, such as food, flowers. But labor, which in many cases has very high value, perishes in the very instant of its production, and therefore has no durability, or permanence, at all. Thus, quantities which have value have all degrees of permanence, or durability. Now, among Bacon's prerogative instances he mentions ultimity, or limit, and says:* "Nor should extremes in the lowest degree be less noticed than instances in the highest degree." This is the doctrine of the law of continuity, which says: "That which is true up to the limit, is true at the limit." From these principles it follows that things which have the lowest degree of permanence, or durability, which is 0, are to be included in economics as well as those which have the degree, *i. e.*, which last forever. Hence it is seen that permanence, or durability, is not necessary to value; it is only the accident of value.

X.—DEMAND THE SOLE CAUSE OF VALUE.

It has now been shown that materiality and durability are in no way necessary to value, but are only in some cases the accidents of value. In what, then, consists the essence of value? The only thing which ancient

* Nov. Org., Bk. II., Aph. 34.

writers, Aristotle, the author of the "Eryxias," the Roman jurists, and in modern times the physiocrates, the Italian economists, Smith, Condillac, Whately, and hosts of others have observed—exchangeability. Each of the quantities in the table of instances may be bought and sold, or their value may be measured in money; each of them possesses the attribute of exchangeability, and that is the sole attribute which is common to all the classes of quantities, and to each separate quantity in each class. Hence, as the ancients unanimously held for 850 years, exchangeability is the sole essence and principle of wealth. Thus, by strictly and reverently following the precepts of the mighty master, by rejecting and excluding all accidental and intrusive ideas, we have at last obtained an affirmative issue.

Now, what is necessary in order that any quantity may be exchangeable? Evidently that someone else should demand it. If I offer something for sale, what is necessary that it should be sold? Simply that someone else should desire or demand it. It is, therefore, clear that demand is the sole cause of value, or exchangeability. Aristotle said long ago that it is *χρεία*, or demand, which binds society together. The author of the "Eryxias" over and over again points out that demand is the sole cause which constitutes anything wealth; and that anything is wealth, whatever its nature may be, so long as it is wanted and demanded, and no longer. He pointed out that the local money of different states is only wealth where it has power of purchase; where it has no power of purchase it is not wealth. It has been shown that the Greek word *χρῆμα*, which is one of the most usual words for wealth, is derived from *χράομαι*, to want, or demand; and that *χρῆμα* simply means anything which is "wanted and demanded"; and that things are only *χρήματα* where they are *χρήσιμα*, or wanted and demanded; and that where they are not *χρήσιμα*, they are not *χρήματα*.

Here it is quite evident that we have got to the origin, form, or cause, of value; it is demand, pure and simple. Value is not a quality of an object, nor is it the labor bestowed on obtaining it; it is an affection of the mind. The sole origin, form, or cause, of value is human desire. When there is a demand for things, they have value; when the demand increases (the supply remaining the same), the value increases; when the demand decreases, the value decreases; and when demand altogether ceases, value is altogether gone.

XI.—CREDITS, OR DEBTS, HAVE VALUE BECAUSE THEY WILL BE PAID IN MONEY.

The importance and the bearing of this investigation on our present subject is obvious. For it is the fatal doctrine that labor is the cause of all value, and that all wealth is composed of the materials of the globe and the product of land, labor, and capital that is at the root of all the difficulty to apprehend the subject of credit. If it be laid down that labor is necessary to all value, how could the notes of the Bank of England or any other bank have value? Or how could the bills of a solvent merchant have value? Everyone knows that a credit in a bank or a bank note has value because the bank will pay it in gold; a bill on a solvent merchant has value because he will pay it in gold when it becomes due. And the gold with which the banker or merchant pays his notes or bills is their value. So Mill, who is a devotee of Ricardo, says:* "An order or a note of hand, or bill payable at sight, for an ounce of gold, while the credit of the giver is unimpaired, is worth neither more nor less than the gold itself." So Smith, Say, and Mill all class bank notes as under the head of circulating capital. Smith himself acknowledges that if money were not exchangeable it would have no value, as the author of the "Eryxias" showed.

We have already frequently shown that all jurists class rights of action, whether written or unwritten, as goods, chattels, commodities, merchandise, which can be bought and sold like any materials, chattels, or like money itself. And this species of goods, chattels, commodities, merchandise has value for exactly the same reason that any other merchandise or money has value, because it is exchangeable. Money has value only because it is exchangeable for products and services, and credits, or debts, have value because they are exchangeable for money. Thus we see that so long as ideas of value are mixed up and founded on labor, the subject is plunged into inextricable difficulties and contradictions. But as soon as we adopt exchangeability as test of value and the sole essence and principle of wealth, as the ancients unanimously did for 850 years, and modern economists are at last coming to do, all difficulties and obscurities are cleared up and dispersed like a fog before the morning sun.

XII.—ON THE ERROR OF THE EXPRESSION "INTRINSIC VALUE."

We have now to say something about an expression which has been the cause of enormous confusion in economics, which has been one of the chief stumbling-blocks in the apprehension of the subject of credit, and which must be cleared away. All ancient writers, as well as modern economists until Adam Smith's deplorable confusion on the subject, clearly understood that the value of anything is some other thing external to itself, and there is not to be found in any of them the slightest trace of any such confusion of ideas as the expression "intrinsic" value. It is not easy to determine when the unfortunate expression intrinsic value came into use, but it seems to have arisen in this way: When unreflecting persons thought about value they thought of the quality of the thing which made it desirable, and they called that its value. They therefore gradually began to speak of intrinsic value. So long ago as 1696, an able writer (Barbon) pointed out the confusion which had arisen from mistaking the absolute qualities of an object for the quantity of things it would exchange for. He says:† "There is nothing which troubles this controversy more than for want of distinguishing between

* Principles of Political Economy, Bk. III., ch. xii.

† A Discourse Concerning Coining the New Money Lighter, p. 6.

virtue and value. Value is only the price of things, and that can never be certain; because it must be there at all times and in all places of the same value; therefore nothing can have an intrinsic value. But things have an intrinsic virtue in themselves, which in all things have the same virtue—the loadstone to attract iron, and the several qualities that belong to herbs and drugs, some purgative, some diuretical, etc. But these, though they have great virtue, may be of small value, or no price, according to the place where they are plenty or scarce; as the red nettle, though it be of excellent virtue to stop bleeding, yet it is a weed of no value from its plenty. And so are spices and drugs in their native soil of no value but as common shrubs and weeds, but with us of great value, and yet in both places of the same excellent intrinsic virtue. * * * For these have no value in themselves; it is opinion and fashion brings them into use and gives them a value." Barbon thus entirely refutes by anticipation the doctrine that utility is the cause of value, which has become rather common in the present day, and puts his finger on the phrase which has caused so much confusion in current economics—intrinsic value—which is to confound an intrinsic quality with an external relation. The following passage from Senior shows how easily even able men are beguiled into the error. He says:* "We have already stated that we use the word value in its popular (?) acceptation, as signifying that quality in anything which fits it to be given and received in exchange, or, in other words, to be lent or sold, hired or purchased. So, defined value denotes a relation reciprocally existing between two objects." Now, the quality of a melon which fits it to be sold is its agreeable flavor; its flavor, therefore, according to Senior, is its value (!); and so defined, he says it means that it costs 5s.! That is, he defines the quality of the melon to be its price! This is exactly the confusion which the economists so carefully provided against. The quality which makes a thing desirable is its value in use, or its utility; and the economists repeatedly explained that economics has nothing to do with value in use or utility, but only with value in exchange, or market price.

This unhappy phrase, intrinsic value, meets us at every turn in modern economics; and yet the slightest reflection will show that to define value to be something external to a quantity, and then to be constantly speaking of intrinsic value, are inconsistent and self-contradictory ideas. Thus, over and over again it is said that money has intrinsic value, but that a bank note or a bill of exchange is only a representative of value. Money, no doubt, is the produce of labor; but Smith himself says that if money would exchange for nothing it would have no value; so he admits that exchangeability is the real essence of value. How, then, can the value of money be intrinsic? How can anything have intrinsic value unless it has the thing it will exchange for inside itself? Money will exchange for anything—lands, houses, corn, books, wine, jewelry, etc.; and each of these is a value of money; but

* Political Economy, p. 13.

which of these is its intrinsic value? Money remains exactly the same in itself wherever it may be placed. A hogshead full of sovereigns has immense value in the middle of London, but if a person had it by itself in a deserted ship in the middle of the Atlantic, or in a barren island, where would its value be? Yet if it has intrinsic value in one place it must have it equally in any other place. A bank note payable on demand is of the value of money; and why is it so? Simply because it is exchangeable for money. Hence, a bank note has value for exactly the same reason that money has—namely, because it is exchangeable for something else. Credit is the right to demand money, and money is the right to demand products and services.

Socrates, in the "Eryxias," shows that it is only when and where that money can be exchanged that it has value; when and where it cannot be exchanged it has no value. So, when a bank note or a bill of exchange can be exchanged it has value; when it cannot be exchanged it has no value. Hence, the value of money and credits of all sorts is essentially of the same nature, though there may be different degrees of it. A credit, by the unanimous consent of all jurists, economists, and merchants, is an article of merchandise, and an exchangeable commodity, just like money, or any other material chattel; and this whether it exists only in the abstract form of a mere right or whether it be recorded on paper.

Who ever heard of intrinsic distance, or of an intrinsic ratio? The absurdity of these expressions is apparent at once; but they are not a whit more absurd than intrinsic value. If we speak of the intrinsic value of money, we may just as well speak of the intrinsic distance of St. Paul's, or the intrinsic ratio of five. To say that money has intrinsic value because it is material and the produce of labor, and that a bank note, or a bill of exchange, is only the representative of value, is just as absurd as to say that a wooden yard-measure is intrinsic distance, and that the distance between two points one yard apart is only the representative of distance.

XIII.—A STANDARD OF VALUE IS IMPOSSIBLE.

That unfortunate confusion of ideas between value being the quantity of any other commodity which any quantity will purchase, and the quantity of labor embodied, as it were, in the thing itself—which is chiefly due to Smith and Ricardo—has not only led to that mischievous expression, intrinsic value, the source of endless confusion in economics, but also to the search for something which the very slightest reflection would have shown to be impossible in the very nature of things—namely, an invariable standard of value.

It is as well to explain what those economists mean who are searching for an invariable standard of value. If we had a British yard and any foreign measures of length before us we could at once perceive the difference between them; and if we were told the measurement of any foreign buildings, however remote in age or country in foreign measures, we could, by a very simple calculation, reduce them to the standard of British measurement, and compare them with the size of our own buildings. Those economists who want an invariable standard of value want to discover and fix upon some single commodity by which they can compare the value of other things in all ages and countries. But the least reflection will show that such a standard is impossible in the very nature of things. Money, indeed, is termed the measure of value; and so it is in exchanges which are effected at the same time and place. If we are told that a quarter of corn is worth 40s., and that a sheep is worth 40s. at a certain time and place, we should say that they were then and there of equal value. But such matters are not the result of simple perception by the senses, as are the different measures of length and capacity. If a quantity of gold were placed beside a number of other things, no human sense could discern what their value would be. And the most violent changes in their several values might take place in the market without there being any visible sign of such a thing. Value is a mental affection; and values are not perceptible by ocular inspection, but they must be declared by the communication of minds.

Moreover, it is not possible to ascertain the different values of different quantities of gold obtained in different ages and countries. If a quantity of gold coin minted in the age of Augustus, an equal quantity minted in the reign of Elizabeth, and an equal quantity minted in China were placed side by side, what human sense could discern the difference in value between them? And yet that is what those economists require who want an invariable standard of value. They want something by which they can at once decide whether gold is of more value in A. D. 30, in A. D. 1588, or in A. D. 1893, in Italy, in England, or in China, without reference to anything else, just as we can discern the difference between British and foreign measures by laying them side by side. But the only test of value is an exchange; and unless we can effect an exchange there can be no value. How can we exchange an ounce of gold in the year A. D. 193 with one in the year A. D. 1593, or with one in the year A. D. 1893?

A measure of length or capacity is a single quantity, and can measure other single quantities, such as different lengths, or bodies of capacity. But value is a ratio, or a relation; and it is utterly impossible in the very nature of things that a single quantity can measure a ratio, or a relation. It is impossible to say that $a : b :: x$. It is manifestly absurd to say that 4 is to 5 as 8, without saying as 8 is to what; just as it is absurd to say that a horse gallops at the rate of twenty miles, without saying in what time.

XIV.—BUT THERE MAY BE A MEASURE OF VALUE.

But though a standard of value is impossible by the very nature of things, there may be a measure of value.

Value being an affection of the mind, or the desire or demand of a person to acquire some object; the quantity of money he is willing to give to acquire it is the measure of his desire to obtain it, and, therefore, the measure of his value for it. But credit is also equally a measure of value as well as money. Neither a merchant nor anyone else will give more in credit, which he is bound to redeem in money, to acquire any commodity, than he would give in money itself. But if he wants anything, he will give just as much in credit as he would in money. Hence, credit is equally a measure of value, or desire, with money. Hence, money and credit are the measure of value; and, as it is universally admitted by all economists that purchases with credit affect prices in all respects equally with money, it follows that the aggregate of money and credit is the medium in which prices are measured, and that the aggregate of money and credit constitutes the circulating medium, or currency.

XV.—VALUE EXISTS ONLY IN THE HUMAN MIND.

Value, then, like color, sound, and odor, exists only in the human mind. There is neither color, nor sound, nor odor in external nature; they exist only in the human mind.

According to the unanimous doctrine of ancient writers and all foreign economists, demand is the sole origin, form, or cause of value. It is demand, or consumption, and not labor, which gives value to a product. It is not the labor which gives value to the product, but the demand for the product which gives value to the labor. Hence, it is not labor which is the cause of value, but value which is the inducement to labor. It is not the labor of the producer which constitutes a thing wealth, but the demand of the consumer. We conclude, then, that it is not labor, but consumption, exchange, or demand which constitutes a thing wealth; and we trace the progress of a nation in wealth according as their wants and desires increase and multiply. First, the demand for the sustenance required by the body gives value to the material products of the earth, food, clothing, shelter, fuel. Then, as their tastes become cultivated and refined arises the demand for works of literature, art, and science; for painting, for sculpture, for architecture, for the drama, for music. And those who minister to these wants of the mind become wealthy, just as those who minister to the wants of the body do. It is the demand of the public alone which makes these things wealth. Hence, in order to be wealthy, a people must be inspired with strong and various desires and be willing to work to gratify those desires. And this shows the great importance, in an economical point of view, of national education. Heavy taxes can alone be borne by an industrious and wealthy people; and the multiplication of wants and desires multiplies industry, multiplies capital, multiplies incomes, multiplies the numbers of persons able to bear the burden of taxation; and renders the nation capable of great achievements, and of taking a leading position in the councils of the world.

SECTION III.

XVI.—ON THE GENERAL LAW OF VALUE; OR, THE GENERAL EQUATION OF ECONOMICS.

THE last branch of our inquiry is to discover the general law of value, or the general equation of economics. That is, to discover a single general law which governs the exchangeable relations of all quantities whatever their nature may be, at all times, and in all places.

The acknowledged principles of natural philosophy show that there can be only one general law of value, or a single general equation of economics. We have shown that there are three distinct orders of economic quantities, and we have generalized all the fundamental concepts of economics so as to grasp all these quantities. These three orders of quantities can be exchanged in six different ways. Our present inquiry is to investigate a single general equation which shall govern all these six species of exchanges indifferently. Suppose that we make £ the general symbol of an economic quantity—*i. e.*, of anything whatever which can be bought and sold, or exchanged, or whose value can be measured in money, or which has purchasing power and representing these various quantities under the general symbol £—we may say that there are in every country quantities of this sort:

£459,621,340
£278,234,500
£826,342,784
etc., etc., etc.

Now, we affirm, by virtue of the great principle of the community of science, and of the great algebraical doctrine of the permanence of equivalent forms, that whatever can be proved to be true economically of any one of this series of quantities must be true of them all.

Now, looking at the series of quantities placed above, who could tell of what species they are? Some may be land, some houses, some corn, some timber, some cattle, some jewelry, some money, some labor of different sorts, some credit, or debts, some the funds, or other public obligations, some copyrights, some patents, some shares in commercial companies, etc.

Now, as we have shown that materiality, permanence, and labor are only accidentally associated in some cases with economic quantities, and not with all, and that exchangeability is the only quality which is common to all economic quantities, it follows that materiality, permanence, and labor must be excluded from any general concept of an economic quantity, and exchangeability retained as its sole general quality. Having thus obtained these independent economic quantities, the whole purpose and object of the science is to discover the single general law which governs the variations of their exchangeable relations. It is clear that by the principle of the continuity of science and the analogy of all physical sciences, however varied and complicated the different phenomena of value may be, there can, by no possibility, be more than one general law of value, or a single general equation of economics, whatever it may be.

XVII.—FUNDAMENTAL CONDITIONS OF THE GENERAL EQUATION OF ECONOMICS.

Now, let A and B be any two quantities whatever supposed perfectly general, it is quite clear that their exchangeable relations are contained within the following limits:

$$\begin{aligned} \infty\ A &= 0\ B \\ \text{etc.} &= \text{etc.} \\ 2\ A &= B \\ A &= B \\ A &= 2\ B \\ \text{etc.} &= \text{etc.} \\ 0\ A &= \infty\ B \end{aligned}$$

The meaning of which is simply this: Let the exchangeable relation between A and B gradually and continuously change from where the greatest possible quantity of A will exchange for the least possible quantity of B, to where the least possible quantity of A will exchange for the greatest possible quantity of B. Now, the law of continuity says that a quantity cannot pass from one amount to another by any change of conditions without passing through all intermediate degrees of magnitude according to the intermediate conditions. Hence, we affirm by virtue of the law of continuity:

1. That if it can be indubitably proved that any particular law is true at any one point in the range of prices, that same law must be necessarily true at all points throughout the whole range of prices.

2. That as the symbols A and B are perfectly general, if any law whatever can be proved to be true in the variations of the exchangeable relation of any two quantities whatever, that law must necessarily be true in the exchangeable relations of all quantities whatever.

Thus, by the law of continuity we are enabled to affirm that if any law whatever can be proved to be true at any one point in the range of prices, between any two quantities whatever, that same law must necessarily be true at all points in the range of prices, and between all quantities whatever. And, as a necessary corollary from the preceding, we may affirm that if any law can be proved not to be true with regard to the relation of any two quantities whatever, that law cannot be a general law of economics.

Furthermore, as it is a universally acknowledged principle of natural philosophy that that law only is the true one which explains all the phenomena, it may be laid down as an unquestionable truth in economics that if two or more forms of expression will explain or account for any phenomena regarding price, or the change of price, that form of expression only is to be adopted as the true one which explains all the phenomena in the science, and not that particular case, or class of cases only.

Economics is a physical science because it is a pure science of causes and effects. There being three orders of exchangeable quantities, and, therefore, six different kinds of exchange, the object of the science is to determine the laws of the phenomena of these exchanges—that is, to determine the laws which govern the changes in their numerical relations of exchange. Hence we have a new order of variable quantities; and the laws which govern this new order of variable quantities must be in strict harmony with the laws which govern the relations of variable quantities in general. The same general principles of reasoning which govern the relations of the stars in their courses must govern the varying relations of economic quantities. The fact is that astronomy is the physical science which is the type of economics. The fundamental problem of economics is identically the same as the fundamental problem of astronomy. The astronomer sees a number of quantities—the heavenly bodies—moving in all sorts of directions—sometimes advancing, sometimes apparently stationary, sometimes retrograding—and his object is to discover a single general law which accounts for and governs all these varying relations. So the economist sees a vast multitude of quantities constantly changing their numerical relation to each other, and his object is to discover a single general law which governs all these varying relations. Economics, like astronomy, is a pure science of ratios.

XVIII.—LORD LAUDERDALE'S LAW OF VALUE.

Now, how is the great general law of astronomy determined? In this way: Let the heavenly bodies at any given instant be in any position. They then change their positions; the problem is to discover the law which governs these changes of relation. We must proceed in exactly the same way in economics. Let any number of economic quantities at any given time have any given relation to each other. They then change their relations to each other; then the problem is to discover the single general law which accounts for and governs these changes of relation. Lord Lauderdale states the case in this way: Take any two quantities, A and B, which may vary with respect to each other. First let A remain constant while B varies. Then the ratio of B to A will change from four causes. It would increase in value—1. From a diminution of quantity; 2. From an increase of demand. It would diminish in value—1. From an increase of quantity; 2. From a diminution of demand. Now, as the variation of A with respect to B will be governed by exactly the same four causes, it is quite clear that the variation of both quantities will be governed by eight independent causes; and if these be connected in the form of an equation, that will manifestly be the true general law of value, or the true general equation of economics. And as it is in the form of a fraction containing no less than eight independent variables, it at once shows the supremely complicated nature of the science.

Lord Lauderdale has thus the credit of having established the true general equation of economics. This comprehends the whole science of pure, or analytical, economics; exactly as the great law of Newton's governs the relations of the heavenly bodies. This complicated equation is the full expression of what is popularly known as the law of supply and demand. All economists admit that it is true when the prices of things are very low; they also admit that it is true when the prices of things are very high; they therefore admit that it is true at the extremes of prices; and, therefore, as it is true at the extremes of prices, the law of continuity affirms that it is necessarily true at all points in the range of prices between the extremes; that is, that it is universally true; and therefore that it is the true general law of value, or the true general equation of economics.

XIX.—REMARKS ON THE GENERAL EQUATION OF ECONOMICS.

The general equation of economics is, therefore, a compound ratio of a very complicated nature; and to apply it to particular cases requires a profound knowledge of the circumstances of the case; but yet it is demonstrably true; and the whole science must be constructed, taking that equation as the basis. In obtaining this general equation, we have followed the method invariably used in all physical science. We have obtained the independent variables, and connected them by a general law, or formula. This insures certainty to the science; but it is on the last point that the real difficulty arises; namely, in giving precision, or numerical amounts, to the co-efficients. It is absolutely impossible to say what numerical variations in supply and demand produce definite variations in value. This has been attempted in some cases, as in that of corn; but it is manifestly impossible to obtain exact numerical data; and in fact, though the same general law is true in all cases, it is perfectly well known that it varies in every particular case; and that the same absolute variation in supply and demand in various quantities will produce great differences in the variations of their numerical values.

It is this impossibility of giving exact numerical values to the co-efficients which makes many persons suppose that it is impossible to make economics an exact science. It is sometimes supposed that for a science to be an exact one, it is necessary that its laws should be capable of exact quantitative statement. This, however, is an error which has been specially pointed out by Comte, who well shows the difference between certainty and precision in science. To constitute an exact science, it is not necessary that its laws can be ascertained with numerical precision; but only that the reasoning be exact, or certain. He says that a dangerous prejudice has sprung up; that because the precision of different sciences is very unequal, their certainty is so too. This tends to discourage the study of the most difficult; precision and certainty are perfectly distinct. An absurd proposition may be very precise; as that the angles of a triangle are equal to three right angles. On the other hand, a certain proposition may not be precise; as that a man will die. Hence, though the different sciences may vary in precision, that will not affect their certainty. This observation applies most forcibly to economics. Some persons are apt to despise it because it does not bring out its results with the same precision as mathematics. This, however, is a grievous mistake. In economics the causes of phenomena can be ascertained with absolute certainty. This is all that is necessary to constitute economics an exact science; because, the method of producing a required result being pointed out with absolute certainty, it has only to be put into force until the result is produced.

In considering the general equation of economics we see the application of Bacon's aphorism:* "That which in theory is the cause, in practice is the rule." No other quantities but demand and supply appear on the face of the equation; it is therefore certain that no other causes influence value, or changes of value, except intensity of demand and limitation of supply. It is certain that neither labor nor cost of production have any direct influence on value; it can only be by affecting the demand or the supply; and that no change of labor, nor of cost of production, can have any influence on value, unless they produce a change in the relation of supply and demand. By this means, we are enabled to create a rigorously exact theory of economics; and by reverently following the precepts of the mighty prophet of inductive philosophy, and the immortal creators of the various inductive sciences, it is seen that economics, as a moral science, is fitted to take rank with mechanics and optics as a great positive inductive physico-moral science; and it is the only moral science capable of being raised to the rank of an exact science.

In interpreting, however, the general equation of economics it is necessary to make an observation. It is sometimes supposed that value is only affected by the actually existing quantity of produce which is brought into the market. This, however, is not so. The expected quantity which may be brought into the market has a most important influence on the value of the existing quantity. If there were a general failure of the coming crops, that would

* Nov. Org., Bk. I., Aph. 3.

exert a most potent influence on the present value of the existing stock. Or if prices had been very high in consequence of great scarcity of supplies and the coming crops promised to be very abundant, that would exercise a most potent influence in diminishing the value of the present stock. Hence, the word quantity in the general equation must denote the quantity, actual or expected. Similarly the word demand must denote the demand, actual or expected.

CHAPTER VI.

THE THEORY OF CREDIT.

SECTION I.

WE have now to explain the organization of the great system of credit—that is to say, the creation—the circulation, and the extinction of credits, or debts—the great marvel of modern commerce. What the steam-engine is in machinery, what the differential calculus is in mathematics, that is credit in commerce.

In the following chapters we shall explain the great juridical and scientific principles of the theory of credit, and show how they are applied to the practical business of banking.

I.—ORIGIN OF THE SYSTEM OF CREDIT IN EUROPE.

If it were asked how that wonderful people, the Romans, commencing with a petty village, gradually extended their empire over so large a portion of the world, it would probably be said that it was due to their hardihood and their discipline. But probably a cause which has been entirely overlooked contributed in no slight degree to the result—and that is their wonderful and methodical habits of business. The Romans were, as far as we are aware, the creators of the great system of credit in all its branches. When the practice of writing became general at Rome, a very strict custom or law grew up. It was established that every *dominus*, or head of a house, should keep a great family ledger, as strict and exact as those of a modern banker. In this every incident of his life was recorded. In this he was obliged to enter all sums of money borrowed and lent; all trade profits and losses; all his revenues and profits, his outgoings, and expenses of every description.* These family ledgers were the only legal evidence of debt

* Ortolan, *Explication Historique des Instituts*, § 1416.

among Roman citizens receivable in courts of justice. And it was from these family ledgers that the whole of the modern system of bookkeeping and credit has been developed. It seems that every occurrence was noted down day by day in a waste-book, termed *adversaria;* and at the end of the month the various items were arranged under their proper heads in the ledger, which was termed *tabulæ,* or *codex accepti et expensi,* which was intended to be preserved as an heirloom in the family. Every five years, the *dominus* was obliged to swear to the truth of the *codex* before the censors; and it was regarded as invested almost with a species of sanctity.

A great difference was made between the *adversaria* and the *codex.* Cicero says:* "He acknowledges that he has not the sum entered in his ledger (*codex*), but he insists that it is entered in his day-book (*adversaria*). Are you, then, so fond of yourself, and have such an exalted opinion of yourself, as to sue for money, not on the evidence of the ledger, but of your day-book? It is arrogant to bring forward your ledger instead of witnesses; but is it not madness to bring forward your own scraps of writing and notes? If these notes have the same force and weight and authority as the ledger, what is the use of making a ledger? to make entries in it? or to keep it in regular order? or to make a permanent record of old writings? But if we have an established custom to make a ledger because we put no trust in notes, is that to be considered of weight, and approved before a judge, which we ourselves consider weak and unreliable? Why is it that we write notes without much care, and we write the ledger with great care? Because the one is to last a month and the other is to last forever. The former are soon erased, and the others are preserved with religious care; the former preserve the memory for a short time, the latter pledge the good faith and honesty of a man forever. Notes are thrown away; the ledger is kept in order. Therefore nobody produces notes in evidence in a cause, but they do produce the ledger, and read the entries." This family ledger was kept in the *arca,* the chest or safe in the *tablinum,* or apartment opposite the door of the *atrium,* or central hall of the Roman house, where all the records and archives were kept.

II.—THE SYSTEM OF CREDIT.

The great system of credit comprehends: 1. The creation of obligations; 2. The transfer of credits, or debts; and 3. The extinction of obligations; which will be fully discussed in the following sections.

The following is a short sketch of the history of the theory of credit:

Demosthenes, about 350 B. C., first perceived and declared that credit is wealth and capital. But concrete practice has always preceded abstract theory. The Romans invented bookkeeping, and the business which in modern language is technically termed banking; the Roman bankers invented

* *Pro Roscio Comoedo.*

cheques and bills of exchange; and the Roman jurists elaborated the juridical theory of credit. Some of the elementary principles of credit are set forth in the Institutes of Gaius, which was the text-book for students from the age of the Antonines till Justinian. But the jurists Ulpian, Modestinus, Paulus, Javolenus, and Papinian, the greatest jurists the world ever saw, worked out the complete juridical theory of credit—except only on one point. And from the emphatic way in which certain elementary principles are laid down by these writers, it is quite clear that there were silly persons at Rome who chattered about credit, just as there are at the present day. The principles elaborated by these great jurists were incorporated in the Pandects of Justinian and in the Basilica, and have been the mercantile law of Europe ever since. They are contained in every Continental text-book of jurisprudence; but on this subject English text-books are lamentably defective. The doctrines of the Roman jurists were, however, inadequate for the complete theory of credit, as they chiefly regarded the subject from the creditor's side, and only very slightly from the debtor's side. But in every obligation there are two sides; the creditor's, or the active, or positive, side; and the debtor's, or the passive, or negative, side.

Accordingly, for the last 150 years—from the days of Maclaurin, at least—mathematicians have been in the habit of terming debts negative quantities. But very few have given any explanation of what they mean by terming a debt a negative quantity; and those who have done so, from a want of knowledge of the principles of mercantile law and the facts of commerce, have entirely failed in giving an explanation which can be received as suitable for economic science. If the subject had been handled by mathematicians who were well trained in mercantile law and practical business, there never would have been the slightest difficulty. But, unfortunately, it has been treated by a series of literary and mathematical writers who were entirely deficient in the necessary knowledge, and they have fallen into a mass of errors, which are fully provided for in the Digest, and in every Continental treatise on jurisprudence. It is well known that although mathematicians have been in the habit of using the algebraical signs, or their equivalents, for 1600 years, and have given the empirical rules for their combination, it is only within the present century that their scientific principles have been understood, and only within the last sixty years that they have been explained in popular treatises on algebra. We must therefore explain the modern theory of algebraical signs, and their application in mathematics and physical science, and then give an exposition of the principles of mercantile law and the facts of commerce, and then discover the interpretation of these signs which is suitable for the particular circumstances of economics.

By applying the principles of the great modern theory of algebraical signs, combined with the subtlest and most abstruse principles of mercantile law and practical business, I have demonstrated the theory of credit simultaneously from the creditor's side and the debtor's side. One difficulty, however, the Roman jurists were unable to solve, and it had hitherto been regarded as insoluble. In 1888 I at last succeeded in solving this difficulty; and the theory of credit is now absolutely complete. Thus, from the year 350 B. C. to 1888 A. D., it has taken 2238 years to bring the theory of credit to perfection.

The doctrines of the Roman jurists are, of course, expressed in words. But we shall find that jurists working separately, algebraists working separately, and the practice of mercantile men acting separately and independently from their own instincts, are all in perfect harmony with each other. And when we fuse these three together—an exposition of the facts of commerce, an exposition of the juridical theory of credit, and show the application of the theory of algebraical signs to these facts of commerce and juridical principles of credit—we shall find a most beautiful exemplification of the use of these signs strictly in accordance with their use in mathematics and physical science.

III.—ON THE CREATION OF OBLIGATIONS.

Personal credit, or mercantile character, is purchasing power, and, as first pointed out by Demosthenes, and now universally acknowledged, is wealth. But personal credit does not enter into economics until the merchant actually exercises his credit and makes a purchase with it.

When a merchant purchases goods "on credit" it is an absolute sale, just as much as if it had been effected with money. He acquires the actual property in the goods as fully and effectually as if he had paid for them in money. In exchange for the goods he gives his promise to pay their price at a future time. That is, he creates a right of action against himself. This right of action is a credit, or *créance*, or debt, and is the price of the goods, and is the property of the seller. Thus, at the very instant that the property in the goods is transferred to the buyer, a contract, or obligation, is created between the two parties, which consists of two parts: 1. The right to demand payment in the person of the seller, or creditor; and 2. The duty to pay in the person of the buyer, or debtor. These two quantities constitute the contract, obligation, or bond of law between the two parties. The obligation consists of two equal and opposite quantities, and may be denoted by this symbol $\begin{Bmatrix} + £100 \\ - £100 \end{Bmatrix}$; where the (+ £100) denotes the creditor's right to demand payment, and the (− £100) denotes the debtor's duty to pay. Also, if either of these quantities be destroyed, the other is also destroyed with it. Hence, as these two equal and opposite quantities come into existence together, can only exist together, and vanish together, they are analogous to polar forces.

IV.—DIVISION OF OPINION AMONG URISTS AS TO THE POSITION OF THE DEBTOR IN AN OBLIGATION.

We have now come to the most subtle and abstruse point in all economics, which will demand the closest attention, because it is the great Serbonian bog in which multitudes of writers, literary and mathematical, have been swallowed up, from a want of knowledge of the most elementary principles of mercantile law and practical business; and its rectification and elucidation will open up a completely new branch of inquiry of the greatest novelty and interest.

When an obligation has been created between two parties by the sale of money or goods "on credit," the case of the creditor is clear; in exchange for the money or goods he has received a right of action—which is termed a credit or a debt—which is his property, and which he can sell or dispose of in any way he pleases, for other goods, or for money. But a strong division of opinion exists among jurists as to the position of the debtor in the obligation. When a merchant has bought goods "on credit," and has given a bill at three months for them, is he in debt at the present time? Roman jurists and English jurists hold different doctrines on this point. When an obligation was contracted the Roman jurists said *dies cedit;* when it became payable they said *dies venit.* "*Cedere* diem significat incipere deberi pecuniam; venire diem significat cum diem venisse quo pecunia peti possit.*"—"'*Cedit dies*' means the day on which money begins to be owed; '*venit dies*' means the day on which it may be demanded." The Roman jurists held that the money was due from the day on which the obligation was contracted, but that the remedy was suspended until the day of payment came. "*Id† quod in diem stipulamur, statim quidem debetur; sed peti priusquam dies venerit non potest.*"—"That which we agree to pay on a future day is indeed due at once; but it cannot be sued for until the day of payment has come."

Paulus says:‡ "*Præsens obligatio est, in diem autem dilata solutio.*"—"The obligation is present, but the payment is deferred until the fixed day." Ulpian says:§ "*Ubi in diem (quis stipulatus fuerit) cessit dies, sed nondum venit.*"—"Whenever anyone has agreed to pay a sum on a fixed day, the obligation has begun to run, but the day of payment has not come." So it was a maxim of Roman law, "*Debitum in presenti, solvendum in futuro.*"—"The money is due at present, but it is only to be paid in future."

This doctrine throws considerable confusion into the nature of an obligation; and it was probably due to the fact that the jurists had not yet completely emancipated themselves from the idea that *debitum* meant the money actually due, and was only then beginning to acquire the meaning of the abstract incorporeal contract which it means now. But English jurists hold quite different doctrine. As in English law and common usage the word

* Digest, 50, 16, 213. † *Instit. Just.*, III., 15, 2. ‡ Digest, 45, 1, 46. § Digest, 50, 17, 213.

debt (passive) means simply the abstract personal duty to pay, English jurists hold that no debt is created until the duty to pay comes into existence—*i. e.*, until the day of payment has come. It is a maxim of English law that credit unexpired may be pleaded under the general issue, which means that if an action is brought against a person who has contracted an obligation payable at a future time, before the day of payment has come he may reply that he is not in debt at all. Thus Pitt Taylor says:* "In addition to these examples, it may be observed that whenever the defendant can show that in fact no debt ever existed before action brought, he may do so under the plea of never indebted. Thus, for instance, if the action be for goods sold and delivered, he may defend himself under the plea by proving that they were sold on credit which was unexpired when the action was commenced."

To understand the following discussions, the reader will find it very useful to fix these principles in his mind: 1. When a person is only bound to pay a sum of money on a future day, he is not in debt at the present time. 2. That if a person has contracted to pay a sum of money at a future day, his creditor has no right to any of his property; he has no *jus in rem;* it is only a claim against his person, or a *jus in personam.* A few examples will illustrate these principles.

(*a*) Suppose that a tenant takes a house or an apartment, and agrees to pay the rent quarterly. Suppose that the day after he had entered into possession the landlord came and demanded his rent. What would the tenant say? He would say: "My good friend, Mr. Landlord, I owe you nothing. The bargain is that I am to have the use and enjoyment of this house for three months before the rent becomes due and payable. My debt, or duty to pay, does not come into existence till then. Good morning to you."

(*b*) So when a farmer takes a farm on a lease of nineteen years, and agrees to pay the rent half-yearly, the agreement is that he is to have the use and enjoyment of the farm for intervals of six months before each installment of rent becomes due. The successive rents are intended and expected to be paid out of the successive profits made out of the farm. And it is obviously absurd to say that the farmer is indebted at the present time for rent which only becomes due nineteen years hence, and is intended and expected to be paid out of profits which will only come into existence nineteen years hence.

(*c*) The same is obviously true in the case of a merchant who has bought goods, and given in exchange for them his promise to pay money for them three months hence. He is not in debt at the present time. The agreement is that he is to have the property in the goods for three months, and to dispose of them in any way he pleases so as to make a profit out of them; and it is expected on both sides that he is to pay his bill out of the profits

* Law of Evidence, Vol. I.

realized by the goods. No debt, or duty to pay, comes into existence until the bill becomes due and payable; and the amount of the bill is not to be subtracted from his present property.

(*d*) It is commonly said that this country is "in debt" about £750,000,000. The answer is that this country is not "in debt" one penny. For a person to be "in debt" means that he is liable to pay a sum of money on demand. Does anyone suppose that the creditors of the country can call upon her to pay £750,000,000 on demand? What the country has undertaken to do is to pay an annuity of about £7,000,000 quarterly. And as soon as one quarter's annuity is paid she is not in debt until next quarter-day comes round. It would be just as absurd to say that the farmer is in debt at the present time for nineteen years' rent. The sum of £750,000,000 is merely the sum of the present values of the annuity.

(*e*) This principle strongly applies to a case of conscience. Suppose that a kind-hearted instructor engages to prepare a student for one of the public services—say the Indian Civil Service—and on his success agrees to take an obligation payable five years after date. On entering the service the candidate is asked if he is in debt. He most properly and conscientiously replies that he is "not in debt," because he has no sum of money which is payable by him on demand. He is only bound to pay at the end of five years; and it is quite understood on both sides that his obligation to his instructor is to be redeemed out of his annual salary. This case is an example of novation, which will be more fully described in another section. When the candidate has won his appointment in the Indian Civil Service, he is no doubt in debt to his instructors. But if the instructor agrees to take an obligation payable five years after date, that obligation pays, extinguishes, and discharges the debt payable as demand; and no new debt arises until the obligation becomes due. The release of the debt payable on demand is the consideration for the obligation payable five years after date.

The importance of the consideration consists in this: It is commonly supposed that when a person has to make a payment at a future time, the sum due is to be subtracted from his present property, and is a diminution of it. It is usual to denote debts by the negative sign —; and according to this view, if a person possessed £100, and was bound to pay £30 three months hence, and therefore his property would be represented by £100 — £30, it would mean that his property was only £70. On a larger scale it would mean that all the obligations in the nation were to be subtracted from all the property in the nation. But this view is entirely erroneous. In this case the sign — does not mean subtraction. What it does really mean will be shown further on. The debtor has the full property in his £100, to do with exactly as he pleases. His duty to pay has no present existence; it is no subtraction from his present property. The expression is not to be read as if his property were only £70. The debt is a mere abstract personal duty; and a personal duty cannot be subtracted from a material sum of hard money. The expression is to be read in this way

He possessed £100 in money, but coupled with the duty to pay £30 at some future given time. Hence, the sign — does not mean subtraction in this case; it is a mere memorandum that he has to make an exchange, by buying up a right of action, at some future time.

V.—ADVANTAGE OF ADOPTING THE CONCEPTION OF ECONOMICS AS THE SCIENCE OF COMMERCE, OR EXCHANGES.

We now see the advantage of adopting and firmly grasping the conception of economics as the science of commerce, or exchanges; because all the mechanism and phenomena of the great system of credit, which are a hopeless puzzle and an inscrutable perplexity so long as economics is treated as the "production, distribution, and consumption of wealth," become perfectly clear and simple when it is understood to be the science of commerce, or exchanges. Every case of a "loan" of money or a sale of goods "on credit" is an exchange, or an act of commerce. In exchange for the money or the goods a right of action is created, and is the price of the goods. This right of action is a salable commodity, which may be bought and sold like any material chattel, and it has value because it will be paid in money. This right of action may circulate in commerce exactly like a piece of money, and effect exchanges exactly like a piece of money, until it is paid off and extinguished; and then it ceases to exist. The debt was created by one exchange; it then may effect any number of exchanges; and when it is due, the holder of it brings it to the debtor, who gives the money in exchange for the right of action. Thus the debt is created by one exchange, and is annihilated, or extinguished, by another exchange; and thus the whole system and operations on credit are merely a series of exchanges.

VI.—ON THE THREE AMBIGUITIES IN THE THEORY OF CREDIT, OR DEBT.

We have now to notice three perplexities, or ambiguities, in the theory of credit, or debt, which have been the cause of an immense amount of confusion and misconception, which the reader must carefully observe.

First ambiguity.—A debt is not the money owed by the debtor, but the abstract personal duty to pay the money.

We have now to explain the meaning of the word debt, about which there is a great misconception. It is one of the examples of words which, in early jurisprudence and classical Latin, meant a material thing, but has come in the progress of civilization and jurisprudence to mean solely a right and a duty. We think it absolutely certain that in classical Latin the word *debitum* means the material thing, whether money or any other, which is due. And in this we are confirmed by the high authority of Professor H. Nettleship, of Oxford. The idea that the word debt means the money due is very common at the present day, and has greatly impeded the due apprehension of the nature of credit. Many literary and mathematical writers suppose that a debt is the money due; or money in the debtor's possession to which the creditor has a right. This very common error, of which we shall hereafter produce several examples, is expressly provided for in the Digest. It is said:* "*Obligationum substantia non in eo consistit ut aliquod corpus nostrum faciat, sed ut alium nobis ad stringit ad dandum aliquod, vel faciendum, vel prestandum.*"—"The essence of obligations does not consist in this that it makes any specific goods our property; but that it binds some person to pay us something, or to do something, or to guarantee something." Pothier well says:† "The right which the obligation gives the creditor of proceeding to obtain payment of the thing which the debtor is obliged to give him, is not a right in the thing itself (*jus in re*); it is only a right against the person of the debtor for the purpose of compelling him to give it (*jus ad rem acquirendam*). The thing which the debtor is obliged to give continues to belong to him; and the creditor cannot become proprietor of it except by the delivery, real or fictitious, which is made to him by the debtor in the performance of the obligation. And till this delivery is made the creditor has nothing more than the right of demanding the thing; and he has only that right against the person of the debtor who has contracted the obligation. Hence it follows that if my debtor, who has contracted the obligation to give a thing to me, transfers it upon a particular title to a third person, whether by sale or donation, I cannot demand it from the party who has so acquired it, but only from my debtor. The reason is, as the obligation does not, according to our principle, give the creditor any right in the thing which is due to me, which I can pursue against the person in whose hands it may be found."

This doctrine is most true and most important. Suppose a creditor comes to his debtor and demands payment of his debt, and the debtor has the very money wherewith to pay his debt in his hand, he may still, nevertheless, give it away, or spend it under the very eyes of his creditor, and the creditor has no legal right to prevent him. So Gide says:‡ "A debt is not the material object, the money; but the juridical object, the duty to pay." So Williams says:§ "Every person who borrows money on mortgage or not, incurs a debt or personal obligation to repay it out of whatever means he possesses."

The distinction is perfectly plain, and of the greatest importance in economics. If the creditor has the right to any specific money in the debtor's possession, that would be a diminution of the debtor's property; he would have no right to spend or part with it; and there would be only one economic quantity in existence—the money. But as a matter of fact, the whole of the money remains the debtor's property, which he can sell, donate, or exchange as he pleases. And also there is the right, or

* Digest, 44, 7, 2. † *Traité sur les Obligations.* ‡ *De la Novation*, p. 139.
§ Law of Personal Property, p. 304.

property, in the person of the creditor, which he can sell, or exchange, as he pleases; and which may be sold, or exchanged, any number of times till it is paid off and extinguished. Hence, in this case there are two economic quantities in existence, which may each circulate in commerce at the same time. To consider a debt as a sum of money in the debtor's possession to which the creditor has a right, is to confound the distinction between a trustee and a debtor. A trustee merely holds money which is in reality the property of the *cestui que trust;* it is in no sense whatever his property; he has no right to use it for his own purposes; and, therefore, there is only one, and not two, economic quantities in existence. If the creditor's right were the right to a specific sum of money in the debtor's possession, it would follow that a debtor could never be insolvent; because if he had no money, his creditor could have no right. But unfortunately this is far from being the case. In too many cases persons are insolvent—*i. e.,* they are under the duty to pay money, and have no money to pay it with; but the creditor's right to demand exists whether the debtor has any money to pay it with or not. If the creditor's right were the right to a specific sum of money, it would follow that the quantity of credit could never exceed the quantity of money; but this is entirely contrary to fact; every jurist knows perfectly well that credit is itself a marketable commodity, a merchandise, and the amount of it in existence and circulation in this country is about 100 times the quantity of money. Hence, the reader must carefully observe that a debt is simply the abstract personal duty to pay money, and has no reference to any specific sum of money.

Second ambiguity.—The word debt means both the creditor's right of action and the debtor's duty to pay.

The second ambiguity is this: It has been shown that the word debt means in the first instance the debtor's personal duty to pay money, and not the money which is due. But it has long been used both in law and common usage to mean the creditor's right of action as well, and is thus used as synonymous with credit. And a creditor's right of action is termed perfectly indiscriminately a credit and a debt. As has been said above, the word *debitum* in classical Latin denotes the material thing, whether money or any other, which is owed. But in the Pandects the word *debitum* is used as synonymous with *obligatio*, the bond of law, or contract, between the creditor and the debtor; and therefore it includes both the creditor's right to demand and the debtor's duty to pay, In classical Latin, a creditor's right of action was termed *nomen*. But in course of time, while *obligatio* always continued to mean the *nexus*, or contract, between the two parties, the word *debitum* split up into two parts, and was used to mean both the creditor's right of action and the debtor's duty to pay, quite indiscriminately. In the twelfth century, the word *debitum* was commonly used to mean a right of action. In 1194, Richard I. issued instructions for a judicial visitation on financial matters in which it was ordered: *"Omnia debita Judæorum inbrevientur, terræ, domus, reditus, et possessiones."*—"Let all the debts (*i. e.,* rights of action) of the Jews be scheduled, their lands, houses, rents, and possessions." *"Item quilibet Judæus jurabit super rotulum quod omnia debita sua et vadia, et reditus, et omnes res et possessiones suas inbreviari faciat."*—"Also let every Jew swear that he will make a true return of all his debts (rights of action), pledges, rents, and all his property and possessions."

In mediæval charters, the word *debitale* was used in the same sense. Thus in one of 1324 it says: *"In omnibus et singulis bonis * * * dominiis, baroniis, censibus, reddituabilibus, debitalibus, servitutibus, homatgiis."*—"In all and singular goods * * * lordships, baronies, revenues, rents, debts (rights of action), servitudes, homages." In another, of 1374, it is said: *"Acquisiverunt reditus, census annuos, et debitalia in fœdis * * * quorum redditorum, censuum, et debitalium."*—"They have acquired rents, annual revenues, and debts (rights of action) in fee * * * of which rents, revenues, and debts (rights of action)." A statute of the city of Placentia, in 1386, clearly shows that *debitum* and *nomen* were synonymous:* *"Nullus homo Plac. emat vel aliqualiter acquirat aliquod debitum vel nomen seu revisamentum contra comm. Placentiæ."*

Thus, the words *debitum* and *debitale* were already at this period used to mean rights of action, and as synonymous with *nomen,* in public instruments; and if they were so used in public instruments, it is clear that that must long have been their well understood meaning in common usage. In English law the word debt has long been used to mean a right of action. Thus in the statute of Acton Burnell, 11 Edward I. (1283), commonly called the Statute of Merchants, it is said: *"Pur ceo qe merchauntz qi avaunt ces houres unt preste lur aver a diverse genz, sunt cheuz en poverte, pur ceo qe il ni aveit pas si redde ley purvewe, par la quele il poeint lur dettes hastivement recoverir. Le rei par luy par sun conseil ad ordine e establi, qe marchaunt qi veut estre seur de sa dette. E si le meire ne troesse achatur face par renable pris liverer les moebles al creanzur, desqe a la summe de la dette en allowance de sa dette."* By which it appears that at that time the word debt had already acquired in English law the meaning of a right of action; a meaning which it has ever since retained, both in law and common usage. So it is said in *"Les Termes de la Ley,"* first published in 1567: *"Dett est un brief que gist lou ascun summe d'argent est due au un par reason d'accompt."*—"Debt is a writ," etc. So in the Act, 46 Geo. III. (1806), c. 125, s. 3, it is enacted that one debt, or demand, may be set off against another. So, as may be seen in any daily paper, the executors of deceased persons advertise for any persons who have "debts, claims, or demands" against the estate to give in a statement of them.

It is so perfectly well known that in English law the word debt means

* *Papa d'Amico, Titoli di Credito,* p. 89.

both the creditor's right of action and the debtor's duty to pay, that it is used in both senses in the same Act of Parliament. So in the law of Scotland, debts are included under the title of movable rights. And in a Scotch marriage contract it is usual for the bride to transfer to her intended husband "all goods, gear, debts, sums of money, and other movable estate." Accordingly, in the digest of the law of bills of exchange which we prepared for the law digest commissioners we began with this fundamental definition: "Credit or debt in legal and commercial [and economical] language, means a right of action against a person for a sum of money."

We need not further multiply examples. The reader must carefully observe that the word debt is used both in English law and common usage, quite indiscriminately, to mean both the creditor's right of action and the debtor's duty to pay; and it requires constant vigilance to perceive in which sense it is used. The word duty also originally meant a right; thus the King's duties meant his right to levy customs. The word "right" had also this double meaning in English. Thus Lord Shelburne said in the House of Lords: "He would think that America had as good a right to pay taxes as Britain"—*i. e.*, it was as much their duty to do so. The word right is but seldom, if at all, now used in this sense in England at the present day; but it is quite common in Scotland to say, "I have no right to do that"—*i. e.*, it is not my duty to do it. The word χρέος in Greek has also this double meaning; it originally meant the actual thing owed, like *debitum* in Latin, or the duty to pay it; but the Greek jurists used χρέος to mean the right of action. Thus Demosthenes says: "τὴν οὐσίαν ἅπασαν χρέα κατέλιπε."—"He left all his property in outstanding debts, *i. e.*, rights of action." In the Basilica, χρέος is used as synonymous with *nomen, créance*, a right of action.

So in German the word *schuld* properly means a debt or liability; accordingly, *schuldner* properly means a debtor; but Austin says that *schuld* has also the double meaning, and that in German law *schuldner* is often used to mean the creditor.

In French, the words *droit* and *dette* are also used in the double sense of the right and the duty; but in the creditor's case it is termed the *droit* or *dette active;* in the debtor's it is termed the *droit* or *dette passive.*

Thus the student must carefully observe that all these words which denote a contract, or obligation, between two persons—such as χρέος, *debitum, debitale,* right, debt, duty, *droit, dette, schuld*—are used quite indiscriminately with respect to both parties; and it requires constant vigilance to determine in which sense they are used. The explanation of this seeming confusion is this: χρέος comes from χρῆ, it is fit, or ordained; *debitum* means that which is due; right, from *rectum,* that which is ordered; and if one person has the right to demand, and another has the duty to pay, a sum of money, it is equally fit, due, ordained, and right that the one person should receive as that the other should pay; hence they are equally χρέα, debts, duties, and rights. On the Continent it is usual to term a person's rights, simply his *actif;* and his liabilities his *passif;* the word *droit* or *dette* being understood; thus in the accounts of a bank its liabilities are termed its *passif,* and its assets its *actif.*

Third ambiguity.—On the double meaning of the words "lend," "loan," "borrow"; or the distinction between the mutuum, *δάνειον or δάνεισμα, and the* commodatum, *or τὸ χρησάμενον.*

The third ambiguity has been the cause of immense misconception in modern times on the subject of credit. When persons hear for the first time such an expression as "credit is capital," they are apt to be startled; and they think that such a doctrine is as much as to say that if one person lends another his book, or his watch, or his horse, that makes two books, or two watches, or two horses. The whole difficulty arises from a want of knowledge of mercantile law, and from not being aware that unfortunately the English words "lend," "loan," and "borrow" are ambiguous, and are used to denote two different operations of an essentially distinct nature.

It has already been shown that there are two kinds of right—the right of property and the mere right of possession, or of use. And there are two distinct kinds of "loan"; the one in which the right of possession only for a limited time is given to the "borrower," but the right of property remains in the "lender," and there is no new creation of property, and the identical thing "lent" is returned to the "lender." The other, in which the "borrower" acquires the actual right of property in the thing "lent," and the "lender" acquires in exchange for it the right, or property, to demand an equivalent only for the thing "lent," both in quantity and quality, but not the identical thing "lent." In this class of "loan" there is always a new creation of property.

1. The *commodatum,* or *τὸ χρησάμενον.*

There are some things which can be lent, and the borrower can enjoy their use without acquiring the actual property in them; and after having enjoyed their use, he can restore the identical things "lent" to their owner. Thus, if a person "lends" his horse or a book to his friend, his friend can ride the horse or read the book without acquiring the property in them; and after he has enjoyed their use, he can restore the identical horse or book to its owner. In such a case, the "lender" only grants a certain limited right of "possession" and "use" of the thing lent to the "borrower"; but he does not cede the right of property in it to the "borrower." He retains in himself the right of property and possession in the thing "lent"; and can reclaim it at any moment he pleases, without any notice to the "borrower." In such cases, there is no sale, or exchange; and there is no new property created. In such cases, the relation of creditor and debtor does not arise between the parties. And there being no sale, or exchange, there is no economic phenomenon; consequently, such transactions not being acts of commerce, do not enter into the science of economics. Such a "loan" is termed in Roman law a *commodatum*, and in Greek law τὸ χρησάμενον; because the "use" only of the thing "lent" is granted to the "borrower," but not the "property" in it.

2. The *mutuum*, or τὸ δάνειον, or δάνεισμα.

But there is another kind of "loan" in which the things "lent" cannot be enjoyed unless they are consumed, destroyed, or alienated. Thus, if a person "borrows" such things as bread, wine, coals, oil, meat, or other things of a similar nature, he cannot enjoy their use without consuming or destroying them; and they are lent and borrowed with the knowledge and consent of both parties, for the purpose of being consumed and destroyed. Hence, from the very nature of the case, the "borrower" must acquire the right of property in such things when lent; and what he undertakes to do is to return, not the identical things lent, but an equivalent amount of other things of the same nature, equal in quality and quantity to the things "lent." So when a person "borrows" money, he cannot enjoy its use, unless he is able to exchange it away for other things. Hence, the person who borrows money must, from the very necessity of the case, acquire the property in it. And what he undertakes to do is, not to restore the identical money lent, but an equivalent amount of money, at the stipulated time.

In all cases, therefore, of the "loan" of such things as bread, wine, oil, meat, coals, money, and things of a similar nature, the lender cedes the property in the thing "lent" to the "borrower," and he acquires in exchange the right to demand, and the "borrower" incurs the personal duty to render, an equivalent amount of things "lent," but not the identical things. In all such cases a new property is created; a contract, or an obligation, is created between the lender and the borrower; and they stand in the relation of creditor and debtor. All such transactions are sales or exchanges; they are all acts of commerce, or economic phenomena, and they all enter into the science of economics. A "loan" of this nature is termed in Roman law a *mutuum*, and in Greek law a δάνειον, or δάνεισμα. To contract a loan of this nature is *mutuare*, or δανείζειν. A loan, therefore, comprehends two transactions of an essentially distinct nature; but the essential feature of a loan is, that it is always the same person who restores the identical thing "lent" or repays an equivalent.

The Roman jurists said that *mutuum* is derived from *quod de meo tuum fit*—because from being my property it becomes yours. Modern scholars, however, repudiate this etymology, however plausible it may seem. The Romans and the Greeks knew very little of their own language. Modern scholars say that *mutuum* is connected with *mutare*, to exchange; as *deciduus* is with *decido*, and *dividuus* with *divido*. But though the etymology may be fanciful, as are so many others given by Roman and Greek writers, it exactly expresses the fact. In the loan of the *mutuum* there is always an exchange of properties. In all cases of the *mutuum*, or the δάνειον, the property in the thing lent is ceded to the borrower; the relation of creditor and debtor is created between them, and the right which the creditor acquires to demand back an equivalent in exchange for the thing lent is the credit, or debt; or, as Ortolan says, the price of the thing lent. The reader must, therefore, observe that every loan of money whatever, no matter between what parties, public or private, is a *mutuum*, and is a sale, or an exchange, an act of commerce, and, therefore, an economic phenomenon.

VII.—THEOPHILUS ON THE MUTUUM, *δάνειον* OR *δάνεισμα*, AND THE COMMODATUM, OR *τό χρησάμενον*.

This distinction is so important that we may cite a passage from the paraphrase of the Institutes of Justinian, by Theophilus, one of the professors of law who were charged with the compilation of the Institutes, because it is more full and distinct than the corresponding passage in the Institutes:

" A real obligation is contracted by an act, or by the manual delivery of something counted out, and this includes the *mutuum*, or the *δάνειον*. A thing is a *mutuum* where the property in it passes to the person who receives it; but he is bound to restore to us, not the identical thing delivered, but another of the same quality and quantity. I said so that the receiver becomes proprietor of it, that I might exclude the *commodatum* and the *depositum;* for in these latter the receiver acquires no property. But he must be bound to us to exclude the donation; for he who receives one acquires the property, but is not bound to us. I said he must restore not the identical things lent, but others of a similar quality and quantity, that I might not deprive him of the use of the *mutuum*. For a person takes a *mutuum* that he may use the things for his own purposes, and return others instead of them. For if he were obliged to give back the same things, it would be useless to borrow them. But all things are not taken as *mutua*, but only those which consist in weight, number, and measure. In weight, as gold, silver, lead, iron, wax, pitch, tin; in measure, such as oil, wine, and corn; in number, such as money, and in short, whatever we deliver with this intent, in number, weight, and measure, so as to bind the receiver to return to us, not the same things, but others of the same nature and quantity. Whence also it is called *mutuum*, because it is transferred by me to you with the intent that it should become your property (*quod de meo tuum fit*). But the real obligation includes *commodatum*, as if anyone were to ask me to lend him a book, and I lent it. * * * But the *commodatum* differs widely from the *mutuum*. For the *mutuum* transfers the property, but the *commodatum* does not transfer it; and, therefore, the borrower (*commodatarius*) is bound to restore the very thing lent."

So it is said in Roman law:* "But it is called giving a *mutuum*, because from being my property it becomes yours (*quod de meo tuum fit*); and, therefore, if it does not become your property no obligation is created." But on the contrary with respect to the *commodatum:* † "We retain the property and the possession of the thing lent (*rei commodatæ*). * * * No one by lending a thing (*commodando*) gives the property in it to him who borrows it."

Thus the whole misconception which is so common among English writers has arisen from the English words "lend," "loan," and "borrow" being used to denote two operations of essentially distinct natures. The French language is equally faulty; the words *louer*, *emprunter*, and *emprunt* are equally applied to both kinds of loan. But the distinction is clearly

* Digest, XII., 1, 2, 2.

† Digest, XIII., 6, 8, 9.

pointed out both in Roman and Greek law; and the Latin and Greek languages have distinct words for each operation. In the *Code Napoléon* the *commodatum* is termed *prêt à usage,** and the *mutuum prêt de consommation.*† All commercial loans are *mutua,* and not *commodata;* every loan of money is in reality a sale or an exchange, in which a new property is created, which is called a credit, or a debt. And when the loan is repaid it is another exchange, by which the new property is extinguished.

No one who had the simplest knowledge of the elementary principles of Roman and Greek law, or of mercantile law, would ever have committed the mistake of confounding the distinction between the loan of money and the loan of an ordinary chattel, such as a horse, or a book, or a watch. Hence, those things only can be the subject of a *mutuum* which consist in *pondere, numero, et mensurâ;* or which can be estimated generically in weight, number, and measure. Such things are termed in Roman law *quantitates,* because equal quantities of bread, wine, oil, coals, etc., are as good as another equal quantity of the same things of the same quality, or one sum of 100 sovereigns is equal to another sum of 100 sovereigns, or one postage stamp is always equal to another of the same denomination. But, also, the Digest says *mutuâ vice funguntur*—one quantity serves the same purpose as another quantity. From this expression mediæval jurists termed them *res fungibiles,* and in modern English law they are termed *fungibles.* In English law the former kind of loan, or the *commodatum,* is said to be returnable in specie, because the identical things lent are returned; the latter kind of loan, or the *mutuum,* is said to be returnable *in genere,* because only things of the same nature are returned.

It is much to be regretted that the English language has not two separate words to denote these two kinds of loan, like the Latin and the Greek, because the double meaning of lend, loan, and borrow has been the cause of great misconception among uninformed writers as to the nature of credit and banking.

VIII.—ON THE ERRORS MADE BY SOME MATHEMATICIANS IN TERMING DEBTS NEGATIVE QUANTITIES.

The juridical theory of credit worked out by the Roman jurists is sufficient for all practical purposes. They explained how credits, rights of action, or debts, are created, how they may be transferred, and how they are extinguished. But this is not sufficient for the full scientific theory of the subject; because they treated these credits almost entirely from the creditor's side. But in every obligation there are two parties—the creditor and the debtor. Now, when two persons are bound together by an obligation, such as that of debt, it is usual to term the creditor the active, or positive, agent, and the debtor the passive, or negative, agent. Hence, to complete the full scientific theory of credit it is necessary to develop it from

* *Code Civil.*, Liv. III., Tit. X., ch. i., sect. i., § 1875.

† Ibid., ch. ii., sect. i., § 1892.

the debtor's, or negative, side, as well as from the creditor's, or positive, side. Accordingly, for the last 150 years—from the days of Maclaurin, at least—mathematicians have been in the habit of giving debts as an example of negative quantities. But they have entirely failed in giving an explanation of the term negative as applied to debts, which can be received as suitable for economic science. The explanation usually given is this: A man's property may be considered as positive, and his debts as negative. Subtract his debts from his property, and the remainder, if any, is his substance, or capital. And as the national capital is the aggregate capital of all the individuals in it, according to this doctrine, in order to find the quantity of capital in the country all the floating debts in it would have to be subtracted from all the money in it; and the remainder would be the national capital (in money). Now, as we shall show hereafter, it may be conjectured that the floating debts in the country are not less than £6,000,000,000, and no one estimates the specie in the country at more than £120,000,000, it would be rather a difficult matter to perceive how £6,000,000,000 of floating debts are to be subtracted from £120,000,000 of hard money. So Peacock and Tait, two very distinguished mathematicians, say: "If property possessed or due could be denoted by a number or symbol with a positive sign, a debt would be indicated by a number or symbol with a negative sign, or conversely. Such affections of property are correctly symbolized by the signs + and —, since they possess the inverse relations to each other which these signs require; for if to a person there be given a certain property or sum of money with, or added to, a debt of equal amount, his wealth, or property, remains the same as before."

Now, in a certain sense these modes of statement have some semblance of truth; if a person were going to retire from business he would call in and discharge his debts, or liabilities, and the remainder, if any, would be his substance. But, then, this result could not be attained without an exchange, because his outstanding debts could not be extinguished without being brought to him to be exchanged for money. But such a mode of statement is quite unsuitable for economics. Economics is purely the science of exchanges, and has only to do with quantities while they exist; and all exchangeable quantities are economic quantities while they exist and are the subject of commerce. Debts, or credits, are a species of property of the most gigantic magnitude, and are the subject of the most colossal commerce of modern times. They exceed in magnitude every other species of property, except the land itself. And what are they to be subtracted from? The mode of statement by Peacock and Tait is entirely inapplicable to the business of banking.

The fact is, that mathematicians have completely mistaken the application of the signs + and — in economics, from a want of knowledge of mercantile law and practical business. Mathematicians are accustomed to treat of quantities and operations, and as these may each be of opposite or inverse natures, they apply the signs + and — to them. The error which mathematicians fall into in applying the signs + and − in economics is that they apply them to property, whereas they affect persons. Persons may stand in inverse, or opposite, relations to each other as well as quantities and operations; and persons who stand in these inverse, or opposite, relations may be indicated by the signs + and −, as well as quantities and operations. Every student of mercantile law will at once perceive Peacock's error in the above extract, which is shared by other mathematicians, because credits, or debts, are not *jura in re;* they are *jura in personam;* and the passive, or negative, debt is not money owed by the debtor, but the abstract personal duty to pay money.

IX.—ERROR OF EULER IN TERMING DEBTS NEGATIVE QUANTITIES.

Euler says:* "The manner in which we calculate a person's property is an apt illustration of what has just been said. We denote what a man really possesses by positive numbers, using or understanding the sign +; whereas his debts are represented by negative numbers, or by using the sign −. Thus it is said of anyone that he has 100 crowns, but owes fifty; this means that his real possessions amount to 100 − 50; that is to say, fifty crowns. As negative numbers may be considered as debts, because positive numbers represent real possessions, we may say that negative numbers are less than nothing. Thus, when a man has nothing in the world, and owes fifty crowns, it is certain that he has fifty crowns less than nothing; for if anyone were to make him a present of fifty crowns to pay his debts, he would still be at the point 0, though really richer than before."

It will be seen that the statement in the first part commits exactly the error we have just pointed out. Suppose that the person has 100 crowns, and is bound to pay fifty crowns at the end of the year; then his property would, according to Euler, be stated as 100 crowns − 50 crowns. But it would be quite inaccurate to say that his property was only fifty crowns; because he has the 100 crowns, which are his absolute property, to dispose of, or trade with, exactly as he pleases in the meantime; and he is bound to have only fifty crowns at the end of the year to discharge his debt. Moreover, as we have shown, the debt is the abstract personal duty to pay, and it does not come into existence until the time for payment has come. Consequently, the person is not in debt at all until the end of the year; and, therefore, the debt, which does not exist, cannot be subtracted from his property. But the owner of the debt may put it into circulation, and it may be sold, transferred, or exchanged, and produce all the effects of money, any number of times, until it is paid off and extinguished. So that there may be the 100 crowns, and the right to demand the fifty crowns, circulating simultaneously in commerce. Moreover, as the 100 crowns are solid money, and the debt of fifty crowns is only the personal duty to pay money, it is

* Algebra, p. 7.

quite evident that an abstract personal duty cannot be subtracted from a solid sum of hard cash.

Furthermore, by the law of continuity, if we diminish the period of payment gradually and continuously to 0, and the debt becomes payable on demand, that in no way alters the general principles of the subject. A duty to pay, though due on demand, cannot be subtracted from a material sum of money. The debtor's money remains absolutely intact until he voluntarily buys up the right of action against himself of his own free will, giving fifty crowns in exchange for it. The expression is to be read in this way: He possesses 100 crowns, but coupled with the duty to pay fifty crowns at some given time.

In the other case, when the debtor possesses 0 crowns and owes fifty crowns, he is said to have fifty crowns less than nothing. This clearly means that he is under the duty to pay fifty crowns, and has 0 crowns to pay them with. Now, suppose that being in such a position, as Euler says, someone makes him a present of fifty crowns to pay his debt with. He pays the debt; he is fifty crowns richer than he was before, but his property is now 0. This is an example that $+ \times + = +$. Thus Euler is right as far as he goes, but he has stated only one half of the case; because there is another combination of algebraical signs which gives $+$—namely, $- \times -$; and there is another method in commerce of arriving at the same practical result. As any person whatever may give the debtor fifty crowns to pay his debt with, let us suppose that the creditor does so. Then, having received the fifty crowns in a present from his creditor, the debtor hands them back to his creditor in payment of the debt, which is then extinguished. The debtor is now, as in the former case, richer by fifty crowns than he was before, and his property is now 0. The same result may be attained in another way. Suppose that the creditor simply releases his debtor from his debt; then, as in the former case, he would be fifty crowns richer than he was before; and his property would now be 0. Now, if crowns be $+$, and to give is also $+$, then a debt is $-$, and to cancel, or take away, is also $-$. Consequently, to give money is $+ \times +$; and to release, or cancel, a debt is $- \times -$; and the position of the debtor will be exactly the same after each operation. This shows that the release of a debt is, in all circumstances, equivalent to a payment in money. Thus it is seen that in commerce, as in all algebra, $+ \times + = - + -$; an example of the permanence of equivalent forms, and a principle of the most momentous importance in modern commerce.

X.—ERROR OF THORNTON AND CERNUSCHI ON CREDIT.

We have shown the error of distinguished algebraists in their interpretation of the negative sign as applied to debts; we have now to point out the error of a plausible view held by two distinguished bankers.

It has been asserted that credit adds nothing to the resources of the world, because it is neutralized by something else. Any person practically conversant with commerce, and seeing that the enormously greater portion of commercial operations are carried on by credit, would think it a strange doctrine that credit adds nothing to the resources of a nation, or of an individual. It is now universally agreed that the only true definition of wealth is "anything which has purchasing power." The wealth of an individual or a nation is their "purchasing power." And their purchasing power is their money, together with their credit; credit is, therefore, purchasing power over and above, and additional to, money, and hence it must be a resource cumulative to money. Some writers, however, have maintained the contrary doctrine in a very plausible way; which we have now to examine.

Henry Thornton, an able man, a distinguished banker, and one of the authors of the Bullion Report, says:* "Paper constitutes, it is true, an article on the credit side of the books of some men, but it forms an exactly equal item on the debit side of the books of others. It constitutes on the whole neither a debit nor a credit. * * * The use of paper does not, therefore, introduce any principle of delusion into that estimate of property which is made by individuals." So another eminent banker, M. Cernuschi, says:† "The balance-sheet of every individual contains three accounts—existing goods, credits, and debts. But if we collected into one all the balance-sheets of everyone in the world, the debts and credits mutually neutralize each other; and there remains but a single account, existing goods. The totality of goods, therefore, forms the general inventory. There is the first matter of exchange. The debts and credits are subsidiary matters. Debts and credits are reciprocally transmitted as goods are transmitted; but however great or however small they may be, and through whatever hands they may pass—credits for some, debts for others—they add nothing to, and take nothing away from, the general inventory."

The argument of Thornton and Cernuschi is simply this: Suppose A to have £100 in money, and also a three months bill of £50 on B. Suppose B to have £100 in money, and at the same time to have accepted a bill for £50 at three months to A. Then A's property would be stated thus, £100 + £50; B's property would be stated thus, £100 − £50. Now, the argument of these writers is this: the + £50 and the − £50 balance and neutralize each other, and the result is 0; which, according to them, is the same thing as saying that these quantities do not exist at all. This view might, perhaps, at first sight seem somewhat specious; but a very little reflection will show that it is quite erroneous. It alleges that if there are two equal and opposite quantities in existence at any moment, which may neutralize each other's effects, and the result is 0, that that is the same thing as saying that these two quantities do not exist at all. Suppose that two equal and opposite forces act upon a particle at rest; they neutralize

* An Enquiry into the Nature and Effects of the Paper Credit of Great Britain, p. 20.

* *Mecanique de l'Echange*, p 1.

each other's effects, and the result is 0; but it would be highly erroneous to say that, for that reason, they do not exist at all. Suppose that, on a division, the Government has 345 supporters and 300 opponents; the 300 members on each side neutralize each others' effects; and the result is that the practical force of the Government is 45; but that does not imply that the 600 members do not exist at all. Hence, even if it were true that these equal and opposite quantities, credits and debts, neutralized each other's effects, it would be quite erroneous to say that that is the same thing as saying that they do not exist at all. The error consists, as we have pointed out, in supposing that, in the case of obligations not yet due, the debt is an existing negative quantity neutralizing the effect of the credit. The credit, or the right of action of the creditor, is an existent quantity, which may be bought and sold like money, or any other chattel; the debt, or duty to pay, does not come into existence until the credit has expired and the day of payment has come; and consequently it cannot neutralize the credit. And even supposing that it is payable on demand like a bank credit, it is still an economic quantity until payment is demanded and it is extinguished; and the debtor's property remains entire until he voluntarily gives some of it up to buy up the right of action against himself. These considerations are of supreme importance, as we shall see, in understanding the nature of banking. Personal credit is a person's purchasing power over and above his money; hence credit is a resource and wealth cumulative to money; and the whole mass of circulating credits are economical quantities over and above, and additional to, money; and they are in their nature and effects in every respect equivalent to an equal quantity of money.

XI.—ON THE TRUE MEANING OF SAYING THAT DEBTS ARE NEGATIVE QUANTITIES.

Jurists term debts "negative" quantities; but they interpret the sign – in quite a different way to what mathematicians do, for they apply it to the person of the debtor. And then the meaning of the term becomes perfectly clear. A contract, or obligation, consists of two parts: 1. The creditor's right to demand; 2. The debtor's duty to pay. The two quantities are inverse, opposite, or contrary to each other; the first is active, or positive; and the second is passive, or negative. Hence, the creditor's personal right of action is the positive quantity, and the debtor's personal duty to pay is the negative quantity. Hence, if a person has £500 at his banker's, and is also bound to pay £50 at some given future time, or even on demand, and therefore his property may be stated as £500 – £50, it is not to be read as if he had only £450 at his banker's; but it is to be read in this way: He possesses £500 in absolute property, but coupled with the duty to pay £50 at a given time, or when demanded. And his property can only be reduced to £450 by giving up to him the right of action for £50. Hence, in economics, the symbol (+ £100) always denotes the right to money, or the right to demand money, such as bank notes, cheques, bills of exchange, or other securities; and the symbol (−£100) always denotes the personal duty to pay money. We now clearly see the meaning of saying that money is a positive quantity, and debt a negative quantity, because money denotes a right, and debt denotes a duty.

And this exactly corresponds with the usual, but not universal, algebraical doctrine that quantities passing through 0 change their sign. Because when a person has spent all his money, and, therefore, his property is 0, and then incurs a debt, he has exhausted all his right to demand, and has incurred a duty to pay. So when a man's property is said to be £100 less than nothing, it means that he is under the duty to pay £100, and has no money to pay them with. It is now seen how necessary it is to observe the double meaning of the word debt both in law and common usage. When a debt is termed "goods," "chattels," "merchandise," "wealth," it means the creditor's right of action. When a debt is termed a "negative" quantity, it means the debtor's duty to pay. And as the inverse, opposite, or contrary quantities in an obligation are created together, can only exist together, and vanish together, they are exactly analogous to polar forces.

XII.—IF MONEY BE TERMED POSITIVE CAPITAL, CREDIT MAY BE TERMED NEGATIVE CAPITAL.

A merchant's wealth, or purchasing power, consists of his money, his rights to demand money (*i. e.*, the bank notes, cheques, bills of exchange, or other securities he may possess), and his credit (*i. e.*, his right to the future products of his industry). If he buys goods with his money and sells them with a profit, he first replaces the sum he has expended, and the surplus is his profit. If he buys goods with his credit, he creates a debt against himself; when he sells the goods, he first discharges the debt he has incurred, and the surplus is his profit. In either case, his profit consists in the excess of his property at the end of the operation above what it was at the beginning. Now, as Senior says: "Economists are agreed that whatever gives a profit is properly termed capital." If he buys with money he makes capital of the realized profits of the past; if he buys with credit, he makes capital of the expected profits of the future. In each case, he makes a profit; hence, by the definition, money and credit are equally capital; but they are inverse, or opposite to each other; hence, if money be termed positive capital, credit may be termed negative capital.

Money is the property in gold already acquired, and credit is the property in gold which is to be acquired. Therefore, credit is inverse, or opposite, to money; but credit is in every way as real a value as gold. By using money the trader makes capital of the realized profits of the past; by using his credit he makes capital of the expected profits of the future; but money and credit are equally salable and valuable commodities. The fact is, that when we adopt exchangeability as the sole essence and principle of wealth, the whole difficulty vanishes; for money and credit are equally exchangeable quantities.

XIII.—ON THE TRANSFER OF CREDITS, OR DEBTS.

Rights of action, credits, or debts, are now clearly shown to be the name of a certain species of merchandise, goods, chattels, or commodities; and they can be bought and sold exactly like any other merchandise, or commodities.

When it is seen that a bank note passes from hand to hand like money, it might perhaps be supposed that any other debts might be sold and transferred with equal facility. This, however, is a very great error. There is very considerable subtlety about the sale of debts; and it was only by very slow and gradual degrees that debts became freely salable. If it were asked what discovery has most deeply affected the fortunes of the human race, it might probably be said with truth, the discovery that debts are salable commodities. When Daniel Webster said that credit had done more, a thousand times, to enrich nations, than all the mines of all the world, he meant the discovery that debts are salable commodities, or merchandise; that they may be used as money; and that they produce all the effects of money.

SECTION II.

XIV.—ON THE EXTINCTION OF OBLIGATIONS.—ON THE LIMITS OF CREDIT.

WE have now to consider the various methods by which obligations are extinguished. Credit being the right to demand some person to pay or do something, and debt the duty of that person to pay or do something, of course when the debtor has paid or done the thing he is bound to do he has fulfilled and discharged his duty; and therefore the right of the creditor is satisfied and extinguished, and thus the obligation is annihilated and extinguished.

It has been shown over and over again that credit is the name of a species of property, commodity, or merchandise, of the same nature as, but inferior in degree to, money; that it fulfills exactly the same function as money as a medium of exchange and circulation. It is a property, commodity, or merchandise cumulative to money, and is in all its effects on prices and production exactly equivalent to an equal sum of money. Credit is, in fact, to money what steam is to water; and like that power, while its use within proper limits is one of the most beneficial inventions ever devised by the ingenuity of man, its misuse by unskillful and unscrupulous persons has produced the most fearful calamities. Credit, like steam, has its limits; and we have now to investigate the proper limits of credit, and to explain the various methods by which it is extinguished.

Credit, no doubt, is of the same nature as money, being the right or title to a future payment. But there is this difference between them, that there is no time limited in which the holder of money shall demand a satisfaction for it; nor is it limited to any particular satisfaction. He may keep it as long as he pleases himself; or he may transmit it to his descendants; and they may receive a satisfaction at any time they please for the services done by their ancestor. But credit is always created with the express intention of being, or of being capable of being, extinguished at a certain short definite time; at least mercantile credit is, of which alone we are treating here. It is unextinguished credit which produces those terrible monetary cataclysms which scatter ruin and misery among nations. It is chiefly by the creation of excessive credit that over-production is brought about; which causes those catastrophes called commercial crises; and it is the inability of credit shops to extinguish the credit they have created—commonly called the failure of banks—which is the cause of the most frightful social calamities of modern times.

The true limits of credit may be seen by the meaning of the word; because all credit is the promise to pay or do something in future, and that something, whatever it is, is the value of the promise or credit. That something need not necessarily be money; it may be anything else; it may be any other chattel; or it may be a promise to do something. The credits, however, which are the subject of this work are always promises to pay money; and it is just on this point that literary economists are utterly at fault. Because a bill, or note, is an obligation to pay money, many uninformed writers suppose that they must always be paid in money or bank notes, and therefore that the issues of credit must always have a fixed and definite relation to the quantity of money in a country; or, in mathematical language, are a *definite* function of it. Now, it is true that credit must always bear a relation to the money in the country; but it is not a *fixed* relation; it depends to a very great extent indeed on the organization of the system of credit; hence, as the quantity of credit to money varies according to the different methods in which credit is organized, we may say, if we may coin the term, that credit is a *contingent* function of money.

To show how extremely ignorant writers are of the actual organization of the modern system of credit, we may quote a sentence from Colonel Torrens, who was one of the influential sect who procured the enactment of the Bank Charter Act of 1844. He says:* "A bill of exchange may also pass from purchasers to vendors many times a day; but no one of the successive transactions of which it is the medium can be finally closed until the last recipient has received in coin or bank notes the amount it represents." This statement also appears in Mill. No doubt, 200 years ago, as far as we are aware, the vast majority of bills were paid in money or bank notes; but that has long ceased to be the case. At the present day, probably not one bill in 100,000 is ever paid in money or bank notes; but by other methods, which we have now to describe.

Those who imagine that bills and notes at the present day are always paid in money or bank notes have as much idea of the truth as those who know nothing of steam navigation beyond the little Comet of four horse-power which paddled down the Clyde in 1812 have of the triple expansion engines of the Campania; or as those who know nothing of a locomotive beyond Stephenson's Rocket have of the last new locomotive on the London and Northwestern Railway. The organization and expansion of the system of credit has developed *pari passu* with that of the steam-engine. The only real difficulty in the case, as has been frequently observed, is for lay readers

* The Principles and Practical Operation of Sir Robert Peel's Act of 1844 Explained and Defended, p. 79.

and writers to understand that a right of action, a promise to pay, which is a credit, or a debt, is itself independent exchangeable property or merchandise, or a chattel, quite distinct from the money promised itself, and that it circulates in commerce by itself, exactly like money. But of course the value of the promise or right of action is the thing itself; and consequently if the thing itself is not forthcoming, the right of action has lost its value. This consideration at once shows the limit of credit. Assuming the credit to be, what is its best-known form in this country, the right to demand money, it is quite clear that as long as a person has in his possession sufficient money, or what is held to be equivalent to money, to discharge his debt when it becomes due, the credit has not been excessive. The futile nature of the speculations of lay writers on this subject consists in the fact that by the highly organized system of modern credit, it is only an infinitesimal portion of bills that are ever paid in money at all; but they are paid in the equivalents to money. The institution of banks and bankers who create currency by means of their credit, either in the form of deposits or notes, has enlarged the limits of credit at least a thousand-fold; but yet the principle of the limit remains the same. Credit always has to be redeemed; and if this can be done the credit has been sound. Hence, credit is never excessive, whatever its absolute amount may be, as long as it always returns into itself.

XV.—ON THE EXTINCTION OF OBLIGATIONS.

We have now to consider the various methods by which obligations are extinguished. Credit being the right to demand something to be paid or done, and the debt being the duty to pay or do that something, the payment, or the performance of the thing, fulfills, discharges, and extinguishes the duty as well as the right. And thus the obligation is absolutely annihilated and extinguished.

Commercial credit in this country is always expressed to be payable in money; and it is often supposed that bills of exchange are always paid in money, or bank notes. But as has been shown in the preceding paragraph, that is a vital error. There are other methods besides payment in money by which obligations are extinguished. And in this country the amount of bills which are paid in money is absolutely infinitesimal compared with those which are paid in other ways. There are four different methods by which obligations may be extinguished. These are: 1. By acceptilation, or release; 2. By payment in money; 3. By novation, renewal, or transfer; and 4. By compensation, or set-off.

XVI.—ON ACCEPTILATION, *ἀθώωσις*, *ἀκκεπτιλατίων*, OR RELEASE.

We have already described how the *obligatio verbis* and *litteris*, or the oral and written obligations, were created. When the debtor came to repay the loan, the proceedings were reversed. He brought the money to his creditor, and said something of this sort to him: "*Quod ego tibi promisi, habesne acceptum?*"—"Have you received what I promised you?" To which the creditor replied: "*Habes, acceptumque tuli.*"—"I have, and have entered it as received."

In this case the debtor made an entry of money paid in his ledger, termed *expensilatio;* and the creditor made a correlative entry of money received in his ledger, termed *acceptilatio.* These entries of *expensilatio* and *acceptilatio,* when once formally made in their respective ledgers by the parties, were final and conclusive, and could not be questioned. All contracts or obligations created by the mutual consent of the parties may be extinguished, canceled, dissolved, or annihilated by the same mutual consent of the parties by which they were created.

As Gaius says:* "*Omnia quæ jure contrahuntur contrario jure pereunt.*"—"All formal contracts are destroyed by a reverse process." Consequently, if for any reason whatever the creditor chose to release the debtor from his debt without the actual payment of money, it was done by the solemn form of *acceptilatio.* The debtor went through the legal form of question, and the creditor went through the legal form of answer, and then made the formal entry of *acceptilatio* in his ledger; it was then a valid and final release, and it could not be questioned or disputed. So, at present, if a creditor gives his debtor a formal written receipt for money due, it is a valid and final release of the debt. We shall hereafter give some examples of acceptilation which may surprise some of our readers.

For "acceptilation," see Gaius, III., 169–175; Instit. Just., III., 29; Theophilus, III., 29; Digest, XLVI., 4; Basilica, XXVI., 9.

XVII.—THE RELEASE OF A DEBT IS IN ALL CASES EQUIVALENT TO A GIFT OR PAYMENT IN MONEY.

Euler, as we have seen above, says that if a person has nothing, and owes fifty crowns, his property is fifty crowns less than nothing. His property is (– 50) crowns—*i. e.*, he is under the duty to pay fifty crowns, and has nothing to pay them with. He then says that, if any person made the debtor a present of fifty crowns to pay his debt with, he would be fifty crowns richer than he was before, though his property would then be 0. Euler is right so far as he goes; but he has stated only one half of the case, because the same result may be attained in another way. As the same result follows whoever gives him the fifty crowns, we may suppose that his creditor makes him a gift of fifty crowns. The debtor then may give his creditor back his fifty crowns, and so he discharges his debt. The debtor is now fifty crowns richer than he was before, and his property is now 0. Now, if money be positive, +, the gift of money is $+ \times +$, which

* Digest, 50, 17, 100.

equals +. But there is another combination of signs which gives +, and that is − × −; and there is another way of arriving at this result. Suppose that instead of the double operation of the creditor giving his debtor fifty crowns, and then receiving them back in discharge of his debt, he simply releases the debtor from the debt. Then the debtor would be fifty crowns richer than before, and his property would be o. Now, a debt is −, and taking away, or releasing, is also −; hence, releasing a debt is − × −; hence releasing a debt is absolutely equivalent to making a gift of money—that is, − × − = + × + in economics, as it does in every other branch of science, mathematical and physical. This example shows that the release of a debt is in all cases whatever, equivalent to the gift or payment of money—a principle of immense importance in commerce, and the application of which may surprise some readers. So Paulus says:* "*Si quis obligatione liberatus est, potest videri cepisse.*" And Basil., II., 3, 115: "ὁ ἐλευθερούμενος ἐνοχῆς δοκεῖ τι εἰληφέναι."—"He who is released from an obligation has gained." So also: "*Per accepti quoque lationem egens debitor etiam eam pecuniam quâ liberatus est, cepisse videtur.*"—"Even an insolvent debtor being freed by a release has gained the amount of what he is released from." So Pothier:† "A release is a donation." So Ortolan says:‡ "The release from a debt is always classed as a donation in Roman law." So Von Savigny:§ "A simple contract, or the release of a debt, may be the subject of a donation." Also:‖ "The increase of wealth may result from * * * a credit given to the debtor, or the release of a debt." "Every release of a debt enriches the debtor. The amount of the donation is always equal to that of the debt, even though the debtor is insolvent. Although the release from a debt destined never to be paid seems a thing of no consequence, the increase of property does not the less exist. In effect not only does property represent a quantity always indeterminate, but its total value may also be either positive or negative. [Negative property is the inverse of a right, *i. e.*, a debt or a duty.] If, then, property is reduced to a negative value, the diminution of minus is in law a change identical with the increase of plus for a positive value" (that is, − × − = + × +). "The release of a debt¶ always constitutes a gift equal to the amount of the debt, even though the debtor is insolvent." So the release of a debt to a debtor may be a legacy.**

XVIII.—APPLICATION OF THE PRINCIPLES OF ALGEBRA AND MERCANTILE LAW TO COMMERCE.

It has now to be shown how the algebraical doctrine that − × − = + × +, and its legal equivalent that the release of a debt is in all cases equivalent to a payment in money, are applied in commerce.

* Digest, 50, 17, 115. † *Traité des Obligations.* ‡ *Explication Historique des Inst. Just.*, Liv. II., Tit. 7, §543, 557. § *Traité de Droit Romain,* Liv. II., ch. iii., § 142. ‖ *Ibid.*, § 155. ¶ *Traité de Droit Romain*, Liv. II., ch. iii., § 166. ** Digest, 34, 3, 3.

Suppose that I owe £100 to a banker, in how many ways can I pay him? 1. I may pay him in actual money—that is, $+ \times +$. 2. If I happen to possess £100 in his notes, I may tender him his own notes; or if I have an account with him, I may give him a cheque on my account—that is, in either case I release him from his debt to me; that is, $- \times -$. That is, releasing the banker from his debt to me is paying my debt to him. 3. I may pay him £50 in money, and £50 in his own notes, or by cheque on my account. Paying him in money is $+ \times +$; tendering him his own notes, or giving him a cheque on my account, is $- \times -$; and the combined effect of the two is to discharge and extinguish my debt of £100. Thus, I may pay a debt to my banker entirely in money, or entirely in his own notes, or by cheque, or partly in money and partly by notes or cheque, and the effect of these several modes of payment is absolutely identical. Thus it is seen that the doctrine that taking away a negative quantity is absolutely equivalent to adding a positive quantity is absolutely true in all branches of science. That is, in all sciences whatever, $- \times - = + \times +$; and in mercantile algebra it is to be interpreted thus: "The release of a debt is in all cases equivalent to a payment in money."

XIX.—THE RELEASE OF A DEBT MAY BE HELD TO EXTINGUISH AN OBLIGATION IN THREE DIFFERENT WAYS.

There are three different methods in which the release of a debt may be considered to extinguish an obligation.

First Method.—As the obligation was created by the mutual consent of the parties, so it may be canceled and extinguished by the same mutual consent which called it into existence. Now, as we have seen that, by the general principles of the theory of signs, to create an obligation is denoted by $+ \left\{ \begin{matrix} + £100 \\ - £100 \end{matrix} \right\}$, so to cancel, extinguish, or annihilate an obligation is denoted by $- \left\{ \begin{matrix} + £100 \\ - £100 \end{matrix} \right\}$.

Now let us observe the effect of the negative sign on each of the parties to the obligation. The creditor's property becomes $-(+£100)$. But $-(+£100) = -£100$. That is, the creditor has *lost* £100. The debtor's property becomes $-(-£100)$. But $-(-£100) = +£100$. That is, the debtor has *gained* £100. Which shows that to cancel or release a debt is exactly equivalent to making a gift of money.

Second Method.—As the creditor's right of action is simply a piece of merchandise, goods and chattels, or a commodity, it may be the subject of a donation or gift, exactly like any other commodity. The creditor may present his right of action as a donation or gift to the debtor himself. Then the debtor has the right to demand $(+£100)$ from himself, and also the duty to pay $(-£100)$ to himself. Then his property will be $+£100 - £100$. These two quantities cancel and extinguish each other like $+a$, and

$-a$, on the same side of equation. They vanish together; the right is not in abeyance; it is absolutely extinguished. The (+ £100) ceases to exist as well as the (− £100); and thus the obligation is absolutely extinguished. The creditor has lost £100, and the debtor has gained £100. Thus if a person makes another a gift of £100, and also releases him from a debt of £100, the donee has received a gift of £200. When Sir Joshua Reynolds died he held a bond of Burke's for £2000. By his will he released Burke from his bond of £2000, and besides that he bequeathed him £2000 in money. Consequently, Reynolds bequeathed £4000 to Burke.

Third Method.—There is still a third method by which it can be explained. When a debtor is presented with a right of action against himself he fulfills two *personæ*, or characters; he is creditor to himself and also debtor to himself. In his *persona* of creditor, he presents his right of action to himself in his *persona* of debtor. In his *persona* of debtor, he pays the right of action to himself in his *persona* of creditor. Hence the duty is fulfilled and discharged, just as much as if he had paid it to another individual. Thus the obligation is not in abeyance; it is canceled and extinguished.

XX.—WHEN + £100 CANCELS AND EXTINGUISHES − £100, AND WHEN IT DOES NOT.

It must, however, be carefully observed that (+ £100) and (− £100), in the same person, do not always and in all cases cancel and extinguish each other in economics. A person's property may be (+ £100) and (− £100), and therefore for practical purposes, be equal to 0; and yet these two quantities will not cancel and extinguish each other in economics. It is only when the right to demand £100 from *himself*, and the duty to pay £100 to *himself* unite, that both quantities vanish, and the contract or the obligation is extinguished. Suppose that a person has £100 in a banker's notes, and at the same time owes £100 to some *other* person. Then his property will be (+ £100), and (−£100), and in substance will = 0. But in this case the (+ £100) will not cancel the (− £100), and the (+ £100) is not extinguished as an economic quantity. The reason of this is obvious; because his right of action against A is no fulfillment of his duty to pay B. The debtor may pay away the £100 in notes, and leave his own debt unpaid.

Suppose that two bankers each hold £100 of the other's notes. Then so far as regards these notes the property of each banker is (+ £100) and (− £100), and in substance = 0. But in this case, the (+ £100) and the (− £100) held by each banker do not cancel each other; because each banker may pay the notes of the other in commerce; and therefore there are £200 of economic quantities in existence. Each banker has the positive absolute right to demand £100 which is actual property; but he is only under the *contingent* duty to pay £100 if demanded. If, however, they exchange notes, each banker will then have the right to demand £100 from *himself*, and the duty to pay £100 to *himself*. Then each of the obligations is simultaneously extinguished; because each banker has performed his duty of paying the other by releasing him from his debt. Thus the £200 of economic quantities vanish out of existence. Hence it is only when the right and the duty emanate from the same person, and are again revested in the same person from whom they emanated, that the (+£100) and the (−£100) cancel each other; and the obligation is extinguished.

XXI.—ON PAYMENT IN MONEY.

The preceding considerations will explain how a payment in money extinguishes an obligation; which very few persons have ever thought of. Suppose that a person possesses £100, and owes a debt of £30, then his property will be (+£100) and (−£30); that is, he possesses £100, but coupled with the duty to pay £30 at some given time. His creditor's right to demand is (+£30). When the creditor demands payment of his debt, he brings his right of action to the debtor, who gives him £30 in money in exchange for it; that is, the debtor buys up the right of action against himself. The debtor's property is then £70, and also (+£30) and (−£30)—that is, £70 in money; and also the right to demand £30 from himself and the duty to pay £30 to himself. The (+£30) and the (−£30) cancel and extinguish each other by either of the methods described above, the obligation is extinguished, and the debtor's property is now £70. This transaction is therefore a sale, or an exchange. Thus the obligation, or contract, was originally created by the sale, or exchange, of the *mutuum;* and it is extinguished by the sale, or exchange, of payment. Thus an obligation is created by one exchange, and is extinguished by another exchange.

XXII.—ON CONFUSIO, *μῖξις*, MERGER.

When a right of action against a person comes in any way into his own possession, so that he has both the right to demand from himself, and the duty to pay to himself, it is termed confusio, or *concursus debiti et crediti*, in Roman law, *μῖξις* in Greek law, and merger in ours. It was universally agreed that the *confusio*, *μῖξις*, or *concursus debiti et crediti* of a simple debt extinguished the obligation; but how it does so has given rise to much subtle speculation, and for centuries puzzled jurists and divines. The divines alleged that a right once created could never be destroyed; and the jurists said that the right being transferred to the debtor, he could not sue himself; and, therefore, that the obligation is extinguished. This explanation, however, is not satisfactory, because in many cases a man may sue himself: he may fulfill two characters, or *personæ;* and as one character, or *persona*, he may sue himself as another character, or *persona*. Moreover, this would only show that the right is suspended, or in abeyance, and not that it is extinguished; and many eminent jurists seem to take this view.* Moreover, in several cases, a *confusio*, or *concursus debiti et crediti* occurs, in which the right and the duty unite in the same person and are not extinguished, but may afterward be separated.† The considerations, however, which we have presented will give a complete solution of the case. When one party is a creditor and another party is a debtor, they are two characters, or *personæ*. If, then, the right of action comes into the possession of the debtor, he now fulfills two characters, or *personæ*. The two *personæ* exist though they are now united in one individual, just the same as they did when in separate individuals. And these two *personæ* may deal with each other in exactly the same way as when they were separate parties. They may agree to extinguish the obligation by either of the three methods previously described. The obligation, then, is not suspended, or in abeyance; it is absolutely extinguished and annihilated. Thus this perplexity which was held to be insoluble by jurists for centuries is now removed, and the theory of credit is now complete.

XXIII.—ON NOVATION, μετάθεσις, RENEWAL OR TRANSFER.

A contract, or obligation, may also be extinguished by substituting a new obligation for it. The new obligation pays, discharges, and extinguishes the preceding one; and the extinction of the preceding obligation is the consideration for the new one. This is termed *novatio* in Roman law, μετάθεσις in Greek law, and renewal or transfer by us. This *novatio* may take place in two ways: (1) The debtor may give his creditor a new obligation of his own in payment of the former one, which the creditor accepts in lieu and substitution of the former one. The new obligation is the price or payment of the preceding one, and the extinction of the preceding one is the consideration for the new one. As, for example, when a banker agrees to renew a promissory note for a customer, the new note is payment of and extinguishes the former one, and no debt arises until the new note becomes due. Or when a creditor has a debt due to him payable on demand, and he agrees to take a promissory note from his debtor payable in three months, the note pays and extinguishes the debt payable on demand, the extinction of the debt payable on demand is the consideration for the note; and no debt, or duty to pay, arises until the note becomes due. This form of *novatio* is called "renewal" by us. (2) The debtor may in payment of his own debt, transfer to his creditor a debt due to him by someone else. If the creditor agrees to receive this debt due to his debtor in payment of the debt to himself, the new obligation due from the debtor's debtor pays and extinguishes the obligation due from the debtor himself. But the creditor may retain his own debtor as surety in case of the new debtor's failure to pay. A familiar instance of this is where a debtor pays his creditor

* Stair's Institutes of the Law of Scotland.

† Erskine's Institutes of the Law of Scotland. Bell's Dictionary of the Law of Scotland, art., Confusion.

in bank notes. He transfers to his creditor a debt due from the banker in payment of his own debt. If the creditor agrees to receive the notes in payment of the debt, the debtor is discharged, and the creditor agrees to take the banker as his new debtor. So when a debtor gives his creditor a bill of exchange upon another person in payment of his own debt. So, if a creditor and debtor are customers of the same bank, the debtor may give his creditor a cheque on his account in payment of a debt. If the creditor accepts the cheque, he pays it into his own account; the banker transfers the credit from the debtor's account to the creditor's; as soon as this is done the debtor's debt is paid just the same as if it had been by money; the debt of the banker to the transferer is extinguished; he becomes debtor to the transferee; the transferer is released from his debt to the transferee, who accepts the banker as his new debtor. This form of *novatio* is termed "transfer."

This novation, or *μετάθεσις*, is equivalent to a payment in money. When the debtor's debtor agreed to the transfer of the debt he was called *delegatus*, and the transaction was termed a *delegatio*. So Ulpian says:* "*Verbum exactæ pecuniæ non solum ad solutionem referendum est, sed etiam ad delegationem.*" So Basil., 25, 5, 56: "*ῥῆμα τῶν ἀπαιτηθέντων χρημάτων οὐ μόνον εἰς καταβολὴν ἀναφέρεσθαι δεῖ, ἀλλα καὶ ἐς ἔκταξιν.*"—"The word payment includes not only payment in money, but also the payment of a credit." So also: "*Solvit et qui reum delegat.*"—"He pays who transfers another debtor." And: "*Delegare est vice suâ alium dare creditori, vel cui jusserit.*"—"To delegate is to give another debtor instead of one's self to the creditor, or to his order." This operation, when effected by persons living in different places, is known in commerce as "an exchange." A person living in one country may be debtor to one person living in another country, and creditor to another. He may pay his creditor by sending him an order on his debtor, and thus the obligation is extinguished. The mass of reciprocal transactions of this nature which take place between different countries is called the foreign exchanges.

For "novation" and "delegation" see Gaius, II., 38, 39; Institut. Just., III., 29, 3; Digest, XLVI., 2; Codex, VIII., 41; Basilica, XXV., 5, 56.

XXIV.—ON COMPENSATION, *ἀντεξέτασις*, *ἀντέλλογος* OR *ἀντελόγισμος*, SET-OFF.

If two persons are mutually indebted to the same amount at the same time, each may claim that the debt which he has against the other shall be taken in payment of the debt he owes. Each, therefore, is money, or legal tender, with respect to the other. This is termed *compensatio*. Thus Modestinus says:† "*Compensatio est debiti et crediti inter se contributio.*" Basilica, 24, 10, 1: "*ἀντεξέτασις ἐστιν χρέους καὶ δανείσματος ἀντέλλογος.*"—"Compensation is the mutual set-off of debts and credits." If the debts are equal,

* Digest, 50, 16, 187.

† Digest, 16, 2, 1.

each is payment in full for the other; they are weighed and set off against each other. If the debts are unequal, equal amounts compensate each other, and the balance only is due in money. Simple as this may appear, it took a long time both in Roman and English law to arrive at it. In early Roman law, compensation was not allowed as a matter of right; each creditor had to bring an action against the other. Afterward, in the time of Gaius,* compensation was not held to be payment; but the Prætor, or Equity Judge, allowed the counter-debt to be pleaded as a defence to the action of debt. But the absurdity of this became apparent. Pomponius says:† "*Ideo compensatio est necessaria, quia interest nostra potius non solvere quam solutum repetere.*"—"Therefore, compensation is necessary, because it is our interest rather not to pay than to recover back what we have paid." Marcus Aurelius allowed compensation as a matter of right, and thus mutual debts became money, or legal tender, with respect to each other. So it is said:‡ "*Si constat pecuniam invicem deberi, ipso jure pro soluto compensationem haberi opertet.*"—"If the mutual debts are proved, compensation is to be held as payment as a matter of right." So also: "*Compensationes debitorum ipso jure fient.*" Basil., 24, 10, 21: "οἱ τῶν χρεῶν συμψηφισμοὶ ἰδίῳ δικαίῳ γίνονται."—"The compensation of debts is a legal right." Bankers, *argentarii*, however, were always obliged to allow compensation for counterclaims.

For "compensation," see Gaius, IV., 61–68; Instit. Just., IV., 6, 30, 39; Digest, 16, 2; Codex, IV., 31, 4; Basilica, 24, 10.

The rule of the common law of England was the same as the early law of Rome. If two persons were equally indebted, each had to bring his action against the other. Equity, however, which adopted the law of the Pandects and the Basilica, always allowed compensation, or set-off. In many cases, the rule of common law worked great injustice. If a person and a bankrupt were mutually indebted, the person was obliged to pay his debt in full, and only received a dividend on his own from the bankrupt's estate. To remedy this the Act, Statute 4, Anne, c. 17, allowed set-off in cases of bankruptcy; and this was extended by Statutes 2, Geo. II., c. 22, s. 12; and 8, Geo. II., c. 24, s. 4. But now by the Supreme Court of Judicature Act, which enacts that in all cases in which the rules of equity conflict with the rules of law, those of equity shall prevail, compensation is allowed in all cases. Hence, if two persons are mutually indebted, each debt is money, or legal tender, for the other. Both debts, however, must have actually accrued due at the time, to be subjects of compensation. Ulpian says:§ "*Quod in diem debetur non compensabitur antequam dies venit.*" Basil., 26, 10, 7: "τὸ ὑπὸ ἡμέραν πρὸ τῆς ἡμέρας οὐ συμψηφίζεται."—"A debt which is not yet due cannot be compensated." As, for instance, if a banker holds a customer's acceptance not yet due, he cannot retain a balance on his customer's account to meet it, because his customer's debt

* Instit. IV., 61–68. † Digest, 16, 2, 3. ‡ Codex, 4, 31, 4, 14. § Digest, 16, 2, 17.

does not come into existence until the acceptance becomes due. So, if a banker holds a merchant's acceptance not yet due, and the merchant holds notes of the banker, the banker must pay his notes on demand; he cannot set off the merchant's acceptance, because the merchant's debt has not yet come into existence. So, for a similar reason, if two merchants hold each other's acceptances, one of which is due and the other not yet due, they cannot be compensated. If a debt which was not yet due was set off against a debt which had become due, it was called *deductio*.*

The following are examples of compensation, or set-off. (1) Suppose that two bankers issue notes, and each has got possession of £100 in the notes of the other. Then each banker is two *personæ;* he is creditor, and has a right of action (+ £100) against the other; and each is debtor, or has the duty to pay (– £100) his own notes to the other. So long as each banker holds the notes of the other, there are, of course, £200 of rights of action, credits, or debts, in existence. But when they exchange notes each tenders to the other the debt he has against him, in payment of the debt due to him; that is compensation. Each banker still continues to be two *personæ;* but instead of each being debtor to the other, each is now debtor to himself. It is a case of double *confusio.* As creditor he demands payment from himself as debtor; and as debtor he pays to himself as creditor the debt he has against himself. Each debtor has now performed his duty of paying his debt; and so each obligation is extinguished, and the £200 cease to exist as economic quantities. (2) Suppose a banker holds a merchant's acceptance for £100, which has become due; suppose that the merchant holds £100 of the banker's notes, or has an account with him. When the banker demands payment of his acceptance from the merchant, the merchant tenders him his own notes in payment; or the banker simply writes off the amount of the acceptance from his customer's account, and as before, both obligations are extinguished. (3) Suppose that two merchants have issued equal acceptances each payable on the same day. Suppose also that the acceptance of each merchant comes into the possession of the other; on the day of payment each merchant tenders to the other his own acceptance in payment of the acceptance due to him, and thus as before, both obligations are extinguished.

This form of compensation was formerly very extensively used on the Continent before bankers discounted mercantile bills. At numerous centers of commerce—Lyons, Antwerp, Nuremberg, Hamburg, and many others—there were held great fairs every three months. The Continental merchants, instead of making their bills payable at their own houses, where they must have kept large amounts of cash to meet them, made them payable only at these fairs. In the meantime, these bills circulated all over the country like money, and got covered with indorsements. On a certain day of the fair, the merchants met together and presented their acceptances to each other;

* Gaius, IV., 57.

and if their respective claims were equal they were balanced and paid by being exchanged against each other, by compensation. By this means an enormous commerce was carried on and liquidated without any specie at all. Boisguillebert says * that at the fair of Lyons transactions to the amount of 80,000,000 (livres ?) were settled without the use of a single coin. We thus see what a prodigious extension of credit and commerce is effected by the modern highly organized system whose juridical principles were elaborated by the Roman jurists. We showed that in the early stages of society the first use of money was to represent the balances which arose from the unequal exchanges of products. But modern commerce is carried on, not by money, but by credit; and except in small retail transactions, money is only used now to pay and discharge unequal balances of debts. We have now developed the complete theory of credit, and explained the great juridical and mathematical principles upon which it is based. And we have now shown that the principles of commerce may be reduced to the strictest scientific demonstration.

XXV.—ON THE RATIO OF MONEY TO CREDIT.

Credit, then, being clearly understood to be the *name* of a certain species of commodity, or merchandise, of the same nature as money, but of an inferior order, it is of considerable practical importance to discover the ratio which credit bears to money in this country. The difficulties which prevent private inquiries are very great, and the opportunities which are presented by Parliamentary inquiries into commercial crises are very rarely made use of for any but their immediate purpose. In the report, however, of the committee of the House of Commons on the crisis of 1857 there is given an interesting statement by Mr. Slater, of the great house of Morrison, Dillon & Co., which may furnish us with a clue to answer this question. Having analyzed the operations of his house for 1856, he gave in the following table as showing the proportion in which each million of receipts and payments was made in money and various forms of credit:

RECEIPTS.

	£	£
In Bankers' Drafts and Mercantile Bills payable after date,	533,596	
Cheques payable on demand,	357,715	
Country Bankers' Notes,	9,627	
		900,938
Bank of England Notes,	68,554	
Gold,	28,089	
Silver and Copper,	1,486	
Post-Office Orders,	933	
		99,062
		£1,000,000

* *Dissertation sur la Nature des Richesses*, ch. ii.

Payments.	£	£
Bills of Exchange, ...	302,674	
Cheques on London Bankers, ...	663,672	
		966,346
Bank of England Notes, ...	22,743	
Gold, ...	9,427	
Silver and Copper, ...	1,484	
		33,654
		£1,000,000

Here it is shown that in this great house, which may be reasonably supposed to represent commerce in general, specie did not enter into their transactions for little more than two per cent. A similar investigation, instituted by some bankers, resulted in showing that specie only entered into their operations to the amount of four per thousand, or .0025 per cent. These investigations furnish a clue by which we may obtain a rough estimate of the ratio of credit to money.

It is usually considered that the quantity of coin, gold and silver, in circulation in this country may be estimated at not far from £120,000,000; and if we take as a moderate estimate that the quantity of credit is fifty times the quantity of money, as the above figures indicate, it would appear that the quantity of credits, or debts, of all kinds in the country is about £6,000,000,000. This, of course, is only a rough approximate estimate; but it is sufficient to show the enormous magnitude of this species of property, or merchandise, in this country, and its supreme importance in modern times. This credit produces exactly the same effects, and affects prices exactly as so much gold; prices are estimated by the aggregate of money and credit, which constitutes the circulating medium or currency; and it is through the excessive creation of this species of property that all commercial crises are brought about; and through the mismanagement of these, and bad banking legislation, that commercial crises develop into monetary panics. Moreover, when we grasp the conception that all this mass of credit, or circulating debts, and other securities of a similar nature, is so much exchangeable property, or merchandise, which can be bought and sold, donated, pledged, and exported and imported between country and country exactly like any material commodities, it compels a thorough reinvestigation of all the fundamental concepts of economics, and shows how utterly erroneous is the doctrine that labor and materiality are necessary to value, and that all wealth is the product of land, labor, and capital.

XXVI.—TWO BRANCHES OF THE SYSTEM OF CREDIT.

The system of credit is divided into two branches—mercantile credit and banking credit.

In mercantile credit, merchants buy or circulate commodities by means of credits, or debts, payable at a certain fixed date; and these credits may circulate in commerce and effect exchanges exactly like money until they are paid off and extinguished; and mercantile debts are always extinguished when they become due.

In banking credit, bankers buy gold and mercantile debts payable at a future time, by creating and issuing credits, or debts, of their own payable on demand. Thus they turn mercantile debts into ready money. Banking credits are created payable on demand; and must be paid if so demanded. But they are not intended or expected to be extinguished. On the contrary, they are created with the hope and expectation that they will not be demanded and extinguished. There is no necessity that banking credits should ever be extinguished; in fact, if banking credits were extinguished as soon as they are created, the business of banking could not exist. Banking can exist only so long as payment of banking credits is demanded only to a very small extent. Banking credit may be transferred from one account to another in the same bank, and from one bank to another, to the end of time. It is quite possible that much of the banking credit which exists at the present day may have been created by the very first banks founded in this country; and there is no necessary reason why it should not continue till the end of time. Money is a very expensive machine to purchase and keep up; but banking credits cost nothing to create, and they may endure forever.

These two departments of credit are perfectly distinct; they are governed by different principles; and they are, in some respects, antagonistic to each other. The same persons should never carry on both branches of business; that is, great bankers should not be merchants, and great merchants should not be bankers, because the duty of bankers is often contrary to the interests of merchants.

A History of Banking

IN

THE RUSSIAN EMPIRE.

BY

ANTOINE E. HORN,

LATE EDITOR-IN-CHIEF OF THE "JOURNAL DE ST. PETERSBOURG."

NEW YORK.
1896.

BANKING IN RUSSIA.

CHAPTER I.

THE EARLY STAGES OF MONEY AND CREDIT.

SECTION I.

The Policy of State Prescription—The Copper Era and Its Crisis—Debasements of the Copeck—Imperial Trading on the Coinage.

IN examining the credit system of Russia, the fact that first of all strikes us is that it has always been conducted, if not in accordance with invariable principles, yet at least after a uniform method and one which has conformed to the political policy of the Empire.

The State is the great dispenser of favors, the general manager of all affairs of its subjects. It exercises its control according to its own ideas, but with a very sincere desire to further all those interests of which it assumes the care; to profit by the experiences of other countries, while avoiding their mistakes, and to excel them if possible; but its success has been only such as a bureaucracy, more or less intelligent, is capable of attaining. That the intelligence of this bureaucracy has not always been equal to the mission it has undertaken; that its final aims have not remained constant, but have varied with the controlling powers and their advisers; that the highest interests of the State have often been construed in a sense adverse alike to the dictates of wisdom and the economic progress of the country; that the tutelage exercised by the State over commerce and industry has not always been to their advantage,—all of this will be made sufficiently manifest in the history of the Russian banking system which is to be here laid before the reader.

That system is to-day what it has been for more than a century. The issue and circulation of money are entirely in the hands of the State. There have been brief intervals when emancipation from that control has appeared possible, and even in the way of being accomplished; but they have yielded no result.

Before treating of note circulation as it now exists, it may be well to take a rapid glance at the monetary situation in the period when paper money was unknown.

Such information as is procurable upon this branch of the history is fragmentary, and must be culled from certain personal memoirs rather than from records of incontestable historical value. However, aside from the influence of local peculiarities, the history we are about to sketch is parallel to the experience of all countries.

Until the middle of the seventeenth century there was no copper money in Russia, except one small coin called a "poul." There were in circulation some gold and silver pieces of foreign origin and some small silver coins of Russian mintage. The Government, which held a monopoly in more than one branch of commerce, sold its merchandise to foreigners for ducats or thalers, and had the receipts recoined at the local mints to its own great profit. About 1650, three new silver coins were introduced which, according to the statements of all the chronicles of the time, partook very largely of the character of counterfeit money, having the appearance but not the weight of coins of an intrinsic value greater than their own. Russian subjects were forbidden to pay out these coins in the purchase of imported goods, the Government fearing that such a course would result in raising the price of imports. Somewhat later, it was deemed advisable to debase even the copper coins, and the difference between their official and real value soon became so great that farmers refused to bring their products to market. A contemporaneous writer states that for 160 copecks the Czar bought enough copper to make coins officially valued at R. 100, thus giving them a fictitious value about sixty-five times as great as their real value.

According to Meyerberg, the Czar put in circulation more than R. 20,000,000 of this money. This traffic, by which the Czar Alexis is said to have gained R. 20,000,000, produced numerous revolts, resulting in massacres and the execution of some citizens. Yet such is the force of actual facts that even a Czar Alexis could not keep his spurious copper roubles at par, and their price, which, up to March 1, 1659, had been 104 copecks at Moscow and 103 at Novgorod, gradually declined. On January 1, 1663, the quotation at Moscow was ten copper roubles for one of silver, and on June 15th it was fifteen at Moscow and twelve at Novgorod. That is to say, the fictitious rouble was valued at only 6⅔ per cent. of par in Moscow and 8⅓ per cent. in Novgorod. A general increase in prices resulted. Naturally the blame was laid upon speculators and forestallers, and many accused of these offences were convicted. Nevertheless, in 1662, the Government acknowledged the force of accomplished facts; but it consulted its own interests even in the readjustment. The copper coins were called in at 1 per cent. of their nominal value; but, inasmuch as their real value was 1.6 per cent., many citizens preferred to keep their copper and turn it into household utensils; so the poorest citizens, who were unable to bear the expense of this change, were the chief sufferers.

Less than a century later, copper was once more called upon to play the rôle of Providence for the imperial treasury. It is said that Peter the Great boasted of having carried on all his wars without contracting a debt. In order to do so, he had found it sufficient at first to debase all the gold and silver coinage, and afterward to issue large quantities of five-copeck copper pieces. These latter gradually drove out the other coins and remained practically the only form of money in Russia until the beginning of the reign of Catherine II.

At this period our sources of information become more abundant and more authentic. We need merely mention, however, that the official debasement of the currency was all the more disastrous because it had as an ally, or rather as a competitor, counterfeiting on private account. An official report of 1740 accuses Russia's dishonest neighbors, Poles and others, of this treacherous rivalry against the State. No greater indulgence was shown to these malefactors than had been extended a century earlier to those who trafficked in roubles. It was decreed that every person coming from a foreign land and found in possession of copper copecks should be hanged at the frontier. But the culprit usually escaped if he had the good fortune to reach the Senate with an appeal from this grievous sentence. As early as 1730, the depreciation had become so great that the Government itself refused to accept its copecks in payment of taxes; and in 1731 it authorized the public to melt them for domestic uses. There was, nevertheless, some sense of the obligation resting upon the State to redeem at par the copecks it had issued. But the Czar's advisers constantly protested against the burden which such a transaction would lay upon the Treasury; and, in 1744, they made an estimate of the loss, putting it at R. 4,000,000—an amount much beyond the then available resources of the Treasury. Nevertheless, it was imperative that something be done; and, on May 11, 1744, it was announced that, on and after August 1st, the public treasuries would refuse to accept five-copeck pieces except as the equivalent of four copecks, and that, after October 1, 1745, they would be taken for only three copecks; and a further reduction to two copecks was to become effective on August 28, 1746. No further change was made until 1754. Then it was resolved to issue copper money at the rate of R. 8 to the "pood" (about 36 pounds avoirdupois); and, with this end in view, dealers in copper were forbidden to retain more than one-fourth of their stock. This was almost a return to monetary honesty; for, from 1728 to 1740, the pood of copper had been coined into R. 40. In 1755, the last five-copeck pieces of the old mintage were called in at two copecks each. It had been feared that large quantities of counterfeit money would be brought forward for redemption; but an official report of April 8, 1757, shows that there were presented altogether only R. 3,250,000, or R. 205,723 less than the State itself had issued. Evidently, a large number of persons had concluded to pocket their loss and had melted down their copper money. As for counterfeiters, they found their occupation gone as soon as the coins ceased to have a value that made their manufacture profitable.

SECTION II.

INTRODUCTION OF PAPER MONEY.

Beginning of Note Circulation—A Sound Issue of Assignats—An Unsound Issue of Assignats—The Volume Inflated for War Purposes—Ruinous Depreciation of Notes—Hoarding of Silver—A Ukase Against Exportation of Silver—Remedial Measure—Failure to Fund the Assignats—Assignats made a Legal Tender—Count Cancrine's Financing—Origin of the "Credit-Rouble."

NOTE circulation in Russia dates from a rescript issued on December 29, 1768, by the Empress Catherine II. The decree provided for the establishment of two banks of issue, one at St. Petersburg and the other at Moscow, having a right, or rather being commanded, to issue "assignats." As a matter of fact, the assignats were issued by the State, the banks merely putting them in circulation and redeeming them. This redemption was to be made on demand; all State departments were commanded to accept the assignats at par; and of every payment of R. 500 made to the State at least R. 25 was required to be in these bills. Prompt redemption was assured, because each bank was required to keep on hand an amount of silver equal to its outstanding bills, and each bank redeemed only its own issues. The avowed objects of these issues were, (1) the creation of a more convenient form of money than the silver and copper then in use; and (2) an increase of the circulating medium. The assignats were not made a legal tender, and anyone who chose to do so might refuse to accept them in payments. The new undertaking developed slowly. In 1770, the provincial officers having money to forward to St. Petersburg were requested to send it in the form of these notes, and in 1771 each of the banks began to accept the other's bills. In 1781–2, branch banks, each having from R. 100,000 to R. 300,000 in assignats, were opened in the cities of Novgorod, Pskov, Tver, Nezheen, Kiev, Koursk, Kharkov, Tambov, Orel, Toola, Kazan, Archangel, Kherson, Riga, and Revel. Yet in 1786, eighteen years after the ukase of Catherine, the total issues were only about R. 40,000,000; and it has been estimated that there were at this time in the country R. 110,000,000 to R. 120,000,000 in Russian silver and copper money, and some R. 10,000,000 of foreign coin, the total circulation certainly not exceeding R. 180,000,000. This, however, must be taken as merely an approximation.

The year 1786 marks the first departure from the prudent system of note issues previously adhered to. By a manifesto of June 28th of that year, the two banks of issue were consolidated with the loan bank of the Empire. At the same time, a new issue of R. 60,000,000 was decreed, R. 22,000,000 of which were to be employed in loans to the nobility, and R. 11,000,000 in loans to cities. The total amount of assignats, this manifesto declared, should never exceed R. 100,000,000; but their redemption could no longer be demanded of the banks, because the circulation was not entirely covered by a metallic reserve, but was secured in part by mortgage loans. A new form was given to the assignats, and very soon, in addition to those of R. 100 and of R. 50, others were issued of the denominations of R. 10 and R. 5. Soon the necessities of the State, arising out of the wars in Europe and the East, impelled it to overstep the maximum limit fixed by the manifesto of 1786. As early as 1790, there was a new issue of R. 11,000,000, and twenty years later (in 1810), the circulation had reached the formidable volume of R. 577,000,000. Aside from the R. 33,000,000 reserved for mortgage loans, all of this money had been devoted to the needs of the national treasury.

Though there was no law giving to the assignats a legal-tender quality, yet in 1793, when the amount in circulation was only R. 124,000,000, there was a variance between their value and that of metallic money amounting to forty-five per cent. It resulted from this lack of legal-tender power that specie, while it had entirely disappeared from the interior of the country, formed in the frontier provinces, Baltic and Polish, practically the only circulating medium. At St. Petersburg, all prices were quoted in assignat roubles, while at Riga business was transacted upon the basis of the Reichsthaler, assignats being in use merely as a supplementary form of currency. In order to check the variance between the value of paper and metallic money, and to prevent the further disappearance of silver from circulation, a ukase was issued toward the end of 1791, forbidding under severe penalties the exportation of any Russian money. On February 22, 1808, the Governor-General of Little Russia was commanded to take such measures as would prevent the Jews from sending silver money out of the country, and in 1809 the order was extended to include even copper. But naturally these measures neither brought silver into circulation again nor put an end to the premium upon it. From 1786 to 1807, the value of that metal, measured in paper, had varied between 102 and 164; in 1808 it rose to 201½, in 1810 to 401, and finally in 1812 it reached 423, so that an assignat rouble was worth only 23½ copecks in silver.

In his work "Das Russische Papier-geld,"* M. Goldmann notes that while this depreciation of paper money resulted in a general increase in prices, the increase was not in all cases proportional to the depreciation. Thus, in 1808, the value of a "last" (about two tons) of rye at Riga was R.160 and in 1812 it was R. 240; for the same years a "pood" (36 lbs.) of butter was quoted at R.16 and R. 20 respectively, and a "loof" (2 bushels) of wheat flour at R.10½ and R.12; during the interval, however, the rouble had depreciated from fifty per cent. of its nominal value to twenty-five per cent. This variance, however, may have arisen from other causes affecting the value of the articles. Complaints were numerous both on the part of the consumer, who objected to the higher prices, and on the part of the producer, who found the purchasing power of his income less than before. The State also had its grievance, for having determined that the taxes should serve as security for its issues, it was bound to receive the assignats at par; thus the deficit increased in proportion to the amount of new issues, which were intended to stop the increase of deficiencies, but which resulted always in enlarging them. Accordingly, in 1812, the Government resolved to put an end to this "tax-foundation"; in a word, the State refused to recognize its assignats as a legal tender to the Treasury. But, in view of the general situation in Europe, the moment was not favorable for returning to the owners of assignats the whole or any part of the loss which an over-issue had brought upon them.

The lesson had been a severe one. Whatever it could do by decrees and ukases toward helping itself and the people, the State freely did. To begin with, an imperial decree of June 20, 1810, provided that for the future the silver rouble should become once more the only legal money—5 livres 6 zoltonik (about 4½ pounds) of silver, 83⅓ per cent. fine, being valued at R.100. Subsidiary silver coins of a less degree of fineness were likewise to be a legal tender, and regulations were also made with reference to copper money. At the same time there was appointed an imperial Committee of the Public Debt, its duty being to reduce the circulation and prevent all new issues. To this end, the committee received a "special fund," consisting of lands and forests, which it was to sell within five years. It began by the issue of a loan of R.100,000,000 in five series of R. 20,000,000 each, the first being put out on July 15, 1810. This first series was issued in two forms—one falling due in seven years and the other running indefinitely. Subscriptions for the loan payable in 1817 were accepted on the basis of two assignat roubles for one of silver, and the interest was 6 per cent.; for the other, on the basis of 1½ to 1, the interest being 4½ per cent.; in both cases repayment was to be made in silver. The assignats paid in on these subscriptions were to be publicly burned. The promise of repayment at a fixed date resulted in a prompt sale of the new securities, and in May

* St. Petersburg, 1866.

and June, 1812, on the eve of Napoleon's arrival at Moscow, they were quoted at a premium of 42 per cent.

Thus the remedial scheme was apparently a brilliant success. But the money brought into the treasury by these new creditors was taken out through the doors of the various credit and deposit institutions maintained by the same treasury; so that the State was gaining nothing, but was simply converting a comparatively inexpensive debt into another much more burdensome. Only R. 5,000,000 of assignats were burned, and the four remaining series of obligations were never issued. The State having constituted itself the sole dispenser of credit, could not, of course, demand credit of the public. Once having absorbed in the form of deposits all the available savings of the country, it could not call them a second time to its aid. The attempt to do so was simply a bookkeeping operation; the money was taken out over one treasury counter and paid in over another. We shall meet this same phenomenon again and again in the course of the century; the lesson such operations have to teach has not yet been thoroughly learned.

The system outlined in the ukase of 1810 was promptly abandoned, and there was no further attempt to establish the silver rouble as the only legal form of money. Yet some change was imperatively demanded. It was decreed, therefore, that the Committee of the Public Debt should be intrusted, not merely with the redemption of the assignats, which function had now become a sinecure, but also with the management of all the public debts; that it should pay them with the aid of its "special fund," and should use the surplus in the redemption of assignats. Its operations were to be superintended by a council partially composed of merchants and having a Grand Duke at its head.

On April 9, 1812, it was decreed by a ukase, amending that of 1810, that taxes might be paid in assignats at the rate prevailing when payment was due; that all contracts with the State or between individuals might be settled upon the same terms, and that all payments stipulated to be made in silver or any other form of money might, at the option of the debtor, be made in assignats at the current rate. This was a legal-tender act with no circumlocution.

It is needless to say that the years 1812–15, those of the French invasion and of the two great wars that carried the Russian armies to the gates of Paris, were not years in which the circulation of assignats could be reduced. On the contrary, it is estimated that in 1817 their volume had increased to R. 800,000,000; after that time, however, there was no further increase. In view of the depreciation which had already occurred (the rouble was worth about twenty-five per cent.), the legal-tender decree did not prevent metallic money from coming into circulation once more. Its position was established, because the value of the assignat was purely fictitious. It remained at twenty-five per cent. until 1820, after which it rose gradually and reached twenty-eight in 1840; thus its value was practically stable. Everyone had become resigned to the depreciation, and business adjusted itself accordingly. The burden of the loss of R. 600,000,000 out of R. 800,000,000 issued had, to a large extent, ceased to be felt with the passing of the generation that had been its victim.

As to the Government, it had in 1817 made a new attempt to raise its assignats to par. In accordance with a manifesto of April 16, 1817, and of imperial decrees of May 10, 1817, and June 16, 1818, the State was to buy up assignats until they had advanced to par, and to this end the Committee of the Public Debt was to receive R. 20,000,000 annually from the Treasury. It was instructed to invite deposits at six per cent., and to use them all for this purpose. In order, further, to hasten the retirement of the paper money, a manifesto of August 16, 1820, ordered that a foreign loan be placed with Baring & Hope for R. 40,000,000, and that this money also should be used exclusively in the purchase of assignats. By these means the paper circulation was reduced from R. 800,000,000 to R. 595,000,000. But the order for liquidation did not last. M. Cancrine, who became Finance Minister in 1823, considered it his first duty to put an end to what he called the "imprudent system" of transforming such a mass of assignats into an interest-bearing debt. From the memoirs of this statesman, who was at the head of Russian finances for a quarter of a century, we learn that he prided himself on having saved to the Russian treasury in this manner R. 18,000,000 per year. The depreciation continued from that time, and the State thought no more of redeeming the assignats at par. Nevertheless, the general peace of Europe was of great advantage to the economic situation; military expenses were less, and Cancrine says in his memoirs that he reduced the annual public disbursements from R. 114,614,147 silver to R. 100,829,053 silver. In 1830, it was deemed safe to revoke the order forbidding the export of the precious metals. They had begun to return to the country, and Cancrine says that the value of assignats rose to 350 after having been for some time at 400 and 380. These fluctuations resulted in the inconveniences and losses to which we have previously referred, for the common people and small tradesmen fell a prey to speculators, who exploited the situation for their own profit. Communication throughout the vast Empire was so imperfect that local speculation in the medium of exchange became an easy matter. Debts would be contracted in one kind of money and paid in another kind, which had been artificially depressed in the meantime for this purpose, or *vice versâ*. Each province had its own discount, which varied sometimes by ten or twenty per cent. from that of the capital. Decrees were, indeed, issued forbidding all speculation of this kind, but it is needless to say that they were ineffectual, and M. Cancrine himself was at last compelled to admit the necessity of retiring the assignats.

The retirement was accomplished by a series of steps taken between 1839 and 1843. A manifesto of July 1, 1839, amending that of 1810, provided that for the future silver money should be the only legal tender; that all taxes should be estimated and paid in that money, as well as all private debts. At the same time, the ratio between the silver and assignat rouble was fixed once for all at 1 to 3½, and all persons were forbidden to deal with them at any other ratio or to give to silver a higher value under the guise of a fictitious rate of interest; meanwhile, all debtors were at liberty to make payment in either form of money at the official ratio. Finally, the State treasuries were to exchange R. 100 for any individual on demand. In 1841, a further step was taken by the creation of a new form of note, such as it exists to-day, known as the "Credit-Rouble" or silver-rouble. The last of this series of manifestoes was that of June 1, 1843, decreeing the retirement of all outstanding assignats, amounting to R. 595,-777,310, in exchange for the new form of bill, at the rate fixed in 1839, 1 to 3½, the exchange to be completed by January 1, 1848.

As we have just said, the credit-rouble, first issued in 1843, is still the legal tender of Russia. Its chief virtue was that it drove out of circulation a form of money which had become entirely discredited, and the exchange value of which was only 28$\frac{4}{7}$ per cent. of its nominal value. Besides, the new bill was to be exchangeable on demand for specie (silver), and in this respect it was to be on a par with the circulating mediums of other countries.

Has this result been attained? Could it have been? It should be borne in mind that these reforms in Russia's monetary system were being carried forward at the time when the subject of note circulation was being thoroughly investigated in England, and when the Act of Sir Robert Peel was just giving to the Bank of England its final form, such as it has retained to the present moment. Count Cancrine was thoroughly advised of that investigation and its results. Let us see how he turned them to the profit of Russia.

In the first place, notwithstanding that he was a foreigner, a fault which Russia has never forgiven him, he set to work in a truly Russian manner, carefully retaining in the hands of the State entire control of the circulation and of credits. Not only did the State insist upon its exclusive right to issue paper money, in spite of the sad experiences of the recent past, but it claimed a monopoly also of banking operations properly so called; the discounting of paper and the receipt of deposits were confined to the State Bank, and Cancrine in his memoirs says it is a matter for congratulation that when the Bank was unable to use all of its deposits in loans to individuals, the State itself came forward time and again and borrowed from them to build fortifications, canals, and highways, and for naval and other public uses, thereby supplying the deficiencies of the public revenues.

One is constrained almost to admire the empiricism with which Count Cancrine handled a matter so delicate as the redemption of fiduciary money. In the system we are examining—if it be permissible to call it a system—a beginning had been made in 1839 by the creation of bills upon depositories always exchangeable for specie. These deposits having in a short time increased to several millions of roubles, with few demands for repayment, it was straightway determined that one-sixth of the issue would suffice to meet all demands; accordingly, when bills of credit were issued in 1841, it was decreed that one-sixth of the amount should always be covered by a metallic reserve, the total issue being further secured by all the resources of the State. Thus some R. 30,000,000 was thought to be sufficient to secure the circulation. This is the process by which that conclusion was reached. At the time we speak of and long afterward, it was held as a sort of doctrine in Europe that every bank of issue should keep on hand a metallic reserve representing a third of the circulation. To-day that theory merely causes a smile; but half a century ago it was accepted almost as a dogma. In view of the fact that the new bills during their earlier years had seldom been presented for redemption, Cancrine thought that half of the usual reserve would be sufficient for Russia, and thus he fixed it at one-sixth.

This exchangeability secured to the bills ot credit (for such is the name by which they are still known) did not prevent the State from making their acceptance obligatory upon every citizen, that is, from clothing them with a legal-tender power. Thanks to this preventive measure, it has never been necessary to revoke the formula inscribed upon each bill, declaring that it is redeemable on demand. Half a century has gone by since the first issue of bills of credit, and they still bear this promise upon their face, but it is a dead letter. In any event, it could not have been difficult to foresee that the State would not long resist the temptation which the printing press held out to it. In fact, as early as 1849 a supplementary issue of R. 20,000,000 was ordered, and in 1853 another of R. 40,000,000, carrying the total circulation above R. 250,000,000. As a result of the Crimean war and the difficulty of placing loans abroad, a ukase of January 10, 1855, authorized the Treasury to meet all extraordinary expenses by temporary issues of bills of credit; at each new issue the Treasury was to deposit with the issuing office one-sixth of the sum in metal, and these temporary bills were to be retired within three years after the close of the war. It is unnecessary to say that they are in circulation yet. The authority for their issue was rescinded on April 5, 1857, one year after the treaty of peace. The circulation, which had amounted to R. 345,000,000 in September, 1854, to R. 356,000,000 at the end of that year, to R. 509,000,000 at the end of 1855, and to R. 689,000,000 at the end of 1856, had now reached a total of R. 725,000,000. Thus, fifteen years had sufficed to bring to naught the reformatory projects of Count Cancrine. He, however, was no longer Minister of Finance, and the final liquidation of the Crimean war expenses did not devolve upon him.

SECTION III.

FINANCIAL RECONSTRUCTION UNDER ALEXANDER II. AND THE FOUNDING OF THE STATE BANK.

The State Ceases to be a Lender—Emancipation of Serfs Disables Nobles from Borrowing—Redundance of Bank Deposits—The Great Liquidation of 1859—The Creation of the State Bank; Its Functions, Powers, and Limitations; Modeled after the Bank of England; Its Initial Non-success.

THE reign of Alexander II. (1855–1881) was destined to be one of great reforms. It was not merely the emancipation of the serfs, the opening of the courts to the public, the establishment of the jury system and of judicial elections, the abolition of the monopoly in brandies, and the convocation of provincial legislatures (Zemstvo) that made memorable the earlier years of this brilliant reign. Sound ideas seem to have prevailed also in the domain of economics and finance.

The new regime went seriously to work to release the State from its position as the sole source of credit, and to emancipate commerce and industry from governmental tutelage exercised through a system of institutions entirely under control of the State. Moreover, the Government was no longer anxious to loan to landed proprietors now that the security they offered was about to disappear. The basis of landed credit had been the number of "souls," of serfs, dwelling upon the estate mortgaged. The emancipation of these in 1861 was going to put an end to that security, and nothing would be left upon which the State could safely base a loan. The contemplated reforms began vigorously at this point, and the first step was to clear the ground of those institutions through which the State had acted as the chief lender, and also as the chief borrower, of the Empire. These institutions were of two classes; those acting under the supervision of the Minister of Finance and the Committee of Credit Establishments, and those in charge of the Imperial Board of Education.

In the first category were: (*a*) The Sinking Fund Commission, whose duties are indicated by its title; (*b*) the Imperial Loan Bank, which received deposits on interest and loaned them on country and city real estate for terms of ten, twenty-eight, and thirty-three years; (*c*) the Imperial Commercial Bank, which received deposits on interest, both for transfer and for safe-keeping, and loaned on securities, merchandise, and public funds; and (*d*) the bureau for the issue of bills, whose duties are indicated by its name. The Imperial Board of Education had under its charge: (*a*) the trust depositories (*caisses de dépôts et de consignations*) at St. Petersburg and Moscow, receiving deposits on interest and loaning them for long terms on real estate and public funds; (*b*) the widows' banks; (*c*) lombards, loaning on personal property, jewels, etc.; (*d*) the savings-banks. Thus it appears that every transaction having any reference to borrowing or lending was under the control of some State institution, and for all those charitable and credit establishments the Treasury was responsible. It is needless to dwell at length upon the fatal defect of this system. As a matter of fact, the State was in a position of chronic insolvency, for deposits payable on demand or shortly after demand were secured only by long-term loans, not to speak of the very serious inroads which the needs of the State itself had made upon those deposits. The credit establishments having undertaken to pay interest to depositors at a fixed rate, and the war having increased the mass of bills of credit by nearly R. 500,000,000, this strange anomaly presented itself in 1857, that the State had in its coffers some R. 180,000,000 of deposits on interest for which it could find no employment.*

An imperial decree of July 20, 1857, reduced the interest rate from five to four per cent. On January 5, 1859, the various State institutions had outstanding loans aggregating more than R. 1,038,000,000, of which R. 37,900,000 were for less than a year, R. 31,400,000 for one to fifteen years, and R. 969,000,000 for more than fifteen years. The bank reserves aggregated R. 68,800,000, against which individual depositors had claims amounting to R. 725,100,000, while there was due to the national treasury R. 242,000,000, or R. 967,100,000 in all. Thus the reserves represented less than one-fourteenth of the claims against the banks, and even if the State had been willing to waive its demands there yet remained R. 725,000,000 of claims covered by a reserve of R. 68,800,000, or less than ten per cent., and part of it was in public funds. The practice of loaning on mortgage was stopped; the interest on deposits was reduced to two per cent.; and temporary deposits, payable on demand, were changed into deposits for a long term by the issue of four per cent. State bills (March, 1859). This change not proving acceptable to depositors, five per cent. bills were offered to them in September, 1859, payable in thirty-seven years and obtainable only in exchange for certificates of deposit. These measures and a long list of other conversions and new issues, together with a sterling three per cent. loan of £7,000,000, were partially responsible for the floating debt which weighed upon the State through the instrumentality of its various fiduciary establishments. By

* Finance Minister Kniajevitch's report of September, 1859.

the close of 1859, this debt had been reduced by R. 638,555,023, and then stood at R.328,550,000. At this point, the State may be said to have emerged from the worst of its difficulties, for about half of this last amount consisted of deposits belonging to corporations, municipalities, and public institutions, which were not likely to demand immediate payment. A year later (December 31, 1860), these deposits had been reduced to R.191,900,000.

The liquidation of the past being thus nearly completed, the next step was the founding of the State Bank by the ukase of May 31, 1860, in its present form, barring such modifications as were made in 1894. The laws under which it was formed aimed to make it an essentially commercial establishment. It was forbidden to loan on mortgage security, and was to conform closely to the practice of the Bank of England; acting as cashier for the national treasury, but having no other connection with it. There was to be no secrecy about its operations, its balance-sheets were to be published weekly and delivered to all applicants. So great was the desire to make of the bank a credit establishment, modeled after the best European institutions, that it was given a capital stock of R.15,000,000 and a reserve fund of R.3,000,000, in spite of the fact that all its liabilities were guaranteed by the State. A *résumé* of the Bank's regulations is here presented; which need be but brief, as the new regulations adopted in 1894 will be stated on subsequent pages.

In 1860, the State Bank was founded to invigorate commercial undertakings and to consolidate the note circulation (Art. 1); and, to that end, it was provided (Art. 2), with the aforenamed capital of R.15,000,000 and a reserve of R.3,000,000, backed by all the resources of the State treasury. Its profits (Art. 3) were to be devoted to the payment of the five per cent. Bills of Credit and the amount loaned by the State to the former credit institutions, as well as to establish a reserve against possible losses. It was forbidden to use individual deposits for State purposes (Art. 9). Idle funds in the hands of State or provincial departments were to be kept on deposit with the Bank (Art. 12). The Bank was empowered to buy and sell State securities, but the total amount on hand should never exceed its capital stock.* The State was to be responsible, to the full extent of its resources, for all the undertakings of the Bank, and rentes were to be delivered to the latter to enable it to pay the amounts borrowed by the State from its depositors, the Bank being primarily liable for these (Art. 16). Commercial loans and discounts were not to be made for a longer term than nine months (Art. 23). No bills were to be discounted unless they represented a commercial transaction (Art. 27). It was made the duty of the courts to facilitate the sale of goods belonging to insolvent debtors of the Bank (Art. 39). The Bank was authorized to buy gold and silver at home or abroad (Art. 40). It could accept deposits for safe-keeping (Art. 48), or on accounts current (Art. 53), and deposits on interest (Art. 60). Every change in the con-

* This regulation has not been observed. At times the Bank has been in possession of public funds aggregating R.200,000,000.

ditions under which these deposits were received was to be published one month in advance (Art. 63). The Bank could loan on public funds, on the precious metals, and on merchandise (Art. 71); but these loans were not to exceed seventy-five or at most eighty-five per cent. of the value of the security as shown by bourse quotations (Art. 73). Upon certain classes of merchandise, the loans were not to exceed fifty or sixty per cent. of the value; and the term of the loan was to be not less than one nor more than six months (Art. 89). All the executive officers of the Bank were to be appointed by the State; but representatives of the nobility and of commerce were to be admitted to the directory, with a deliberative voice regarding certain transactions.

In order to emphasize the somewhat modernized character of the institution, there was placed at its head, not a public functionary, but an old banker, Baron Stieglitz, a business man whose fortune was such that it should have insured him the utmost independence of action, and who gave up his banking business to accept the position of Governor of the Bank of Russia. He devoted himself entirely to the work, but, unfortunately, it must be candidly said that he was not equal to the task. True, he was no bureaucratist, but still less was he a financier. He was an honest parvenu, humble and timid, very deeply impressed with the importance of his office and the honor conferred upon him, but not sufficiently imbued with a sense of the responsibilities of his new position; or perhaps it would be more accurate to say that he looked at his duty only from one point of view, that of the Government under which he held office. We may dismiss Baron Stieglitz with the remark that he quitted his position in the fall of 1866.

The Baron had as assistant, and afterward as successor, M. Eugene Lamanski, the ablest financier and banker in all Russia; a bureaucratist, indeed, but at the same time a man of education. He was very bold in his conceptions—to some of which we shall have occasion to allude later—but not consistent in their application. Was he the author of the new regulations of the Bank? We believe not; but he was bound to submit to them. The current was then setting in another direction, and M. Lamanski would have asked nothing better than to be allowed to float with it. His aspirations and convictions, founded upon a thorough understanding of the situation, and upon ideas which were entirely modern, had to yield to official exigencies, and he bravely undertook to make of the Bank an establishment modeled, as far as possible, upon European institutions of a like kind. We are about to see him at this work in his first semi-annual report of the business of the Bank. The extract from that report which we present shows that, from the beginning, the Bank was simply a branch of the national administration, and that its commercial business was of very small importance. The former credit establishments were closed, but the Bank had merely taken their place as part of the State machinery, and—the statement is true even at the present time—at thirty-five years from its beginning it has not materially altered its position or its methods.

The next chapter exhibits the condition of the Bank after the first six months of M. Lamanski's management.

CHAPTER II.

METHODS AND OPERATIONS OF THE STATE BANK.

THE "Journal de St. Petersbourg" of August 20 (September 20) contains a report of the operations of the State Bank for the second half of the year 1860. As the document comprises no less than ninety quarto pages, we can here present only a brief condensation of its more important features.

The directors announce that, in publishing an account of the first half-year's business of the Bank, they consider it advisable to enter into certain details touching not only the principles involved and the progress made by the Bank itself, but also the operations with which it was intrusted for account of the Treasury and those which it was authorized to undertake in order to stimulate trade and industry

The business of the Bank is divided into two main categories. To the first belong all its operations for account of the State; to the second, its commercial transactions proper. The Bank having entered upon both in the middle of the year, and having taken over all the accounts of the existing branches and of the Bank of Commerce, as they respectively stood on July 1, 1860, the directors found it indispensable, both for the symmetry of the report and as furnishing a just basis of comparison with the business of preceding years, to place in this document, besides the detailed figures relating to the operations of the Bank, certain totals showing the transactions of the Bank itself and those of the branches.

Before entering into the details of these operations the directors furnish the following figures of the liquidation of the accounts of the former credit institutions. According to the balance-sheet of the Bank of Commerce, the State Bank took over on July 1, 1860, as liabilities:

	ROUBLES.
1. Debts to itself—including: Capital of the Bank of Commerce, R. 8,571,428.57; reserve, R. 1,745,001.05; profits, R. 2,801,965.68, and premiums on the bonds of the Sinking Fund Commission, belonging to that bank, R. 16,605	13,135,000.30

	ROUBLES.
2. Debts to third parties and to public departments: Deposits (for transfer, in trust and on interest and interest on those deposits)	87,773,620.46
Amounts belonging to the Sinking Fund Commission, on account of conversions into bonds of the 4 per cent. Consolidated Loan	2,266,469.45
Amount converted into 5 per cent. Bank bills	91,366,446.69
Debts of the Bank to the branches	19,609,147.81
Debt to the commission for the issue of credit bills, for the bills delivered by it	12,000,000.00
Total	R. 226,150,684.71

On the other hand, the Bank received from the Bank of Commerce, as assets:

	ROUBLES.
Cash on hand (including deposits of gold and silver and exchequer bills deposited for account of transfers)	4,413,481.08
Public funds belonging to the Bank	7,843,639.29
Time loans to various debtors	19,990,356.91
Outstanding credits for protested bills and debts in default	1,630,829.57
Outstanding for extraordinary loans made by order of the Sovereign	1,030,280.00
Owing by the various credit institutions	4,014,121.66
Due to the Bank from the branches	12,254,317.81
Deposits on interest made by the Bank of Commerce with the Loan Bank	174,186,574.06
Sums due on the conversion of deposits into 5 per cent. Bank bills	787,084.33
Total	R. 226,150,684.71

In addition to the accounts of the late Bank of Commerce, which it replaced, and its branches, the State Bank had to take over:

1. All the deposits held by the various credit institutions of the Empire.

2. All the accounts of the 4 per cent. Consolidated Loan for the cancellation of a corresponding proportion of the Treasury debt to the State Bank.

3. All the deposits converted into 5 per cent. bills of the State Bank.

4. The accounts of the Commission for the Issue of Bills of Credit, which now became a department of the State Bank.

5. All the loans made to the Treasury, or to public departments by the credit institutions, to be consolidated into a general account of the Treasury's debt to the State Bank.

6. The capital stock of the Loan Bank, which the State Bank was to turn to the account of its capital and reserve.

During the second half of the year 1860, the State Bank had finished its settlement with the credit institutions of St. Petersburg only. As to the Commission for the Issue of Credit Bills, the R. 704,904,927 of those bills in circulation on the day of the consolidation of its accounts with those of the State Bank were carried to the debit of the latter, and these were carried to its credit, for account of the redemption fund, R. 92,533,777 in gold and silver, coin and bullion, and in public funds. Thc R. 612,371,149 forming the surplus of bills in circulation over the redemption fund were brought into the account as a non-interest-bearing debt of the Treasury. The credit bills issued in 1859 to strengthen the cash accounts of the credit institutions, and charged to them at that time, were stricken out of their accounts in 1860, as an offset against their loans to the Treasury, so that the latter became sole debtor to the full extent of credit bills in circulation. Since then, all the business of issuing, exchanging, and redeeming credit bills has become part of the duty of the State Bank.

The liquidation of the affairs of the Loan Bank and of the Lombard of St. Petersburg gave the following general results:

The State Bank entered on the debit side of its account:

	ROUBLES.
1. Deposits on interest	216,220,192.65
2. Deposits converted into 5 per cent. bills	58,264,764.81
3. Amount converted into bonds of the 4 per cent. Consolidated Loan	30,209,131.57
4. Sundry amounts not belonging to the Bank	129,208.26
5. Interest collected on loans	8,005,153.48
6. Balance of the accounts with the Bank of Commerce	500,000.00
7. Debts assumed in the liquidation of accounts between the banks	9,207,597.41
8. Capital stock of the Loan Bank	15,213,701.47
9. To offset the deposits of the Bank of Commerce by the amounts due from it to the Commission for the Issue of Credit Bills	4,000,000.00
10. Amounts of the accounts current of the Lombard	386,996.89
11. For account of the deposits of the Bank of Commerce with the Loan Bank	162,549,039.05
Total	R. 504,685,785.59

To balance these amounts entered to the credit of the respective accounts, the State Bank received:

	ROUBLES.
1. Claims against the Treasury for loans made to it	262,510,589.17
2. Loans to individuals and public institutions, the Bank having a right to collect the annual payments on account	232,866,399.17

	ROUBLES.
3. Interest-bearing securities belonging to the Loan Bank and to the capital fund of the institutions in charge of the Board of Trustees of the Imperial Foundling Hospital	3,934,996.42
4. Balance of sundry mutual accounts	4,986,803.94
5. Cash on hand	386,996.89
Total	R. 504,685,785.59

As the Bank of Commerce was creditor of the Loan Bank to the extent of R. 174,186,574 on account of deposits, interest included, when all the preceding amounts were transferred to the accounts of the State Bank, that claim of the latter against the Loan Bank was settled by the following items: R. 162,549,039 carried over to the liquidation account as above (No. 11); R. 4,000,000 owing by the Bank of Commerce to the Commission of credit bills in exchange for an equal amount deducted from the deposits of said Bank of Commerce with the Loan Bank; R. 5,285,653 of the interest-bearing funds of the latter transferred to the State Bank; and lastly, R. 2,351,881, being the interest due to the Bank of Commerce on its deposits for 1859; total, R. 174,186,574. Immediately after having finished that liquidation, the State Bank began to separate its commercial business from that transacted for the account of the Treasury; to this end it was necessary: (1) To set aside as capital stock, R. 15,000,000, and as a reserve fund, R. 1,000,000; (2) to carry to the credit of the Treasury all the amounts not belonging to the Bank; and (3) to hold the surplus as a security for such outstanding credits as were considered doubtful, and also to cover loans not sanctioned by the new regulations of the Bank.

	ROUBLES.
After having set aside its capital stock and reserve fund, the Bank had upon that account a surplus of	9,528,476.27
On the profits made before the foundation of the Bank, deducting the sum of R. 2,351,881, mentioned above, R. 28,730 for gratuities made by order of the Sovereign and other expenses, the surplus was	3,537,278.58
The surplus of the amounts received from the Commission for the Issue of Credit Bills, all deductions being made, amounted to	12,000,000.00
Profits accrued to the Bank of Commerce on previous purchases of bonds of the Sinking Fund Commission	16,605.00
Total	R. 25,082,359.85

That sum, carried to a temporary account, was not, however, altogether available, because it had to be used to secure doubtful credits and transactions not authorized by the new regulations, as well as several items of expense to be charged against the Reserve Fund and the profits of the Loan Bank, and the income of the Lombard. By order of the Minister of Finance, there was deducted from that total R. 14,975,835; namely, R. 12,000,000 to counterbalance an equal sum owing by the Treasury for credit bills; R. 1,601,727 for protested bills of exchange belonging to the Bank of Commerce, in order to close that account; R. 175,799 for loans on merchandise not paid to said bank at maturity; R. 1,174,500 for loans contrary to the regulations, but made in accordance with the orders of the Sovereign, and R. 23,809, surplus of expenses arising from loans on merchandise. As a result of these deductions, the amount remaining at the disposition of the Treasury on January 1, 1861, was R. 10,106,524.

The transactions which the Bank undertakes for account of the Treasury have reference to: (1) The credit bills; (2) the repayment of deposits, principal and interest; (3) the payment of coupons and the redemption of the 5 per cent. Bank bills; (4) various conversions into bonds of the 4 per cent. Consolidated Loan; (5) the collection of interest on loans to meet the above payments; (6) the accounts of the Treasury debt and of the Lombard loans.

1. Credit Bills.—On January 1, 1860, there were R. 678,211,187 of credit bills in circulation. During that year, R. 45,679,306 were issued, including R. 7,179,306 against deposits of specie; R. 10,913,924 were withdrawn from circulation, including R. 9,714,322 paid in specie. There were, therefore, R. 712,976,569 of credit bills in circulation on January 1, 1861.

On January 1, 1860, the fund for the redemption of credit bills amounted to R. 95,674,981. This, as has just been noted, was increased by R. 7,179,-315 and decreased by R. 9,969,864 during the year, so that on January 1, 1861, it amounted to R. 92,884,431, of which R. 43,123,731 was in gold coin, R. 8,482,078 in gold bars, R. 32,729,198 in silver coin, and R. 8,549,424 in public funds. This redemption fund being deducted from the total of credit bills in circulation, the balance, amounting to R. 620,092,137, formed the non-interest-bearing debt of the Treasury. During that year 18,847,000 new credit bills were printed for an amount of R. 42,253,000; 7,757,315 old bills, aggregating R. 36,888,950 were burned. The Bank received from boards of finance and local treasuries R. 728,240 of copper coin, and from the national treasury R. 110,000 in subsidiary silver coin, to be exchanged for credit bills. On January 1, 1861, R. 38,876 of the former and R. 15,250 of the latter still remained in the hands of the Bank.

2. Deposits at interest; Deposits with former credit institutions and the Bank of Commerce.—On July 1, 1860, the sum total of deposits with the State Bank, including those received from the Bank of Commerce, the Loan Bank, the Lombard, and the balance of deposits after conversion into 5 per cent. bills of the Bank, amounted to R. 288,978,318. Of that amount, during the second half-year R. 97,058,000 were converted into bonds of the 4 per cent. Consolidated Loan and into 5 per cent. bills of the Bank. There remained on January 1, R. 191,920,318 of deposits originally made with various credit institutions of St. Petersburg, but for which the State Bank was now liable. Prior to 1860, the branches of the Bank of Commerce at Kiev and Odessa were the only ones receiving deposits on interest, and on January 1st of that year they had R. 33,683,084 of deposits. All the branches having then been authorized to accept such deposits, the receipts for 1860 were R. 16,568,711 by the branches in Moscow, Archangel, Kharkov, Kiev, Riga, Catherinebourg, and Odessa; the withdrawals were R. 20,307,436, so that there remained R. 29,944,359 in the branches of the State Bank on January 1, 1861.

3. Deposits with the State Bank.—In accordance with its regulations, the Bank receives interest deposits on certain conditions at rates of interest fixed by itself according to the state of business and the length of time for which the deposit is to remain. The acceptance of deposits under the new conditions began at the Bank at its opening, and later at its branch in Moscow. At the other branches it did not begin until 1861. In 1860, the Bank received deposits amounting to R. 29,982,319, of which R. 2,174,757 were withdrawn during the year; so that at the beginning of 1861 there was a balance of R. 27,807,561. That amount was made up as follows: deposits to be withdrawn at will and bearing three per cent. interest, R. 19,038,352; deposits for three to five years and yielding four per cent., R. 2,409,509; deposits for six to ten years and yielding four and a half per cent., R. 6,359,698.

The branch at Moscow received deposits aggregating R. 4,217,072, of which R. 44,030 was withdrawn during the year; balance on January 1, 1861, R. 4,173,042. Among those deposits appeared a certain number of bills of former credit institutions and even bills of the Lombard of Moscow and of several public charitable establishments. After settlement had been made with these establishments and with the Lombard, the Bank (on January 1st) was still their creditor for R. 667,359, and its Moscow branch for R. 545,012.

The old Bank of Commerce kept a special account for interest due but unclaimed by the depositors, on which account the State Bank was debited with R. 13,594,228; on the same account R. 3,115,924 was carried to its credit as profits of the Bank of Commerce. That account must henceforth change its form, and the amount of unclaimed interest accumulated to January 1, 1860 (the date at which the payment of compound interest was stopped), must be carried to the deposits account, when the liquidation of the transfer to the Bank of all the deposits of the other credit institutions is completed.

4. Five Per Cent. Bills of the State Bank.—Before the first of July the Bank of Commerce had converted into five per cent. bills of the State Bank deposits amounting to R. 91,223,545; together with those that were transferred to it for purposes of this conversion in the second half-year by the Loan Bank, the Lombard of St. Petersburg, and the branch at Odessa, the total amount of those deposits being R. 155,114,910. On January 1, 1860, the branches of the Bank of Commerce at Kiev and Odessa had R. 6,327,652 of deposits converted into five per cent. bills of the Bank, and the conversions made during the year were R.3,785,166. While this conversion was proceeding, the Bank received in sundry small amounts R.148,516, and repaid (R.31,165 deposited anew being deducted) R.1,134,862 to the depositors.

Up to January 1, 1861, the total value of the five per cent. bills of the State Bank exchanged against deposits on interest amounted to R. 276,578,500. During the second half-year, the Bank exchanged R.10,740,200 of these bills for the same amount in bills of other denominations.

5. *Bonds of the Consolidated Loan.*—It is the duty of the Sinking Fund Commission to provide for the interest on these bonds, but the State Bank is intrusted with the collection of the amounts paid for them, with the conversion of the deposits of credit institutions into said bonds, and with the delivery of the bonds themselves. The total amount collected by the Bank from the Sinking Fund Commission, the Loan Bank, and the Lombard of St. Petersburg for these purposes and also for the continuation of the exchange until January 1, 1861, was R.59,609,340. The total amount of deposits converted into these bonds must form a new debt registered in the ledger of the Public Debt, and must be deducted from the debt of the Treasury to the Bank. The latter, not having yet received the total amount of the subscriptions, had a claim of R.109,313,487 upon that account on January 1, 1861.

6. *Debt of the Treasury for Loans from Credit Institutions.*—The Bank received from the Loan Bank and from the Lombard of St. Petersburg claims against the Treasury aggregating R. 262,510,589; it recovered in cash (R. 23,856,297) and by offsetting several accounts, R.158.612,170, which leaves a balance of R.103,898,418.

7. *Long-Term Debts of Individuals and Corporations to the Old Credit Institutions.*—The Lombard of St. Petersburg remains intrusted with the recovery of these debts for account of the State Bank, and they constitute a guarantee fund for the payment of its five per cent. bills. The total thus carried to its credit, both from the Loan Bank and the Lombard, amounted (unpaid arrears included) to R. 232,876,418. The Bank has recovered R.1,492,671; balance due, R. 231,383,746.

8. *Loans to Credit Institutions.*—On July 1, 1860, claims against the credit institutions amounting to R.4,014,121 were transferred to the State Bank; during the second half-year the Bank made further advances to them of R.21,331,598; of that amount, R.19,290,281 was settled by a balance of accounts, so that, on January 1, 1861, the claims of the Bank on that score amounted to R.6,055,438.

9. *Interest on Long-Term Loans.*—As a fund for the payment of interest on deposits and on its five per cent. bills, and of certain expenses for account of the Treasury which formerly had to be deducted from the profits of the Loan Bank, the interest on all loans made by the credit institutions must be remitted to the Bank; but it is carried to the credit of the Treasury, on

account of which the above-mentioned payments are made, and the balance, if any, goes to reduce its debt to the Bank. During the year 1860, the Bank received only interest on loans made by the credit institutions of St. Petersburg, although the payment of coupons of the five per cent. bills fell almost entirely upon it. The Bank will recover the remainder when it makes its final settlement with the credit institutions outside of St. Petersburg. The amount the Bank collected for interest during 1860 was R. 17,690,946, from which have been deducted R. 5,285,643, the interest due the Bank of Commerce from the Loan Bank at the time of the liquidation, and R. 238,702 for sundry expenses on Treasury account.

10. Interest Paid to Depositors.—During the second half of 1860, the State Bank paid to depositors interest amounting to R. 3,432,439; the Bank of Commerce had paid R. 13,817,673 during the first half of the year.

11. Payment of the Coupons of the Bank's Five Per Cent. Bills.—The first coupon of these bills was due on November 1st; up to the end of the year R. 7,043,168 of these coupons was paid by the Bank or brought into its account for payments made by the branches and by local treasuries. Thus, coupons upon about R. 93,000,000 were not presented and will have to be paid during the succeeding year. This statement is not entirely accurate, however, because some coupons paid in 1860 in the provinces were brought into the account of the Bank at the beginning of 1861.

12. Collections for Treasury Account.—The doubtful debts having been deducted from the amounts carried to the credit of the Treasury, the latter is credited with all the collections since made by the Bank on debts of that kind. Up to January 1, 1861, those collections amounted to R. 21,167.

13. Profit and Loss Account of the Treasury.—According to the balance-sheet of the Bank of January 1, 1861, the following items were carried to the credit of the profit and loss account of the Treasury:

1. Amounts carried provisionally to the credit of the Treasury	R. 10,106,524.29
2. Balance on hand on January 1, 1861, on account of interest on loans	12,166,589.74
3. Recoveries on doubtful debts	21,167.89
Total	R. 22,294,281.92

The same account was debited as follows:

1. Interest paid depositors	R. 3,432,439.90
2. Payment of coupons of five per cent. bills	7,043,168.29
3. Charges for handling State securities	26,035.26
4. Interest due depositors on January 1st	3,253,677.04
Total	R. 13,755,320.49

So that there was a surplus of R. 8,538,961 at the disposal of the Treasury. That amount cannot, however, be carried definitively to the credit of the Treasury for the following reasons: (1) A very considerable quantity of coupons of the five per cent. bills due in 1860 have not yet been presented by their holders; (2) several doubtful debts due the branches of the Bank have not been deducted from the amounts with which the Treasury was credited;* (3) certain expenses for account of the Treasury, to be charged against the reserve fund of the late Bank of Commerce, had not been settled at the close of 1860.

The directors proceed next to the commercial transactions of the Bank, taking them up in the following order:

1. Transfers of Cash Accounts.—When the State Bank began business its cash capital was represented by R.3,629,947. The changes in the cash accounts during 1860 are presented as follows:

At the Bank itself:

	RECEIPTS.	EXPENSES.
First half-year..............	R. 213,902,191	R. 212,373,483
Second half-year...........	271,661,620	265,601,855
Total.......................	R. 485,563,811	R. 477,975,338
Total receipts and expenditures.........		R. 963,539,149

At the branches during the whole year:

Receipts..	R. 107,975,525
Expenses..	105,491,300
Total...	R. 213,466,825

Furthermore, R.368,355 was transferred from the account of the Bank to the account of trust deposits. On January 1, 1861, the cash on hand amounted to R.10,104,891, or R.6,475,143 more than on July 1, 1860, and R.7,221,613 more than on January 1, 1860. The branches had cash on hand amounting to R. 9,265,666, or R. 2,484,225 more than on January 1, 1860. Thus the total business of the Bank and its branches represents R.1,177,-005,977.

2. *Capital Appropriated to the Branches.*—Of the fifteen millions of capital, R.7,400,000 has been appropriated to the branches, in the following proportions: R. 4,000,000 for the branch at Moscow, R.1,000,000 for the branch at Odessa, R.550,000 each for the branches at Riga and Archangel, R.500,000 for the branch at Kiev and a like amount for that at Catherinebourg, and R.300,000 for the branch at Kharkov. In the year 1860, R.500,000 was placed at the disposal of each of the temporary offices which the branches established during the fairs at Irbite, Rybinsk, Nijni-Novgorod, and Poltava.

* The total of these debts, since transferred to the Bank to be carried to the debit of the Treasury in 1861, is R. 2,266,663.

3. *Deposits in Trust.*—The total of these deposits, in articles of gold and silver, in Treasury notes and cash (including those existing on January 1, 1860), amounted during the year to R. 801,541, of which R. 433,186 has been returned; so that, at the opening of the year 1861, there was a balance remaining of R. 368,355, which sum was subtracted from the cash account, in which manufactures of gold and silver appear for R. 56,355; the balance consists of Treasury notes. The acceptance in trust of interest-bearing securities not having begun until September 13, the Bank, up to January 1, 1861, had received but 8909 of such deposits, of a nominal value of R. 2,971,412. Of these, 331, valued at R. 76,950, were returned, leaving a balance of 8578 deposits, valued at R. 2,894,462, consisting mostly of public funds.

4. *Deposits for Transfer.*—Before the introduction of accounts current, which occurred shortly after the State Bank was established, the place now occupied by them was filled at the Bank of Commerce by deposits for transfer; these deposits were availed of both to transfer funds through the medium of the Bank and to secure the safe-keeping of Treasury notes under pretence of transfer. On July 1st the State Bank received from the Bank of Commerce R. 1,739,456 of those deposits, and before the opening of its accounts current this sum had been increased by R. 4,480,247. Repayments, transfers to the branches, the buying of transfer duties, and, finally, the transference of Treasury notes to accounts current have reduced that sum by R. 6,215,918. When accounts current were opened, the account of deposits for transfer was closed, and the balance carried to a new account under the name of:

5. *Accounts of Sums Held in Trust.*—This was debited with R. 3876. This sum, together with new deposits made since by individuals having no accounts current (withdrawals being deducted), leaves a balance on that score amounting on January 1, 1861, to R. 13,134.

6. *Accounts Current of the State Bank.*—These accounts, now introduced for the first time in Russia, furnishing, as they do, by the use of cheques, such great facilities for prompt payment and the safe-keeping of money, have increased with remarkable rapidity from the beginning. Not only individuals and corporations, but public departments also have taken advantage of the services of the Bank in this regard. On January 1, 1861, the number of accounts current was 133. Since the month of September, when the practice began, the Bank has received in accounts current R. 102,314,127, and has paid against cheques deposited with its branches and those turned into the Bank itself for transfer from one account to another, R. 72,000,936, so that on January 1, 1861, the Bank was debited in accounts current with R. 30,313,190, or R. 28,479,667 more than the deposits for transfer in the Bank of Commerce at the beginning of 1860.

7. *Account of Transfers with the Branches.*—During the second half of 1860, the branches were credited at the Bank with R. 44,031,160 arising from transfers (including their credit on July 1st), and debited on the same account with R. 26,678,505, leaving at the beginning of 1861 a balance to

their credit of R. 17,352,655. The changes arising out of transfers between the Bank and its branches produced the following results during the first and second half respectively of the year 1860: During the second half-year, the transfers from the Bank to its branches, made by order of individuals, showed an increase, as compared with the first half-year, of R. 3,750,000, namely, R. 12,997,758, against R. 9,244,995; the transfers from the branches to St. Petersburg increased by R. 800,000, namely, R. 2,153,731, against R. 1,273,019; and, finally, the remittances in silver from the Bank to its branches to strengthen their cash accounts, decreased by nearly R. 9,500,000—that is, R. 11,277,250, against R. 20,734,750. These favorable results were attributed partly to the reduction of the rate of discount on transfers and partly to the increase in the cash resources of the branches arising from the interest deposits of individuals and from deposits by local treasuries of their unemployed funds for Treasury account. Another result of the reduction of the discount rate on transfers was an increase in the profits of the Bank from that source, notwithstanding the fact that no discount is charged on transfers made for the Treasury.

8. Transient Accounts.—For the regularity of its bookkeeping, the Bank opened an account in which are entered all sums received by mail until they are in regular course carried to the proper accounts, and also the sums ordered to be paid, but not yet actually delivered to the payee. For the second half-year that account showed R. 23,576,880 of receipts and R. 23,052,432 in disbursements.

9. Discount of Bills of Exchange.—According to its balance-sheet of January 1, 1860, the Bank of Commerce then had on hand R. 27,556,351 in bills of exchange, of which R. 13,459,371 were in the Bank itself and R. 14,096,980 in its branches. During the first half-year 8559 bills of exchange were discounted for R. 9,737,499.03; during the second half-year, 10,380 bills for R. 15,557,954.80, and coupons of 5 per cent. bills for R. 65,237.41. Total, R. 25,360,691.24. The eleven branches of the Bank discounted within the year 23,991 bills of exchange, aggregating R. 46,670,539. Thus the total was 42,930 bills, valued at R. 72,031,230; an increase of R. 24,402,950 over the transactions of 1859. Of the total of bills discounted (deduction being made of protested and duly honored bills, and of offsets for loans made by special order), the Bank and its branches had still in their portfolio on January 1, 1861, bills for R. 32,141,619, or R. 4,585,267 more than on January 1, 1860.

10. Protested Bills of Exchange.—The face value of the bills protested during the year (including bills for R. 2,400 on which extensions were granted by the branch at Catherinebourg) was R. 475,648; together with those brought forward from the preceding year, the sum total of due debts unpaid was R. 3,269,855, but this was reduced to R. 2,932,691 by the collections made during 1860. Of the protested bills of exchange belonging to the Bank of Commerce and its branches, accumulated since the year 1818, the sum of R. 2,899,362 was carried to the account of profits and balances put at the disposal of the Treasury, leaving on January 1, 1861, at the State Bank and its branches, R. 33,328 in protested bills of exchange; this amount was balanced by profits of the Bank at the closing of its profit and loss account of 1860.

11. Loans on Merchandise.—During the year, the Bank and its branches advanced on merchandise R. 5,583,154; the amount due at the end of the year was R. 3,020,358. Including amounts previously overdue, the holdings of the Bank on that class of loans, not paid at maturity, amounted, at the close of the year, to R. 1,211,760.

12. Loans on Deposits of Gold and of Receipts issued by the Managers of the Oural and the Altai Mines.—The total value of the loans made on these securities during 1860 was R. 6,311,387, and on January 1, 1861, there remained in the Bank and its branch at Catherinebourg, R. 4,334,642 of these pledges.

13. Loans on Deposits of Public Funds.—Of these loans there were issued during the year, R. 13,556,054, of which all but R. 23,371 was repaid at maturity. At the same date, the bank and its branches had out R. 6,747,889 of time loans made on this class of securities.

14. Loans on Railway Stocks and Bonds Guaranteed by the Government.—The total value of these loans was R. 10,512,452. On January 1, 1861, the Bank and its branches held notes aggregating R. 3,893,865 for time loans made on these collaterals; of those that fell due during the year R. 461,258 were not paid at maturity. That large proportion of unpaid engagements consisted principally of loans made upon the stocks of the Grand Railway Company, and especially upon those that were not fully paid up, for the reason that the Bank of Commerce had loaned on those securities 90c. on the rouble of their nominal value, with no special regard to their market price; and whenever an assessment was made on those shares they were abandoned to the Bank. The new regulations of the State Bank put an end to that difficulty.

15. Loans Contrary to the Regulations of the State Bank made before it came into existence.—The Bank of Commerce had made loans of this kind during the first half of 1860 and earlier, amounting to R. 3,000,000: R. 1,000,000 to the Bank of Finland, R. 1,650,000 to the Bank of the Nobility of Esthonia, and R. 350,000 to the Russo-American Company. Of these amounts, R. 1,950,000 had been repaid before July 1st, and R. 1,050,000 in bonds were delivered to the State Bank.

16. Loans made by order of the Sovereign.—The loans and offsets carried to that account in 1860 amounted to R. 1,229,780, of which R. 30,000 had been repaid, and R. 25,280 carried to the account of loans on merchandise security; balance at the end of the year, R. 1,174,500.

17. Account of Arrears and Deficits on Loans.—An amount of R. 25,586 remaining due on July 1, 1860, for loans on merchandise security has been deducted from the funds placed at the disposal of the Treasury. All doubtful debts and those made contrary to the regulations of the State Bank, and all the previous arrears, amounting together to R. 5,242,499, were either deducted from the balance-sheet of the Bank when its accounts were opened, or have been transferred by the branches to the Bank to be deducted in 1861.

18. Interest-bearing Securities Belonging to the Bank.—On January 1, 1860, the Bank of Commerce owned R.7,843,639 in public funds, consisting almost entirely of perpetual six per cent. State bonds; the whole of this sum was delivered to the State Bank. At the time of the liquidation of the Loan Bank, the State Bank had also received R. 2,340,025 in bonds of this class. By order of the Minister of Finance, all these bonds were delivered to the Sinking Fund Commission against R. 5,100,000 deposited by the latter with the Loan Bank, and transferred to the State Bank, and R. 5,011,450 deducted from the account of the four per cent. Consolidated Loan. After these transactions, the Bank had only R.72,214 in public funds. During the second half of 1860, there were left in possession of the Bank by borrowers R. 852,878 in stocks of the Grand Railway Company. This raises to R. 925,092 the value of the interest-bearing securities in its possession on January 1, 1861.

In addition to the transactions named above, the Bank had bought and sold interest-bearing public securities on commission. Thus it was intrusted (during the second half of 1860) with the sale of R.14,000,000 of exchequer bills, out of the five series authorized to be issued; and it succeeded in disposing of nearly all of them, thanks to the great diversity of methods it adopted for the purpose. It made these bills so popular, in fact, that at the time of the last subscription opened by the Bank there was a demand for no less than R.306,000,000. The Bank undertakes also, for a commission of $\frac{1}{10}$ of one per cent., the sale and purchase of these five per cent. bills for the public.

In closing their report, the directors of the State Bank sum up as follows the profit and loss account of the Bank for the second half of 1860:

All the profits made by the Bank of Commerce up to July 1, 1860, including the interest on its funds deposited with the Loan Bank, were placed at the disposal of the Treasury. At the closing of the profit and loss account of the Bank its gross revenue for the second half of 1860 was found to be R.1,333,715, including the net profits on the discount transactions of the temporary offices at Nijni-Novgorod, Rybinsk, and Poltava, amounting to R.192,068. From that total was deducted R. 425,836, viz.: R. 92,794 for various expenses of the Bank and its temporary offices; R. 23,807 for protested bills of exchange and unpaid loans secured by public funds and stocks; and lastly R. 309,234 for that part of the interest on loans and discounts belonging to 1861. This leaves for the Bank itself a net profit of R. 907,878.

The net profits of the branches for the year 1860 amounted to R. 722,830, giving a total profit of R.1,630,708, or a little over ten per cent. of the capital stock of the Bank. During the first half of 1860, the net profits of the Bank of Commerce had been R. 338,646, or R.569,232 less than the profits of the second half-year.

CHAPTER III.

BANKING VICISSITUDES FROM 1862 TO 1875.

Attempts at Currency Reform in 1862—A Loan of £15,000,000 to Strengthen the Reserve against "Bills of Credit"—The Polish Insurrection Intervenes—Failure of Resumption of Specie Payments; Causes of that Failure; Its Disastrous Effects—Prostration of Commerce and Credit—Creation of Joint-Stock Banks—Communal Banks—Banking on the Mutual Principle—Railroad Construction Financed for the Benefit of the Bank; Metallic Reserve thereby Increased.

IN 1862 the Bank was called upon to conduct the very serious undertaking of putting an end to the legal-tender power of bills of credit and re-establishing a metallic currency consisting of gold and silver. It should be noted at this point that the trebling of the circulation between 1854 and 1857 had not adversely affected the value of paper money. In April, 1857, the paper rouble was quoted at 403 centimes, even above the par value, which was 4 francs. But such a situation could not last. We have seen that on January 1, 1861, the Bank had in its possession a fund of R. 92,900,000, of which R. 8,500,000 was in State securities, against a note circulation of R. 713,000,000. The value of the rouble was bound to be affected by this state of affairs; and it is interesting to notice that the depreciation had been comparatively small, very small indeed, relative to what it has been at various times since (as, *e. g.*, in 1866, 1879, and 1887), to which reference will be made later on. Evidently, the financial world had great confidence in the economic situation of Russia and in the sincerity of her desire for progress in every direction. And such a desire did exist; it was real and sincere, though somewhat naïve and inexperienced, as is shown by the history of the reform undertaken in 1862. The first conception of this reform undoubtedly originated in the fertile imagination of Eugene Ivanovitch Lamanski. As proof of this, the author may cite a pamphlet which appeared anonymously in 1860, and of which only fifty copies were then issued, and those without authority of the censors—that is to say, in manuscript. "The Causes of the Depreciation of Our Circulating Medium and the Means of Remedying It"—such is the title of this tract, the authorship of which there can be now no reason to conceal. After summing up the various steps taken between 1857 and 1859 to retire a large part of the floating debt, M. Lamanski treats of the reform of the Bank, as he understands it, and of the resumption of specie payments. He thus sets forth and sums up his conclusions upon the subject:

"1. Let his Majesty graciously declare that his government renounces forever the privilege of issuing circulating notes to meet the needs of the Treasury. Extraordinary demands can be met by means of loans in regular form and by the issue of exchequer bills with no legal-tender quality and for short terms.

"2. The bills of credit now in circulation should be replaced by bank notes not bearing interest, and exchangeable for specie on demand.

"3. The right to issue such notes for the whole of Russia, except Poland and Finland, should be granted to the State Bank for twenty-eight years, or until 1890. The Bank should be empowered to issue notes to the full extent of all the circulation retired, whether in the form of bills of credit, outstanding bank notes, or four per cent. specie bills; and in exchange for gold or silver bars or specie, it should be allowed to issue notes to an unlimited extent.

"4. In order that the Bank may have the means of redeeming its bills, let the State turn over to it all the metallic funds now held in its vaults. The other R. 600,000,000 needful to this end should be guaranteed in the following manner: (*a*) One-third (R. 200,000,000) should be supplied to the Bank in the form of R. 10,000,000 of five per cent. State rentes, in denominations of R. 5 of rente (representing a capital of R. 100) and upwards. That sum should be immediately placed at the disposition of the Bank; the Bank should receive: (*b*) an irrevocable credit against the State of R. 200,000,000, which should bear no interest, but be repaid at the rate of one per cent. per year for a hundred years, and the yearly sum of R. 2,000,000 should be annually employed in the redemption of bills of credit; the remaining third should be guaranteed (*c*) by all the public lands, forests, factories, and railroads belonging to the State; the latter should continue to collect the revenue from these sources; but, in case of need, the Bank should be allowed to sell any of the pledged property with the consent of the proper minister, who should in turn be empowered to repurchase the property so sold at the price for which it was pledged. Armed with these guaranties, let the Bank begin immediately the redemption of bills of credit in specie, gold, or silver, and that in the following manner:

"As a starting-point should be taken, not the legal value of the demi-impériale (R. 5.15), but the actual exchange value as measured in paper money. During the whole of 1862, the Bank should exchange the demi-impériale for R. 5.70 in paper; during the first six months of 1863, for R. 5.50, and for R. 5.35 during the last six months; let the exchange value be R. 5.25 for the whole of 1864, and from the beginning of 1865 let the demi-impériale be paid out at its legal value of R. 5.15. During this transition period, which may be abridged if necessary, the Bank should have the right to buy the precious metals at the prices named above.

"5. The Bank should be authorized to sell the R. 200,000,000 of five per cent. rentes to be turned over to it, but only after notifying the Finance Minister of its intention.

"6. The Bank should be separated from the Finance Department, and should be amenable only to the Commission of Credit Institutions, which should be increased by new members named by the Government, the nobility, and commerce. At any time after 1865, the Bank should be allowed to establish a share capital of R. 20,000,000 and have stockholders to that extent. As fast as the capital is paid in, an equal amount of the property pledged by the State should be released. The profits would thus be shared by the State and the stockholders, and that part belonging to the Government would be used to redeem its guaranty given to the Bank. The latter should be compelled to increase the number of its branches to forty within the next fifteen years.

"7. The acceptance of deposits payable on demand should cease immediately; deposits for a definite term should continue to be accepted until 1865, but only from individuals and charitable institutions, not from the State. From July 1, 1862, interest at the rate of one per cent. only should be paid upon outstanding bank bills, and from the beginning of 1863 all interest upon them should cease. To this rule there should be no exception, save in cases where the owner of the bills has parted with them temporarily and is not in a position to present them for redemption. Time deposits should be used for the purchase of mortgage bonds, but only by order and on the responsibility of the Finance Department.

"8. If it should become necessary to increase the circulating medium, the Bank should have a right, six months after the beginning of redemption in specie, to issue R. 20,000,000 of new bills against deposits of short-time bills of exchange.

"9. Inasmuch as the Bank is no longer to accept deposits, savings-banks should be opened in all places where there may be need of them.

"10. Bourses for dealing in public securities should be established in St. Petersburg, Moscow, Odessa, and Riga."

We come now to the conditions under which the return to specie payments was to be accomplished. In pursuance of a ukase of April 14 (26), 1862, a loan of £15,000,000 sterling was placed with the London house of Rothschild, the intention being that the proceeds should be used exclusively to build up the fund reserved for the redemption of bills of credit. On the 25th of the same month, a second ukase ordered that the proceeds of the loan should be devoted to the strengthening of the metallic reserve and to the gradual resumption of specie payments. It was provided in the first of those ukases that "the printing and issuing of the bills of credit shall be done by the State Bank and under its authority, and under no circumstances shall they be issued except in exchange for gold or silver." The outstanding bills were to be redeemed at a gradually increasing valuation, and a notice issued by the Bank, on April 29th, contained the information that, on and after the first of May, the exchange value of the demi-impériale, gold (intrinsic value, R. 5.15), should be R. 5.70, and that of the silver rouble, 110½ copecks; and that, after August 1st, the values should be, respectively, R. 5.60 and 108½ copecks. Thereafter, the valuation was to be as follows:

	Gold Demi-Imp. Roubles.	Silver Rouble. Copecks.
September 1, 1862, . . .	5.56½	108
October 1, " . . .	5.54	107½
November 1, " . . .	5.51	107
December 1, " . . .	5.49	106½
January 1, 1863, . . .	5.46	106
February 1, " . . .	5.43	105½
March 1, " . . .	5.41	105
April 1, " . . .	5.38	104½
May 1, " . . .	5.36	104
June 1, " . . .	5.33	103½
July 1, " . . .	5.30	103

When the redemption began, the Bank had in its coffers R. 79,000,00 and the circulation aggregated R. 722,000,000, of which the Bank held R. 15,000,000. At first, the demand for redemption was small, amounting to only R. 10,037,000 between May 1 and December 31, 1862. This latter date was just on the eve of the Polish insurrection. In April, 1863, the chief European powers intervened by diplomatic notes, and it was well known that Napoleon III. was eager to interfere by force of arms, provided England and Austria should offer him other than mere paper support. Then the metallic resources of the Bank melted like snow. From January to the end of July R. 45,000,000 of gold were withdrawn; and between the 1st and 3d of August the demands amounted to R. 4,405,000. A loan was impossible. The Bank, therefore, resolved to stop paying gold and to continue the redemption only with silver. At the same time, however, it was selling to the public drafts on foreign countries at the same rate at which it had undertaken to redeem its bills. In this way, the proceeds of the Rothschild loan were soon exhausted, though still at the Bank's disposal abroad. On November 1 (13), 1863, the rouble was almost at par (397c.); but it was upon this date that the Bank was forced to suspend the redemption of its paper. It continued the sale of foreign drafts for a few days longer, but this did not prevent the rouble from losing eight per cent. of its value by November 19th; and when on this date the sale of drafts ceased in turn there was a further fall of four per cent., and the rouble was quoted at 350 centimes.

The experiment had failed; and its most obvious result may be summed up thus: On December 1, 1863, the note circulation amounted to R. 642,800,000, of which the Bank held R. 8,000,000 in addition to R. 68,000,000 of specie. Since May 1, 1862, therefore, the note circulation had decreased by R. 79,300,000 and the specie holdings of the Bank by R. 11,000,000. If we take account of the Rothschild loan of R. 96,000,000, the experiment had cost R. 107,000,000 of metal; and as only R. 45,400,000 of the redeemed bills had been destroyed (on June 11, 1863), the net result of the undertaking was an actual loss of R. 62,000,000, not counting the numerous and severe indirect losses attending the failure.

Did this failure arise solely from the Polish insurrection, the public fear of renewed hostilities, and the impossibility of replenishing the metallic reserve by the method outlined in the imperial ukase and M. Lamanski's pamphlet? Such was the official explanation; but the impartial student cannot accept it. One needed simply to be on the ground in order to witness the extreme eagerness with which paper money was presented to the Bank for redemption. The true explanation is that the circulation had been increased almost threefold within less than ten years, and that this increase was not demanded by any commercial or industrial need, but simply by the necessities of the Treasury. Then, again, the Russian Government had made the mistake of issuing in the form of a floating debt what was simply a substitute for note circulation, a proceeding that had been of considerable service to it at times, but which had now become a great burden. Thus, there had been issued in denominations of R. 100 nearly R. 100,000,000 of so-called "metallic bills" drawing interest at four per cent. Exchequer bills had also been issued, of R. 50 each, bearing interest at 4.32 per cent.—that is to say, 18 copecks per month—and redeemable in eight years. These, in view of their small denominations, were simply bills of credit, except that they bore interest. In ordinary times, the capitalist kept them in his safe and the merchant took them readily because the Treasury would accept them in payment of certain taxes. But the moment specie grew scarce these bills circulated just like bank notes, and the only concession made to the taker was that he had the benefit of the one or two months' interest due upon them. Thus the public had ample opportunity to exhaust the metallic reserve of the Bank. Not to have thought of this before issuing the ukase of April, 1862, was one of the most serious mistakes made by the authorities, but it was by no means the only one. Thus the attempt to resume specie payments was a failure in 1863, and no other effort has been made since. It will be our duty hereafter to examine the causes which have made all further efforts in this direction impossible up to the present moment. But first we shall make some further examination of the past, for the history of the Bank of Russia cannot be written except in connection with the financial transactions of the Empire, so close is the connection between them.

It is not merely the ukase of April 14, 1862, decreeing a return to specie payments, that makes that year memorable in the annals of the Russian Bank. The same year signalizes another very important reform. M. de Reutern had been only a few days at the head of the Finance Department when he published the first budget of the Empire. Up to that time nothing of the kind had been known in Russia, and the figures the Author was able to quote in the earlier part of this work, bearing upon the expenses of the years 1823 to 1827, were taken from the memoirs of Count Cancrine. Without casting any reflection upon the memory of M. Reutern (obit 1890), we may say that his first budget did not furnish a full account of the situation; it did not even include all of the national receipts and expenditures. In fact, it was several years before the budget became what it ought to be. A central auditing office for the accounts of the Empire had, it is true, long been in existence, but in a condition calling loudly for reform. This reform was accomplished by Tartarinow* (obit 1871); and since his time the annual publications of that institution are of real value and very helpful to all students of Russian finance. The same may be said of the reports of the Finance Ministers, accompanying the provisory budget at the first of January of each year. But at the time of which we speak there was no publication of this kind, and no information was to be had regarding the state of Russian finance except from the annual report of the Commission of Credit Institutions, and there is no reason now to conceal the fact that that information was very meager in its details. It is hardly more instruc-

* Tartarinow had as successors in office several men of great ability, such for example, as Greig and Abasa, who afterward became Ministers of Finance.

tive to-day; but then it has been a long time since anybody has thought of paying any attention to the tiresome document crammed with figures with which that Commission annually honors the official files. The very precise and accurate reports of which we have just spoken render it altogether superfluous now. But, at the time of which we write, it was the only document giving any information concerning the management of Russian finances, and it could have been made of great value.

The Author has a very distinct recollection of the eagerness with which he pored over the first report of that Commission which fell under his eyes, now thirty-three years ago. It was the "Address of the Finance Minister to the Commission of Credit Institutions, presenting the report of those institutions for the fiscal year 1861." I studied it with the greater ardor because it was part of my duty at that time to write the Russian chapter for the "Annuaire des Finances Publiques," published at Paris by M. J. E. Horn. The more we sought to sound the depths of that document the more signal was our failure. All we could be certain of was that the chapters did not agree with one another and that the report was not true to its title, because it did not show even the whole of the public debt. Russia had a press censorship even at that time; but as the administration seemed desirous of illuminating those places that were in need of light, we made known our difficulties in an article sent to the "Journal de St. Petersburg," of which we were financial correspondent. The Commission condescended to reply in a note which we have preserved, and a translation of which we here present. There can certainly be no indiscretion in publishing it at this late day; and no one will accuse me of egotism, for clearly it caused the Commission no pangs to snub an intermeddler who had dared to call in question the value of an official report read by a minister. But the reader may possibly conclude that as early as 1862 the Commission of Credit Institutions had outlived its usefulness, if, indeed, it ever had any. Here is the official document:

"Observations.—The statement does not pretend to set forth the general financial situation, as M. Horn appears to think, but it is a mere introduction to the very voluminous reports of the credit institutions—reports which are annually printed as soon as the committee appointed by the Council for the purpose has verified their correctness.

"1. The sum of R.716,000,000 makes up the total of the deposits particularly described at the end of the report. As to the sum of R.712,000,000, it consists of the following items:

1. Treasury debt	R.160,017,496
2. Credits extended to the Lombard of St. Petersburg	153,575,872
3. Credits to the former Loan Bank	63,941,148
4. Credits to the Lombard of Moscow	177,136,394
5. Debts owing by the management of public charities	90,786,425
6. Discount of bills of exchange	39,284,198
7. Loans on merchandise	4,415,195
8. Loans on stocks	16,479,340
9. Loans on various interest-bearing securities	6,833,729
Total	R.712,469,797

"The sums named under Nos. 1–5 are to be found under corresponding headings in the report. As to the particulars of the sums under Nos. 6–9, which belong to the business of the State Bank, it was not supposed to be necessary to repeat them, the more especially as all the figures relating to them may be found in the monthly statements of the Bank, and in view of the further fact that the report of all these transactions, which was presented to the Commission of Credit Institutions in May, 1862, is to be published very soon.

"2. In order to estimate the comparison made by the author at its proper value, it should be noted, first of all, that the address delivered by the head of the Finance Department in submitting to the Commission of Credit Institutions the reports of those institutions should not be a mere bookkeeper's statement, and that it does not set forth any figures or facts except those of the first importance relating to the business of the fiscal year. It is for this reason that the foreign publications named by the author cannot serve as a model for the address in question, and are to be compared only with the reports of the Sinking Fund Commission and other credit institutions.

"3. It is not proper to place in the same category the loans which go to make up the State debt and the liabilities of credit institutions arising out of interest-bearing deposits. State loans, properly so called, differ widely from deposits with the Bank, both as to their origin and as to the manner of repayment. Being contracted to meet Government needs, the loans are repaid in annual installments which are a charge upon the State budget; whereas the liabilities merely guaranteed by the Treasury are covered by enforceable obligations, and the guaranty is altogether nominal, because the income of the credit institutions is sufficient, and more than sufficient, to pay their debts, principal and interest, and no part of them is charged against the budget. It should be evident, therefore, that the fusion of these two accounts, so totally different, while it might be of some statistical interest, could produce no result of any practical value.

"4. The total of the bills of credit in circulation is not omitted from the report. It appears therein stated at R.713,000,000. It should be observed that in citing the bills in circulation as a State debt our author ought to have taken account of the reserve fund, amounting on January 1, 1862, to about R. 98,000,000.

"5. That part of the circulation which consists of exchequer bills has no proper place in the document in question, because the aim of the report is simply to set forth the transactions of the credit institutions, and not those of the Treasury. Moreover, the introduction to the report (sections 1 and 2) does state the amount of exchequer bills recently issued, in order to bring to the attention of the Commission of Credit Institutions the fact of their issue.

"6. The amount of so-called metallic 4 per cent. bank bills issued in 1861 is R.36,000,000, as appears from a *résumé* of the report of the State Bank recently issued. Besides, the issue of these bills to the extent named had already been announced in a report of the Finance Minister made in October, 1861.

"7. The public must not expect to find complete and detailed information as to the financial situation of the whole Empire in a document which is simply a succinct abridgment of the reports of the credit institutions alone; and the whole financial situation is not to be thoroughly grasped except by a conscientious study of the full reports of those institutions and of the State budget as well."

As we have said, the reports of the Commission and the Commission itself have now merely an archæological value. The State Bank is the only institution that interests us at this time, and it has learned to put its reports in a form which is not only intelligible but has almost the precision of a mercantile balance-sheet. This it has succeeded in doing in spite of the complicated network, interweaving its own operations with those of the State and detracting greatly from the simplicity of its accounts. But, in 1862, the Commission might have made its reports of great value if it had not, as its note shows, considered it beneath its dignity to satisfy the curiosity of the public and its desire to know the truth about Russian finance.

It is true that, at the time we are now considering, publicity as to the Bank's transactions had not been attended with flattering success; and the failure that crowned the work of 1862 almost seemed to justify the secretive policy of the Public Debt Commission. Rarely has there been a more disastrous failure or keener disappointment than was involved in the closing of the Bank's wickets on November 3, 1863. It was followed not only by a steady depreciation of the rouble, but by a permanent Treasury deficit, so that several loans became necessary between 1863 and 1866. In 1864, a loan was floated in Holland of 70,000,000 florins, or £6,000,000 sterling; and in 1864 and 1866 domestic loans of R. 100,000,000 each, on lottery and premium bonds. Meanwhile, exchequer bills were increased by R. 99,000,000, issued in thirty-three series of R. 3,000,000 each. The credit of the Empire did not improve, and the reader can get some idea of the opinion foreigners had of the situation by glancing over these few lines from an article which appeared in the "Berliner Reform" of September 24, 1865: "Anyone who examines the situation in this country (Russia) must be forcibly struck with its financial and economic condition. That condition is immeasurably sad, not to say hopeless. Paper money is depreciated by one-fifth, despite its legal-tender value; gold and silver have disappeared; there is practically no credit; discount rates are high; there is an annual deficit; trade is nearly at a standstill, and capital is exhausted almost to the last penny; prices are immoderately high; the nobility is ruined, the capital city and trade centers are in visible decay."

Meanwhile, the State Bank had ceased to be the sole credit institution of the vast Empire. In 1865, a group of capitalists had obtained permission to establish at St. Petersburg the joint-stock "Bank of Commerce" (such is its title still), with a capital of R. 5,000,000 in shares of R. 250 each. The people were so unaccustomed to rashness of this kind that the State was compelled to encourage the enterprise by taking shares for R. 1,000,000, agreeing not to sell them for ten years. But very soon the public became more courageous, and in a few years St. Petersburg and other cities had a large number of these share banks. In fact, that class of banks became so numerous that, in 1873, the State considered it to be its duty to check the movement; it refused to charter any more banks for the capital, the result being simply that, in order to get around this obstacle, banks were set up in the little towns nearby, such as Viborg and Cronstadt, with branches in St. Petersburg.

But, two other palliatives had been found for the State Bank's inability to satisfy the needs of credit. One of these had been, if not exactly created, at least actively promoted by the State. M. de Reutern had hardly been installed in his office before he had a law enacted for the establishment of communal banks. Any commune furnishing a capital of R. 10,000 could found a bank, with ample powers in all directions, except as to the issue of notes. The great partiality that Russia has always had for the *Mir* (municipal autonomy), and the hostility in certain quarters to enterprises in which shareholders pocket all the profits, made this ukase very popular. It was useless to point out the fact that a commune or city is, of all corporate bodies, the one least fitted for banking affairs, that its responsibility is illusory, and fraud inevitable; in spite of conservative protest and warning, these banks sprang up on all sides. A fair sample of them was that at Skopine. To the bank in that little city of the province of Riasan, deposits flowed in from all parts of the Empire, the inducement being a promise of interest at the rate of six or seven per cent. The Mayor (*Golova*), M. Rykow, had become an extremely popular man. He devoted a liberal share of the bank's profits to public improvements and works of charity. His annual reports and his appeals to the public were perfect gems of puffery. Rykow knew how to realize upon his merits, and his breast was soon covered with decorations. When at last the Government awoke to the danger and amended the law so that a communal bank could not accept deposits exceeding ten times its capital and reserve fund, the bank of Skopine went right ahead with its business and its public appeals, declaring ingeniously that a law could have no retroactive effect and that the new restriction affected only such banks as should be thereafter established. One day, however, about 1875, the bubble burst; Skopine could not pay its deposits, then amounting to about R.7,000,000. There were disgraceful revelations as to the way in which the money had been spent, and Rykow was condemned to Siberian exile. Government agents were appointed to investigate the business of communal banks, and since then their transactions have been merely local. Further on will be found their balance-sheet for 1893.

Another new form of institution was to some extent a result of the great conflagration which, in the spring of 1862, had destroyed the greater part of the Tchoukine-Dvor of St. Petersburg, which may be called the little bazaar, as distinguished from the Gostinoi-Dvor, or great bazaar. The merchants affected by that disaster had need of credit, and the State Bank, the only banking institution then in existence, could not supply it, because its regulations required three signatures on all paper. In this juncture of affairs, M. Lamanski, then vice-president of the Bank, conceived the idea of founding, upon the model of the Société Général of Belgium, an association in which mutuality should be the controlling principle. It took him more than a year to find two men willing to subscribe an amount which should represent the maximum of their credit at the proposed bank, and to pay in ten per cent. of it. Evidently this was to be an association of very small importance; it was, in fact, so unassuming that its offices were established in one room of the State Bank, where M. Lamanski managed its affairs with the purest disinterestedness. Yet, five years later, that association controlled the fluctuations of the St. Petersburg Bourse, and indirectly, those of all Russia. Instead of confining itself to the discounting of its clients' paper, it had begun to loan upon public funds, and as it was always able to rediscount its paper at the State Bank, thanks to the common management of the two institutions, this financial conspiracy had promptly led to an excess of speculation, resulting in 1869 in a serious crisis upon the Bourse, of which the independent bank, the only one then in existence, had to bear its part. Both institutions escaped from the crisis in safety, but there was a serious run upon both of them as a result of it—one upon the Bank in 1872, which imperiled its existence and which for nearly twenty years, or until 1890, kept its stock among the lowest of those quoted on the Bourse; and another upon the Mutual Association in 1875, which compelled it to levy an assessment upon its members, then numbering more than seven thousand. Many of the members retired from membership; nevertheless, the association survived the disaster it had brought upon itself, and returned the assessment to its members; but it never recovered the commanding position it had previously held. We shall see later on that the association is still in existence and that it has had a number of imitators in the provinces. But the enthusiasm for that form of association was exhausted after a short trial.

The attempt of the State Bank to resume specie payments having failed once (in 1863), no further effort in that direction had been made; but it must not be inferred that the Bank had altogether abandoned the idea of final resumption. Beginning with 1867, railroad charters, with or without a State guaranty of interest on the bonds, were granted with considerable frequency. At that time, a guaranty of interest was regarded as a purely formal matter, tending to further the enterprise, but not likely to become a burden on the public treasury, and the State was not niggardly in such patronage. Generally its guaranty covered only the bonds, which formed two-thirds of the nominal capital, and which were made payable in specie that they might meet with a readier sale abroad. As to the capital represented by stock, it usually served some other purpose than construction of the road or the purchase of materials. The fewer the calls upon the stock for aid in building the line, the more urgent the necessity for selling the bonds at whatever price they would bring, and a foreign market was found for them, especially in Germany. Finally, the Finance Minister took alarm at this state of things. Five per cent. bonds guaranteed by the State were as good as Russian rentes, and the sale of the latter was greatly impaired by the competition arising from the sale by the railroad companies of guaranteed bonds. For this reason it was determined that the State itself should issue the bonds and pay the proceeds to the companies; and, as the major part of the sums borrowed was to be used in Russia for construction and materials, the Government paid the companies in paper money at prevailing rates and used the specie for its own purposes. Part of it was used in making foreign purchases and in payment of interest on the public debt abroad, and part of it went to swell the metallic hoards in the vaults of the fortress of Peter and Paul in St. Petersburg. This is the explanation of the seven consolidated railroad loans, each of £15,000,000 sterling, made between 1868 and 1875; and it was by this means that the metallic reserve, which we found to be only R. 69,000,000 at the close of 1863, had reached R. 229,400,000 in 1875, of which R. 28,300,000 were in silver, the gold having amounted to

R. 126,900,000 at the close of 1869, to R. 128,500,000 at the close of 1870, and to R. 175,600,000 at the close of 1872. The value of the paper rouble (the rate of exchange), which in 1866 had gone as low as 270 centimes, had advanced again to 370, notwithstanding the fact that the circulation during the whole of 1875 had been R. 797,300,000, or nearly three and a half times the metallic reserve. Confidence had returned. The budget no longer showed a deficit, and M. de Reutern, at the end of twelve years of power, was on the point of bringing exchange once more to par and resuming specie payments. The State Bank was already selling silver and gold at current rates. During the years 1873–5, when the first effects of silver depreciation following Germany's adoption of the gold standard were felt, the Bank was even compelled to defend itself against attempts that were made to deliver silver to it at the value hitherto officially maintained.

CHAPTER IV.

THE EASTERN WAR PERIOD.

Further Increase of the Circulation—Reduction of the Circulation Attempted but Fails—Refunding Operations—So-called Temporary Issues—New Regulations of the Bank—Increase of State Bank Capital from R. 15,000,000 to R. 50,000,000—A Monometallic Symptom—Metallic Resources of the Bank—Report of the Council of State—Agreement with the Bank of France—Charges upon Deposits.

AT the period reached at the close of the last chapter, there appeared to have been a recovery in all respects from the disaster of 1863, when the revolution in Bosnia, the Servian war, and, finally, the Russian campaigns of 1877–8 in the East, once more brought to naught the whole splendid prospect. When the war was at an end the metallic reserve of the Bank (July 1, 1878) was only R. 130,300,000 gold and R. 17,500,000 silver. The circulation had been reduced to R. 726,900,000; but, in addition to this, there was an issue of R. 429,600,000 appearing under the misleading title of "bills issued on account of the branch banks." In fact, the Treasury had used up that sum during the war, and, in addition to this, three large loans, known as "Oriental loans," had been made, aggregating about R. 700,000,000. Professor Wagner had at this time very charitably urged Russia to part with the gold lying unused in the vaults—gold, as he said, being the proper money for States with an established credit. This advice of the learned German was not followed, but it was ten years before Russia's metallic treasure had again reached the figure of 1875.

No new taxes had been levied to meet the expenses of the last Eastern war. There was a desire not to make the war unpopular, and it had been expected that the campaign would be short and decisive. All attempts of M. de Reutern to persuade the Imperial Council to sanction a levy of additional taxes had been fruitless. The only concession he had been able to get was a ukase issued in November, 1876, directing the payment of customs duties in gold. When that step was taken it amounted to an increase of only 12 to 15 per cent. in the paper cost of imports, but later, owing to fluctuations in the exchange rate, the increase rose to 40 or 60 per cent. It is true, however, that between 1877 and 1887 the specie thus secured was of great assistance to the State.

There was less opposition to an increase of taxation when the war was over. That unpopular duty devolved upon General Greig, who had succeeded M. de Reutern on the very day the treaty of Berlin was signed, July 1st (13th). As to the State Bank, it could obtain no help, nor could it do anything alone toward reducing the circulation to its volume on the eve of the war. It was not until January 1, 1881, that an imperial decree, issued at the instance of M. Abasa, who had succeeded M. Greig in August, 1880, prescribed a series of measures having that end in view. The R. 417,000,000 of bills of credit issued for the purposes of the war were to be retired within eight years, R. 17,000,000 immediately and the remainder at the rate of R. 50,000,000 per year, and the State was to supply the Bank with the funds necessary for this purpose. This arrangement was only partially carried out. Though there have been no other wars, and the only military operations called for have been those, relatively inexpensive, required in Central Asia between 1880 and 1886, still the international situation in Europe has necessitated heavy expenses, which M. de Bunge, who succeeded M. Abasa in 1881, found it difficult to meet. When he quitted the post at the close of 1886, the value of the rouble was 60⅔ copecks in gold. The provisions of the ukase of January 1, 1881, were modified by a second ukase of December 9, 1894. The latter states that of the R. 417,000,000 of paper money to be retired, R. 87,000,000 had been destroyed; R. 63,750,000 had been transferred from the account of temporary issues to that guaranteed by the fund available for redemption, which, meanwhile, had been increased by R. 40,000,000 of gold taken from the funds of the Bank proper—that is, from the proceeds of its commercial transactions; that R. 92,750,000 had been retained under the heading of provisional issues, and were offset by the amounts due the Bank from its customers, and that the remaining R. 173,500,000 had been covered by rentes delivered to the Bank, upon which it had not yet realized. The important fact is that only R. 87,000,000 had been destroyed. By this ukase, then, it was ordered that the R. 266,250,000 (R. 92,750,000 + R. 173,500,000) should remain permanently part of the circulation; we have just seen that R. 63,750,000 had previously been disposed of in the same way.

Here we must take a momentary glance at the past for the purpose of noting that in spite of the delicate position of international relations, in spite of the fact that the Bank of Germany and the Seehandlung of Berlin were forbidden to loan on Russian securities or purchase them, in spite of the increase of military expenses and other public charges in all countries, a remarkable phenomenon had appeared in the markets of all European capitals; the price of silver had fallen everywhere, and this had produced a favorable effect upon the credit of the various governments. Refunding operations became fashionable, and M. de Bunge himself, about a year before quitting his place, had been on the point of concluding an extensive arrangement with certain German houses which would have resulted in reducing to four per cent. the interest upon a large part of the Russian public debt, and that, too, barely two years after it had been somewhat difficult to find a foreign market for a loan of R. 50,000,000 at six per cent. We may note in passing that that loan, so uncomplimentary to the credit of a great empire, was the last transaction managed by Baron Stieglitz, who retired from the management of the Bank in 1866. The refunding operation undertaken by M. de Bunge did not succeed, but no one can regret its failure who knows the burdensome, not to say humiliating conditions under which it was to have been made. His successor, M. Wyschnegradski, was a man of a totally different character. Though formerly a professor, like Bunge, he had for some years been in control of important enterprises, and had thus acquired, what had been entirely lacking in his predecessor, the art of managing men and conducting business affairs, boldness of decision and rapidity of execution. He had, in addition, the good fortune to be at the head of affairs during four years of very abundant crops and of an export of cereals such as had never been known before. He entered immediately upon the task of refunding the debt, and he was able to interest the French market in the undertaking, though it had up to that time avoided Russian securities almost entirely. He began with the pledge certificates of the Mutual Credit Foncier, which the State had finally guaranteed, and the interest on which had been reduced from 5 to 4½ per cent. at the same time that the premium of R. 20 secured upon their repayment had been withdrawn. Inasmuch as the Rothschilds had taken part in the issue of these securities, they were called upon to assist in this first conversion, and since then they have had a share in other refunding operations which M. Wyschnegradski carried on upon a large scale, and which his successor, M. de Witte, afterward took up and is still carrying forward. It is not merely loans issued directly by the State that form the subject of the refunding operations; besides the securities of the Mutual Credit Foncier, of which we have just spoken, railroad bonds also were included. During the past ten years, and especially between 1888 and 1894, the State has bought a large number of important railways, and has very materially reduced the burdens imposed upon it by the payment of subsidies and the guaranty of interest.

The subject of these refunding operations will be more fully treated in a subsequent chapter. What especially interests us just now with reference to them is their influence upon the condition of the Russian Bank. We have just seen what disposition was finally made of the circulation called into existence by the Eastern war of 1877-8. Notwithstanding the fact that only R. 87,000,000 of the R. 417,000,000 so issued had been paid, there came a time in 1889 when, as a result of the very great increase of exportation coincident with the fair of Nijni-Novgorod, the circulation was for the moment insufficient. M. Wyschnegradski had no hesitancy in authorizing the Bank to make a supplementary issue of R. 25,000,000; but he stipulated that the Treasury should deposit with the Bank a like sum in gold as a guaranty. A second issue of R. 25,000,000 was afterward approved upon the same terms; and it should be stated that these issues were in fact only temporary and were retired at the end of a few months. As a practical matter, the specie deposit carried from the Treasury to the Bank was of no avail. The holders of the "provisional" bills had not, any more than holders of ordinary bills, a right to demand their redemption in gold. The most important result of that temporary measure was that circumstances soon induced M. Wyschnegradski to repeat and extend it; when the famine of 1891 required exceptional sacrifices of the Treasury, the so-called temporary issue was several times doubled and even trebled, so that at times it reached R. 150,000,000; but the credit of Russia was not seriously impaired thereby. Thanks to the prompt recovery from the economic crisis of 1891, and to the boldness with which M. de Witte, the successor of M. Wyschnegradski, has continued the refunding operations; thanks also to the constant decrease of interest rates in the money markets of the world, the Russian rente stands to-day at a figure which, six years ago, the most optimistic hardly dared to hope for.

Inasmuch as the present system plainly consists in intrusting to the State the largest possible share in the economic affairs of the people, the regulations of the Bank were revised on June 24, 1894, and made even more emphatic in the direction indicated. We shall merely cite such of these modifications as are peculiarly characteristic of the new methods. In the first place, in addition to commerce and manufactures, the agricultural classes also are to share the favor of the Bank. Chapter II of the law treating of commercial operations provides in Art. 77 that the Bank shall accept for discount "not only paper resting upon a commercial basis (a completed transaction, paper already in existence), but also paper drawn in view of commercial or industrial transactions yet to be entered into." As an offset, however, to this privilege, it is stipulated in Art. 85 that "the Bank may at any time demand of its clients a detailed balance-sheet, a complete account of their affairs, and such extracts from their books and other information as may be needful to give it a full insight into all their transactions." Art. 89, treating of manufacturing and agricultural loans, provides that the Bank "shall give credit and make loans upon such bills drawn to order as may be secured: (*a*) by a real-estate mortgage; (*b*) by a chattel mortgage upon agricultural or manufacturing tools and machinery; (*c*) by a guarantor; (*d*) by any other security which the Finance Minister may hold to be sufficient." Art. 93 prescribes that when the loan is secured by new machinery the Bank shall pay the amount of the loan, not to the borrower, but to the seller of the machinery, and shall see that the purchase is delivered. Art. 97—Loans to any single enterprise shall not exceed R. 500,000, and those to a small tradesman shall not exceed R. 600. Art. 100 provides that loans and credits (upon one-name paper) intended to provide any undertaking with money for current needs, shall not exceed seventy-five per cent. of the sum necessary for the financing of the business. Art. 119 stipulates that when the value of any class of merchandise shall have decreased as the result of exceptional circumstances, the managers of the Bank may grant an extension to the debtor and may refrain from demanding even partial payment or additional security. Art. 124 states that in making advances upon paper bearing only one signature and secured by a pledge of personal property, the Bank, if it has full confidence in the borrower, may allow these concessions: (*a*) it may accept as collateral articles of merchandise not named in the official list set forth in Art. 109; (*b*) the pledge may remain in the hands of the borrower; (*c*) the amount of the loan may be as great as seventy-five per cent. of the estimated value of the guaranty. Art. 135 permits call loans to be made, either on collateral securities or on such paper as would be accepted for discount. The conditions of these loans are that the borrower shall repay them at any moment on demand, or else at a fixed time. Art. 138 provides that, at any time when its resources are sufficient, the Bank may extend its credit to provinces, districts, and communes, upon conditions to be approved by the Ministers of Finance and of the Interior. In accordance with Articles 165–8, the Bank may sell bills drawn to order, may buy and sell foreign bills of exchange, gold and silver, securities issued by the State or guaranteed by it, and securities not so guaranteed if they form part of the collateral of one who has defaulted in his obligations to the State; this latter transaction the Bank enters into only upon express instructions from the Minister of Finance. Articles 178 and 179 set forth the services which the Bank is required to render to the public treasury. There is no change in this respect from the original regulations, which have already been set before the reader; we shall not, therefore, repeat the provisions of those sections. Suffice it to say that in addition to all the duties pertaining to the circulation, to the issue of loans, and to the care of the funds of the State, the Bank is required to furnish such sums as the national pawn-offices may need; to assist in caring for the ransom of the serfs—that is to say, in administering the annuities owing by these peasants; and to liquidate the affairs of the former credit institutions of the State, in so far as this duty rests upon it under existing laws. When we have called attention to the fact that "the capital" of the Bank has been increased from R. 15,000,000 to R. 50,000,000 we shall have set forth the whole series of reforms to which that institution has been subjected. At this point, we may introduce the last balance-sheet issued by the Bank, that of August 16 (28), 1895:

Balance-Sheet of the Bank of Russia and of Its Nine Agencies and Ninety-eight Branches, August 16, 1895.

I.—Exchange Fund and Credit Bills.

ASSETS.

	Roubles.
1. Cash on hand:	
Gold at nominal price	375,000,000
Silver	....
2. Open account of the Treasury for bills of credit	671,281,634
3. Gold at nominal price as guaranty for temporary issue of bills of credit (imperial ukase of July 28, 1891)	75,000,000
Total	1,121,281,634

LIABILITIES.

1. Bills of credit in circulation	1,046,281,634
2. Bills of credit issued temporarily by imperial ukase of July 28, 1891	75,000,000
Total	1,121,281,634

II.—Commercial Transactions.

ASSETS.

	August 1. *Roubles.*	August 16. *Roubles.*
1. On hand:		
a. Bills of credit	74,059,289.00	67,598,048.00
b. Gold and silver	63,218,608.37	....
c. Silver, full weight and standard	....	5,448,513.75
d. Subsidiary coin	5,395,070.35½	5,251,833.78¾
Total	142,672,967.72½	78,298,395.53¾
2. Bills discounted	172,474,883.80	174,462,445.51
3. Advances on special account, secured by bills	15,733,647.50	16,598,521.72
4. Advances on special acct., secured by public funds.	18,457,090.12¾	18,146,960.63¼
5. Advances on special acct., secured by merchandise.	169,047.29	169,047.29
6. Advances on merchandise	27,875,839.94	28,471,539.94
7. Advances on public funds	28,368,272.28½	28,228,636.69½
8. Advances on stocks and bonds	4,794,808.00	4,761,736.00
9. Advances to owners of rural estates (law of Jan. 24, 1884)	27,274,315.26	27,661,372.26
10. Advances to manufacturers	5,048,101.78	5,274,101.78
11. Amounts remitted the Lombard of St. Petersburg for loans on pawn	3,065,000.00	3,100,000.00
12. Amounts remitted the Lombard of Moscow for loans on pawn	1,471,000.00	1,470,000.00
13. Unpaid bills	792,641.42	823,216.42
14. Public securities belonging to the Bank	39,724,344.03	43,059,962.82
15. Public securities bought on order	460,572.53	298,607.46
16. Gold belonging to the Bank	....	62,965,902.57
17. Administrative and other expenses of the Bank and the branches	69,082,329.93¼	69,641,459.55¼
18. Account of the Bank with its agencies and branches.	58,168,236.55½	58,599,516.92¾

	August 1. Roubles.	August 16. Roubles.
19. Amounts abroad	20,309,769.09	20,946,473.90½
20. Premium on the gold taken out of the general funds and held in reserve, together with the exchange fund as a special guaranty for the credit bills issued temporarily by virtue of the imperial ukase of July 28, 1891	25,860,000.00	25,860,000.00
Total	661,802,867.26½	668,837,897.02

LIABILITIES.

	Roubles.	Roubles.
1. Capital stock	50,000,000.00	50,000,000.00
2. Reserve	3,000,000.00	3,000,000.00
3. Capital designed for the construction of buildings for branches of the Bank	495,066.07	495,066.07
4. Deposits at interest on time	34,346,675.58	34,317,575.58
5. At sight	92,264,395.13¼	89,247,383.29½
6. Accounts current:		
a. Of State establishments, private institutions, private banks, and individuals	137,818,293.49½	138,506,668.50¼
b. Of the Treasury Department	72,884,452.03	73,360,205.79
c. Of local treasuries, on account of State revenue	22,016,698.72	23,208,840.74
d. Of local treasuries on account of deposits	153,608,431.14½	157,648,907.79½
e. *Des sommes des opérations*	8,489,268.51¾	8,812,749.13½
7. Transitory amounts	25,628,430.45½	25,604,821.34¼
8. Promissory notes and telegrams	106,471.58	106,471.58
9. Accounts of the agencies & branches with the Bank	31,750,000.00	34,580,000.00
10. Interest collected on transactions of 1895	13,774,985.46½	14,329,508.11½
11. Net profits for 1893	4,877,227.04¼	4,877,227.04¼
12. Profit and loss for 1894	10,742,472.03¼	10,742,472.03¼
Total	661,802,867.26½	668,837,897.02

Besides deposits for safe-keeping :—

	Roubles.
a. Belonging to individuals and private institutions on August 16, 1895 :	
Gold and silver as valued by depositors	8,455,170.89
Deeds and documents	1,315,280,447.33¾
b. Gold and silver belonging to the Treasury at its nominal value	115,852,416.95
c. Public securities for collection at their face value	2,233,595.94
d. Coin held as a guaranty for the payment of the Bank's due-bills	209,403.50

THE GOVERNOR OF THE STATE BANK : ED. PLESKE.

It appears from this balance-sheet that, at the time it was issued, the circulation amounted to R. 1,121,300,000 (R. 75,000,000 being "temporary") and the metallic reserve to R. 450,000,000 of gold, R. 75,000,000 of this also being a temporary reserve. If we subtract this R. 75,000,000 from both sides of the account we have left R. 1,046,300,000 of paper money secured by R. 375,000,000 of gold. Moreover, the Bank included under "cash," on August 1 (13), R. 63,200,000 of gold and silver. Fifteen days later, that important sum no longer appears among the "cash," but we find it a little further on under the heading "Gold belonging to the Bank," which amounts to nearly R. 63,000,000. We cannot explain that change in the entry; but a comparison of the two totals will show that silver made up only about R. 250,000 in the first column, while it does not appear at all in the second. This shows that Russia has turned her face resolutely against bimetallism and that she accords to silver no higher position than that of a subsidiary coinage; a fact, moreover, which has been officially declared.

In view of the summary of the Bank's new regulations which has just been placed before the reader, it would be useless to insist further upon the extent to which the affairs of the Bank and those of the State are intermingled, an intermingling more definite and pronounced than that existing under the regulations of 1860. It is more difficult than ever to understand why a capital stock should be thought necessary, or what place the capital of R. 50,000,000 provided by the new regulations can have in the economy of the Bank. But it is precisely because these intimate relations do exist that the value of the circulation cannot be predicated upon the relation it bears to the cash of the Bank. The State is responsible to-day, as it was thirty-five years ago, as it was also a century ago, for all the agreements of the Bank; and because this is so it becomes important to know that the metallic resources of the Treasury (including those of the Bank) amounted at the close of 1892 to R. 493,900,000; at the close of 1893 to R. 598,000,000, and at the close of 1894 to R. 598,600,000, in gold. On June 30 (July 12), 1895, the "Bulletin Russe de Statistique Financière" published a table showing that, on that date, the total metallic reserve amounted to R. 580,800,000, of which R. 4,666,000 were in silver and subsidiary coin, and the remainder in gold. Upon the strength of such a reserve, equal to more than half of the circulation, the Russian Government has deemed it safe not to insist upon a rigid enforcement of the legal-tender law, and it has given its sanction to the transaction of domestic business upon a gold basis. When it was first proposed, this measure aroused strong opposition. Though discussed at frequent intervals for some years, it was always vigorously resented as an attack upon the credit of the State, or rather upon the fiction that this credit was undisputed within the Empire and that foreigners alone evinced any doubts of Russia's solvency by refusing to accept the paper rouble at its nominal value. M. de Witte (Finance Minister since 1893) was courageous enough to dissent from that Jesuitical position; but even he was desirous of stopping half-way and of granting the right to deal upon a gold basis only to certain classes of society; his view was like that held in some other countries, where certain classes are denied the privilege of dealing upon the Bourse or making time contracts, lest advantage be taken of their ignorance. It is very interesting to follow the Council of the State as it discusses the question, settles it in a very enlightened manner, refutes the apprehensions of the Finance Minister, and finally determines that its own deliberations upon the matter are of sufficient importance to be given to the public, an occurrence which is very rare in Russia. As this report teaches a valuable lesson and also furnishes one of those rare instances in which we are able to take the measure of the Council, it has seemed to us advisable to publish the document just as it appeared:

"By the terms of the laws now in force (Art. 1540 of the Civil Code and Art. 71 of the statute concerning bills of exchange) all accounts, agreements, and transactions of every kind, both those among individuals and those between individuals and the State, must be settled in silver coin, with the understanding, however, that in settling domestic transactions credit-roubles cannot be refused if they are offered instead of silver or gold roubles. These laws, together with several reasons of an economic nature, have resulted, since the Treasury has ceased to cash bills of credit on demand, in the gradual disappearance of coin from circulation. Serious difficulties have followed upon the exclusive use of paper currency thus brought about. To obviate these, the Ministry of Finance has presented to the Council of the Empire a project the object of which is:

"1. To authorize the use of Russian gold coin in all payments when both parties to the contract agree, and to allow all persons, with the exception of the peasantry and the lower order of tradespeople (non-privileged inhabitants of the country and the towns), to contract engagements specifically in gold roubles, with the understanding always that debtors shall be allowed to make payment in paper money at the valuation existing on the day of payment; which, if there is any dispute, shall be taken to be that of the St. Petersburg Bourse; but the State Bank must pay its gold deposits in gold.

"2. To empower the Minister of Finance to authorize certain taxes, namely, excise duties (indirect taxes), license fees and transfer duties, to be paid in gold, at the current rate, in localities where he may deem it expedient, and to fix the valuation at which gold shall be received and paid out by the Government treasuries; provided, however, that public notice shall be given of the valuation thus established, and that it shall also be telegraphed to the respective treasuries and shall become immediately effective.

"During the discussion of that proposition at a session of the various departments of the Council of the Empire, Privy Councillor De Witte showed that the palpable defects of our present inconvertible paper currency have inspired in all those successively intrusted with the direction of Russian finances a desire to change that system and gradually to adopt a metallic currency. With that end in view, several steps have been taken during the last two reigns (such as the collection of customs duties in gold, the proposed restriction in 1881 of the issue of credit bills, etc.) tending to prepare the ground for the re-establishment of a metallic currency. The proposition now brought forward belongs in the same category. It does not in any manner affect the fundamental basis of our monetary system; nor does it furnish any ground upon which to predicate the adoption of a gold standard, or commit the State to any particular method of redeeming the bills now outstanding. Its object is far less pretentious, being simply to facilitate the circulation of gold, which, so to speak, has now no right-of-way among us, and almost all of which, despite our own large production, finds its way abroad. Thus it promises an effective remedy for one of the principal vices of note circulation, its lack of elasticity. It is well known that, in countries having a metallic circulation, the supply of money always answers almost exactly to the demand; if money is scarce, its value increases, and this causes the metal of other countries to flow in; if, on the contrary, there is an over-supply, the consequent depreciation drives the metal to foreign markets, where it has more value. Very different is the situation in countries in which paper is the only currency. When the demand increases in such countries, there are no importations of specie to bring the circulating medium to the required volume, because specie forms no part of their circulation. This explains why the periodical need of increased circulation in Russia, for the purpose of moving the crops, cannot be met by means of gold brought from abroad, and why trade and industry have no other resource in such cases than the State Bank, that reservoir into which are poured all the bills not demanded by current needs. In view of the Bank's inability to defend its stock of bills by raising the rate of discount, these extraordinary demands place it in a difficult position even in normal years, exhausting its notes and interrupting its ordinary course of business. When a demand arises which is at all exceptional, the Financial Department of the Government is compelled to have recourse to new issues of bills of credit, secured by gold deposits, notwithstanding the disadvantages of such a measure. Although these issues are called 'temporary,' their withdrawal presents such serious difficulties that of the R. 200,000,000 so issued in 1891, 1892, and 1893, only R. 125,000,000 have been canceled and R. 75,000,000 are still outstanding. The legalizing of contracts expressed in gold roubles aims, first of all, to put a stop to that abnormal situation, which retards the economic improvement of the country. There is reason to hope that, when our domestic markets demand unusual quantities of a circulating medium, the fact that gold coin can be used as an instrument of exchange will attract foreign gold and will thus absolve the Government from the necessity of making new issues of bills. But even if this result should not follow in the beginning, the demand for increased circulation might be met either by putting out the gold belonging to the Bank or the Treasury—a thing which is not now possible because gold coin is not recognized as a legal form of circulating medium—or by issuing special deposit receipts expressed in gold roubles, which the Bank would be required to redeem in gold at sight. Thus the power to use gold in business transactions would give to our circulation the elasticity it lacks. Besides, that measure, by removing difficulties which are now inevitable, could hardly fail to attract foreign capital to us. Finally, it will bring our financial system into better repute abroad, where the efforts made by the Government to improve its circulating medium will be appreciated at their full value, and this result alone makes the project worthy of serious consideration.

"As for the fears aroused by the proposal to legalize gold contracts, they may be dismissed as altogether unfounded. In view of the fact that all questions relating to the circulating medium are highly technical and involved, so that many persons of education know little about them and the masses still less, this suggestion of possible distrust is likely to be a subject of dread and to give rise to unfounded comments. Such lack of confidence as there may be in the Government's position upon this question will arise from a familiarity with the existing state of things and from a vague fear of the unknown consequences that may wait upon a change. These are the only grounds for the public apprehensions arising out of such hints as the press has given of the Government's intention to authorize the circulation of gold. Nevertheless, the very fact that the proposal has aroused such fears among those who will determine to a very large extent the public attitude toward the law, renders it necessary that great care be used in fixing upon the exact terms of the enactment. Everything must be kept out of it which is not absolutely necessary to the end proposed, or which is likely to be misinterpreted. For this reason it would be well to omit the provision authorizing payments to be made by mutual consent in Russian gold coin at the current rate of valuation. There is no legal objection to such payments now, and a law authorizing what is not forbidden might very easily give rise to misunderstandings and to a false interpretation of the end in view. Again, authority to stipulate for payment in Russian gold should be limited to written contracts, which alone are of any real importance in view of our present object; then, after such contracts have become common, verbal agreements calling for payments in gold will follow without any special authorization, in all cases in which there may be any call for them. In the next place, only those taxes should be allowed to be paid in gold which fall upon persons who, from the nature of their business, will readily become accustomed to this form of payment; for this reason the measure should, in the first instance, be made applicable only to the payment of excise duties. Finally, that part of the plan which proposes to authorize the various public treasuries to pay in gold must be abandoned altogether, that there may be no ground for a supposition that the Government is taking advantage of the privilege to pay its debts at a rate of exchange fixed by itself and unfair to its creditors. These amendments being made, there is reason to expect that the proposed measure will not be received with disfavor by the public, and that its beneficent effects will become manifest in the near future to the full extent now hoped for.

"The departments regard the question from a double point of view. In the first place, they see in the proposed measure a possible prelude to further legislation looking to the reorganization of our monetary system, and they can appreciate it as an integral part of such reorganization. But the proposition is of such a character that it may equally be regarded as an isolated measure, having its own aim, and not in any way foreshadowing future action. From this second point of view the discussion of the measure must turn upon the results it may be expected to produce in and of itself; we must seek to learn whether it will answer the end proposed, what are its strong and its weak points, and under what conditions it will attain the highest measure of success.

"It appears from the explanations offered by Privy Councillor De Witte that the proposed measure must not be taken as in any way indicative of the final direction of our financial policy regarding the circulation. The departments find that position well taken, for it thus becomes possible to consider the proposed measure without being engrossed with various questions which are closely connected with it and which might give rise to discussion, such, for example, as whether the Government is to be bound to exchange its bills of credit for silver, or for gold, etc. The departments are of opinion that the proposal to legalize contracts expressed in gold roubles, considered by itself, is worthy of adoption. It is likely that the measure, under favorable conditions, will bring gold gradually into circulation. As it will thus become possible to make contracts expressed in foreign gold coin—contracts now authorized by law (Art. 97 of the chapter relating to notaries, General Code, Vol. XVI., Part I., edition of 1892)—it is certain that foreign gold will circulate among us when money is most in demand; and there is such a demand in our markets every autumn by reason of the heavy transactions peculiar to that season. The amount of business transacted upon this basis would, of course, never become very great, except in the absence of important fluctuations in the exchange value of the credit-rouble; for, if there were such fluctuations, Russian traders or producers would not be inclined to contract engagements in gold coin and thereby expose themselves to the risk of a fall in credit-roubles. But the steadiness which the credit-rouble has recently maintained leaves little room foı fear on that score. Furthermore, our Financial Department holds a considerable stock of the yellow metal, amounting in round numbers to R. 670,000,000, a fact which makes the stability of the credit-rouble practically certain. Moreover, the improvement of our financial system cannot fail to contribute to the steadiness of our circulating medium.

"Admitting, upon the grounds here set forth, the possibility of adopting the measure proposed by Privy Councillor De Witte, the departments are constrained to share his views as to the necessity of using special care in drafting the law, so that there may be no room for misapprehension as to the Government's aim and no misleading comments upon it, which may tend to depreciate the credit-rouble. It is needless to dwell at length upon the power of public opinion in all questions relating to credit, or upon the difficulty of restoring a confidence once lost. It is to the interest of the State and the community alike that the value of the credit-rouble be not lessened either in Russia or in Eastern countries. Therefore, the departments have fully approved the modifications proposed by the Minister of Finance tending to prevent the measure from producing an unfavorable impression on the public mind.

"Proceeding to an examination of the particulars of the proposed law as presented by the Minister of Finance, the departments have discussed the section which, provisionally at least, prohibits peasants and small tradesmen not members of a guild from contracting obligations payable in gold. The object of that proviso was to protect the unenlightened portion of the community against the wiles of people eager to take advantage of their ignorance of monetary questions. But aside from the fact that State guardianship, in matters arising under the civil law and in industrial and commercial transactions, is of very doubtful utility, it has seemed to the departments that to declare the present law inapplicable to the lower classes, forming more than eighty per cent. of the population of the Empire, would give rise to unpleasant comments on the employment of different kinds of money among different classes of society, and on the establishment of a special privilege for the benefit of the upper classes and to the detriment of the peasantry and lower order of trades-people.

"Pursuing their examination of the details of the law, the departments understand it to be a general rule that contracts expressed in gold must be paid in gold. Still, it is well to make specific mention of that obligation, providing at the same time that such contracts may be settled in credit bills at the exchange rate prevailing on the day of settlement, or, in case of disagreement, at the rate last received from the St. Petersburg Bourse in the city or place where payment is to be made. On the other hand, there is no need to prescribe that the State Bank shall return gold to depositors of gold, because that is already made obligatory by Art. 148 of the law governing the Bank. If this stipulation should be introduced into the new law, it might become the basis of a mistaken view that gold deposited with other credit institutions or intrusted to individuals could be repaid in bills of credit at the ruling rate. While the departments see no objection to allowing the Minister of Finance to accept gold coin in payment of excise duties, in all cases in which the tax-payer wishes to pay in gold, they are of opinion that he should not be authorized to fix the rates at which gold is to be accepted and telegraph them to the various collecting offices, except upon condition that the rates so determined shall be immediately posted in all public places in the towns or cities in question for the information of those interested, and that they shall become effective only after a lapse of six hours from the time of their receipt.

"Finally, the departments have asked themselves whether it might not be advisable to specify in the present law how the stamp duties are to be reckoned on deeds and documents expressed in gold roubles. In the absence of a specific provision on this point, misunderstandings might arise, before the question was settled, as to whether the duties should be estimated as on deeds of an equal amount in credit-roubles, or whether the difference in value between the gold and credit rouble should be taken into account.

"Upon this question, considering that the law (General Code, Vol. V., Art. 28 of the chapter on tax-duties, edition of 1893), in fixing taxes to be paid on bills of exchange drawn in marks of Finland, or in foreign money, estimates those moneys according to a schedule which gives the credit-rouble the value of the gold rouble, the departments think that the stamp duties to be paid on documents and deeds expressed in terms of the gold rouble should be based on the nominal amount; and in order to remove all doubt upon the question, it should be expressly so provided in the law. For the reasons here set forth, the assembled departments of Economy, Laws, and Civil and Religious Affairs have decided to add to the laws now in force upon the subject the following:

"1. Any written agreement authorized by law may be contracted in Russian gold coin.

"2. Agreements contracted in Russian gold coin may be settled either in gold roubles to the amount specified or in credit-roubles at the rate of valuation prevailing on the day of payment. In case of dispute as to such valuation, the last average rate of the Bourse of St. Petersburg received at the place of payment shall be law for the parties.

"3. The stamp duties payable on deeds and contracts expressed in gold roubles shall be the same as on contracts in credit-roubles of an equal nominal amount.

"4. It shall be the duty of the Minister of Finance (*a*) to authorize the public treasuries, in places where he may deem it expedient, to accept gold coin, at the option of the debtor, in settlement of excise duties, at the valuation fixed by him, it being understood, however, that it shall be his duty to inform the Senate of his decision in order that due publication may be made; and (*b*) to telegraph his decision to the treasuries concerned, whose duty it shall then become to post up in their offices the contents of the telegram and put the order in force on the day following its reception."

As a result of that legislative measure, the State Bank published on July 14 (26) and July 26 (August 7) the two following notices, laying down its regulations for the acceptance of specie deposits, and the price at which the yellow metal was to be bought and sold by it:

By-laws Governing the Issue by the State Bank of Certificates of Metallic Deposits.

1. In accordance with the provisions of section 148 of the statutes, the State Bank will accept on deposit the articles and securities specified in paragraph 3 of these by-laws, and will deliver against them Certificates of Deposit expressed in gold roubles and payable by the Bank in Russian gold coin.

2. The Certificates of Deposit will be issued by all of the agencies and branches of the Bank. The Minister of Finance will designate for each of the establishments of the Bank the particular securities of those named in paragraph 3 in exchange for which that establishment shall be authorized to deliver Certificates of Deposit.

3. The Certificates of Deposit are to be delivered against these metallic securities: (*a*) Russian and foreign gold coin, on the terms indicated in the table annexed to these by-laws; (*b*) gold bars of high standard duly stamped by the mint or an assay office, the zolotnik of fine gold being valued at R.3.63767, gold; (*c*) such foreign bank notes payable in gold as may be selected by the Minister of Finance; (*d*) drafts which have been delivered by the Department of Mines in exchange for gold deposits, these to be accepted at their face value; (*e*) coupons of Russian bonds payable in specie and of loans guaranteed by the Government, as well as such of said bonds as have been drawn for redemption, with the usual discount of interest; (*f*) those drafts on foreign countries which the State Bank is authorized by its regulations to purchase.

4. All the securities named in paragraph 3, above, are to be accepted at their value in gold roubles.

5. The Certificates of Deposit will be made payable only to bearer, and will be of the following denominations: 1 demi-impériale, 1 impériale, 3 demi-impériales, 5, 10, 50 and 100 impériales, the impériale being estimated at 2 zolotniks* 69.36 dolei* of fine gold, and the demi-impériale at 1 zolotnik 34.68 dolei. These certificates are payable in Russian gold coin, the limit of toleration not to exceed that provided by section 21 of the monetary statute.

6. If the value of the security deposited, calculated according to the rules laid down above, cannot be exactly expressed in figures corresponding to the denominations of the certificates as set forth in paragraph 5, the surplus is to be paid in credit-roubles at the rate fixed for the purchase of Russian gold coin.

7. Certificates of Deposit of the various denominations enumerated in paragraph 5 are to be issued in series of 10,000 each, every certificate bearing the letter of its series and a number showing its place therein.

8. The Certificates of Deposit are to be issued in a form approved by the Minister of Finance.

9. The State Bank will set aside a special guaranty fund consisting of Russian gold coin, equal in amount to the certificates issued and to be reserved exclusively for their redemption. Foreign gold coin at a valuation calculated according to the table annexed may form part of the aforesaid fund.

10. Certificates of Deposit will be accepted on a par with Russian gold coin in all payments to be made in gold either to the Imperial Treasury or to the State Bank. Individuals may accept or refuse the certificates when offered in settlement of amounts stipulated to be paid in gold roubles.

11. Certificates of Deposit will be redeemed by the agencies of the State Bank in St. Petersburg, Moscow, Warsaw, Riga, Odessa, Rostov-sur-Don, and by such others as may be specially authorized. Other agencies of the Bank will redeem the certificates whenever the cash on hand will allow them to do so.

12. All branches and agencies of the Bank are authorized to exchange Certificates of Deposit of one denomination for those of another.

13. Holders of the certificates may deposit them with any branch of the State Bank and demand that any other branch shall issue certificates to a like amount in exchange for them. No charge is to be made for these transfers, except the cost of the dispatch when they are made by telegraph.

The State Bank will accept gold coin in exchange for Certificates of Deposit on the following terms:

* The dolia equals 0.68578 grains; the zolotnik is 96 dolei, or 65.83488 grains.

Description of Coins.	Minimum Weight.		Value in Gold.		Reduction of value for every dolia of abrasion in gold copecks.
	Zol.	Dol.	R.	Cop.	Cop.
Demi-impériale, old mintage..................	1	50	5	15	
Russian Tschervonets (ducats)...............		87	3	9	
Impériale, new mintage.....................	3	1	10		3½
Demi-impériale.............................	1	48	5		
F. 20, French, “ “ Italian, “ “ Swiss, “ “ Belgian, ...	1	48.2	5		
Fl. 8 of Austria...........................	1	48.2	5		3½
M. 10 of Germany..........................		89.2	3	8	
£1, English...............................	1	82.7	6	30	
$10, U. S	3.864		12	95	
10 Crowns, Austria........................	75.9		2	62	

REMARK.—Foreign coins of larger or smaller denominations than those named in the table are to be valued upon the same basis.

Rules Governing Accounts Current in Gold Roubles opened by the Bank against Deposits of Gold Coin.

1. The State Bank is prepared to open accounts current in gold roubles for individuals and private establishments against deposits of Russian gold coin. The branches of the State Bank which redeem Certificates of Deposit will also accept such certificates and carry the amount for which they are drawn in accounts current. Amounts deposited in gold coin to the credit of an account current must be repaid in gold coin.

2. A person or institution wishing to open with the Bank an account current in gold roubles must present on a prescribed form a fac-simile of his or its signature and of the signatures of the persons authorized to sign checks in the name of the depositor.

3. The State Bank and its branches and agencies may refuse to open an account current without assigning any reason for the refusal.

4. The deposits are to be entered as soon as received in a special bank-book delivered by the Bank to the depositor. Each deposit is to be attested by the signature of the officers of the Bank.

5. Each deposit in an account current must be accompanied by a special declaration.

6. The depositor may withdraw his deposit by means of checks signed by him or by his attorney in fact (§ 2); a check-book will be delivered to him by the Bank, together with the bank-book wherein his deposits are entered. Checks must be drawn in round figures, and they may be paid in demi-impériales of the new mintage.

7. The drawer of the check may write after the printed words "to bearer" the name of the person to whom he transfers the check.

8. Interest may be paid upon accounts current expressed in gold roubles, the rate being fixed by the Directors of the Bank with the approval of the Minister of Finance. No interest will be paid upon such of these accounts as are opened to the credit of those whose accounts in paper roubles do not bear interest.

9. If a drawer should lose a check the Bank will not be liable for a wrong payment unless it has prompt notice of the loss.

10. Accounts current in gold roubles may be closed at any time, in the discretion of the Bank, but the depositor shall have seven days' notice of the intention. Whenever an account is closed the depositor must return to the Bank all unused checks in his possession.

Let us here take note of one further measure, destined, if not to increase the business of the Bank, at least to facilitate dealings abroad in Russian securities. We refer to the arrangement concluded between the Finance Minister of Russia and the Bank of France on April 11 and May 1, 1895, in virtue of which the Bank of France undertakes to accept at Paris or at its branches any negotiable evidences of the Russian debt deposited by holders who wish to have them registered. The Bank of France agrees to deliver registered bonds to such holders upon their payment of the stamp duties. It will also keep itself informed as to the drawings of bonds to be paid, and if any are drawn that are registered with the Bank it will inform the holder and make the collection for him. It pays the coupons as they fall due, and for these services it makes no charge against the bondholder, but looks to the Russian Government for all claims except those arising out of stamp duties. This arrangement went into operation on July 1, 1895.

A notice published on September 1 (13), 1895, by the Bank of Russia puts in force a new set of rules relative to the safe-keeping of funds and documents deposited with it by the public. It provides that thereafter the Bank and all its branches will charge upon deposits left for safe-keeping:

1. Upon the deposit merely for safe-keeping: (*a*) of securities and valuable documents, for one year, in advance, 5 copecks for each document and 1-50 of 1 per cent. (20 copecks on R. 1000) of its value; all fractions above 5 copecks shall be regarded as 5 copecks, and the minimum charge on a deposit shall be 20 copecks (§ 34); (*b*) on securities deposited for six months, 1-50 of 1 per cent. (20 copecks per R. 1000) of the value of the deposit, for each six months, payable in advance; on envelopes containing documents deposited for six months, R. 1 (§ 39); (*c*) on envelopes containing documents or wills, and deposited for an unlimited term, R. 5 once for all (§ 44).

2. On deposits both for safe-keeping and management (at any branch or agency rendering such services), 1-50 of 1 per cent. (20 copecks per R. 1000) of the value of the deposit, per year, in advance, and 10 copecks in addition for each deed or security, the minimum charge upon each deposit being fixed at 30 copecks.

3. Upon the deposit of other valuable articles (where such articles are accepted at all), for each half-year, in advance: On each chest or box not more than one archine (28 inches) in width and length and 1½ archines in height, with a maximum weight of 1 pood (36 pounds), R. 2; 2 poods, R. 4; 3 poods, R. 6; 4 poods, R. 8; 5 poods, R. 10, with an additional charge of 1-20 of 1 per cent. (50 copecks per R. 1000) upon the value of the deposit, the minimum charge being 50 copecks. Chests or boxes of larger dimensions or of greater weight will not be received except at double rates, and then only when it is convenient for the establishment in question to accept them (§ 41).

With reference to this publication, it should be stated that the custom is widely prevalent in Russia of depositing valuables not only with the banks, but also with the local treasuries. On January 1, 1895, those treasuries held thus on deposit R. 17,600,000 of securities payable in specie, and R. 228,600,000 payable in credit-roubles. The State Bank had R. 217,400,000 of the former and R. 1,941,700,000 of the latter. Taken all together, deposits of this kind aggregated R. 2,405,300,000 on January 1, 1895, against R. 1,967,900,000 on January 1, 1894, for the State Bank and the treasuries.

The reader is thoroughly informed now as to the duties and the methods of the Bank of Russia. It had been the Author's intention to dismiss the subject at this point, but we have just had our attention called to the following notice published on August 24 (September 5), 1895. It brings out so strongly the "philanthropic" aims of the institution and its solicitude for the agricultural classes that we feel called upon to transcribe it:

"NOTICE.—The St. Petersburg office of the State Bank hereby informs the public that its charges until further notice will be as follows: (1) For the discount of paper having three months or less to run, 5 per cent.; six months, 5½ per cent.; nine months, 6½ per cent.; twelve months, 7 per cent.; (2) upon special accounts current, guaranteed by bills, 6½ per cent.; (3) loans on collateral: 4 per cent. rentes, 5½ per cent.; lottery bonds of the Banque Foncière of the Nobility, 4 per cent., and other securities, 6½ per cent.; (4) on special accounts current secured by 4 per cent. rentes, 6 per cent.; on those secured by lottery bonds of the Banque Foncière of the Nobility, 4 per cent., and on those secured by other collateral, 7 per cent.; (5) loans on the security of cereals: on those made directly by the Bank to the borrower, 5½ per cent., and on those made through brokers, 4½ per cent.; to railroads on cereals deposited in their warehouses, 4½ per cent., and on shipments *en route*, 5 per cent.; loans on any other merchandise taken in pledge, 6 per cent.; (6) loans to farmers to furnish them either with funds necessary for current needs or to be used in the purchase of agricultural machinery, 5½ per cent., and (7) loans to manufacturers, 6 to 7 per cent."

CHAPTER V.

PRIVATE BANKS.

Joint-stock Banks; Their Classification and Transactions—Legal Regulation of Private Banks—Banking Decree of June, 1894.

PRIVATE joint-stock or non-Government banks, as we have previously said, did not come into existence until 1865. The shares are legally fixed at R. 250 each, except in the case of the Bank of Kama-Volga, which has shares of R. 1000 as well as those of R. 250. The following, according to the "Bulletin de Statistique Financière," is a schedule of all the stock companies as they existed on January 1, 1894:

DESCRIPTION OF COMPANIES.	Capital of R. 50,000 or less.	No.	Capital of R. 100,000 or less.	No.	Capital of R. 300,000 or less.	No.	Capital of R. 500,000 or less.	No.	Capital of R. 800,000 or less.	No.
1. Foncier banks	......	...	......	..	......	..	339,691	1	554,460	1
2. Mortgage loan companies (cities)	......	...	......	..	490,858	2	......	..	1,703,538	2
3. " " " (country prop.)	......	...	......	..	......	..	......	..	......	..
4. Discount and Crédit Mobilier banks.	......	...	......	..	300,000	1	2,500,000	6	1,350,000	2
5. Mutual Credit associations	951,947	37	1,974,294	27	4,042,346	23	1,199,005	3	1,797,552	3
6. Municipal banks	2,805,046	104	4,908,425	68	8,890,148	50	3,351,538	9	4,899,899	8
7. Banks of villages, etc.	234,343	8	51,749	1	276,312	2	......	..	......	..
8. Loan & sav'gs banks & associat'ns.. 9. Loans on pledge }	......	...	......	..	200,000	2	1,375,000	3	2,427,558	3
10. Insurance and transp'n companies..	......	...	......	..	......	..	2,957,000	5	600,000	1
Total	3,991,336	149	6,934,468	96	14,199,664	80	11,722,234	27	13,333,007	20

DESCRIPTION OF COMPANIES.	Capital of R. 1,000,000 or less.	No.	Capital of R. 3,000,000 or less.	No.	Capital of R. 5,000,000 or less.	No.	Capital of above R. 5,000,000	No.
1. Foncier banks	1,898,479	2	17,297,400	8	4,000,000	1	32,976,900	4
2. Mortgage loan companies (cities)	996,087	1	2,690,592	1	3,294,764	1	......	..
3. " " " (country property)	......	..	......	..	......	..	8,733,473	1
4. Discount and Crédit Mobilier banks	6,000,000	6	39,145,310	12	3,400,000	1	59,000,000	5
5. Mutual Credit associations	837,660	1	2,564,571	12	7,392,791	2	......	..
6. Municipal banks	......	..	1,300,000	1	......	..	......	..
7. Banks of villages, etc.	......	..	......	..	......	..	......	..
8. Loan and savings banks and associations 9. Loans on pledge }	1,000,000	1	3,375,000	2	......	..	......	..
10. Insurance and transportation companies	5,000,000	5	13,200,000	7	8,000,000	2	......	..
Total	15,732,226	16	79,572,873	43	26,087,555	7	100,710,373	10

The same official publication prints another collective table concerning all non-Governmental credit institutions *engaged in short-term transactions.* This table is so comprehensive that a summary of it must suffice. All of the joint-stock banks together had in January, 1894, a capital of R. 116,957,000, a general reserve of R. 32,000,000 (27½ per cent.), and a reserve for special purposes of R. 4,200,000. The Municipal banks had a capital of R. 28,400,000, a general reserve of R. 5,500,000, and a reserve for special purposes of R. 945,000. The Mutual Credit associations had a capital of R. 21,400,000, a general reserve of R. 4,400,000, and a special reserve of R. 1,666,000. Thus these various institutions had a total capital of R. 166,750,000, a general reserve of R. 42,000,000, and a special reserve of R. 6,800,000. *Perpetual deposits,* which, outside of the State Bank, are not found except in Communal banks, aggregated R. 13,100,000. *Time deposits* aggregated R. 203,100,000; of sight draft accounts there were R. 47,250,000, and in accounts current, R. 237,400,000. Deposits with the branches (for such banks as have branches) were R. 74,000,000; interest due to depositors, R. 6,600,000; profits, R. 10,300,000, of which R. 6,000,000 belonged to Share banks, R. 2,900,000 to Communal banks, and R. 1,400,000 to Mutual associations. On the credit side of their accounts were: Cash (including sums subject to cheque), R. 67,700,000; loans on securities and the precious metals, R. 83,200,000; discounts, R. 337,200,000; loans on pledge, R. 120,400,000; call loans (special accounts current), R. 191,300,000; loans on realty, R. 24,500,000 (of which R. 2,600,000 was on country property); loans to municipalities, R. 2,100,000; debts in default, nearly R. 7,000,000, of which more than R. 4,000,000 were held by the Municipal banks. The balance-sheet of all these associations shows a total of R. 1,092,169,000, the proportions being: R. 801,000,000 for the Share banks; R. 180,600,000 for the Municipal banks, and R. 160,600,000 for the Mutual Credit associations.

With reference specially to the stock banks, the information is more recent, coming down to January 1, 1895. Those of St. Petersburg, ten in number, had then a share capital of R. 83,237,000 (including the branch of the Crédit Lyonnais, with a capital of R. 16,000,000), a general reserve of R. 13,000,000, and a special reserve of R. 2,600,000. Their deposits subject to sight draft and accounts current aggregated R. 131,000,000, and their time deposits were R. 26,400,000. They had borrowed upon securities and in the form of rediscounts, R. 21,300,000. They had earned in the form of interest and commissions R. 14,250,000, and their total transactions represented R. 464,166,000. Among their assets were R. 14,100,000 in cash; R. 19,800,000 in accounts current (of which R. 17,500,000 were in the State Bank); R. 15,100,000 in Russian funds; R. 8,200,000 in other bonds; R. 2,900,000 in foreign drafts; R. 500,000 in single-name paper; R. 14,600,000 in loans on bonds; R. 5,500,000 in loans on merchandise; R. 128,100,000 in special accounts current, guaranteed; and R. 86,600,000 in paper bearing two signatures.

Moscow has only four stock banks, with a total capital of R. 19,000,000 and reserve funds of R. 8,000,000. Their total transactions aggregated R. 133,100,000. The city of Riga has three private banks; Warsaw and Kiev have two each, and there are eighteen in the other chief centers of the Empire. The total transactions of all the private banks in Russia, at the close of 1894, represented R. 887,788,000. Among their assets were included R. 100,600,000 in the hands of their correspondents, and of this amount R. 41,700,000 were over-drafts. Their expenses for the year were R. 8,000,000; the property belonging to the banks was valued at R. 7,700,000 (of which R. 6,900,000 was in real estate); the total of paper held for collection was R. 15,200,000; merchandise for sale, R. 305,000; cash on hand, R. 27,100,000; accounts current, R. 24,300,000; stocks and bonds, R. 61,000,000; drafts, R. 209,600,000; loans on collateral, R. 66,900,000; special accounts current, guaranteed, R. 198,100,000. On the debit side of the account we find R. 140,500,000 of share capital; R. 38,900,000 of reserve; deposits subject to cheque, R. 194,100,000; sight draft accounts, R. 14,000,000; time deposits, R. 112,300,000. The discounts and collateral loans by banks aggregated R. 44,700,000, and the interest and commissions collected were R. 27,700,000.

It is scarcely needful to cite at length the regulations of the class of banks just considered. Suffice it to say that these regulations, like those of all stock associations, must be approved by the Government. Latterly, this control has been extended to include even private banking firms and exchange offices. A decree adopted by the Imperial Council on June 3 (15), 1894, and promulgated on July 5 (17) of the same year, puts in force a series of restrictions, of which the principal are these: Anyone wishing to open a banking house or exchange office must make a formal declaration to that effect, specifying the particular kinds of transactions in which he or they wish to engage. This declaration is forwarded to the Minister of Finance, who may demand further information and explanations. The Minister may order examinations to be made of the books and business affairs of the establishment. After such an examination of a banking house, he may forbid it to sell lottery bonds on time, to borrow on collateral deposited with it a greater sum than it has loaned thereon, to accept deposits of any kind, or to open accounts current. Any banker guilty of having engaged in a transaction forbidden by the Minister is liable, for the first offence, to a fine of R. 100 to R. 1000; for a second offence, to a fine of R. 1000 to R. 3000, and, upon conviction of a third offence, he is to be fined R. 300 to R. 3000 and imprisoned for a term of from two to eight months, his establishment is to be closed and the offender is to be forbidden ever to open another bank.

This moralizing of speculation has been inspired by the best intentions. It has been elsewhere shown what results it had produced one year after the promulgation of the decree. (See chapter on the Bourse.)

MUTUAL CREDIT ASSOCIATIONS.

The origin of the first Mutual Credit association and its rapid development have already been described. Thirty years later (on January 1, 1895) their number was ninety-three, of which two were in St. Petersburg (one in the city and the other in the district) and one in Moscow. These three associations together had 10,494 members, of whom 6127 were in St. Petersburg. The capital cities of the provinces had forty-five Mutual associations, and the capital cities of the districts had the same number. The whole number of members was 56,629, of whom 2200 were in Moscow, 30,318 in the capitals of provinces, and 15,837 in the capitals of districts. Thus the total number of these associations, which were expected to produce such important results, does not exceed that of the branches of the State Bank, and it is rather interesting to note that only one of these associations, that of the capital of the district of Gomel, was established in 1894; all the others are at least ten years of age, and the greater part of them fifteen or twenty years, or more. The enthusiasm which followed upon the establishment of the original association in St. Petersburg has very greatly abated, if, indeed, it has not entirely died out. For this result there are two reasons. Faith in the creative force and earning power of mutuality has been impaired by several serious mistakes; and, secondly, the great amount of aid extended by the State has paralyzed the efforts hitherto made in the direction of self-help. The capital of the associations is R. 21,700,000; their reserve, R. 5,100,000, and their funds reserved for various special purposes, R. 1,700,000. Of this total of R. 28,500,000, St. Petersburg has R. 4,700,000; Moscow, R. 4,000,000; the capitals of provinces, R. 14,400,000, and the district capitals, R. 5,400,000. On January 1, 1895, all of these associations together had in ordinary accounts current, R. 41,800,000; in conditional accounts current, R. 8,000,000; in conditional deposits, R. 1,750,000, and in deposits repayable at a fixed time or on demand, R. 58,000,000. The debts of the associations aggregated R. 14,600,000; their profits, R. 6,100,000, and their total transactions, R. 169,100,000. They held deposits for safe-keeping amounting to R. 12,800,000. Included in their assets were R. 2,600,000 of available cash, R. 56,200,000 of paper bearing two signatures, R. 23,900,000 of bills drawn to order and guaranteed by deposits, R. 20,500,000 of loans on collateral, R. 31,100,000 in special accounts current (on call), and R. 5,900,000 of bonds and stocks. Their debts in default aggregated R. 1,600,000, their real property was valued at R. 2,500,000, their losses amounted to R. 57,600. As mentioned above, their paid-up capital was R. 28,500,000; the capital subscribed but not paid in was R. 187,775,100.

LAND CREDIT INSTITUTIONS.

Until the emancipation of the serfs in 1861, the land credit business of Russia was conducted under the auspices of the State Bank. The process then was quite simple, and no land registry system was required. The terms of credit were based on the number of serfs, or "male souls." Of course, this unit of reckoning disappeared when emancipation was decreed, and the whole business came to an end. In order to secure outstanding debts, the amount which land-owners owed the Bank was deducted from the so-called "liberation fund," and this altered debt was laid upon the emancipated serfs, who were to wipe it out in forty-nine years, with interest at five per cent., by an amortization rate of one per cent. yearly. Some of these charges are still current.

Then, for many years, the most varied plans were tried for supplying land-owners with credit. Direct help from the State was not considered; nor even State guaranty of interest. But there were tendencies along these lines. The Kingdom of Poland and the Baltic Provinces had long since made shift for themselves; for in those countries there were joint-stock land credit companies, whose mortgage bonds also found a ready sale abroad. It is true that the countries in question had a land registry system; and, be it added, they were in the *habit* of helping themselves. Such advantages were quite lacking in the Empire at large. To have drawn up land registry books would have consumed too much time; but there were at least efforts at self-help. Let us first mention the Joint-Stock Land Credit Company which was organized at St. Petersburg in 1866–7, under the directorship of the energetic Marshal, Count Bobrinsky (later, Minister of Public Works). The company was to issue five per cent. mortgage bonds, payable in coin, so as to be acceptable abroad. Loans, interest, and amortization dues were to be paid in coin, and amortization should be complete when the rates had amounted to 125 (it should be explained that in those days exchange was 20 to 25 per cent. below par). These feats were difficult; and the State stepped in, or rather it was adroitly drawn in, to help.

When Count Muravieff was appointed Governor-General of the so-called Western Provinces, in 1863, with headquarters at Vilna, one of the watchwords of the time was the "Russification," or "Muscovization," of that western region; and R.5,000,000 was assigned for this object. But either the Russians were not pleased to settle in that Polish environment, or else the scheme dragged by reason of bureaucratic indolence; for, when Muravieff left his post at the end of 1866, the R.5,000,000 were still intact. Under the triumphant banner of Count Peter Schuvaloff, then at the zenith of his power, the aristocratic party had again got breath, to the discomfiture of Muravieff and Milutin; so that Count Bobrinsky succeeded in anchoring the loose R.5,000,000 as a State advance, free of interest, in behalf of his credit colony. It was argued that if the prostrate Russian proprietors were assisted to their feet again, they could transplant themselves to the western and southwestern provinces (Volhynia and Podolia), thereby obviating the necessity of replacing Polish nobility by promiscuous, unlineaged ragamuffins. Thanks to this contribution, the company was now presentable in the European money market; and Rothschild, with alacrity, engaged to place the mortgage bonds to the amount of R. 50,000,000, or even higher. Meanwhile, the provinces also bestirred themselves, and local companies were formed, which issued bonds at five, six, and seven per cent. One of the earliest and most substantial of these companies, that of Kherson, flourishes still. Besides the companies, joint-stock mortgage banks were organized; but all, with an exception to be treated below, were based on paper capital, so that their market generally remained local and restricted. Most of these banks are still in existence, having hitherto withstood the wrenching violence of political agitations; but they have in nearly all cases reduced interest on their bonds to five per cent., which reduction was facilitated by the favorable situation of State credit.

Central Land Credit Bank.—We now come to the exception referred to above. This was the Central Land Credit Bank, initiated in 1873 by capitalists of St. Petersburg, Berlin, and Vienna, with a capital stock of R. 5,000,000. This concern contained germs of decay in its very incipiency, for it originated just at the time of the financial crash in Vienna; nor did the founders enjoy the satisfaction of raising the shares even temporarily above par. This bank's object was to buy up most of the six per cent. mortgage bonds issued by the local banks and replace them by five per cent. bonds payable in coin, which might be marketed abroad and make good the abatement of one per cent. The process continued until the war in the East, and for so long as the rate of exchange stood between eighty-five and ninety. Losses began in 1877, though at first they could be covered out of the reserve fund, as yet scarcely five years old. The loss for 1877 was R. 797,000; then it reached as much as R. 1,292,000 for single years, and showed a total of R. 10,997,000 from 1877 to 1893. This had reduced the capital stock of R. 15,000,000 to barely R. 4,000,000; though down to 1887 it was partly revived by State advances amounting to R. 4,100,000, which relief then ceased. Thanks to the State reinforcement, the capital stock was still as great as R. 7,400,000 at the beginning of 1894. The State has now transformed the R. 44,700,000 of outstanding mortgage bonds into three per cent. rentes; the bank is dissolved, and the shareholders receive the R. 7,400,000, or about equal to fifty per cent. of their stock.

The Pomestchik, or Proprietors of Large Estates.—No class had been more prompt to welcome the Eastern war, in 1877, than the great landed proprietors. In 1875, the paper rouble had risen to 90 per cent., the Imperial Bank had a considerable coin reserve, and Finance Minister Reutern entertained serious hopes of a speedy solution of the financial problem. But the export trade was imperiled; Odessa could no longer pay high prices for crops, when twenty francs brought only six roubles instead of eight. So a little war, with obligatory increase of paper currency exempt from extra tax, was the *Pomestchik*, or manorial, ideal; and it was shortly realized. The note circulation of the Bank of Russia rose from 715 to 1140 million roubles, and the rate of exchange fell all the more persistently because at the same time the Bank's coin reserve had been materially reduced, and at the end of the war was only R. 120,000,000, or somewhat over ten per cent. of the circulation. Could the wholesale producer of grain wish anything better, especially as for full ten years after the war the rate of exchange kept sinking and sinking, and at last twenty francs brought not only eight, but even nine and ten roubles?

However, the sunny situation became gloomy with clouds. American harvests began to influence the grain market of Europe more and more perceptibly, and prices fell. Then, too, the Russian proprietor now had to pay 7½, 8, and even 9 paper roubles in interest and amortization rates on 100-rouble mortgage bonds, instead of 6 or 6½ roubles, as was the case before the war. (The bonds had been issued on a hard money basis.) This went against the grain in more ways than one; and the "poor" *Pomestchik*, or lords proprietors, pathetically exclaimed that the Eastern war, which they now said they had never approved, and the Nihilistic outrages, which they abominated, were ruining them and society. In other words, the State must assume their burden; as it gradually did. One step in this direction was the institution of the *Bauernbank*, or "Peasants' Bank," in 1882.

Peasants' Bank.—There were wide complaints that the peasantry, in certain districts, had received too little land at the time of the emancipation in 1861; and in particular governments this was quite true. The general lot of the peasant class was therefore far from enviable; especially as the *mir*, or agricultural communes, by their periodical redistributions of land, prevented any properly individual ownership, with its promise of better farming. Moreover, the former serfs had come to hold the opinion that each new Czar ought to favor the peasantry by undertaking a fresh distribution of land; and this idea became so fixed in their minds that Alexander III., on the occasion of his coronation in May, 1883, invited six thousand peasant commune chiefs to Moscow, provided for their hospitable entertainment, and assured them, in a stately address, that their ideas, or the current rumors, in regard to his intentions were altogether erroneous. However, the Peasants' Bank should liberally supply the rural population's urgent needs of capital, and incidentally facilitate the sales of the large proprietors. The Peasants' Bank, a strictly State institution, paid eighty per cent. of the price whenever there was a conveyance of land from the large proprietors to the peasants, and the latter paid, or failed to pay, the remaining twenty per cent. in cash. Of this, more anon. The acquisition of land might be either personal or collective and communal. Without entering into too many critical details, let it suffice to say that the defects of the plan, both at the start and now, some twelve years later, may be referred to the fundamental mistake of artificially raising the price of land at a time when American competition and other causes were bringing prices down. The peasants readily consented to pay what was asked without analyzing the market situation. At the most, they had to pay only one-fifth, and even this the seller would willingly throw off, as he generally had a pretty good bargain in the eighty per cent. paid by the State. The interest and amortization of the debt to the State should be discharged in 24½ or 34½ years. The results have been as follows:

By the end of 1893, 11,440 advances had been apportioned between 943,477 persons. In a word, the debts were mostly collective, and the *mir*, or communal system, still prevailed. The conveyances embraced 2,047,000 Russian *dessiatines*,* and the proceeds amounted to R. 89,600,000, of which the bank paid R. 70,333,000, and the remaining R. 19,250,000 were paid out of the buyers' "own resources." About R. 9,750,000 are bonded for 24½ years and R. 60,500,000 for 34½ years. The status of these debtors may be learned from the following official communication, which was published in connection with the "Act of Grace" on occasion of the Czar's accession to the throne on November 26 (14), 1894:

"Since its institution, the Peasants' Bank has loaned money at 5½ per cent. (without amortization or other charges), and has also issued bonds at this rate. Although since the end of last year the bank has converted its debt into 4½ per cent. bonds, and issued no more bonds at 5½ per cent., the annual payments of the bondholders could not be correspondingly canceled, since many of the latter were not in a position to meet their obligations. Their arrears increased, and they finally made over their land to the bank in default of payment. The bank is therefore subject to heavy losses, the extent of which may not be estimated even approximately, since the lands have not yet been sold. It was purposed to cover a part of the loss by fixing a higher rate of interest; but inasmuch as the imperial manifesto has decreed a reduction of interest by one per cent., the losses will fall upon the State." At the close of 1894, the debt amounted to R. 63,016,796.

Other Mortgage-credit Associations.—We must return to the large estates and *their* banks. The Central Credit Bank, which was founded in 1873, soon succumbed, as we have seen, to adverse conditions of exchange, and its liquidation was to be completed by the end of 1895. Its older and greater companion, the Land Credit Company, had no shareholders. This, too, was paternally adopted by the State, which in 1885 assumed the guaranty of interest on the mortgage bonds, but at the same time reduced the rate from 5 to 4½ per cent. The amortization bonus (120 to 100) disappeared, as the new bonds were redeemed at par.

Titled Nobility Bank.—The Company was itself transmuted, in 1886, into a purely State "Aristocracy Bank," and its plebeian patrons had to find other accommodations within five years, meanwhile paying one per cent. higher interest than the aristocracy. By January 1, 1889, after three years of

* One dessiatine = 1.0925 hectares, or 2.6997 acres.

activity, the bank had arrears to the amount of R. 4,900,000 on loans amounting to R. 170,000,000—that is, the arrears amounted to 46 per cent. of the annual charges. Advances in sums above R. 100,000 reached a total of 25 per cent.; in sums between R. 10,000 and R. 100,000, 66 per cent., and 9 per cent. for sums under R. 10,000. Manifestly, the State had done too little for its distinguished clients; but its omissions were made good by the ukase of October 30 (18), 1889, providing for the issue of a lottery loan of R. 80,000,000. As the lots of the two earlier issues (1864 and 1866) were quoted at 240, these new lots at 5 per cent. (though the rate was actually no more than 4¾ per cent., on account of a 5 per cent. tax on coupons) were offered at 215, payable within six months. The resultant enthusiasm was fairly unbounded; instead of 800,000 lots, over 26,000,000 were demanded, but the price soon fell, and payments were far from punctual.

The State Aristocracy, or Titled Nobility Bank was none the worse for these diversions. Most of the proceeds (R. 172,000,000) were turned over to the bank; and as it paid only three per cent. interest thereon, the interest on its own advances was forthwith reduced from 5 to 4½ per cent., with reactionary effect on all loans contracted within the preceding four years. After this, the bank paid R. 100 per bond, and not R.98, as it had formerly done. The period of amortization was also lengthened from 48⅔ to 51¾ years for borrowers whose annual rate was ½ per cent.; from $36\frac{7}{10}$ to 38⅓ years where the rate was 1 per cent. At the same time, it was ruled that on and after May 1, 1890, the regulations of the bank should be strictly enforced. Events, however, ruled otherwise, for there came the famine of 1891; and the inaugural manifesto of 1894 granted the same grace to the noble debtors as to the peasants, both being equally brought low by debt and equally helpless to meet their obligations. A six months' respite, or prorogation of debts, was allowed in case of estates forfeited to the Nobility Bank, as it was impracticable to sell them. An aristocracy bank may not sell estates to commoners, and there is nothing for it to do but exercise aristocratic patience toward its debtors. We summarize the condition of the bank's affairs for 1893:

	ROUBLES.
Amount of 14,935 mortgage loans on 11,671,326 dessiatines of land, with an appraised value of R. 714,000,000	402,500,000
251 loans of less than 1,000 roubles	196,000
3,284 " from 1,000 to 5,000 roubles	10,100,000
2,833 " " 5,100 to 10,000 "	21,100,000
3,106 " " 10,100 to 20,000 "	45,400,000
1,568 " " 20,100 to 30,000 "	38,900,000
1,532 " " 30,100 to 50,000 "	59,900,000
1,123 " " 50,000 to 100,000 "	77,100,000
491 " " 100,000 to 200,000 "	68,400,000
171 " " 200,000 to 500,000 "	47,600,000
36 " of more than 500,000 "	33,800,000

				ROUBLES.
Amount of	38 advances for terms of	11 to 25 years		500,000
"	103 "	34½	years	5,400,000
"	741 "	36 and 38	"	15,800,000
"	197 "	44	"	8,000,000
"	120 "	48⅔	"	2,000,000
"	10,552 "	51¾	"	289,600,000
"	2,644 "	66½	"	87,333,333

At the close of 1894, the claims of the Nobility Bank amounted to R. 468,000,000, of which about R. 117,000,000 had come over from the original institution and included loans to commoners. The Nobility Bank had by no means driven out private credit concerns, nor even seriously checked their activity. We shall proceed to illustrate this by official data, first remarking that the Nobility Bank simply facilitated the acquisition of debts, and (if we may make so bold), it disaccustomed people from the art of paying. The official data are as follows:

On January 1, 1895, the circulation of mortgage bonds was R. 1,530,000,000, including R. 87,600,000 payable in coin, and 7,200,000 German marks. Of the total circulation, R. 282,000,000 belonged to the Nobility Bank; R. 62,900,000 to the Peasants' Bank, with interest reduced from 5½ to 4½ per cent.; and the remaining bonds, amounting to R. 1,185,100,000, were issued by private banks.

The latest returns of *Other Land Companies* show, in their latest published statements, the following amounts of mortgaged bonds outstanding:

The Bank of Kherson, a mutual liability company, R. 103,800,000; the ten joint-stock banks of Kharkov, Poltava, Tula, Moscow, Bessarabia, Samara, Kiev, Vilna, Yaroslavl, and Don have, unitedly, R. 506,100,000; five *municipal credit companies*, R. 374,700,000, distributed as follows: St. Petersburg, R. 179,900,000; Moscow, R. 125,500,000; Odessa, R. 56,200,000; Kiev, R. 10,100,000, and Cronstadt, R. 3,000,000; total, R. 374,700,000. Credit Company of the Kingdom of Poland, R. 117,500,000; Warsaw Credit Company, R. 41,600,000; four other Polish cities, R. 11,400,000; Esthonian Nobility Credit Company, R. 2,000,000 and 7,250,000 marks; Livonian Land Credit Company, R. 30,700,000; Courland Land Credit Company, R. 17,000,000 and R. 1,700,000 payable in coin; five Baltic cities, R. 29,000,000; City of Tiflis, R. 9,100,000, and two Nobility Banks of the Caucasus, R. 17,800,000. Leaving out of account the municipal banks, Peasants' Bank, and the Polish institutions, we find that the total mortgage obligations on January 1, 1895, amounted to R. 1,164,500,000, against R. 654,400,000 on January 1, 1887; an increase of some R. 510,000,000, or nearly eighty per cent. in eight years. For the Nobility Bank alone there was an increase from R. 208,800,000 to R. 468,000,000, or nearly 124 per cent. In this instance, moreover, the value of the mortgaged property rose from $30\frac{70}{100}$ to $31\frac{25}{100}$ roubles per dessiatine; the total average increase being from $25\frac{1}{100}$ to $26\frac{12}{100}$ roubles per dessiatine. In other words, the banks loaned more than before, although the decline in prices of crops would seem to have encouraged a contraction in the loan business. But it was necessary to compete effectually with the Nobility Bank; and thus the State subsidy stimulated running into debt. In May, 1894, the third, or so-called "third," demand addressed to backward State debtors involved no less than nine per cent. of the aggregate estates mortgaged by the Nobility Bank. We have seen that a respite was granted in November, 1894.

The Land Credit banks cleared an annual average net profit of fifteen per cent. for the period 1888–92. The following are specimens of the dividends:

Kharkov, 13.8 per cent.; Poltava, 17.1 per cent.; Tula, 9.6 per cent.; Moscow, 16 per cent.; Bessarabia, 14.1 per cent.; Samara, 16.6 per cent.; Kiev, 19.4 per cent.; Vilna, 15.9 per cent.; Yaroslavl, 6.7 per cent., and Don, 14.8 per cent. The capital stock of these ten banks was R.33,250,000 in 1888, R.36,600,000 in 1892, and R.41,600,000 at the close of 1894. Their net profits in 1894 were R.7,580,687, or 18.2 per cent.

We have had occasion to speak of the Czar's inaugural ukase, with its large concessions to debtors. The abatement of ½ per cent. annual interest to the nobles and peasants implies an inevitable expansion of the State budget; and this begins to assert itself in the case of the Nobility Bank whenever the loans increase by R.42,000,000. The Nobility Bank was to assist in lightening the burdens of its customers, which office it discharged by paying on their account R.212,000,000 to other banks, and loaning them 112 millions in cash. Meanwhile, had the debts on landed property decreased at private banks? They had increased by R.217,000,000.

Before the emancipation of the serfs, the estates of aristocratic landowners, with a serf population of 5,000,000 "male souls," were mortgaged to the amount of R.328,000,000 to the State Bank. This amount was then converted, at the emancipation, into a bonded debt redeemable in forty-nine years by the liberated peasantry. The only land credit concerns regularly operative in Russia were those of Poland and the Baltic Provinces; and as late as 1869, the total mortgage debt was not above R.117,000,000. In 1874, it was R.335,000,000; R.511,000,000 in 1879; R.617,000,000 in 1884; R.930,000,000 in 1889; and, as we have seen, some R.1,530,000,000 in 1894. The liberation debt of the peasants is not included in the foregoing figures. On January 1, 1893, it amounted to R.716,000,000, and after an abatement of R.183,250,000, granted by the State on sundry occasions, it still amounts to more than R.532,000,000. Under the item of emancipation, the State has paid the noble proprietors R.572,000,000 in mortgage bonds, R.6,000,000 in cash, and R.316,000,000 in the way of canceled debts; a round total of R.900,000,000. The arrears of the peasant communes for emancipation dues are locally as high at 300 per cent. of the annual charges; so it is no hard matter to understand the State's frequent practice of canceling back accounts. The end is perhaps not yet.

According to a publication of Mr. Golubov, Secretary of the Committee of Land Mortgage Banks, the mortgage indebtedness for the period 1889–94, was as follows:

	January 1.	Number of Estates.	Extent in Dessiatines.	Amount of Debt in Roubles.
State Nobility Bank	1889	5,919	5,041,083	173,452,300
	1894	12,562	10,023,571	335,209,768
State Nobility Bank*	1889	8,110	7,306,485	196,155,364
	1894	7,693	5,664,686	167,091,722
Peasants' Bank	1889	5,241	1,249,445	47,907,883
	1894	10,764	1,838,727	58,435,153
Mutual Liability Company of Kherson	1889	3,368	3,192,241	63,765,893
	1894	3,805	3,266,657	86,726,888
JOINT-STOCK BANKS.				
Kharkov	1889	3,229	1,309,736	39,371,469
	1894	4,255	1,436,692	49,188,281
Poltava	1889	2,448	687,459	28,021,169
	1894	4,272	1,092,805	39,492,035
St. Petersburg-Tula	1889	1,774	991,848	17,649,538
	1894	2,777	1,159,285	24,558,924
Moscow	1889	3,406	2,278,618	57,600,945
	1894	4,614	2,243,234	51,084,718
Bessarabia-Taurida	1889	699	736,732	21,140,129
	1894	906	851,276	29,423,586
Nijni-Novgorod	1889	1,138	3,159,868	25,529,053
	1894	1,078	3,171,836	24,468,622
Kiev	1889	1,757	1,165,368	38,046,223
	1894	2,423	1,200,286	43,600,488
Vilna	1889	3,345	2,432,265	40,451,744
	1894	5,559	3,996,026	59,361,344
Yaroslavl-Kostroma	1889	243	216,262	2,362,330
	1894	218	181,690	1,463,396
Don	1889	769	508,273	10,271,669
	1894	1,670	905,609	21,411,574
Total	1889	41,441	30,275,628	756,415,689
	1894	62,596	37,330,084	986,516,449

The average loan for each dessiatine of land was 24 roubles and 90 copecks in 1889; 26 roubles and 13 copecks for 1894.

SAVINGS-BANKS.

We come now to the Savings-Banks. A new law concerning them went into force on June 1 (13), 1895. Its main provisions are as follows: The State shall assume the responsibility for all sums deposited, and "these are not to be used toward defraying the general expenses of the State" (Art. 2). Deposits cannot be attached except by judicial order. The funds of savings-banks are to be turned over to the State Bank, which shall pay on them a rate of interest less by at least ½ of 1 per cent. than that paid upon sight draft accounts, but never less than ½ of 1 per cent. per annum. The funds are to be invested in State securities or in securities guaranteed

* These data represent what was brought over from the Nobility's predecessor.

by the State. The surplus is to be turned into a reserve fund until the latter amounts to ten per cent. of the deposits held on December 31st of the year last past. Such profits as may yet remain are to be carried to the credit of the Treasury as a budgetary receipt (Art. 9). On the other hand, if the profits are not sufficient to pay the interest due to depositors the State will make up the difference (Art. 10). The limit of interest-bearing specie deposits is R. 1000 for an individual and R. 3000 for a corporation. If this limit is passed, interest ceases on the whole of the specie deposit in that account. Notice is thereupon sent to the depositor, and if, at the end of a month, he has not reduced his deposit within the legal limit, the surplus will be invested in State securities for his account (Art. 35). The rate of interest paid to depositors is to be fixed from time to time by imperial decree (Art. 43). When any account has not been increased or drawn upon for thirty years it becomes the property of the savings-bank (Art. 52).

It is yet to be seen what measure of success these reforms may have. On January 1, 1894, the number of savings-banks under the management of the State Bank was eighty-six, and their deposits aggregated R. 287,500,000, of which R. 260,400,000 was in ordinary savings-banks, and R. 27,100,000 in "postal banks." The provinces of St. Petersburg and Moscow appear in this total for R. 40,800,000 (14 1-5 per cent.); the five provinces of the north, for R. 13,500,000 (4.68 per cent.); the six provinces of the east, for R. 28,900,000 (10.05 per cent.); the seven provinces of the manufacturing districts of the interior, for R. 46,300,000 (16.11 per cent.); the nine provinces of the Terre Noire, for R. 48,900,000 (17.01 per cent.); Little Russia (three provinces), for R. 15,100,000 (5.24 per cent.); the three Baltic provinces, for R. 9,500,000 (3.31 per cent.); the six provinces of the northwest, for R. 14,900,000 (5.17 per cent.); the three provinces of the southwest, for R. 13,700,000 (4.76 per cent.), and the six provinces of the south, for R. 23,700,000 (8.14 per cent.). This makes for European Russia, properly so called, R. 255,300,000, or 88.67 per cent. of the whole. Of the 11⅓ per cent. remaining there were R. 8,750,000 in the ten provinces of the Vistula; R. 13,100,000 in Caucasia and Transcaucasia, and R. 10,333,000 in Asiatic Russia.

On April 1, 1894, the various social classes were represented among the depositors thus: Agriculture and trades closely allied with it, 241,636 depositors, representing R. 51,100,000; trades-people of the cities, 101,593 depositors, with R. 14,700,000; the mill and factory classes, 83,039 depositors, with R. 11,250,000; domestic servants, 125,959 depositors, with R. 19,800,000; the commercial classes, 123,250 depositors, with R. 20,900,000; soldiers, 72,302 depositors, with R. 12,100,000; Government employees, 95,949 depositors, with R. 21,100,000; personal servants, 119,992 depositors, with R. 22,300,000; all other classes, 281,476 depositors, with R. 61,600,000; and corporations, 112,025, with R. 35,200,000. There were altogether, therefore, on April 1, 1894, 1,357,221 depositors, with an aggregate of R. 270,050,000, or an average of R. 198.97.

The monthly savings-bank report of June 1, 1895, puts the number of these banks at 3,388, the number of depositors at 1,746,309, and the total deposits at R. 350,125,000. Between January 1st and June 1st of that year the savings-banks increased by 198, the depositors by 91,417, and the deposits by R. 14,600,000.

SMALL CREDIT INSTITUTIONS.

We turn now to the examination of a new species of credit institution of very recent origin. The "Messager Officiel" of June 17 (29), 1895, publishes the text of an order of the Council of State, approved by the Emperor on June 1st (13th), authorizing the establishment of institutions for "small credits," in whose behalf the State Bank will open special credits for the formation of their capital. From the regulations drawn up for the management of these institutions, it appears that they are to be of the following classes: (1) Credit associations; (2) credit and savings associations; (3) commercial or savings banks of rural communes, of bailiwicks, or of Cossack villages (*Stanitsas*). The Commission, whose duty it was to draw up rules for these institutions, had before it the task of erecting, in the midst of the rural population, a type of credit establishment which should meet the wants of small tradesmen without demanding of them advances from their own resources. To this end, and also to avoid the defects which the practical working of existing credit and savings societies for the past thirty years has shown to exist in them, the new law establishes credit institutions whose working capital shall be furnished by the State Bank under the guaranty of all who share their benefits. Nevertheless, these societies may, if they wish, be established upon a capital furnished by provincial councils (*Zemstvos*), or by individuals. If the capital is supplied by the State Bank, the direct management of the institution is with the Bank or its branches, whose agents superintend the business of the enterprise, the management of its affairs, the stockholders' meetings, etc.; they have a right also to discharge or to prosecute such employees as may be guilty of neglect of duty or malfeasance in office. This same privilege belongs to representatives of provincial councils or agents of individuals who may have furnished the funds necessary for the establishment of one of the new credit institutions. The profits of these institutions are not to be paid out in dividends but are to be used to furnish a capital which shall belong to the institutions themselves.

CHAPTER VI.

THE BOURSE.

Its Small Beginnings and Rapid Development—Wholesome Influence of the Finance Minister—An Imperial Warning Against Speculative Excesses—Conservative Counsels from the "Journal de St. Petersbourg"—A Lesson from the Minister of Finance.

IN 1856, the dealings upon the St. Petersburg Bourse comprised only the following items: Exchange on London, Hamburg, Amsterdam, and Paris; under the heading of public funds, one six per cent. and two five per cent. loans; the securities of sixteen corporations, including: The Russo-American Company (dissolved in 1868 as a result of the sale of Alaska to the United States); three fire insurance companies; three maritime insurance companies; one mineral-water company; one cotton-spinning corporation; one Volga navigation company; one company accepting goods on storage and in pledge; and the St. Petersburg-Zarskoe-Selo Railroad Company, with a line 16⅔ miles in length. This was not an extensive showing. By April, 1862, however, there were upon the official list eleven public loans; the bonds of the Crédit Foncier of St. Petersburg; the 5½ per cent. bills of the State Bank and various 4½ per cent. railroad bonds; the stocks of five fire insurance companies; twelve shipping companies, four railroad companies, etc.; in all, thirty-seven different issues. To emphasize the unimportance of the Bourse of those days, we have but to recall the fact that, in 1860, the "Gazette de la Bourse" suspended publication during eighteen consecutive days; for throughout all of Holy Week and Easter Week, and up to the following Tuesday, the Bourse was closed. Ordinarily, it was open only on two days of the week, Tuesday and Friday, and then only from four to five o'clock; for the prices of merchandise and securities dependence was placed mainly on advices from Amsterdam, London, Hamburg, and especially from Berlin. It is so no longer. Since 1872, the Bourse has been open six days in the week, every day; that is to say, except Saturday.

It must not be inferred from this that the Jewish element is predominant on the St. Petersburg Bourse; on the contrary, the Jews have always been less prominent there than in other money markets. Moreover, during the last few years, the Bourse has been open on Saturdays, as it is elsewhere. On December 30, 1878, the Bourse dealings represented four issues of five per cent. bank bills; sixteen classes of public securities, including guaranteed railroad bonds; fifty-nine series of mortgage bonds (issued by cities and provinces); the shares of twenty-five commercial and ten foncier banks; the shares of about twenty manufacturing and fifteen insurance companies; the stock of twenty-one and the bonds of five navigation companies; the shares of thirty-six railroads, and the bonds of twenty-four.

At the close of 1890, there were in all Russia:

Crédit Mobilier and discount banks	38	Chemical manufacturing companies	15
Cotton manufacturing companies	48	Paper mills	18
Sugar refineries	73	Corporations engaged in making loans on pledge	11
Mortgage banks	17	Gas companies	8
Insurance and transportation companies	19	Mineral-water companies	9
Petroleum companies	9	Tramway companies	9
Steamboat companies	26	Engaged in the manufacture of silk	9
Metal-working and machine-manufacturing companies	22	Cement companies	4
India-rubber companies	2	Engaged in the preparation of food supplies	8
Engaged in the preparation of beverages	28	In the manufacture of tobacco	3
Linen manufacturing companies	15	In the preparation of skins, leathers, etc.	5
Engaged in the finishing, dyeing, and printing of fabrics	13	Dealing in wood	7
Woolen companies	18	In asphalt	2
		And about twenty others.	

The important transactions looking to the reduction of interest on Government loans, the purchase of railroads by the State and its refunding of their obligations, which went on from 1889 to 1894, gave to the St. Petersburg Bourse a wholly new bearing, and brought to it business of an importance previously unknown. It is a well-established fact that a country which has need of foreign capital is not in a position to hold a commanding place among either the money or security markets of the world. Nevertheless, there have been several instances in recent years in which countries thus situated have persuaded themselves that they were able to declare their independence of the real money markets of London, Paris, Amsterdam, Berlin, and Frankfort. Between the close of 1893 and the close of 1894, this emancipation on Russia's part was specially pronounced. Even the death of the Czar Alexander III. did not arrest it. One circumstance peculiar to Russia has greatly aided the emancipation. Ever since M. de Witte has been at the head of the Finance Department he has exerted himself to put an end to speculation in exchange, and on several occasions he has made special efforts in this direction. The speculators have finally taken him at his word and have devoted themselves with the greater ardor to stocks and securities paying a fixed rate of interest. As proof of this may be cited the prices of the shares of a few banking and other corporations as they were quoted on December 31, 1893, and December 31, 1894, respectively:

	Par Value. Roubles.	Quotations. Dec. 31, 1893. Roubles.	Dec. 31, 1894. Roubles.
Russian Bank of Foreign Commerce	250	330	464
Discount Bank	250	490	658
International Bank	250	509	675
Volga-Kama Bank	250	915	1015
Azof-Don Bank	250	528	758
Foncier of Kharkov	200	498	548
Foncier of Bessarabia	250	570	720
Russian Insurance Company	250	330	480
Mills of Briansk	100	131	388
Mills of Poutivl	125	75	178
St. Petersburg Tramway	100	61	190
Rybinsk Railroad	100	89¾	132

This upward tendency became so much more pronounced in January, 1895, that the Government, in its solicitude for the public welfare, felt constrained to warn its subjects of the dangerous path they were treading, declaring at the same time that it could afford them no assistance, but relied upon their own wisdom and foresight. The effect of that appeal was only temporary. Those who deal upon the Bourse are always confident that the storm will not reach them or that they will be under cover when it breaks; so the ministerial admonition was little heeded. On August 1, 1895, the majority of shares were much higher than they had been eight months earlier, as will appear from the following comparative quotations:

	Dividends. 1893. Roubles.	1894. Roubles.	Quotations on August 1. 1889. Roubles.	1892. Roubles.	1895. Roubles.
Private Bank of St. Petersburg	25	27.50	370	315	603
Discount Bank of St. Petersburg	28	37.50	672	470	812
International Bank of St. Petersburg	30	34	532	436	676
Bank of Foreign Commerce of St. Petersburg	20	24	248	253½	524½
Volga-Kama Bank of St. Petersburg	50	55	705	710	1235
Bank of Commerce and Manufactures of St. Petersburg	..	10	....	212	420
Bank of Azof-Don of St. Petersburg	30	40	365	490	730
Bank of Warsaw	26	27.50	325	353	547
Bank of Siberia	35	35	475	525	660
Foncier Banks—					
Bessarabia-Taurida	38	39.40	450	500	726
Vilna	38	38	550	590	636
Kharkov	28	28	350	447	535
Bavarian Brewery	20	22	250	335	450
Nevski Tramway	10	12	97	140	205
Insurance Companies—					
Company of 1827	90	90	1185	1195	1550
Russia Second	20	20	285	257	362
Salamander	27.50	30	520	440	570
Rossia	17.50	20	280	280	456
Capital Insurance	12.50	12.50	210	235	240
Railway Stocks—					
Rybinsk-Bologoë	5.25	7.25	79¾	63¾	175½
Southeastern	8.72	9.50	167¾	134¼	192½

The months of July and August were signalized by a remarkable advance in prices; a very decided reaction followed during the second half of the latter month; and yet on August 31st (September 12th) the quotations were as follows: The private bank, 595 to 600; Discount Bank, 875 to 868; the International, 712 to 719; Bank of Foreign Commerce, 537 to 533; Volga-Kama, 1320 to 1300; Azof-Don, 720 to 728; Warsaw, 536 to 537; the foncier bank Bessarabia-Taurida, 680; Vilna, 655; Kharkov, 530 to 535; the Insurance Company of 1827, 1600; the Second Insurance Company, 370; Rossia, 440 to 450; the Rybinsk-Bologoë Railway, 179; the Southeastern, 190 to 191. Three days later, on September 2d (14th), at the date of the last quotation, we have seen as we bring this chapter to a close, the Discount Bank had gone down still more, to 840; the International, to 703 to 685; the Volga-Kama, to 1285, etc. Nevertheless, in its monthly bulletin of the Bourse, published on September 3d (15th), the "Journal de St. Petersbourg," which has always been very conservative, stated that the downward tendency had been brought about partly by the scarcity of money, but more especially by undue speculation in the shares of new concerns having as yet no actual existence; and it added:

"After numerous fluctuations in both directions, the majority of speculative shares are still considerably above par. After the great advance they have enjoyed, a retrograde movement was inevitable. Nevertheless, the downward tendency of these shares, all things considered, is of slight importance; for, the great public, which, for the last two years, has been the dominant factor upon the Bourse, always favors a rising market, and it will probably not fail to return to the charge at the first favorable opportunity."

Dealing upon the Bourse in Russia is greatly facilitated by certain practices to which the independent banks lend themselves. Elsewhere (in Austria, for example) it has been made a reproach to these institutions that they carry accounts for dealers and allow speculators for a rise to deposit in their hands those shares whose prices they wish to put up or sustain. In Russia that practice is disguised under the name of "call loans." This is a transaction to which reference has been made in our chapter on banks. Calls loans, as the term is understood in Russia, are loans in the form of accounts current guaranteed by securities or other valuables (including even real estate and mere personal security), which loans may be called in at any moment after six hours' notice, or a notice of three or four or five days, as the case may be. The minimum interest on call loans is generally above that paid by the State. Thus, during the latter half of 1888 it varied between 6 and 8 per cent.; in 1889, between 4½ and 8; in 1890, between 4½ and 7; in 1891, between 4 and 8; the same in 1892, and in 1893, between 4 and 7 per cent., whereas during those same years the interest paid by the State Bank on accounts current subject to cheque was only once as high as 3.6 per cent. (from September 3, 1888, to March 30, 1889), and for the remainder of the time it was between 1½ and 3 per cent. The "Bulletin Russe de Statistique," which we have previously mentioned, in speaking of this subject calls attention to the fact that in Russia money loaned for a short term brings in a larger return than that invested in funded securities, which is precisely the opposite of the rule elsewhere. It adds that the banks find call loans to be very profitable, and that they often employ in this way nearly all the money they hold subject to cheque.

The downward tendency that had begun in August was even more pronounced in September. The Government felt called upon to set itself right upon the subject. In a country where the granting of credit is entirely a State function, and where everything centers in the State, it was altogether natural that speculation should demand of it aid and succor in the shape of new issues of paper money. The Minister of Finance had the courage to refuse such aid and to leave speculation to its own devices, holding that the well-being of the State or of the community was in nowise dependent upon a high quotation for banking shares and for the stocks of a few industrial concerns. He explained his position in an official note, inspired by sound principles, which shows that the guardianship assumed by an absolute government sometimes appears to it extremely onerous. As a declaration of sound canons of finance the document may merit reproduction here.

"SPECULATION AND THE SCARCITY OF MONEY.

"The further sudden decline in the security market toward the middle of last week was not unexpected. On several different occasions the 'Journal du Ministère des Finances' has pointed out the probable consequences of the stock exchange game which has grown to such dimensions in the last year and a half, and has called attention to the abnormal inflation of prices in a series of securities listed upon the Bourse. This is not the first time facts have confirmed its predictions. Unfortunately, neither warnings nor the sad experience of heavy losses is sufficient to deter speculative amateurs, lured by the irresistible bait of prompt and easy gain, from intrusting their means, often very limited, to the hands of skillful players.

"Everybody knows that there is no game at which all can win; it is always the rule that some win, while others inevitably lose. The stock exchange game is managed by those who know all the sinuosities, while the inexperienced public, allured by the hope of gain, furnishes the means necessary to keep the game going. Evidently in such a game the winners will be invariably those who direct it—men who thoroughly understand the game and know how to take advantage of the people's ignorance of it—while the unsophisticated, trusting public always loses in the end and so finds itself punished for its unwise desire to gain wealth quickly, easily, and without labor. Yet, in spite of the absolute certainty of the truth of these statements, in spite of the constant teaching of experience and repeated warnings, there are always persons seeking to make their fortune at the game and intrusting their savings to agents for this purpose.

"Some there are who think that industrial progress bears a steady relation to speculative activity; that while some of the new enterprises which spring up during such activity come to grief afterward, others, more substantial, live and grow, and the net result is a national gain though some investors must inevitably lose. Admitting that this is true, and that we are now in the midst of an industrial revival such as is always accompanied by failures which it is not to the national interest to prevent, still we cannot refrain from declaring that the speculation now rampant upon our Bourse, against which we have continually warned the confiding, inexperienced public, and which, as a matter of conscience, we always shall oppose, has not the slightest connection with the upbuilding of any new enterprise. This speculation is concerned chiefly with a certain small class of securities, to which new additions are made from time to time. The prices of these securities fluctuate violently and often reach a height out of all proportion to the income produced by the shares. The fact is, that it is a pure game of chance, played, too, by some who have very small stakes invested through the agency of banks or other intermediaries, and that no account is taken of the real situation of the enterprises whose stocks are speculative favorites. All kinds of false reports are circulated to put up the price of these securities, and the establishments accept orders at a loss in order to give color to their claims of growth and activity; then, when the shares have found their market among the public, the owners of the enterprise, whether it has been long in existence or has newly sprung up, abandon it. For them its usefulness is over, and they go in search of a new enterprise of like kind. What is there about all this that savors of a renewal of industrial activity? Certainly it is desirable that small savings seek investment in industrial undertakings, but transactions of this kind keep them out of such investments by encouraging a passion for foolish gambling, for which amateurs always pay dearly in the end. The facts prove the truth of these assertions.

"This is the third time recently that securities, especially those in which speculation is most active, have suffered a sharp decline. The fall was especially severe on September 22d and October 4th. Some attribute this to the scarcity of money. Let us see what foundation there is for that claim. It is true that in the fall, when the greater part of our agricultural products come to market, the demand for money increases and the cash in the banks generally decreases for a while. But it should be noted: (1) That the crops of all kinds this year, according to preliminary forecasts, are less abundant than last year; and (2) that the ruling price of grain is generally supposed to be too low, in view of the probable demand, and sales have been very limited; farmers have sold only so much of their cereals as was necessary to provide them with money for their actual needs. Moreover, the exports this fall have not only been less than those of last fall, but less even than those of the summer.

"On the other hand, all needful steps looking to an increase of the circulation were taken in due time. One-rouble silver pieces previously held in reserve have been put in circulation, and the Bank has been authorized to issue the gold belonging to its reserve fund. Thus, every provision has been made to meet an increased demand for money. If in spite of these precautions money is found to be so scarce that some have been compelled to sell their securities in order to obtain it, this scarcity has not arisen out of any commercial demand for money, which, on the contrary, is less than it usually is at this time of year; the scarcity is due to the speculation which has had such an extraordinary development recently upon our public bourses and upon clandestine bourses as well, drawing into the game not only the citizens of the capitals, but also, and to even a greater extent, the inhabitants of the provinces.

"We have merely to place side by side various quotations of those securities on which speculation thrives in order to show the remarkable and absolutely senseless advance scored by many of them in a comparatively short space of time. Let us look at a few of those securities. The shares of the Mills of Briansk (quoted at R. 130 in January, 1894, these shares gradually rose to R. 550 in August, 1895, and then went down to R. 450 on October 5th); the shares of the Mills of Poutivl (R. 75 in January, 1894, R. 180 in September, 1895, R. 130 on October 4th); those of Sormovo (R. 175, R. 370, R. 310, on October 4th); the shares of the Société des Mines d'Or (R. 100, R. 420, R. 400, on October 4th). As to this last company, nobody knows as yet what kind of showing its first balance-sheet will make, nor is anything known with any degree of certainty concerning the extent of the company's operations. This, then, is simply a case of betting on a rise, with no guide to go by.

"The shares of the Russian Bank of Foreign Commerce, quoted at R. 330 on January 3, 1894, went to R. 534 on August 1, 1895, only to fall sharply to R. 500 by October 4th. Shares of the Discount Bank advanced during the same time from R. 490 to R. 880, and fell back to R. 800 on October 4th. The shares of the International Bank of St. Petersburg and of the Volga-Kama Bank of Commerce have likewise been subject to considerable fluctuations; the former went from (R. 498 to R. 725, and then back to R. 680, while the latter went from R. 905 to R. 1375, and fell suddenly to R. 1290.

"Glancing over the balance-sheets of these banks, we notice that accounts current 'on call' and credits opened with correspondents of the banks, which are mainly secured by collaterals not guaranteed by the State, make up the main part of their business. In one of the large banks of

St. Petersburg credits of this kind constitute sixty per cent. of the total business, while commercial transactions constitute barely ten per cent. If we add the fact that banking institutions engage largely in rehypothecation, we may form some idea of the extent to which speculation is carried on. In comparison with the enormous sums necessary to keep this speculation alive, the amount of money demanded for commercial needs is absolutely insignificant. Here, then, is the real cause of the scarcity of money. Last year, though the demand for money on the part of exporters was greater than now, it was not necessary to have recourse to a supplementary issue of bills of credit; but speculation at that time was far less active than it is at present.

"But people do not confine themselves to declaring that money is scarce (that scarcity, if it existed, would be due to speculation on the Bourse, as we have shown above); some advise a new issue of bills of credit in order to lessen the damage caused by speculation. This advice seems to us as ill-founded as the notion of the artless public that it is possible to deal upon the Bourse with no risk of loss.

"What is the meaning of the term 'scarcity of money'? Money becomes scarce in the market whenever too large a part of our available resources have been invested in merchandise so that they are locked up until the merchandise can be sold. When such a state of affairs arises in a country with a proper form of circulation, the demand for money causes an influx from neighboring countries having a greater abundance. In this manner money is secured with more or less difficulty, and the temporary embarrassment is promptly ended. On the contrary, countries that have a fiduciary circulation not current elsewhere, and which are in this respect cut off from other countries, experience in such cases monetary disturbances which are hard to quell. A new issue of bills of credit, by satisfying the temporary demand for money, appears for a time to ameliorate the situation, but as soon as specie is once more plentiful new difficulties arise, producing on the one hand an increase in the price of goods, and on the other a decrease in the purchasing power of money.

"Besides, each new issue of bills of credit serves, first of all, as fuel for speculation, and speculation is an enemy to the common weal because it leads to stock-jobbing, to the enrichment of a few persons by means for which there is no justification, and to the ruin of most of the other participants. If we take into consideration the further fact that it is generally a very difficult matter to withdraw these temporary issues (witness the fact that for fear of unsettling the money market we have not yet consigned to the fire the R. 75,000,000 of bills of credit issued under a gold guaranty), we shall have a clear understanding, both of the uselessness of these issues and of their harmful effects. As a matter of fact, notwithstanding all the issues hitherto made, we still feel the lack of money every time the demand for it becomes a little brisk.

"What, then, in its final analysis, is the advice given by that large class of persons who trace the cause of all our troubles to the lack of new issues of paper money and demand that such issues be made? They act as one who should advise a doctor to administer poison to a patient, as a sedative, during the crisis of his disease, with the result of complicating the malady, when a regular and hygienic course of treatment would have brought the patient back to his normal state and resulted in a complete cure. We are advised, in fact, to stir up further trouble in the money market and to furnish additional supplies to the speculation whose baleful effects have never been more acutely felt than now. Suppose that by supplying this additional means of speculation we should save certain overbold speculators from loss, is it not evident that others, less expert, would meet with reverses rendered all the greater by the very fact that the day of settlement was postponed? Is it advisable, for the sake of results so unsatisfactory, to disarrange our monetary circulation and all legitimate business by further complicating, through a new issue of paper money, a system which even now is highly unsatisfactory? The need of regulating our monetary system by the re-establishment of a metallic circulation is an urgent one. Our Finance Ministers and far-seeing statesmen have long been waiting impatiently for a moment propitious for the change.

"Our Finance Department has just entered upon a series of measures tending to establish among us at last a sound and healthful monetary circulation, the lack of which paralyzes every branch of our domestic economy. It is not to be supposed, then, that that department, after having felt impelled to find some way out of the anomalous situation which has continued so long, and after having actually decided upon the preliminary steps, will turn back again, even temporarily, to the very devices which caused the trouble and which have long been condemned both by experience and by a knowledge of the normal conditions of national life.

"Finally, the real needs of commerce do not demand recourse to a supplementary issue of paper money. By legalizing transactions in gold; by putting into circulation from the large reserves accumulated by the State Bank gold enough to supply the needs of commerce and industry; by issuing metallic receipts for our people, who are accustomed to handling only paper money; by placing in circulation, for convenience in small transactions, silver of standard weight and fineness taken from the Bank's reserve—by all these various means there have been placed in circulation, not a fixed quantity of monetary signs as was the case when supplementary issues of paper money were made, but precisely that quantity for which there was a real need. Another important advantage of this system is that the withdrawal of this circulating medium will be effected without any difficulty and in the exact proportion in which the demand for money grows less, because specie always flows back into its strong-boxes when money becomes plentiful in the market.

"If we are not yet accustomed to the use of gold money because it has so long been out of circulation among us, that is a defect that time will cure. The value of the credit-rouble has been so stable during the last few years that even in transacting business with foreigners our merchants have ceased to protect themselves by a purchase of credit bills on time, as was formerly their custom, in order to avoid loss in the exchange. There is reason to hope that before long transactions will be concluded directly in Russian gold coin, at a fixed valuation and for long terms. It is certain that confidence in the fixity of the exchange rate, and in the possibility of exchanging at any moment at such fixed rate bills of credit against gold roubles, is not far in the future. And then our first aim will have been attained, that of giving greater elasticity to our monetary circulation."

CHAPTER VII.

THE PRECIOUS METALS.

Paucity of Statistics—Production of Gold and Silver—Regulation of Coinage—Relative Values of Coins—Operations of the Mint.

STATISTICS running back over any considerable length of time are always to be received with caution, and this is particularly true of Russian statistics, because the official publications of the country date back only about thirty years; and of all Russian statistics, those relating to the production of the precious metals and to dealings in them are least worthy of implicit confidence, because there enter into them so many elements, all tending to obscure the truth. Suffice it to recall the fact that all dealings in gold dust are there prohibited, and that this prohibition gives rise to all manner of fraudulent and illegal traffic. Nevertheless, in 1861, M. Tarassenko-Otreschkow, an old officer of the Commissary Department of the army, who had taken part in the siege of Sebastopol, and had afterward devoted himself to the study of economic questions, entered upon that new vocation by the publication of a book entitled "Production of Gold and Silver in Russia," and treating of the production, importation, and exportation of those metals. We should be sorry to speak disrespectfully of a worthy man deceased for twenty-five years, but in view of what we have said above, we cannot accept as of any great authenticity the information contained in a book whose author, while he was unquestionably a most conscientious man, was not in a position to estimate at its proper value the information he had collected.

So much being premised by way of reservation, we may say that, according to the statement of Narcissus Tarassenko-Otreschkow, silver mining in Russia dates from about 1704, and gold mining from 1745. Between these dates and January 1, 1825, the total production of the precious metals was R. 110,804,540, or F. 443,218,160. The minute exactness of these figures, referring to a period not distinguished for precision, furnishes in itself food for reflection, and we do not insist upon their accuracy. During the reign of the Emperor Nicolas I., from 1825 to 1855, the mines produced R. 360,-103,480 (F. 1,440,413,920), and from January 1, 1855, to January 1, 1860, R. 120,000,000 (F. 480,000,000); making a total for the three periods of about R. 591,000,000 (F. 2,364,000,000). The author places the average annual production of gold at 1500 poods (a pood being equal to 16⅓ kilograms), of the value of about R. 20,000,000, and the average annual production of silver at 1000 poods, worth R. 951,000; making a total annual production of R. 21,000,000 (F. 84,000,000). During the thirty-five years, 1825–1860, there were mined only R. 480,000,000, or an average of only R. 13,000,000 per year. Finally, for the last three years of his epoch, M. Tarassenko-Otreschkow makes the following detailed statement:

1857..........	1680	poods	32 zolotniks gold,	and	1091	poods	silver.
1858..........	1638	"	.... "	"	1061	"	"
1859..........	1452	"	.... "	"	906	"	"

This makes, he says, a value of about R. 23,000,000 per year. The coinage at the St. Petersburg mint in 1857 was R. 27,200,000; in 1858, R. 22,200,000, and in 1859, R. 23,700,000; making a total of R. 73,100,000. The importations for those three years were, respectively, R. 8,800,000, R. 6,600,000, and R. 2,800,000; a total of R. 18,200,000. The exportations were, respectively, R. 23,700,000, R. 30,800,000, and R. 28,600,000; a total of R. 83,100,000. The exports exceeded the imports, therefore, by R. 64,-900,000. We may add that from 1825 to 1860 Russia received from abroad in payment of trade balances R. 100,000,000. At this point we may dismiss these citations, whose value is purely archæological. There can be no doubt that during the years immediately following the Crimean war and the Peace of Paris (1856), a number of events conspired to cause a large exportation of the precious metals from Russia. We need only recall what we have previously said about the abundance of paper money, and bear in mind these two facts: that immediately after the war heavy purchases of all kinds were made abroad, and that a large number of Russians, whom the war had kept at home, left the country after it was over, taking considerable sums of money with them.

We have also seen how, as part of the plan of establishing a metallic currency in 1862, R. 100,000,000 were brought into Russia by a foreign loan of £15,000,000, and with what rapidity it went out again at the end of eighteen months. We have described, further, how from 1868 to 1875, as a result of railway loans, for which the State became responsible, the precious metals, and especially gold, were heaped up in the vaults of the fortress of St. Peter and St. Paul in St. Petersburg, and under what pressure arising out of the Eastern war of 1877–8 and the issue of R. 400,000,000 of new bills by the State Bank, this fund was depleted in its turn. Lastly, we have passed in review the series of fortunate events—notably the debt conversions and an excess of exportations over importations—as a result of which the metallic holdings of the Government have once more been restored, in 1895, to about R. 600,000,000. But we have no hesitancy in declaring that no reliable information is to be had as to the production of the precious metals in Russia prior to 1876. In 1894, however, there was issued by the Finance Department a table showing the production of gold from 1877 to 1893. From this it appears that, during those 17 years, the mines of Russia produced R. 477,793,862; that the largest production of any year (R. 33,000,000) was that of 1893, amounting in weight to 2343 poods 6 livres 14 zolotniks 47 dolei;* that the smallest production of any year was that of 1891, a little more than 1052 poods, valued at R. 14,374,720.

During the same period, the mints issued to individuals, in pieces of R. 10 (impériales), R. 5 (demi-impériales), and R. 3 (ducats), R. 54,000,000; to the Emperor's private treasury, R. 2,167,655; to the fisc (Imperial Treasury), R. 17,636,855, and to the State Bank, R. 324,882,687. The Bank also received R. 124,845,914 in bars, and medals were struck for public institutions and individuals to the value of R. 1,712,867. Putting these sums together, we find that the R. 477,793,862 produced by the mines somehow becomes R. 525,000,000. But it is to be remembered that the production is estimated in fine gold, while the coinage was of a fineness of only $\frac{11}{12}$ until 1886, and of $\frac{9}{10}$ since that date. The mintage during those seventeen years was as follows, in millions and tenths of millions of roubles:

YEAR.	FINENESS.	IMPÉRIALES. (R. 10)	DEMI-IMP. (R. 5)	DUCATS. (R. 3)	TOTAL VALUE.
1877	$\frac{11}{12}$	....	33	0.1	33.1
1878	"	....	34	0.6	34.6
1879	"	....	36.1	....	36.1
1880	"	....	31	0.3	31.3
1881	"	....	27	0.1	27.1
1882	"	....	22.7	....	22.7
1883	"	....	28.2	....	28.2
1884	"	....	24	0.1	24.1
1885	"	....	26.7	0.1	26.8
1886	"	....	16.8	....	19.2
1886	$\frac{9}{10}$	0.6	1.8		
1887	"	9.8	16.3	....	26.1
1888	"	0.2	26.3	....	26.5
1889	"	3.4	21	....	24.4
1890	"	0.2	28	....	28.2
1891	"	....	2.7	....	2.7
1892	"	0.1	0.6	....	0.7
1893	"	....	3	....	3

A brief official table has been issued for 1894 placing the production of that year at 36,312¾ kilograms of fine gold, of the value of F. 125,070,797

* A dolia = 0.68578 grains; a zolotnik = 96 dolei; a livre = 96 zolotniks; a pood = 40 livres.

(R.31,250,000); the export of bars at 60 3-5 kilos; the export of Russian gold coin at 53¼ kilos, and the export of foreign gold coin at 48,512½ kilos, the kilogram being estimated at F.3444½. The imports are estimated to have been 899 3-5 kilos of bars; 43 4-5 kilos of Russian coin, and 140,373¼ kilos of foreign coin. Thus the imports aggregated 141,317 kilos, against 48,626 kilos of exports, a difference of 92,691 kilos, which, at F.3444½ per kilo, amounts to F.319,273,149. The imports of manufactures of gold, which should be deducted from this sum, aggregated F.1,500,000. The gold used in the arts was 8027 1-5 kilos, of the value of F. 27,600,000; the gold coinage aggregated F.12,000,420, consisting of 1007 impériales (R.10) and 598,007 demi-impériales (R.5), having, together, a gross weight of 3871 1-5 kilos and a net weight of 3484 $\frac{1}{10}$ kilos.

As for the production of silver, which has never been very great in Russia, an official table informs us that in 1894 it amounted to 8,578,641 kilos, of a value of R.1,906,774½; that the exports were 155,717 1-5 kilos in bars, 31 3-5 kilos in Russian coin, and 511 $\frac{1}{10}$ kilos in foreign coin, a total exportation of 156,259 kilos, besides manufactured articles of a value of F. 224,912. The importations were 500,491½ kilos in bars, 657 kilos in Russian coin, 8878 kilos in foreign coin, and manufactured articles to the value of F.1,182,682. In the arts were used 137,338 kilograms of fine silver, valued at F.30,500,000. There were coined 3000 one-rouble pieces $\frac{9}{10}$ fine, and 3,000,000 smaller coins (10-copeck pieces) $\frac{5}{10}$ fine. The silver production of Russia for the six years, 1887–92, is officially estimated at 5015½ poods, as follows: 939 poods in 1887, 924 in 1888, 846 in 1889, 889 in 1890, 838 in 1891, and 579½ in 1892.

Russia's part in the international movements of the precious metals in recent years has naturally been very considerably affected by the great depreciation of silver on the one hand, and on the other by Russia's extensive conversions of debts held abroad, necessitating large gold movements. The following official table shows the imports and exports of gold during the last twenty-four years:

YEARS.	IMPORTATIONS.	EXPORTATIONS.
1871	R. 6,345,000	R. 16,861,000
1872	8,111,000	6,649,000
1873	2,500,000	14,309,000
1874	6,552,000	17,054,000
1875	1,721,000	27,576,000
1876	1,488,000	101,845,000
1877	9,403,000	13,502,000
1878	10,249,000	6,806,000
1879	7,388,000	5,322,000
1880	7,046,000	25,876,000
Total, 10 years,	R. 60,803,000	R. 235,800,000

YEARS.	IMPORTATIONS.	EXPORTATIONS.
1881	R. 5,371,000	R. 66,925,000
1882	4,489,000	68,136,000
1883	3,014,000	19,212,000
1884	2,412,000	3,034,000
1885	2,489,000	5,336,000
1886	2,401,000	14,293,000
1887	2,191,000	18,890,000
1888	21,007,000	35,001,000
1889	2,688.000	17,451,000
1890	15,801.000	16,915,000
1891	72,322,000	616,000
1892	104,363,000	232,000
1893	13,195,000	172,000
1894	109,124,000	37,528,000
Total, 14 years,	R. 360,867,000	R. 303,741,000

For the whole of the twenty-four years the importations were R. 421,-670,000, and the exportations, R. 539,541,000, a difference of R. 117,871,000. It is needless to say that that difference would have been much larger but for the fact that the last four years of the series alone show imports aggregating nearly R. 300,000,000, against R. 38,500,000 of exports.

Another official publication, which appeared in 1894, shows the movements of the precious metals, bullion, and specie during the seven previous years (1887–93), from which we quote merely the totals, with this word of explanation, that in returning bullion and specie under the same heading, 100 poods of coin has been reckoned as the equivalent of ninety poods in bars.

	GOLD EXPORTS.			GOLD IMPORTS.		
YEARS.	Frontiers of Europe and Finland.	Asiatic Frontier.		Frontiers of Europe and Finland.	Asiatic Frontier.	
	POODS.	POODS.	TOTAL POODS.	POODS.	POODS.	TOTAL POODS.
1887	1,178.8	16.9	1,195.7	103.8	34.8	138.6
1888	2,188.0	36.6	2,224.6	1,268.5	62.4	1,330.9
1889	1,233.3	9.3	1,242.6	125.4	66.0	191.4
1890	1,131.5	72.9	1,204.4	1,028.2	96.9	1,125.1
1891	12.6	31.3	43.9	5,045.9	103.6	5,149.5
1892	11.0	5.5	16.5	7,388.3	42.7	7,431.0
1893	4.1	8.1	12.2	865.6	73.9	939.5

The following table gives the like facts concerning silver:

	EXPORTS.			IMPORTS.		
Years.	Frontiers of Europe and Finland.	Asiatic Frontier.		Frontiers of Europe and Finland.	Asiatic Frontier.	
	Poods.	Poods.	Total Poods.	Poods.	Poods.	Total Poods.
1887	74	3,213	3,287	3,525	845	4,370
1888	34	4,565	4,599	11,106	1,271	12,377
1889	130	4,177	4,307	10,811	1,263	12,074
1890	2,764	2,957	5,721	8,939	1,570	10,509
1891	25	7,599	7,624	9,446	1,588	11,034
1892	32	6,218	6,250	9,640	3,752	13,392
1893	9	10,171	10,180	20,206	5,611	25,817

The coinage of silver has always been of two kinds: that of standard fineness ($\frac{9}{10}$), and that serving merely for small change, which, previous to January 1, 1867, was coined to represent seventy-five per cent. of its nominal value, but since that date, only fifty per cent. It is needless to say that, for many years, silver coins in Russia, as elsewhere, have not been worth the amounts inscribed upon them. The silver rouble is to-day a depreciated coin, like the pieces of 50, 25, or 10 copecks, with merely this difference, that the proportion of silver contained in it is forty per cent. greater than that contained in the smaller coins (90 per cent. as against 50). With this explanation, we may state that from January 1, 1860, to September 30, 1894, the St. Petersburg mint coined silver of standard fineness ($\frac{9}{10}$) to the value of R. 34,780,529¼; subsidiary silver coins to the value of R. 127,944,847.10; and copper to the value of R. 8,571,928.34. The recoinage is not included in these figures. For the same years (1860–94), it aggregated R. 24,500,000 in pieces $\frac{9}{10}$ fine, and R. 20,500,000 in subsidiary coins. During the same period of thirty-five years the mintage of coins less than a rouble has consisted of 83.7 millions of 20-copeck pieces, 35 millions of 15-copeck pieces, 14.5 millions of 10-copeck pieces, and 2.2 millions of 5-copeck pieces, a total of 135.4 millions of subsidiary coins, of which 7,725,000 pieces were coined abroad and the remainder in Russia.

Russia is not, any more than other countries, proof against counterfeiters. It has even been said that the counterfeiting of Russian bills of credit has developed into a regular business in various foreign lands. There is nothing astonishing about this, for the more extensive any country is, the greater the ease with which a large number of counterfeit bank bills may be circulated in it before the authorities become aware of the fact. We accept, then, merely as a minimum the figures contained in an official table and purporting to show that the amount of counterfeit Bills of Credit put in circulation between 1879 and 1893 was only R. 1,312,189.

CHAPTER VIII.

FOREIGN EXCHANGES.

THOSE who have never had any experience of a circulation with an enforced legal-tender quality do not know, cannot even imagine, the uncertainties introduced into every business transaction by variations in the rate of exchange. In the first instance, only foreign commerce appears to be affected, and no harm seems to result except to importers who buy foreign goods on credit and do not know what amount of depreciated currency they must put aside against the day of settlement, to pay a debt contracted in francs, pounds, or marks. The domestic producer appears, for his part, to have no concern in the matter; he may even congratulate himself on the fact that the depreciation of the national currency, as measured in foreign money, affords him protection in addition to that furnished by the import duties, and enables him to sell his goods without fear of competition from abroad. But his joy and his profits are transitory. We have seen above, in our allusions to the Crédit Foncier, that Russian farmers were very well satisfied with the depreciation of the rouble caused by the Eastern war of 1877–8, making it possible for them to sell their grain at a higher price, or rather, to get a larger number of roubles for it. But we have seen also that the necessity which the depreciation of the rouble imposed upon these same farmers of paying seven or eight, or even nine roubles per year, as interest and contribution to the Sinking Fund upon every R.100 of the specie debt they had contracted with the Société Foncier soon made them plead poverty; and this they did so loudly and so successfully that the Government soon took upon itself a part of these payments, and later assumed the whole burden by transforming the Société Foncier into a State mortgage bank, that Bank of the Nobility, of the unsatisfactory management of which we have had much to say above.

Our present purpose is simply to call attention to the very wide fluctuations through which the circulation, the fiduciary money, passes in a country that has once abandoned a specie basis, the only true foundation upon which to establish a circulation. The following table, which we borrow from an official publication, shows the great changes in value to which the rouble has been subjected, not only during the long period of twenty-five years, but often within the space of a single year.

THE GOLD ROUBLE, CREDIT ROUBLE, AND SILVER ROUBLE.

VALUE OF THE DEMI-IMPÉRIALE.				AVERAGE OF THE YEAR.		
Years.	Average value.	Highest.	Lowest.	Value of R. 1 gold in credit roubles.	Value of R. 1 credit in copecks, gold.	Value of R. 1 silver in credit roubles.
						Coined silver of full weight & fineness.
1870	6.63	7.10	6.38	1.2874	77.66	—
1873	6.10	6.19	6.00	1.1844	84.43	—
1874	5.93	6.13	5.88	1.1515	86.84	—
1875	6.00	6.25	5.85½	1.1650	85.83	—
1876	6.39	6.98	6.20	1.2408	80.59	—
1877	7.64	8.80	6.54	1.4835	67.41	1.444
1878	7.97	8.89	7.40	1.5476	64.62	1.4814
1879	8.16	8.30	7.65	1.5845	63.11	1.4733
1880	8.00	8.32	7.59	1.5534	64.37	1.3673
1881	7.84	8.16	7.58	1.5223	65.69	1.3344
1882	8.16	8.44	7.91	1.5845	63.11	1.3658
1883	8.33	8.46	8.12	1.6175	61.82	1.3780
1884	8.12	8.44	7.77	1.5767	63.42	1.3378
1885	8.13	8.45	7.73	1.5786	63.34	1.3132
1886*	8.49	8.85	8.08	1.6485	60.66	1.2651
1887	8.98	9.21	8.44½	1.796	55.68	1.3710
1888	8.41	10.00	7.45	1.682	59.45	1.2768
1889	7.59	7.95	7.30	1.518	65.88	1.1067
1890	6.89	7.37	6.11	1.378	72.57	1.0908
1891	7.49	8.65	6.69	1.498	66.76	1.0706
1892	7.93	8.22	7.48	1.586	63.05	1.1082
1893	7.66	7.89	7.50	1.532	65.27	1.0438
1894	7.46	7.57	7.36	1.492	67.02	—

Let us examine a few of the figures in this interesting table. Take the year 1876: war is not yet declared, but it is expected and dreaded; the value of the demi-impériale ranges from 620 copecks to 698, a variation of about sixteen per cent. We have seen above that during that same year gold exports attained their maximum—R101,800,000. But that value, 698 copecks, which marks the maximum depreciation for 1876, was not reached again for some years, except once at the beginning of 1877 (654 copecks),

* Before 1886, the demi-impériale was worth F. 20.67 (and was the equivalent of R. 5.15); since 1886 it is worth F. 20 or R. 5.

while the war was still in the future. Thereafter, up to and including 1889, the most favorable valuation was never below R. 7 for the demi-impériale; and in 1888 we reach a maximum of R. 10, or 168 copecks, paper, for R. 1 gold. The year 1888 was the year of Boulanger in France, of the death of the Emperor William I. in Berlin, and of the publication of the treaty of alliance between Austria and Germany. Now, observe the two figures standing, respectively, at the right and left of that maximum of R. 10. The average value was 841, and the lowest was 745. The explanation of this is that after the anxiety caused by the events we have named, William II., just after ascending the throne (June 18th), had paid a visit to St. Petersburg, and confidence had been restored by that fact. But what a margin such fluctuations furnish for speculation, for stock jobbers, and with what ruin they menace the honest merchant! It is in 1890 that we find the most favorable valuation of the rouble (611 copecks for the demi-impériale). The reason is that M. Wyschnegradski was then most busily engaged in his refunding operations, and a series of letters appeared in the "Berliner Boersen-zeitung" declaring that the re-establishment of a metallic circulation was at hand. As a matter of fact, however, we know that the Minister had never given the subject a moment's thought. Accordingly, the increased valuation of the rouble was not maintained. Even as we write (October 20, 1895), though the metallic reserve is twice as great as it was in 1890, and though the circulation of gold is officially authorized and encouraged, the paper rouble is, notwithstanding, lower than in 1890; the demi-impériale is quoted in St. Petersburg at 740 copecks in paper.

As to the silver rouble, which is still officially regarded as the legal tender of the Empire, it has been acted upon by two opposing forces—by the depreciation of paper money, tending to increase its value, and by its own depreciation, as silver, tending to lower its value. The table on page 421 shows the direction in which the silver rouble has moved during the past thirty-five years.

The last column of this table furnishes an interesting study for those who believe that the State has merely to put its impress upon a piece of metal in order to ensure it a fixed intrinsic value. During those years in which Russian credit was severely strained, the silver rouble was more valuable than the paper rouble, the difference being at times as great as forty per cent. But as the credit of the Government improved, silver depreciated as compared with paper money, and in 1893 the difference between them was only 1⅓ per cent. In other words, silver has not succeeded in Russia, any more than elsewhere, in holding out against the depreciation forced upon it by the universal law of demand and supply; it follows that bimetallism has not the slightest chance of revival in Russia. The Imperial Government has never had the least predilection for it, under any event, and we have already shown in our examination of the State Bank that its vaults contain the largest amount of gold and the smallest amount of silver of any on the continent of Europe. Moreover, in 1893, the Russian Government dissociated itself, to a certain extent, from the silver rouble, which had been its legal tender, by inserting in the "Messager Officiel" of August 12th

YEARS.	Price, in Pence, of a Standard Ounce of Silver in London.			Ratio of Gold to Silver.	Bourse of St. Petersburg exchange on London. Value of £10 in credit roubles.	Average Price in Credit Roubles	
	Average.	Highest.	Lowest.			of the amount of fine silver contained in R.100, silver, calculated according to the London price of silver and St. Petersburg sight exchange on London.	of R.100 in coined silver (Russian coinage) at the St. Petersburg Bourse.
1860	61 11/16	62 3/8	61 1/4	15.29*	67.15	107.96	——
1861	60 13/16	61 3/4	60 1/8	15.26	70.42	111.61	——
1862	61 7/16	62 1/8	61	15.35	69.12	106.51	——
1863	61 3/8	61 3/4	61	15.37	65.68	105.81	——
1864	61 3/8	62 1/2	60 5/8	15.37	74.09	118.51	——
1865	61 1/16	61 7/8	60 1/2	15.44	76.05	121.03	——
1866	61 1/8	62 1/4	60 3/8	15.43	80.99	129.02	——
1867	60 9/16	61 1/4	60 5/16	15.57	73.66	116.27	——
1868	60 1/2	61 7/8	60 1/8	15.59	73.01	115.12	——
1869	60 7/16	61	60	15.60	78.66	123.90	——
1870	60 9/16	62	60 1/4	15.57	80.67	127.33	——
1871	60 9/16	61	60 3/16	15.57	74.93	118.27	——
1872	60 1/4	61 1/8	59 1/4	15.65	73.35	115.18	——
1873	59 1/4	59 15/16	57 5/8	15.92	73.98	114.24	——
1874	58 5/16	59 1/2	57 1/4	16.17	72.05	109.50	——
1875	56 3/4	57 5/8	55 1/2	16.62	73.24	108.33	——
1876	53.05	56 5/8	47	17.77	77.82	107.55	——
1877	54.71	57 1/2	53 3/4	17.22	92.30	131.19	144.40
1878	52.55	55	49 5/8	17.92	97.96	134.16	148.14
1879	51.32	53 9/16	49 1/2	18.37	98.97	132.38	147.33
1880	52.21	52 13/16	51 3/4	18.06	95.73	132.62	136.73
1881	51.83	52 7/8	51 1/4	18.19	95.28	129.12	133.44
1882	51.72	52 1/4	50	18.25	99.21	133.73	136.58
1883	50.75	51	50 1/8	18.58	101.18	133.83	137.80
1884	50.63	51 1/8	49 7/8	18.62	98.46	129.92	133.78
1885	48.48	49 7/8	46 15/16	19.45	99.21	125.35	131.32
1886	45.34	46 7/8	42 5/8	20.79	102.74	121.41	126.51
1887	44.61	47	43 11/16	21.13	112.15	130.39	137.10
1888	42.71	44 1/8	41 13/16	22.07	107.49	119.65	127.68
1889	42.64	44 3/8	42	22.12	94.57	105.10	110.67
1890	47.71	54 1/2	43 5/8	19.77	85.82	106.71	109.08
1891	44.93	48 3/4	42 3/4	20.98	91.25	106.85	107.06
1892	39.58	40 7/8	37 7/8	23.83	99.07	102.20	110.82
1893	35.33	38 9/16	30 1/2	26.69	95.22	87.68	104.38
1894	28.80	31 3/4	27 1/16	32.74†	93.02	69.82	——

* Read : 100 kilograms of gold are worth 1,529 kilograms of silver.
† " " " " " " " 3,274 " " "

(24th) of that year the following comments upon an imperial decree of July 8th (20th):

"In view of a depreciation so rapid and so great, it became the duty of the Government to take such steps as would lessen, at least, if they could not neutralize, the disastrous consequences arising from the depreciation of a metal which, in legal contemplation, serves as the basis of our monetary system, though, as a matter of fact, the silver rouble of full weight and fineness (18 grams fine)* has entirely disappeared, and the credit-rouble (paper money) has become our real monetary standard.

"As a result of various steps on the part of the Government tending to the establishment of a fixed relation between gold and the credit-rouble a belief has arisen that the credit-rouble is no longer an equivalent of the silver rouble. The collection of customs duties in gold roubles, the acceptance of gold deposits as a guaranty for the issue of bills of credit, and the fact that the coinage of gold is much larger than that of silver have led the public to believe that the credit-rouble represents a specific value in gold. This conviction betrays itself in the lack of correspondence between the fluctuations of the credit-rouble and of silver; on the one hand, owing to certain political and economic disturbances, the credit-rouble has at times been of less value than 18 grams of fine silver; and on the other hand, the depreciation of the white metal has failed to affect the valuation placed upon the credit-rouble in London, Paris, Berlin, and other money markets. In 1891, before the promulgation of the Sherman Act, 18 grams of silver were worth less than a credit-rouble; in June, 1893, when the ounce of silver, which had recently been quoted at 37d., fell to 30d., and 6 per cent. Mexican bonds went down to 59, there was no change upon the Paris or Berlin Bourse in the value of the credit-rouble or of Russian funds expressed in credit-roubles. It is very fortunate that the silver rouble (of full weight and fineness) has practically gone out of circulation; otherwise the depreciation of the white metal would have been followed by serious losses in Russia. The Treasury will not be seriously damaged by the return to it of the twenty or twenty-five millions of coins outstanding which it will be obliged to accept at par (that is, as the equivalent of credit-roubles) notwithstanding that 18 grams of silver are now of less value than the paper rouble.

"The situation would be very different if there was free coinage of silver. Until we are able to adopt gold as our monetary standard, the silver rouble will continue to be our legal tender, and as such it must be received at par both by individuals and by the public treasuries, and inasmuch as the purchasing power of the rouble is greater than that of 18 grams of fine silver,† everybody would make haste to have as many roubles coined as possible, and our stock of silver roubles would soon become enormous. Not only would this result in a serious depreciation of our paper money, but the value of the credit-rouble would follow the rapid fluctuations of the white metal. It was to prevent this result that the further coinage of silver for private account has just been forbidden."

---

* More exactly, 17.996 grams, or 0.62555 (approximately 5-8) of a standard ounce.

† Including the cost of coinage, which is considerable; for silver it was 6 2-3 per cent.

CHAPTER IX.

THE DEBT AND FINANCES OF RUSSIA.

ON January 1, 1870, the "Annuaire des Finances Russes" estimated Russia's public debt at R.1,854,475,793.29. This sum comprised all the interest-bearing debt, foreign and domestic, including R.216,000,000 of exchequer bills (seventy-two series of R. 3,000,000 each, in denominations of R. 50, bearing interest at 4.32 per cent. per annum), and including also of the fiduciary circulation of R.721,788,189 the unsecured part, amounting to R. 567,972,166.30. In this total, the specie debt was estimated at the rate of 29⅝d. per rouble, the rate prevailing on December 31, 1869.

Twenty-five years later, on January 1, 1895, another official publication shows the same debt to have reached the total, in credit-roubles, of R. 5,776,828,440; that is, R.1,882,872,438 payable in specie (estimated at the rate prevailing during the last few years, 160 copecks, paper, for R.1 of specie, making R. 3,012,600,000 credit-roubles), and R. 2,764,627,539 payable in paper. Nominally, then, the debt has more than trebled during the quarter-century, having increased from R.1,854,500,000 to R. 5,776,800,000. Have the expenses of the Government increased in the same proportion? In the budget of 1870, we find under the heading of "interest on the public debt," in credit-roubles, R.78,375,496. That we may not have to return to this subject, let us say at once that, in addition to this amount, there was R.6,500,000 representing a charge upon guaranteed railroad debts. For 1895, we find the interest charge to be R. 74,094,913, upon the specie debt (or, in credit-roubles, R. 118,551,861), and R.129,647,261 on the debt payable in paper money, a total of R. 248,199,122 in credit-roubles. If we take account of the fact that this sum includes interest due on the bonds of railroads purchased by the State, we find, in the first place, that while the debt has increased more than threefold, the annual interest charge, which for

1870 was R. 85,000,000 (including the R. 6,500,000 upon guaranteed debts), has not increased in the same proportion. This relative lightening of the burden has resulted evidently from a saving of interest by refunding operations. At this point, it is worth while to examine in some detail the various items composing the public debt. Thus we shall find that the formidable increase between 1870 and 1895 has not arisen entirely out of so-called unproductive outlays—that is, outlays made necessary by wars and by the maintenance of large armies in time of peace; though these, in Russia as elsewhere, make up, unfortunately, a heavy total in the annual expense account. It is often difficult to distinguish clearly between loans which are for a productive use and those which are not, because any given loan may have been made entirely or mainly for the construction of railroads, for example; then as the State bought in the roads it issued rentes against them, and these in the public debt statement are indistinguishable from loans made purely for administrative purposes. Nevertheless, from the large total of the public debt payable in specie (R. 1,882,900,000), we can separate the following items:

	Millions of Roubles.
4 per cent. loan of the Nicolas Railroad	145.2
" " bonds of the Tambov-Saratov R. R.	7.2
" " " " Grand Railway System	28.9
" " " " Kursk-Kharkov-Azov R. R.	54.8
" " " " " " " "	7.7
" " " " Orel-Vitebsk R. R.	11.4
" " " " Orel-Griasi R. R.	17.9
" " " " Dvinsk-Vitebsk R. R.	19.1
" " " " Donets R. R.	6.9
" " " " Riga-Dvinsk R. R.	9.5
3 " " " Transcaucasian R. R.	52.1
" " " " Grand Railway System	12.2
" " " " Morshansk-Syzran R. R.	2.7
" " " " Riajsk-Viazma R. R.	3.3
5 " " " Transcaucasian & Poti-Tiflis R. R.	16.7
" " " " Riajsk-Morshansk R. R.	4.5
" " " " Tambov-Koslov R. R.	1.9
" " " " Riga-Mitau R. R.	1.1
" " " " Donets R. R.	1.3
" " " " Riga-Dvinsk R. R.	2.3
" " " " Orel-Vitebsk R. R.	27.0
" " " " Losowo-Sebastopol R. R.	6.8
4½ " " " Grand Railway System	31.7

This gives us a sum of R. 326,000,000 devoted directly to railroads. But there remain also the large total of R. 560,300,000 of four per cent. consolidated bonds and a four per cent. gold loan of R. 455,500,000, a large part of which were used by the State in the purchase of railways. We are certainly justified in placing at least half of these two sums (or more than R. 500,000,000) in the railway account; and this, together with the R. 326,-000,000 named above, leaves but little more than R. 1,000,000,000 under the heading of unproductive expenses, or of expenses which can in any sense be so called.

We come now to the debt payable in paper roubles. In the total of R. 2,764,600,000 named above under this heading, we find also the bonds of some railroads that have been purchased by the State, namely:

	MILLIONS OF ROUBLES.
4 per cent. bonds of the Kursk-Kharkov-Azov R. R.	9
" " " " Orel-Griasi R. R.	4.7
" " " " Grand Railway Co. of 1893	9
" " " " Orenburg R. R.	10.1
" " " " Libau-Romny R. R.	4.6
" " " " Tambov-Koslov R. R.	3.5
" " " " Riajsk-Morshansk R. R.	3.4

These figures make a modest total of R. 44,300,000; but to this must be added two domestic (or non-metallic) railway loans, one of R. 74,600,000 made in 1890, and one of R. 74,800,000 made in 1892, and also two issues of five per cent. railway bonds, that of the Oural line, R. 10,200,000, and that of the Riga-Dvinsk line, R. 1,800,000. These four sums together amount to R. 161,400,000, which, added to the R. 44,300,000 above, makes a total of R. 205,700,000 of loans for productive purposes. Adding also the R. 100,-000,000 of five per cent. rentes issued for the railway account, we have R. 305,700,000 to be deducted from the total of the debt payable in paper money, which leaves $\frac{8}{9}$ (R. 2,459,000,000) of that sum as the amount devoted directly to State purposes.

It was between 1888 and 1894, as we have already learned, that very important conversions of Russian 6, 5½, and 5 per cent. loans into four per cents. were made, as well as a large number of purchases of railways, the result being an increase of budgetary expenses on the one hand, and on the other a decrease in the amount of interest guaranteed. The net result of these operations the official tables sum up thus: Upon loans payable in specie the interest charge was R. 61,881,281 in 1887, and R. 74,094,913 in 1895, an increase of R. 12,213,632; the interest on loans payable in paper was R. 122,514,658 in 1887, and R. 129,647,261 in 1895, an increase of R. 7,132,-603. Altogether, therefore, the refunding operations and the purchase of railway lines added to the annual interest charge more than the equivalent of R. 26,000,000 in paper. But this amounts virtually to a decrease if we take into consideration the disappearance of a large amount of interest guaranteed by the State.

In an article recently published (September, 1895), the official organ of the Finance Department presents an estimate of the amount of the public debt on January 1, 1896, and of the interest charges. The totals are practically the same as those we have quoted for January 1, 1895. The addition of the 3½ per cent. gold loan of R. 100,000,000 made in 1894, and other small sums, brings the specie debt to R. 2,038,284,210. The debt payable in paper money will be increased from various causes by about R. 55,500,000, and will amount to R. 2,820,069,317. The two debts together will make a total, reckoned in paper, of R. 6,081,200,000, the metallic rouble being taken as the equivalent of R. 1.60 paper. We are told that the interest upon the specie debt for 1895, which we have estimated above at R. 74,094,913, amounted in fact to R. 74,274,913, and that the sinking fund for that debt required R. 9,268,561, making a total of R. 83,543,474; for 1896 the interest charge will be R. 79,817,708, and the sinking-fund requirement, R. 10,183,001, a total of R. 90,000,709 in specie. As for the debt payable in paper, the interest charge named above is also slightly increased and becomes R. 130,267,281; its sinking fund will demand R. 13,270,312, a total of R. 143,537,593. While the interest charge upon the specie debt is greater for 1896 than for 1895, there will be a reduction in the charge upon the debt payable in paper; interest on this part of the debt will be only R. 123,040,125, and the sinking-fund requirements, R. 11,087,761, a total of R. 134,127,886. To sum up: the requirements of 1895 are R. 83,543,474, specie (the equivalent of R. 133,669,000 in paper), and R. 143,537,593 payable in paper, making altogether an equivalent of R. 277,200,000, paper. For 1896 the specie requirement is R. 96,000,000 (the equivalent of R. 144,000,000 paper), and the paper requirement R. 134,000,000, or R. 278,000,000 in all. Thus the charges for each year are practically the same.

It is claimed that more than half of these expenses entailed by the public debt are met by revenues imposing no burden on the tax-payers. We present the figures upon which this theory is based, without intending to make ourselves responsible for the soundness of the theory itself.

Out of the gross revenue of R. 179,800,000 produced by the State railways, there is set apart under this heading the

	Millions of Roubles.
Net profit of	51.2
Annual payments of serfs previously belonging to individuals, for their emancipation	39.9
Payments by the Southwestern Railway	16.0
Extra charges for fast freight service	7.3
Annuities payable by railways	14.8
The State's revenue from private lines	1.6
Payments to be made by the Bank of the Nobility	6.5
Five per cent. interest on certain loans	6.0
War indemnity	3.4
Total	146.7

There is more than one item in this table whose title to the character it assumes might be contested. For example, the payment of redemption money by the serfs is certainly felt by those who pay it, and so of the fast freight charges. On the other hand, we may be permitted to ask whether absolute dependence can be placed on all these sources of income. It is altogether possible, for instance, that the Bank of the Nobility may meet with some disappointment in its collections, or that some of the former serfs may allow their payments to fall into arrear, especially as they are somewhat accustomed to delays of this kind, like their former masters of a higher social grade. But let us not insist upon these points. We have seen above that the total public debt is estimated at R. 2,038,000,000 payable in specie, and R. 2,820,000,000 payable in paper. Is that the whole of it? It appears to us that the paper money issued by the State ought to have a place in this category. Inasmuch as these issues aggregate about R. 1,100,-000,000, while the metallic reserve in the Treasury is nearly R. 600,000,000, which, at the usual rate (R. 1.60), represents R. 960,000,000 in paper, there remains only about R. 150,000,000 paper to be included among the debts. Then, on the other hand, we must take account of the State's assets. Upon this point we have no official information corresponding to the dates for which we have stated the debt. We have not as yet the report of the Comptroller-General for the year 1894; it will not appear until the end of 1895. In his report for 1893, published in 1894, the various arrearages and credits of the State are reported thus, in millions and tenths of millions of roubles:

	Gold.	Credit Roubles.
1. War indemnity	181.5	1.0
2. Loans by the former credit institutions	....	26.8
3. Loans made by the Treasury	7.2	186.8
4. Due in payment for lands allotted to the former serfs	....	1,646.7
5. Sums due from purchasers of State lands	....	8.2
6. From railroads	303.7	929.0
7. Other credits and arrearages	....	146.6
Total	492.4	2,945.1

This, the report says, amounts to R. 3,683,800,000, estimating gold roubles at the current rate. Compared with the balance-sheet of 1893, this shows a decrease of R. 268,100,000, resulting principally from the abolition of the debts charged against the Orenburg, Moscow-Kursk, Baltic, and Donets railway lines purchased by the State, and against the Baltic shipyards, likewise purchased by the State. We may add that in 1894 and 1895 the State bought a number of railway lines, so that the sums named above as railroad credits, R. 303,700,000 specie and R. 929,000,000 paper, have been considerably diminished; but, on the other hand, the property of the State has been increased to a proportional extent. Properly speaking, there is no occasion to make a critical examination of the market value of the R. 3,683,800,000 of credits held by the State as an offset against its debts. The credit of a State is not to be estimated upon the basis of such claims, on the greater part of which it cannot realize, and least of all at a time when the public treasury is in need of funds. These are the statistics of an amateur; the future of a nation is in nowise involved in them.

The credit of a State depends upon an established financial policy and conscientious fidelity in meeting its obligations. As to Russia, its conduct toward foreign creditors has always been above reproach. Certain stock exchange rumors having been recently circulated concerning a series of proposed refunding operations alleged to be contrary to the express agreement of the Government, an official note was published on October 13 (25), 1895, denying these imputations. As it presents a clear exposition of the Imperial Government's views upon the subject, we place it before the reader:

"Certain newspapers, Russian and foreign, have raised the question of the Russian Government's right to anticipate the payment of the 5 per cent. (specie) loan of 1822, the 4 per cent. bonds of the Nicolas Railroad, the issue of 1867–9, and the 4 per cent. Consolidated Russian Railway loan of 1880.

"For this reason it has seemed advisable to the Bond Department of the Government to call the attention of the public to the fact that the answer to this question may be found in the imperial ukase of November 8, 1888, which orders:

"'That steps shall be taken, as soon as the state of the money market will allow, to refund the public loans and the debts guaranteed by the State into new obligations at a lower rate of interest; provided always, that these three points be kept in mind:

"'(*a*) The owners of outstanding bonds shall have the option of accepting payment at par in specie, or of exchanging their bonds for those of the new issue.

"'(*b*) The following descriptions of bonds are not to be refunded: those which by the conditions of their issue were to be repaid at more than their par value, and those in respect to which the Government has ever waived, either temporarily or permanently, its right to refund them.

"'(*c*) Three months at least shall always be allowed, after official publication of the intent to refund, during which the bonds may be presented for repayment, and interest upon the bonds so called in is to cease only at the expiration of this time.'

"Accordingly, there can be no conversion of loans payable with a premium, that is to say, above 100 per cent.; nor of lottery bonds, nor of bonds the anticipatory payment of which the Government has waived, even at the date of their issue.

"From the application of this law to the four classes of loans named above, it follows that—

"(*a*) The 5 per cent. loan of 1822 cannot be refunded, because the evidences of that loan carry upon their face this provision: '§25. No one can be compelled to accept, without his own consent, the whole or any part of the money invested in the permanent debt' (that is, in the debt having no definite date of payment, not payable at a time fixed in advance).

"(*b*) The three other loans, namely, the 4 per cent. bonds of the Nicolas Railroad, the issues of 1867–9, and the 4 per cent. Consolidated Russian Railway loan of 1880, sixth series, the Government can refund or pay before their due date, because there is no stipulation upon these bonds denying its right to do so, and no prize or premium is secured upon their repayment.

"It is to be noted that during the conversions made between 1888 and 1891 of the 5 per cent. and 4½ per cent. loans, though these loans were in nowise distinguishable, except as to the rate of interest, from the 4 per cent. bonds of 1867, 1869, and 1880, the law quoted above gave rise to no question or misunderstanding, either in general or in any specific case.

"Up to the present moment the 4 per cent. bonds of 1867, 1869, and 1880 have never been quoted at the Bourse above other Russian 4 per cent. bonds, though frequently they have been quoted below them. This fact proves that neither the public in general nor those persons specially interested in bonds have ever supposed that either of those three issues enjoyed any special privilege arising from the fact that its payment could not be anticipated.

"We are justified, then, in supposing that the question raised with regard to this matter did not arise out of doubts honestly entertained by any *bona fide* holder of bonds."

A History of Savings-Banks

IN

THE UNITED STATES.

BY

JOHN P. TOWNSEND, LL.D.,

PRESIDENT OF THE BOWERY SAVINGS BANK, OF NEW YORK.

::

NEW YORK.
1896.

HISTORY OF SAVINGS-BANKS

IN THE

UNITED STATES.

I.

ORIGIN AND GROWTH OF SAVINGS-BANKS.

THE birth of the savings-bank idea must be credited to England, where, in 1797, the first publication on the subject was issued by Jeremy Bentham, in whose plans for the management of paupers was included a system of "frugality" banks. Mr. Bentham's writings interested many philanthropic people, and in the later years of the last century and the early years of this, many well-intentioned plans were evolved in Great Britain, some of which seem queer in the light of the present, but all of which aimed to aid the poor to independence and self-respect. Among others who were interested in this evolution were Samuel Whitbread, Patrick Colgeshoun, Rev. Joseph Smith, Lady Isabella Douglas, and Mrs. Priscilla Wakefield. The latter was, in 1801, the superintendent of a "friendly society for the benefit of women and children," which combined with it a bank for savings for their benefit. It was not until 1810 that Rev. Henry Duncan, who has been called the father of savings-banks, established at Ruthwell, Scotland, in his own parish, "a savings and friendly society." It is true that Mr. Duncan's effort resembled more nearly the modern savings-bank plan than anything which had been previously established, and the publication of his ideas and work stimulated an interest in savings institutions. When, in 1817, the first act of Parliament was passed which established the system in England and Ireland under Government control, there were seventy-eight private societies distributed through England, Ireland, and Wales which received and invested the savings of the laboring poor. In Scotland, where Rev. Mr. Duncan had worked so successfully as a pioneer, these savings institutions were not recognized by law until 1835. It is worthy of mention in passing, that the savings-bank theory was established in Switzerland, at Zurich, in 1805, and the first bank in France was opened at Paris in 1818.

To America belongs the honor of first incorporating and regulating by law a savings-bank. This bank was the Provident Institution for Savings, which was incorporated in Boston, December 13, 1816, the year before the British savings-banks were sanctioned by act of Parliament. The ideas and hopes which possessed the founders of the bank in Boston were well expressed in their appeal for recognition to the Legislature of Massachusetts, as follows: "It is not by the alms of the wealthy that the good of the lower class can be generally promoted. By such donations, encouragement is far oftener given to idleness and hypocrisy than aid to suffering worth. He is the most effective benefactor of the poor who encourages them in habits of industry, sobriety, and frugality." Though this Boston bank was the first savings institution in the world regulated by law, it was not the earliest savings-bank in the United States, for in a previous month of the same year, 1816, a bank for savings opened its doors in Philadelphia. This latter society was not incorporated until February 15, 1819.

THE BASIC IDEA OF THE SAVINGS-BANK.

In looking back, it seems strange that eighteen centuries of time were required before savings-banks came as a practical aid in solving the problem impressed on human intelligence by the words, "The poor you have always with you." Charity had been taught and applied from the first, but the benefits which flow from the blending of business and benevolence in the savings-bank system were unknown prior to the opening of the present century. Speaking broadly, the history of the first savings-bank is the history of all. The basic idea was the desire to aid the poor in a practical way, and benevolent men associated themselves together in this effort to improve the condition of those who, under conditions then existing, were unable to help themselves. These men recognized the fact that pauperism and crime were allies; that public morals became more lax as poorhouses and workhouses increased. To help the poor individually would decrease the public tax burdens for their support. This was the end hoped for. It is probable that the men who in 1817 developed the savings-bank plan had no conception of the power they were generating. Even so late as 1834, when the Bowery Savings-Bank, the fourth in New York City to be incorporated, was established, so little was its use anticipated that the total amount of deposits allowed by its original charter was limited to $500,000. When it is said that to-day the deposits of this one bank exceed $55,000,000, and it has more than 112,000 open accounts, with assets at market value of $63,000,000, the contrast of the promise of A. D. 1834 with the realization of A. D. 1896 can readily be understood. Yet so simple was the theory of the founders, so full was it of a knowledge of human nature, that in the test of sixty-two years of actual practice it has suffered no essential change, only development and expansion, guided by the wisdom and safeguarded by the conscience of the men who have been identified with these institutions in later years. It may be said here that the general law of the State of New York differs in no essential particulars from the original charter granted to the Bowery Savings-Bank in 1834. The secret of the success of savings-banks is found in the truth that "self-preservation is the first law of nature." They furnish the opportunity in business for the outworking of this law in the individual.

While savings-banks teach the poor lessons in thrift, they at the same time pay to the poor a premium for accepting the lessons. In efforts to elevate humanity, the hope of reward is a more salutary force than the fear of punishment. Every savings-bank is a monument to that enlightened self-interest which is the corner-stone of all progress—material, intellectual, and spiritual. It is worth noting that the inception of savings-banks occurred in that era in the last quarter of the eighteenth century when Europe and America were shaken by a Vesuvius of democracy. Out of the battle-fires kindled at Bunker Hill in 1775, and rekindled with fiercer flame on the other side of the Atlantic when, in 1789, the Bastile fell, the spirit of liberty and equality rose an inspiring sight, illuminating the political, social, and commercial world. For centuries the poor had been enslaved. The rich and powerful ruled the Church and State alike; the many were kept in serfdom that the few might luxuriate in wealth and power. A few years of appalling struggle changed all this. The declaration of independence in America, the eloquence of men like Chatham and Burke in England, and the teachings of Franklin impressed new ideas on Europe and America. Freedom came, greater responsibility for the individual, and with greater liberty, more self-respect. One method of expression of this sense of greater responsibility was found in the organization of savings-banks. They, in the financial world, reach down to the people as the ballot-box does in the political world. The ballot-box enables a man to assert himself in the politics of the nation, and savings-banks furnish him the opportunity of sharing in its prosperity. It was, therefore, natural that when equality came into political life, the savings-bank should quickly follow it in financial life, each in its own way tending to uplift the individual and strengthen the nation.

FAILURES OF OTHER PHILANTHROPIC SCHEMES.

The charitable spirit had been previously displayed in the colonial history of this country, and had found expression in efforts to fix by law the price of articles of necessity, and the wages of mechanics and laborers; but experience demonstrated that such regulations were detrimental to the interests of the people; afterward lotteries with charitable designs were legalized, as well as charitable societies for the protection and support of members who might be in need of assistance, by reason of sickness or accident, and for the relief of destitute widows and orphans of deceased members. In 1803 a petition was presented to the Legislature of the State of New York, praying that sundry persons might be incorporated into a society, with power to build workshops and purchase materials for the employment of the poor. The present political society of Tammany, or Columbian Order, in the city of New York, was incorporated in 1805 as a charitable institution, for the purpose of affording relief to the indigent and distressed members of the association, their widows and orphans, and others who might be found proper objects of its charity. Many benevolent and charitable societies were incorporated in the New England and Middle States in the next decade; some of them fulfilled the designs of their founders to a limited extent, but all failed to accomplish anything for the permanent well-being of those they intended to benefit. Instead of helping the beneficiaries so that at some time in the future they would take care of themselves, they ministered to present wants only, which were ever recurring but never fully satisfied; with every succeeding dispensation the receivers became more dependent, finally lost their own self-respect, and really became paupers. The disease had been aggravated by improper remedies. Experience demonstrated that, in most cases, temporary relief resulted in entire dependence, and the number of poor, instead of decreasing, steadily increased. As soon as it became known in a community that anything could be had without labor; that soup, fuel, clothing, or shelter could be had without cost, then the moral standard of the neighborhood was lowered, and all further efforts on the part of recipients to earn their own living were abandoned, not only for the part gratuitously offered, but all honest work was given up, and ingenious schemes were resorted to in order to obtain the greatest amount possible. Time and labor were wasted which, if they had been directed by honest efforts, would, in most cases, have comfortably supported the degraded persons and their families. Having learned this plain lesson taught by experience, a class of philanthropists resorted to the system of helping others to provide for themselves by teaching the poor to acquire habits of thrift in laying aside some part of their earnings in a time of prosperity, to provide for future wants in the days of adversity or old age.

In addition to the savings-banks opened in 1816 in Boston and Philadelphia, there were others in the United States prior to 1820. The Savings-Bank of Baltimore was incorporated in December, 1818; the Salem (Mass.) bank in the same year; the Bank for Savings in New York, March 26, 1819, and in the same year also, the Society for Savings in Hartford, Conn.; the Savings-Bank of Newport, R. I., and Providence (R. I.) Institution for Savings. All of these institutions are still in existence, and the latest annual reports show them to be in a flourishing and prosperous condition, the results of honesty and common sense in their management, which have characterized them from the beginning.

THE AIMS OF SAVINGS INSTITUTIONS.

The aims and objects of savings-banks do not seem to be well understood by the general public. Even among men of affairs the amount of misinformation regarding the savings-bank plan is remarkable. For example, in a recent magazine article a Western financier referred to the "owners of savings-banks"; and oftentimes when men are approached with an invitation to become trustees the question is asked, "How much stock will I have to buy in order to be elected a trustee?" or, "What pay do trustees receive for attendance at meetings?" It is such questions as these that cause one to welcome the opportunity of explaining the beneficent purposes and philanthropic operations of savings-banks. They are really institutions organized and managed for the purpose of aiding the people of the poorer classes, so called—those who have no knowledge of investments, or whose savings are so small that they cannot be invested, with profit, by the individual. The smallest sums are received. Savings-banks will open an account for a person with one dollar; some accept an account where the initial deposit is only ten cents. As a further inducement for the depositor to save, his money, when the amount to his credit aggregates five dollars, begins to draw interest. And these little savings which amount to the enormous sum hereinafter indicated, belonging to more than four million depositors, become great factors in the financial operations of the country. The different States and the various municipalities, when about to borrow money, send their prospectus to the savings-banks, and so high is the reputation of these institutions that the price the savings-banks will pay for the securities fixes in many instances their market price, or the rate at which money can be borrowed upon them.

Later in this article will be given a digest of the New York law governing savings-banks, as the best way of making entirely clear the operation of these institutions as they attain to perfection to-day.

In the old systems of public economy, mankind were divided into two classes—the capitalist and the laborer; but through the agency of savings-banks, in these later years, our political economy must be written anew, for behold, the laborers have become the capitalists in this new world! The millions of the earnings of the poor are loaned to the rich on bond and mortgage in this State. Is a local improvement projected, the savings-bank is the capitalist who advances money. Nor should we lose sight of the character in which savings-banks are thus revealed as a sort of co-operative union of the industrial classes. Their savings, aggregated as capital, minister to these public enterprises; but these public enterprises demand laborers for their prosecution, and thus return to labor in the form of wages what they have borrowed from it in the form of capital. The laborers get better wages for the facility with which, through savings-banks, the requisite capital can be procured, which is equivalent to having their capital returned to them in full, with extra dividends, by installments called wages, while at the same time they hold in their pass-book the original certificate which entitles them to have it again returned to them, with ordinary dividends called interest. What other capitalist is able to make so safe and at the same time so profitable an investment of his money? Other "unions" are formed as combinations of labor against capital, but here is a combination of labor and capital. The former seeks to control the price of labor by arbitrary dicta; the latter affects the price of labor favorably to the laborer through the operation of natural laws. The former has a fund which offers a premium to idleness by contributing to the support of a laborer while on a strike; the fund of the latter incites to industry by flowing into the channels of enterprise which demand labor for their prosecution.

In view of what the savings-bank system has done and of what it is to-day, it claims fair treatment and credit according to its performance. Because savings-banks hold hundreds of millions of money securely, because they help those who try to help themselves, because they are giving aid to thousands of men in business or owning houses partly paid for, because the system has been perfected by disciplinary experience and corrective legislation, and because it is rooted in many ways directly—and remotely, too—in the material and moral interests of the people, the savings-bank system deserves the considerate support and demands the patient and sympathetic attention of those who study economical and social problems with the purpose of promoting public welfare and of doing the greatest good to the greatest number.

II.

SAVINGS-BANKS IN THE STATE OF NEW YORK.

The nature and methods of savings-banks can be best understood from a description of them as they exist in the State of New York, as the laws of that State provide a plan on which, with some modifications, all true savings-banks are operated in the New England and Middle States.

The law of the State of New York provides that thirteen or more persons, two-thirds of whom are residents of the county where the projected bank is to be located, may become a savings-bank by executing and acknowledging a certificate in duplicate, one certificate to be filed in the office of the clerk of the county, and the other in the office of the Superintendent of Banks, within sixty days, setting forth: (1) The name selected for the corporation; (2) the place where its business is to be transacted; (3) the name, residence, occupation, and post-office address of each member of the corporation; and (4) a declaration that each will faithfully discharge the duties of trustee in such corporation.

After a notice of the intention to organize has been properly published in the newspapers, and the duplicate certificate filed with the Superintendent of Banks, this officer ascertains from investigation: (1) Whether greater convenience of access to a savings-bank will be afforded to any considerable number of depositors by opening a savings-bank in the place designated in the certificate; (2) whether the density of the population in the neighborhood designated for such savings-bank, and in the surrounding country, affords a reasonable promise of adequate support to the enterprise; and (3) whether the responsibility, character, and general fitness for the discharge of the duties appertaining to such a trust, of the persons named in the certificate, are such as to demand the confidence of the community in which such savings-bank is proposed to be established. If the Superintendent of Banks is satisfied upon these matters, he issues a certificate of authorization for the proposed savings-bank, and transmits it to the County Clerk, who attaches it to the Certificate of Incorporation previously filed with him. If the Superintendent of Banks fails to be satisfied with the necessity for the bank, or the competency of its organizers, he notifies the County Clerk of his refusal to issue the Certificate of Authorization.

The savings-bank corporation thus prepared for work must begin business within one year or forfeit its rights. In addition to the usual powers conferred by the general corporation law, savings-bank corporations have the power to receive on deposit any sum of money that may be offered for that purpose by any person, or society, or corporation, and to invest the same, and declare, credit, and pay dividends thereon, subject to limitations which will be explained hereafter. The number of persons to organize a savings-bank cannot be less than thirteen, as the law provides that there shall be a board of not less than that number, who shall have the entire management and control of affairs, and who shall elect from themselves or otherwise, a president and two vice-presidents, and other officers within their discretion. The thirteen persons named in the certificate of authorization constitute the first board of trustees. This board has the power of filling any vacancy which may occur in it, but no man can be elected a trustee who is not a resident of the State, and whenever a trustee removes from the State, he thereby forfeits his trusteeship. The constant supervision of the management of the savings-bank is ensured by the law, which prescribes that all the by-laws and rules and regulations of the bank, as drafted by the trustees, shall be transmitted to the Superintendent of Banks, and that no change or amendments can be made without his knowledge.

Trustees of banks must meet as often as once a month, and in order to secure the faithful performance of duty upon the part of officers and agents of the bank, they are permitted to ask bonds from such subordinates. As indicating the sedulous care which the State of New York exercises over the management of its savings-banks, the following two paragraphs are worth quoting entire:

"Whenever a trustee of any savings-bank shall become a trustee, officer, clerk, or employee of any other savings-bank, or when he shall borrow, directly or indirectly, any of the funds of the savings-bank in which he is trustee, or become a surety or guarantor for any money borrowed of or a loan made by such savings-bank, or when he shall fail to attend the regular meetings of the board, or perform any of the duties devolved upon him as such trustee, for six successive months, without having been previously excused by the board for such failure, the office of such trustee shall thereupon immediately become vacant; but the trustee vacating his office by failure to attend meetings or to discharge his duties, may, in the discretion of the board, be eligible to re-election.

"No trustee of any such corporation shall have any interest, direct or indirect, in the gains or profits thereof, nor as such, directly or indirectly, receive any pay or emolument for his services, except as hereafter provided; and no trustee or officer of any such corporation shall, directly or indirectly, for himself or as an agent or partner of others, borrow any of its funds or deposits, or in any manner use the same except to make such current and necessary payments as are authorized by the board of trustees; nor shall any trustee or officer of any such corporation become an indorser or surety, or become in any manner an obligor, for moneys loaned by or borrowed of such corporation."

Regarding the repayment of deposits, the power regulating the time and method of payment is vested in the board of trustees, but the regulations must be of a permanent character, and must be conspicuously posted in the place of business of the corporation. The trustees are also authorized to limit, at their discretion, the aggregate amount which any person or society may deposit, and they may also refuse to receive any deposit or at any time return all or any part of any deposit. Lest the opportunity of savings-banks for safe investment and sure interest should be used too freely by the rich, for whom they are not intended, the law provides that the aggregate amount of deposits to the credit of any individual at any time shall not exceed $3000, exclusive of deposits arising from judicial sales or trust funds or interest; and that the amount to the credit of any society or corporation at any time shall not exceed $5000, exclusive of accrued interest.

THE PROTECTION OF DEPOSITORS—INVESTMENT OF DEPOSITS.

The advantages and protection which savings-banks offer to minors and to women are of much interest. It is provided that when any deposit is made by or in the name of a minor, it shall be held for the exclusive right and benefit of the depositor, and be free from the control or lien of all other persons except creditors, and shall be paid, together with dividends and interest thereon, to the person in whose name the deposit is made, and the receipt and acquittance of the minor who so deposits is a valid and sufficient release of such deposit or any part thereof. In all actions in any court of the State of New York against savings-banks by a husband to recover for moneys deposited by his wife in her own name, or as her own money, the wife may be examined and testify as a witness just as if she were an unmarried woman. One other section (116) of the savings-bank law of the State of New York may be quoted entire in order to give adequate information as to the manner in which the interests of depositors are guarded. The trustees of the savings-bank can invest the moneys deposited therein and the income derived therefrom only as follows:

(1) "In the stocks or bonds or interest-bearing notes or obligations of the United States, or those for which the faith of the United States is pledged to provide for the payment of the interest and principal, including the bonds of the District of Columbia.

(2) "In the stocks or bonds or interest-bearing obligations of this State, issued pursuant to the authority of any law of the State.

(3) "In the stocks or bonds or interest-bearing obligations of any State of the United States, which has not within ten years previous to making such investment, by such corporation, defaulted in the payment of any part of either principal or interest of any debt authorized by the Legislature of any such State to be contracted.

(4) "In the stocks or bonds of any city, county, town or village, school district bonds and union free school district bonds, issued for school purposes, or in the interest-bearing obligations of any city or county of this State, for the payment of which the faith and credit of the municipality issuing them are pledged.

(5) "In the stocks or bonds of the following cities outside of New York State: Philadelphia, St. Louis, Boston, Baltimore, Cincinnati, Cleveland, Pittsburg, Detroit, Milwaukee, Minneapolis, Louisville, St. Paul, Providence, Allegheny, Worcester, Toledo, New Haven, Paterson, Lowell, Scranton, Fall River, Cambridge, Grand Rapids, Reading, Trenton, Hartford, Des Moines, and Portland, Me. If at any time the indebtedness of any of the said cities, less their water debt and sinking fund, shall exceed seven per centum of its valuation for purposes of taxation, its bonds and stocks shall thereafter cease to be an authorized investment for the moneys of savings-banks, and the Superintendent of the Banking Department may, in his discretion, require any savings-bank to sell or retain such bonds or stocks of said city as may have been purchased prior to said increase of debt.

(6) "In bonds and mortgages on unincumbered real property situated in this State, worth at least twice the amount loaned thereon. Not more than sixty-five per centum of the whole amount of deposits may be so loaned or invested. If the loan is on unimproved and unproductive real property, the amount loaned thereon shall not be more than forty per centum of its actual value. No investment in any bond and mortgage shall be made by any savings-bank, except upon the report of a committee of its trustees charged with the duty of investigating the same, who shall certify to the value of the premises mortgaged, or to be mortgaged, according to their best judgment, and such report shall be filed and preserved among the records of the corporation."

The savings-banks are permitted to invest in real property to the extent of owning their own bank building, which, with the lot, shall not cost more than twenty-five per cent. of the net surplus of the corporation, and of retaining for a time such property as may come into possession of the bank at sales upon the foreclosure of mortgages owned by it, or on judgments or other methods of settlement for debts due to it. Five years is the limit of time for which savings-banks can retain such property, other than their own banking house, unless they receive permission anew from the Superintendent of Banks. Even before they purchase the site of their bank building they must submit the plans of the building to be erected, with the estimate of the cost of the lot and building, to the Superintendent of Banks for his approval. The trustees are permitted to keep uninvested an available fund for current expenses, but this fund must not exceed ten per cent. of the whole amount of the deposits in the bank. This sum may be deposited in any bank organized under the law of this State, or of the United States, or in a trust company incorporated by any law of the State whose paid-up capital and surplus aggregates at least four times the amount of money deposited with it by the savings-bank. Another method of use for this current expense fund is provided by the law in the following words: "Such available fund, or any part thereof, may be loaned upon pledge of the securities, or any of them, named in the first four paragraphs of section 116, but not in excess of ninety per centum of the cash market value of such securities so pledged. Should any of the securities so held in pledge depreciate in value after making any loan thereon, the trustees shall require the immediate payment of such loan, or of a part thereof, so that the amount loaned shall at no time exceed ninety per centum of the market value of the securities pledged for the same."

CAUTIONARY PROHIBITIONS AND LIMITATIONS.

The savings-banks in New York State are expressly prohibited from loaning money on notes, bills of exchange, drafts, or any other personal security whatever, and in all cases of loans upon real property, a sufficient bond, secured by a mortgage on the property, shall be required from the borrower, who must also pay all expenses incident to the transaction. The bank is further protected in its realty investments by the requirement that the mortgagor insure the property, and assign the policy to the bank, which also has the right to renew the policy of insurance from year to year, as it may expire, charging the expenses of the renewal in every case to the mortgagor. The only exception to the prohibition against dealing in commodities is that which permits banks to sell gold or silver received in payment of interest or principal of obligations owned by them, or from depositors in the regular course of business, or they may pay regular depositors, when requested by them, by draft upon deposits to the credit of the bank in the city of New York, and charge current rates of exchange for such drafts. No savings-bank can make or issue any certificate of deposit payable either on demand or at a fixed day, or pay any interest except regular quarterly or semi-annual dividends upon any deposits or balances, or pay any interest or deposit, or portion of a deposit, or any check drawn upon itself by a depositor, unless the pass-book of the depositor be produced and the proper entry be made therein at the time of the transaction. Within their own discretion and subject to the approval of the Superintendent of Banks, savings-banks are permitted to make payments in cases of loss of pass-book or other exceptional cases where the pass-book cannot be produced without loss or serious inconvenience to depositors.

REGULATION OF INTEREST TO DEPOSITORS.

The trustees must regulate the rate of interest or dividends, not to exceed five per centum per annum, upon the deposits in such manner that depositors shall receive, as nearly as may be, all the profits of such corporation, after deducting necessary expenses and reserving such amounts as the trustees may deem expedient as a surplus fund for the security of the depositors, which, to the amount of fifteen per cent. of its deposits, the trustees of any such corporation may gradually accumulate and hold, to meet any contingency or loss in its business from the depreciation of its securities or otherwise. The trustees may classify their depositors according to the character, amount, and duration of their dealings with the corporation, and regulate the interest or dividends allowed in such manner that each depositor shall receive the same ratable portion of interest or dividends as all others of his class. The trustees cannot declare or allow interest on any deposit for a longer period than the same has been deposited, except that deposits made not later than the tenth day of the month commencing any semi-annual interest period, or the third day of any month, or withdrawn upon one of the last three days of the month ending any quarterly or semi-annual interest period, may have interest declared upon them for the whole of the period or month when so deposited or withdrawn. Only upon an aye and nay vote by the board of trustees can dividends or interest be declared; and should any interest or dividend be declared and credited in excess of interest or profits earned by and credited to the savings-bank, the trustees voting for such dividend are liable for the amount of the excess. At least once in three years, all savings-banks whose surplus amounts to fifteen per cent. of its deposits must divide equitably the accumulation beyond such authorized surplus as an extra dividend to depositors, in excess of the regular dividend authorized.

In determining the per cent. of surplus held by any savings-bank, its interest-paying stocks and bonds must not be estimated above their par value or above their market value if below par. Its bonds and mortgages on which there are no arrears of interest of a longer period than six months must be estimated at their face, and its real property at not above cost. The Superintendent of Banks must determine the valuation of such stocks or bonds, or bonds and mortgages, as are in arrear of interest for six months or more, and of all other investments not herein enumerated, from the best information he can obtain, and he may change the valuation thereof from time to time as he may obtain other and further information.

The trustees of the bank who are chosen as officers of the institution, and whose duties require regular and faithful attendance, may receive such compensation as the majority of the trustees deem reasonable. When the vote is passed by the trustees fixing such amount, the trustee for whose services compensation is being allowed cannot vote, and trustees, as such, cannot receive any compensation whatever for their attendance at meetings of the board.

SUPERVISION, INSPECTION, AND REPORTS.

At all times, savings-banks are under the scrutiny and control of the Superintendent of Banks, and if it appears to him from an examination made by or reported to him, or from a report made by any such corporation, that it has committed any violation of its charter or law, or is conducting its business and affairs in an unsafe and unauthorized manner, he directs a discontinuance of such illegal and unsafe or unauthorized practices. Constant and thorough knowledge as to the assets of each savings-bank on the part of the trustees is required by the provision of the law that the trustees of savings-banks, by a committee of not less than three of their number, on or before the first day of January and July in each year, shall thoroughly examine the books, vouchers, and assets of their savings-bank, and its affairs generally. The statement or schedule of assets and liabilities reported to the Superintendent of Banks for the first of January and July in each year shall be based upon such examination, and shall be verified by the oath of a majority of the trustees making it; and the trustees of any savings-bank may require such examination at such other times as they shall prescribe. The trustees shall, as often as once in each six months during each year, cause to be taken an accurate balance of their depositors' ledgers, and in their semi-annual report to the Superintendent they shall state the fact that such balance has been taken, and the discrepancies, if any, existing between the amount due depositors, as shown by such balance, and the amount so due as shown by the general ledger.

That the expenses which negligence on the part of savings-banks causes to the State may fall upon the savings-banks themselves, it is provided that for the purpose of defraying the expenses incurred in the performance by the Superintendent of Banks of the duties imposed upon him with respect to savings-banks, other than the examination thereof, each such corporation shall annually pay five dollars into the treasury of the State, and the residue of such expenses, to be apportioned among them by the Superintendent, shall be paid into the treasury of the State by savings-banks whose deposits exceed one hundred thousand dollars, in proportion to the amount of assets severally held and reported by them. Whenever any State bank or trust company becomes insolvent, its debt to savings-banks becomes a preferred liability, and is paid immediately after provision has been made for the payment of the circulating notes of the bank or trust company, if it has any, unless, in the case of a trust company, other preferences have been provided for in its charter. The interest of the State in savings-banks is further shown by the decree that no bank, banking association, individual banker, firm, association, corporation, person or persons can advertise or put forth a sign as a savings-bank, under penalty of severe punishment.

It requires the affirmative vote, properly recorded, of not less than two-thirds of the whole number of trustees, at a meeting called for the purpose, to close a savings-bank, and all moneys due depositors must be paid in full, or unclaimed deposits turned over to the Superintendent of Banks. The Superintendent then has the power to pay out such moneys to the depositors entitled to them upon satisfactory identification, and he must annually report to the legislature the names of all closed savings-banks, with the sum of the unclaimed or unpaid deposits to the credit of each of them.

OFFICIAL REPORTS OF CONDITION.

Under the law of New York State, there can be no doubt as to the thoroughness with which the conduct of each and every savings-bank is scrutinized. The details already given of the intimate relations between these institutions and the State can be verified upon examination of the law regarding the reports which savings-banks must make semi-annually to the State. These reports must be made on or before the 20th day of January and July in each year, and must contain a statement of its condition on the mornings of the first days of January and July preceding. The report states the amount loaned upon bond and mortgage, together with a list of such bonds and mortgages, and the location of the mortgaged premises, as have not been previously reported, and also a list of such previously reported as have since been paid wholly or in part, or have been foreclosed, and the amount of such payments respectively; the cost, par value, and estimated market value of all stock investments, designating each particular kind of stock; the amount loaned upon the pledge of securities, with a statement of the securities held as collateral for such loans; the amount invested in real estate, giving the cost of the same; the amount of cash on hand and on deposit in banks or trust companies, and the amount deposited in each; and such other information as the Superintendent may require. The report also states all the liabilities of such savings corporation on the mornings of the first days of January and July; the amount due to depositors. which must include any dividend to be credited to them for the six months ending on that day, and any other debts or claims against such corporation which are or may be a charge upon its assets. It also states the amount deposited during the year previous, and the amount withdrawn during the same period; the whole amount of interest or profits received or earned, and the amount of dividends credited to depositors, together with the amount of each semi-annual credit of interest, and the amount of interest that may have been credited at other than semi-annual periods; the number of accounts opened or reopened, the number closed during the year, and the number of open accounts at the end of the year; and such other information as may be required by the Superintendent. The president and cashier or treasurer of the savings-bank must take oath to the completeness and accuracy of the report, the failure to make which is punishable by a forfeit to the people of the State of one hundred dollars for every day that the report is withheld. Any savings-bank failing to make two successive reports forfeits its charter.

An additional report which must be made to the Superintendent of Banks concerns the accounts of depositors of amounts of five dollars or more which have been dormant for twenty-two years or more from the first day of May preceding—that is, accounts which have not been increased or diminished by deposits or withdrawal, exclusive of interest credits. This report must be made by the first of June of each year, and negligence regarding it is punishable in the same manner as in the case of the main report of the bank.

III.

METHODS OF OPERATING IN DIFFERENT STATES.

The method of operating savings-banks is not the same in all the States where they exist. In some they take the form of a society, with power to add to their membership, and with perpetual succession, a certain number of members are yearly chosen by ballot to act as managers; these managers elect their own officers, make rules and by-laws, and alter or rescind them at pleasure. In others the corporators are a limited number, and are themselves trustees, with power to fill vacancies, and are responsible for the management to State authority, to which they report for publication at regular intervals. In some they do business under special charters, in others under general laws to which every institution in the States conforms. This last system is growing in favor, as supervision is simplified so that superintendents or commissioners familiar with the one law can easily determine if investments have been made in prohibited securities or in too great amounts on permissible ones. The laws in the six New England States in relation to savings-banks are very similar, although in some banks the managers are more conservative in their practice than in others. All invest to some extent in United States bonds, in bonds and mortgages on real estate, in national or State bank stocks, State, county, city, town, or village bonds, loans on personal security, in railroad bonds, and some in railroad stocks.

In addition to the investments permitted by the laws of the State of New York, there are permitted to savings-banks, under the laws of the States of Maine, New Hampshire, Vermont, Massachusetts, Rhode Island, and New Jersey, investments in the county bonds of other States; and New Hampshire, Vermont, and Rhode Island permit bonds and mortgages in the Western States. Maine permits bonds and mortgages beyond its own boundaries only, in the cities of the State of New Hampshire. Maine, New Hampshire, Vermont, Rhode Island, Connecticut, New Jersey, Pennsylvania permit investment in bank and trust company stocks; Maine, New Hampshire, Massachusetts, Rhode Island, Connecticut, New Jersey, Pennsylvania, and Ohio in railroad stocks and bonds; Maine, New Hampshire, and Rhode Island in the stock of water companies; New Hampshire, Rhode Island, and

New Jersey in gas company stocks; Maine, New Hampshire, Vermont, Massachusetts, Rhode Island, Connecticut in promissory notes; Connecticut allows investment in bonds and mortgages in four States outside its own jurisdiction; the State of Maryland allows savings-bank funds to be invested in stocks and bonds and mortgages without specifying exactly their character or location.

The limitation on deposits in Maine is $2000, and in Massachusetts the largest amount on deposit permitted to any one account is $1600. In no other State except New York is there any limitation placed upon the amount of deposits. In one savings-bank in Rhode Island there is one deposit amounting to $169,000, which, however, constitutes a fund intended for philanthropic purposes.

DIVIDENDS AND TAXATION.

The limit of dividends allowed in the State of Maine is 5 per cent.; in Vermont, 4½ per cent.; in Massachusetts, 5 per cent., and in the others there is no limit set up. The annual dividends paid in the year 1894 averaged, in Maine, 3.86 per cent.; in New Hampshire, 3.51 per cent.; in Vermont, 3.95 per cent.; in Massachusetts, 4.06 per cent.; in Rhode Island, 4 per cent.; in Connecticut, 3.86 per cent.; in New York, 3.53 per cent., and in New Jersey, 2.86 per cent.

Deposits in savings-banks are taxed, in Maine, seven-eighths of one per cent.; New Hampshire, one per cent.; Vermont, three-fourths of one per cent.; Massachusetts, one-fourth of one per cent.; Rhode Island, one-fourth of one per cent.; Connecticut, one-fourth of one per cent., and in the other States deposits are untaxed.

In Massachusetts the laws really forbid deposits above $1000, but allow interest to accumulate to the amount of $600 additional, making a total of $1600, the largest possible amount held in one account.

The official reports for 1894 show that the number of savings-banks in eleven Eastern and Middle States was 626, and the number of depositors 4,296,133. The average to each depositor was $367.39; the total amount of deposits was $1,578,352,728.00; and the total assets were $1,733,227,013.00; showing the surplus of assets over liabilities, $149,073,165.00.

The following statement of number of depositors and amount of deposits in the Eastern and Middle States and Ohio is compiled from the latest official reports for 1894:

Compiled from the latest Official Reports of 1894.

States.	Number of Banks.	Number of Depositors.	Average to each Depositor.	Deposits	Surplus.	U. S. Bonds and Loans on same.
Maine..........	51	155,704	$350.22	$54,531,223.30	$3,195,833.54	$1,106,800.00
New Hampshire.	70	169,510	416.59	70,616,943.66	4,186,579.49	164,900.00
Vermont........	22	65,329	310.37	20,276,126.73	1,239,955.33	255,750.00
Massachusetts...	185	1,247,090	334.20	416,778,017.53	25,342,154.25	2,383,175.00
Rhode Island....	35	131,623	511.65	67,444,117.14	3,881,656.81	2,564,787.50
Connecticut. ...	90	337,254	461.51	136,928,858.49	5,505,431.78	727,950.10
Total, New England...	453	2,106,510	363.91	766,575,286.85	43,351,611.20	7,203,362.60
New York......	125	1,615,178	398.63	643,873,574.43	91,574,734.76	107,109,050.00
New Jersey......	24	127,842	253.42	32,397,632.34	3,266,115.54	5,200,496.75
Pennsylvania....	14	261,128	258.68	67,550,365.17	8,651,717.27	8,187,459.50
Maryland.......	9	137,013	327.19	44,829,132.51	No report.	No report.
Ohio (Cleveland Society for Savings).........	1	48,462	477.21	23,126,737.10	2,228,987.08	2,725,209.37
Grand Total....	626	4,296,133	$367.39	$1,578,352,728.40	$149,073,165.85	$130,425,578.22

States.	Bonds and Mortgages.	R.R. Stocks and Bonds and Loans on same.	Bank Stocks and Loans on same.	Total Assets and Liabilities.	Largest Single Depositor.
Maine..........	$7,120,688.94	$16,424,277.59	$2,764,711.80	$57,761,918.46	No report.
New Hampshire.	25,108,808.27	9,632,210.85	2,519,222.65	76,203,054.78	"
Vermont........	11,580,457.70	No report.	399,021.04	21,520,930.79	"
Massachusetts...	183,344,058.68	49,756,962.55	30,675,324.53	442,391,264.81	"
Rhode Island....	27,324,466.24	11,965,040.99	2,511,973.41	71,364,527.67	$169,148.21
Connecticut.....	55,296,853.66	28,462,855.75	6,773,661.46	146,020,795.48	112,271.60
Total, New England...	309,775,333.49	116,241,347.73	45,643,914.89	815,262,491.99	....
New York......	310,788,531.64	....	....	735,863,598.94	40,643.11
New Jersey......	15,212,934.84	5,080,000.22	11,500.00	35,679,253.08	15,899.27
Pennsylvania....	17,870,153.19	20,483,244.25	64,582.25	76,236,813.22	No report.
Maryland.......	No report.	No report.	No report.	44,829,132.51	"
Ohio (Cleveland Society for Savings).........	8,355,487.00	849,348.30	No report.	25,355,724.18	No report.
Grand Total.....	$662,002,440.16	....	....	$1,733,227,013.92	....

The following statement of number of depositors and amount of deposits in the United States in 1894 and 1895, respectively, is taken from the Statistical Abstract issued by the Treasury Bureau of Statistics:†

States, Territories, and Divisions.	1893–94. Number of Depositors.	1893–94. Amount of Deposits.	1893–94. Average to Each Depositor.	1894–95. Number of Depositors.	1894–95. Amount of Deposits.	1894–95. Average to Each Depositor.
EASTERN.		Dollars.	Dollars.		Dollars.	Dollars.
Maine	153,922	53,261,309	346.03	155,704	54,531,223	350.22
New Hampshire	169,510	70,616,944	416.59	163,702	66,746,703	407.73
Vermont	92,239	27,966,855	303.20	94,994	29,430,697	309.81
Massachusetts	1,214,493	399,995,570	329.35	1,247,090	416,778,018	334.20
Rhode Island	130,610	69,053,724	528.70	131,623	67,444,117	512.40
Connecticut	335,879	133,967,220	398.95	337,254	136,928,858	406.01
Total	2,096,653	754,861,622	360.03	2,130,367	771,859,616	362.31
MIDDLE.						
New York	1,585,155	617,089,449	390.50	1,615,178	643,873,574	398.63
New Jersey	137,897	34,266,298	248.49	144,160	36,149,920	250.76
Pennsylvania	248,244	66,025,821	265.97	264,642	68,522,217	258.92
Delaware	18,264	3,693,311	202.22	18,648	3,765,784	201.94
Maryland	144,218	43,758,875	303.42	148,342	45,490,279	306.66
District of Columbia	1,258	72,667	57.76	1,356	95,300	70.28
Total	2,135,036	764,906,421	358.26	2,192,326	797,897,074	363.95
SOUTHERN.						
West Virginia	3,522	236,025	67.01	....	....	....
North Carolina	*8,750	416,695	47.62	*6,039	291,744	48.31
South Carolina	*23,246	3,939,976	169.49	17,418	4,578,838	262.88
Georgia	*7,196	836,823	116.29	5,747	741,596	129.04
Florida	881	175,115	198.77	*1,148	205,710	179.19
Alabama	*2,590	102,347	39.52	....	....	....
Louisiana	7,786	2,057,845	264.30	9,918	2,687,934	271.02
Texas	2,450	301,648	123.12	....	....	....
Tennessee	9,664	1,412,840	146.19	8,703	1,112,491	127.83
Total	66,085	9,479,314	143.44	48,973	9,618,313	196.40
WESTERN.						
Ohio	77,533	27,403,922	353.45	86,183	34,753,222	403.25
Indiana	13,967	3,165,214	226.62	15,636	3,667,312	234.54
Illinois	83,802	22,870,005	272.90	94,724	24,357,400	257.14
Wisconsin	1,219	152,300	124.94	1,439	179,877	125.00
Iowa	*72,397	26,230,214	362.31	*77,809	28,158,488	361.89
Minnesota	38,493	8,954,575	232.63	42,777	9,471,799	221.42
Total	287,411	88,776,230	308.88	318,568	100,588,098	315.75
PACIFIC STATES AND TERRITORIES.						
Oregon	*1,732	753,080	434.80	1,803	662,229	367.29
Utah	5,528	963,227	174.24	6,271	1,142,215	182.14
Montana	1,240	347,476	280.22	2,844	812,910	285.83
New Mexico	182	37,476	205.91	217	37,951	174.90
Washington	*11,595	2,415,669	208.34	*5,512	1,148,104	208.29
California	172,225	125,420,765	728.24	*168,638	126,830,513	752.08
Total	192,502	129,937,693	674.99	185,285	130,633,922	705.04
Total United States	4,777,687	1,747,961,280	365.86	4,875,519	1,810,597,023	371.36

* Partly estimated.

† This Treasury report includes not only all the savings-banks which the Author has taken into consideration, but also the savings-banks of the West and South; which are organized with capital, have stockholders, take any amount on deposit, and invest the funds in many instances as the directors please. Those institutions are not to be classed with the true savings-banks of the Eastern and Middle States, which have no capital, and whose assets and surplus are held for the benefit of depositors only.

IV.

SPECIAL FORMS OF SAVINGS FUNDS.

In addition to the regularly incorporated savings-bank, two railroads have established savings funds. The Baltimore & Ohio Railroad Company has established a savings fund in order to afford to employees and their near relatives an opportunity to deposit savings and earn interest thereon, and to enable employees to borrow money at moderate rates of interest, and on easy terms of repayment, for the purpose of acquiring or improving a homestead, or freeing it from debt. The company guarantees the repayment of deposits and the payment of interest at the rate of at least four per cent. per annum, unless changed by notice. If the net earnings of the savings fund exceed the guaranteed interest, dividends may be declared, and, as a matter of fact, depositors have regularly received no less than five per cent. on their investments. During the year ending June 30, 1895, the interest paid to depositors reached 5½ per cent. The rules governing the savings fund give: (1) An employee of the company, his wife, child, father, or mother, or the beneficiary of any deceased member of the relief feature, the privilege of depositing with the company any sum of money not less than one dollar and not more than $100 in one day, for the repayment of which, with interest, the company becomes the guarantor. Any person ceasing to be employed by the company may continue a depositor if his balance is fifty dollars or more at the time of leaving. (2) Any adult employee of the company, who is a member of the relief feature and has been continuously in the service not less than a year, may borrow from the funds of the savings feature sums not less than $100, at the interest rate of six per cent. per annum, payable monthly. It is, however, provided that every borrower must carry life insurance in the relief department equal to the sum loaned him; or, if the regulations of the relief feature prevent this, the borrower must hold a policy of equal amount in some regular life insurance company. The only purpose for which money can be borrowed is for acquiring, improving or releasing a lien, upon a home situated, except in large cities, within a mile of the railroad company's lines. No loan is paid directly to the borrower, but is applied to the payment of bills approved by him. The repayment of loans is provided for by deductions from the monthly wages of the borrower of $1.50 for each $100 of the debt. If the borrower leaves the service of the company he must make the monthly payments at his own risk.

The plan of the Pennsylvania Railroad Company's savings fund differs from that of the Baltimore & Ohio in several particulars, the chief difference being that the Pennsylvania makes no provision for loaning money to employees. Deposits may be made of sums, in even dollars, not exceeding $100 a month. The privilege of depositing is limited to the period of employment in the service of the company. If a depositor's connection with the company be severed, his accounts must be settled within thirty days. According to the report of June 30, 1894, the savings fund of the Baltimore & Ohio was in debt to 1825 depositors to the amount of $780,668.42. The outstanding loans to the employees were $667,334.75. The deposits during the year were $227,861.11; the amount loaned within the year, $206,081.56. From August 1, 1882, when the savings fund was inaugurated, to June 30, 1894, the total deposits amounted to $2,220,334.28, and the total sum loaned to employees equaled $1,526,842.35. The money thus loaned was used upon houses—in building 813, buying 714, improving 159, and releasing liens on 329. The report of the Pennsylvania Railroad Company, December 31, 1894, shows that 4112 employees of that road were depositors in its savings fund. The total amount of the fund on that date was $1,354,748.33, and of this sum $1,300,000 had been securely invested in four per cent. bonds of the Pennsylvania Company or its allied lines. The company established the fund December, 1887.

The Paymaster-General of the United States Army reports that the United States Army savings fund has about $1,017,000 on deposit at the present time. It is impracticable to give the actual number of men who deposited, as some would deposit small sums regularly every pay-day, while others would not deposit more than once or twice a year, or perhaps during their whole period of enlistment. The fund, he believes, tends to lessen desertion, and in its operations is conducive to better discipline. Four per cent. interest is guaranteed to the depositors.

The Penny Provident Fund of the State of New York has 50,359 depositors, with a total of $31,000 to their credit, an average of sixty-one cents to each depositor. Of these deposits about $25,000 are invested in securities paying nearly five per cent. per annum. The balance is deposited in trust companies at three per cent. interest. The fund has two hundred and ninety-six stations, and pays no interest to depositors. This fund being chiefly used by children, is of great value in inculcating lessons of thrift and self-restraint. Savings in them are frequently made for special purposes; to buy shoes, hats, or clothing, or books, but more often recently, to save five dollars with which to open an account in a savings-bank.

The school savings-banks in the United States, which are located in sixty-nine cities, towns, and villages in the States of New York, Pennsylvania, Massachusetts, Ohio, Vermont, Maine, Indiana, New Jersey, North Dakota, Colorado, Kansas, and Michigan, comprise 1204 constituent banks, and have deposits amounting to $100,837.82. The plan has been introduced into 290 schools, located in twelve States. Though these banks pay no interest to depositors, their salutary influence has been amply proved, teaching the children, as they do, the uses and value of money. The 25,972 depositors in these banks comprise nearly one-half of the number of pupils attending the schools where the banks are located. When the depositor's balance amounts to a sufficient sum, an account for the pupil is opened in a neighboring bank.

BENEFICENT RESULTS OF SAVINGS-BANKS.

As before stated, the savings-banks in the State of New York are managed upon a system which illustrates the welding of business and philanthropy into a great financial bulwark for the protection of the poorer classes, and the security of the community at large. It is because of the excellence of this plan as well as its general use in other States that its details have been dwelt upon at length. Savings-banks are essentially the banks of the poor; they were established for the benefit of the plain people, and for the purpose of concentrating and utilizing for the general welfare the odds and ends of money which would otherwise remain hidden away unused at the bottom of a trunk or other hiding-place. They are managed by trustees without salary, who can have no interest in the profits of the business, and who administer their affairs with disinterestedness and remarkable ability, sustained in their work of benevolence by a unanimous public opinion. Their funds are wisely and safely invested, the net earnings being credited to the depositors, whose savings are thus augmented by compound interest. The proceeds of labor converted into active capital by depositors are made in this way to produce a revenue without impairing or endangering the original sum, and to go on increasing while the owner is engaged in the production of other surplus savings. The beneficial results of savings-banks are both individual and communal, as well as direct and indirect. The direct benefits both to the individual and to the community must be evident from what has already been said. Indirectly, savings-banks are a great factor in the moral as well as the material growth of the people. The man or woman with a bank account, however meager its proportions, is usually a good citizen. Especially in this country, where opportunities are more nearly than elsewhere equal for all, do savings-banks exert a certain moral influence. The cares which accompany their use sharpen the mental faculties and tend to increase the moral perception of the individual; education is encouraged; patriotism is promoted; family honor, as well as local pride, is engendered; commercial enterprise stimulated; and much which makes for higher spiritual life secured.

The statistics of the number of depositors and the amount of their savings in the regular savings-banks of the eleven States, in the Pennsylvania Railroad, the Baltimore & Ohio Railroad savings funds, in the United States Army fund, in the Penny Provident Fund of the State of New York, and in the school savings-banks in twelve States, was as follows: Deposits, $1,581,636,981; depositors, 4,381,401. These figures prove the steady growth in the past years of the savings-bank principle and practice. The exact percentage of growth in the regular savings-banks between the years 1880 and 1895 is shown by the following table, giving savings-banks statistics in the eleven States for these fourteen years:

	1880.	1894.	Per Cent. of Increase.
Number of depositors......	2,416,280	4,296,133	$77\frac{8}{10}$
Deposits.....................	$824,515,162.51	$1,578,352,728.40	$91\frac{4}{10}$
Surplus........................	62,567,044.32	149,073,165.85	$138\frac{3}{10}$

V.

DECREASE OF DIVIDENDS AND INCREASE OF DEPOSITS.

On account of the cheapness of money, the returns on savings-bank investments have decreased in the past fourteen years, so that the average dividend paid to depositors has diminished from four and five per cent. in 1880 to three and one-half and four per cent. in 1894; but the deposits to the credit of individuals have increased owing to the accumulation of capital by the plain people, induced and fostered by opportunities furnished through the savings-banks, so that while in 1880 the average was $341.25 on each open account, it was in 1894, $367.39, and the number of open accounts increased from 2,416,280 to 4,296,133. The total deposits increased from $824,515,162 to $1,578,352,728. The surplus fund grew from $62,567,049 to $149,073,165. Investments in bonds and mortgages nearly trebled, increasing from $269,021,908 to $662,002,440. Because of the decreased income from United States bonds, investments in and loans on the same fell off from $199,675,922 to $130,425,578. The total assets were increased from $891,666,424 to $1,733,227,013. The number of banks increased but little; in 1880 there were 594, and in 1894 there were 626 savings-banks. The teachings of the savings-bank system have extended, as will be seen, for there are now a much larger number of people using them, the number of open accounts having increased by 1,879,853, and they are continuing in the same direction. This increase in the number of people who are able to deposit funds in savings-banks seems to contradict the theory that the "poor are getting poorer." On account of the concentration of deposits in the older and larger savings-banks, the percentage of the expense of management to the total deposits does not increase. In the State of New York nearly one-half the deposits in savings-banks are in New York City, where are located twenty-five banks, and of these twenty-five, four banks have about one-half of the total deposits of the city.

In the State of New York there has been organized among its 125 savings-banks an association for mutual benefit, and delegates from every bank have elected an executive committee, which considers matters of benefit to all. Bills offered in the Legislature affecting savings-banks are considered by the executive committee of this association, and recommended or opposed according to their respective merits. The quality of securities proposed to be authorized by law for investment are discussed; and the safeguards attending the issue of bonds or other evidences of indebtedness issued by cities, counties, municipalities, etc., have lately attracted the attention of this association, and on account of the present lack of system regarding the issue of them, it has been recommended that the validity and genuineness of each and every such issue shall be certified to by a responsible trust company, in order to give proper guarantees of their validity. Bonds engraved by a responsible bank-note company have been recommended as another means of guarding against counterfeiting, to which printed and lithographed bonds are liable. In instituting such reforms as the foregoing, the association secures protection for officials who are responsible for savings-bank funds, as well as security for the investors, as a low rate of interest on valuable property is preferable to higher rates under questionable conditions.

UTILITY OF LARGE SURPLUS FUNDS.

Recently there have been some criticisms of the large surpluses held by some of the more successful savings-banks, and it has been suggested that this surplus money should be divided among the depositors. The framers of the law of the State of New York seem to have foreseen the possibility of such criticism, and to have wisely anticipated it by providing in Article III., Section 123, of the savings-bank law the following: "The trustees of any such corporation whose surplus amounts to fifteen per cent. of its deposits, at least once in three years, shall divide equitably the accumulation beyond such authorized surplus as an extra dividend to depositors, in excess of the regular dividends authorized." The critics seemed to have overlooked both this law and the fact that no bank in the State at the present time has a surplus large enough for distribution under the law. A good-sized surplus in a savings-bank is not only a very desirable feature in itself, but is also valuable in its advantages and its influence. As a monument to the success of the institution, it gives confidence to depositors and encourages others to enroll themselves upon the bank's ledgers. In case of sudden financial depression or of any unforeseen disturbance which might cause a run upon the banks, a surplus becomes a source of strength both to the bank and to the community. Moreover, in the year by year operations of the bank, the surplus plays a most important part. To-day the banks that pay the highest rate of interest, even paying four per cent., are the banks that have the surplus, because they could not take the moneys deposited with them now and invest them properly, and secure at the utmost more than 3¾ per cent. on the average. They are enabled to pay to depositors after all expenses of the bank are deducted, a higher rate of interest, simply because they have a surplus which earns interest for their benefit. Another reason that makes a surplus requisite is that it is needed to meet contingent losses in the depreciation of the value of securities. Hence the wisdom of the law which permits its accumulation to the extent of fifteen per cent. of total deposits.

SOUND CURRENCY.

The number of savings-bank depositors in the eleven States in which those institutions are located is equal to one-fifth of the total population; and the localities in which each of these institutions is located are freer from pauperism and crime than in other less favored communities; and to lessen the confidence of depositors in their places of financial trust by unwise legislation like the passage of a free coinage law by Congress, which would lessen the value of the dollar, would be a blunder on the part of law-makers which would tend to undermine a system which it has taken eighty years to build up. After the legal-tender act of 1862 was passed, deposits in savings-banks decreased largely, whilst after the resumption of specie payments in 1879, the percentage of increase was even greater than the withdrawals of seventeen years before. Confidence is a thing of slow growth; and in educating, it is necessary to show by example the teacher's faith in the principles striven to be inculcated, viz., that honesty and thrift are the best policy; and as these lie at the foundation of savings-banks, the depositor must be made to feel that his self-denial will be rewarded by a return, of the full amount at least, of the money which he has denied himself the pleasure of spending in temporary gratifications; but if he finds that, owing to a depreciation of the currency, a fraction of its value only is given back when he calls for it, because the law has stepped in and confiscated for the benefit of a few any part of his savings, the fruit of the good principles inculcated will be blasted in a moment. The first effects would probably be a run on the bank, followed by extravagance and riotous living with the money withdrawn, which would end by lowering the moral tone amongst the class of people who up to that time had been so largely benefited.

WHAT SHOULD BE THE RATE OF DIVIDEND?

As has been said, the average gross income which a savings-bank can earn on *new* deposits to-day does not exceed three and three-quarters per cent., and from this the expense of management must be deducted, say one-third to one-half per cent., leaving the net income for depositors about three and a quarter per cent. If more than this is paid, it is out of the earnings of the surplus fund which has accumulated on the undivided earnings of older deposits. Most of the banks have a surplus, and because of it they do pay an average of three and one-half per cent. dividends; but this cannot continue indefinitely, unless a larger range of investments is authorized which will pay an increased rate of interest on the money put into them. The desire to continue or increase the present dividends has induced some bank managers to favor the amendments which authorize the purchase of city bonds in certain States outside of New York. But it may be questionable if it would have been better policy to prohibit savings-banks from paying more than three per cent. interest per annum, except that if one accumulates a surplus of ten per cent. on its deposits (estimating its securities at par value if they are worth it, or the market value if they are worth less), then, once in three years, it should pay an extra dividend on the balances of all accounts which have been in bank for that length of time. Let us consider the latter course. A savings-bank is prohibited by law from receiving on deposit from any individual, or paying interest on, a greater sum than three thousand dollars. The charge is made, and is not disproved, that large sums, in many cases three thousand dollars, are deposited by one individual in each of the several banks, or he opens accounts in trust and thus gets in one bank more than the law intended. This is not prohibited by law, but it enables a well-to-do person who should make his own investments to put the burden on trustees engaged in a benevolent work, and he secures the advantage of investment in first-class securities, and obtains more interest than if he attended directly to the management of his own capital. Now, savings-banks are not designed as resorts for capitalists when prime investments pay low rates of interest elsewhere. They may be likened to kindergarten schools, where the young, the helpless, and the uninformed may learn the advantages of economy and thrift, the good results of which are shown by the increased balances which added interest exhibits each half-year, and who should learn by a study of the results secured by wise and prudent management how they themselves may care for the accumulations when their sum surpasses the limit (not a small one) fixed by statute. This was the theory of the founders, and is the theory of the present law of the States, in forbidding the payment of interest on sums over three thousand dollars. Savings-banks are practically freed from taxation, because they are engaged in a purely benevolent work, for the good of the masses, and it is an evasion of the spirit of the law for the depositors of large sums to use them. An indication that they are using them is shown by an analysis of the following statements taken from the official reports of the Superintendent of the Banking Department of the State of New York for three decennial periods.

	Total Deposits.	Number of Depositors.	Average to each.
January 1, 1868.......	$152,127,562	537,466	$281.18
" 1, 1878.......	312,823,058	844,550	370.40
" 1, 1888.......	505,017,751	1,325,062	381.12
" 1, 1896.......	691,764,503	1,695,787	407.93

At the first date, 1868, about twelve per cent. of the population were depositors in savings-banks; in 1878, seventeen per cent.; and in 1888, twenty-three per cent. were depositors. The average amount to the credit of each had increased in twenty years from $281 to $381, averaging a hundred dollars increase for each depositor. The returns up to January 1, 1896, show a still increasing average. Now, it will not be claimed that the wage-earners, those dependent on salaries and wages, have increased from twelve to twenty-three per cent. of the population, nor that all together have been able to lay up thirty-five per cent. more of their earnings in 1888 than in 1868. Wages, salaries, and expenses were about on the same plane at the two periods, but first-class investments outside of savings-banks paid six to ten per cent. in 1868, while in 1888 the same class of investments paid but two and three-fourths per cent., and the same money deposited in savings-banks paid the depositor three and one-half per cent.

There is in England a law which prohibits a person from having an account in more than one savings-bank, under penalty of forfeiting his deposit. There is no such law in any of our States, and therefore there is no way of preventing investors with large capital from taking advantage of the savings-banks, which were designed solely for the benefit of the poorer classes. A shrewd investor of some thousands of dollars who insists upon gilt-edged securities only, at the highest obtainable rate of interest, and who wishes to avoid the fluctuations of the market in buying or selling, and at the same time to keep his money on call, deposits in the savings-bank. There he finds all his conditions complied with, the law of the State protects his property, and holds the bank's trustees to a strict accountability. There appears to be a growing tendency to receive deposits of considerable amount, which cannot fairly be considered savings, of the kind for which savings-banks are chartered. This tendency, if unchecked, may result in changing the nature of the banks, and induce the Legislature to tax deposits, which will lower the rate of interest paid. The evil may then be cured, of course, by the applied remedy, but the principle having been violated, the result will be disastrous to the benefit of communities, the inducement will be taken away for the poor to save. and the acquisition to the ranks of good citizenship will be diminished.

GOOD RESULTS OF THE LAW OF 1875.

Savings-banks have prospered since the general law of 1875 was enacted, because under it they have been well and conservatively managed. No failures have occurred since the old wrecks came ashore which met with disaster before the law was enacted. We have had twenty years of prosperity, and no future calamity is feared, unless a reduction of dividends might be so classed. With first-class securities this is unavoidable, the rate of interest tends downward as the country increases in wealth. It seems, therefore, preferable that the regular rate of interest or dividends paid should be reduced to three per cent., rather than to further increase the range of investments. The rule for savings-banks should be, not to pay a higher rate of interest to individual depositors than the aggregate of deposits invested in large amounts can earn when put into strictly first-class securities. The rate suggested is a sufficient inducement for people to save, and inspires a feeling of the utmost security for the safety of their principal.

In addition to the examination of the books of the savings-banks as required by law, a practice has been instituted in this country by the Bowery Savings-Bank of having its books examined at regular intervals by a firm of public accountants. The practice has been found an excellent one. It makes "assurance doubly sure." In closing their last semi-annual reports, submitted January 9, 1896, these public accountants write as follows: "We examined all vouchers for expenses and found same in order. During the past six months we have examined in detail the ledger balances representing the amount due to individual depositors, as on October 1, 1895, and, with the adjustment of some small clerical errors in interest, found the same in order and in agreement with the general ledger. There are no overdrafts to report on at December 31, 1895. We also compared some 9500 bank pass-books with the corresponding accounts in the depositors' ledger, and found same in agreement. In our last report we mentioned that the president had instituted some excellent changes in the general routine of the business of the bank. We are pleased to testify that these changes continue to bear good fruit, and that the work of the bank is in excellent order."

The employment of public accountants has been in vogue in England for some years, but has never been generally adopted in this country in connection with the work of savings-banks so far as known. As the merits of the plan become clearly understood, the employment of public auditors to supplement the work of the trustees of the bank and of the State Bank Department—that is, to examine the examination—will become a general custom.

It may be said that the depositors in savings-banks are relatively the best paid investors in the community. Their security is as nearly absolute as wisdom and law can make it, and the returns from the investments are regular and certain, subject to little or no fluctuation and untouched by the many causes which bring depression to holders of railroad and manufacturing stocks. Savings-bank depositors are the real capitalists of the community. Their money it is which is largely loaned on first mortgages at 4½ per cent. and upwards on the apartment and tenement houses in which they dwell, the churches they attend, the clubs, business stores and factories, the theatres and places of amusement they frequent. It is largely their money which is loaned to the city on its bonds for the construction of public buildings and docks, the purchase and improvement of public parks, and paving streets.

In many cases a parent or relative opens an account for a child at birth, the fact being kept a secret from the beneficiary, and not developed until the death of the person who has performed the good deed. It often becomes capital for a young man to commence business with; or, in the case of a daughter, it may serve as a marriage portion. While it is running, the identity of the beneficiary of the account may be quite unknown to the savings-bank; but if legislation should be enacted to deprive him of his rights, the bank could easily find a way to apprise him of the danger of loss.

The accumulations of interest on these accounts is surprising in many instances, as the following memorandum, taken from the books of a well-known bank, will prove:

"In 1835, an account was opened in the bank by a deposit of $5. Further deposits were made up to April, 1849, when the total amounted to $705. At various other times between 1835 and 1850, $253.89 were withdrawn, leaving a balance (with accumulated dividends of $47.89) of $499. From 1853 to 1855, $500 was withdrawn, but when the last draft was made, the depositor's book appeared to be overdrawn to the extent of $1, which may have caused him to lose his regard for the account, but he had overlooked the fact that there was due him at that time dividends amounting to $100.01, which had not been entered in his pass-book, and the bank really owed him a net balance of $99.01.

"This balance went on accumulating dividends for twenty years until 1875, when it became a dormant account and ceased to draw interest. The amount then due him was $343.25. Efforts were made from time to time to discover the owner of the account, but without success, until 1889, when he was found, a very old man, unable to work and living on the bounty of his children, totally unaware of the snug sum due him by the bank. This balance of $343.25 was paid to him in November of that year to his great delight and satisfaction."

It does not seem to be generally understood that there are many savings-bank accounts that have been in existence and little used for even more than twenty years; but they exist, and every bank has a large number of them. Because of the fact that they do exist, legislators have been led to suppose that such accounts had no legal claimants, and bills are offered yearly making inquiries about these old accounts. Even the Constitutional Convention in the State of New York two years ago seriously thought of putting a clause in the new constitution confiscating to the use of the State moneys which had been unclaimed for twenty years or more. The Banking Department of the State of New York, at the request of the convention, made inquiry, at the time, of each of the banks of that State; and when it was found that the number of accounts without claimants within the twenty-year limit was comparatively few, the idea was abandoned.

The secrecy which depositors wish to have observed with regard to their transactions with savings-banks does not seem to be taken into account by legislators in their eagerness to enact laws. Existing notions with regard to these accounts have caused many of the savings-banks to seek out the owners of these old accounts, and request them before the expiration of twenty years to make a deposit or a draft, so that the accounts may be revived and not become "dormant."

CAUSE OF INCREASE IN DEPOSITS.

The increase in the average amount of individual deposits is caused by the banks' receiving large amounts from individuals. There is no doubt that many people who formerly invested in stocks and bonds, and on bond and mortgage, have divided their funds by putting into each bank as much as would be taken, and thus swelled the aggregate of all the banks. This proceeding is unavoidable, as there is no prohibition against one person opening an account in every bank that will receive it; and one person may have the legal limit in every bank and thus have many thousands on deposit when they are aggregated, although he is prohibited from having more than $1000 to $3000 in any one bank. The limit in the United Kingdom is £300 sterling, or $1500; in France, the limit is F. 2000, or $400; and if the same person has a deposit in more than one bank the penalty is, in the United Kingdom, forfeiture of the whole deposit or benefit to the Government; in France, the deposits will be returned without interest and the depositor will be forever excluded from the savings-banks.

For the reason that, as has been said before, new deposits can only be invested here to earn from 3⅝ per cent. to 3¾ per cent. interest, it has been suggested that deposits of many years' standing should be allowed a greater rate of interest than more recent ones, because they helped the bank to earn the surplus which enables it to pay high rates of interest; but as it would require very complex calculations, the idea has never been put in practice.

Within the past few years investments in railroad and other securities have become so precarious that many people have striven to place their accumulations in savings-banks, so good was the reputation of these institutions. Here they could secure the greatest safety as well as the highest rate of interest—the savings-banks, on account of their surplus, being able to pay depositors a higher rate of interest than their money alone could actually earn upon investments made to-day. This condition of things, however desirable in itself, gives rise to danger. People are attracted to savings-banks for whom the banks were never intended to be used. Large sums are offered to the savings-banks, and although some of the institutions consent to receive them, it is a matter of doubtful expediency. Not alone does the accommodation of such people divert the forces of the savings-bank from the true channels, but it also makes the bank liable to sudden drains upon its available money. These depositors, who use the savings-bank purely for investment, are always ready to avail themselves of a better investment if one appears, and in the case of a panic, when all securities go down in value, they come eagerly to the bank to secure their money, in order to buy securities which are selling below their value, and which must, as soon as the panic subsides, return to their higher and normal value. It is at just such times that the bank itself needs ready money. Large depositors should be discouraged, because, as a rule, they come from a class who know how to invest their own money, and they should not ask trustees who serve as benefactors to invest their money for them, nor should savings-banks, which were founded for philanthropic purposes, and which in carrying out their purpose are relieved of taxation, permit their institutions to be used for speculative purposes. This question is easy to manage when the amount of the deposit received is kept down. When only small sums are received at a time, savings-banks are, as a rule, serving the class for whose benefit they were intended—that is, those who have not sufficient knowledge of financial affairs to invest their money for themselves profitably.

During the last twenty years there have been but few important failures among the savings-banks of the East. In their rapid increase previous to the War of the Rebellion it is not surprising that many errors and abuses crept in—for which atonement has long since been made in loss and disaster. The multiplication of savings-banks in the early sixties was stimulated by the evidence of prosperity, and the competition for patronage became more and more active and demoralizing. In the management of some institutions the old landmarks of safety seemed to be altogether obliterated. The question of security seemed to be secondary, or to have been lost sight of altogether. Young institutions, conducted more in accordance with the requirements of such a trust, were feebly maintained at the expense of the trustees, or showed a deficiency of income, which enlarged from year to year. But the real conditions of weakness and premature decay were obscured by the glamour of apparent prosperity elsewhere prevalent. The shock which came just previous to the panic of 1873, and the protracted trial which followed, from which we have not yet fully emerged, have rudely dispelled the illusion with which so many were beguiled.

What more natural, what more inevitable than that this period of trial should prove disastrous to the fortunes of very many savings-banks? The wonder is, not that some score or more in New England and New York were forced into liquidation, but that any could survive the tests of this protracted season of financial depression. At the time, much intemperate speech was indulged in concerning trustees, whose only crime was that in their ignorance they had accepted a trust the responsibilities and difficulties of which they understood little, but the duties of which they had endeavored to discharge, at no small cost to themselves in time, labor, anxiety, and money. Of course, not all were so innocent and guileless. This season of trial became a judgment-day not only for institutions weak from their inception, weak from very necessity, but for those which, once strong, had been made weak by inexcusable faults in their management.

In whatever aspect viewed, the employment of industrial force in promoting public improvements and in the creation of public wealth, confers lasting benefits upon society, if integrity and economy govern in the administration of affairs. Whatever, then, facilitates this employment is a social force to be respected and honored, to be protected and surrounded by safeguards. Savings-banks, as reservoirs of capital, are this social force. They make it possible to borrow these tokens of industry offered for practical uses, and thereby to summon industry to further conquests in behalf of the good of mankind.

INDEX.

PART I.

HISTORY OF BANKING IN GREAT BRITAIN.

PART II.

HISTORY OF BANKING IN RUSSIA.

PART III.

SAVINGS-BANKS IN THE UNITED STATES.